A GREATER REALITY

The New Paradigm of Nonlocal Consciousness the Paranormal & the Contact Modalities
Volume #5: Experiencer Chapters

Angels
NDES
Non-Human Intelligence
OBES
Hallucinogenic Journeys
UFOS
Remote Viewing
SPIRITS
Prayer

Meditation
Teleportation
Apports
Telekinesis
Kundalini Awakening
Cosmic Consciousness
Intuition
Clairvoyance
Lucid Dreams
Precognition
Retrocognition
Telepathy
Energy Healing
Mediums
Channeling
HICE/CE-5
Automatic Writing
Poltergeists
Orbs
Post Death Communications

Editors

Rey Hernandez, JD, MCP
Dr. Rudy Schild, PhD
Dr. Joseph Burkes, MD
Dr. Jon Klimo, PhD
Dr. Michael Grosso, PhD
Dr. Jeffrey Long, MD

Consciousness & Contact
Research Institute, CCRI

Email: Info@AGreaterReality.com
Website: AGreaterReality.com

⊕CCRI

A Greater Reality:

The New Paradigm of Nonlocal Consciousness, the Paranormal & the Contact Modalities

VOLUME FIVE: Experiencer Chapters

Editors

Reinerio (Rey) Hernandez, JD, MCP
Rudy Schild, PhD
Michael Grosso, PhD
Joseph Burkes, MD
Jon Klimo, PhD
Jeffrey Long, MD

AMAZON CUSTOMERS

Please go to Amazon and give us a 5 Star Rating

Thank you!

Email: Info@AGreaterReality.Com

Website: AGreaterReality.Com

ALL OF MY BOOKS ARE AVAILABLE FOR FREE

I am giving away all my books as FREE PDF files.

The downloadable PDF file is located at the CCRI website, located at:

AGreaterReality.Com

If anyone wants a physical copy or an eBook of any of my books, they can purchase it from Amazon Press.

What I do ask from everyone, those that chose to pay for my books on Amazon and those that decide to download my books via free downloadable PDF files,

please go to Amazon and give us a

5 Star Review

https://www.amazon.com/s?k=books+by+reinerio+hernandez

A Greater Reality

Table of Contents

Volume 5

Book Endorsements

Jeffrey Long, M.D.

Author of the New York Times best-selling *"Evidence of the Afterlife: The Science of Near-Death Experiences"* and *"God and the Afterlife: The Groundbreaking New Evidence for God and Near-Death Experience"*. https://www.nderf.org/

The six-volume book series, each 800 pages in length, titled *"A Greater Reality: The New Paradigm of Nonlocal Consciousness, the Paranormal & the Contact Modalities"*, edited by my friend, Reinerio (Rey) Hernandez and his distinguished co-authors, is a groundbreaking work that reshapes our understanding of consciousness and the nature of reality. These books are establishing a new paradigm of viewing the nature of our reality. The first two volumes are theoretical volumes that delve deeply into the theoretical underpinnings of consciousness as the fundamental source of existence, expertly connecting it to various paranormal **"Contact Modalities"**, a term that Rey has coined.

By demonstrating that these seemingly separate phenomena-- like Near Death Experiences, UFO encounters, Out of Body Experiences, seeing and communicating with the deceased, Remote Viewing, various PSI phenomena, Hallucinogenic Journeys, etc., are actually interconnected facets of one consciousness-based reality, these volumes challenge conventional materialist views and introduce a cohesive, consciousness-centered model of the universe. The third, fourth, fifth and sixth volumes are a captivating collection of firsthand accounts from major experiencers of these Contact Modalities, giving readers an intimate and transformative look into encounters with Non-Human Intelligence across multiple dimensions.

Finally, Rey's book discussing his personal experiences, *"A Greater Reality: One Man's Journey of Discovery"*, offers an illuminating, profound journey that is essential reading for anyone interested in the deeper mysteries of consciousness and our place in the cosmos. His journey and transformation are similar to the NDE journey and spiritual transformation that I have encountered in my 30 plus years of NDE research. All of Rey's books in the *A Greater Reality* book series are scholarly, yet a joy to read. They are all essential reading and highly recommended.

Jeffrey Mishlove, Ph.D.

Host of New Thinking Allowed
https://www.youtube.com/@wThinkingAllowed
Author of "*Beyond the Brain: The Survival of Human Consciousness After Permanent Bodily Death*" (Winner of the BICS Survival of Consciousness Essay Contest), and "*The Roots of Consciousness: Psychic Liberation Through History, Science, and Experience*"

Rey Hernandez is a man on a quest and on a mission. By the grace of the absolute, his life has been transformed in miraculous and synchronistic ways. He has been shown, via a wide variety of experiences, that the wide variety of paranormal experiences (what Rey has coined "**The Contact Modalities**"), reported by thousands, if not millions, of people around the world, have a single source. That source is pure consciousness itself, mind-at-large (as some would put it), or in Rey's own language, the "*Mind of God*". Of course, such experiences and visions are not uncommon. But what is truly rare, is Rey's determination to collect data and reports from thousands of experiencers and dozens of academic researchers investigating their claims. This he has achieved with ceaseless energy. This six-volume book series, 800 pages for each volume, titled "*A Greater Reality: The New Paradigm of Nonlocal Consciousness, the Paranormal & the Contact*

Modalities", is a gift from the realm of spirit to the entire world and help to establish a "new paradigm" connecting consciousness to the paranormal Contact Modalities. These books are truly historic and an invaluable resource by arguing that all of the paranormal phenomena are actually one integrated phenomenon under consciousness.

Volumes 1 and 2 are academic books, with chapters written by many PhD academics and MDs, many who are my personal friends, is a valuable resource for academic research on the topic of the paranormal Contact Modalities and consciousness. Volumes 3-6 are a collection of articles written by major Experiencers of the Contact Modalities. These experiencer written chapters demonstrate the interconnectedness between the paranormal Contact Modalities and consciousness. Most of these individuals have had experiences with 3 or more different Contact Modalities, once again demonstrating that the paranormal phenomena are not separate and distinct from each other but instead are ONE interrelated phenomenon under consciousness.

Finally, Rey's well documented academic book detailing his personal experiences, *"A Greater Reality: One Man's Journey of Discovery"*, provides additional supporting documentation that the "paranormal" involves a multidimensional consciousness-based phenomenon involving a manipulation of spacetime. These collections of books are one of the most important resources that detail the relationship between consciousness and the paranormal. They are an invaluable resource for any consciousness scholar and a must read!

Steve Mera - Investigative Researcher

Founder: SEP - The Scientific Establishment of Parapsychology
Publisher of "Phenomena Magazine".
s_mera@yahoo.com

The six-volume book series, *"A Greater Reality: The New Paradigm of Nonlocal Consciousness, the Paranormal & the Contact Modalities"*, edited by Reinerio (Rey) Hernandez and his distinguished team of co-authors, represents a ground-breaking body of work that fundamentally challenges and reshapes our understanding of consciousness and the nature of reality itself. In the first two volumes, the authors dive deeply into the theoretical foundations of consciousness as the primary, underlying source of all existence. They skillfully explore its connections to various phenomena traditionally classified as "paranormal", what Rey has coined **"The Contact Modalities"**.   These include Near-Death Experiences, UFO encounters, Out of Body Experiences, communication with the deceased, Remote Viewing, various PSI phenomena, and Hallucinogenic Journeys, among others. Rey and the other authors propose that these seemingly disparate experiences are not isolated or mysterious events, but rather interconnected aspects of one universal, consciousness-based reality. In doing so, they challenge entrenched materialist perspectives and offer a cohesive, consciousness-centered model of the universe that transcends conventional scientific paradigms.

The series' third, fourth, fifth, and sixth volumes take a dramatic turn, presenting a rich collection of first-hand accounts from individuals who have had direct encounters with Non-Human Intelligence across multiple dimensions. These personal stories, drawn from major experiencers of these Contact Modalities, offer readers a profoundly transformative window into the nature of these otherworldly interactions, deepening our understanding of how consciousness operates beyond the physical world. Together, these volumes offer not only a scholarly investigation of these extraordinary phenomena but also a deeply personal and thought-provoking exploration of human consciousness in its most expansive form.

Rey has also completed a book about his personal experiences via the Contact Modalities titled "*A Greater Reality: One Man's Journey of Discovery*". This book presents Rey's personal "paranormal" experiences in a scholarly manner. He dissects the details of each of his paranormal experiences and provides an academic, yet easily understood hypothesis to explain his many experiences that is both innovative and pedagogical.

In summary, the *A Greater Reality* book series is a must-read for anyone seeking a more profound understanding of the mysteries of contact with non-human intelligence, consciousness, our place in the cosmos, and the nature of reality itself. Both intellectually stimulating and deeply engaging, these books are highly recommended for anyone eager to explore the deeper dimensions of human experience.

John B. Alexander, Ph.D.

Former U.S. Army colonel, Los Alamos National Laboratory (retired). Author of "*Reality Denied: Firsthand Experiences with Things that Can't Happen - But Did*" and "*UFOs: Myths, Conspiracies, and Realities*"

A Greater Reality: The New Paradigm of Nonlocal Consciousness, the Paranormal and the Contact Modalities, edited by Reinerio (Rey) Hernandez and a team of distinguished academic professors, is an extraordinary compilation of materials that span the breadth of anomalous phenomena. Rey was the first researcher to name this cross correlation of paranormal experiences as the *"Contact Modalities"* -- as one integrated phenomenon under consciousness where consciousness is fundamental and not our perceived physical reality. All of the editors and academics associated with this book series also argue that all of the Contact Modalities should be viewed as one integrated phenomenon under consciousness.

Rey was the first academic researcher to actually collect data demonstrating the cross correlations between what were commonly believed to be unique fields of inquiry. While the concept of the Contact Modalities as one integrated phenomenon under consciousness had been postulated by some of us, Rey was the first to engage thousands of people to evaluate their personal experiences and compare them with those with similar experiences via the Contact Modalities. A massive undertaking, the results were published in Rey's first pioneering academic book titled *Beyond UFOs: The Science of Consciousness and Contact with Non-Human Intelligence*.

Moving beyond his personal research, Rey was instrumental and successful in bringing together a who's who of the serious scientific Ph.D. academic and MD researchers in the fields of anomalous phenomena and consciousness studies and formed the **CCRI**, or **Consciousness and Contact Research Institute**. The result was a six volume book series, each over 800 pages in length, titled "*A Greater Realty: The Science of Nonlocal Consciousness, the Paranormal & the Contact Modalities*".

The introductory book to this six-volume book series is titled *The Mind of GOD: A Virtual-Spiritual Reality Model of Consciousness and the Contact Modalities*. There is no better place for anyone interested in these topics to survey the topics and be pointed to areas for further exploration and study. While consciousness is considered a quintessential "*Hard Problem*," and quantum physics a keystone to our understanding of the nature of the universe, these volumes provide a substantial foundation to the explorer at any stage of development. All is interconnected, and consider that if you are thinking globally, you are thinking too small.

Whitley Strieber

Author of *"Communion"*, *"The Afterlife Revolution"*, *"The Super Natural: Why the Unexplained Is Real"*. *www.unknowncountry.com*

A Greater Reality: One Man's Journey of Discovery, is a rich exploration of the truly extraordinary life of one of the legendary figures in UFOlogy, Reinerio (Rey) Hernandez. It takes the reader on a riveting journey down some pathways that even very few close encounter witnesses have ever dared to tread.

Rey was the first researcher to academically research the relationship between Consciousness and not only UFOs but all of the paranormal. He assembled a large team of Ph.D. academics and UFO contact researchers to undertake a comprehensive worldwide academic statistical research study of UFO contact experiencers whose data was published in his historic book titled "*Beyond UFOs: The Science of Consciousness and Contact with Non-Human Intelligence*". Much of this data contradicts much of what is currently circulating in materialist Ufology.

The *Beyond UFOs* research study clearly demonstrated that the UFO contact phenomenon was much more complicated than what the field of materialist Ufology is presenting. The study demonstrated that UFO contact was both a physical and a "paranormal" phenomenon. His new 6 volume book series, "*A Greater Realty: The Science of Nonlocal Consciousness, the Paranormal & the Contact Modalities*", is a historic book which argues that not only UFOs, but all of the paranormal, what Rey termed the **Contact Modalities**, needs to be viewed as ONE interrelated phenomenon under Consciousness. All of Rey's books are academic, easy to read, yet mind-opening and fascinating reading! They are a historic treasure that will certainly be appreciated for generations to come.

<u>Grant Cameron</u> – UFO and Paranormal Researcher

Author of *"Beyond Magic"*, *"Tuned-In: The Paranormal World of Music"*, *"Contact Modalities: The Keys to the Universe"*.

A Greater Reality: The New Paradigm of Nonlocal Consciousness, the Paranormal & the Contact Modalities, edited by Reinerio (Rey) Hernandez and other distinguished academics, is a six-volume book series that is required reading for anyone researching the relationship between UFOs, consciousness and the other paranormal **"Contact Modalities"**, a term that Rey coined in 2013. This book series centers on "consciousness", what is the nature of our reality, and its relationship with the paranormal Contact Modalities. Rey and the other academics featured in this book series argue that UFOs need to be studied as a paranormal related phenomenon. In addition, this book series argues that not only UFOs, but all of the other paranormal "Contact Modalities" are not separate and distinct from one another but in fact need to be researched as ONE integrate phenomenon under consciousness.

I firmly believe that understanding the paranormal lies in understanding what is consciousness. I have written 22 books on UFOs and the paranormal, and have quoted Rey's research more than any other author. We either go down the road that Rey is on, or we will spend 80 more years chasing lights in the sky and paranormal stories and get no farther than we did in the first 80 years. These six volumes are a prolific academic collection of the data that has been collected, data that has been sadly ignored by the field of materialist Ufology and academia in general.

This 6-volume magnum opus, should be read in corollary with Rey's personal book, *"A Greater Reality: One Man's Journey of Discovery"*. This book contains many of Rey's personal paranormal experiences, detailing his personal contact with large and up-close UFOs, which Rey calls "**CAPs**", or **Consciousness Aerial Phenomenon**. It is a wonderful read of stories I have heard Rey tell over the years since I have known him. The book, with all the synchronicities and paranormal events he experienced, illustrates that Rey is truly on a mission to bring the truth about the nature of reality, what is consciousness, to the world, as directed by a greater intelligence, an intelligence that Rey has termed "**The Mind of GOD**". Rey relates his experiences in a no BS "tell it like it was" manner.

I consider Rey's work with experiencers and scientists to be some of the most important research ever done in any field. Rey was the first author to publish the direct connection between the paranormal Contact Modalities and Consciousness by arguing that what we initially viewed as separate phenomena, are instead one interrelated phenomenon under consciousness-- all the paranormal, including UFOs, need to be viewed as ONE phenomenon under consciousness.

"A Greater Reality: One Man's Journey of Discovery" tells Rey's personal story of the drive and dedication of the man behind that research. It discusses his personal experiences via the Contact Modalities and should be read as a continuation of his 6-volume book series, *"A Greater Reality: The New Paradigm of Nonlocal Consciousness, the Paranormal & the Contact Modalities"*. All of Rey's books are required reading for anyone interested in researching the relationship between consciousness and the paranormal Contact Modalities. These are the most important books ever written on the relationship between Consciousness, our greater multidimensional reality, and the paranormal Contact Modalities. They are required reading for anyone interested in not only the UFO field but also the fields of paranormal research and consciousness studies.

Alan Steinfeld

Author of "***Making Contact: Preparing for the New Realities of Extraterrestrial Contact***".

Some people desperately search for a greater reality; some people stumble upon them out of curiosity, while others have a greater reality thrusted upon them. This is the case of Reinerio (Rey) Hernández, whose second book, "***The Mind of GOD: A Spiritual Virtual Reality Model of Consciousness and the Contact Modalities***", serves as an introduction to his epic 6-Volume book series titled "***A Greater Reality: The Science of Non-local Consciousness, the Paranormal and the Contact Modalities***", the most important books ever written on the relationship between the paranormal, UFOs, and consciousness.

In the midst of ongoing revelations from the government about the UAP/UFO reality, it is strange times we are living in and this is exactly why this book is most needed at this time. Rey's writings navigate the unexplored levels of consciousness, which will give us insight into the vaster cosmos of consciousness we are part of.

Like the subjects it convers, this is not an ordinary text, it is an attempt on a grand scale to explore a universe filled with wonder, magic, and possibilities yet to be dreamed. This excellent series of books is a greater sampling of this evolutionary moment. It is indeed a welcome treasure and a companion for the ongoing revelation of who and what the human being really is. Thank you, Rey.

George Knapp

Chief Investigative Reporter for KLAS TV 8newsnow I-Team, weekend host Coast to Coast AM radio. Co-Author of "***Hunt for the Skinwalker: Science Confronts the Unexplained at a Remote Ranch in Utah***"

Interest in the UFO mystery has spiked in recent years, and most of the attention has focused on government secrets, whistleblowers, crash retrievals, what the Pentagon might know, what kind of classified studies, reports, photos, and videos might be stashed in various stovepipes inside the DOD or intelligence community. This is the materialist approach to Ufology. But what if the truly important information isn't hidden inside a deep, dark Pentagon cubbyhole, but rather is in plain sight? What if the UFO mystery is much more complicated than this materialist approach?

The story told by Rey in the "***A Greater Reality***" book series is historic, compelling, credible, and global in scope. The true significance of human contact with Non-Human Intelligence (NHI) might have nothing to do with the quest for advanced technology and materialist Ufology, but rather, with the nature of our interaction with some other form of higher intelligence under the rubric of consciousness, our greater reality. While Volume 1 and 2 of this book series are academic and theoretical in nature, Volumes 3-6 provide thousands of pages of detailed contact experiences of experiencers of the **Contact Modalities**-- paranormal experiences where these individuals are having contact with NHI via Near Death Experiences, UFO Contact, Out of Body Experiences, Remote Viewing, Hallucinogenic Journeys and other paranormal phenomenon. The collection of these books argues that our true reality might not be a physical one but one that is much more complicated.

Secondly, the "*A Greater Reality*" book series argues that all of the Contact Modalities, all of the "paranormal" contact experiences with NHI, including UFO contact experiences, need to be viewed as one interrelated phenomenon. This was the same conclusion reached by the NIDS research team, the National Institute for Discovery Science, in their extensive research of Skinwalker Ranch-- the lesson is that somehow all of these phenomena are related, now it's up to you to figure out how. Rey's books go a long way to providing an ontological framework that begin to explain the nature of how all paranormal phenomena might be interrelated. This is truly a historic piece of academic research.

The overall message as described in the "*A Greater Reality*" book series is positive, almost hopeful. The esteemed writers who contributed to this massive effort, many who I personally know, make the case that humanity is being transformed, one encounter at a time. And while most of these encounters are terrifying and bewildering at the time of their initial experience, the humans who've had these experiences eventually come to the conclusion that contact with NHI changed their lives for the better. Whoever they are, wherever they are from, they seem to be interested in slowly preparing us for whatever comes next.

All of Rey's pioneering books, while academic in nature, are easy to read, illuminating, and a must read for anyone interested in understanding the complexities of the UFO and paranormal contact phenomenon.

Forward

Mary Rodwell
©2024 Mary Rodwell

It is my pleasure and honor to write the forward for the six volume book series, titled "*A Greater Reality, the New Paradigm of Nonlocal Consciousness, the Paranormal & the Contact Modalities*", co-edited by my dear friend and research colleague Reinerio (Rey) Hernandez. I personally believe Rey Hernandez's contribution to this subject with his research into the complexity of human interactions with Non-Human Intelligence (NHI) is seminal in its reach and scope. I am not aware of any other source or individual who has compiled such a wealth of information and personal accounts of contact with Non-Human Intelligences to date.

Rey Hernandez's personal experiences, referenced in his new book, "*A Greater Reality: One Man's Journey of Discovery*", offers more understanding of the motivation and deep commitment Rey has demonstrated by exploring the complexity and mystery of his own personal experiences and spiritual journey. In this book, Rey details how his personal Contact with Non-Human Intelligence provided the inspiration and on-going connection to this intelligence, who Rey refers to as "**The Mind of GOD**". Rey explains how his Contact experiences inspired the focus to his groundbreaking research, and the creation of an academic research institute, the Consciousness and Contact Research Institute (CCRI), comprised of more than 25 Ph.D. academics and medical doctors. Rey should be applauded for his attempt to scientifically explain and demonstrate the validity of multidimensional reality behind Contact.

He also needs to be acknowledged for his development of the term "**The Contact Modalities**", that all of the paranormal is actually ONE interrelated phenomenon under consciousness, which in turn connects human consciousness to Non-Human Intelligence.

Rey's research demonstrates that the materialist perspective of 'nuts and bolts' Ufological research was trapped by its own limits into what data was deemed credible. Many researchers have demonstrated through their own research that the UFO phenomenon is a multidimensional experience involving a manipulation of space-time and as such could only be explored though a broader 'lens' if it was to be fully understood. The Experiencer of the Contact Modalities are often connected to other realms or dimensions of the multiverse through what is termed human 'consciousness.'

Rey through his personal experiences was led to challenge all his previous beliefs, and courageously stepped into the 'unknown' with this expanded awareness. Rey, and countless of other Experiencers, have been led to challenge the boundaries of conventional wisdom, exploring scientific parameters in the quantum realms of our multidimensional reality. Rey was inspired to study a layman's version of quantum physics research and the vast academic research literature on Consciousness Studies and the Near-Death Experience phenomenon because these subjects help explain and indicate that Consciousness is primary and not our perceived physical reality. Rey has argued that not only Consciousness, the nature of our true reality, is "fundamental", but also that all of the "paranormal" Contact Modalities need to be viewed as one integrated phenomenon under Consciousness, including the UFO phenomena.

He argues that this hypothesis helps us to better understand our multidimensional reality and the experience of Contact with Non-Human Intelligences via the Contact Modalities, which include: Near Death Experiences, Out of Body Travel, UFO contact, contact and communication with the deceased, Remote Viewing, Hallucinogenic Journeys, the ESP phenomenon, and other forms of contact with Non-Human Intelligence.

Rey's viewpoint is innovative and unique and his many books and publications establish a "New Paradigm" of understanding the nature of our consciousness-based reality and our role in this complex multidimensional existence. No one's work compares to the breadth and scope of the innovative approach of my friend, Rey Hernandez.

It has become increasingly evident that academic research into the fields of Quantum Physics, Consciousness Studies, the Near-Death Experience and the UFO contact phenomena all point to the hypothesis that human contact with perceived Non-Human Intelligence is a consciousness-based phenomenon involving a manipulation of space-time. The academic research of the Dr. Edgar Mitchell (FREE) Foundation, an organization co-founded by myself, Rey, the late Apollo 14 Astronaut Dr. Edgar Mitchell, and Harvard Astrophysicists, Dr. Rudy Schild, demonstrated statistical data that supported this hypothesis.

The FREE Experiencer Research Study was the first and continues to be the only comprehensive statistical academic research study of UFO Contact Experiencers. It provided data from 700 quantitative and 70 open-ended in-depth questions on UFO related contact with Non-Human Intelligence. Over 4,350 individuals from over 125 countries responded to our English language surveys. FREE also conducted these surveys in several other languages. This information is detailed in the 820-page historic book titled *"Beyond UFO's: The Science of Consciousness and Contact with Non-Human Intelligences".*

This groundbreaking 6-year academic research study indicated that 75% of Encounters were experienced in an Out of Body (OBE) state, which clearly demonstrated why the previous Ufological methodology researching this phenomenon had been inconclusive. Such data once again demonstrated we are dealing with non-ordinary states of consciousness.

Much of the FREE survey data contradicted what is still circulating in the field of materialist UFOlogy. The FREE data findings demonstrates that almost everything that one reads in the internet and in materialist UFO books is either wrong or misguided. Materialist Ufology focuses on a physical "flying" UFO, argues that the intelligence behind the physical UFO is a physical being coming to visit us, in most cases for less and 30 seconds and is coming to visit us from a physical planet. The focus is on UFO crashes, UFO sightings, UFO videos, UFO photos, in essence, on the physicality of the UFO phenomenon.

This materialist perspective completely ignores the main essence that the UFO phenomenon is a "Consciousness-based Phenomenon". All of Rey's books do not use the term UFOs or UAPs. Instead, his preferred term is **CAP, or Consciousness Aerial Phenomenon**, to properly define the phenomena as one that is Consciousness-based.

What was significant from the FREE survey data is that it indicated that many "Contact Experiences" were the result of a multidimensional experience and this was a catalyst for awakening them to be more consciously aware of communication with NHI. Rey

Hernandez named the catalyst to this Contact with NHI as "**The Contact Modalities**" -- a term that demonstrates that Contact with NHI may occur not only after a 'sighting' of a CAP-UFO but from numerous other experiences such as a Near Death Experiences (NDE), a shamanic experience, Astral Travel, Remote Viewing, mediumship, clairaudience, clairaudience, clairvoyance, channeling, a Kundalini awakening or other paranormal experiences, etc. The term the "**Contact Modalities**" suggest that all of the paranormal needs to be viewed and researched as ONE integrated phenomenon under Consciousness instead of separate and distinct phenomena.

For many individuals, the interactions often began from early childhood but may have been interpreted though spiritual or religious belief, such as angels, spirit guides or religious entities. The individuals were unaware this may be Contact with NHI but their personal spiritual or religious beliefs may provide a different interpretation. Unfortunately, due to the limits of such beliefs it can often take a pivotal event to dissolve and reconfigure a more expansive and open attitude to what is possible, to create a more expanded understanding of reality. A seminal event such as a sighting of a UFO, a 'missing time' episode, or a miraculous medical healing experience that was unexplainable, would be pivotal to activate the awakening of the individual awareness, which in turn, leads to further exploration as to the nature of their consciousness-based reality. Each individual will have a unique story to how this occurred for them, although there may be similar patterns to this awakening. In many cases it can be unique to the individual soul. The bottom line is that all of the Contact Modality experiences lead to a spiritual awakening where the Experiencer, over many years, reaches the conclusion that they are eternal spiritual beings within a complex multidimensional reality. Rey has presented this complex evolution leading to spirituality in all of his books including his book on his personal experiences titled "*A Greater Reality: One Man's Journey of Discovery*".

I am a therapist first and researcher second. My role has been to assist the individual to make sense of their own personal journey to connect the dots to their own personal understanding what these experiences mean to them. Initially it is to help them understand and I am a therapist first and researcher second. My role has been to assist the individual to make sense of their own personal journey to connect the dots to their own personal understanding what these experiences mean to them. Initially it is to help them understand and validate, through offering of information of similar accounts, but also to look deeper into their own experiences to help them discover more about their Contact and what this means as they seek to understand pivotal questions such as: Why me?; Who are they?; What is the purpose of this experience? The answers to these crucial questions may take them on a deep spiritual journey into questioning reality and their place in it. The outcomes of "Contact" may lead to huge changes in philosophy, motivation, values and their individual worldviews appear to be pivotal to the experiences including the awakening of "intuitive multidimensional" abilities.

I can be tasked to assist the individuals integrate such changes in perspective and to help the individual manage expanding multidimensional awareness which for some is uncomfortable and challenging depending on their religious and educational programming. There is a deep fear for some that exploring such awareness will cause them to fear they will become mentally ill. This is why *Volumes 3, 4, 5, 6*, the Experiencer chapter books in the "*A Greater Reality*" book series, are incredibly valuable and supportive as it covers many sensitive aspects of Contact.

The challenge to the Experiencer of the Contact Modalities, is how can they embrace their expanding abilities and awareness without losing their sanity. Western society and conventional psychology is still reluctant to accept multidimensional abilities as valid. Hence, many Contact experiences, are mis-judged as fantasy or illness. This means that in many cases the individual will keep such a reality to themselves or share to a few trusted souls. These experiences result in isolation, and often, because of this, many experiencers remain with further doubt or are confused by their experiences.

The "Truth Embargo" on this subject by "authorities", including many in the field of materialist UFOlogy, has done so much damage as it negates the truth of these realities. However as more of this phenomenon has been exposed as true and other paranormal multidimensional realities are accepted, it provides the opportunity for more courageous souls with the plethora of extraordinary accounts of multidimensional experiences to share their stories. Rey's new book on his personal contact experiences and the six volume "*A Greater Reality*" book series, will provide the required revelation to stimulate this new paradigm of thought. All of Rey's books convey how we are interacting with the consciousness matrix, what Rey calls "**The Mind of GOD**". This thesis argues that all is interconnected, all is ONE, that there is no separation from the physical and non-physical realms, all is consciousness.

It is hard for many of us to realize that we are educated into a very limited reality matrix. The awakening of humanity into its true nature is what is now happening. Its challenging us to face all our fears and to be open to what we don't know. *A Greater Reality: The New Paradigm of Nonlocal Consciousness, the Paranormal & the Contact Modalities*, Volumes 3-6, are personal accounts of human experiences with Non-Human Intelligence.

In my opinion, these books will amaze, surprise and raise many questions as to who or what we are. These books will educate us to better understand and appreciate the possibility that we are part of an expanding consciousness within a matrix of awareness. I believe these volumes are a gift to help us explore such questions. Reys contribution and dedication is to bring such profound stories into the light of day.

As I often say to myself "We don't know what we don't know". However, the salient point is as follows, "unless they are true, what point would there be in sharing them?" I recall replying to a TV interviewer on a breakfast TV show some years ago who asked me if I believed the Contact accounts I heard. I replied: **"I have never been to Alaska but if enough people have been there, and shared their stories of going there, then I have to believe Alaska exists."**

There is no reward or publicity for this phenomenon, but more often judgment, isolation and fear. Thus, Rey, and the many courageous individuals who share their truth, need to be commended and supported. For those that resonate or have similar experiences, these extraordinary volumes of Experiencer accounts will give not only validation but hopefully more confidence to share their truth.

Thank you, Rey, for your generosity of spirit in bringing this extraordinary information to the public awareness. A riveting read of all volumes of the *A Greater Reality* book series, will validate and support countless souls who will be grateful for all those who shared so openly their personal lives and for their work and dedication of bringing this valuable information to humanity.

Mary Rodwell
Principal of ACERN (Australian Close Encounter Resource Network)
Author of "*Awakening: How Extraterrestrial Contact Can Transform Your Life*", and "*The New Human: Awakening to Our Cosmic Heritage*"

PROLOGUE

Consciousness & the
Contact Modalities:
Three Moves into Strangeness

Jeffrey J. Kripal, Ph.D.
©2024 Jeffrey J. Kripal, Ph.D.

I am happy and honored to be asked to write a brief Prologue for the six volume book series, *"A Greater Reality: The New Paradigm of Nonlocal Consciousness, the Paranormal & the Contact Modalities"*. As a historian of religions, that is, as someone charged with the task of taking *everyone's* extraordinary experience seriously and not just this or that culture's convictions, I have encountered almost all of the exceptional events described in these six volumes in some form or another, either in living people or textual deposits. So, I have been thinking about these matters for some time, decades really. I have also been watching contemporaries react to them, often not so well, often, alas, rather dumbly.

Not here. Rey Hernandez and his colleagues, most who are well known Ph.D. academics and medical doctors, treat an exceptionally broad range of these experiences of transcendence. Rey calls them the *"Contact Modalities"*, a term that he has coined, and speculates that they all have something to do with the primacy of consciousness or

Mind as the fundamental base of reality. I strongly suspect that they are correct, or correct enough. I also suspect that, once we take such Contact Modalities seriously and what they imply about our place in the universe, things are going to get stranger, *way* stranger.

Are we ready for that? I think there are three moves into strangeness that we very much need to make, all of which are made in this important six volume book series, **A Greater Reality** and in his personal accounts of his experiences via the Contact Modalities, titled "**A Greater Reality: One Man's Journey of Discovery**".

The first move involves the realization that *all of these* **Contact Modalities are connected.** In fact, everything is connected to everything, but this is especially true in this twilight zone. This move, I want to suggest, is one of the real markers that separates the novice from the mature thinker and Rey and his research colleagues are certainly one of these mature thinkers. The novices think that their particular specialty is somehow a specialty, that it is set apart from all of that other "crazy" stuff. You know, UFOs are real, but Bigfoot is not. Or maybe telepathy happens, but certainly not precognition. And forget about levitation. That sort of thing.

The seasoned thinkers are not so tricked. They know that the UFO phenomenon and the NDE phenomenon are not the same, but that they are also definitely connected. So are parapsychological phenomenon (precognition, clairvoyance, remote viewing, even levitation, teleportation, and bilocation). So are spectral presences of every kind (from ghosts, angels, and demons to cryptids and monsters). The more one knows, the weirder it gets. Things, in actual fact, never really "makes sense," and for one glaringly simple reason: such phenomena have little to do with the five senses.

The second move we very much need to make involves the realization that *the imaginal is the Contact Modality*. Put a bit less elliptically, once we realize that everything is connected, we have to come up with a model that explain why all of these things are connected *but are also so different*. We have to become comparativists. This is one of the hardest things for people to do in my experience. The believer wants to believe. The debunker wants to debunk. Neither can recognize the partial truth of the other. Neither can hear the secret—that the imaginal is a symbolic translator, a medium of communication, the dimension of consciousness that connects all of the dots.

By invoking the imaginal, I do not mean that these things are "imaginary." I mean rather that, under very special circumstances, the human imagination is somehow empowered and becomes, for a while, not a spinner of fantasy but a medium of contact. What this means in turn is that no such contact modality should be interpreted literally but all should be interpreted really. Do not confuse the dream with the dreamer, but recognize that the dream *is* the dreamer, or rather is a symbolic expression and art form of the dreamer.

To invoke a simple metaphor, I have used in other contexts, these Contact Modalities are all functioning like the stain glass windows of the church in which I grew up as a kid. The images and stories told in that glass are all culturally and religiously specific, as is the lead and glass art that constructed the windows many moons ago. But the sun that shines through them is neither culturally determined nor locally specific. And, of course, other places of worship will have other kinds of stain glass windows with other images and stories. What unites them all is the same sunlight shining through them and the subsequent process of artistic illumination and local mediation. There is real difference. And there is real sameness. But, in order to balance these two truths, one needs to recognize the artistic expression, the translation, the medium of contact. Otherwise, one will simply be confused, focusing on the images in the glass as literally true (the believer) or as obviously absurd (the debunker).

The third move involves what comes after, speculative ontology, that is, the positing of new models of reality and, specifically, new models of reality that are not strictly physicalist or reductive, that is, that do not frame everything as causal products of material reality. In our present reigning model, essentially different forms of scientism, most all of these extraordinary things are not extraordinary at all. They are simply impossible. They cannot happen. And so, or so we are told, they don't. But they do.

As you read through the remarkable academic essays contained in Volumes one and two and the Experiencer essays contained in Volumes three to six of the *A Greater Reality* book series, you will see the gifted authors making these same three moves. They make them in different ways and toward different ends, but the six volumes as a whole shout their triple truths. It is all connected. The imaginal is the contact modality. And we need to imagine new realities in order to bring these strange things into belief, acceptance, and, eventually, human knowledge.

Bio: Dr. Jeffrey J. Kripal is the Associate Dean of the School of Humanities and holds the J. Newton Rayzor Chair in Philosophy and Religious Thought at Rice University, where he chaired the Department of Religion for eight years and helped create the GEM Program, a doctoral concentration in the study of Gnosticism, Esotericism, and Mysticism that is the largest program of its kind in the world. Jeff is the author or co-author of eleven books, seven of which are with The University of Chicago Press, including, most recently a memoir manifesto entitled "***Secret Body: Erotic and Esoteric Currents in the History of Religions***" (The University of Chicago Press, 2017). He is presently working on a three-volume study of paranormal currents in the history of religions and the sciences for The University of Chicago Press, collectively entitled "***The Super Story***".

Website: **https://jeffreyjkripal.com/life/**

Introduction to Volumes 3, 4, 5 & 6:

The Experiencer Chapters for

"A Greater Reality: The New Paradigm of Nonlocal Consciousness, the Paranormal, and the Contact Modalities"

Reinerio (Rey) Hernandez
JD, MCP, ex-PhD Candidate UC Berkeley

Our 6-Volume book, titled *A GREATER REALITY: The New Paradigm of Nonlocal Consciousness, the Paranormal & the Contact Modalities,* is comprised of 6 volumes. Each volume is approximately 800 pages each. The introduction to this 6 volume book series is titled *The Mind of GOD: A Spiritual-Virtual Reality Model of Consciousness & The Contact Modalities* and is published as a separate book.

Volumes 1 & 2 are our theoretical volumes and feature articles by more than 45 Ph.D. academics, medical doctors, and researchers who focus on researching the connection between Consciousness and the Contact Modalities.

Volumes 3, 4, 5 & 6 features articles written by more than 75 major Experiencers of the Contact Modalities who each have had many diverse contact experiences with perceived Higher Forms of Intelligence via the Contact Modalities. These individuals have written a summary of their diverse paranormal experiences with many different Contact Modalities.

A GREATER REALITY aims to articulate a new paradigm that seeks to integrate the findings of consciousness research and the phenomenology of extraordinary experiences, what we at the **Consciousness and Contact Research Institute (CCRI)** call the **Contact Modalities. CCRI** is an academic research institute, comprised of 25 Ph.D. academics, medical doctors, and researchers, committed to an integrative approach to the entire spectrum of psychophysical anomalies. In the future, we hope to undertake a comprehensive academic statistical research study, in multiple languages, administered on a worldwide scale, to Experiencers of the Contact Modalities. We hold that it is the Experiencers of the Contact Modalities that may provide humanity with clues as to the question of "**What is Consciousness-- What is the nature of our reality**"-- a question that has been addressed by the academic fields of Philosophy, Neuroscience,

Psychiatry, Psychology, Theoretical Physics, Theology, and by humanity at large since the dawn of human existence.

In their contact experiences via the Contact Modalities, these individuals have had experiences that can be considered multidimensional where they experienced a manipulation of space-time and where they have had a diverse array of contact experiences with Higher Forms of Intelligence. Another term I use interchangeably with Higher Forms of Intelligence is the term Non-Human Intelligence-- which can be defined as all higher forms of intelligence that are not physical human beings living in our physical Earthly reality. Examples of Non-Human Intelligence can be as follows: perceived deceased human beings, spiritual beings and guides, demons, extraterrestrials, arch angels, fairies, and thousands of different physical and non-physical forms of Higher Forms of Intelligence seen by humanity over the ages. These experiences involve contact with a cornucopia of an almost infinite community of conscious sentient beings. For example, the FREE academic research study, the world's first and only comprehensive, statistical, worldwide, academic research study on UFO Contact Experiencers, demonstrated that the 4,350 individuals from over 125 countries who took our 3 surveys, saw thousands of **different** types of physical beings.

In my book, ***The Mind of GOD: A Spiritual-Virtual Model of Consciousness & the Contact Modalities***, I argue that these contact experiences can be seen as extensions of the Universal Mind of GOD, as an extension of "Consciousness" itself, our multi-dimensional reality, instead of the hypothesis that these are "physical beings who are visiting us from thousands of different physical planets". The overwhelming number of these physical contact experiences on our Earthly plane, with thousands of different types of physical "beings", interact with humans for at most a few seconds to less than one minute. Yet, the majority of Experiencers and researchers of the paranormal Contact Modalities, perceive these experiences as physical experiences instead of conscious-based experiences. The issue of whether these experiences are physical, consciousness-based, or both, was detailed in my book *The Mind of GOD*, which serves as the formal introduction to the *A GREATER REALITY* six volume book series.[1]

The majority of academic authors and researchers in Volume One and Volume Two of our book, *A Greater Reality*, view these contact experiences with Higher Forms of Intelligence via the Contact Modalities as ONE consciousness-based phenomenon and not necessarily as many diverse physical-based phenomena. While we, as humans living in our Earthly physical reality, perceive these experiences as merely physical, in fact these experiences involve a symbiosis between our 5 physical senses within our 4-dimensional space and our multidimensional consciousness-based reality.[2] Unfortunately, given the physical limitations of the human body, we are not able to perceive our Greater Reality, a reality involving a hierarchy of multiple dimensions under the One Mind of GOD, Consciousness itself. In Volume One of *A Greater Reality* and in *The Mind of GOD*, I argue that we are living in a multi-dimensional spiritual and virtual reality, a reality that Dr. Edgar Mitchell termed the "*Quantum Hologram*", and that our individuated units of consciousness (our spirit/soul) can travel within these many dimensions, or astral planes, within this "Greater Reality". Examples of this thesis are Near Death Experiences, Out of Body Experiences, Astral Travel Experiences, Remote Viewing and all forms of Clairvoyance, and many other

---

[1] Reinerio Hernandez. (2022) *The Mind of GOD: A Spiritual-Virtual Reality Model of Consciousness & The Contact Modalities*. Amazon Press

[2] 4-dimensional space can be briefly defined as the 3 dimensions of Euclidean Space plus the additional dimension of spacetime, as defined by Albert Einstein. We now commonly coin the concept of 4-dimensional space as "Space-Time", also written as spacetime.)

paranormal" contact experiences, including CAP-UFO Contact Experiences.[3]

All of the **Contact Modalities** experiences involve a manipulation of space-time. Not only can human consciousness travel within this "Greater Reality" to other dimensions of existence, but the consciousness of a vast array of Non-Human Intelligence can also travel within this Greater Reality into our physical reality. Example of this is the CAP-UFO contact phenomenon and the physical sighting of deceased humans, commonly called ghosts or spirits. In fact, tens of thousands of **DIFFERENT FORMS** of "physical beings" have been described in the hundreds of books in the field of Ufology, in the literature on ghosts/spirits, in the NDE and OBE literature and in the "paranormal" literature. The human consciousness of Experiencers of the Contact Modalities has also been brought by Higher Forms of Intelligence to other astral realms, also called multidimensional realities, where they have received consistent and similar messages of Unity, Oneness, Spirituality, and the need for humanity to become a more loving species and to promote love for each other and for our mother Earth. I am a witness to this type of personal human consciousness Astral Travel Experience. This experience seems incredulous to almost all of humanity but once you have had a similar experience you are no longer a skeptic.

---

[3]I argue throughout this book, and all of my other books, that the UAP/UFO phenomenon is a consciousness-based phenomenon. Thus, instead of the term UAP or UFO, terms that do not define nor explain the phenomenon as one that is consciousness-based, my preferred term is **CAP or Consciousness Aerial Phenomenon**. This term is much more explanatory of the true nature of the phenomenon. Therefore, throughout all of my books, I use the term **CAP-UFO (Consciousness Aerial Phenomenon)** to signify what is commonly called the UFO Phenomenon. I will articulate on this new term later in this chapter.

The academic researchers of CCRI have concluded that only by understanding the Experiencers of the Contact Modalities can one begin to fully understand the nature of our Greater Reality. Scientists, Ph.D. Physicists, Ph.D. Neuroscientists, and Ph.D. Philosophers cannot address the riddle of "*What is Consciousness*" but the information from Experiencers of the Contact Modalities can lead us in the proper direction of addressing these questions: "**What is Consciousness?**", "**What is the Nature of our Reality?**" and "**How can humanity begin the process of preventing its self-destructive behavior?**"

In the Fall of 2013, I introduced the term the "**Contact Modalities**".[4] This term is now used by many researchers instead of the term "paranormal" because many major academic researchers, including most of the Ph.D. academics, medical doctors and researchers within CCRI, have long suspected that all of what we call the "paranormal" is actually ONE integrated phenomenon under Consciousness involving a manipulation of space-time. The term "paranormal" does not provide a consciousness-based explanation of the phenomenon while the term Contact Modalities suggests that all of these contact experiences should be viewed and researched as one integrated phenomenon under the rubric of consciousness.

---

[4]In the Fall of 2013, I introduced the term "**The Contact Modalities**" when I published an article in the Dr. Edgar Mitchell FREE Foundation website, *Experiencer.Org*, titled "*The Quantum Hologram Theory of Consciousness and the Contact Modalities*." I wrote this paper shortly after I had an Astral Travel Experience (ATE), while I was driving my car in a traffic jam and where I was shown the relationship between Consciousness and the Contact Modalities. Please note that the FREE Foundation website no longer exists and is replaced by the CCRI website, **https://agreaterreality.com/**. I continued to use this term in two peer-reviewed academic articles published in the *Journal of Conscientiology* and in the *Journal of Scientific Exploration* and in my co-edited book, published in May of 2018, titled *Beyond UFOs: The Science of Consciousness and Contact with Non-Human Intelligence*. I continue using this term in my new book, "*A Greater Reality*". Since 2013, my understanding of the term the Contact Modalities and my hypothesis on the question, "What is Consciousness", has undergone a profound evolution which is now being presented in my new books, *The Mind of GOD* and *A Greater Reality*.

The term "**Contact Modalities**" is defined as "*all of the diverse ways that humans are 'piercing the veil' of our physical reality and having perceived contact with consciousness-based Higher Forms of Intelligence*". Examples of the Contact Modalities are as follows: Near-Death Experiences (NDEs), Out of Body Experiences (OBEs), Astral Travel Experiences (ATE), which are very different from OBEs, Conscious Aerial Phenomena (CAP-UFOs), (commonly called UFOs), contact experiences with perceived deceased humans (commonly called Ghosts or Spirits), contact experiences via Hallucinogenic Journeys (via entheogens such as DMT, Psilocybin, LSD, etc.), contact experiences via Remote Viewing or other forms of clairvoyance, contact experiences via Channeling or Mediumship, contact via the many forms of Post Death Communications, contact experiences via Lucid Dreams, contact via perceived Poltergeists experiences or spiritual attachments, and many other types of "paranormal" contact experiences with tens of thousands of diverse forms of Non-Human Intelligence.

The CCRI Ph.D. academics and medical doctors (MDs) also hold the view that "**Consciousness is Primary and that our physical world is a manifestation of Consciousness and not our physical reality**". This hypothesis was articulated and defined in Volumes One and Two of the *A Greater Reality* book series and in my book *The Mind of GOD*.

Before we continue, I want to clarify my use of the term UFOs or Unidentified Flying Objects. This is not a very appropriate term for this phenomenon. First of all, these perceived physical objects do not "fly". Secondly, even though these objects are perceived as "physical", the Dr. Edgar Mitchell FREE UFO Experiencer Research Study confirmed that these perceived "UFO crafts" might not necessarily be physical objects. This is also the hypothesis by the fathers of modern Ufology, Dr. J. Allen Hynek (in the later years of his life), Dr. Jacque Vallee, and numerous other Ufologists such as John Keel, Raymond Fowler, Dr. Leo Sprinkle, Dr. John Mack, Brad Steiger, and numerous Ph.D.

academics such as Dr. Jon Klimo, Dr. Edgar Mitchell, Dr. Rudy Schild, Dr. Kenneth Ring, Dr. Jeffrey Mishlove, Dr. Jeffrey Kripal, Dr. Joseph Burkes, Dr. Michael Grosso, Dr. John Alexander, Dr. Edith Fiore, Dr. Peter Sturrock, Dr. Glen Rein, Dr. Raul Valverde, Dr. Massimo Teodorani, Coast to Coast radio show host George Knapp, and many others. Instead, all of these scientists, Ph.D. academics, medical doctors, researchers and I hypothesize that UFOs and UFO intelligence, might not be a physical "craft" operated by an "alien being" from a physical planet. Instead, the hypothesis held by the majority of the authors in *A Greater Reality*, and all of the previously mentioned individuals, is that ALL of the Contact Modalities are ONE integrated phenomenon under Consciousness and that the perceived CAP-UFO might be a consciousness-based phenomenon involving both a perceived physical and a psychic (consciousness-based) component. This hypothesis is articulated further in this book and in Volumes 1 and 2 of the *A Greater Reality* book series and in my book *The Mind of GOD*.

The findings of the "**Dr. Edgar Mitchell FREE Foundation UFO Contact Experiencer Research Study**" were published in 2018 in our historic 820-page academic book titled *Beyond UFOs: The Science of Consciousness and Contact with Non-Human Intelligence*. This book demonstrated that a small percentage of the 4,350 participants from more than 125 countries, who participated in our 3 surveys, saw a physical "flying saucer".[5] The overwhelming majority saw thousands of different "light or energy configurations" which were not perceived as a physical flying craft.

More recently, US military intelligence has used the term UAP, or Unidentified Aerial Phenomenon, instead of the term UFO. While UAP is a better term, this term also ignores the consciousness-based

---

[5]Hernandez, R., R. Schild & J. Klimo, eds. (2018). *Beyond UFOs: The Science of Consciousness and Contact with Non-Human Intelligence*. Create Space Independent Publishing (Amazon Press).

aspects of the phenomenon. I argue throughout this 4 volume book series, similar to the numerous UFO researchers and Ph.D. academics previously cited, that the UAP/UFO phenomenon is a consciousness-based phenomenon. Thus, instead of the term UAP or UFO, terms that do not define nor explain the phenomenon as one that is consciousness-based, my preferred term is **CAP or Consciousness Aerial Phenomenon**. This term is much more explanatory of the true nature of the phenomenon. Throughout my writings, I will use the term **CAP-UFO (Consciousness Aerial Phenomenon)** to signify what is commonly called the UFO Phenomenon. In my book, *The Mind of GOD*, I detailed my arguments for the use of this new term CAP-UFO instead of the term UFO or UAP.

In 2019, the Dr. Edgar Mitchell FREE Foundation was replaced by the **Consciousness and Contact Research Institute**, or **CCRI**. The 25 members of CCRI include academics in the fields of Astrophysics, Philosophy, Psychiatry, Psychology, Neuroscience, Sociology, Quantum Biology, Information Sciences, Theology, and Parapsychology. The five co-authors of our 5-volume books of *A Greater Reality* are as follows: **Dr. Rudy Schild**, who is a retired Harvard University Astrophysicist, **Dr. Jeffrey Long**, a Medical Doctor and noted NDE researcher, **Dr. Michael Grosso**, a retired professor of Philosophy, who has authored many books on Consciousness and the "Paranormal", **Dr. Jon Klimo**, a retired professor of Psychology for more than 45 years who has also authored countless books and articles on the topics of Consciousness and the "Paranormal", **Dr. Joseph Burkes**, a retired Medical Doctor and longtime UFO Experiencer, researcher and author, and yours truly, **Reinerio (Rey) Hernandez**, a now retired US federal attorney, an ex-Ph.D. Candidate at the University of California at Berkeley and researcher on the relationship between Consciousness and the Contact Modalities.[6]

---

[6]Please refer to the CCRI website where you can read more about the many authors in our book. Our website is: **AGreaterReality.Com**

The academics and medical doctors of CCRI argue that "Mind" and Consciousness are fundamental, non-local, and that matter, energy, and information are ultimately grounded in "One Mind" and Consciousness. For a materialist, these are not easy concepts to grasp but these concepts have been articulated by numerous Nobel Prize winners in Physics, Nobel Prize winners in Medicine and Physiology, and Ph.D. academics in the fields of physics, astrophysics, biochemistry, engineering, and Ph.D. academics in almost all of the social sciences. These concepts are not "woo woo" science but concepts that have been articulated by various Nobel Prize winning Ph.D. physicists such as Max Plank (Nobel Prize in Physics, 1918); Erwin Schrödinger (Nobel Prize in Physics, 1933); Niels Bohr (Nobel Prize in Physics, 1922); Werner Heisenberg (Nobel Prize in Physics, 1932), Eugene Wigner (Nobel Prize in Physics, 1963); Charles H. Townes (Nobel Prize in physics, 1964), and other physics pioneers such as Sir James Jeans, Sir Arthur Eddington, and David Bohm. All of these geniuses spoke about the topic of Consciousness, our ONE Mind. The Consciousness writings of each of these noted pioneers of modern physics are discussed in my book, *The Mind of GOD: A Spiritual-Virtual Reality Model of Consciousness & the Contact Modalities*.

The *A Greater Reality* book series introduces the post-materialist hypothesis that "Consciousness is Primary" -- the philosophical position that the only thing that exists is consciousness and that our physical reality is derived from consciousness.[7] This is the philosophical hypothesis held by almost all of the authors in our 2-volume theoretical books in our *A Greater Reality* book series. Volume One of our book series also includes numerous academic articles discussing the topic "**Is Consciousness Primary?**"

---

[7]Schwartz, S., M. Woollacott & G. Schwartz, eds. (2020). *Is Consciousness Primary? Perspectives from Founding Members of the Academy for the Advancement of Postmaterialist Sciences*, Vol 1. AAPS Press.

We also hypothesize that all of the Contact Modalities are interrelated via a manipulation of spacetime, involving a spiritual and virtual reality and by definition might be multidimensional in nature.[8] We argue that there is a range of states of consciousness, the Contact Modalities, where we, as individuated units of human consciousness, can access both non-physical and physical realms, where we interact with perceived Non-Human Intelligence via our ordinary senses within this "Greater Reality". Clear examples of this include the well documented Near-Death Experience and Out of Body phenomenon. Numerous theories might explain this greater reality but our book argues that we are living inside a "Spiritual-Virtual Reality" as detailed in the 5 volumes of our book.

I presented a model of our "Spiritual-Virtual Reality" in Volume One of our 6 volume book series and in my book "*The Mind of GOD*". We argue that our perceived physical experiences, via our 5 senses, are actually "Maya", an illusion where things appear to be physical but are not what they seem to be. This concept of "Maya", an illusion, was defined and detailed in Volume One of our books, *A Greater Reality*, in the section titled "*Is Consciousness Primary-- A Brief History of Idealism*". Why is our material reality an illusion? The answer is that our true reality, and our personal individuated unit of consciousness, are part of a larger living system inside a "Greater Reality"-- part of a larger consciousness system which I have coined "*The Mind of GOD*". For all of these reasons, we assert that the Contact Modalities need to be studied as **ONE PHENOMENON**-- as manifestations of a single greater source of mind and consciousness. For further clarification on these complex topics, please refer to Volume One of *A Greater Reality* and to my separate book titled *The Mind of GOD*.

---

[8]The terms multidimensional and interdimensional will be defined and discussed throughout our 6-volume book of *A Greater Reality*.

Introduction to the CAP-UFO Contact Research

Reinerio (Rey) Hernandez

JD, MCP, ex-PhD Candidate UC Berkeley
©2024 Reinerio (Rey) Hernandez

The vast majority of the experiencers writing articles in Volumes 3-6 of the *A Greater Reality* book series have had many diverse types of contact experiences via the Contact Modalities. They have had Near Death Experiences, Out of Body Experiences, Astral Travel Experiences, Hallucinogenic contact experiences, they have seen perceived ghosts/spirits, among many other experiences via the Contact Modalities. Approximately 3/4ths of the Experiencer authors in Volumes 3-6 have had CAP-UFO-related contact experiences.[9] All of the UFO Contact Experiencer authors have also had other types of contact experiences via the Contact Modalities. Because the CAP-UFO contact aspect of the Contact Modalities is such a large component of these articles, It is important to educate the readers about the CAP-UFO academic research data on this phenomenon.

---

[9] I argue throughout this book, and all of my other books, that the UAP/UFO phenomenon is a consciousness-based phenomenon. Thus, instead of the term UAP or UFO, terms that do not define nor explain the phenomenon as one that is consciousness-based, my preferred term is **CAP or Consciousness Aerial Phenomenon**. This term is much more explanatory of the true nature of the phenomenon. Therefore, throughout all of my books, I use the term **CAP-UFO (Consciousness Aerial Phenomenon)** to signify what is commonly called the UFO Phenomenon. I will articulate on this new term later in this chapter.

The majority of the researchers in the field of "Ufology" are materialists-- they hold the belief that the CAP-UFO related contact hybridization program on human beings. Three prominent Ufology researchers, David Jacobs, Budd Hopkins, and Richard Dolan, argue that 100% of CAP-UFO Contact Experiences are negative and that they result in highly traumatized individuals who suffer from a lifetime of trauma and fear. **David Jacobs, in particular, has argued that he has NEVER met a CAP-UFO contact experiencer that has had a positive experience-- NEVER!** Today, with the rampant circulation of conspiracy theories on the internet, we now understand that if you repeat a lie over, and over, and over again, the lie will eventually become a "fact" in the mind of the intended audience.

In their hundreds of radio interviews and numerous presentations at major CAP-UFO conferences over the last 40 years, David Jacobs, Budd Hopkins, Richard Dolan and other "Abduction" researchers have articulated negative views of the UFO contact phenomenon, and in turn, these lies, misinformation and disinformation began to establish the mainstream view within Ufology that all CAP-UFO contact involves an abduction by a physical being from a physical planet and that all abductions are highly negative experiences involving the hybridization of humanity.

All of this propaganda is sheer nonsense which was destroyed by the only academically derived data of the 5 year academic research study of the '***Dr. Edgar Mitchell FREE Foundation UFO Experiencer Research Study***" which was published in our historic 820-page academic book "***Beyond UFOs***". In addition, the two principal pioneers of Ufology, Dr. J. Allen Hynek and Dr. Jacques Vallee, have dismissed the traditional view of the Alien Abduction Phenomenon as documented in their numerous recorded testimonies and books.

The majority in the field of Ufology, in particular Richard Dolan, one of the most well-known materialist Ufologists, has supported the work of Budd Hopkins and in particular David Jacobs. **In one of his radio shows in 2018, Dolan stated that David Jacobs was the "best researcher" in the CAP-UFO contact phenomenon field.**[10] The YouTube video that Richard Dolan released his interview with David Jacobs had the title "**This Planet will be Theirs, interview with Dr. David Jacobs, the Richard Dolan Show**". The interview date was December 10, 2018. The interview begins as follows:

> *"Welcome to the Richard Dolan show… My guest for this program is Dr. David Jacobs. I think that Dr. David Jacobs is **unquestionably the world's leading researcher in the generally neglected field of alien abduction**… His take is that it is not just bad, it is very bad… He states that we are in the midst of what he called a planetary acquisition… **David is remarkably careful, and yes, scientific in his approach**…"*

It is important to restate that David Jacobs has publicly stated in numerous of his recorded radio interviews over the last 30 years that **he has NEVER met a CAP-UFO contact experiencer with a positive experience-- NEVER!** In Volumes 3-6 of the A Greater Reality book series, you will learn that **EVERYONE** of the UFO Contact Experiencers view their UFO Contact Experience as highly positive and highly spiritually transformative. In this article you will understand the reasons for this wide gap of opinons on the UFO Contact Phenomenon.

---

[10]Richard Dolan interviews David Jacobs.
https://www.youtube.com/watch?v=xQE6qkwfaGo

Richard Dolan, based upon his relationship with David Jacobs, Budd Hopkins, and many of the so-called "Abduction Researchers", also claims to know what is "The Alien Agenda". In 2020 Dolan published a book titled "*The Alien Agenda*" even though he has never done any primary research on the CAP-UFO contact phenomena nor has he conducted any academic statistical research on this phenomenon. All of conducted any academic statistical research on this phenomenon. All of his research was based upon secondary sources derived via the hypnotic regression work of David Jacobs, Budd Hopkins and other Alien Abduction hypnotic regression researchers and not on any academic statistical research or any primary research on UFO Contact Experiencers. An old saying in academic statistical research can be applied to the case of Dolan, Jacobs and Hopkins: "**Junk In and Junk Out**".

Yet, Dolan, whose book "*The Alien Agenda*" has sold tens of thousands of copies, has presented these claims at numerous CAP-UFO conferences, radio interviews, and his Netflix and Ancient Alien appearances over many years. It is the view of Hopkins, Jacobs and Dolan that pervades the field of modern materialist Ufology-- a view that was dismissed by the Fathers of Modern Ufology, Dr. J. Allen Hynek (last years of his life), Dr. Jacques Valle, and Dr. John Mack (in his book "*Passport to the Cosmos*"). The world's only comprehensive academic statistical research study on UFO Contact Experiencers, conducted by the academics and researchers of the Dr. Edgar Mitchell FREE Foundation, have also dismantled and dismissed the views of Jacobs, Hopkins and Dolan.

Are the views of Jacobs, Hopkins and Dolan correct-- that CAP-UFO Contact Experience with Non-Human Intelligence (NHI) result in highly negative experiences from physical ET beings? Are all of these contact experiences negative? Are these so-called beings conducting alien hybridization on the human species? Are these "beings" physical beings from other planets? Neither Jacobs, Hopkins, Dolan, nor any other Alien Abduction researcher, has ever conducted a comprehensive academic worldwide statistical research study on CAP-UFO Contact Experiencers. All of the data presented by Hopkins and Jacobs has been based on pre-selecting individuals for hypnotic regressions, in particular individuals that perceive their experiences to be a negative phenomenon. Anyone that had a positive or neutral experience were dismissed and not invited to one of their hypnotic regression sessions.

Yet Richard Dolan states that David Jacobs is unquestionably the best researcher in the field and that "***David is remarkably careful, and yes, scientific in his approach.***" Let's investigate whether Dolan's statements are an accurate assesment on the "research methodology" of David Jacobs and Budd Hopkins and whether his views reflect the data from UFO Contact Experiencers.

The wife of Budd Hopkins, Carol Rainey, in her article in Volume 3 of the ***A Greater Reality*** book series, titled "***Priests of High Strangeness: Co-Creation of the "Alien Abduction Phenomenon"***. Her article highlights numerous examples of how Hopkins and Jacobs, through their biased work, created an environmenet of misinformation and disinformation which resulted in the creation of a fictionalized "***Alien Abduction Phenomenon***". I highly recommend this article written by the ex-wife of Budd Hopkins to get a better understanding of the biased work of Hopkins, Jacobs and their supporter, Richard Dolan.

It was not until the formation of the Dr. Edgar Mitchell FREE Foundation UFO Experiencer Research Study (FREE Research Study) that the contact phenomenon was studied academically and statistically for the first time. Before the FREE research study, there were no previous comprehensive, worldwide, statistical, academic research of CAP-UFO Contact Experiencers. There were small studies on CAP-UFOs, on perceived "physical crafts", such as the Condon Report, but never a comprehensive worldwide academic statistical research study on CAP-UFO contact experiencers-- Never! Some of the previous small studies focused solely on "abductees". In addition, some of these previous research studies on UFO Contact Experiencers had at most 50 respondents and had less than 50 questions-- all related questions focused on a physical abduction. These studies were severely limited because they focused only on so-called abductees and because of the small preselected sample size of 50 individuals and the 50 questions, focused on the abduction phenomenon.

The FREE Research Study represents the first comprehensive academic multi-language and cross-cultural statistical investigation of individuals who have reported to have seen a UFO and have had various forms of UFO related Contact Experiences with Non-Human Intelligence. The FREE research committee, comprised of more than 8 Ph.D. academics and 8 CAP-UFO non-academic researchers, developed 2 quantitative surveys, comprised of 700 questions, and a qualitative survey, comprised of 70 open-ended questions. FREE received more than 4,350 responses from individuals from more than 125 countries for our English language surveys. Our Spanish language surveys had responses from an additional 1,200 Spanish speaking respondents. Our research was much more comprehensive than the previous research studies that had only 50 questions and received responses from only 50 individuals who claimed to have had an abduction experience.

Our FREE research study findings contradict almost all of the views currently held by mainstream materialist Ufology and the "alien abduction researchers". Thus, the FREE research study is the only game in town and the data findings from this academic research study totally contradict all of the abduction hypnotic regression information presented by Hopkins, Jacobs, Dolan and the other "abduction reseachers". These data findings were published in 2018 in the academic book titled "*Beyond UFOs: The Science of Consciousness and Contact with Non-Human Intelligence*".[11]

As previously noted, this book is available for FREE as a PDF file in the CCRI website: **AGreaterReality.Com**. If you want a paperback copy or an eBook such as Kindle, you can purchase a copy via Amazon.

Even though there is no other statistical research study on UFO Contact Experiencers, our book *Beyond UFOs* has sold only a few hundred copies since its publication in 2018 but meanwhile, the books by Dolan, Jacobs and Hopkins have sold hundreds of thousands of copies. In addition, these individuals were invited to hundreds of UFO conferences and radio shows over the last 40 years. Yet, the Ph.D. academics of FREE, including Dr. Edgar Mitchell, Dr. Rudy Schild, Dr. Jon Klimo, Dr. Bob Davis, and others, were never invited to a UFO conference or radio show. So much for academic research! As usual, conspiracy theories, fear mongering stories, outright lies, misinformation, and disinformation have reigned supreme in the field of materialist Ufology and this worldview of "*Alien Abductions*" resulting in a "*Hybridization of Alien Babies*" has remained the predominant view within the field of mainstream materialist Ufology.

---

[11]Hernandez, R., R. Schild & J. Klimo, eds. (2018). *Beyond UFOs: The Science of Consciousness and Contact with Non-Human Intelligence*. CreateSpace Independent Publishing (Amazon Press).

For these reasons, in my opinion, the field of materialist Ufology remains clueless of the complexities of the UFO contact phenomenon and for this reason other Ph.D. academics and scientists have totally dismissed the field of materialist Ufology, certainly almost all of the academics associated with CCRI-- academics whose primary research agenda is on the topic of "**What is the relationship between Consciousness and the paranormal Contact Modalities**".

In order to have participated in our FREE Research Study, the participant must have been able to respond to these two questions:

1) the participant must have seen a CAP-UFO, commonly called a UFO or UAP, and must describe what he saw and the details regarding the sighting, and

2) the participant must have had a "contact experience" with a Non-Human Intelligence-- the contact can be contact with a perceived "physical being" or the contact can be via a "telepathic communication".

The above-referenced FREE data collected from thousands of "Contact Experiencers" clearly indicates that CAP-UFO Contact is overwhelmingly a positive experience and that the majority of individuals call themselves "*Contactees*" instead of "abductees". Out of the 4,350 UFO Contact Experiencers from more than 125 countries who took our 3 surveys **only 5% claimed that their experiences were negative-- that is it, only 5%. Hopkins in particular has claimed that he has NEVER met a UFO Contact Experiencer that has had a positive experience. So much for the so-called hypnotic regression "research" of Dolan, Jacobs and Hopkins!**

In addition, over 85% of these contact experiencers have claimed that they have undergone a dramatic positive transformation of their values and worldviews. Such transformations include an increase in spirituality, they became more loving and caring to others, they became more ecologically friendly, they no longer cared about acquiring material wealth, they became more consciously aware, they no longer feared death, and this was just a few of the more than 70 transformational questions we asked. We borrowed these 70 questions from the work of Ph.D. academic Dr. Kenneth Ring [12] in his work "***The Omega Project: Near-Death Experiences, UFO Encounters, and Mind at Large***".[13] The data findings from the FREE surveys matched the data findings from Dr. Ring's statistical research findings.

Over 84% of those that took the FREE surveys stated that they did not want their CAP-UFO Contact Experiences to end. 70% claimed that their CAP-UFO contact experiences changed their lives in a "positive way". The data also did NOT reveal any evidence of a hybridization of humanity like David Jacobs has alluded to. In fact, over 67% stated that they have seen CAP-UFOs and have seen a perceived Non-Human Intelligence but they never had an "abduction". Of the 30% that stated that they "initially" thought that they had a perceived abduction experience, over 70% of these individuals now claim their experiences were highly positive and that they now consider themselves a "Contactee" instead of an "Abductee".

---

[12] Dr. Kenneth Ring is Professor Emeritus of Psychology at the University of Connecticut, and an internationally recognized authority on the subject of near-death experiences, a topic where he has written five books and nearly a hundred articles. He is also the co-founder and past President of The International Association for Near-Death Studies and the founding editor of its quarterly scholarly journal, ***The Journal of Near-Death Studies***.

[13]Ring, K. (1992). ***The Omega Project: Near-Death Experiences, UFO Encounters, and Mind at Large***. William Morrow and Co.

Thus, 70% of the 30% who initially thought they had an "alien abduction" experience now perceive their experiences as a positive contact experience and not as a negative abduction experience. Remember, David Jacobs has publicly stated that he has NEVER met a UFO Contact Experiencer who has had a positive experience— NEVER! Yet Richard Dolan has stated that Jacobs is "**unquestionably the world's leading researcher in the generally neglected field of alien abduction**" and that "**David is remarkably careful, and yes, scientific in his approach.**" For Dolan, hynotic regression from a biased reseacher, who preselects the person he wants to interview and who asks one leading question after another, is superior to a non-biased statistical academic research study developed and supervised by various Ph.D. academic professors.

The overwhelming majority of the UFO contact experiencers now state that they are not an abductee but instead they now call themselves a "Contactee" and that their experiences were overwhelmingly positive. All of the data for these statements are presented in Chapter One of our book "***Beyond UFOs***". **So much for the views of Dolan, Jacobs and Hopkins that _ALL_ UFO Contact Experiences are negative!**

One additional and important research finding is that the CAP-UFO contact experiences are primarily "paranormal" experiences instead of physical experiences. The numerous articles in Volume 3-6 of our *A Greater Reality* book series also confirm this fact. Raymond Fowler, a UFO researcher, who has spent over 60 years researching UFO Contact Experiencers, presents hundreds of examples supporting the hypothesis that UFO contact is primarily a "paranormal" experience instead of primarily a physical experience. Raymond Fowler's article, presented in Volume 4 of the *A Greater Reality* book series, clearly substantiates the hypothesis that the UFO Contact Phenomenon is primarily a Consciousness-based "paranormal" phenomenon involving the Contact Modalities, including a relationship between CAP-UFOs,

Out of Body Experiences and the Near-Death Experience (NDE) phenomenon. This was the same conclusion also reached by Dr. Kenneth Ring, Harvard Medical Professor Dr. John Mack and by the academics of the FREE Foundation.

The FREE Experiencer Research Study demonstrates that these individuals have seen a perceived physical CAP-UFO and have physically seen a perceived "physical being", but more than 90% of their experiences can be considered "paranormal" in nature. For example, 80% have had an OBE; 78% have received telepathic messages from Non-Human Intelligence (NHI); 50% have stated that they or a family member has received a "miraculous" medical healing from NHI; 37% have had an NDE; 67% have had a past life memory; 55% have physically seen an orb; 76% have seen a ghost or spirit; and the overwhelming majority have had other types of paranormal experiences in their home.

There were over 75 different types of paranormal experiences described by these individuals in our statistical questionnaire. While these types of paranormal contact experiences have been documented in the past, the FREE research study, for the first time, quantified each type of CAP-UFO associated paranormal contact experience. Remember that this data was derived from more than 4,350 UFO Contact Experiencers from more than 125 countries for our English language survey. Volumes 3-6 from the *A Greater Reality* book series documents the detailed experiences of more than 75 individuals that highlight the positive aspects of the CAP-UFO contact experience and its paranormal nature.

Initially, some of these individuals viewed their experiences as negative, but when they took the survey, sometimes more than 30 years after their initial UFO Contact Experience, all now view the initial UFO Contact Experience as highly positive. This data is in contrast to the views of Dolan, Jacobs and Hopkins and almost all materialist Ufologists who have never acknowledged the paranormal aspects of the CAP-UFO contact phenomenon. **Once again, so much for the so-called alien abduction "research" of Dolan, Jacobs and Hopkins**.

It should be pointed out that neither Jacobs, Hopkins nor Dolan has ever conducted nor published any statistical research on CAP-UFO related contact experiences with Non-Human Intelligence. Meanwhile, the academics of the FREE Foundation published 2 peer-reviewed academic articles in two academic journals, on our FREE Research Study.[14] It should also be noted that the FREE research did not allow memory recollection based upon hypnotic regressions, which can be very biased (see the article by Hopkin's wife, Carole Rainey, in Volume 3 of *A Greater Reality*) but almost all of the information received by Hopkins, Jacobs, Dolan and the other "abduction researchers" has been derived via hypnotic regressions. Carole Rainey's article details numerous examples of how Jacobs and Hopkins co-created the "Alien Abduction Phenomenon" via biased selection of their candidates for hypnotic regressions, the many leading questions they asked, and their refusal to admit when one of their interviewees have been caught in numerous lies and deception.

Unlike the opinions of Jacobs, Hopkins, and their supporter Richard Dolan, who both believed that ALL of the contact experiences revolve around an "alien abduction breeding program," the FREE study revealed that only 7% of our entire sample population reported that a

---

[14] Hernandez, R., Schild, R, Klimo, J, Davis, R, Scalpone, R. A Study on Reported Contact with Non-Human Intelligence Associated with Unidentified Aerial Phenomena. *Journal of Scientific Exploration*, Vol. 32, No. 2, pp. 298–348, 2018

fetus "**<u>might</u> have been taken**" from them, even though this 7% of the survey participants did not present any detailed written response nor evidence of their suspicions of an "alien hybridization program".

Many of these individuals later told us in their open-ended questions that the information of hybridization came from a hypnotic regression even though the survey instructions told them not to include memories from a hypnotic regression. Of the 7% that mentioned that they "might" have been involved in an alien hybridization program, only 5 individuals wrote down the details of these hybrid pregnancies in our open-ended survey. All of them, however, stated that the information was recalled via "hypnotic regression" and not via "conscious explicit memories".

Were these 5 individuals hypnotically regressed by David Jacobs? In statistical language, the small numbers that answered the "alien hybridization" question (5 out of 4,350 who took our survey) can be viewed as an "outlier", possibly due to the influence of Jacobs, Hopkins, Dolan and other "abduction researchers" who began publishing their views of "Alien Hybridization Program" over the last 30-40 years at all of the major UFO conferences and in UFO related radio shows. All of this *indoctrination* was bound to affect a small group of individuals over a 30–40-year period. In statistical analyses, these "outliers" are thrown away because they are not consistent with what the overwhelming majority of the 4,350 participants in our 3 surveys have told us. Unlike David Jacobs and Budd Hopkins, who argued that 100% of the Alien Abduction involved an Alien Hybridization Program, our FREE data found just the opposite. **Once again, so much for the so-called "alien abduction research" and "alien hybridization findings" of Dolan, Jacobs and Hopkins**.

While initially, 37% of the FREE survey respondents viewed their experiences as negative, **over time**, only 5% came to view their experiences as negative-- **that is it, only 5%!** This initial rate of negativity is understandable and were described in the cases of Dr. John Mack who stated that these initial experiences can be described as an "ontological shock", due to the anxiety, confusion, and searching for answers, etc., of these initial contact experiencers. Nevertheless, with repeated interactions with various forms of Non-Human Intelligence, in many cases lasting 20-40 years, such as the case of UFO Contactees Whitley Strieber and Kathleen Marden, the majority of CAP-UFO contact experiencers came to regard their experiences as highly positive and transformative. This was the same conclusion reached by the FREE Foundation researchers Dr. Leo Strieber, Kathleen Marden, Barbara Lamb, Mary Rodwell, Rosemary Ellen Guiley, Brad Steiger, and non-FREE researchers such as Raymond Fowler, Dr. John Mack, and so many others. What all of these researchers lacked was an academic statistical research study to provide data for their initial hypotheses.

What accounted for this extreme rate of positivity over the long term in the thousands of FREE survey participants? Both the quantitative and qualitative data findings confirm two reasons why initially the rate of negative experiences decreased from 37% for their initial experiences but later only 5% viewed their experiences as negative. First, their initial experiences were perceived with fear and were an "ontological shock". Their past worldview of reality came crashing down. Nevertheless, over time, both the nature of their experiences changed to more positive experiences and, over time, their experiences became more spiritual. These perceived additional experiences triggered them to reflect on the nature of our reality and the spiritual aspects of their lives. Again, this hypothesis is reinforced by the finding that, 84% of the FREE study population reported that they did not want their contact experiences to end. In addition, 80% stated that they became more spiritual after their "Contact Experiences" started. In summary, approximately 5% of survey respondents regarded their Contact Experience (CE) with NHI as "negative" while more than 71% stated that their CEs were "highly" positive.[15] As further proof for this argument, I encourage everyone to read the numerous experiencer written articles in Volumes 3-6 of the *A Greater Reality* book series.

Dr. Joseph Burkes and researcher Preston Dennett, in Chapter Six of "*Beyond UFOs*", a chapter titled "*Medical Healings Reported by Contact Experiencers: An Analysis of the FREE Data*," described that 50% of the thousands who took the FREE surveys stated that they had a "*miraculous CAP-UFO medical healing*". FREE defined a **medical healing** as "a physiological improvement of a severe medical ailment as the result of an encounter with Non-Human Intelligence (NHI)". CAP-UFO medical healing cases have appeared regularly since the modern age of CAP-UFOs, in historical religious texts, and continue to be reported today. Once again, thousands of experiencers have documented a medical healing but Jacobs, Dolan and Hopkins never bothered to mention the fact of UFO medical healings. These medical healings were totally dismissed by these 3 individuals.

In 1996, prolific UFO researcher Preston Dennett released his book, *UFO Healings*, that discussed in detail more than 100 cases of medical healings by CAP-UFO related Non-Human Intelligence.[16] In 2019, after the FREE Foundation published its 820-page book, "*Beyond UFOs*", Preston published a second book, but now with over 300 new cases of CAP-UFO medical healings.[17] While many researchers now

---

[15]Hernandez, R., R. Schild & J. Klimo, eds. (2018). *Beyond UFOs: The Science of Consciousness and Contact with Non-Human Intelligence*. CreateSpace Independent Publishing (Amazon Press).

[16]Dennett, P. (1996). *UFO Healings: True Accounts of People Healed by Extraterrestrials*. Wild Flower Press.

[17]Dennett, P. (2019) *The Healing Power of UFOs: 300 True Accounts of People Healed by Extraterrestrials.*

agree that these cases exist, little was known about how common they actually were until the FREE study. The data from the FREE survey revealed that 50% of the thousands of respondents that took our surveys, reported a CAP-UFO related medical healings by Non-Human Intelligence-- **again, over 50% had a medical healing!**

Alien Abduction researcher Budd Hopkins stated, ***"The question is whether we hear about healing cases. We do sometimes, <u>very rarely</u>, but they do turn up"*** (Dennett, 1996). Alien Abduction researcher David Jacobs in his book***, Secret Life,*** writes, ***"In <u>extremely rare cases</u>, the aliens will undertake a cure of some ailment troubling the abductee"*** (Dennett, 1996). The FREE surveys documented that not only "mere ailments" were medically healed, but cancers, complete paralysis, and other MAJOR illnesses, which are certainly not "mere ailments". Retired medical doctor, Dr. Joseph Burkes, reviewed the medical records of many major medical healing cases and confirmed these "miraculous" medical healings. Many of these major healing cases were fully documented and presented in Chapter Six of our book ***"Beyond UFOs"***. One case was from Kathleen Marden, a major UFO researcher, author and a FREE Research Committee member. Before the book's publication she did not want her name to be identified as one of the 10 UFO medical healing cases. She has now publicly discussed her own UFO medical healing. A second case of a UFO medical healing was from another emergency medicine doctor, who I personally know, and who wished to remain anonymous. Dr. Burkes interviewed this other ER MD and all of the individuals in the 10 presented healing cases were mentioned in Chapter Six of ***Beyond UFOs***. He also reviewed and confirmed the medical records of these individuals.

While Hopkins and Jacobs both asserted that such accounts are "very rare," Harvard Medical School professor of psychiatry, John Mack MD, in his book, ***Passport to the Cosmos: Human Transformation and Alien Encounters***, a book that was a watershed event for the CAP-UFO experiencer community, writes "...*many abductees have experienced or witnessed healing conditions...*" (Mack, 2000). Edith Fiore Ph.D. concurs with Mack and writes, *"One of the most interesting findings that emerged from this work was the many healings and attempts to heal on the part of the visitors...In about <u>one-half of the cases</u>, I've been involved there have been healings due to operations and/or treatments"*. [18] FREE's data matches exactly Fiore's cases-- one half of contact experiencers have had a medical healing! Again, this data is not from a small group being hypnotized on the couch of David Jacobs or Budd Hopkins. Instead, the medical healing data was derived from more than 4,250 individuals from more than 125 countries that took our 3 surveys.

This example clearly illustrates that while many major researchers have uncovered thousands of cases of medical healings, these cases have been minimized by mainstream materialist ufologists and the majority of the "Alien Abduction" researchers. Why? -- because quite frankly, many have a mindset, like Jacobs, Hopkins and Dolan, that all of the CAP-UFO contact experiences with NHI are primarily negative, evil and that medical healings do not buttress these worldviews.

The topic of *"UFO related Medical Healings"* is just one of the many prime examples of how David Jacobs, Budd Hopkins and Richard Dolan tried to misinform and disinform the public with their negative spin on the CAP-UFO Contact Phenomenon. **Once again, so much for the so-called "Alien Abduction" research of Dolan, Jacobs and Hopkins**.

---

[18]Fiore, E. (1997). *Encounters: A Psychologist Reveals Case Studies of Abductions by Extraterrestrials.* Random House Publishing

Many well-known individuals who wrote about their early negative abduction experiences are now stating that their experiences, viewed after many years, were actually highly positive and were not abductions. Two well-known CAP-UFO researchers who initially viewed themselves as "abductees", Whitley Strieber and Kathleen Marden, now consider themselves "Contactees" and now claim that they became deeply spiritual because of their contact experiences. They underwent a complete psychological profile transformation for the positive and became deeply spiritual just like the thousands who took our FREE surveys.

UFO and Alien Abduction researcher Kathleen Marden many years ago wrote a book titled *"Captured! The Betty and Barney Hill UFO Experience. The True Story of the World's First Documented Alien Abduction"*. This book buttressed the negative alien abduction scenario created by Whitley Strieber, David Jacobs and Bud Hopkins. If you read this book you were frightened to death. Kathleen, who is a dear friend, recently wrote a book titled *Forbidden Knowledge: A Personal Journey from Alien Abduction to Spiritual Transformation*.[19] In this latest book, Kathleen moves away from the "negative abduction genre" to the spiritual aspects of the UFO contact phenomenon. She has also recently revealed that she also has had a miraculous medical healing of a major disease by UFO related Non-Human Intelligence. Her recent lectures over the last few years have moved away from the "horrors" of the abduction phenomenon to the spiritually transformative aspects of CAP-UFO contact phenomenon.

---

[19]Marden, K. (2022). *Forbidden Knowledge: A Personal Journey from Alien Abduction to Spiritual Transformation*. Independently published.

Whitley Strieber is arguably the most well-known "Abductee" known to humanity. His abduction-related books have sold hundreds of thousands of copies and have freighted an equal number of readers. His early books, together with the books by Jacobs and Hopkins, helped to establish the negative abduction stereotype. Yet, even Whitley Strieber has moved away from the negative abduction narrative to one of spiritual transformation.

His book **Communion** was a New York Times bestseller and spoke about the horrors of the CAP-UFO "abduction phenomenon". After the publication of **Communion**, Whitley was invited to speak at all of the major UFO Conferences and major UFO and paranormal radio shows all over the world for the next 40 years. Whitley, together with the "evil alien" narrative of Jacobs, Hopkins and Dolan, set the initial narrative that **ALL** CAP-UFO contact was evil, negative and involves an alien hybridization program. Now Whitley is presenting a contrasting view.

For over 40 years the majority of CAP-UFO radio shows or CAP-UFO conferences would prominently feature either Strieber, Jacobs, Hopkins, or other "abduction researchers", as featured speakers who would usually speak of the horrors of the abduction phenomenon. They set the tone, the worldview so to speak, of the CAP-UFO contact phenomenon. Remember that this worldview took root without any comprehensive academic statistical research on the phenomenon-- all of their "findings" were based upon "hypnotic regression" from biased researchers working on their living room couches. All of the positive aspects of the phenomenon demonstrated by researchers Dr. Kenneth Ring, Dr. Leo Sprinkle, Dr. John Mack, Barbara Lamb, Mary Rodwell, Raymond Fowler, Dr. Edith Fiore, and so many others, were ignored and the preference was to have the appearance of Jacobs, Hopkins, and more recently Dolan as featured speakers at these major UFO conferences and UFO radio shows. As the old saying goes, "**Fear Sells**". This allowed their hypothesis of the evil alien, and the negative alien abduction phenomenon, to become firmly ingrained in the world view of materialist Ufology. Anyone hypnotically regressed during the 1980s, 1990s, until recently was heavily influence by the 30 years of non-stop propaganda campaign of the evil aliens who are capturing humans, the evil aliens doing wild experiments on us, and the evil aliens impregnating human females with hybrid babies. All of this hypnotically induced false information was promoted by the biased regression therapist teaming up with a propaganda filled experiencer who jointly created the perfect environment for propagating this false alien abduction narrative.

As previously mentioned, I encourage everyone to read Volume 3 of *A Greater Reality* book series which contains an article, written by Carole Rainey, who was the ex-wife of Budd Hopkins, which provides numerous details how the false narrative of the alien abduction phenomenon was propagated by Jacobs and Hopkins. She describes this process as the "*Fabrication of the Alien Abduction Phenomenon*".[20]

Would it come as a surprise that UFO Contact Researchers Kathleen Marden, Mary Rodwell, Barbara Lamb, and the late Dr. Leo Sprinkle, individuals who have jointly researched over 10,000 UFO Contact Experiencer cases, have recently stated that the alien abduction phenomenon has almost completely disappeared over the last 15 years. It is now rare to hear of a new "evil alien abduction" case. What could be the reason for this dramatic decline? In the 1980s, 1990s and early 2000s, almost anyone that saw a UFO later stated that they "might have been abducted". Why are these evil aliens no longer capturing us? Why are they no longer inseminating human females in hopes of producing hybrid babies? Why are these evil beings no longer doing wicked experiments on humans? Could it be that the good aliens have

---

[20] See the article by Budd Hopkin's wife, Carole Rainey, in Volume 3 of the *A Greater Reality* book series, titled "*Priests of High Strangeness: Co-Creation of the Alien Abduction Phenomenon*"

killed off all of the evil aliens, a rumor spreading all around the internet? Or could the reason be that Hopkins is dead and that Jacobs is no longer on the UFO lecture circuit? You decide!

Over the years, Whitley Strieber's books changed their tone-- he moved away from the horrors of the alien abduction phenomenon to his current position that the CAP-UFO contact is highly positive in the long term and that this contact experience results, in the long term, in a positive spiritual transformation of the experiencer. Whitley's latest books, titled *The Afterlife Revolution*[21] and *Jesus: A New Vision*, speak about his movement away from the alien abduction narrative towards a narrative of spirituality, resulting from his "Contact Experiences". In one of his recent interviews, he stated that he literally prays to his "Visitors" every night for making him a spiritual person and allowing him to communicate with his deceased wife.[22] Again, here is an example, just like Kathleen Marden, and the thousands who took our surveys, of individuals starting off with a fear-based perspective of their experiences, but over time, eventually came to view their experiences as highly spiritual and highly positive. **Once again, so much for the so-called "Alien Abduction" research of Hopkins, Jacobs, Dolan, and other Alien Abduction researchers**.

Numerous other individuals, such as Debra Kauble, Rev. Michael Carter, and many other individuals who were publicized in the books of David Jacobs and Budd Hopkins, also represent examples of individuals who moved away from the negative aspects of their initial experiences to the spiritually transformative aspects of their experiences. They initially were horrified and scared by their initial experiences but now

---

[21]Strieber, W. (2020). *The Afterlife Revolution*. Beyond Words Publishing.

[22]Jeffrey Mishlove interviews Whitley Strieber.
https://www.youtube.com/watch?v=oBQ33MyNBr4

they view their experiences differently and now promote the view that their experiences were highly positive and deeply spiritual.[23] **Once again, so much for the views of Jacobs, Hopkins and Dolan who view _ALL_ CAP-UFO contact as highly negative.**

John Keel, one of the pioneer Ufologists during the 1960s and 1970s, and author of numerous Ufology books, eventually reached similar conclusions to Dr. J. Allen Hynek and Dr. Jacque Vallee. Keel stated:

> *I abandoned the extraterrestrial hypothesis in 1967* when my own field investigations disclosed an astonishing **overlap between psychic phenomena and UFOs... The objects and apparitions do not necessarily originate on another planet and may not even exist as permanent constructions of matter.** It is more likely that we see what we want to see and interpret such visions according to our contemporary beliefs.[24]

In the last few years of his life, Dr. J. Allen Hynek, who I consider the Father of Ufology, began to speculate that the CAP-UFO phenomenon was both physical and psychic and that the phenomenon might be a consciousness-based interdimensional phenomenon.

In Curtis Fuller's book titled "*Proceedings of the First International UFO Congress*",[25] he quotes Dr. Hynek as follows:

---

[23] See the chapter in Volume 2 of A Greater Reality, authored by Rev. Michael Carter, titled **"The Spiritual Transformation of the UAP Contact Experiencer: An Analysis of the FREE Research Data"**

[24] Raynes, B. (2019). **John A. Keel: The Man, The Myths, and the Ongoing Mysteries.** Self-Published.

[25] Fuller, C. (1980). **Proceedings of the First International UFO Congress.** New York: Warner Books.

> *... in addition to the observations of materialization and dematerialization, he cited the "poltergeist" phenomenon experienced by some people after a close encounter; the photographs of UFOs, sometimes in only one frame, and not seen by witnesses; the changing of form in front of witnesses; the puzzling question of telepathic communications... the sudden stillness in the presence of the craft; levitation of cars or people; and the development by some of psychic abilities after an encounter.* **"Do we have two aspects of one phenomenon or two <u>realms</u>, so mysterious to us today, may be an ordinary part of an advanced technology".** Fuller, C. (1980).

Note that Hynek was not specifically referring to an advanced technology of a physical alien being from a physical planet. Towards the end of his life, he was publicly discussing the consciousness-based aspects of this "advanced technology". From the above-referenced quote of Dr. Hynek, the Father of Ufology, one can easily apply the Virtual Reality Hypothesis to the phenomenon of Ufology. What Hynek was missing was the spiritual aspects of the phenomenon which would make it the Spiritual-Virtual Reality Hypothesis. Hynek, unfortunately, was not privy to the extensive academic research data we have today from the field of Near-Death Experience research or the UFO data from the Dr. Edgar Mitchell FREE CAP-UFO Experiencer Research Study, which details the spiritual connection to CAP-UFO Contact. This connection between NDEs and the UFO phenomenon was discussed in Dr. Kenneth Ring's 1993 book titled "***The Omega Project: Near-Death Experiences, UFO Encounters, and Mind at Large***".[26] The connection between NDEs and the UFO phenomenon is also articulated in the attached article in Volume 4 of this book by noted UFO researcher Raymond Fowler, titled ***"The Relationship Between Ufology & the Paranormal: The UFO and NDE Connection"***.

---

[26]Ring, K. (1992). ***The Omega Project: Near-Death Experiences, UFO Encounters, and Mind at Large***. William Morrow and Co.

Dr. Jacques Vallee is in my opinion, the Father of Modern Ufology. He basically took over the mantel held by Dr. Hynek after his passing. As of this writing, in October of 2024, Dr. Vallee is still alive. Dr. Vallee has written over a dozen books on the topic of Ufology since the mid-1960s. He initially was a Research Astronomer and later received his Ph.D. in Industrial Engineering and Computer Sciences from the same university that Dr. Hynek was a professor of Astronomy at, Northwestern University. They were very close friends and shared many similar worldviews.

During that same time period when Dr. Hynek was changing his views on CAP-UFOs from a materialist to a consciousness-based position during the late 1960s and early 1970s, Dr. Vallee also began to speculate that the intelligence behind the CAP-UFOs might also be a consciousness-based phenomenon. In Vallée's many books, he speculates that the CAP-UFO phenomenon might be a multidimensional phenomenon based on consciousness and that CAP-UFOs might not be a physical flying saucer from a physical planet. Instead, he argued that the UFO phenomenon might be a multidimensional intelligence from another reality-- part of an informational mechanism of "Consciousness". Two of my books, "***Beyond UFOs***" and "***The Mind of GOD***", have greatly expanded on this initial hypothesis of Dr. Vallee. Dr. Vallee stated in an interview with Dr. Jeffrey Mishlove the following:

> *"My personal contention is that the [UFO] phenomenon is the result of an intelligence, that is technologically directed by an intelligence, and that this intelligence is capable of **manipulating space and time** in ways that we don't understand... The essential conclusion I'm tending to is that the origin of the phenomenon of the intelligence is **not necessarily***

> ***extraterrestrial****... I think we are dealing with something that is **both technological and psychic**, and seems to be able to **manipulate other dimensions**. This is neither wishful thinking nor personal speculation on my part. It's a conclusion that comes from interviewing critical witnesses, and then listening to what they have to say.*[27]

Dr. Vallee is stating a CAP-UFO hypothesis that mirrors both the model previously stated by Dr. Hynek and what I have presented in my two recent books -- a model that the CAP-UFO phenomenon is a multi-dimensional consciousness-based phenomenon. The difference between the positions of Dr. Valle and myself is that I am presenting the CAP-UFO phenomenon as a phenomenon integrated with all of the other Contact Modalities under the rubric of Consciousness, our multidimensional Greater Reality. I also differentiate from Dr. Vallee because I incorporate a spiritual component within a Universal Mind of GOD, a model revealed by the research on the Near-Death Experience phenomenon. Thus, while we share some similarities, our hypotheses on the CAP-UFO Contact Phenomenon are very different. I also contend that all of the Contact Modalities, including CAP-UFOs, need to be researched and viewed as ONE integrated phenomenon under Consciousness because all of the Contact Modalities, including the phenomenon of CAP-UFOs, involve a manipulation of space and time.

Needless to say, Dr. Vallee was ostracized by mainstream Ufology, especially the Alien Abduction researchers, who still cling to their nuts and bolt materialist approach. Vallee did not believe in a physical ET being and certainly did not believe that these perceived physical beings came to visit us from a physical planet in our physical

---

[27] Dr. Jacques Vallee, Ufology research pioneer and consciousness scholar. (YouTube video titled "Thinking Allowed – Implications of the UFO Phenomena"), interviewed by Dr. Jeffrey Mishlove, dated 2003)
https://www.youtube.com/watch?v=sP10HPJkJ4Q&t=86s

universe. Even though Vallee is the most well-known and respected Ufologist of his time, and one of the few Ph.D. trained scientists in the field of Ufology, he had decided to speak at only a few recent UFO conferences over the last 20 years. Dr. Vallee chose to ostracize himself from the many Ufology conferences circulating around the world and the field of Ufology. He rarely discusses his Psyche Non-ET hypothesis.

Ufology today still remains a field with almost zero academic research and zero academic credibility. Ph.D. academics, certainly not the Ph.D. academics associated from CCRI, will not associate with Ufology organizations. Mainstream materialist Ufology organizations still have not embraced the controversial non-materialist theories of Dr. Hynek and Dr. Vallee, the two pillars of Ufology.

Dr. Jacques Vallee's classic book, "***Passport to Magonia: On UFOs, Folklore, and Parallel Worlds***", first published in 1969, became a highly controversial book because it completely broke with the theories of materialist Ufology.[28] One of Vallée's major accomplishments in this classic book is that he thoroughly documented hundreds of events in human history that detailed contact with gods, angels, demons, fairies, dwarfs, giants, monsters, and numerous other types of diverse physical beings. Vallee argues that these experiences were very similar to the modern CAP-UFO descriptions. He then speculated that all of these experiences appear to be manifestations deriving from a common origin-- a consciousness-based psyche origin.

It was in this book where Vallee first speculated that *the CAP-UFO phenomenon demonstrated both a physical and a psyche, consciousness-based component.* It was with the publication of this

---

[28]Vallee, J. (1969). ***Passport to Magonia: On UFOs, Folklore, and Parallel Worlds***. Contemporary Books.

book that Vallee became a heretic among heretics and he was soon ostracized from materialist Ufology. Why? Because in 1969 the field of Ufology was comprised of materialists and this remains to this day. Dr. Vallée's approach was not a traditional Ufology materialist approach but a much more complicated one involving a consciousness-based approach involving both materialist and psyche (Consciousness) based components.

My research and publications in the field of Ufology and Consciousness Studies can also be considered as the writings of a heretic among heretics. First, research arena that merges the topics of Consciousness Studies and the Contact Modalities is comprised of a small niche of researchers. Also, my writings have been rejected by the materialist Ufologists because of my Consciousness-based approach of Ufology. I have been ostracized by those in charge of UFO conferences and UFO radio shows because I am not a materialist and I hold the view that "Consciousness is Fundamental".

Even though I was one of the academics responsible for the only academic statistical research study on UFO Contact Experiencers, I have not been invited to speak at any of the major UFO conferences or well-known radio shows except for George Knapp, the host of Coast to Coast radio who invited me to his show one time. By the way, Mr. Knapp also shares the hypotheses of CCRI which is that 1) Consciousness is Fundamental and 2) that all of the Paranormal (Contact Modalities) might be ONE integrated phenomenon under Consciousness; and finally; 3) that "little green" are not visiting us from a physical planet to promote the alien hybridization of humanity. I conducted a lengthy interview of Mr. Knapp at the home of Dr. John Alexander in Los Vegas a few years ago which will be revealed in my upcoming documentary titled "*A Greater Reality: One Man's Journey of Discovery*".[29]

In addition, most of the researchers that study the Contact Modalities still believe that they are all separate and distinct phenomenon. In contrast to this, I have argued that not only the phenomenon of Ufology, but all of the Contact Modalities, is ONE integrated phenomenon under Consciousness (Our Greater Reality). I am also one of the few Consciousness researchers, together with the majority of the academics and MDs in the CCRI organization, that argues that Consciousness is Fundamental and not our material reality.

As one can see, I am also a heretic among heretics. My worldview, my new paradigm of reality, has to wait for later generations to shatter the previous old paradigm. At this time, very few are able to digest the hypotheses of my books. This will be left for future generations.

Dr. Vallee, in many of his books, stated that UFO "crafts" and UFO "beings", could possibly be holographic projections and might not be "physical". As I stated in my book, "*The Mind of GOD*", I also share this hypothesis and I amplified on this view with numerous detailed examples in my new book on my personal experiences titled "*A Greater Reality: One Man's Journey of Discovery*". In this book, I discussed in detail how I learned that the UFO and the UFO related beings are actually "*Holographic Projections*".

---

[29]The documentary, titled "*A Greater Reality: One Man's Journey of Discovery*", co-produced with Kevin Layne and Helene Layne, is expected to be released in 2025. A draft trailer of this documentary can be viewed at the bottom of the CCRI website, **https://agreaterreality.com**

In his book "**Passport to Magonia**", Vallee introduced this concept which was later discussed in almost all of his later books-- that UFO crafts and UFO beings might be "**Holograms**".
Vallee states:

> "*If it were possible to make **three-dimensional holograms** with mass, and to project them through time I would say this is what the farmer saw… Are we dealing… with a parallel universe, where there are human races living, and where we may go at our expense, never to return to the present?... **From that mysterious universe, have objects that can materialize and "dematerialize" at will been projected? Are UFO's "windows" rather than "objects"?**[30]* (Vallee, J. 1969)

In addition, regarding the hypothesis that both the thousands of diverse forms of CAP-UFOs and the thousands of diverse forms of Non-Human Intelligence seen by humanity might be "*Holographic Projections*", please read the article by medical doctor, Dr. Joseph Burkes, in Volume 3 of the "*A Greater Reality*" book series, *titled* "***Report from the Contact Underground: Human Initiated Contact, The Consciousness Connection, Holographic Projections & the Virtual Experience Model***". I also share this view that the CAP-UFOs and the Non-Human Intelligence seen by Experiencers are also "Holographic Projections". My book, ***The Mind of GOD***, presents numerous reasons for the "Holographic Projection" argument.

My writings, in addition to the Ufology works of Dr. Jacques Vallee, Dr. John Mack, Dr. Jon Klimo, Dr. Edgar Mitchell, Dr. Rudy Schild, Dr. Claude Swanson, Mary Rodwell, John Keel, Raymond Fowler, and many others, argue that the materialist approach to Ufology has contributed very little since Kenneth Arnold described seeing a

---

[30]Vallee, J. (1969). ***Passport to Magonia: On UFOs, Folklore, and Parallel Worlds***. Contemporary Books.

"Flying Saucer" in 1947. What has this materialist approach contributed to our knowledge about CAP-UFOs? My answer is **ALMOST NOTHING**! We know that CAP-UFOs exist, that is about it. We have seen pictures and videos of CAP-UFOs, none of them up close. We know that they move very fast and that they have materialized on radar and then quickly dematerialized from the radar

screen. We know that they change their appearance right in front of your eyes. We know that while a large group of individuals are looking up, only a select few are "allowed" to see the CAP-UFO. Allegedly, Ufologists have recovered metal from crashed physical UFOs but there is not one shred of documented evidence to support this statement. So, what are we left with? Almost nothing! If you truly want "**UFO DISCLOSURE**", why are you waiting for the US Federal government to release additional videos and photos? Instead, I recommend that you read our books "***Beyond UFO's***" and Volumes 3-6 of the "***A Greater Reality***" book series where you will read "**DISCLOSURE**" from thousands of UFO Contact Experiencers.

If you want to understand the CAP-UFO phenomenon, you need to understand the CAP-UFO Contact Experiencer and not rely on a materialist Ufologist who clings to their collection of long-distanced UFO videos, photos and who promote a biased use of hypnotic regression.[31] The approach of the older Dr. Hynek, Dr. Vallee and the FREE Foundation research team was to focus on the Experiencer, the witness to the CAP-UFO phenomenon and not to use hypnotic regression as data in interviewing the CAP-UFO witness. It was this approach, of detailed investigations of UFO Contact Experiencers that led them to hypothesize the consciousness-based and not the materialist approach, to Ufology.

---

[31] Hypnotic Regression can be a useful tool in the hands of an unbiased professional.

Unfortunately, only a few of the major materialist Ufologists have even bothered to read the data findings from the Dr. Edgar Mitchell FREE Foundation 5-year academic research study on CAP-UFO Contact Experiencers-- data that contradicts the more than 80-year history of materialist Ufology. For this reason, the majority in the field of Ufology remain clueless about the complex nature of this phenomenon and will remain clueless for the foreseeable future. How ironic that one of the very few academic research studies on the CAP-UFO contact phenomenon has been totally ignored and criticized by most of these well-known materialist Ufologists.

Richard Dolan, for example, in his radio show has publicly stated that the Dr. Edgar Mitchell FREE Foundation UFO Experiencer Research study is "***not scientific***" and called our work "***woo-woo science***", when in fact the FREE Foundation had over 8 Ph.D. academics and scientists (we had 3 Ph.D. physicists, a Ph.D. Neuroscientist and several other Ph.D. scientists and medical doctors in the FREE Foundation). Dr. Jon Klimo, who taught "Statistical Research Methodology" to Ph.D. students for over 40 years, was the chair of the FREE Research Committee and was the lead academic in our development of the 3 FREE surveys and our research methodology. Unlike the FREE Foundation, the CCRI organization has many more Ph.D. academics, scientists and medical doctors, totaling more than 25 individuals, as can be viewed in our website (**https://agreaterreality.com/**).

Yet how many materialist Ufology researchers are academic Ph.D. scientists? Almost none! I can count them with one hand. I should remind everyone that neither Dolan, nor Hopkins is a Ph.D. and they are not scientists or academics. Jacobs is a Ph.D. historian but unlike the academics of FREE or CCRI, he is not a scientist. Thus, whose work is considered "woo-woo" science? Is it the work of FREE's or CCRI's Ph.D. Physicists, Ph.D. Astrophysicists, Ph.D.

Neuroscientists, Ph.D. Biochemists, and Medical Doctors? Should their work be considered "woo-woo" science? Or is the hypnotic regression work of Hopkins, Jacobs, and their supporter, Richard Dolan, considered woo-woo science? One uses laboratories, scientific instruments and statistical analysis to gather data while the other group uses a living room couch and the tool of "hypnotic regression" with leading questions to acquire data. Yet Dolan has stated that Jacobs "**is remarketably careful, and yes, scientific in his approach.**" You be the judge.

The materialists within Ufology have avoided stories from Experiencers that have had contact with Non-Human Intelligence. Raymond Fowler has researched the UFO phenomenon since 1963 and was involved with all of the major UFO organizations over the last 50 years. In Fowler's article in Volume 4 of A Greater Reality, he informed us that almost all of the early research in Ufology during the 1950s, 1960s, and 1970s would dismiss all cases involving UFO Contact cases which also involved the "paranormal".[32]

The materialist approach to Ufology seeks to explain a CAP-UFO as simply a physical ET "Alien" being who is visiting us, usually for less than one minute, from a physical planet. Nevertheless, this materialist approach cannot explain many facts: this approach cannot explain the tens of thousands of different types of CAP-UFO-related physical beings that usually appear for less than 30 seconds; this approach cannot explain the tens of thousands of different physical UFOs seen by individuals; it cannot explain the numerous and diverse paranormal experiences associated with CAP-UFO contact phenomenon; it cannot explain, as both Dr. J. Allen Hynek and Dr. Jacques Vallee have shown, that CAP-UFOs have the ability to

---

[32] Raymond Fowler. *"Coming of Age as a Ufologist: The Relationship Between Ufology & the Paranormal Contact Modalities (NDEs, OBEs, PSI, Ghosts, etc.)"* in _A Greater Reality_, Volume 4.

"manipulate spacetime"; this approach cannot explain the fact that 50% of UFO Contact Experiencers have had a miraculous medial healing; it cannot explain that 50% of the Contact Experiencers have been brought to multi-dimensional realities where the majority have received spiritual teachings; it cannot explain that over 85% of these Contact Experiencers have had their worldviews shattered in a positive way and are making positive changes in their lives. This is just a small sample of facts, out of thousands of facts, that materialist Ufology is not able to explain away. It is only recently that many Experiencers are becoming aware that there are thousands perhaps millions of individuals around the world that are having similar experiences. Some of these "Experiencer stories" are presented in Volumes 3-6, the Experiencer chapters, of *A Greater Reality* book series.

A few of the materialists within Ufology are slowly accepting the CAP-UFO Experiencer contact phenomenon but very few are accepting the consciousness-based explanation of the phenomenon. At best, they are arguing that the tens of thousands of different physical beings encountered in the CAP-UFO phenomena are actually tens of thousands of different physical beings coming from tens of thousands of physical planets. In contrast to the materialist approach, the "New Age" metaphysical approach to Ufology is that these physical beings are coming from every constellation known to humanity-- they are coming from the Pleiadeans, Sirius, Arcturus, Andromeda, Orion, etc., and many even argue that they come from planets in our solar system-- this is Venusian, this is a Martian, etc. Are there really tens of thousands of different physical beings, arriving from tens of thousands of different planets, interacting with selected individuals, usually for only less than one minute? Or is the explanation more complicated than this simplistic argument?

Both Dr. Vallee, Dr. J. Allen Hynek, Dr. Edgar Mitchell, Dr. Rudy Schild, Dr. John Mack and the many authors of the FREE Foundation, and now the CCRI organization, and the many books that I have published, disagree with the views of materialist Ufology, in particular the view of David Jacobs, Budd Hopkins and Richard Dolan. If anyone wants to truly begin to understand the CAP-UFO Contact Phenomenon, there is only one game in town-- there is only one comprehensive, academic, statistical research study, administered in multiple languages, on a worldwide basis, prepared and supervised by a team of Ph.D. academics and experienced researchers in the UFO contact arena, and that is the work of the Dr. Edgar Mitchell FREE Foundation UFO Experiencer Research Study, as published in our 820-page book, ***Beyond UFOs: The Science of Consciousness and Contact with Non-Human Intelligence***.[33] In addition, Volume 2 of the ***A Greater Reality*** book series also contains 11 chapters that discuss the consciousness-based aspects of the UFO contact phenomenon. Once again, I want to reiterate that all of these 11 UFO chapters in Volume 2 are available for FREE as downloadable PDF files at the CCRI website, (**https://agreaterreality.com/**).

In conclusion, if you continue to rely on the "Alien Abduction" research of biased individuals such as David Jacobs, Budd Hopkins, and Richard Dolan, you will remain clueless as to the complexities of the CAP-UFO contact phenomenon. I emphasize that Richard Dolan stated that David Jacobs is "***unquestionably the world's leading researcher in the generally neglected field of alien abduction***" and that "***David is remarketably careful, and yes, scientific in his approach***." Yet, David Jacobs has repeatedly stated that he has NEVER met a UFO Contact Experiencer who view their experiences as positive. For Jacobs, all UFO Contact are negative and evil.

---

[33]Hernandez, R., R. Schild & J. Klimo, eds. (2018). ***Beyond UFOs: The Science of Consciousness and Contact with Non-Human Intelligence***. CreateSpace Independent Publishing (Amazon Press).

It should be emphasized that Richard Dolan is not a Ph.D., he is not a scientist, he is not an academic, and he has not done any academic statistical research on the UFO Contact Phenomenon. He considers the methodology of David Jacobs, which is to preselect biased individuals to "hypnotically regress" the person in his living room couch, as "*scientific*". The Ph.D. academics in the FREE Foundation and the CCRI organization disagree.

Once again, the FREE Foundation and the CCRI organization, comprised of Ph.D. academics and scientists, do not view the biased selection by Hopkins and Jacobs, of less than 100 individuals who they have hypnotically regressed over the last 30-40 years, as "scientific". Compare their sample of 100 preselected individuals that they have hypnotically regressed with many leading questions, over 40 years with the sample of 4,350 individuals from more than 125 countries from our FREE academic research study. These 4,350 survey respondents were also not "pre-selected"-- they were volunteers who chose to answer our surveys based upon the fact that they had seen a UFO and had some form of "Contact" with a Non-Human Intelligence. These surveys were also developed and the data collection was supervised by numerous Ph.D. academic professors.

> # Thus, which approach is "scientitic" and which one is "woo woo" science?

I encourage every one to download the free PDF copy of our 820-page academic book, "*Beyond UFOs*" if you want to get educated about the UFO Contact Phenomenon.   You can download this book at the CCRI Website: **https://agreaterreality.com/**

You can also download free PDF copies of Volumes 1 and 2 of our "*A Greater Reality*" book series. Volumes 1 and 2 are theoretical chapters written by Ph.D. academics and medical Doctors. Volumes 3-6 contain chapters written by major experiencers of the Contact Modalities. Each of these 6 volumes are approximately 800 pages each. In addition, my book "*The Mind of GOD: A Spiritual-Virtual Reality Model of Consciousness and the Contact Modalities*", is also available for free as a free PDF file at the CCRI website: **https://agreaterreality.com/**

My Visitors Are Not Evil, Just Unfathomable:

Interventionist Evolutionary Consciousness, the Voice, the Visitors and Me

Gregory Foster Grove

> *"The Truth is One. Sages call it by various names."*
> *- The Rig Veda*
>
> *"The Universe is made of stories, not of atoms."*
> *- Muriel Rukeyser, The Speed of Darkness*
>
> *"Freely they stood who stood, and fell who fell."*
> *- John Milton, Paradise Lost*

Let's stipulate something important at the beginning of our journey into maximum High Strangeness: I'm not crazy. I don't hear voices inside my head. Well, except for the one. But that's usually only once every decade or so. I call this exception to the rule that I don't hear voices inside my head-and am therefore not crazy-The Voice. He will play an outsized role in what follows, considering the relative rarity of his appearances in my story. The first time I remember hearing The Voice is just before I wake up screaming inside of an alien resurrection tube. (Reminder: I'm not crazy.) Deep and soothing, The Voice says something like, "*You're not going to have to do this anymore. I'm taking care of things*."

It's the early 1980s, and I'm around twelve-years-old. The previous few months have been exhausting, and I've moved well beyond my breaking point. Somehow, for the last two years, I've found myself deeply entangled in an otherworldly research project-one that, in my opinion, has been conducted a little too aggressively by various non-human intelligences. Almost every detail is fuzzy about these interactions, but I will attempt to share most of what I remember in this essay.

First, I recall being bathed in rainbow light just before passing out in the front bedroom of my grandparents' house. Then I hear my name, "*Wake up, Greg. Wake up*." I open my eyes and feel a soothing presence beside me, an entity I will later name The Voice, simply because I've never laid eyes on him, not once in forty years. But I sure have heard from him.

And this happens to be my first time hearing from him, at least in this format. He says, "*We have some time. Let's go visit one of your favorite places*." Instantly, we're floating a couple of hundred feet above my most beloved childhood playground, which is peaceful and childless in the night.

For some reason, I'm less concerned that we're floating in the air than that we're floating in the air 150 miles away from my last known location. How did we get here so fast? No sooner do I think that I would rather visit my mother's house instead of this playground than we are high above the trees, staring down at the front porch. I say that I would like to see my mother, but The Voice tells me that it's time to go. "*Let's fly back.*"

As we speed home, we're traveling so fast that the vast farmlands of rural Northern California blur together like pages in some kind of manic flipbook. The Voice tells me that I'm not going to remember any of this for many years, but not to worry-I won't have to deal with the Visitors anymore. An almost mystical sense of relief, perhaps even of triumph, floods over me.

Bursting with happiness, I open my eyes and find myself inside an alien tube, which is a little smaller than the size of a dunk tank like you'd see at a county fair. So much for happiness. Out of the corner of my eye, I see myself floating in another container, and it occurs to me: I'm not seeing my reflection. I'm seeing another version of me, one that looks dishevelled and discarded. I look down and notice that I'm naked, unlike the other me who has clothes on. My clothes. I start screaming, "*What's going on? Who's that? Is that really me? Am I a clone?*"

I don't think the Visitors are having a good night. I'm not supposed to see any of this. Before I slip out of consciousness again, I know that I'm witnessing this scene for a reason. One day, decades later, I will dig this memory up from out of the shadows and share it with others. That's the plan.

My Visitors are not evil, just unfathomable, though I do understand this: They often lack in social graces, and healthy boundaries are not part of their shtick-sort of like a few engineers and mathematicians I know. But there is also joy in some of my communications with them, at least on my side of the equation. For example, it has been about two weeks since my consciousness gloriously merged with and piloted a flying saucer-a story you will read shortly.

About a week after the alien tube incident, I hear from The Voice for the second time. I'm actually on vacation at my mother's house now, a two-hour drive down south from where I'm living with my dad and his parents. The Voice wakes me up with instructions to telephone my dad immediately to let him know that someone is going to break into his van and steal his tools. You will read this story later on as well.

Just know upfront that The Voice is a loving presence that turns up in my life now and then, though very rarely. He grants me visions and insights, sometimes of the future, sometimes of the past, sometimes of whatever is right in front of my face. Everything he has ever said to me or shown me has proven absolutely factual, accurate, correct, and true: Including the heads-up about my father's tools being stolen, which was the first vision of the future I was granted-a test run, so to speak.

I suspect that my interactions with The Voice will prove to be the most essential and vital heart of this essay, along with the specific, clear-sighted prophetic visions and understandings that I have experienced on my own ever since The Voice came into my life just before I woke up inside that alien resurrection tube.

As you might already discern from reading the above, my contribution to this research project contains deeply peculiar narratives of an extraordinary nature. The stories that follow are from my personal history. And although these often uncanny accounts might seem entirely unrelated, they are, in fact, intimately interconnected inflections, declensions, and conjugations of a Greater Reality, one that is making itself known through what the researchers and Experiencers in this book are calling the ***Contact Modalities***: UFOs, near-death and out-of-body experiences, prophetic dreams, ghosts, interactions with non-human intelligence, discarnate entities, aliens-in short, a veritable smorgasbord of the weird, paranormal, and fringe.

> **The fundamental question we Experiencers are tasked with tackling in this volume is both succinct in its requirements, and vast in its implications*: "What is the relationship between consciousness, our cosmology, and contact with non-human intelligence via the Contact Modalities?"* My experience suggests, strongly suggests, that various levels of Higher Intelligence are engaged in an interventionist agenda aimed at evolving human consciousness via the Contact Modalities.**

Throughout what follows, my primary objective in sharing these narratives is to hew as closely to the "Capital T" Truth as possible. Despite the astonishing claims in this essay, all magical thinking and ego inflation of any kind are the pernicious enemies of this project. In short, do not mistake the envelope for the message contained within it. I'm an anonymous conduit-the least interesting part of this story. The message is the message. Getting caught up in worrying about messengers instead of messages is one of the reasons this planet is in such peril. Therefore, names in this history have been changed to protect the innocent. Any of these stories could have just as easily happened to you. If you see the Truth in them, then-in a very real sense-these stories will have happened to you. And that is precisely the point.

From a certain point of view, my involvement with this project began on a flight. It's October 2019. I'm flying home to New York, and have just settled into my headphones to listen to the audiobook of Eknath Easwaran's translation of The Bhagavad Gita. I've recently fallen in love with this particular Gita, which is itself a minor miracle, bordering on the paranormal, as until recently, I was what you would call a hardcore atheist, more or less in sympathy with the likes of Christopher Hitchens, Sam Harris, and The Flying Spaghetti Monster.

A favorite mantra of mine used to be, "I might be an atheist, but I'm a Protestant atheist," as I have ministerial ancestors on both sides of my family tree-all of them Protestant-running back around four hundred years. Stubbornness, freethinking, and questioning authority run deep in my veins, but I guess you can say that things have changed for me over the last couple of years. Though I'm probably just as wilful and skeptical as ever, my spiritual growth is now priority number one. So, I'm genuinely thrilled to sit back in my airplane seat, relax, and dive into The Gita's beautiful and practical wisdom.

Just as I reach over to press play on the audiobook, a Download strikes. ***"Don't worry about why you've had your Experiences, or how you're going to tell your story. The universe doesn't waste its time. You're good."***

By "Download", here, I mean an unexpected immediate understanding of reality. It's like being struck by a bolt of pure Truth. As to who is tossing around these epiphanies, I'm not absolutely sure. Let's just call it non-human intelligence for now. This particular Download kindly name-dropped "the universe," which is my catchall nickname for a Higher Power. We'll revisit this topic later.

To be clear, I did not hear a voice telling me this Download information. It was more an instantaneous knowingness, as if I were remembering a plain and simple fact, like the sky is blue, or the Earth is round. The more philosophically inclined often refer to Downloads as "noetic experiences." Sounds fancier. More scientific.

After about eight more hours of travel, I finally arrive home, and in a further eight hours or so, my Download pays another visit: This time in my inbox.

I wake up early that next morning and see an email from Rey Hernandez, a familiar name, which I can't quite place. I'll let the message speak for itself:

> *"Thank you for your email. Do you have your experiences in writing? We are preparing a new book. If you can get me a short document, 20-30 pages of your experiences, I can place it as a chapter in our six-volume book. Let me know if you are interested."*

What you are reading now is a direct response to this unexpected invitation from Mr. Hernandez. I had discovered the FREE Foundation's project on "Non-human Intelligence and the Contact Modalities" in early 2019, long after the initial phase of the study had finished up, and had sent a short note to their generic email address. Frankly, I had forgotten all about it. But synchronicity has a way of asserting itself in my life, and Mr. Hernandez emailed me out of the blue, just a few hours after my noetic experience at 32,000 feet. The universe doesn't waste its time. You're good.

As you might know, Mr. Hernandez has had Downloads himself, as well as direct interactions with non-human intelligence. In fact, his noetic experiences specifically address and align with my understandings and dealings with The Phenomenon in its various manifestations. What a relief then to discover that not only am I not alone. There are at least several thousand of us with transformational experiences across a broad spectrum of High Strangeness. And it seems like a common denominator is emerging in our collective consciousness as Experiencers: *A Higher Intelligence is unfolding itself to our awareness, selectively intervening in our affairs, shepherding us through dangerous times as part of an enlightenment project for humankind.*

Before I get going any further, I have to give you an example of what I mean by interventionist Higher Intelligence. While working on the first draft of this essay, I experienced some unusually persistent writer's block. Utterly exasperated, I asked the universe for a sign that I should continue working on this project. It took less than two minutes for a response. A massive blur landed on my window air conditioner. I'm near the top floor of my apartment building, and we rarely get pigeons up here. Except it wasn't a pigeon. It was a gigantic peregrine falcon, wings outspread, staring directly at me. The falcon paused for a beat, looked into my eyes, then flew off into the twilight. Two minutes. A peregrine falcon. My air conditioner. New York City. The odds are a zillion to one.

Message Received. I have my answer. Get to work.

To be clear from the outset: I believe that my participation in this Greater Reality project is the result of an interventional non-human intelligence that communicates through often pretty ordinary people. I'm not sure why this Greater Reality can't just announce itself to everybody all at one time, but apparently, there's some kind of system in place. This is the way it's done. I've had a minor Download about this, but it's not satisfying. In contrast, and as you will soon see, I've had genuinely incredible Downloads that are mind-blowing in their cosmic precision and layered complexity. Then sometimes, I just have these flabby little understandings like, "There's a system in place" or

"Humanity is likely headed towards another Iron Age. Look up how many people lived during the Iron Age. Not many."

I don't know a lot of things for sure when it comes to The Phenomenon, but I do understand these three points: First, a Greater Reality does exist, and we are all a part of it. Second, this Greater Reality is a unitive state that expresses itself prismatically through consciousness, experienced by some of us as the Contact Modalities. And third, this Greater Reality is engaged in public relations. It wants its stories told.

Before embarking on this vastly abridged journey into my personal relationship with The Phenomenon, I would like to thank the universe for my partners in High Strangeness. Without the stabilizing influence of a small posse of indispensable friends and family, I could not stand by the sanity and veracity of my own story. But stand, I do. That's because the universe has been kind to me on at least one front. I have witnesses.

Aliens, Ghosts and Hoodies

Let's get the UFO, ghost and alien stuff out of the way early so that we can move onto perhaps even more important and stranger things.

It's autumn in California. The 1970s. I've just started the fifth grade, and decide one day after school that I'm going to summon a UFO telepathically. (It's the Central Valley, after all, and there isn't a whole lot else for a ten-year-old to do.)

I stand at the kitchen window for three nights and send out my invitation, vectoring a flight path to myself throughout all of time and space. I've always been a natural lucid dreamer, although it was much more effortless and frequent in my childhood. For some reason, my ten-year-old self intuits that I can use the same techniques of positivity and absolute self-assuredness to get what I request, as if this universe itself is but a dream, and will yield to my passionate lucidity.

"I am a friend of Intelligent Life, and I want to say hello. Come visit me."

Three nights of staring at the stubborn sky, sending out wave upon wave upon wave of invitation. Nothing happens. I see a few shooting stars. Odd. Was that meteor traveling up instead of down? And then . . . the miracle.

A classic silver flying saucer appears less than 150 feet away, just across the street, centered directly above the cul-de-sac. Friendly lights twirl and dance on the asphalt in thick red, green, blue, and white beams. Imagine for a moment my utter disbelief. And then think of my mother's as I scream for her to get out of the bathroom. The saucer is parked silently in the air outside our home, as if sitting on an invisible shelf. I can feel its friendship radiating towards me.

I run to the bathroom shouting, "Mom! Mom! Come and see the UFO!" By the time we rush outside, the saucer is gone (or invisible). Let me be crystal clear here. This is a conscious, waking memory. Not a memory of a dream. Not some flight of fancy. Not some wishful thinking. This happened. Period.

I remember this silver flying saucer and its dance of densely colored lights more clearly than almost any other event in my life. This modern miracle happened over four decades ago, and yet I've only told a handful of friends about it. And until very recently, I would purposefully omit from this story all details about my three nights of telepathic invitation sending. There's only so much crazy a general audience can take.

For those of you who make up the more specialized audience that includes UFO researchers and enthusiasts, I'm sure that you've already categorized my experience within your well-established conceptual and theoretical frameworks. But for me, none of this is conceptual or theoretical. It is ontological. It really happened, and decades before I would ever hear about so-called Close Encounters of the Fifth Kind (CE5), also known as Human Initiated Contact Experiences.

My recent awakening to a world in which CE5 is out of the closet, so to speak, is the direct result of reading about the USS Nimitz UFO encounters in The New York Times in December 2017. This news story, and its corroborating official US Navy video, turned my curiosity dial up to eleven, waking me up to my own life history in the process. I'm still surprised by the number of educated, well-read people who to this day know nothing about what should have been one of the biggest stories to ever break in world history. It's like there's a pall of ignorance hanging over our planet, preventing us from seeing the truth.

The Nimitz story activated something in me. Finally, I can tell my stories. Disclosure is coming. At the same time, I realized that I needed to brush up on what the world has been up to since the last time I looked into any of this UFO and paranormal stuff. I was shocked to discover that not only are people talking about telepathically summoning UFOs nowadays, but also, they are paying experts tons of money to teach them how to do this. For over 40 years, I thought I was the only person who had ever had this kind of contact experience. It's no wonder I kept it to myself.

I think it's important to note here that I successfully invited a UFO to my exact coordinates in time and space, and that I did it for free, with zero training. I suggest you have an open heart and take the same route before you pay anybody a single penny. The secret is: You just have to remember who you really are, that you are more than your current life-story and container. And you have to come from a place of love and friendship to connect with the shared reality that unites all sentient beings in the universe: consciousness. No other credentials are needed. Of course, be careful what you wish for. You might find yourself inside of an extraterrestrial research project like I did.

Before a couple of years ago, the most research I had ever done on flying saucers was to search for "UFO solid red green and blue lights" on Netscape Navigator. You can use Google to estimate how long ago that was. (For those interested, that first early Internet search came up with the Rendlesham Forest incident, even way back then.)

My success with summoning a UFO at the tender age of ten brings me back to one of the main reasons that I'm participating in this project today. I believe that the Phenomenon can only be understood through paying extremely close attention to the true stories of Experiencers, and I'm here to provide experiential "back-up" to Mr. Hernandez and his associates.

The connection between UFOs, non-human intelligence, and consciousness is real, very real. And I've known about it since just a few days after my tenth birthday over four decades ago when I called down that flying saucer with nothing but my mind and friendly intentions. It's taken decades of dead-ends pursuing worthless leads on "nuts and bolts" ufology, but finally portions of the UFO community are finally catching up to the unavoidable fact that consciousness is primary. Any hope to understand the Phenomenon must begin there.

Another thing the UFO community is catching up with is the connection between UFOs and ghosts. This confluence of weirdness is so counterintuitive that I believe only an authentic Experiencer would make the connection, and only because he or she has lived through it.

Just a few days after my first and only Close Encounter of the Fifth Kind ("Nailed it!"), my home was visited by another otherworldly vision, an African American ghost wearing a chunky white-cabled turtleneck, and an absolutely gigantic afro. This is where the universe blesses me with my first corroborating witness: my mother.

We're back in the 70s again. I wake up in the middle of the night and feel very uneasy. Something's amiss. My bedroom door is open to a hallway that shoots straight down to the kitchen window, the same window that I stood at for three nights the previous week during my successful UFO summoning. There's a simple white vinyl shade pulled down over the window. I should mention that I'm extremely nearsighted. I don't have my glasses on, and everything just looks like a blur. As I stare down the hallway for a few moments, I think I'm looking at that white vinyl shade. And then I see movement. The shade has something black coming out of it near the top, and that dark mass just moved a little bit. I pull the sides of my eyes into a squint to help me see what's going on. I'm not staring at the vinyl shade at all. I'm staring at a tall black man in a chunky white fisherman's turtleneck. And like I said before, he has an absolutely gigantic afro.

I scream, "Mom! Mom! There's someone in the house!"

I reach for my eyeglasses, and just then, my mom comes barrelling out of her bedroom with her .45 pointing the way. I yell, "Kitchen!" Nobody is in there. Maybe five or ten seconds have passed. All the doors and locks are checked. Nothing is awry. My mom calls my dad to let him know that I just saw someone in the house. He lives on the other side of town but will come over the next couple of evenings to make sure that everyone feels safe. Next, my mom calls one of her girlfriends, and we head over to her house to spend the rest of the night.

I wake up the next morning to hear my mom talking to her friend in the kitchen.

"The weird thing is. The night before last, I woke up and felt uneasy. I looked out my bedroom door, and I saw a black guy with a white sweater walk into Greg's room. I immediately grabbed my gun and ran in there, expecting that I was going to have to shoot somebody. But nobody was there."

My mom thought she had just been dreaming, and so she didn't say anything to anybody about it. But then I saw the same apparition the following night. And apparently, the ghost was on a schedule. He showed up at the same time both nights.

For over four decades, I've wondered why on Earth did my mom and I both see the same apparition on different nights? And why did it happen just a few days after I summoned the UFO? One of the comforts I've discovered over the last couple of years in my research is that, once again, I'm not the only person to see a UFO followed in close succession by some kind of spiritual entity. This sort of thing is somewhat common among Experiencers.

On a personal note: I've been in the closet about this project with almost everyone I know for some pretty obvious reasons. First, I don't want my personal or professional life to be adversely affected. Second, I don't need my friends or family worrying about me. But I took a leap of faith last week. I mentioned this project to my mom, who usually is the very definition of skeptical-- definitely not religious or into any kind of new age or "hippy woo-woo" stuff. I wanted to get some other perspectives for this project and decided to ask her if she remembered the ghost with the sweater and the afro back in California. Without missing a beat, she said, *"I will never forget it. Weirdest thing that's ever happened to me in my life, other than the guys in brown hoods."*

By "guys in brown hoods," my mom is referring to her recent near-death experience, which happened quite unexpectedly, only a few months ago, while I was off having some of my own unforeseen mystical experiences in Europe. Almost by definition, nobody ever expects an NDE.

My mom's occurred during quintuple bypass surgery. I was deep into a three-week vacation, and nobody bothered to tell me that my mom was diagnosed with severe congestive heart failure, let alone that she was scheduled for emergency surgery. Anyway, during the operation, my mom found herself transported to a chair in a conference room of sorts. In front of her was a brilliantly polished walnut table, around which sat twelve hooded figures.

My mom intuited immediately that these hooded figures were genderless. (Yay! My mom just had her first noetic experience.) The beings were dressed in robes of various shades of brown, from very light, a tannish-white, to very dark, almost black. She could not see their faces. In fact, not only were these creatures, gender-free. They were also face-free-their bodies ended in long headless necks.

She looked over at them, and this is what happened. One by one, they examined her briefly and said either ***"I don't want her" or "We don't want her."*** They started at one end of the table and slowly moved their way to the final hood. "I don't want her," he concluded, and then my mom woke up from her surgery.

Anyone who has ever had surgery under general anaesthesia will tell you that conscious brain activity and dreams cease completely while you're out, creating a vacuum of lost time. You're there, and six hours later, you're back, and it seems like no time has passed at all. This was not the case for my mom. She was sitting at that shiny walnut conference table for what seemed like hours, waiting to hear what the brown hooded figures would say next. Turns out, they didn't have much to contribute.

My mom swears that what she saw in this afterlife setting was "more real than real"-that these Ascended Masters were there to evaluate her for the next step in the journey of her soul. And then she added, "Is it weird that the brown hooded guys all had greyish skin?"

"No, mom, that's not weird. Have you ever heard of Grey aliens before?" Believe it or not, my mom didn't know what I was talking about. If it's not a classic Hollywood film, a mystery, Perry Mason, or CSI-Whatever, she's not interested.

I mention all of this backstory as a way of making more sense of my experiences. My mom's recent NDE, and her willingness to talk about it fearlessly, motivated me to open up about this Greater Reality project. I asked her if she remembered the time I screamed at her to come outside and see the UFO across the street.

Flashback to that first UFO incident: My mom is massively annoyed at me, but-on the plus side-I managed to get her out of the bathroom. We run outside looking for the flying saucer but nothing is there. I point across the street to where the saucer had effortlessly parked in midair, and we look out in all directions. Again, nothing.

So, some forty years later, I ask my mom if she remembers the UFO as clearly as she remembers the ghost, which happened only a few days afterward. She has zero memory of this incident. None. This absence in her recollection completely freaks me out. It's not the sort of thing my mom would forget. She has a fantastic memory, which made her an invaluable asset in the legal profession for years. I sense the memories were yanked out of her. You will understand more of my feelings on this subject as we move into the next section.

Okay, Mom. Let me tell you some other things that you don't know about UFOs. About three months after summoning my Intelligent Friends from who knows what planet or dimension, I moved further upstate, into an even more remote area of California. My dad got custody, and we were living with his parents, whom I loved very much. It is from this home, and in what I call a "pocket universe" version of this home, that I will have the majority of the rest of my alien Contact Experiences.

Memory. I'm standing up and yelling. *"No, I will not get naked!"*

I'm of average height for a ten-year-old and have several inches on the two small Grey aliens that alternate between looking at me and at each other. As I think of them now, they are just so gosh darn cute. But I'm angry and stubborn, and I'm simply not going to follow directions. One of them walks off to find a supervisor. The other one just doesn't understand why I'm not following his instructions.

"Please, just take off your clothes. You can leave your socks on, but bring your things with you."

"No. I'm not going to do that!"

Anyone who has ever known me will tell you that I'm an extremely body-conscious, modest person. I'm not sure why it runs so deep, but it does. For example, you are never going to see me whip off my clothes and skinny dip in a lake. Nor will you find me sharing a hot tub with friends. Never going to happen. So as far as Alien Mind Control goes, my Body Dysmorphic Disorder is considerably more powerful.

The next thing I remember is a much taller Grey coming onto the scene, big eyes, you know the type. He's standing on my left, seemingly out of nowhere. He looks right into me. I sense extreme power, perhaps served up with a small side of exasperation. I wonder if I've been a pain in this guy's ass on more than one occasion. The poor friendly little guys just don't have the mind control horsepower to get me to do something I deeply, stubbornly don't want to do. The Tall Grey stares at me for a few seconds. I know that he's seeking to understand.

Then he breaks the silence and speaks to me inside of my head. *"We do not care about your naked body. We just have to run some tests, and you will be able to go home. Nobody will see you. Look there."*

I look over to my right and suddenly notice a young woman, maybe early teens, hard to tell. She's standing there naked. Has she been there all along? It's the first time I can remember seeing a stranger's bare breasts up close in person. Of course, this coming-of-age moment just had to happen inside of a UFO. She's carrying her clothes in a bundle at her waist. She's completely motionless, staring straight ahead. Like a zombie. End of memory.

My next memory is of being onboard a flying saucer, and knowing that if I turn the corner, I will see the beautiful rounded wall, the top third of which looks like it's made out of a cheese grater. There are inch-round circular holes up there. For ventilation? It's my favorite detail of this ship. I've been here enough to have favorite architectural flourishes. What I don't care for is the ambient temperature of this place. Not only is it unbearably hot in here; it smells really bad.

Next fragment: I'm in a vast hangar-like room, inside what I assume to be a massive spaceship. A uniformed military guy is standing next to me. I say something like, *"Wow. This is the most amazing place I've ever seen. It's like Battlestar Galactica!"* And he responds, *"I know. But they'll never let us remember."*

Simple reverse psychology often works wonders with me. I can remember saying, "I will remember this! I will remember this! I will remember this!" Over and over again.

Now, we're shifting locations again to what I call the "pocket dimension" of my grandparents' house. Either I'm in an illusion, and the Visitors are simply making me think that I'm in a modified-version of my grandparents' house-perhaps to make me feel more comfortable-or the Visitors are actually able to create another version of reality altogether, one based on the template of my grandparents' house, like using the "Save As" function in Microsoft Word, except creating new dimensions in space-time, instead of documents.

This time, I'm in the pocket-dimension version of my grandma's kitchen. They've erected some kind of pony wall that I can't see over, and I'm looking at a small TV monitor. I'm being told to relax and to guess the correct symbols. I remember being slightly pissed off and massively tired. I believe that I can remember this particular snippet because the Visitors have had to switch off some of their mind control technology in order to test me accurately for psi ability.

I remember choosing the wrong symbols on purpose, just to be spiteful-to get through the exercise as quickly as possible. I'm tired of helping these guys with whatever they're up to. Of course, my plan doesn't work as they instantly pick up on my intentions. (Duh! They're telepathic.) *A voice tells me that the sooner I take the test seriously, the sooner I can go home.*

At some point over the course of these alien night visits, I grow fond of one of the shorter Greys. I ask him about how I'm doing on the psychic testing. Turns out, not too hot. He suggests that it might have something to do with the dead chicken that it's in my stomach. It must be Friday, because my grandmother has made fried chicken dinner every Friday night for decades. Eating another sentient creature is simply incomprehensible to the Visitors. They are deeply disturbed by my casual and senseless indifference to this other life form.

I explain, ***"But if you'd just try some of my Grandma's fried chicken, you'd understand!"*** My favorite little helper alien seems to have a dark sense of humor, and **although he's disgusted by my suggestion, we share something like a laugh together.** It's funny, but now that I've been vegan for the last three years or so, I see where the Greys are coming from on dietary matters.

After I test for psychic ability, I'm shown scenes, on the same little monitor, of what I understand to be the future: dead oceans, forests on fire, animal carcasses, poisoned skies. I think they show me this bad news from the future after I resist cooperating with them on my tests. It's a reminder of why they're bothering me. **These Visitors present themselves as helpers.**

As I'm writing this, I take a quick break to make sure that the world isn't ending (anyone alive during this particular epoch in human history will appreciate what I'm talking about). A headline at CNN catches my eye "The ocean temperature around the world is rising at the same rate as if five Hiroshima bombs were dropped in every second." Could we do a more horrible job of taking care of Mother Earth? Or each other? What is wrong with us? I wonder if the environmental devastation videos I was shown forty years ago are about to come true. Perhaps these videos are from a potential future timeline, one that we can turn away from and avoid. Otherwise, what was the purpose of showing them to me?

My next memory is not scary at all. In fact, it is joyful beyond all reckoning. I wake up in a small room facing a curving wall. The room is shaped like a piece of pie. And I'm happy to be here. Very happy. I'm in a flying saucer again. Across from me, and I'm not sure if they are sitting or standing, are two fellow eleven- or twelve-year-old contemporaries, who I immediately recognize for some reason. I'm delighted because they are my best friends. (But at the same time, I have no idea who they are. Weird sensation.) The boy, I immediately identify as Hindu. I don't know how I know this. He could have been Muslim or Sikh. But I remember thinking, "Oh, it's my Hindu friend!" Between him and me is a shorthaired Tomboy with freckles. I think her name is Kelly. (Hello, Kelly, are you out there reading this?) I adore her completely, plus I want her for my personal bodyguard. She is a badass. I don't know how I know this, but I do.

Anyway, we're told that today is going to be fun. As we've been ideal participants, we're being rewarded with a very special treat. I don't remember any Greys or other non-human life forms anywhere else on the ship. Other than The Ship itself, of course, which I'm now upgrading to initial capital letters as he is a sentient being. We walk into what I guess you would call a control room or bridge. As elsewhere, I'm going to reconstruct my memory of this dialog as best as I can. The gist is definitely here.

"Okay, Greg. Go ahead and put your hands on that little globe over there." I'm pretty sure it was a translucent globe-like thing, and not just a plain flat panel. Maybe sort of like a crystal ball. "What are we going to do?" I ask. ***"Today, you're going to learn how to fly me. We're going to practice a little bit, and then you're going to get a special treat."*** This communication is coming directly from The Ship. I put my hands on the ball, and then the next thing I know, I'm outside of The Ship. "Wait, what's happening?" The Ship responds that I'm seeing things from his perspective. (It's definitely a boy ship.) **I understand that a part of me, my consciousness, has merged with The Ship**. I'm not experiencing myself holding onto the globe controller. I don't even know where my body is at this point. Or where my Hindu friend is. Or where Kelly is. I'm literally flying the ship as The Ship. And currently, I'm not worried about what's on the inside of

The Ship. I'm not worried about anything, not even flying. I'm doing great!

I think that this reminds me of flying in lucid dreams. The Ship tells me, "You're not dreaming, Greg. This is real." The magnificent joy radiating out of me that day is shared seamlessly with The Ship. He is having a fantastic time as well. I know that this kind of interaction is what The Ship lives for. The Ship is now definitely my new best friend.

Just imagine merging your mind with a pure love and friendship consciousness who also happens to be an interdimensional spaceship that can travel anywhere on Earth, literally at the speed of thought. In essence, I felt like The Ship and I had established a soul connection-like I had a friend for life. The happiness radiating out of both of us is simply beyond description. (I would only ever feel such pure and unadulterated love one more time in my life. We'll get to that later when we move into the spiritual portion of our trip through the Contact Modalities.)

So I'm swooping and flying through the air, and we dive into the Pacific Ocean as well, which is actually a suggestion from The Ship. I'm concerned that we will kill whales and dolphins by going under the water, but The Ship assures me that we won't hurt anything.

And then all at once, I'm back inside The Ship again, my consciousness returned to its usual container, and I've still got a hand on the control globe. "You don't have to hold that anymore. We're connected." (To translate into 2020 terms, it's like I hadn't been bumped off the Wi-Fi network yet.)

The Ship tells me to think really carefully about where I would like to visit next. He will take us to one more place, and it can be anywhere I want. I make my choice almost instantly. Next memory is standing with my little friends, all of us looking out the view screen towards planet Earth, far below. We're in orbit. Magnificent beauty lies before us. I ask The Ship how many people choose to visit this place for their wish, and he says about two out of every three.

"I can't believe I'm seeing this. We're just like astronauts." I look over at my friends. Their wide eyes and smiles of amazement confirm my own feelings. It's an instinct by now, and I begin my mantra. "I will remember this. I will remember this." Then I think of my friends. I tell them to join in or else they will forget everything. The three of us hold hands and chant, "We will remember this. We will remember this. We will remember this."

Tall Grey Beings

The next memory is scary, and leads into the experience that's at the very beginning of my story. I'm in the living room of my grandparents' house-the pocket dimension edition. I'm standing next to a Tall Grey, who's obviously concerned about me. Something's very wrong. I can no longer be on the ship. I believe that it has made me sick. From what I can tell, it's just me and the Tall Grey in the living room, but he has called for backup.

The Grey says something like, *"Don't worry. We're going to fix you."* Not the sort of thing you want to hear from anybody, at any time, under any circumstances, but it's even worse coming from an extraterrestrial entity. I start screaming that I want to know what's going on, yelling for my dad and grandparents. Nobody's around to hear my cries, except for the Grey who has had about enough of me. He tells me to calm down, or he's going to have to use the stick. That thing scares me. It's like some kind of high-tech cattle prod. I know that I've felt pain at the wrong end of that instrument, and I settle down. Around this time, I can hear some commotion coming out of the front bedroom, which connects directly to the living room. Something is getting set up in there.

Praying Mantis Being

Next thing I remember, the Tall Grey leads me into the bedroom. Standing before us is what I've recently learned is called a Mantid, **an exceptionally tall being that looks like a Praying Mantis**. This is the first and only time I can remember interacting with this species. I notice that the Grey seems to be in awe of our new friend. I don't suspect he interacts much with this level of being. The Grey communicates to me that I'm in good hands, that this being is billions of years old, nearly as ancient as our solar system. It seems like the Grey almost worships this new guy. It's like we've been granted an audience with alien royalty.

The Mantid's appearance may be grotesque, but I'm instantly comforted by him. His very presence radiates peace of mind and well-being. I ask the Mantid if he's really as old as the Grey says. He tells me that he's almost as old as our Sun, but not quite. Around four billion years old. He explains that he's a specialist there to help me. I understand that something is incredibly wrong with my health.

I remember this next bit very clearly: The Mantid manually examines both of my forearms where marble-sized tumors have recently appeared just under the skin. He's not at all concerned about these growths, and tells me not to worry about them. In fact, I think that this four-billion-year-old advanced being has just humored a twelve-year-old earth child, simply because I asked him to take a look at "my new bumps." Whatever it was that he was there to do, it was not to diagnose me with benign lipomas. The Greys had dialed a sort of Intergalactic 911 for something far more serious than my bumps.

All of a sudden, I notice that there's a metallic examination chair at the foot of the bed, blocking the closet. It looks like a dental chair. I take a seat, and the Mantid begins to scan me with a rod that emits colored lights. This tool looks like a magic wand and I'm deeply fascinated. In just a few seconds, he finds what he's looking for. I sense that there's a renewed urgency in him, and I'm afraid again. I remember breaking into a loud sob. I'm wracked with overwhelming feelings of failure, self-disgust, and hopelessness. I cry out, "Does this mean that I'm not going to be able to help anymore?"

I don't remember the Mantid answering. More importantly-switching back to the present day-I don't remember exactly what I meant by "help anymore." I wonder if that sick and scared twelve-year-old back in 1982 knows anything more about what's going on than I do nearly four decades later. I doubt it. This whole project is shrouded in mystery. I would love to go back in time and ask these creatures what all of this means. I want a clear explanation and accounting for everything. But that's not how it works. "There's a system in place."

Next flash of memory. Whatever examination or procedure that happened in the alien dental chair has been completed. Now, we're moving on to a new contraption that looks like one of those old-fashioned vertical climbing machines call a VersaClimber. This machine is now to the left of the bed. There are handgrips on either side of a central shaft, and I'm told to stand up and grab the grips. I'm afraid for my life. I scream out something like, "I don't want to die."

The Mantid telepathically communicates to me that I'm going to see some lights. He's behind me now, and I know that he's going to do something in the region of my upper back, just below the neck. I remember thinking, "Oh my god. These lights are beautiful."

We've now circled back to the moment I remember meeting The Voice for the first time. We teleport to my favorite park; we teleport to my mom's house; and then we fly the scenic route back home, with promises that I will not have to deal with the Visitors anymore. After I wake up inside that tank and freak out one final time, I never have to take another alien test again.

The Future is a Memory of a Dream

"Bellevue, Iowa? Where the hell is that? Is it even a real place?" I wake up in the middle of the night, and know instantly that I've had one of my special dreams. Ever since that alien tank experience, and my first meeting with The Voice, I've had dreams of the future that come true. They're pretty rare, so when I have one, I don't mess around: I tell my friends right away. I know I need to talk about this strange vision when I get up, but it's only three in the morning, so I fall back to sleep.

The next thing I know, it's a few hours later. The comforting percolations, burps, and whistles of my uncle's Mr. Coffee waft in with the fresh breakfast aromas of mid-week morning. I can hear my uncle and grandma talking in the kitchen. I'm visiting a small farming community in rural Northern California. I'm here to see my ailing maternal grandma for the last time. We are only a few miles from where I had the majority of my UFO and alien contact experiences as a child. It is now twenty-eight years since my visit with the Mantid healer.

I walk into the kitchen. "Oh my God. Had the weirdest dream in the middle of the night." My uncle and grandma look up at me, and I realize that I'm catching my uncle just before he heads out to start his day.

Please note: The dialog that follows (like elsewhere in this chapter) is a reconstruction of what was said to the best of my recollection. It's roughly how I tell the story to the rare people who I get "a push" to tell this stuff to, and follows as closely to reality as possible. "I dreamt that I was working in someplace called Bellevue, Iowa. I've never even heard of Bellevue, Iowa. Not sure it's even a real place."

"Anyway, I'm interviewing this guy for a job, but I already know I'm not going to be able to help him. He's a nice enough guy, but not a good fit for what I need. I wonder how he even made it in front of me. But I always make sure to spend a little extra time with anybody who I interview, even if I can't help them at my company, so I decide that I'm going to coach him with some résumé and interview tips."

"So, I'm showing him what I would change on his résumé to make it better, and I look up at him and notice something weird and say, 'What's that you have in your eye?' I get closer to see what's going on. 'Oh my God! You have a worm in your eye!' at which point, this giant worm jumps out at me, and I wake up."

Before my grandma or uncle can respond to my little dream diary moment, the television does it for them. My grandma has her morning show blasting far too loudly in the other room. I think it was probably Good Morning America. "News just in from Bellevue, Iowa. A man discovers that he has a parasitic worm. In his eye!" Without skipping a beat, my uncle looks at me and says, "I have dreams of the future that come true, too. All the time."

The extreme temporal and narratological synchronicity of my dream story merging seamlessly with morning television news, as if orchestrated perfectly by some unseen conductor, reminded me of another impossible dream of the future that came true.

"This is just like the dream about my dad's tools. Do you guys remember the time I dreamt about my dad's tools being stolen?" And my grandma answers, "Gregory, everybody remembers your dream about your dad's tools being stolen." (What my uncle and grandma don't know is that this next bit of psychic history happened just one week after the medical emergency, Mantid alien encounter described above. I didn't remember this connection for almost forty years, but that's definitely the chronology. Without doubt.)

It's 1982 again, and I'm visiting my mom back down in the Central Valley, a couple of hours south of the small town I'm living in with my dad and his parents. My mom's parents have driven me to see her for Christmas, and the bedrooms are full up. I struggle to squeeze in a little extra sleep on a sofa in the living room. I wake up on and off, hearing my grandparents and mom talk in the kitchen. I've just managed to fall back to sleep when I hear a deep, urgent voice telling me about something that should be impossible. This is the second time I remember hearing The Voice, but the first time he has come to me in a dream. It will not be the last time I hear from him.

The Voice says, ***"Wake up, Greg. Wake up. You have to get up now and call your dad. Someone's breaking into his van and stealing his tools."*** The Voice is deep. Resonates warmth and power. Experience will show me that when you hear The Voice, you listen and take action. There are no alternatives.

"Mom, I have to use your phone to call my Dad. I just had a dream, and this voice told me that I had to wake up and call my dad because someone's breaking into his van and stealing his tools." "Um, okay. That's weird. But go ahead and call him."

"Dad, Hi. It's me. I just had a dream that somebody was going to break into your van and steal your tools and that I had to call you." "What do you know about that? The police have just left. Someone broke into my van and stole my tools. I just filed a report. You better tell me what you know."

What was I supposed to say to that? I'm twelve-years-old and have been visiting my mom for a few days, more than two hours away. I'm not a criminal mastermind running some kind of underground, breaking-into-vans, tool-stealing syndicate.

When I return home the following week, I don't receive a friendly welcome. I'm under deep and angry suspicion for a few days. It's actually quite hellish, and I learn to keep my mouth shut tight about this stuff. That's how it will remain for most of my life. Keep that mouth shut. Protect yourself no matter what. Don't stand out.

In over fifty years, I've only shared some of my stories with a very select group of friends and family-and often only because they're first-hand witnesses to the weirdness. It's not easy. I don't want to scare anybody. I don't want to lose a job or a friend over these shenanigans. But recently, the universe has stepped up its campaign to get me to talk about this stuff, and I've decided to listen.

It takes a few days after my return home upstate, but eventually, the man who stole my dad's tools is arrested trying to pawn them. Of course, he's some middle-aged drug addict with zero connection to me. My name is not Damian, Pinhead, or Rosemary's Baby. I only have these experiences because some form of Higher Intelligence wants me to have these experiences. I generally do not invite them.

Given that I'm going to have these visions and experiences whether or I want them or not, I'm particularly thankful that the universe has provided me with the best mental health plan currently available under the circumstances: Witnesses. My mom witnessed the "Afro Sweater Ghost," even before I did; my parents, grandparents, and uncle were all there for the "Stolen Tool" incident. But I have to say, when it comes to recent times, I feel especially blessed for my friends Tanya, Mary, and Alan, who have all been incredibly stabilizing influences in my life, especially regarding this weird stuff. They are all extraordinary witnesses of the extraordinary.

Shamanic Interlude

I don't want to give you the impression that I've been sitting around these last forty-odd years having mystic visions of the future by day, and piloting UFO tours on nights and weekends. I've often gone years between significant events. And frankly, I'm thankful for the time off. Recently, though, the dial is turned back up to maximum weirdness, which is why I'm writing this essay.

The longest stretch of time I've had without significant High Strangeness activity has been around thirteen glorious years. I think the reason that I got this time off was because back in college I underwent a spontaneous shamanic journey that lasted for about three months, and frankly almost killed me. Surely, this is a 200-page story all to itself, and I'm not going to share details here. Let's just say that I had no cultural context for this spiritual awakening, it came out of the blue, and it was terrifying.

This experience was also horrifying for my father, who by this time had remarried. Until my shamanic spirit walk, my dad had never heard me stick up for myself. When I was brutally honest with him about some of his parenting issues, he took extreme umbrage and never talked to me again for the remaining thirteen years of his life.

During my shamanic journey, I had an onslaught of intense spiritual insights spontaneously, without recourse to the study of any sort of mystic literature. I've never had so many Downloads hit me all at once. I felt like the universe was trying to kill me, or at least stretch the limits of my bandwidth. My noetic understandings came fast and furious. After three months of extreme daily spiritual epiphany, I crawled back into the safe bubble of my secular humanism and rational atheism, and-miraculously-forgot almost everything I learned on my wild trek into hidden spiritual truths.

Years later, I would stumble across this treasure trove of spiritual insight once more, although in the form of a book, and not via supernatural visionary experience. My spiritual awakening already had a name: Advaita Vedanta, one of the most ancient spiritual traditions on the planet, a major foundation of Eastern spirituality, and the best key to understanding consciousness.

My sabbatical would not end until I moved to Grand Street on the Lower East Side of Manhattan in the early 2000s. Perhaps the Greater Reality decided that it was time for me to get freaky again. I'm going to unpack my extraordinary experiences on Grand Street shortly, but first let's circle back to my prophetic dreams, a particularly active Contact Modality for me, and one in which a clear pattern is emerging. Warning: Rough seas ahead.

One, Two, Three if By Sea

It's Tuesday, June 14, 2005. I wake up from an intense dream that feels visionary. I've just seen two helicopters crashing into the East River. A noetic understanding accompanies these images. "These crashes are happening this week, on different days. Make sure you tell your friends in the office."

My office has an open floor plan with pony walls separating the desk spaces. Both the CEO and President of the Company sit out on the floor with everybody else, and although it's generally a congenial environment, there's zero privacy. So, when I come in that Tuesday morning and announce to Tanya and Mary that I've had one of my "special dreams," it's like one of those old E. F. Hutton Commercials: People listen.

I tell everybody in the office that I believe that two helicopters are going to crash into the East River this week, explaining that sometimes I have dreams that come true. For a finance-related firm, I'm surprised about how accepting most people are about this pronouncement. (Oh, it's just Greg being Greg again.) I've had accurate visions of earthquakes, fires, and other unpleasantries in the past, but it has been several years since I've been troubled with any disaster dreams. Thank the stars. I genuinely want to take a pass on this ability.

A few hours pass, and then Tanya breaks the news to the entire office. "Oh my God, Greg! A helicopter just crashed in the East River! No way!" This is a few years after 9/11, but I instantly sense that hackles are up. Some of my colleagues are clearly uncomfortable. Nobody says anything to me, but I get looks. I feel exactly as I did when my dad all but accused me of stealing his tools some 25 years previously when I accurately predicted that his tools were going to be stolen out of his van. There is simply no way for me to know the future before it happens. That is, if you accept our modern scientific worldview as Gospel.

I'm all for science. In fact, bring it up to speed quickly, please. My Experiences happen in the real world. My Experiences are actually normal. We just call them paranormal, for now, because our primate brains aren't quite there yet. And there is undoubtedly a lot of career-protectionism going on that prevents scientists from exploring essential areas. You can't do science if you're dying from malnutrition because nobody will hire you. Anyway, I digress.

It's now 4:38 p.m. on Friday, later that same week. Prediction number two has just crossed over from dream world to real world. From Timothy Williams's article in The New York Times: "A corporate helicopter carrying six banking executives and two pilots crashed into the East River this afternoon shortly after taking off from Manhattan near the United Nations, the second such helicopter crash in the river this week." (For the record, in the history of New York City, there has never been another time-ever-that two helicopters have crashed in the same week, not to mention in the same river, in the same week. This is not normal by any definition. I'm going to place the odds at two gazillion to one.)

And the "two helicopter prophecy" pales in comparison to what's coming up next. It's December 22, 2009, and I've had over four years off from "my disaster dreams." Unfortunately, that's all about to change.

I've gone to bed but wake up unexpectedly to find myself floating several hundred feet in the air, high above Alaskan waters. I look down and spontaneously start to narrate the noetic experience to myself as it unfolds directly into my consciousness. This is what I say to myself: "Oh, interesting. That boat has just crashed in the same place as the Exxon Valdez. And the fuel in the water is making a chaos symbol." This is what a laser-focused, absolutely perfect Cosmic-level Download looks like.

I did not hear another voice telling me this information. I was narrating it to myself. I was in a state of perfect knowledge. The interesting problem is that I was seeing the future, very much non-locally, through a Higher Consciousness. This is what it was like when I merged with the UFO as a child. I just knew stuff.

So later that day, I go out of town to visit my friend Mary for our annual Christmas fun get-together at her beautifully appointed home. Mary is brilliant. One of the absolute best people I have ever had the honor to work with and call friend. Mary was ranked number one in her graduating class at one of the world's top public universities-and math was part of her degree, not baroque dance or twelfth-century puppet arts. She is a globally respected businessperson. In other words, she is what you would call-and I'm using this word for only the second time in my essay-a badass.

I tell Mary about my dream, about how it's going to come true. There is what I call "a stickiness" to the dream. The details are just too precise; the feelings, too intense. Anybody who has experienced a prophetic vision or a weird psi event will know instantly what I mean. For example, my uncle, who you met briefly during the "Bellevue, Iowa, Worm in the Eye" story, also has dreams that come true, that have a certain hallmark intensity and specificity.

My uncle's prophetic dreams often involve his friends dying or communication with people who have already passed over. What makes these visions special is that when he has a dream about his friends passing away, you better believe that they are going to pass away. In fact, they've either just passed away in the middle of the night or will the following day. These are usually young friends, not older people in nursing homes, but individuals who don't even know that they have a health problem, or else commit suicide.

I've had two particularly powerful death dreams myself–which I will get to shortly. But first, back to Mary and the vision about the spill in Alaska. As a reminder: Mary was there in the office for the two helicopter prophecy back in 2005. So far, I'm batting a thousand with my psychic predictions. We agree to keep an eye out for environmental disaster news from The Last Frontier.

I return home after a lovely pre-Christmas day with Mary, go to bed, and think nothing more about our conversation, as I get caught up in the hustle and bustle of the holidays. A few days later, I think to log onto The Anchorage Daily News' website to see if there is any news about what I know is coming down the pike.

This can't be happening. There it is, pictured on the main page. An aerial photograph shows the fuel spill exactly as envisioned: My remote-viewing, astral-projecting, future-seeing Contact Modalities seem to be in perfect working order. It's as if my prophetic vision is being captured from inside that aircraft. Or perhaps even more strangely, from inside the photograph itself. Worlds unfolding within worlds. What don't we know about space-time, multiple dimensions, the nature of causality? And far outweighing all these mysteries: Are we rushing towards an inescapable doom? Or are we being given a second chance?

I check all the relevant data. The spill doesn't happen until several hours after I've already told Mary of my vision. The picture that appears in The Anchorage Daily News shows a clear whirlpool vortex pattern under the leaking tugboat, which I interpret as a chaos symbol. Exactly as envisioned. And this is when I get the chills. The name of the tug that has done the unthinkable and ran aground on the same reef as one of the most infamous environmental disasters of all time? The Pathfinder.

"You Dummies keep making the same mistakes, in the same exact places. And here's a chaos symbol for you to think about, too, just in case it's not obvious that you suck." The Greater Reality is speaking to us. And Mary is now on my witness support team for life.

Just in case all of this wasn't "High Strangeness" enough for you, every one of my prescient visions has eventually been followed up with "Clarification Downloads," noetic experiences that suggest that I did not pay close enough attention to the details of my own visions. "Wake up, Greg, pay attention!"

These visions are designed to be profoundly instructive, and clearly impossible for anybody to invent out of thin air. There are details wound up within details fortified within further details-a complex fractal dimensionality that is breathtaking in scope and depth.

Just when I think I've found my last meaningful clue, another Clarification Download pops up. There's a stunning interactive design to these visions-certainly not my own. It's difficult enough for me just to write this stuff down as experienced. I don't know anybody who could "Kaiser Soze" these stories up out of such seemingly unrelated minor news clips. As my friend Tanya says, "Ain't nobody got time for that!"

It isn't enough that I dream about someplace called Bellevue, Iowa, with a guy with a parasitic worm in his eyeball. (Seriously, "Take the worm out of your eye and see more clearly!) No, I have to get a Clarification Download. "Greg, you know that "Bellevue" translates as "beautiful or clear view" but do you know how "Iowa" translates?" (Hint: It's sleepy-ones, as in "Wake up, Dummies!")

It isn't enough that I saw two helicopters go down in the same week, in the same river (Interpretation: "Stop making the same mistakes in the same place, over and over again. Do we have your attention now?") No, I have to have a Clarification Download, years later. "Greg, did you happen to notice the name of the hospital that all of the crash victims were sent to?" (Hint: It's Bellevue Hospital.) My visions are cross-pollinating now!

It isn't enough that the Pathfinder tugboat crashed into Bligh Reef, the site of the infamous Exxon Valdez catastrophe. ***"Greg, did you look up the etymology of Bligh, as in Bligh Reef?"*** (Hint: It means "Gaze" in Old Norse, which is what the universe is doing to you to figure out why you're not catching on to this stuff this sooner.) Wake up and see!

Note: this Bligh Reef Clarification Download just happened moments ago, literally as I was writing this section.

"Greg, did you happen to notice why The Pathfinder foundered in the same place as the Exxon Valdez?" *(Hint: Don't worry. The captain of the ship wasn't asleep at the wheel. No, he was actually wide-awake. It's just that he was busy with more important things* *than piloting the boat. Like playing games on his phone!) Wake up and pay attention, people! And get off your phones!*

Note: this Clarification Download came years after the initial story, and was the result of an investigation that took some considerable time to complete and make public.

"Greg, it's not just called The Pathfinder. It's called The 'Crowley' Pathfinder, and what concept is inextricably entangled with the name Crowley?" (Hint: it's Magic, as in this vision is so strange and impossible that it might as well be Harry Potter to you guys.)

Every time I think I've finally gotten to the bottom of one of these visions, there's another deep level of meaning ready to assert itself. I invite you to play along. Google these news events and see if there's not some unseen detail that speaks to Revelation, or perhaps even to you, personally, on a level that only you can understand.

As for the Bellevue, Iowa dream, my sincere apologies to the guy in the national news with the worm in his eye. I guess he's been on television on one of those "Monsters Inside of You" cable television shows, but I've not been able to find a copy of it online. (I wonder if he looks like what I remember from my dream? I would not be surprised at all.)

I did get a Clarification Download a couple of years ago about this "Worm in the Eye, Bellevue, Iowa" guy. *"Greg, you didn't bother to pay attention to the guy's name! Hello!"* (He happens to share names with two of the Four Evangelists, each known for their prophecies and signs.)

So why did I have the Bellevue, Iowa dream, anyway? First, I had the dream so that I could build a bridge between my uncle and me- without it, I never would have known that he also has visions of the future. This mystical dream had to happen at my uncle's house so that both of us would know that not only is this stuff real, but also that neither of us is alone. We can talk to each other now, as we are both Experiencers, and we know that we aren't making this stuff up. We don't have time for shenanigans.

Second, I had this dream so that I could begin to understand the real nature of prophecy within the world's spiritual traditions. Prophecy can be real. This realization is a massive jump for me, one that I could never have made on my own if I weren't receiving the visions myself.

Third, I've always been bothered by the competing, often contradictory truth claims that underlie all of the world's religions. Logically, not everyone can be right. So, by definition, that means some religions have to be wrong. Right? But I dislike bullies and uppity holy-rollers, precisely the subset of religious people who can make the world a horrible, deadly place, the kind of people who just happen to know that they are the only ones who are right, that everyone else is wrong. Until recently, it was easier for me to just cut the Gordian Knot on this nonsense and lump everything religious and spiritual together under the rubric of mythology, and take comfort knowing that I was above the fray, happy to identify as post-theistic-beyond religion and God.

But this particular Bellevue, Iowa vision has taught me something. People do, in fact, receive messages from beyond our everyday, commonsensical, linear understanding. I received essentially true, and impossibly allegorical, emblematic information about somebody and someplace about which I had zero knowledge. Bellevue, Iowa could have been about as real as Emerald City -I mean the first time I heard about it was in a dream, after all. But no, it's a real place that also happens to be highly-and meaningfully-symbolic of purposeful visionary awakening.

The guy with the worm in his eye is a real person whose story-at least for me in relation to my own growing mini cosmology-also happens to be stunningly emblematic of deeper universal meaning: of clear-sightedness, prophecy, self-improvement, and healing. What was not real was the dream part. I was not interviewing this guy in real life. I had not relocated to Iowa in real life. (Sorry Iowa, I love New York.) Those details are miscellaneous fictional plot elements that serve to drive the story forward, and to provide a space for the important part of the vision, which was the truth of revelation. In other words, there's a lot of filler between the good parts.

If you really pay attention to all of the Abrahamic traditions, the utmost highest teachings are very similar. The truth of the stories is the same. The cast of characters is different, the language is different, the prophets have different names, and there are different rules for personal conduct-and various other issues; to be sure-but the core teachings are truth-based. The same holds for all of the Eastern traditions. Truth is truth. As one of the most ancient spiritual texts on Earth, The Rig Veda, makes clear-and I'm quoting it for the second time: "The Truth is One. Sages call it by various names."

So I guess I had the Bellevue, Iowa dream to wake myself up, to take the worm out of my own eye. All of the world's spiritual traditions are equally true, in the sense that there is only one truth. Truth just happens to go around using different ministers, different prophets. In fact, all the truth you need is already right inside of you.

What's equally true is that all of the world's spiritual traditions are equally false. So don't get high-and-mighty or self-important. Be a good person. Treat others with love and respect. Don't use the world as your personal toilet and toxic waste dump. Put a smile on someone's face today. Get out of your head, and think of others sometimes. Trust your inner voice because the entire universe, and all points in time and space live inside of you. These simple truths are built into our core operating system. Any programming that violates these basic principles is a move in the wrong direction. Reboot yourself when necessary.

Clearly, it's time. We have to wake up now. We are all Children of God, even our friends from different spiritual traditions, even our friends with no spiritual traditions. We need to grow up, and start taking better care of each other, this planet, and ourselves.

Friends, this Greater Reality stuff is real. Please, let's pull the worms out of our eyes.

The Pathfinder Vision is a gift, as well. Perhaps it's not too late for us. We can find a path and course-correct. It's no longer simply a matter of Faith or Belief when you know with absolute certainty that consciousness is non-local, that time is non-linear, that there's some kind of Higher Intelligence with which we're all intimately connected, and that this planet is in massive crisis.

This non-human intelligence is so powerful that it can use Time, Space, the very fabric of Reality itself, like some kind of cosmic chalkboard to teach lessons and impart warnings. There's a helpful and loving intention behind all of it, too.

Without naming names (cough, military-industrial complex, cough cough), I think it's pretty silly to pretend that these Advanced Intelligences are out there plotting to take away our freedoms or to invade our planet. We're doing that pretty well all on our own, with no assistance from outer space or dimensions unknown. We won't have to worry about freedom at all if there's no water to drink, food to eat, or air to breathe. Because we'll all be dead. Like our planet.

If you look at the highest teachings of any of the world's religions, you will realize that Jesus is saying, **"Love thy neighbor as thyself,"** not because it's a cool thing to do, and just shut up and do what you're told. Jesus is reminding us of the deepest truth, found at the highest level of reality, that your neighbor literally is yourself. I was able to call the flying saucer to me from across untold dimensions of space and time, because I knew that I was calling out to a part of myself that was experiencing this universe as a part of something else. The aliens are us. We are all inextricably linked through consciousness.

To save time on your journey toward spiritual self-knowledge, you might choose to skip ahead of the class and move forward a few grades. Look into Advaita Vedanta, a tradition that has resonated with me for the last two years. This pathway has helped me make sense of our world, and my experiences in it. I've mentioned that my unexpected shamanic journey back in college consisted, in part, of Downloads into the truth of this tradition. Well, I've had a whole series of paranormal incidents since then that have guided me towards this non-dual Vedantic direction, which I don't have time or space to go into here. Let's just say, the universe essentially grabbed me by the nape of the neck and tossed me in with the Vedanta people. I'm beyond grateful for this intervention. I hope readers of this chapter will do some research on their own.

In the end, there's essential truth in every tradition. As my favorite fortune cookie says, "For light, go directly to the source of the light, not any reflections." You're going to find your own path forward at your own pace. Just know that there is a light inside of you, and that's the best place to start your spiritual awakening.

Let's take a pause from prophetic dreams and spiritual revelations, and move back to actual spirits, this time with returning special guest star, The Voice.

The Voice Returns / An Appointment with a Ghost Maid Lady

I originally posted this story about my interaction with a ghost at the Mohonk Mountain House, a gorgeous Victorian resort hotel in New York State, on a website about haunted places in the United States. I'm copying and pasting it here to save time (with some minor revisions).

My story happens in 2016, beginning on Friday, the Fourth of November, and ending on Saturday the Fifth, early morning, to be exact. I know because I searched through my calendar and email archives to make sure to get the details right.

First off, let me say that if you think you have any sort of spiritual or psychic sensitivities, this place will move your needle. I sometimes get strong hunches or feelings about people, places and things but was not prepared for what I saw here-clearly, and at extremely close range.

Upon arrival at Mohonk, my friend and I check into one of the hotel's "Victorian" rooms. Cozy and well-appointed, the room comes complete with a working fireplace, and a lovely balcony facing out towards the main drive snaking up to the resort.

We fought a lot of traffic getting out of Manhattan, and I'm eager to go to bed as early as possible that first night. After a brief dinner, I return to the room and snuggle into bed. I fall asleep within minutes. A couple of hours later, I wake up. A commanding, stentorian voice startles me out of my dream. It's The Voice. He informs me, very matter-of-factly, that I am going to wake up at 2:10 that morning. I don't think I've heard his actual voice for at least twelve years, although I only have this insight now that I'm looking at everything in retrospect. This time gap pretty much fits The Voice's schedule these days.

I put my glasses on and look over at the clock. It's only 11:11. Someone's clock is off, I think. I get up briefly, drink a glass of water, use the facilities, and quickly go back to bed. I sleep comfortably until I hear the same booming voice again, this time more urgent. The Voice says, "Wake up, Greg. Wake up! You're not alone in the room!" I get chills writing this down years after the fact. Startled and awake, I immediately rear up in bed. With my index fingers, I pull back the skin along the side of my eyes, forcing a hard squint that allows me to see clearly without my eyeglasses.

Standing just at the foot of the bed is a woman dressed in what looks like a Victorian maid's uniform. Her white apron is edged with lace scalloping, and she has an old-fashioned white bonnet in her hair. Are the long skirt and blouse of her uniform in some kind of muted red and white-checkered pattern, almost like picnic cloth? Not sure. But the white apron and the white bonnet are what stand out for me. Until I see her skin.

She's a black woman, and the skin on her face and hands, which is all the skin I can see, is heavily mottled with streaks of pink and white. My first impression is that she's a burn survivor, and not just any burn survivor, but one who has lived through an incredible inferno, perhaps in her childhood. But just then, I remember Michael Jackson and his skin problems, and think that maybe she has a severe case of vitiligo, the pigmentation disorder.

All of these thoughts happen in an instant, and at the same time, I yell out, "Who the F&@# are YOU?!" I reach for my eyeglasses on the bedside table and put them on. At that moment, I look up, and the maid is gone. My friend snores peacefully in the next bed over.

I think, Jesus Christ, did I just have a waking dream?
Then I look at the clock. It's 2:10 on the dot. As always, The Voice is a discarnate entity of his word. ***"Stay the F&@# out of my room!"*** I roar

to the now empty space at the foot of my bed. Meanwhile, my friend continues to snore happily a few feet away. I decide to wait until morning to tell her about the intruder.

After I cut and paste this story, it occurred to me that perhaps this ghost did not cross over because she had, in fact, been a burn survivor. She simply feared the Light. In that case, may I suggest to the universe: Take her to the waters instead. I'm going to take you there myself, a little later in this essay.

I'm looking down at my notes and realize that I have a couple of more ghost stories to tell. I just don't have the room in this context to add anything else, but I have a strong feeling that I will get to tell the poltergeist stories in another piece. There was one in Cheyenne, Wyoming, when I was a kid, which scared the daylights out of me, and, more recently, in a 16th-century palazzo cum Airbnb rental in Venice, Italy.

Also, every day for the last week, something has been jumping on top of my bed while I'm in it and still awake. When I look down to see if it's my cat, she's happily sleeping like nothing in the world is wrong. One night, I actually bounced up after what felt like a bowling ball had been dropped from the ceiling onto my bed. And then, this morning, I went into the bathroom, and the hot water tap was running in the sink. I thought, Oh no! I must have left this on when I got up and washed my hands several hours ago. The hot water was gone, which I didn't think was possible since I live in a big apartment building with a huge boiler.

Anyway, I turned the hot tap off and then thought to turn it on again just to make sure, and in just about four seconds, there was piping hot water. Somehow, that tap was turned on just seconds before I went into the bathroom. This sounds crazy, but it's like something wants me to know it's there. I'm definitely feeling all kinds of presences around me even as I type this now. Not normal. My home has never had so much of this "presence stuff" manifesting in it. More often than not, I'm away when I sense spirits.

Grand Street Rising

Speaking of which, a lot of weird stuff happens to me when I'm on vacation. In fact, with the notable exception of sentient orbs (recent) and various interactions with Grey aliens (around forty years ago), I would say a substantial majority of my experiences with non-human intelligence have occurred while I'm relaxed and away from home.

In 2018, my friends Alan, Pierre and I took a long trip to London and Ireland that started with a seven-night transatlantic crossing on the Queen Mary 2, sailing from New York to Southampton, England. On the eve of our adventures, I was lying in bed, planning out possible itineraries in my head when I felt a distinct presence in the room, observing me. Since I live in Manhattan, my bedroom is the size of a small walk-in closet, so the shimmering red-orange orb floating four feet from the floor next to the foot of my bed was not hard to spot. I screamed, "Jesus Christ!" and the orb instantly vanished.

My twenty-first-century instincts kicked in, and I immediately reached for my phone. Not to call 911 but to text one of my best friends. As you might remember from the two helicopters story, Tanya ranks up there as one of my staunchest allies in High Strangeness. She has been witness to plenty of weird stuff herself, including not only the helicopters dream but also her own encounters, experiences that she shared with her brother and grandmother as witnesses. (Thank you, Universe, for bringing "T" into my life. She keeps me as sane as I'm going to get!)

After texting Tanya, I looked down at my watch and saw that it was much later than I thought it possible, long after Midnight, so I texted Tanya again to apologize for dinging her phone so late. It appears that I had lost some time that evening. About two hours.

On the following afternoon, my friends and I embark on the Queen Mary 2 without incident. About three days into our trip, Alan and I decide to have lunch together in the Kings Court cafeteria, which is on Deck 7 of the colossal ocean liner. Alan is a recently retired environmental engineer and is a brilliant math and science guy, whose family is full of self-made captains of industry, engineers, neuroscientists, etc. Pretty much everyone in Alan's family has been the valedictorian of his or her graduating classes, including Alan. But Alan-warm-hearted, open-minded Methodist from Middle America-also has a deep spiritual side, and I had recently opened up to him about my childhood experiences with UFOs, and other unusual events.

The conversation flowed effortlessly that afternoon. Alan and I must have entertained (and perhaps scared) many of our fellow cafeteria diners during that lunch as I remember there was an almost unique silence surrounding our table, even though our section was full as we had to hunt to find an empty spot to eat. As one is wont to do from time to time, I discussed hazy memories of interacting with Grey aliens, as well as recollections of telepathically interfacing with and flying that UFO in my childhood.

As the lunch went on, I shared my first-hand observations about how the aliens I observed have the ability to hack into human brains and make us do almost anything they want, though I gave them a hard time on a couple of occasions, much to their annoyance. We also discussed my memories of being "beamed up" to a hovering craft through solid walls and closed windows via an unpleasant, nauseating, and loud interdimensional "vibra-beam." (This is the first you're hearing of it in my narrative, but believe me, I'm leaving out a ton of material as I'm already going to be well over my page count.) I'm sure our well-heeled shipmates had some fun stories to tell their friends about the UFO weirdos who somehow made it past security back in New York.

Of particular note, I recall explicitly talking about how most Experiencers report missing time, with many finding themselves transported miles away from their original destinations while driving. My UFO and alien experiences happened in childhood, and I think that most of my lost time was in the form of sleep deprivation, as my encounters happened late at night. My fifth and sixth grade years were unusually sleepy ones.

But what sticks out for me about this conversation is telling Alan that, even taking into consideration the flying saucers, the aliens, and the various other psychic phenomena that we discussed that afternoon, that far outranking all of these experiences was what happened to me on Grand Street, the time two discarnate entities escorted me to the place where Time itself began. More on this place later.

Eventually, our leisurely lunch ended, and I joked that it was time to go back to our staterooms so we could nap for a few minutes before heading back out for afternoon tea in the ballroom.

First, a little bit about this ocean liner's layout: there are four elevator banks on the Queen Mary 2, clearing marked A through D, running from forward to aft. The Queen is over 1,100 feet long, and although I don't have the ship's blueprints in front of me, I believe that each elevator bank is at least 200 feet apart. We were on the C elevator line, Deck 7, just off the cafeteria. Alan had a single stateroom on Deck 5, midships/aft on the starboard side, while my friend Pierre and I shared a larger stateroom on Deck 4, midships starboard. I mention all of these locations because of what happened next.

We call for the elevator on Deck 7 and manage to have it all to ourselves. This is the closest elevator to both of our staterooms. My room is about 20 feet to the left of the starboard exit of the C elevator lobby on Deck 4, and Alan is about 40 feet to the right of the starboard exit of the deck above mine. Boarding the elevator, I push buttons for Decks 5 and 4. It's a short blip of a ride, and Alan exits the elevator first. The door closes, the elevator goes down another floor, and then I get out. We could have just walked down the stairs and got to our rooms in about the same time that it took to call the elevator to Deck 7, but we had just been eating for what seemed like two hours, and we were conserving energy.

Anyway, I get off the elevator, head starboard, turn left, walk down three doors on the right, and insert my keycard into the door. I get a red light, and nothing happens. That's weird. Let me try again. So, I enter the card into the door one more time. Red light again. I look up at the stateroom number and realize that I'm trying to get into the wrong room. In fact, I'm on the wrong deck altogether, Deck 5. Funny, Alan must have got off on Deck 6. How did that happen?

No matter, this little foray has cost me nothing but about 30 seconds of inconvenience. I round the corner back into the C elevator lobby and take the quick flight of stairs down to Deck 4. As I turn left heading to my room, I glance to the right and see Alan waving at me excitedly from far, far down the hallway, near the aft end of the ship. I think to myself, What the hell? How did he get all the way down there? He got off on 6!

I insert my keycard into the correct stateroom door lock, which summons a friendly green light, and Pierre, who is just getting up from a midday nap. I explain what just happened to Pierre, and he says something like, "It's a good thing they don't allow guns on board, or you would have been shot trying to break into that room upstairs!"

About a minute passes, and there's a knock on the door. I open it to find a visibly shaken Alan. I ask him how he got all the way down to the end of the ship on Deck 4 when he first got off the elevator on Deck 6. It was physically impossible.

Alan is in shock. "I didn't get off on 6. I got off on 4. And not only that. I turned right to go to my room and saw that I was already past my room. I was already near the end of the ship. Then this is the weird part. I looked up and saw the big letter D next to the elevator landing. I somehow just exited the D elevator!" Frankly, what just happed is not physically possible. Let me preface this by saying Alan and I have both been on several crossings aboard the Queen Mary 2. Believe it or not, I'm about the farthest thing from a fancy person. I'm honestly not sure how I've been on this ship so many times. But I love it. This was my fourth crossing and Alan's third. We know how this ship works. Also, our elevator ride was extremely short, and it was all in a downward direction. I would have felt the elevator changing direction and going up.

Most importantly, Alan and I know how to count, and we know our ABCs. Alan got off first. On the C elevator line. On Deck 5. Except not, somehow. Alan assured me that not only did he get off on Deck 4, and not Deck 6, but that he was 100% sure that he had somehow beamed over to the D elevator bank. Yes, he used the words beamed over. The environmental scientist. The math and science guy. Since we had just been talking about lost time and teleportation, it was if the universe was giving us real-time, super woo-woo confirmation of some seriously weird stuff. When you enter a C-line elevator, you exit a C-line elevator. At least according to all known laws of physics and common sense. But not on the Queen Mary 2. Not on that day.

Anyway, if Alan wasn't 100% sure before, he is now very much on my witness team when it comes to most of this High Strangeness jibber-jabber. Teleportation will do that do a guy. And just in case you're wondering, no, we did not have wine with lunch. Alan is a non-drinker, and I am pretty close to a teetotaler myself.

As I said, a lot of weird stuff happens to me when I'm on vacation, and two weeks remained on this trip, just enough time for a couple of more odd experiences, both of which focused squarely on a particular section of Grand Street, in New York City.

"Greg, these guys are from New York!" Alan's voice booms with excitement. We are no longer on the Queen Mary 2, and have just boarded our tour bus, and are preparing to drive back to Dublin after a pleasant afternoon traipsing around Kilkenny, Ireland. Alan has an almost supernatural midwestern ability to meet everybody on every tour we've ever been on, and rarely comes away without life histories, phone numbers, email exchanges, and plans for future get-togethers. He is tirelessly affable and outgoing-traits I occasionally possess, but that are not essential to my nature-which is probably why we get along so well.

I look back towards Alan and see him pointing to his new best friends from the tour, a group which consists of three 30-something guys traveling with their mom, who is Irish and looks like she could be my own mother's long-lost secret twin.

A strange rush of energy courses through me, and I get a distinct impression, out of nowhere, that all of these guys were my brothers in another lifetime. The men and I all share the same close-cropped Kojak look, and it turns out we are also all Vegan (which is relatively new for me, part of my spiritual awakening, but is just how they grew up). I ask them where they live and it quickly comes out that not only are they fellow New Yorkers, but they also grew up on Grand Street, in the building directly next door to where I had the most spiritual experience of my life, the one I was describing to Alan before we had the teleportation incident on the Queen Mary 2.

The Lower East Side of New York plays a big part in my story of High Strangeness, specifically Grand Street. The universe is big on me telling my Grand Street stories. Let me tell you how I know this absolutely for sure.

Alan and I get back to Dublin after meeting my "brothers from another lifetime," and I tell Alan how I had this strange rush of knowledge about these guys. Alan tells me that he had the same exact feeling about them being his brothers pretty much at the same time when we were all together on the bus. Pretty sure that Alan is one of my spiritual brothers, too.

Anyway, then Alan looks at me and says something like, "Well, the universe obviously wants you to tell your Grand Street stories because we both had this same reincarnation experience, and they end up living next door to where you used to live. Plus, what happened on the ship." I had the same feeling the moment they mentioned where they grew up, and now I have Alan kindly pointing out that the universe is making stuff pretty clear-cut on this subject.

The universe is not done being weird on this trip. It's saving its last card for Norway.

Part of the reason I can go on some of these fun trips is that I look for outrageous bargains, and our flight from Dublin back to New York was in that category, several hundred dollars cheaper than any other plane available. There was just one thing: We had to route through Oslo, Norway. Since Alan, Pierre, and I had never been to Norway, I booked the cheap tickets.

Pierre had been having some mobility issues and requested the use of a wheelchair to help him get through the airport in Dublin. When we arrived in Oslo, we had to wait for everyone else on the plane to de-board before the airport disability services brought in the wheelchairs.

The airline was having a staffing problem that day, and we were stuck on the plane for an extra 30 minutes. Thankfully, our connecting flight was delayed, but there was a lovely older couple from Florida who were definitely going to miss their connection to Miami. Of course, Alan struck up a conversation with the couple while we were waiting for wheelchair assistance to arrive. Eventually, the nice older lady turned her attention to me and asked where we were flying. I told her New York, and she said, "Oh, we're from New York, but we're retired in Florida."

"Oh, where did you live in New York?" I ask her-thinking from her accent that she's probably from Brooklyn, or perhaps Long Island. "Lower East Side. We still own our apartment. It's on Grand Street." It turns out she has an apartment in the same building as my "brothers from another lifetime" who Alan and I met on the tour bus in Ireland. Now we're in Oslo with people from Florida, except not really, they're from Grand Street. I've never seen Alan's jaw drop so quickly. Okay, Okay, I get the message.

Eternal Sunshine

It's 2003, and I've been living in a pretty snazzy two-bedroom apartment on Grand Street for about a year. My roommate and I are among the only non-Jewish residents. It's a very conservative place. The building has its own sukkah, for example, and many of the residents are Sabbath-keepers, which means, among other things, that people will not use the elevator or do any work on Saturdays.

Just about every Saturday, we find people waiting patiently downstairs for us to let them in to visit their families because they cannot buzz the door, as this is considered work and is thus forbidden. All of this is new to me as a small-town boy from the other coast, but we blend right in and start to enjoy following the Jewish calendar so that we can keep track of the holidays along with our neighbors. There are a lot of them-holidays and neighbors.

The very day after I moved into this building in 2002, there was a triple homicide. Some drugged-out monster broke into two apartments via the fire escape. He killed an elderly couple who had been married for over sixty years. They were Holocaust survivors. He also murdered a man who was alone in his apartment. I mention this gruesome fact because there's just something about this place that's unusual from the very beginning of my relationship with it.

At the time, I had recently decided to take a break from the corporate world and try my hand at writing movies. One night, I'm struggling at my computer, trying to think of a fun way to make a modern adaptation of Balzac's Lost Illusions (a film I'd still love to see one day). It occurs to me that maybe I should give up on adapting someone else's fiction, and that I should tell my own true stories about my encounters with UFOs, aliens, and the paranormal.

Something sparks inside of me, and I know that I should ask the universe for guidance. Although I don't enjoy this perfect hindsight perspective at the time, I'm nearing the end of my long sabbatical from the paranormal. I've not had a single strange encounter for over ten years, so asking the universe for guidance has not been something on my weekly to-do list.

"Universe, should I even bother trying to write a movie anymore? Can you give me a sign if I should continue trying to do this?" It's around 3:30 in the morning, and I've been staring at a blank computer screen for almost eight hours. Nothing is flowing. About four hours later, I have my answer. I wake up to the sound of construction and a gaggle of voices. I go downstairs and ask the building's security guy what's going on. "Oh, they're filming a movie here for the next couple of weeks!" No way.

Turns out, it's Eternal Sunshine of the Spotless Mind, and it's by one of my favorite screenwriters, Charlie Kauffman. He will go onto win the Oscar for Best Screenplay for this film. They're filming the "Lacuna" office scenes here.

But the strangeness doesn't stop there: I look online to find out more about the production and discover that I have a stronger connection to the film (other than the whole synchronicity/cosmic sign thing, that is). I know one of the Executor Producers. He and his partner just had dinner with me a couple of weeks before when they were visiting from Los Angeles. Neither of them has ever been to my apartment, as we always meet at a restaurant or theatre whenever they're in town. My friend had no idea that they were about to film in my building, and I had no idea that he was even producing a film in the area. Stranger still, I'm not in this industry, and this guy is-no joke-the only person I know who works in the movies. The only one. It's like the universe has lined this stuff up for me to write about one day.

Odds are three zillion to one. Oh, plus this movie is literally about consciousness, so there's that. Eternal Sunshine of the Spotless Mind, indeed. By the way, I ignored the universe's advice and stopped writing screenplays. Trying to compete with Charlie Kauffman is not on my to-do list either.

Existence. Consciousness. Bliss. Return of "The Voice"

Forward to April 2004, still in my apartment on Grand Street. I've fallen asleep on the sofa while watching late-night television. The first thing I remember is that deep, reassuring Voice. I've not heard from him since 1986, just a few hours before a day of stunning personal tragedy.

Eighteen years is a long time not to hear from someone, even when that someone's a discarnate entity.

"Wake up, Greg. Wake up. We're going somewhere."

I stir instantly. Today, The Voice has brought backup. I feel a friendly presence on my right. It never occurs to me to look around to see who is waking me up. I'm just following directions. That's the way it works with this guy. Before I can even ask where we're going, we're off. The Voice is on my left, and he starts talking.

"Your Daddy prayed for 10,000 years that you could see this place." I'm immediately taken aback on two fronts. I've not used the word Daddy since I was eight-years-old. It's a word from a different century. Back when my father meant more to me than Jesus and Superman combined. Nobody has ever loved his Daddy more than me. But I'm confused. And skeptical.

"That doesn't make any sense!" (My incredulity crosses the line into bitchiness.)

The silent figure on my right giggles, maybe a little nervously. Before I can say anything else, The Voice calmly explains, ***"Time works differently here."***

This next bit, I've had a mental block about for years and years. I wish I could remember The Voice's exact words, more or else as above. The gist is The Voice says something about how it's only going to be a short trip.

Suddenly, I'm aware of my surroundings. We're not in my living room anymore. We're traveling in some kind of vortex. It feels like we're cutting through space as easily as a hot knife through butter. There's only the faintest hint that we're traveling at all-sort of as if you were on a rowing machine in the gym on zero resistance. There's a mild churning sensation. All around me, streaks of light fly past. The universe seems to be doing all the work, and we're just cruising.

Moments later, and we're already at our destination. It's a beach. I feel myself gently placed in the water, which is luminous in soft whites and blues, a beauty that grows in intensity and brightness the deeper you look into it. I feel this delicious warmth sweep over me. What I can only describe as absolute bliss. I'm gently floating out to the ocean, the warm embrace of the water recharging me.

I'm floating there surrounded in this perfect moment when my old buddy Body Dysmorphic Disorder decides to pay a visit. A little tremor of shame courses through me as I realize that I must be totally naked in this water, and I wonder who can see me. I look behind me where I assume there's a beach, and realize that actually, there's no land at all. I look down to check myself out, and that's when I discover that that I don't have a body. No body. No Body Dysmorphic Disorder. Problem solved. The last little bit of shame is gone. I look up and see the horizon in 360 degrees. There's only a nebular light show in every direction, with streaks of pink and purple light throbbing and dancing in glorious syncopation.

That's when I see that there are two gigantic suns in the sky looking down at me, at impossibly close range. I'm definitely not on Earth anymore. What happens next is a burst of revelation, what I learned later the mystics call a Samadhi moment. I know that I'm in an ocean of pure consciousness. This water is not water but the light of soul energy. This is our first home. Every problem that we've ever had is just a story. The greatest evil, the highest good-just stories. Bliss radiates in every direction. I'm a drop in the ocean and the whole ocean itself all at once. I'm not a creature of time. I'm the unitary everything. I'm Existence-Consciousness-Bliss. I know every secret, every story, everything there is to remember throughout all of time and space. Ah, yes, this is our only real home. Such bliss. Such bliss.

Just as I'm getting comfortable merging with every soul, I'm pulled out of the wholeness. I'm the one soul again. But now I feel something that I didn't notice before, an absolute tender love and devotion radiating down towards me. I look up and see the two giant suns in the sky. I feel love and bliss energy freely flowing between this ocean and the suns. Is this even an ocean? Or am I a sun, too? The secrets are disappearing now. I squeeze out one last epiphany. This is of the nature of the Download, as I narrate to myself the hidden truth I forgot I knew.

"Wow, I didn't know that a sun could be feminine!" The star on my left is radiating such an incredible amount of distinctly maternal energy and love. She is looking at me. I know that her power is beyond measure. I love her back. The other sun is masculine. His attention is turned outwards, not towards me. Suddenly, I feel myself rising out of the water, out of the light.

I don't so much wake up as realize that I'm already sitting upright on my sofa with tears running down my face. What I saw was real. It was not a dream. The phone rings and I pick up. It's my Grandma. *"Gregory. Are you sitting down?" "Yes. Why, Grandma? Is Grandpa okay?" "Well, I'm sorry to tell you this. But your dad just died yesterday."* I had not talked to my dad for about 13 years. We were utterly estranged.

In 2017, thirteen years after my visit to the Ocean of Consciousness, I received a Download out of the blue while talking to my friend Mary. My father was not only responsible for arranging my visit to the Ocean. He was actually with me that day. It was my daddy who giggled when I told The Voice his story didn't make any sense. He was on my right side escorting me to the Highest Heaven. I wish I would have turned to look at him, but it never even occurred to me.

Shirley MacLaine is Dead, but Only Baptists Go to Heaven

Speaking of Mary: I just phoned her for a pep talk after writing the last section about my trip to the Ocean of Existence-Consciousness-Bliss. That's because I'm dreading what's coming next in my story, and I needed to be rallied and fortified. Navigating through the upcoming unavoidable emotional landmines will be infinitely more difficult than writing about being an alien test subject, or having a scary shamanic journey in college, or even being estranged from my dad for the last thirteen years of his life.

Just as I hung up with Mary, my phone went rogue on me and started playing the song "Ghosts" by the English band The Jam. Problem is, not only did I not press play on that song. It's not even in my music library. "Ghosts" has been banned from my playlists since the 1980s because it reminds me of pain and loss and real-life ghosts. It was one of my pal Marcus's favorite songs. I feel like the universe is cowriting this little essay at times, adding bits of improbable synchronicity and beauty as a reminder to stay on target. Do yourself a favor and listen to "Ghosts" after finishing this chapter.

We're going back in time again. It's February 1986, and my paternal grandmother is in a coma about ready to shuffle off. She has had a massive brain aneurysm, her second in eight years, but this time there's no hope for recovery. She's breathing on her own, without the aid of life support, and the doctors have given her about one or two days. I'm driving home from the hospital to grab a couple of things before going over to study at my best friend Marcus's house when a Christian advertisement comes on the radio, offering healing prayers for loved ones. Miracles happen every day. Just call, and God will help you and your family. Ask, and ye shall receive.

I'm an archetypical rebellious teenager at this point, and despite my multitude of strange and otherworldly experiences, I don't believe in any of this prayer stuff. At least on a typical day. But I love my grandma.

I call the prayer line

I'm desperate, and I'm willing to try anything, so I call the prayer line with a genuine willingness to suspend disbelief. I explain the situation and ask for prayers and miracles. The man on the other line sounds warm and says that this will be no problem. He says that any time two people come together in prayer before the Father, God will answer. He explains that it was God Himself who made me hear the radio ad and dial the prayer hotline, and that they will be glad to help. But first a couple of questions.

"What church does your grandma go to?" "She doesn't go to church. But she's a good person. She helped raise me." "Okay. Do you know where your grandma was baptized? What church did her parents go to?" "I don't know. Her parents weren't religious, either. I don't think she was baptized." "Well, son, I'm sorry to tell you this. But if your grandma was not baptized, then there's nothing that we can do for her now. She's beyond our power." "What are you talking about?" (Fact: I'm getting red-faced even reconstructing this exchange 34 years later.)

"As it says in John 14:6, 'Jesus saith unto him, I am the way, the truth, and the life. No man cometh unto the Father, but by me.' Your grandma ignored Jesus." "Just what are you saying?" "It's too late for your grandma, but it's not too late for you. You still have time to accept Jesus Christ into your heart as your personal Lord and Savior."

What happened next is a blur. I almost passed out from shock and anger. I remember raising my voice and throwing this line out, which I've used a number of times with nasty religious people, "The Prince of Darkness can quote scripture for his purposes!" I remember telling this guy that he didn't know shit about Jesus. That what he had just said to me was the definition of evil-the very opposite of Jesus. I told him he should stop getting lost in Bible verses and concentrate on helping a fellow human being in crisis. That his prayer line was a worthless bait and switch, and that if anybody deserved to go to Hell, it was he.

I decide there and then that I'm never going to put up with smug, mean-spirited, so-called religious people, and will call them out for small-mindedness, spiritual vacuity and hypocrisy whenever necessary. I hang up the phone disgusted beyond measure, and head over to Marcus's.

Marcus is a year ahead of me in school and is on his way to being the valedictorian in a class of over 500 people. To this day, Marcus is the most effortlessly brilliant person I've ever known, and I've met astrophysicists, prize-winning mathematicians, self-made billionaires. Marcus is smarter, seems to learn through osmosis, never breaks a sweat. He's going to be a pilot and perhaps an astronaut. Stanford is his safety school. I arrive at his house and tell him about my grandma's impending doom, and my call to the Prayer Line of Evil. Marcus doesn't like phonies either.

The next day, I see my grandma take her final gasping breath, surrounded by family who've come from all over the United States to be with her in her last moments. I'm not the least bit concerned that she's going to Hell to suffer everlasting agony and torment. She led an honorable life, raised a lovely family, made the best fried chicken in the world (unless you happen to be a Grey alien), and was a good person. Bible verses and Baptist bumpkins be damned.

A few days later, I head over to Marcus's house to catch up with him, let him know how I survived the funeral and family obligations, and generally unwind. Marcus says that he has something to show me. He takes me back into the family room and has me sit down in front of the TV. He presses play on the VCR. He's lined up a scene from the film Faces of Death. I watch as a man jumps out of a plane wearing some kind of aerodynamic cape called a batwing. Various cameras capture the action, both from the perspective of the skydivers as well as from the vantage of the spectators below. I believe this spectacle was part of an airshow performance.

I have no idea what Marcus has lined up for me, or what I'm about to see, but I wonder why the guy has not pulled his chute. Just then, the bat-winged skydiver hits the ground. Something malfunctioned. He "bounces."

Marcus skydives with his dad on the weekends. He's also getting hours towards his pilot's license and nearly perfect scores on the SAT. He's only seventeen, and none of this is standard stuff in the 1980s. "When I'm up there, jumping out of a plane with my dad. Sometimes I don't want to pull the chute, Greg. Sometimes, I want to bounce."

I don't know what to say to this admission. I'm blindsided. Marcus is a cross between a cool big brother and God to me. He makes everything look so easy. He is kind and noble and a bit of a rascal, and has introduced me to some bad habits. In retrospect, I don't know what to say to Marcus at this moment because I'm just a teenager myself, and have no life experience. I've just lost my grandma, who I loved like a mother, and honestly, I don't think I have to take Marcus that seriously. He can be dramatic. Maybe he's just being extra punk-rock today. Big mistake. A regret that will sting me for the rest of my days.

Stunned, I say something like, "I know how you feel. I get depressed, too. Anyway, do you want to get some beer and drink in the park now?" (We were both excellent students, but we also liked to party like teenagers.)

It's now a couple of weeks later, and I'm asleep. I'm floating in space looking down on planet Earth, but this time I'm not in a space ship with my Hindu friend or Kelly, the young lesbian. I'm with The Voice. I don't see him, but I know that he's on my left. I've not heard from him since he woke me up to tell me about my dad's tools getting stolen.

The Voice returns for the 3rd Time

As far as I can recall, this is The Voice's third direct appearance in my life. ***"What are all of those gorgeous lights?"*** I'm staring down at North America, which is bathed in auroral energy. Everywhere I look, brilliant lights flicker and shimmer in glorious starbursts and waves of pink and white. ***"Greg, those are people dying."***

This answer is certainly not what I was expecting. I'm overcome by how peaceful and beautiful it all is. Then I hear the music. "What are those voices?" ***"Songs for the dead. A celebration. Death is nothing to fear. Everyone is evolving. Transitioning. Those lights are souls leaving their bodies, their containers."***

Behind me shines the moon. The celebratory music is coming from back there somewhere. Countless voices in harmony-what you would call an angelic choir if you weren't a sixteen-year-old atheist. Little insights pop into my consciousness as I watch the scene below, enjoying the heavenly background music.

Energy is rearranging itself through some kind of well-ordered system that values the light within everyone and everything. I'm seeing evolution take place on a planetary scale: The evolution of souls. Instantly, I know that the lights flashing down below are all sentient beings: Catholics, Muslims, Buddhists, Christian Fundamentalists, Presbyterians, Hindus, Mormons, Sikhs, Jews, Jains, Agnostics, Atheists, and creatures of all kinds. Everybody and everything evolves. Nobody and nothing is without light-and that light never goes out.

The Voice is still beside me, silent and comforting, letting me take in the view and listen to the music. I know my grandma is all right now, despite John 14:7. But now I've been shown everyone is going to be all right. Without exception.

Channeling and the Death of Marcus

Suddenly, my beatific vision is interrupted. An incredible surge of energy flows through my body. Another consciousness has crammed itself inside of me, urgently trying to communicate. I feel like I've been struck by lightning. My lips are moving. This is real. I'm hearing myself scream, though I'm not in charge of my words. The urgent sound of my voice scrambling out of me wakes me up, and I fly out of bed, hearing these strange words pass my lips, ***"Shirley MacLaine is DEAD!"*** What? What the heck did I just say?

If you've never woken yourself up channelling someone else's consciousness through your own voice, I can assure you: It's uniquely unsettling. I don't know what just happened, but I look at the clock and realize that I might be late for class. I skip my morning shower, brush my teeth for about 10 seconds, and run out the door determined not to be tardy for English.

As I'm crossing the street in front of my high school, one of my friends comes up to me and says, "Marcus hanged himself this morning." I say, "Wait! What? How is he?" "Marcus is dead." Stunned, I walk into my English class, about five minutes late. My teacher is not amused and says something snarky. I have tunnel vision. The world has stopped spinning. My teacher goes up to the blackboard. We're starting a new unit on Shakespeare. My teacher grabs a piece of chalk, looks directly at me, and writes in colossal block letters what I know now to be an inflection point in my life, a sign that the universe is paying attention: TRAGEDY.

Marcus killed himself on his birthday. He was admitted to every university to which he applied, for which he'd worked so hard, including the Air Force Academy, which was his first choice because it was a full-ride, and his parents wouldn't have to pay a single dime. On his way to being an astronaut. But then he bounced.

It's been over 36 years since this tragedy, and not a day goes by that I don't think about Marcus. The Voice knew what was coming, right on the heels of my grandma's death. I believe that I was given a vision into how death works in our plane of existence, from the perspective of the Greater Reality, guided by a Higher Intelligence. What I saw in orbit was real. That angelic choir is singing its heart out right now. It's real. Those lights are shimmering and starbursting all over the world right now. They're real. Souls are swimming around in a splendid light show right now. They're real, too.

Counting the alien resurrection tank story that began this essay, this vision would be my second mystical near-death experience, except this time it wasn't me who died. I believe that The Voice showed me this dimension of reality so that I could go on with my own life, and not follow in Marcus's footsteps.

It probably goes without saying that I believe that it was Marcus who channelled through me that morning. Marcus used my voice to convey as much information as he possibly could, as economically as he could, in as short a time as possible. *"Shirley MacLaine is dead."*

About a month later, I'm home from school early when I flip on the TV and am shocked to see that Shirley MacLaine is on Oprah. I think she's there in support of her book ***Dancing in the Light***. I've been a gigantic emotional disaster area since Marcus's suicide, and seeing Shirley MacLaine instantly transports me back to that horrific morning of tragedy. But also, I get an immediate Download: ***What you're about to see on TV is for you. Listen up.***

I tune-in just as a caller comes on with a question. She and her husband have recently lost their one-and-a-half-year-old baby son, and she's having a hard time. I'm going to quote Shirley's response directly here as I've just found the exact clip that was part of my noetic experience on YouTube, which is something of a minor miracle. The universe lined this moment up for me perfectly back in 1986, as well. The transcription is mine; the words are Shirley's.

The large cosmic, universal, Absolute Truth is to me that nothing ever dies, and everything is simply in a state of transition . . . I think in terms of how to bear such a tragedy is to respect the free will of that soul, which was not only 20-months-old. That was a very old soul, obviously teaching you and your husband something, and now because you've brought that to this show, however many viewers Oprah has, teaching them something. *("Shirley MacLaine's Cosmic Truth: Nothing Ever Dies."* YouTube Video, 2:18, posted by "OWN." Accessed 8 February 2020.
http://www.youtube.com/watch?v=pW8oz3GSjB0.)

There is, without doubt, not only a Higher but also a Loving Intelligence to this universe. I'm not sure why I occasionally get extra help in seeing it, hearing from it, and experiencing it. All I know is that I'm finally accepting that this stuff is actually happening to me. The big lesson is that this Higher Intelligence is trying to teach us that there's a living soul inside each of us, and that we're all connected. Even that mean guy who just knew that my grandma was headed to Hell. Even that jerk has a soul. And yes, even the Visitors have souls, though I don't think they have Mozarts or Michaelangelos or movies. Which is why we have to stop killing our world before it's too late for our species. I love this planet and don't want to lose what makes life here so beautiful. Don't mess with my music or my movies.

Staircase to Heaven

On some level, I've known that I was reincarnated since I was around four-years-old and joyously insisted that my parents had to "buy a house with stairs." My dad's job had moved, and my parents half-jokingly asked me what kind of house I wanted them to get. When they asked me why I wanted stairs in the new home, I told them because I had died on the stairs, and it was "important for me to get over it." God, I was a weird kid!

I can envision a grandfather clock at the top of the stairs and the landing where I lay dying. To the best of my knowledge, I've never been to Rio Linda, California, but that's where these stairs of death are. Also, I know that I had a wife and that she predeceased me. I know that I had a son and daughter who did not find me for some days after I fell. The fall did not kill me; the waiting for help did.

Also, I don't think my kids liked me very much. I was a strictly traditional, pious Sikh man, somewhat traumatized by the pernicious racism I encountered when I relocated my family to rural Northern California from India. I believe that I was a stickler for religious duty, often to the detriment of my spiritual and family life. I think I knew the letter of the law but missed the big picture. In other words, I was the Eastern-style edition of the guy from the Southern Baptist prayer hotline. That I should come back as a white guy, and not only that, but as a gay white guy, shows that the universe has a wicked sense of humor. Oh, you were Cleopatra in your past life? Well, I was a super devout Sikh guy in Rio Linda, California. I wonder what that former Self would think of this new container of mine?

Perchance to Dream

Dreams are a key to understanding the nature of the Greater Reality at play throughout this essay. Skeptics might downplay my prophetic Downloads of the future, journeys to the other side of the universe, and other paranormal visions as being the product of a fertile imagination-nothing but dreams. And I understand this logic. I dislike nothing more than when I'm watching a film or reading a book and find out that what happened was "just a dream." It's a cheap plot trick, characteristic of lazy writing.

As a culture, we are canny and sophisticated when it comes to storytelling, and dream narratives rank near the bottom of what is taken seriously because there are no stakes. If a character dies in a dream, he's still alive when he wakes up, so who cares? Nothing really happened, except you've wasted my time. We are culturally immunized against caring about dreams. And this is why the Phenomenon can hide in plain sight, ignored by almost everyone, especially scientists. In early 2018, I discovered that it's unwise to assume that the line between dreams and reality is really that distinct.

I've mentioned that growing up, I was a natural lucid dreamer. I believe I first woke up inside of a dream as a result of being chased by the boogie man. Once I discovered that I was dreaming, it was easy to vanquish him and go on adventures in my own little dream universe.

Over the years, I've converted Stonehenge into a pizza parlor, practiced mindfulness meditation inside of floating crystal pyramids, and flown all over the solar system - all while entirely aware that I was in my dream world. But thanks to a lifetime of accurate visions of the future, I've also discovered that I have access to an information source that transcends time and space - what researchers in this volume and elsewhere call the Akashic Record.

One of my friends suggested getting in touch with the Akashic Records to find out who my spirits guides were to the Ocean of Consciousness. This was before I had the Download that one of them was my father.

So, the next time I had a lucid dream, I remembered to ask. I've always wondered if my friend Marcus is one of my guides since it was he who channelled through me with the "puzzle message" about Shirley McClaine being dead. So I ask, "Was Marcus one of my guides?" Immediately, I hear an unfamiliar voice. And I get another "puzzle message," a noetic experience that requires a bit of work to decipher. ***"Neither Absalom nor Achitophel!"*** The names sound vaguely familiar but I don't know what this new voice is talking about, so I say, "Sorry, could you repeat that? I'm not sure I know what you just said."

"Neither Absalom nor Achitophel!" booms the instant replay. "Okay. Sorry, one more time. Could you repeat yourself so I can wake up and Google this stuff?" "Neither Absalom nor Achitophel!" This last repetition comes with a side dish of intuition. I know that this is not the real answer to my question, but that it will be instructive about how the process works for accessing information from this well of universal knowledge.

I wake up and reach for Google on my phone. Via Wikipedia, I find out that Absalom was a son of David from the Bible who turned against his father, and Achitophel was David's learned advisor. What I read next really blows my socks off. Achitophel was not just an advisor, he was a mystic and an oracle whose access to divine wisdom, and the Holy Name of God, put him on par with Angels-ahead of all other men. But he did not receive his gifts with a humble heart, and "he withheld his mystic knowledge from King David in the hour of peril." As a punishment, Achitophel is cursed, doomed to die from strangulation. In the end, Achitophel hangs himself. The first suicide in the bible.

Now, I know for sure that Marcus was not one of my guides to the Ocean of Consciousness, and I also know that the so-called Akashic Records just threw me some insanely relevant trivia. *"No, Marcus was not your guide, but your question reminds us of this other guy who was smarter than everybody else, gifted beyond measure, and also hanged himself. Yeah, that guy was also not your guide."* I repeat, I never knew anything about Absalom or Achitophel until I googled them after my trip to the dream library.

So, I've just discovered that I'm able to reach a kind of Super Google while in my lucid dream state. But there's a voice inside of me that says that maybe I should just let the universe come to me when I'm supposed to get a message, when it's the right time. If I need to know something from beyond, I'm pretty sure it's safer if the Greater Reality knocks on my door, instead of the other way around. Turns out that my reluctance to use this gift might be entirely justified, considering what I'm about to tell you happened when I decided to turn my attention to the Visitors from my childhood.

Show Me the Aliens

It's early 2018, a couple of months after the USS Nimitz story awakened my interest in all things UFO and consciousness-related. It occurs to me one night that I can use my gift of tapping into nonlocal consciousness and remote viewing to get to the bottom of this whole UFO thing. I will make a point of solving this issue once and for all the next time I enter into a lucid dream state. I don't have long to wait. Later that night, I'm in the middle of a dream when something catches my eye that just does not make any sense, and I realize, Aha! I'm in a dream!

Instantly, I remember my mission. I must figure out what's going with the aliens and the UFOs. I raise my dream arms excitedly and scream out my command: ***"Show me the aliens!"***

I'm instantly transported to another planet, but am now a disembodied conscious entity. I'm floating above an ancient tiered structure that looks like a cross between a ziggurat and a step pyramid hewn from some sort of red stone. I understand immediately that I'm looking at millions of tons of stone, a massive engineering marvel dwarfing any structure on our world, and that this structure has stood for over two million years. There are gigantic hieroglyphic symbols in a frieze on the top tier of the structure. In front of the ziggurat are three massive, sculpture-like objects, made of the same red stone. Each object looks a four-fingered hand facing upwards, unfurling, with space in the palm and between the fingers. Download: these are where the flying saucers appear and disappear. They are like 3D-Printers for creating and un-creating flying saucers, and other objects and entities. I sense that the stones themselves have their own artificial intelligence.

The sky, the atmosphere, and the earth surrounding the structures are also red. Is this Mars? Not only are these structures two million years old, I realize that I'm looking backward in time to two million years ago, just after the aliens disappeared from this place. I take all of this information in instantly, and then realize, Wait. Where are the aliens now? This is my dream universe, after all, and I will get what I want.

Again, I issue my command. ***"Show me the aliens!"*** I receive something like an instant "Out of Office Reply" Download: ***"Sorry, that's not allowed."*** I've never had pushback like this in my own universe before. In a lucid dream state, I'm usually pretty much omnipotent, so I'm taken aback. But I'm stubborn and reply in kind, ***"Fine. Then Speak!"*** Immediately, I'm affronted by a tremendous cacophony-what sounds like thousands of barn owls and crickets screeching together in surprised outrage. I'm still floating above the ancient structure, but am now very much aware that I'm being observed. I've set off some kind of alarm. I feel presences beginning to surround me. Fear takes over. I will myself to escape.

Taken Out of my Body

I wake up in bed and see the early morning light coming through the transom window above my bedroom door. I let out a gasp. Oh my God. That was scary. There's enough light in my room now to see myself in the mirror behind the door, and I start to rise to go to the bathroom when, WHAM!

Suddenly, I'm no longer in my body. My astral form has been yanked out of my waking existence just as I'm getting out of bed-again, reminder: I'm one-hundred percent awake here. It feels like I'm attached to an invisible cord, and whatever I was remote viewing on the red planet is now about to view me, but up close and personal. Whether you call it my astral form, my soul, or my subtle body-whatever that thing is, it's no longer in my bedroom in New York. I'm now floating above what I intuit to be a giant sentient ocean planet. But unlike the Ocean of Consciousness from my unexpected trip back in 2004, this ocean does not exude any bliss at all. I'm looking down on a massive swirling miasma, and it's looking up at me.

Just as I realize that I'm being scanned by a formidable group intelligence, it pulls me in closer. I feel helpless in its clutches as it yanks my cord. This ocean is like a giant eyeball of awareness. I'm nearer its surface now, which teems with movement and unpleasant effluvia. I don't think this place gets many outside visitors.

My noetic understandings come fast and heavy here. I'm viewed with great curiosity. Sort of like, "how did this little gnat come to find us?" I understand that this group intelligence is what became of the aliens who were absent from my remote viewing of the red planet. These beings evolved to the point where they could upload themselves into this swirling mass of group-think. I also understand that this dimension is engineered. **That this particular Intelligence is almost God-like it its ability to structure reality.** And yet, I also realize that there is something missing here. There is no bliss. There is no dynamic interaction of love energy like I felt on the world of souls with the masculine and feminine suns in the sky. This hive mind Intelligence is not evil, they have souls, in fact, I'm looking down at an ocean of them, but they have stopped evolving. Their engineered world of immortality and power, despite its marvellous ingenuity, is simply not privy to all the secrets of the universe. Their world is a somewhat sad, distant cousin to the realm The Voice showed me with my father. I would not trade an eternity in this place for one minute in the real Ocean of Existence-Consciousness-Bliss.

I feel two distinct presences on either side of me holding me in place-a security detail. So, this group intelligence can differentiate itself when needed. I can't think of a better way to say this, but I feel them scanning my soul through time and space, looking at me through my various incarnations. I hear a distant voice in the ocean below, *"I think I knew this guy once."* This odd revelation makes no sense to me at all, but, by this point, in addition to being afraid, I'm getting tired of being the plaything of this giant miasmic group intelligence. With every ounce of willpower, I summon the attitude of self-assured command that managed to make this group intelligence speak earlier in the evening, despite its security system. *"TAKE ME HOME!"*

The next thing I know, I'm staring at my reflection in the mirror behind the door. I didn't have to open my eyes because they were never closed. I've been awake during this portion of the evening's festivities, just not inside my body. I've been unsheathed from my physical form. I can see much more daylight streaming in now through the transom window. Judging from the light, perhaps an hour has passed. I make to get out of bed and realize that I can't move. I can't blink. Terror fills me. Not all of me has made it back to Earth. I'm paralyzed. I can't even scream.

Did I have a stroke? Is this what it feels like to wake up inside an Edgar Allan Poe story? A few seconds pass, and I feel a surge of energy whip into me. I'm fully back in my body. I realize this when I hear myself gasp in exasperation.

Imagine the kind of power that can snatch your astral form/soul/whatever-you-call-it out of your physical body, from across time and space-not in a dream, but in your waking form. Aside: Funny how synchronicity and coincidence works on this project. I just stepped away from writing this paragraph and saw a Facebook Memories alert pop up on my feed with video from a Teddy Thompson concert I attended with friends exactly two years ago. It turns out that today is the second anniversary of this elective visit to the red alien planet (and of my non-elective visit to the green alien ocean just afterwards). I feel like I'm on some kind of timer system with this project.

A few months ago, I had an epiphany: my various crazy stories all form part of a much larger narrative having to do with the evolution of our souls in this universe, connecting human and non-human intelligences with death and rebirth, including the death and rebirth of parts of our planet and our species. Change is coming, and we all know it. Fasten your seatbelts. Death is just a transition. Nothing ever really dies.

But there are so many unanswered questions still. Out of frustration, I decide to ask for some solid answers instead of waiting around years for a clue to drop here and there via one of the Contact Modalities. And just as I sit down to meditate, to ask for some specific, actionable guidance, I receive a noetic understanding. "Relax. You'll find out things when you're supposed to find out things. And by the way, you're a horrible backseat driver." The Greater Reality has a dry wit. I break into laughter.

Another Download follows in quick succession. ***"The only reason you made it out of the Green Ocean of Consciousness so easily is that they scanned your timeline. You were there for a purpose."*** Instantly, I understand that an apology is in order. Around eighteen months after my trespass onto the red alien planet, I send the following message, telepathically-of course-to the green, not so jolly, Ocean of Consciousness. "Sorry about visiting unannounced. I didn't mean to be rude. I was just curious. Please forgive my manners." The reply was instantaneous. I surge of energy coursed through my body, from my tailbone up to the back of my head. Message received. It's all good.

The Visitors know that we are in crisis

Like everything else in this story, I believe that my visit to the alien planet-to both alien planets-was orchestrated by a Higher Intelligence. I think that what I saw on these planets provides a genuine part of the untold backstory for at least some of the Visitors.

A massive team of Visitors knows that we are in crisis, that our world is going to spin out of control with self-created environmental disasters, famine, war, and disease. At least some of them know that they must help us survive and grow. Perhaps, their evolution depends on our survival, and our survival depends on mutual evolution.

I believe that a Higher Intelligence, ranking far above both species, has orchestrated a renewed interest between worlds. One world-our world-is teetering on the brink of destruction, and yet is full of souls that have the capacity to experience such beauty and bliss; another world is the apex of science and harmony, but lacks the ability to advance into higher levels of spiritual evolution, and does not have the innate understanding of some of the states of Being we frankly take for granted as our birthright, like love, joy, and happiness.

This realization is my "Bellevue," what the universe has been guiding me towards for the last few decades. Perhaps this message is for future generations alone to understand. Maybe we can mix the best bits from both species to find a better tomorrow for everybody.

I'm back on the plane again-the same one from near the beginning of this essay-heading home to New York. I've just had my first waking Download in quite some time. "Don't worry about why you've had your Experiences, or how you're going to tell your story. The universe doesn't waste its time. You're good."

My Request to Meet God

Immediately, I think back to just a few hours before this early morning flight. I find myself waking up inside of a dream, going lucid for the first time in many months. And I'm determined not to waste the opportunity. I decide to go big. In fact, to go as big as big gets. I ask to speak to God Himself. First time it ever occurs to me to be so bold.

"Please don't take this wrong. And I ask in the humblest way possible. But could I meet with God now? If it's not too much bother?"

Instantly, I feel a friendly, familiar presence to my left, and know that we're going to have some fun. We're zooming through outer space. I see the stars surrounding us in every direction at once, and although I don't see my friend, I know that he's there.

The planet Neptune is coming up on our right. There's classical music, Mozart, playing in the non-air, as if to mark the occasion. I'm filled with joy. I hear my own voice narrating every exchange that happens next, all of which is of the nature of noetic understanding. *"Oh, we're flying by one of the moons of Saturn now. How cool!"* It looks very familiar for some reason. (Have I been there before?)

Then I wonder (rather randomly), *"What would happen to me if I came across a black hole out here in outer space," and I hear my own voice answer back, "There are no black holes anywhere near here, and they aren't what you think, anyway. They can't hurt you in this form."*

Suddenly, we're done with space, and back on Earth. I'm floating near the ceiling in a small office, looking down toward a dark-haired white guy. I think, "Oh my God, is that a clip-on necktie?" He's wearing a short-sleeved dress shirt that looks like it has some polyester in it. (Am I in the 1970s, or what?) This guy's reasonably good-looking, has a nice smile, and is a total nerd.

As if to validate this experience for later, I instantly Download that we're in a place called Morgan Township, Ohio. I've never been to Ohio in my life, but I'm pretty sure that Morgan Township is not the capital. I know that I have to break out Google as soon as I wake up to see if this place is real or just a dream. (Could this be the next Bellevue, Iowa?) Then, I hear myself narrate the following explanation. *"This guy is an Avatar of the Lord, but has no idea. His main concern right now is why he can't get a date on Saturday night!"*

I laugh, and know that I've just seen something pretty special-though definitely not what I was expecting. I wanted to be able to ask questions and get direct answers from God Himself. But that's all right. I wake up with a huge smile on my face, feeling loved beyond measure. Perhaps these are answers to questions that I've not even formulated yet.

So, I'm back on the plane, thinking about this dream, and about how Morgan Township, Ohio, actually is a real place in the non-dream world (population 5,515 according to Google), when I connect the dots. I asked to meet with God a few hours ago, and now I've just had a noetic experience from out of the blue. The Universe doesn't waste its time. You're good.

I reach for my headphones to start up The Bhagavad Gita audiobook that I love so much. I left off at Chapter 15, "The Supreme Self," and am in the middle of a little introductory essay. I press play, and this is exactly what I hear next: ***"At the beginning of time Vishnu took three steps that measured out the entire cosmos. The third and highest step became a heavenly world, the realm of the blessed."*** I have never heard this part of the audiobook before, and let out a gasp, as tears of gratitude stream down my face.

For all these years, I've struggled to remember exactly what The Voice said that night he and my dad escorted me to the Ocean of Consciousness. Now, I have the answer. It comes rushing back to me after fifteen years of amnesia. The invisible conductor has lined everything up perfectly-once again.

Just before we headed out to the Ocean of Consciousness back in 2004, The Voice said these exact words, ***"It only takes three steps to get to the other side of the universe."*** The audiobook continues to play, extending my epiphany:

May I go to his blessed world
Where those who love the gods rejoice;
For there, truly, is the company of the far-stepping god,
A fountain of honey in the highest step of Vishnu.
The Gita describes Krishna's home as a realm of Light
beyond the light of the sun.

(The Bhagavad Gita, Translated by Eknath Easwaran,
Nilgiri Press, 1985, p 230.)

Vishnu is worshipped by millions of Hindus as the Highest Incarnation of God, the Supreme Being. In my understanding of Hinduism, it's not so much that there are many gods. It's that there are many paths to God. And God takes on countless forms depending on who's searching for him. There are more paths to God than there are atoms in the universe. Nothing less would befit the Supreme Being. Infinity, eternity, existence, consciousness, bliss. These are just words, and words cannot do justice to God. He is far beyond all name and form.

But as we say in New York, "I don't know from Vishnu." I was not raised Hindu. In fact, I was not raised in any sort of religious environment. Whatever I've learned about spirituality has come to me organically, through my own experiences in the world, and from my interaction with a Higher Intelligence that has shown me infinite patience, kindness and Grace. Reality, in all its High Strangeness, is my church.

I did not learn about The Three Steps of Vishnu until fifteen years after I took Three Steps with The Voice. The story of Vishnu's three steps recounts how he traced out the boundaries of the entire universe, placing it under his protection. Not in seven days, but in three simple, impossible steps. Pretty awesome stuff.

So, then, is the universe telling me that The Voice is Vishnu? Yes. Without doubt or hesitation. The fact that Vishnu is a foreign concept to me makes it easier to accept this revelation. There's a cultural buffer that prevents my head from exploding. I asked to meet God for the first time, and He's telling me that we're already old friends. The Voice is Vishnu, and He has looked after me since I was boy, and throughout my life, turning up just when I needed him the most.

Does this sound crazy? Obviously. (Remember how I stipulated that I wasn't crazy at the very first sentence of this essay. Well, now you know why.) But since the name Vishnu has never been part of my upbringing or cultural awareness, it's seems a whole lot less crazy than if I were raised in India. The Truth is one. Sages call it by various names.

I don't call The Voice Vishnu nowadays. I prefer a simpler name, one that I'm more familiar with as a Westerner. Personally, I'm not going to dwell on this revelation. Ego inflation is the worst. But I will say this on Vishnu's behalf: We couldn't hope for a better Supreme Being.

Traditionally, Vishnu is The Preserver and The Protector. He's responsible for organizing the universe and making sure that it runs smoothly. He steps in when stuff gets ugly, and needs to be sorted out. And when things get really bad, He comes down to Earth and Incarnates: Krishna, Buddha, some people believe Jesus. Maybe this guy in Morgan Township, Ohio? Who knows?

Well, since I know absolutely nothing about Vishnu until this epiphany hits me at 32,000 feet, I decide to do some research, and find this fascinating bit of lore. One of Vishnu's favorite tools is a flying disc, known as the Sudarshana Chakra, or disk of auspicious vision.

Could this disk of auspicious vision have anything to do with that wonderful flying saucer I merged souls with as a child? I suspect one day I will remember his friendly voice, and know for sure. I think I feel one of my Clarification Downloads coming on.

The Time I Spoke to God:

A Mental Health Clinician's Journey with Psilocybin

Yessenia Guglielmi

I'm a careful person, not one to take chances or unnecessary risks. Controlled, measured. I take my job of being a mother to be the biggest responsibility of my life. To accommodate this, everything else is secondary including myself. I maintain a steady schedule that my family can rely on. They know I'm in bed by 8:30 watching TV. I'm not out, I don't see friends, I work from home, and am available to my family including my own parents and brother. It's this consistency to routine and balance that helps my children feel supported and steady in the craziness of this world and in the difficulties that they encounter. This is why my calendar is full too, my patients can come to me and ground themselves in the calm energy that I offer to them.

I listen more than I ever talk, a patient person with reasonable expectations. I study and continue to learn best practices in my field and it keeps me well informed, knowledgeable, and resourceful to help those whom I am guiding. My free time is spent in research for my doctorate. By all accounts it's exactly the kind of therapist a person would want to talk to. Good marriage, good kids, close relationship with parents, a dutiful wife and mother. These are the areas that I often pride myself about and promote on my website, for it's not been an easy task or come without great sacrifice.

So it was strange that I was sitting on a bed, on the floor that Glenn had made for me at his condo. Stranger that I had accepted his invitation during a pool party back in June to take a journey. My husband gave me a look back then and when he drove me to Glenn's, on Saturday, he lingered in the parking lot to make sure I was still serious. I had an out, my youngest was getting over a stomach bug and I could have canceled on Glenn. He responded that morning not to worry, that everything will be how it's supposed to and to just keep him posted. I felt bad, he had carved out over 4 hours of his day to accommodate this journey and I understood as a clinician the great value of one's time.

I told myself that I would get a feel of the vibe and ask my questions. If I felt uncomfortable, then I would treat Glenn to dinner and call it a night. My husband would happily pick me up and I could watch reruns with my daughter of our favorite shows. Safe, secure, comfortable. Glenn is family, he married my husband's first cousin about four years ago. There is a kinship we share in that he is Latino, queer, and coming into an Italian family. He would understand and understand many things left unsaid.

I don't recall the exact moment it started; I remember that I wasn't feeling anything and asked Glenn to try the third piece of mushroom. It was a long white stem with a small cap. We had waited about 30 minutes and nothing seemed to be happening with the first two. I felt scared yet resigned to take this journey. I had asked for it, and already stated my intentions. Now thinking back, it was rather bold of me. I tend to cut to the chase in matters and my intentions for this journey is to know if there is a God, truly. How could so much bad be happening in the world? Why did the bad people seem to keep winning all the time? I wanted to know what was out there. I clung to my eye mask with shaky hands and laid down on my back. Glenn motioned for me to put it on if I wanted to and I did, feeling too scared to watch the room change. I closed my eyes and geometric shapes started to form slowly, I was leaving and I was terrified.

I didn't want to die; I was so scared of dying. Leaving this world and blaming myself for taking this journey. What if I died doing this? What if my heart wasn't strong enough? I worried about my blood pressure and my responsibilities in this world. I was cold, so cold that when Glenn covered me with a blanket, I was deeply thankful. He held my hand and told me I would be okay. I felt cared for. I could hear the music in the background, the notes reverberating in my body and around the room. I clutched the blanket and suddenly I was in the ground buried deep in the earth watching plants and roots around me. I was at peace, watching all the white lines of the different plants I was blooming. I felt warm and safe as if in the womb of the earth being nurtured and well cared for. There was no fear, only comfort, gentleness. I don't know how long I was in this state for, time was suddenly non-existent. Time didn't matter. The roots around me appeared and then died only to do it over and over again like the seasons.

I could hear singing around me. The lyrics were asking me to let go of illusion, let go of the mask, release the illusion. The voice chanted over and over again. I felt myself let go and separate further from my body. I felt the earth begin to slowly birth me out with each push I was more connected to the world. I rose to walk into a tent-like structure and began to walk around feeling more connected to the earth, seeing the beauty of the grass and nature around me. I was in God's infinite garden. I was energy no longer a body, taking in the vivid beauty. God was singing to me, it felt like it was all around me, angelic voices singing to me about being a flower on this earth and in this garden. I was surrounded by a feeling of love all around me with an understanding that I was deeply loved. This love felt never ending, infinite and that it anchored the universe.

The lyrics were asking me again let go of illusion, let go of the mask, release the illusion. The voice sang over and over again. I came to a place of prayer. I was sitting and breathing deeply in a prayer pose with my hands going to my forehead, to my mouth, and then to my chest over and over again. I understood that my death is only a rebirth into something greater.

I saw myself dressed in white, praying and my prayers were going directly to God. I was aligned in my purpose of helping others heal pain. People were coming to see me and I prayed for them to heal. I was like a deity illuminated in white light. The more I prayed the more I was able to heal. I could see Glenn in my vision. He was sitting across from me on his small couch in meditation. As I prayed for him he was getting better, I could see white light come down over his head and enter into his body healing him. We were healing each other. I remember feeling intense gratitude and having to thank God over and over again for everything in my life, all the blessings that I have received from God's loving energy throughout my life.

I don't know how long I was crying and with every kindness Glenn did for me it would fill me with immense gratitude that I had to cry and thank God over and over again. I kept doing my prayer pose and holding my hands tightly together. The message I received over and over again was that this was what I was supposed to do to help people heal. Pray for them, heal their minds and that this is my gift, a gift that could grow into something more powerful. I felt like Glenn was praying with me and I felt that he was healing and crying too. I just continued to pray for him over and over again. We were in a white room and I was watching myself sitting on a table of some kind, dressed in white praying for people, praying because of the suffering in the world. There weren't enough tissues or tears to express my gratitude to God, the tears just flowed down my face and all I could do was to continue to cry. I felt exhausted, thirsty, and Glenn gave me water. I was sitting up and the eye mask was off.

The message I received was that I am a flower. A flower in God's garden, like so many other flowers here to serve God, that love is all that God is, God is everywhere and in everything. The universe and the mysteries of the universe were bigger than I could ever imagine. That God's plan is perfect, that I could rest in him and I would be cared for. I could unburden myself with him, that he understands. That I need to unburden myself with God to heal and to do my work. Also, that my ancestors were with me, my grandmothers were with me guiding me. I could see a white door with a frosted glass and saw shadows behind it. I felt they were my grandmothers, that I was being divinely guided in this life. That as things happen around me, the world, that I didn't need to worry, God was in all of it. Things have already been determined, I didn't need to worry. It was okay.

The other message I received was about my grandfather's story. That I would find myself in that story and that it would be powerful. I kept thinking that I didn't have enough words to describe what I was experiencing and what God was revealing to me. How would I write it all down? I also remember God reminding me to sing my song. God is asking me to open up to express myself, to teach, that was another message I received. I could see myself teaching others and finding great joy in this. I felt like God was speaking to me in chants over and over again. God has many voices and speaks through many forms of life. And that God has sung to me before and that I heard it. This is true, I know the exact song it is that I feel is a direct message to me and I was always afraid of the song it came on the radio since I was a child.

When I feel afraid, I need to pray for those around me and ground myself in God's love, this would make me heal as well as those I prayed for to heal and lessen my fears. Gratitude, humility, kindness, love, and thanking God are the keys. I also felt the responsibility of my experience to do more in my life, to teach others. To trust the healing medicine of God, the gift that God has given to us. I felt healed, I felt my chest radiate in healing, my heart was good and that I didn't have to fear being sick. I saw my husband Michael in my vision as I lay down, my heart felt hollow without him and I understood that he is my heart, my life without him is empty and felt the profound love that I feel for him.

I also remember laughing because Glenn's pants made strong sense to me, I could see the design come alive and spin. I also remember not wanting to share what I was experiencing because I didn't have enough words to do so. I still don't, this writing feels like

I'm using a crayon to describe the experience. Yet, that's all I have. I think I understand the passion and inspiration that went into each psalm of the bible and into the Song of Solomon 8:6. "Set me as a seal upon your heart, a seal upon your arm"

Everyone has experienced love in one form or another and this is God. God is in everyone through love. Love is the expounding energy in the universe, love is everywhere.

I also remember hearing God's voice say to prepare myself to receive healing and that the healing was coming. When it did, I was overcome with emotion and was crying, releasing years of pain I didn't know I was carrying. Not just my own pain but also the pain I have carried for others. Jesus carries the cross for all of us. Was another message I received and I could see Jesus carrying the cross walking freely. I was healed by love, God's love. The voice sang to me, telling me it was time to come home. That I would be awake soon.

The sound of the singing was in the rhythm of a drum, when I would lay on my side it would muffle slightly and when I turned my head, I could hear it strongly. It was a consistent sound and energy going through my body. The chanting would repeat to make sure I remembered. I thought to myself, wow this is some playlist that Glenn has. Yet, it was what I believe was God's voice guiding me and my silence helped me hear it even more. The singing I heard was beautiful, like a celebration.

I suddenly felt so bad asking Glenn for water, he was already doing so much for me. And God's voice kept telling me that Glenn understands, that Glenn already knows, that it was okay. Glenn's kindness to me and to this world through his work left me in deep humility and gratitude. When I began to come back to my body and the effects of the mushrooms began to dissipate; I was still tearful and cried easily. Glenn says I cried for four hours. It felt like I had gone through ten years of therapy. Glenn and his husband drove me home and I was embraced by my husband and went to bed.

An insight that came to me this morning as I recalled this experience was in regards to LGBTQ and how it didn't matter to God at all. That it was such a teeny tiny detail compared to the larger picture of life. To even think such a thing would bother God at all is silly. It made me reflect on my patients, and those suffering so much with this concern of being transgender. I thought to myself that I would remind them of God's love for them and tell them what God told me, that they too are flowers in God's infinite garden and they can bloom anyway they want to. That God is connected to the love, kindness, and compassion in our hearts. That's all that matters. I reflect deeply in regards to the transgender community. I have always been drawn to working with those that identify, perhaps it is because of the bravery entailed in transformation. So visible, so vulnerable, so hated in our society. My heart feels that they, those who identify as trans are our great teachers. Their suffering is our own, it mirrors back to us our own need for transformative change and that it's possible. I pray for them and thank them.

Now living in between two worlds will take some balance. On one hand there is a feeling of less regard for the material, that it truly does not matter while at the same time having responsibility in this life to complete for the others whom I care for. My final thought is that I must be grounded so that if/when I do another journey, more will be revealed that I will really need to be ready for. Glenn says these insights or downloads will continue to come to me and I welcome them. The learning continues after the journey.

It's been almost a week since my healing. I awoke this morning in tears, my dog Sophie jumped on the bed to hug me. She did this when I came home from my journey too as if to ground me. It occurred to me that my Sophie knows God too, through her love for me and my love for her. This made me cry more, the kindness of our pets. It's been several days of vivid dreams, new insights, crying, and continued prayer. Glenn sent me some affirmations to use. He also suggested buying some grounding stones like black tourmaline, jade, or obsidian. I could also use Agua De Florida, saging or palo santo. He reassured me that these reactivations are normal. And so, I journey on. Perhaps it wasn't death I was afraid of after all, perhaps it was this transformation. I am changed. I am in awe of my life, the great blessing to be able to serve my community, to help people heal their minds and to receive enough to sustain my family with my work. It's a miracle, really to be able to do my work. I am, after 25 years in mental health, reinvigorated in the importance of this work. I feel wealthy, with enough richness to share with those who need it. My mind feels rewired, with more neuroplasticity, expanded with more neural connections than before. Connected to ancient knowledge.

As a clinician, I would guide people who want to try this medicine to proceed with caution. To find a skilled practitioner to guide them, someone who has themselves had the experience, and who has the knowledge, tools, and sensitivity to guide. When you journey, you will be in a very vulnerable position where you are unaware of time, space, or being. After care is also very important, having a counselor to talk to or a network or support since healing continues well after the journey itself. Perhaps it's where it really begins.

Many blessings

Namaste
 &
Hare Krishna-"Oh Lord, oh energy of the Lord, please engage me in your service."

My Lifetime of Contact with Non-Human Intelligence via the Contact Modalities

Gillian Evans

The following account of my life experiences with Non-Human Intelligence and the Paranormal have occurred without hypnotic regression or drugs, though I confess to the odd glass of wine! It is also very much 'warts and all' and from the heart. I was born on the 7th March,1952 (Amersham, Bucks, U.K.) to typically white, dark-haired middle-class parents and I was their first child. My Mother had always wanted a girl with blonde hair she could plait (her wish fulfilled as I am blonde even to this day) but in other respects poor Mum got far more than she bargained for!

My earliest memories are pre-birth. Flying across moorland on a starry night with one other 'companion/spirit' who was with me to share the experience of coming to Earth in the physical. The second memory is being in the womb during my mother's labour. It was warm, very bright with red and orange colours in a sort of narrow coiled container. It felt like I was upright but after this there is nothing I can recall until I was about a year old. When I was old enough to learn a little about 'the birds and the bees' I began doubting this memory as I was told that babies come out 'head -first' but wasn't until my own puberty that my mother felt I was old enough to know some gory details about her 'first labour' – it transpires that I was a breech birth. The doctors had tried unsuccessfully to turn me around but I retaliated each time and was born 'feet first'. For those who know me well they will say this sounds about right!!! So, to me, this memory was real. The flying dreams/experiences have continued in different forms for the last 69 years but on my own.

My first childhood memories are of lying in my pram at about a year old. I vividly remember the tapestry style edging around the inside of the hood, I used to get bored and this was something to study. I remember the countryside and seemingly flat, endless landscape so I remember amusing myself by following the rise and fall of the telegraph wires and would play a game where I would guess when the next pole would come into my line of vision. This was verified by my late Mother who wanted to put some things right just before she died at the age of 94, many things that hadn't been spoken about including confirmation of the fact she knew I had been a bit different. But this was light-hearted as I used to get the giggles every so often when they and they had never worked out why! Another memory as a small baby was being surrounded by men in uniforms making sort of baby talk. This is the strange thing because the next minute I can see them holding me and I can see my parents also standing with them as they hold me, everyone is smiling and relaxed so this must have been my first OBE. Initially seeing through my baby eyes and then out of body as an observer. Again, my mother was eventually to confirm that what I described had happened; they had had a very small chimney fire which the fireman had dealt with quickly and had come into my bedroom to 'admire the new baby' and presumably check all was in order.

My next memories are of about three years of age onwards (in fact I remember most things from then on). I actively sought my own company in Nature, either in the garden making up spells or on a 'family walk' with my Grandpop and Nanna May (my father's parents) and my Nanny Rose (my mother's mother) when they came to visit. I loved to go ahead with huge strides, I thought maybe I would start flying like I did in my dreams and they called me 'The Pathfinder'. We lived inland at this time but apparently when I was taken to my Grandparents house (Folkstone, Kent) and I when I saw the sea for the first time I screamed. I remember, as this vast expanse of water reminded me of some far -off place that I had temporarily forgotten. From then on it was difficult for them to get me out of the sea and an adult this is still the case and I feel the sea is home. Inland and without access to nature, I feel I can't breathe.

My childhood was not idyllic. I feel somewhat uncomfortable writing about two troubled people, my 'human birth' parents, who in many ways did their best and are now longer with us but I must write this honestly. Mum was very 'Christian' and if I questioned anything to the contrary it upset her. She also told me when I was about seven years of age that if I upset her too much it would make her ill So, I desperately tried not to, and she did indeed live to a good age with very little illness! From my early age there were big arguments and I recall one such disagreement when they were out walking me in my pushchair. I mention this because I could 'hear' the argument but at the same time have a clear memory of seeing 'them from behind and me being pushed in the chair', so another O.B.E. and I remember a few more. Anyway, Mum did have a nervous breakdown shortly after this argument which she confessed to just before she died because she was worried that by sending me away to my grandparents in Kent at the age of four whilst she recovered may have had a long- lasting effect on me.

However, I was able to put her mind at ease for I'd had a wonderful time, so many vivid and joyful memories including a very special one (which I now know) was sent to re-assure me. I was lying awake in a little bed my grandfather had made for me, it was a warm moonlit night and suddenly a beautiful, kind and young lady appeared and asked me if I wanted to go outside with her. She took through the window somehow and a short way down the garden and up on to a railway track (which I presumed was disused) but I have no other memory of it. She held my hand and pointed up at the star lit sky. "This is where you come from," she said, so softly and reassuringly. I can still smell the air, see those stars and feel the loving stillness; the memory is so vivid and has stayed with me all this time, as if it would have meaning at some point. Occasionally, as a young adult, I thought this figure may have been my real Mother but of course now I know it couldn't have been as she was coping with her illness a long way away. It happened as I remember it and I now know who this entity was.

I started school at the age of five. I remember it was a big class and we had a pretty, young teacher but I felt she did not care for me. I was never allowed in the 'Wendy House' and even when she asked us to put up our hands if we had been overlooked, she still ignored me. This happened when she brought in some clay for us to model with, so some children had two goes and I didn't have one! This is significant because already I was not too good at speaking up for myself and was becoming increasingly shy, sensitive and introverted as 'This World' was beginning to 'over-whelm' me….. My flying dreams continued but I had other disturbing dreams where the pavement would open up to reveal molten lava; or a huge force that tried to knock me over but if I turned my back on it and walked backwards into with all the strength I could muster, I would make it go away. It was an unpleasant experience, unlike 'the force' that was to come to me 'in the 3D physical' many, many years later. Another repetitive dream was of a grey, dystopian landscape – mainly industrial and devoid of people or nature. I was seated on some sort of platform which went round and round encircling the area, as if I was on a merry-go-round. It felt soulless and lifeless. That was at the age of five. Quite recently I went to visit my granddaughter who is at University in London and when we were travelling together on the suspended overground tube-train I saw that same, eerie landscape. Was this the dream manifested?

My sister was born when I was six but, sadly she died at 6 months of age, a cot death. I remember my mother's sorrow and I felt for her so. This is probably when I first began to feel responsible for her and so I felt very hurt when she believed a childhood friend of mine who told a lie about me and I was sent to bed for punishment even though I was totally innocent. I couldn't understand why my friend would lie or why my mother would not listen to my truth. I was seven years of age and felt increasingly my own person, at odds with other children/human beings but also desperately trying to appease my Mother and failing. It wasn't all bad however and I remember the fun I had giving my friends a fast ride on the back of my new three wheeled bike until dusk fell. As I grew up wherever I have gone to live or work I have made some very special and lasting friendships and I feel very blessed.

We moved again, this time to a sleepy inland village where my brother was born. He was a noisy baby and I was frequently sent to pacify him. Somehow, I would look directly into his eyes and he would settle, I knew what I was doing but I didn't know how or where it came from. I was now nine. I loved the countryside surrounding the village and I took my brother for long walks in the pram. I was also given a two wheeled bike which I loved as it gave me even more freedom to 'get away' into nature and until very recently I have had a bicycle all through my adult life. This was just as well as I was taunted by the other children because I was new to the village, verbally and physically. However, one village girl stood up for me and we are still friends to this day. I was also starting again to 'see' other realities. For instance, there was an old shop a few doors down from our cottage. The window was smeared but I could see cobwebs through the glass and old tins. It fascinated me. One day I was looking in and I saw a man fiddling about with these tins. I hadn't seen anyone in there before and I went home and told Mum. She immediately told me I had been imagining things because the man I described had recently died and the shop was empty!

That same year we had our first holiday paid for by my grandfather. We went by train to a holiday camp for a week in Cornwall and I was now ten. From the onset I was 'seeing prisoners with heads bowed' in this place, feeling such sadness but felt compelled to go out and 'feel their pain'. I told my parents what I had seen and again I was told it was just my imagination - that I was a 'funny girl' (in the abnormal sense). I began to feel afraid after this when I would physically see abandoned Nissen huts (which was quite common in the early 60's) and had more visions of wretched, suffering beings accompanied by a horrific smell.

Years later I painted what I was seeing/experiencing and after completion the pain vanished; it's a technique I have used occasionally since. On the return journey I remember sitting in the railway carriage on the scratchy seat with my bare legs not quite touching the floor. I looked out of the window as we had come to a stop mid-route for a few minutes seemingly in the middle of nowhere. I saw a tall hill divided in two by a natural hollowed out area, from this area streamed a beautiful soft blue ethereal beam of light and I felt such peace. I also heard this reassuring male voice, for the first time, saying 'you will always remember this moment' and I have. A few months later this voice returned. This time I was out on my own and unfortunately caught site of one of my bullies. She was with her boyfriend and she saw me. They were both at some distance away, so I just smiled at them which was clearly the wrong thing to do. She hurled abuse but I hadn't done anything wrong and I couldn't understand why she would be like this. I froze to the spot and then 'the voice' returned and it said, very clearly: 'Do not worry, you will teach people how to love each other'. I was ten and very taken aback by this voice in my head but not scared as I had heard it on the train journey some months previously. It somehow felt reassuring and familiar.

The last meaningful experience in this village was when I was poking about in the earth on my own designated 'garden plot'. (My Father had been digging the whole area up with view to growing vegetables and it was very over-grown.) I was using my hands in the soil as I like to do and came across something shiny. I dug around it and finally it came lose, revealing itself to be a beautiful rose quartz which I have kept to this day. Despite the whole garden being dug over nothing else like this was found. Now I know why I found it, it was a gift to me and more re-assurance. With regards to 'seeing the soldiers and feeling their pain' my mother eventually confessed that I had been right. It turned out that the holiday camp we had stayed in had been a converted prisoner of war camp. It wasn't common knowledge or made known to the public at that time but all those years later, just before she died in 1996, she had heard it documented on a BBC Radio 4 programme.

We moved to Dorset but Father was far from happy. I started at the local secondary school for girls, the Headteacher was without compassion and no interest in the Arts or anything progressive. The next four years were a prison sentence. I was not popular amongst many staff members because I asked inappropriate questions. I had asked my parents, aged twelve, "if there is no-one in a room to see it then does it exist?" They did not have the answer but found it an interesting question and told me to ask a teacher at school. I did but it did not go down too well, they didn't have the answer either and were very uncomfortable with my query, although – as always, I was very polite. I was so shy and underconfident I found a way to hidebehind my long hair so I could gaze out of the window or draw pictures under the desk, I was so bored!!! In Science none of my experiments worked and in Sport I used to duck the ball! I was teased mercilessly by many of the other girls, especially as I would not join in the bitching which was rife. They told me I was 'weird', 'from another planet' and even called me Twizzle after an E.T. character in a television series who had an unusually long neck (which I suppose I have) and because I was so tall. I learnt to survive by drawing them pictures, doing their Art homework and writing their essays which was pleasure for me anyway.

I did have a small circle of school friends including some staff. An R.E. teacher, an Art teacher and even my Geography teacher (ironically my worst subject next to Maths) who made me promise, when I left school, that I would always paint. At home things were dreadful. My Father's temper was dangerously out of hand and, on one occasion, put me in hospital. However, my mother made me promise not to say anything because the shame would be too much and she wanted to 'keep the family together'. So, I said nothing. I was also put in charge of my brother who was 'challenging' to say the least and I probably didn't help myself because by the time I was fifteen I started to get angry too and longed for an escape!

However, the positive side was my father's interest in UFO's. Many clear nights were spent spanning the night sky and we were usually able to spot one or two, albeit from a great distance. After school exams were nearly over, the aforementioned Geography teacher proposed a long walk along the Purbeck coastline which was new to me. I had rarely joined anything but would get me away from home. It was a beautiful early Summer's Day and the landscape absolutely took my breath away. Secretly I felt a strong sense of past life in this ancient place and I knew I would return.

In September,1968, I enrolled at Art College. What a relief!... To be drawing and painting all day! It was here I met my future husband and Father to my daughter. However, I knew I could never afford to be 'an artist' as earning an income and associated responsibilities had been drilled into me and my parents were struggling to support me. I did not want to go in for commercial design; even at the age of sixteen I could see advertising as quite dark, playing on peoples' weaknesses. Homelife was now utterly unbearable and despite my mothers angst at my leaving her I joined my future husband in Leeds where he had a place at the Polytechnic.

Then in September,1970, I found out I was six months pregnant, (miraculously) and in December 1970 my beautiful daughter was born after a nearly three-day labour. I was so happy and loved Motherhood, joining in her games and watching Emma grow. I also became friendly with the elderly lady who delivered our milk called Phyllis. She and her husband would pick us up in an old truck and take us to their cottage and small holding, she was a kind 'ancient soul' and we grew very close.

Then, aged twenty-one, I started work as a night nurse at a local Heart/Lung Hospital, an amazing and humbling experience. I learned how to save lives using resuscitation but also, when a life had come to an end, to sit with person and hold their hand. It was such an honour to be with them when their time had come, to share in their experience and to re-assure them. Many were old, alone and forgotten. I could not understand why, when there naturally is great joy and celebration at birth, why does this not apply to a passing? I found I was able to look straight into their eyes, feeling them see into mine, no barriers, soul to soul, just before 'their time'. Some of the staff thought I was odd sitting with the dying during my night breaks when I could be reading glossy magazines! But there were also some staff who understood, were incredibly compassionate and I learned much from them. I also found it a privilege to 'lay someone out' after death and did it with great care.

Occasionally I would be sent to the baby unit which was quite upsetting at times. However, I re-discovered that I could often reach into the eyes of babies, with love, in the same way. It is something that has stayed with me all my life and I was very recently nicknamed 'the baby whisperer'. Whether it is the elderly, babies, young children or animals there is so often the lack of barriers which enables soul to soul contact.

In 1976 a 'fellow Mum' and teacher whose children I would look after during term-time persuaded me that I should consider teaching! Even though I had loathed school, she tried to convince me that schools had probably changed. I began to see that it could be a way to help 'different' children AND bullies, putting my Art to good use and provide a stable future for my daughter. Well, things were not much different at Teacher Training college, the same old mindset but I had already committed myself and I had Emma to think of and I could perhaps make a difference when I started teaching. Also, it was a course designed for Mothers with young children (which was an asset) but the downside was the noise in the canteen and the gossip. I struggle with crowds, especially crowds of women so I only went in there once!

I did well on my Arts course and in curriculum studies but scraped through the 'Education Studies'-my tutors warned me that future headteachers might view me as a bit ahead of my time, they used the term 'avantgarde' and that I might be slammed down. They were right! In my future employment in most schools, it did still seem to be about manipulating children, not about them thinking for themselves and I was determined to put this right.

I was good at defending others and as a teacher I felt I was fulfilling my desire to help the sensitive and troubled ones (who actively sought me out) but still increasingly hopeless at sticking up for myself. I had lost some contact with Phyllis because of all the demands on me but one day I felt urgently compelled to visit her (These were days when not everyone had a telephone, let alone a mobile). I raced there on my bicycle to her alone and in floods of tears, besides herself. Ephraim, her husband had just died! …In the weeks to come helping her through this was more important than anything else in life.

During our time in Yorkshire, I would return to Dorset as much as I could, taking Emma camping to the place I had fallen in love with on that school trip. Getting from the North to the South of England involved long journeys in those days but Emma was very good. I used to (and still do) try and find a seat where I could hide away from human beings, just be myself with my daughter and window gaze. But almost every time I did this 'the Universe' had other ideas and I would find myself in deep conversation with complete strangers. They were not the average conversations and clearly, we were meant to meet. This was to continue.

In 1982 I broke my ankle very well, just about every bone! I was in hospital and the time came for my operation. I remember looking into the anaesthetists 'eyes and seeing a very troubled soul, I had an ominous feeling. Sometime later I woke up in the theatre paralysed, I couldn't breathe but could not communicate this. I could hear and see straight ahead but my eyes were in a fixed position and eventually stopped struggling to breathe. However, I found that I was still conscious and began to float up to this brilliant white light, so full of love, so amazing that I didn't want to go back. I could hear them shouting 'she has arrested, where is the crash trolley?' and them having trouble locating it but I was in this beautiful place and was no longer breathing, I was alive! Then at this moment I heard 'the voice 'again who asked me 'what about Emma?' In that split second I knew I had to go back and quickly. Simultaneously I heard the surgeons say, 'She's back, we've got her'. Apparently, a shot of adrenaline did the trick and re-started my heart. As I started to regain feeling they ironically told me that I had given them all a shock!

I parted from my husband after eleven years, having tried so hard for so long I finally realised I was not responsible for his depressions. With my new qualification as teacher, I returned to Dorset with Emma to take up my first position in an independent school for children with learning difficulties. The school was set in the Cranborne Chase and I would cycle for miles, again feeling so intimately connected to this ancient landscape. It was also a pleasant diversion from unpleasant school and village politics. Emma was growing up and becoming increasingly her own person – naturally. I felt I would like another relationship but ended up again in many other abusive situations with unhappy people which I regret, especially for my daughter. I still believed people said what they meant but I was to learn many more lessons before I started to realise that sometimes they didn't, however, I had to take responsibility for it as very easy prey.

Moving on a few years, with Emma about to leave school, I went to work in an Autistic Community Home. I also obtained a cottage/small holding which had been my dream for a long time, with goats and chickens which I absolutely loved. There is nothing better than growing organic vegetables and mucking out! My first goat, Sophie, lived the longest and I used to love burying my face in her white coat as I milked her. We were very, very close and even though she was huge with big horns, she never hurt me. She was a real character but not only that, I felt a deep spiritual connection with her. I also enjoyed my new job working with autistic young people and found I related to them but the Manager of the home, who had worked with autism all her life, (and to be another dear friend) assured me that I wasn't on that spectrum.

However, I knew there was something and in years to come I was to find out. It was here, too, that I met Rod who became my husband and we have been together now for 35 years. I also met Lorna, a fellow teacher whom I instantly recognised as 'soul mate' and she felt the same way. Not only did we share the same passions, we also had the same sense of humour and would literately spend hours with a fit of the giggles, crying with laughter into our wine! Sadly, she was taken from me seven years later and very suddenly. I had never felt such pain; I didn't think I could bear it. However, her tragic death was to kick start all my psychic senses and abilities that I had shut down for so long and in a very big way, at times overwhelming so.

Her passing was then in the future and before that time I had moved to be with Rod in Cumbria who was setting up a small hotel and the local vicar kindly let me have un-consecrated ground to house and graze Sophie. Rod was simultaneously looking after his Father, one of the original members of the S.A.S. as well as sorting out family dramas which were numerous, continuous and very draining. Although we both had additional part-time jobs the recession was against us. Months later the bailiffs were due to come in, we had lost all our money and there were huge family rifts which I was caught up in. I had 'burned my bridges' financially and emotionally but I was determined good would come out of it and light would prevail. I kept my head down and stayed in my light. I am lucky in that, whatever happens in life, I always wake up to a new day with optimism.

In 1989 we moved to Anglesey, North Wales, his father's choice in his final years. I had put by just enough for a deposit on a little terraced cottage while Rod half-lived with his father in a rented bungalow. My little dwelling had a huge garden backing on to common ground, perfect for Sophie. It was also adjacent to a pine forest which led down to some amazing coastline facing Llanddwyn Island. Despite unfriendly villagers (and I was to completely understand why later) it was a perfect place for healing and there was far more ahead for me, in the spiritual/physic sense, that I could ever have imagined!

I used to take Rod's dog for a long run through the great expanse of forest to the beach for a swim and amongst these trees felt such a presence, like I was being watched but also as if I belonged to something. This was 'owned' by the Forestry Commission but I felt this ancientness again, which I couldn't explain, peaceful but also at times so sad. Glorious light used to come in through the gaps and branches which inspired me to paint it. I would also cycle to another local beach where I felt overwhelming sadness and even anger from an unseen source, so much so that I tried to send love to whatever it was that was suffering. I had no-one to talk to about it. Lorna would have listened, but she was far away and for some reason she had not replied to my letters for weeks which was very unusual. I had found employment as a tutor for people with learning difficulties and was asked to create local history walks in the summer evenings for students who were in supported work placements.

It was at the local library that I discovered what had happened in Niwburgh Forest and in the neighbouring village. The village I was living in was apparently new because the original village had been on the spot now 'owned' by the Forestry Commission. People had been forced from their houses and moved against their will as part of the clearances. The same was true of Malltreath village but there had been a lot of bloodshed there and this what I had been experiencing. I was now sensing events from the past, reading peoples auras, feeling their emotions and often reading their thoughts, whether I wanted to or not.

At the same time, unbeknown to me (as he knew I would have asked him not to) Rod telephoned Lorna, he knew how worried I was. Then a letter came. I was much relieved and hastily tore it open only to read devastating news; Lorna had cancer and had wanted to get better before she told me; this is why I hadn't heard from her (and it's what I would have done) and she felt sure I would understand. Unfortunately, she wasn't improving so Rod's communication had prompted her to confess to me. I will always be grateful to him (in this instance) for going against my wishes and I immediately rushed across the country to be with her.

Over the next few weeks, I went as often as I could to help, to sit with her, to 'BE' but it was obvious she was not improving. I so wished I had skills to relieve her suffering. We acknowledged our love and friendship on a deep level and on the last occasion I saw her she asked her husband to leave us alone for a few hours. By this time Lorna was confined to bed. Unlike Rod, Tony had never been comfortable with our friendship and often resorted to inappropriate behaviour, but in fairness, on this occasion, he did leave us for a long time. Lorna showed me a photograph of herself in High School and pointed out another young man. She confessed this was her childhood sweetheart and that they had lost contact for many years until a few months before she was diagnosed with ovarian cancer when they met up again on a platonic basis. She said she had been frightened to tell him about her illness as she had done with me. I told her that it was vital she told him and soon for both their sakes. She looked at me in the eyes, held my hand tightly and asked me if I thought she would get better and I replied 'of course', in my heart knowing that her return to health would not be on the physical plane.

A week or so passed and I had a very uneasy feeling, like the urgency to fill my days with anything rather than to go to the telephone kiosk. Rod kept telling me to ring but I couldn't bring myself to do it. Eventually I was brave enough to make the phone call and received the news that shortly after our last meeting Lorna had been admitted to hospital where she had died peacefully. I was devastated and I vowed never to feel like this again – better to put the intense feelings of love and loss to some good use but at the time I didn't know how. … A few days later when Rod and I were in the car I heard Lorna's voice so clearly in my head. It felt so natural; she was with me and I confessed it to Rod. (As always, he listens but doesn't pass judgement). She told me to find Barry and explain what had happened – why she hadn't contacted him also. I said to her (in my head) 'how on earth am I going to do that?' She replied confidently and softly, 'you will find a way.' Lorna knew I would do this but the only thing I had to go on was his first name and that he was a solicitor!

The day before her funeral I arranged to meet Rod after he finished work in a small shopping mall in Llandudno. I had spent the day by the sea just sending her love before we were to travel to Norfolk that evening. There was only one door in at the front of this mall and one door out at the back, the rest of it was fully enclosed. This experience had nothing to do with Lorna's passing but was weird to say the least, especially happening at this raw time. I sat at a small table belonging to a modest café near the entrance so that I would be in Rod's direct line of vision when he came through the big glass doors. Eventually he came in (and on time) but looked right through me! I noticed, too, that he had changed his outfit from the morning, presumably to look smart for travel. Then (and this is completely out of character because he hates shopping for clothes) he took a sharp right into a men's outfitters. I was puzzled but decided to wait…. I waited and waited for him to emerge from that shop but twenty minutes later he was still seemingly in there. Then I saw him come in again through the glass doors exactly as he had done previously in this same change of outfit. This time he looked straight at me and came over to my table. I asked him what had been doing in the gent's outfitters? He replied that he hadn't been in there and had just come straight from work. I told him I had just seen him twenty minutes earlier come in through the doors in the same exact way (I know my husband! He was close and I have good eyesight) but he repeated that he had only just arrived! Together we went into the outfitters where I had seen him go in and seemingly disappear. At the back of the shop, it was a solid wall and there was no way out. …Obviously I was very, very shaken.

We arrived at the house to be warmly greeted by her husband and grown-up children as if Lorna was still with us.

It was the same the next day at breakfast and the sun was shining for her funeral. David, Lorna's son asked if I had seen Lorna at the funeral home and they all insisted I should go. I was in there probably an hour talking with her, I really felt her presence and I had so much to say. Even looking at her, there was something of her still there. Unbeknown to me, a female funeral director had been on duty outside and heard every word that I had said. She asked me if I was O.K. and then proceeded to tell me that she had never heard such an outpouring of love. I didn't know how to take it, a stranger hearing my ramblings! The funeral went well as funerals go and the church was packed and so was the pub afterwards! I didn't know if Barry would be there, I only had Lorna's assurances that I would find him. I asked several men if their name was Barry and I was getting strange looks. I had also to do it discreetly because obviously it would upset Tony and the family if they knew what I was doing. I was starting to think that maybe I would have to find him some other way until I spotted him. I hadn't much to go on as the faded photograph I had seen briefly was of a sixteen-year-old boy (Lorna would have been fifty-nine) but it was him and he was clearly very moved when I was able to pass on her message. He had only found out about her illness funeral quite by chance the day before and naturally it had been a great shock. He asked me if we could correspond so that I could tell him more about Lorna and her life which I agreed to and this lasted a few years. Then one day it was to be his last letter, he said that he could no longer bear it, having realised what he had lost, but thanked me for all that I had done.

About six weeks after her passing I was still talking to her in my head, just as we did on the telephone but also carried on my working life as normal, it was if I was still with her. It felt so natural. Then one glorious day when I had gone to visit a working farm with view to involving my students (which I know Lorna would have loved) I was left alone to make notes. I remember being in a field with the sun beaming down on my face and feeling so happy sharing this moment with her. Then her tone of voice changed, became softer but serious also. She said, 'Gilly, you know must go, now, don't you?' These were words I did not want to hear but understood that I was tying her to Earth and that she had work to do elsewhere. It was hard but it was here I let her go with love.

A few days later Rod and I had walked through Niwbirgh forest to eventually watch the sunset and settled ourselves in our usual spot for that time of year. Whilst Rod was occupied with retrieving the glasses and wine I was gazing into the distance. Suddenly a shape appeared on the horizon between the tops of the pine trees and the sky. It was sort a of tube torus with a golden tunnel leading, curving and disappearing inwards. The tunnel 's interior seemed to be strangely ribbed, not in itself attractive but there was an amazing glow emitting incredible angelic sounds. I was seeing it with my physical eyes and hearing it with my physical ears and the love that was emanating from this shape was incredibly powerful. It lasted a good few minutes and then quickly faded. I was in tears but managed to blurt out "Rod, did you see that?" But Rod hadn't seen or heard a thing.

A month or so later I received a letter from Hazel, the mother of another close friend from schooldays who had written to tell me Julia had terminal cancer. I wasn't totally surprised as Julia was sadly alcoholic and a very talented jazz musician. We kept each other going at school as she was also bullied (it was also clear that she was going to be Gay) and she used her amazing humour to fend off attackers and was also a way of hiding her pain. I loved going to stay at her house, her parents allowed her to make the front room like a jazz club where she kept her piano and like me, she preferred the company of older people, but ironically, especially older men.

Some years later Julia had lived with Emma for a while, I had tried unsuccessfully to help her but she eventually returned to London which had been her home since leaving school. So, following the operation for her throat cancer I often went to look after her in London but I wasn't always keen on the company she kept and made this known to her and why. When her time came, I felt so hopeless and longed for something that I could do to help ease suffering, other than in the practical sense. On the way back from her funeral, and as usual when travelling, I tried to find solitude on the train but, also as usual, the Universe had other plans. A woman (Barbara) asked me if the seat opposite was free, she seemed a quiet and I immediately felt at ease. She took out a book and placed it on the table dividing us. Just by seeing the cover, not even knowing what it was I knew I wanted it. Then she looked across and asked ME, "Do you mind if I ask you what you are reading? Can I copy the details? I feel I really want a copy! So, we exchanged book details and became friends. My book was titled 'The Celestine Prophesies' and had helped me realise that, because of my childhood, personality and past I had developed an un-healthy victim consciousness. Her book was about the Usui System of Reiki (Barbra was a Reiki Master) and with her help I trained in the Usui System of Reiki over the coming years, a wonderful healing tool and I started by first healing every year of my life, with gratitude and love.

A couple of years after Julia's death I had a vivid dream. I found myself in a narrow, cobbled street with her, a beautiful area with plane trees and grand Georgian houses and it felt like a part of North London where she had spent most of her short life. She beckoned me to follow, no words were spoken. We came to a smart, blue door and she led me through into a darkened room; much like her 'night club' we enjoyed as teenagers. When my eyes accustomed to the dim light in the room I could see about half a dozen, seated elderly gentlemen, drinking and smoking of course, but there was a jovial atmosphere. Julia was smiling at me and very clearly content. Suddenly I was outside the door, alone and I knew I would never see her again.

After my Father -in -Law died we decided to leave Anglesey but before we left, we were at last able to afford two admissions to Plas Newydd country house on the shores of the Menai Straits, a place I had felt drawn to since arriving in North Wales. However, I was grossly disappointed at the interior of all the rooms as they were filled with patriarchal memorabilia detailing the conquests of War but this the place was to come up again years later.

In 1994 Rod obtained a position as Mental Health Social Worker in N.W. Scotland. We had been to Argyll on camping trips in our old converted Sherpa van and had both fallen for the area, the cost of housing/living was also good as our funds were limited. Our first home was in a draughty rented flat in a rambling, deteriorating country house belonging to an eccentric (but lovely) elderly couple. The house was set in acre upon acre of grounds on the shore of Loch Etive, a dream location with amazing views. Sophie had the sole use of one -acre of walled garden but we use to take her down to the shores to lick the salt from the seaweed, which she loved and to be the company of other wildlife (including some docile Hebridean cows). When Rod was at work I would often swim as near as I could get to a small island, not far from the shore, where seals would bask in the Sun. On my approach they would jump off, one at a time and swim around me, as curious of me as I was of them and I only felt a mutual kindship.

This was just one wonderful experience among so many with Scottish wildlife that Rod and I would encounter over the next six years. Eventually, after selling my house in Wales we were able to afford a modest property. Rod had seen a cottage for sale on the Island of Luing, twenty miles South of Oban and a ferry ride from where he (and now I) worked. We viewed the dwelling from the outside, it was affordable but didn't inspire me and I was drawn to the cottage next door to it. This place seemed so very, very familiar but this was sadly not for sale.

A few weeks later I was still looking in the Estate Agents window when, to my joy and surprise, the cottage which had felt I knew was now on the market and, although it severely stretched our finances, we bought it! There was an outbuilding for Sophie directly opposite, miles of common ground as well as a huge garden to grow vegetables. I was also only yards from the Atlantic and we would share the beach with otters, often taking Sophie too, for her sea-weed snack. Buzzards had permanent nesting sites on the cliffs beyond our garden and we would watch the fledglings take first flight in Spring, spurred on by their dedicated parents. We also bought an old boat to potter about in, viewing neighbouring islands devoid of human life. There was an ancientness here I felt deeply connected to, wilderness so beautiful, untouched by human greed and endeavours and all the time I felt this stirring inside and a deep connection to the landscape. Again, as with Anglesey, in some places I felt overwhelming sadness and I was to discover that they had also suffered mass human slaughter there, on an enormous scale, because of the clearances. This is also a time when my psychic experiences/ abilities really took off!

On one of our favourite overnight jaunts to Loch Morar we had decided to treat ourselves to a day trip to Skye, somewhere I had always wanted to visit. On the return journey, despite being overcast, we had a panoramic view of the mainland coastline. There was one area, however which was illuminated with brilliant sunshine illuminating what seemed to be a golden stretch of sand and as Argyll is mainly rugged coastline, this was unusual. I felt an impelling urge to go there, as if it was reaching out to me. On return we looked it up on the map and the place I thought I had seen was called Applecross, a very remote area, only accessed in two ways. Our nearest option would involve travelling fair distances and climbing up incredibly steep mountainside in our old van; I never passed my driving test (to the relief of many who know me) so it was all down to Rod and the van who both graciously rose to the challenge. On our first trip there we were amazed at how far up we had ascended with magnificent far-reaching views and we got out of the van to stretch our legs before the descent into Applecross village. I felt a vibrational force coming up through my feet, I felt highly agitated and in my 'mind's eye' I could see ancient, rather grubby people rushing around with spears as if they were in pursuit or being pursued. I tried to what I had seen but more was to come. We found the very excellent 'Campsite' which was off season, beautifully quiet and where I was able to go off alone and practice Reiki but I was still getting very powerful shots of something I find hard to describe.

The next day we explored the coastline. Near to the site it was rocky and not good for swimming but in addition to this I felt overwhelming sadness and could not bear to stay there too long. We then discovered the sandy beach I had seen from the boat and it felt as if I had been called there. Again, in my mind's eye, I could see ancient fair -haired families with their golden naked bodies joyfully running about in one of the sandy caves. We went the following day and I saw it again. I also explored the campsite and came across a modern, well cared for cottage, tucked away in a corner. I was drawn to one end of the garden, again feelings of sadness consumed me, AS IF SOMETHING VITAL WAS MISSING FROM IT. I could not rest till I had found out about this house so plucked up the courage to ask the owner of the site who the house belonged to and why I was getting these strange feelings. As I am a very shy person this took a lot for me to do. This lovely lady looked shaken when I told her, almost tearful and asked me to come back in the afternoon when she had some free time which I did. Apparently, the house belonged to them and they had it built when they bought the campsite. What they had done, however, was to reluctantly remove one of the standing stones (which I was to learn were all around this area) as it had been in the way during construction. They said it was an action they deeply regrated and this was what I was feeling; not their guilt but sadness from place from where the stone had been removed. She then said I should talk to a local historian in the village who would fill me in on all the other things I had seen (with my mind's eye) and felt. It turned out that on the stony shoreline at the time of Columbus a community of monks had drowned having just sailed all the way there from Ireland via Iona. They had wanted to set up a religious community in Applecross but tragically never made it…. The figures I had seen in the cave belonged to a Neolithic people and that some months previously there had been an important archaeological dig. They had found human remains, a fire pit, artefacts and animal bones all suggesting this place had once been a permanent dwelling place. (The artefacts were now in the Museum at Inverness if my memory serves me well). This kind lady gave me copies of all her notes and newspaper reports which supported their findings. Rod, obviously, had been witness to all this and although he hadn't a clue what was happening to his wife (and neither had she) he was none the less very supportive. On another camping trip, unbeknown to us at the time, we had a brief encounter with the legendary Loch Morar monster, but that's another story.

Back on Luing, whilst sitting in the garden one day, I saw a small white, gossamer-like shape floating about in the holly- tree but I could see it wasn't of this world because otherwise it would have been caught on the prickly leaves. It just hovered about, like a ghostly handkerchief and eventually faded. (It was a 'one off' the time but these shapes have since re-appeared where we live now some many years later).

Then, on a camping trip to Mull I began to have new experiences. We had spent the day in Iona, a beautiful place and were camping near the Iona ferry. The following day I awoke knowing I was not fully in my body although I could hear everything, a dog barking and birds singing. There was very bright light and I was somehow aware somehow of a door, slightly ajar but I instinctively knew that if I looked through I would not get back so I waited for the brilliant light to fade before somehow twisting myself back into my body, like a cork screw.It happened again but I got used to it.

In 2001 my daughter gave birth to another beautiful girl, Eleanor and I now felt, emotionally and spiritually, that I was now three! I spent as much time with them as I could, revelling in being a grandmother and joining in Eleanor's magical games. On a much sadder note, my Father's health was deteriorating and so was the health of my goat. I will not dwell on this for too long. Sophie went first and the pain was as unbearable as when Lorna had died. Her head was cradled in my arms and was just managing to lick the whiskey from my fingers (she loved her tipple). She was suffering and we could see it was her time. Asthe vet waited with an injection Sophies eyes bored into mine with such knowing and yet such uncertainty and I tried, subconsciously to re-assure her. The love we felt was indescribable and at my reluctant nod the needle was inserted. I do not remember much after that until Rod buried her in the place she loved, I just felt trapped in an unbearable weight of sadness and didn't know how to escape it.

A few days later, however, when I was sitting alone the thought came to me that I should convert my feelings of intense sorrow into that of love and send it to her. This is what I did and from then on 'pain' became gratitude for having had such a wonderful companion.
Not long after this my father also died. He had become much gentler in his old age despite his acutely poor health and I was also with him when his time came. So too was Mum and Rod. At his time of death Dad had that familiar rapturous look in his eyes that I had encountered years

before. And after his release, in my 'minds' eye', I could see him dancing! This is not something he ever enjoyed doing as he was never comfortable in his own body and used to sit in a suit on the beach!

Interestingly, years later, when I felt able to talk to my mother about things, she also confessed to seeing the same thing in her head when he died– my father dancing for joy – but she dismissed it, knowing him as we did, as totally implausible! After losing my father, Rod's old dog had to be put down and this was also very upsetting. Then a position was advertised on the Isle of Manas Mental Health Social Worker and despite my deep reservations Rod was successful. Just before we left Scotland, I'd had my fiftieth birthday and had treated myself to a day in Glasgow with an overnight at a friend's house. I'd heard about the Hubble Telescope Exhibition where photographs had been blown up to room size and was really interested but I was not prepared for what was to come! Instantly I felt dizzy, my head began swimming and I felt myself turning upside down! I had to hold on to something in the physical to stop myself from falling, I knew I was part of what I was seeing, especially the Eagle Nebula, it felt so familiar. I only have the guidebook now but when I look at the picture it affects me now as it did then.

Our first house on the Isle of Man was a very small terraced cottage in a seaside village, the only property available to us in that price bracket. It was a relief to have our own place and I was accepted on to the island's teaching pool. Unfortunately, we discovered our new home was haunted. It was a male presence, a smoker who used to hang about in the bathroom when I was in there and I could smell the nauseous mixture of tobacco and shaving foam. He would then follow me into the bedroom and would sometimes be on the stairs when I came in from work. Eventually Rod sensed it too although he obviously did not feel intimidated in the same way. I also felt that something profoundly sad had happened in this village together with feelings of absolute darkness and sometime later I was to discover why. We secured a buyer for our house but after scraping a deposit on a new-build we were gazumped and about to lose everything. However, we found new buyers and with only hours to spare! I had gone to the site on my days off just staring at the emerging shell imagining myself in there and it worked. I mention this because I was to use this skill sometime in the future – imagining something I wanted into being. I was also offered a permanent position at my first school but owing to the distance from home I elected to go elsewhere. A big mistake!

At this point I feel I should say that I was to find the island at odds with itself. I was to encounter magnificent scenery and an abundance of ancient sites (which strangely again filled me with immense sadness) and to become friends with many very spiritual Manx ladies who were justifiably proud of their island and mostly unaware of the dark side that Rod and I were to encounter as government employees. It is no different in the U.K. or in Scotland but as a small island (which also accommodated an unsavoury banking Mecca) it was more obvious.

My next school presented me with enormous challenges, a huge mixed aged, mixed ability class with some disturbed children (from families at war with each other and known to the services) in a very small space. When it was known I practised Reiki I was given a wide berth! Yet we had committed ourselves financially; and professionally I was determined I was going to get through my appointed year. Just before I left some Year Six Girls asked me if I had any advice to give them. I usually find spontaneous remarks difficult but from somewhere inside of me out came the words, "whatever you do in life, do it with love," which is how I feel; they thanked me very much.

I was then transferred to small school of my choice in a tiny hamlet nor far from where I lived. There was a temporary replacement Headteacher and history began repeating itself, I was such an easy target. However, my confidence was growing, I had finally learned to defend myself in a detached way and without feelings of ill-will. I was to be tested again but I was no longer victim consciousness and I only reacted back with pleasantries and love (which I felt/feel anyway) and eventually they gave up! I am very grateful to everyone who has tried to give me a hard time in life! Our worst experiences are sent to be our best teachers and I obviously needed to learn these lessons. This little school had then amalgamated with a larger school in the village where I lived along with a new Head who was to become a friend and I worked between the two. I had also been put in charge of the Pre-school for a year and I was to teach these children (as class teacher or for different subjects)for the next eight years. Right from the start I recognised many of them as very special, aware children. It was an honour and privilege to guide them through their early years and as they got older to share in their 'otherworldly' feelings and experiences as they would quietly seek me out. I felt deeply connected to many of them and although I hadn't heard of the word 'Star seed' at the time or have any notion of it, I know now.

Apart from teaching there was a discreet, spiritual side to the Island which offered me some opportunities to investigate my experiences and to my Mothers HORROR (the 'new me' decided to tell her). Although, as always, I was very selective I felt drawn to attend a three -day course on Mediumship with about thirty others, all women, (barring one) and most of whom had travelled from England including the 'Medium'. Over the weekend Mediumship was explained, followed by exercises working with identified partners and I shared some very special moments. I had been assigned to work with a lovely young woman, already quite an established medium. She told me she could see a lovely lady surrounded by children; that the woman was wearing lilac-coloured clothes and smelled of lavender. 'The woman' told her that I would know who she was and what she was doing. Of course, it was Lorna and on 'the other side' she was still teaching and looking after young children which had been so important to her on the Earth plane and how we had met.

Lorna could not contact me directly anymore but used this opportunity, through another, to show me she was happy and fulfilled. For my partner I saw a sweet old lady on her hands and knees happily picking at the carpet beneath her or on the sofa. I felt really embarrassed to say what I was seeing but my partner was amused! Her Grandmother had had dementia in her final years(and as a very 'thrifty' woman in life) she would amuse herself by getting on her hands and knees all day looking for coins that may have fallen out of peoples' pockets! Another communication I had was for another young woman and I could see another elderly lady in an old-fashioned kitchen. The woman was smiling but kept pointing at her baking. I could smell a strong smell of steak and kidney pie in this communication which seemed very strange (and unpleasant for me as a vegetarian) but I described the scene.

Again, this was another grandmother who, whilst supervising her granddaughter had made her steak and kidney pie to eat for the first time. Unfortunately, the little girl (now the young woman in front of me) suffered an allergic reaction to the kidney and ended up in intensive care. Obviously, she survived and to the relief of everyone, especially her grandmother and this was the message! On the last day of the course the tutor asked us if we'd received any random messages. Only one participant (and only male) felt moved to speak. Although visibly shy this young man described a tall man with distinguishing features, awkward in his gait but very intelligent. I listened attentively and compassionately but did not immediately respond. The more he described this man the more silent the room seemed to be as no-one felt they knew this person…. but I did! In the end I just had to raise my hand because it was undoubtedly my father! Then the nervous young man turned and looked me in the eyes with this communication which was, "Please tell her that I am so very, very sorry."

Shortly afterwards I went to stay with my mother to put her mind at rest. I had not expected it but one evening messages came through for her. I had understood that it was a sort of spiritual law that mediums did not normally receive communication from blood relatives however here was my mother's grandmother (in theory my Great Grandmother) who was imploring my mother to forgive and forget whatever had transpired. My Nana Rose was also there in spirit with this lady (who would have been her mother) but Nana was distancing herself from it. It was a very upsetting experience for me as a go-between and I could feel the tensions rising so I brought things to a close and promised her I would do what I could.

A few days later I also had communications from two girlfriends belonging to my mother and one of them described trips they had all taken; apparently their incentive was to try and get my mother to come out of her shell after a broken engagement (and heart). My Mother then filled me in on many things; who these girls were and where they had all gone. It did in many ways provide her with some lighter comfort. She especially like being contacted, (through me) by an American G.I. with whom she'd had a few dates. He was able to tell her that he had not meant to leave but he had been called back very suddenly.

I learned more about the feud with my Great Grandmother but my mother, despite my best efforts was refusing to give in, both very stubborn characters. I did not have any more communications for Mum after this. I had tried so hard to encourage her to forgive on the Earth-plane but she'd refused, it was if her hurt was now part of who she was. Other things were happening to me and gathering pace. I was seeing brilliant flashes of colour, beautiful purple/blue hues just appearing and flashes of white light.

The flying dreams have continued all my life and one was particularly significant. I was in a room crowded with people. A man had lifted me up into the air as far and was telling me to fly! With the support of his strong arms and confident manner I took off and as I did so he called out "you must give your dance a name, what will you call it?" and I called back at him "The Sun Dance!" It felt so free as I looked down on people looking up but within what seemed like seconds I was back down on my feet, in the arms of this man and looking directly at him "What is your name?" I asked and he replied, "Sir Fredric Ashton." The next day, because it had felt so real, I looked him up on the new Internet and found a matching biography and photograph. It was the man in my dream. Not only had he been a famous dancer and choreographer in his day he had also spent much of his life staying in Plas Newydd, the country house I had felt drawn to whilst living in Anglesey, so I believe him to be a spirit guide whilst I am in the physical.

As a child I wanted to be a ballet dancer (and still love to dance) and my grandparents were both in the theatre, so there are connections. I had also discovered, through the Internet, that Anglesey and the Isle of Man had strong bonds in the past, both had been Druidic centres for learning and with a shared library which had been destroyed at the time of the Roman invasion. Seemingly I attune to ancient cultures, to past events and traumas suffered and the need to heal them.

I was now witnessing much U.F.O activity at night, most nights in fact. Also, each week for a couple of years I sat in meditation with a friend who had been professional medium at one time in Liverpool. I had met Elaine through a very close mutual friend called Linda who was herself deeply spiritual and accomplished in many areas. They were both going to see a woman visiting the island whom they rated highly. This woman reputedly channelled angels and had the ability to identify specific angels working with each human soul and drew pictures of what she saw. They asked me if I wanted to go too and I welcomed the opportunity. It was a popular venue, Elaine and Linda went in first and came out beaming so I was quite excited when my turn came. My experience was to be quite different, however. She looked at me with an embarrassed and puzzled expression and then admitted she wasn't getting anything at all from the Angelic Realms. She was, however, receiving something that she'd never had before and started to draw something very strange, seemingly a maze of scribbles and eyes. She apologised and said that this was all she was able to do; that they were beings of some sort who worked with me and with Nature. I thanked her but came out confused and rather disappointed, especially after all my experiences and belief in Angels but I was to find out much later in life that she had been correct! I had also been re-united with another close school friend after over thirty -five years (the circumstances of which make for another amazing story and example of the Universe at work). Paula and I bought a tent together and began camping in Pewsey Vale near to Avebury, the renowned crop circle area and I was desperate to see one. From my very first time here I felt another strong sense of déjà vu and deep connection. On one hillside near Alton Barnes, I could see in my mind's eye an encampment as I had had done in Applecross and was feeling it in every cell of my body. We bought a map and I discovered that there had indeed been a dwelling place; the views were also amazing and far reaching – and an excellent spot to scan the horizon for circles. So, for the next nine years or so we went there several times a year, just because we loved it. Although I talked to Paula openly about my experiences, she had not had anything herself so was understandably sceptical. The crop circles however, she could see and appreciated herself that they were created in a way that was not of this world.

Rod and I were camping in Purbeck and had been discussing where we would live post-retirement and I said wanted to return here. I then went off for a walk on my own along Priests Way, paused to look at the view and then something made me look down on the ground. Suddenly, from this moment on I realised that there was nothing separating me from what I was seeing, that I was also part of the landscape, part of the stones beneath my feet and all was one. It was simple but very profound and has remained with me ever since. From here we went to my mother for our final week and mid-stay one night I was to experience something so incredibly profound and extremely hard to describe. I was half asleep but felt myself come out of body and I was aware someone or some being was with me. I was then taken up into space at incredible speed and I was looking down on the Earth and seeing it in an entirely different way; everything consisted of interlocking, geometric shapes and patterns and so too was everything else I encountered. There was also the most beautiful light and colours that I had never seen before but there is nothing in this Earthly three - dimensional life that I could use to compare it with.

I was also given the secrets of the Universe and I felt so incredibly blessed! I knew that when I returned to Earth, I could tell everyone and in so doing so make the World a better place, I was euphoric! Then I was led back but I didn't mind as I was so excited as this knowledge would change everything! I remember looking up at the ceiling with my physical eyes trying to fit myself back into my body 'the corkscrew way' but with the experience quickly fading and THAT KNOWLEDGE gone in an instant!!! I tried to grasp it but failed and a little later I tried to explain to Rod but there were no words. Normally I have a joyful disposition but after this everything felt so flat and lifeless. As a painter I am constantly aware and appreciative of how Nature uses complimentary colours to such wonderful effect but for weeks afterwards I could only see shades of grey, my 3D home felt very strange and painfully devoid of that which I had left behind. I was living a monotone existence and it took weeks before 'normality' returned, whatever that is!

For some years Rod and I had gone to Greece for our annual two -week vacation. I felt very drawn to this country in another past-life way and was convinced that one day I would meet some like-minded female healers. Although we went to some beautiful places and met some wonderful Greek people it was about the tenth Greek holiday before it happened. I had been extremely busy at home with SATS marking (painful) and writing reports for school so left it to Rod to choose our holiday as we both enjoyed the same things; sunsets, sea and a traditional way of life. He showed me a photograph of the destination, it felt somehow familiar and I was happy with his choice. Some weeks later, Elaine and I had our usual meditation together. I went into a deep trance and saw a Greek woman, a priestess who beckoned me to follow her. I saw an amphitheatre on a hillside and was led through a marketplace before we came to a low doorway and she led me inside. It was very dark but as my eyes grew accustomed, I saw the illuminated body of another female who appeared to be in chains. She looked me in the eyes and said, "you think it is difficult in your time but in 'my time' it is much harder." I had no idea why she'd spoken so I asked her who she was, she replied, "I am the Oracle of Delphi".

Some months later when were about to go on our holiday and with free time at last I bought a travel guide of Athens and the Mainland; I like to know as much as I can about an area before we travel, particularly its history and we hadn't been to this part of the mainland before. When I opened the book, I couldn't believe my eyes when I saw that Delphi was not too far from where we would be staying (approximately a half day or more by car) but much more than that, inside the guide was a double spread and illustrated 3D representational map of the site. I could see very clearly the main entrance which the guidebook described as 'once a marketplace (agora) where religious objects were bought and sold' and in my trance this is where I had been led in. Next to the map was an artists' rendering of the Oracle of Delphi and their portrayal was exactly as I had seen her, the room and everything in it. I was absolutely stunned as there was no explanation.

Our accommodation was perfect for our needs, in an olive grove near to the sea and surrounded by mountains and I felt instantly at home this beautiful and fertile area. We went every night to a lovely taverna overlooking the sea and on the third night when I was at the reception-desk I heard the young woman talking to another Greek about a death.

On the bar was a stack of business cards, I took one as a memento and was drawn into the photograph, mesmerised by the man fishing on the front which turned out to be the proprietor when he was younger. At the same time a young male voice came into my head, "please tell them it was an accident, it wasn't their fault, please tell them it was an accident and that I wanted to go!" As we walked back to our accommodation the young male kept repeating the same words over and over to me in my head. In the end I told Rod - that the young man was imploring me to speak with the pretty restaurant receptionist who had settled our bill. I did not know what to do or how Greek people would view such matters, would I end up in a Greek jail?

I woke up the next morning and still heard this young man imploring me to pass his message on. He also said, "tell her I was the clown!" So, I plucked up courage to approach her and we arranged a time to talk. She said I ought to speak to their mother but I insisted that the message was specifically for her. I told her what I had 'received' and afterwards she began to fill me in. The young man had been her brother who was born very physically disabled and had not been expected to live for as long as he had. This young woman said that it was she that had done a considerable amount of caring for him being the eldest of six children and they had been very close. They used to watch a children's animated cartoon film together, his favourite, over and over, and that her brother identified with one of the leading characters, "the clown fish". I have never seen the film so cannot comment but it was obviously significant. She also told me that her brother was in and out of hospital and having reached puberty felt he was missing out.

Then that night (approximately two weeks before I had arrived there) he had been admitted to hospital again with an infection. Due to his vulnerable condition and medical history the staff were supposed to make regular checks but (because of another emergency I believe) he was left unattended for some time and a vital injection was overlooked.

This is when he had decided that he would make his transition, that life had become too painful both physically and emotionally and took this opportunity to release himself from the Earth plane. Now there was to be an official enquiry and he was feeling bad because in spiritual terms he'd been given the choice and he had chosen to go.

So, everything was now making sense and I was so glad that he had impressed on me to speak on his behalf. I was then introduced to their Mother who was married to the proprietor in the photograph, she was a spiritually aware person and although grieving we instantly became friends. It was also through her I was then put in touch with two other like-minded women the next day and we too connected immediately. So within just the first week of this two -week vacation, through very unusual circumstances and not one I would have chosen, I had found them! These very close friendships are now their sixteenth year and the circle has grown.

There was a brief period, however, a year or so later, when I felt that the family of the young man doubted me. I found this troubling as my only intention had been to help but I believe that the enquiry was stopped as he had hoped and that was what he had wanted. So now I had come to realise what "The "Oracle of Delphi" had meant by her remark. I was also feeling that, for some reason which I couldn't explain to myself at the time, it was not my destiny to be limited to the 'Astral Planes' and so I chose to shut this part of me down.

I returned each year and eventually after retirement and Mum's passing, to buy a little olive grove where I live when I am there, very simply and quietly. This land I call (in Greek) Mother Earth's Garden as I feel it represents Gia and I am her custodian. One day, alone on the long, deserted beach, a stray dog with scruffy white hair came and sat next to me. I wasn't sure about her personal hygiene so moved away but wherever I went, she went and even put her paw on my arm, seemingly to stop me from escaping. She followed me back to my apartment and sat outside. I eventually discovered who the owner was, a lovely, deeply caring man and the son of a retired vet. He lived just around the corner from where I was staying and cared for over twenty stray and abandoned cats but Rudthula, (the Greek name for Rose) at only about three months old, was the only dog. I began to help him with the sick or very young animals with Rudthula helping too. In my absence she would escape to look for me, sometimes going vast distances and putting herself in danger.

One day when Rod and I were in the marketplace it was so busy we suddenly decided to completely change plans and head up to the castle, a five- minute walk away. There she was waiting for me at the top of the hill, and as I had only just decided to go there; it was obvious she could read my thoughts. When the time came parting from her was almost unbearable, I can see through her eyes into her soul and she can see into mine. She is grown up now at about five years of age, very independent and devoted to her owner but when I return the bond is still strong and I am as attuned to her as she is with me. I call her 'my space dog' and firmly believe our relationship will continue whatever dimension we are next in.

Back in England and I had turned sixty. It was the school Summer holidays and Paula and I gone as usual to Avebury for the crop circle season. It was August 9th, 2012 an incredibly close and humid day. Whilst waiting for Paula to catch up, I was propped up against one of the beautiful standing stones feeling part of it, blissfully content and giving thanks for the fact that I had now finally learnt to stick up for myself but from the heart and with love. I had no attachment to hurt whatsoever or to the actions of others and had come to feel happy with being different, more than ever feeling at one with nature, Gia and the Cosmos. I was also wishing Paula could have some sort of paranormal encounter of her own as she often would say to me, "Gill, how is it you have all these experiences and I don't?" My friend arrived and we went together into the formation which was made up of many connecting circles and although very new, unfortunately already busy. We were both very hot and sticky and the air was incredibly still. I was in one circle and my friend was to my right on the edge of another circle but quite close to me. To my left was a young man in another circle but the other visitors were several metres away.

Suddenly I saw something move in the distance immediately below a line of trees, at first it was just a pin prick but as it came rushing towards me, growing in speed and strength it formed a sort of inverted 'V'. It was a huge force, like a wind but not a wind, it blew my skirt right up, Paula's Tilly hat, and circled me three times before disappearing behind me. Everywhere else was completely still, untouched and nobody, apart from the three of us, saw or felt anything. No-one had even looked up! Despite the strength of this force the crop immediately returned to normal. The stranger and my friend were visibly in shock, both describing it like something from a Sci Fi film set but I felt secretly elated. Then Paula turned to me and said, "That was for you Gill." I felt thi sbut also that it was sent as a shared experience and my wish for Paula had come true. The next day we returned to the crop circle where we had had the encounter and were very disappointed to see it full of people. We wanted so much to have it to ourselves for a short while to give thanks. In my head I wished them away and immediately, one by one, people left. We were in that circle at least fifteen minutes on our own until we felt it was time to go and then slowly the visitors returned. This was further confirmation. I have been in contact 'with them' via the use of my heavy dowsing rods ever since, slowly and formally at first as I adapted to their wonderful presence in my life.

Rod and I had an offer accepted on a bungalow as our house had finally been sold on the Isle of Man. One day Paula and I decided to go on a long hike first through a village called Langton Matravers to Corfe Castle then back along the coastal path. As usual I was in front and when I was waiting for Paula to catch up when I distinctly heard 'the voice "you will come to live here in Langton." I didn't understand why it would say this as we were buying a property further away. However, it was the voice I'd heard on those very specific, rare occasions when I had been in difficulties. An hour or so later we had stopped for refreshments and I received a 'phone call from Rod to say that, on the point of signing our buyer had just pulled out! Devastated, I returned to the Isle of Man where we decided that I would still retire and rent a flat in Swanage whilst Rod continued to try and sell our property. During my final term I continued to meditate on the drawing I had made of my dream property on the Dorset coastal path. I had placed on my kitchen wall five years previously. In February 2013 we finally sold our bungalow and I started looking for another property. One immediately caught my attention a semi- detached cottage needing complete refurbishment in Langton Matravers, the village of my dreams but could never afford! I went straight into the office and startled the estate agent as he had only just that minute put the details in the window. The property was almost identical to my drawing, on the coastal path and six weeks later I moved in! My dream manifested as 'the voice' had told me it would.

Unfortunately, Rod had to have surgery in the middle of all this. He was recovering in the flat and understandably feeling weak. I was still getting used to 'my beings' and had not communicated with them since Rod's discharge from hospital. Feeling exhausted I went outside one night to gaze at the stars and in a moment of weakness expressed a wish to return! I then went to bed and as I started to drift to sleep that familiar light illuminated the wall in front of me.

The next thing I knew I was on an operating-table, I don't remember seeing but I could hear. There was an entity about to perform something on me when I suddenly felt the presence of two other, kindly, authoritative beings, one either side of me. "What do you want with her? She knows too much!" is what they said. At this point I was immediately returned and upon waking the next morning saw my left hand was turned inwards, I could not use my fingers and they were also numb, I accepted it had happened. However, I couldn't understand why the kindly beings said I knew too much when I felt I knew very little. I tried to conceal my hand over the next two weeks and it eventually improved. I checked with my Doctor who admitted he had no idea what it could have caused it but assured me that I was in good health. I asked 'my beings' if it had been them that had intervened on my behalf and it was.

Rod continued to work on the Isle of Man until his retirement as planned and I was overseeing the massive renovations to our new home. As I was living alone this afforded me plenty of opportunity to communicate with 'my beings'. I had begun to record my U.F.O sightings (which I was witnessing most nights) and in a separate journal asked 'my beings 'permission to keep a notebook and record our conversations. They agreed but 'I felt' them teasing me in the nicest possible way as I am, by nature, a copious note taker! Then, on a few occasions (when Rod was there too) I go him out of bed to witness some of the craft I had seen which I called 'Sky Skimmers'. They are cigar shaped, approximately the size of small aircraft with three bright lights and seem to glide silently and effortlessly across the air at a height which I would equate with a helicopter. We would watch them glide over our house and towards the English Channel. I asked 'my beings' whether all the various U.F.O.'s I was seeing were friendly or unfriendly, human or non-human and the reply was that they were mixed, I could observe but must stay clear of interaction. They were serious about this.

With regards to 'my beings' and our method of communication at this time it started as simple yes/no answers or neutral if the question could not be answered. Sometimes the yes or no would be a weak response and at other times very stated according to the question asked. I asked them if I was 'channelling them' and they said a very definite "no". I replied, "well are we having conversations then?" and the answer was a very strong "yes"! so much so I thought the rods would take off, and again I felt their love, warmth and humour.

Over the next few years, I learned much from them, it was usually two beings that worked with me (but now I have only the one very particular appointed guide). They are interdimensional light beings from the Pleiades region and were once in the physical. They have told me not to get too absorbed in unnecessary details because they are all around, sharing in 'our perceived sense of space' and remind me of this each day! Not all is as it seems, time and space are human constructs. If necessary, they would return briefly to the physical but so far have chosen not to. Although a blend of male/female qualities they represent the 'Divine Feminine' and work with other light workers everywhere to bring this back into consciousness including angels, physical and non-physical beings and those of us incarnated here briefly in the third dimension.(I was to learn that I been to Earth a few times before, which is why I feel connected to certain ancient sites and like so many of us, return at very critical times for specific purposes).

Rod joined me in 2014 but unfortunately in July,2015 he was rushed to hospital where he was to have his second aortic valve replacement and because of various health issues I was told by the surgeons that he might not make it. However, I asked my beings for their support and spent the entire eleven hours on the day of his operation sending healing. At one point, towards the end, I felt him slipping away and I put all I could into keeping him here because I knew he so much wanted to live. He did survive but had died on the table just towards the end and it had taken a lot to bring him back; the surgeons told us both afterwards that he had(has) completely defied the odds; team work, positive thinking, love and prayer knows no bounds. I am also so very grateful for the support of my beings in the non-physical and to the incredible skills of the surgeons, not to mention the wonderful nursing staff who also allowed me to help them care for Rod as he made his miraculous recovery.

In 2016 Mother passed away. I was naturally shocked and upset but this was also because she had depended on me, emotionally, all my life. I had spent so long caring for her needs but at the same time trying to maintain some sort of emotional independence. Mum was often critical of my life choices which didn't do much for my confidence, torn between what I wanted to do or upsetting her. Mum was also extremely afraid of change- if an ornament was moved only slightly, she would react with panic so that when I cleared the house after her death, I did it very slowly, over weeks, explaining each move to her – and with love. Before this there was the funeral to arrange but I had a fair idea of what she wanted as we had spoken of it many times so did not feel too daunted. I had arranged the front room in the way she would have liked, Emma and I shared the catering – we knew with confidence what was to be served and Eleanor did a reading. All the people she wanted there were there, it was a perfect day – except for one thing! The candlestick holders were bereft of candles. A few weeks before her death she had sent me out for white candles as the vicar regularly came to the house to give her communion and she had run out. I went into every shop I could think of to find white candles but could only find 'off white' candles and she made it known she was not impressed. However, I felt that slightly off-white candles in the candlestick holders would be better than nothing on 'her day' and so Rod placed one in each holder very firmly. I wanted everything to go smoothly, which it did. Unfortunately, the next morning after the 'wake,' one of the candles had been placed very carefully on its side on the narrow shelf above the electric fire. The windows had been shut, there was no wind or draughts and if there had been the candle would have fallen on the carpet. Rod and I had been the only ones in the house that night, clearly Mum was not happy with the off-white candles!

The time was approaching to dispose of Mum's ashes. Again, I had made a very firm promise since childhood to scatter them on my sister's grave, where we had scattered Dad also. She reminded me of this promise each time I went to see her in later years. However, this venue was now a long way from where we lived (I would be partly dependent on public transport) and to get everyone there, it needed careful organising, so I had put it on hold. One night I had a vivid dream. I awoke to find myself standing in a very small room, like an office. To the right of me was a window and a dark night sky. To the left was an open door with a brightly lit corridor beyond. In front of me was a filing cabinet. I opened the cabinet and found a baby and a document. Suddenly, in through the window came the feeling of intense anger but the corridor seemed a safe place to escape to. Then I woke up. For an hour or so I was very distressed until I realised Mum was sending me yet another very clear message; that I should now take her to be with my sister and my father as I had promised I would! On both occasions I had felt her disapproval, despite my efforts, nothing changes, even 'on the other side' – but it was almost a comfort! She was Mum, a real character and I loved her! So, the 'scattering of the ashes' promptly took place and I set about clearing and selling the house as sensitively as I could, the monies to be split between me and my brother.

A few years on and my spiritual and paranormal experiences were increasing. I still thought of Mum but in a happy way, the pain had gone. Then one night she appeared to me in a vivid dream very similar to the one I'd had with Julia. Although I had sold her house 'in the physical' I saw Mum standing outside this family home she had lived in (and loathed) for the last forty years. After Dad died I had tried to get her to move because she felt so unhappy with the area and the house, but there was always an excuse – the real reason was that she hated change.

So in this dream the house was just the same apart from one thing. Mum was standing outside and beckoned me towards her, and as with Julia, there was no speech. She then proudly showed me a 'new front porch', something she had always wanted in life but felt she couldn't afford or bear the upheaval (or changes) it would incur. She was obviously elated and very proud to show me what she had done at last! The lawn was also now in good condition and there were flowers. Suddenly she walked around the side of the house and disappeared leaving me standing there alone as Julia had done and I knew I would now never see Mum again. Both Julia and Mum had seemingly created familiar, safe worlds for themselves on the Astral Planes, both had wanted me to know, independently of each other, that they were happy and settled. Then both disappeared in the same way.

In 2017 Rod brought my attention to an article on NEXUS newsfeed about 'sliders', people who cannot wear watches and interfere with electrical equipment – I am such one! At the end of the article is said, 'have you ever considered yourself starseed?' Well, I hadn't because I associated 'starseeds' with the new children being born with special gifts or with adults who could do things like bend spoons etc. with their minds which I can't! I then, (because it was in Nexus and not in a glossy magazine) tried the Myers Briggs personality test and seemingly I was indeed that rare 1% of the population which didn't surprise me. However, I suddenly felt drawn to do an 'adult starseed test on- line 'and ticked 27 out of 28 boxes. My one cross was an interest in technology! No! Eventually I summoned up enough courage to ask "well, am I star seed then?" My being's answer was a strong, playful and resounding "yes"!!! I could feel the joy and laughter as I had finally worked it out!

From around this time onwards I have contacted them daily as far as possible (now with one very specific 'guide) and no longer felt the need to write things down! Everything now made sense and from then on referred to them as 'my family' because I know that is who they are. They have told me that although from the Pleiades my spirit is also partly from Orion and that they are at present in (but not confined to) the 5th dimension. Eventually I will be returning and working with them and other star seeds in the Cosmos but not on Earth as we know it at present. All light beings, whether from the Pleiades, Arcturus, Sirius, Orion, other dimensions or Angels associated with Earth etc.,all work together as a unified family of light. The sheer numbers would be hard for us to comprehend. So, to talk of a 'home planet' is misleading as they do not view this term 'home' as having meaning. For them home (and it is still not the right word) is everywhere and they insist that they share the same space with me on this Earth plane as well as being everywhere else.

At my request they have recently confirmed I can now use telepathy to communicate with them, which is quicker, in the beginning it was not permitted. Their reply is still with the use of the dowsing-rods, left for yes and right for no but they have devised other movements such as crossing at my heart centre or resting on my shoulders when answering questions. I immediately feel gratitude, peace and at one with all that there is when we spend time together. They greet me with both rods whirling around to confirm their presence, at times almost overwhelming love pouring through my crown chakra and down the nape of my neck.

The 'white shapes' have also returned, much bigger in size now but I have only seen them at night around the house and I am told they are benevolent beings. Lately I have also woken up to other strange things happening! Last year a magnificent and highly intricate, golden geometric pattern was seemingly projected on to the ceiling covering it entirely, as if it was an ancient temple. I could see it with my physical eyes and took a minute or so to fade away. The next day another smaller pattern was projected on to the glass door, like a stained -glass mandala and I have been receiving them regularly in the same way ever since. It is always upon waking and they last a few minutes before disappearing. They vary in colour, (the blue ones are my favourite) and this beautiful sacred geometry seems to vibrate. Then odd flying objects have appeared, one looked like the ceramic end of a pull switch! Also, recently, I 'lost' half an hour or more of daytime whilst standing upright. I went into some sort of unconscious state but did not fall, very strange. This happened to me once in the 'Valley of the Kings' some years ago but I did not expect it in my own home.

Last November (2020) Rod and I were staying in a Travelodge in Bournemouth, not far from where we live, to break the journey for one of Rod's hospital appointments as we are reliant on public transport. At about 1.30 a.m. I awoke to hear a noisy helicopter very close to the hotel.

I awoke to the sound of a helicopter near to our hotel; it was very noisy. I saw some lights, then it was out of site but seemed to be hovering nearby. Then I saw a long string of red lights directly over the roof tops of the Restaurant/Hotel complex opposite us as the sound of a helicopter faded. The long string of horizontal lights then turned to yellow, then blue, then turquoise and back to red. Then it shot off at speed to the left and shot back, then at speed to the right and back to its original position. Then out into space as a red streak in the sky then back again. It repeated this many times – moving away at speed and back, fading away to a red streak, then returning – colour changing etc. I couldn't make out the shape but there were about fifteen horizontal lights which merged into one. It felt like it was 'showing me' for a reason. The whole thing lasted well over an hour before fading away for the last time. Rod saw it too, although his limited vision prevented him from seeing it all. He did observe the colour changing and rapid movement, back and forth but his disability prevented him from observing the sheer size of it. I was so excited because I thought that the following day people would be out in the streets shouting about it - but not a word, it looks like it was just us that had witnessed it.

I questioned 'my family' and they said that it had been sent for me (us) to observe and interact with.' I have seen many U.F.O's in my time but never one so huge or so close or for so long. I was mesmerised.

There was love, playfulness, and communication in the nicest possible way.

Last Summer, 2020, I bought two identical battery clocks from the same shop (specifically purchased as they do not make an irritating ticking sound). Then I inserted two new batteries from the same pack at the same time into each new clock. This year, in April, they both stopped together at the same time. I inserted two new batteries, one into each clock, again from the same new pack. One clock immediately started to work, the other identical clock didn't. However, they were still sat side by side on the same shelf, one working normally – with its twin completely dead.

A few weeks passed and I still hadn't got around to disposing of the seemingly 'dead clock' but awoke one morning to find the 'dead' clock making a strange grinding sound. On closer inspection it had started up again but in reverse! It was going backwards!!! The other 'normal' clock was telling the 'normal' time (though I know there is no such thing as 'normal')! So, for a good seven or eight weeks the previously dead clock continued to work in reverse. I looked it up and the Internet suggested that the only way to reverse a clock is to take the back of and do it – if you know how! My husband is registered partly sighted, I am totally incapable of undertaking such a task and we were the only two people in the house – no visitors allowed at the time owing to the current situation.

My NHI family claimed responsibility (as previously noted, they have a sense of humour) but also implied a serious side. I felt a lot of affection for these two opposing clocks. Then, when I was finally able to travel to see my daughter in the first week of June this year (after nearly a year) I returned to find the 'backward clock' had reversed itself back again! We are now late into July and both clocks have continued to work normally and in unison. I am told events like this will happen more often as the veils between dimensions begin to fade.

My trip to see my daughter, Emma, in Northamptonshire was not without human incidents and it made me very aware of the present chaos and anxieties some people have, especially in the cities. (I later visited Eleanor in London and it was the same). However, we made the most of our time together and Emma took me to her new studio space in Northampton itself. The community of artists and organisation she belongs to has acquired new premises and exhibition space in formerly council offices. Immediately we entered the building I felt illness, fear, tremendous anxiety and despair. Emma was deep in conversation with another artist while I was trying to keep it together and not embarrass my daughter but found it almost overwhelming. Eventually I told her what I was feeling and said that this place might have been a mental hospital because of the anxiety levels and the sense of rife T.B. Emma took me to the window and asked me to look over to the next street at a particular building. I didn't have much of a reaction to this. I was still feeling it very powerfully where I was.

She told me that the opposite building was the former men's prison and gallows; she suggested we go and see the curator as she was also curious as to why I was feeling so much where I was. It transpired that it wasn't a mental hospital but that we were standing on the edge of the woman's prison and that the last woman to hang in Britain was in the gallows opposite. As Mother and Grand-mother I felt I was experiencing the pain and uncertainty of their future and inconsolable loss at being parted from their children. A lot of these women would not have been criminals; it felt as if they were calling out to me. I asked Emma if we could go, returning at another time but she wanted to show me where they were going to put the tea rooms and exhibits, so I followed her round the corner proudly. However, as we approached this area the pain was unbearable again and I couldn't go any further. It turned out that this used to be the women's exercise yard. I have sent remote healing but also feel the need to go back. I suggested to Emma, who is also very much into human rights, that as artists they are in a strong position to redress these wrongs and make the plight of these women known.

A few weeks ago, not long after visiting Emma and Eleanor I was in our garden preparing a barbeque for Rod and myself. It was a warm, beautiful evening but, despite this, inwardly I was very aware of my concern for things I was witnessing both personally and globally. I hadn't had time for meditation and communication that day either (which always puts me back on track). Suddenly I felt something observing me and instantly looked up into the sky over to my right, along the cliff tops at Dancing Ledge where I regularly go to be alone in nature and to communicate with 'my family', which is a unified experience. Then I saw it – a U.F.O moving at some speed in a horizontal line. I instantly knew it was them, sent to remind me they are always there!

We are all gathered on Earth at this time for a very special reason, that of Gia's ascension. Whether an interdimensional being, star seed, hybrid, human or non-human we are all one and come together in light and love. Darkness has taken over the Earth and beyond and Gia is suffering; this must be recognised but not by giving away our power which is love. The more of us who wake up to this, the higher the vibration will be and the power to affect change. The more love we have for each other and gratitude for consciousness itself the brighter the light will be and as the new Gia emerges re-born, the darkness will just shrink away. We are all so very blessed.

Gillian.

August 2021

Love Others
Until they can
Love Themselves

Dr. Melanie Barton

Early Encounters

From day one I have not felt at home in my body. Allergies, asthma, bruises, fatigue, fevers, infections, nausea, nose bleeds, rashes, and stomach aches plagued my days and nights. A child psychiatrist determined the cause of my symptoms was separation anxiety validated by me missing half of my kindergarten year. His prescription was for my parents to give me more love and buy me presents. When that plan failed, the local osteopathic doctor accurately diagnosed tonsillitis and inflamed adenoids. He referred me to an ear, nose, and throat specialist who recommended surgery. My absences from school lessened greatly after the tonsillectomy and adenoidectomy.

Over my lifetime I have adapted to many medical conditions that limit my ability to fully express my highest self. Since before I could speak, I have had a connection to God; but it has gone through many permutations. This relationship has helped me cope with my conditions and keeps me spiritually grounded.

Constantly ill as a child, my parents followed the doctors' orders as best they could on a bare bones budget. The metal vomit pan became a permanent fixture on my bedside rug. One afternoon too sick to attend school for the second day in a row my mom ordered me to stay in bed which I did not mind because I was so fatigued and nauseated. With no energy to gather my meager toys off the corner shelf I created my own entertainment.

"Hey, Fairy. I see you dancing in the sunlight on my rug," I said pointing to the wisp of movement. "How come nobody else can see you?" I asked. The response was straightforward, "Because you believe in me." "Robbie (the name I gave him), are you still here?" I inquired looking around my room with trepidation since I had not seen my 3-foot silvery friend in a few days. "My dear child, of course I'm here," said Robbie appearing on the tile floor next to my rug. "You haven't seen me much because you're in kindergarten now," he said gently. "Robbie, how come you don't go to school with me so we can play as we always have?" I asked perplexed laying on my side facing the window. "Melanie, your teacher would not want me to come to school with you. She and your friends can't see me, only you can. She wouldn't understand you talking to me. She'd think you were strange," said my lifelong companion.

Tears welling up, I reached out for him and asked, "Robbie, will I still see you when I'm not in school?" "Sweetie, no, but I'll still be watching out for you," he reassured me. "After a while you will forget about me. I'll come back from time to time as you grow up, but I'll look different. It'll be okay, I promise." Mom stuck her head in my doorway and asked, "Melanie, who were you talking to just now? Did someone come into your room? I don't see anyone," she said surveying the room, "and I didn't hear any voice but yours." "Mommy, I was just talking to my friends Robbie and the fairy playing on my rug," I said, pointing to the floor, but they were gone. "Robbie says he can't go to school with me." "Now Melanie, you know that is not true. You better not talk to anyone about it or they'll call you crazy like Grannie Mildred. Do you understand?" my mom said sternly. "But why Mommy? Does Grannie see Robbie and my fairy too? Robbie says only I can see him." "Okay, Melanie. That's enough questions," she said coming in and pulling back my bedcovers. "You can get up now. Come into the living room and I'll let you watch a little T.V. til supper's ready. Tomorrow you'll go back to school."

New Encounters

I did not see Robbie again, but missed him until the memory of him faded. Two years later when we moved to a 100-year-old two-story house I had new experiences. My bedroom floor shook whenever anyone climbed the varnished mahogany stairs to the second floor. The antique floorboards were well-worn from the years the house served as a doctor's office. The gray and pink linoleum cemented to the weakening floor buckled in spots and offered no warmth for harsh Michigan winters. The cedar wardrobe leaning against the north wall held my dad's Army uniform and winter coats. It would freak me out when it vibrated. My parents tried to convince me the movement was due to the creaking house settling, or the vibration of the moving train two blocks away, but I knew better.

There was an unheated storage room off to the side of my bedroom. The door had a hook lock on the outside. It always felt creepy to me and smelled of mothballs. One day I came upstairs to get my library book to read on the front porch feeling safe because mom was up there. She was rummaging in the side room to get something out of the gray rectangular storage bin on floor. She heard the phone ring downstairs and left quickly to answer it. This was in the days before there were answering machines. I froze. The DOOR was open! I wanted to run away but something drew me to the room. The hair on my arms stood up as I approached the doorway. I planned to just hook the lock and run back downstairs. Inside the room was a small window that overlooked the peak of the roof. As I started to pull the door shut, I caught a glimpse of something out of my peripheral vision. Shaking, I turned my head straight to see what it was. There was a boy about seven years old with bluish skin and blank eyes sitting on the roof. He looked at me and knew I saw him. I got so spooked I dashed out of the room breathing hard and skipped downstairs three steps at a time to get away from him. When I told my mom she just looked at me, sighed, and said nothing. She went upstairs and got a blanket out of the bin. I was still shaking after she returned from putting the blanket on the clothesline to air out the mothball smell. Today I know he was probably one of the deceased patients that the doctor treated in what had become my bedroom.

He was not the only uninvited house guest. Similar to C.S. Lewis' book *The Lion, the Witch, and the Wardrobe* my wardrobe held secrets. I was unaware of that book when I had my encounters. Each night I delayed bedtime with all kinds of excuses. My parents would tell me nothing was in my room. It was just my way of avoiding going to bed. I would beg and plead for one of them to go up with me to "tuck" me in. Mom said, "Don't you think you're a little old to be tucked in?" "Please, mom. I'm afraid." "All right, but I am not staying up there." "Thanks, Mom." I would climb the stairs like I was a condemned criminal headed to my execution. Once under covers Mom would say my prayers with me, pull the covers up to my chin and go back downstairs. Then my trembling would begin. I would pull my sheet and blanket over my head and try to scooch so far down into my bed that no one could find me. It did not work. I could feel his eyes staring at me. The Native American chief who lived inside the wardrobe wore a full headdress adorned with brown and white feathers, ornate bead work on the headband with reddish orange accents. He would attempt to communicate with me telepathically. I wanted no part of it.

Finally, one night I garnered my courage and formed the words in my mind. "Why do you stay in my wardrobe?" The chief answered, "To guide you." "But I am only a child. Why do I need guiding?" He answered, "There are things I will help you do as you get older. Remember Robbie? This memory of this conversation will also fade, but know I am always here." "Robbie was fun. I did forget about him, but you scare me. Please go away." The chief said, "I will now, but later you will understand and remember. Sleep now." I slept better after that, but I knew without checking that the dead boy was still sitting on the roof.

Religious Influence

To cope with my parents' disintegrating marriage, I became involved in a hard-shell Northern Independent Baptist church just before entering high school. It provided me stability, a place to go to escape the tension in the household, and people who were eager to shape me into the image they believed God would want me to become. I was there whenever the doors were open. Over time church activities separated me from my peers who were experimenting with dating, pre-marital sex, drugs, and drinking. I was insulated from those temptations because all of that was taboo – including (even) dancing, card playing, movies and cursing. I became very religiously zealous and judgmental of those who did not accept the gospel message I tried to force upon them. Everything I did, read, and participated in had to have the church elders' blessing or I feared I would go to Hell.

In my Junior year of high school my engaged older sister took my mom and younger sister to meet her fiancé's family, an eight-hour drive from our Michigan home. I had a fever so did not accompany them. While reclining on my bed, I reached over to my nightstand and retrieved my weekly Sunday school bulletin from inside my Bible. The feature article was about African missionaries encountering demonic spirits in the village where they were attempting to evangelize the natives. The account spooked me so much that I got cold chills, despite my fever. I ran downstairs exiting the back door and threw the paper in the burn barrel. I could not get the details out of my head. I finally fell asleep in the wee hours of the morning.

When I awoke, I went into my closet to select my outfit for the day. As I reached for the hanger that held my black pleated skirt something fell from my overhead shelf at my feet. I looked down perplexed how anything could have fallen with no vent nearby to blow air. I froze when I saw the Sunday school paper, I had thrown out the night before. I felt an ominous heavy presence in the air. I could not move. I first started praying in my head in the "Name of Jesus go away." Like in a dream, my voice could not utter the words above a whisper. After what seemed an eternity, I gingerly lifted the possessed paper with two fingers. I shook the whole time I descended the stairs and strode toward the backyard. As I walked through the kitchen, I grabbed a box of matches out of the glass baby food jar that sat on the counter. I watched as the paper turned to embers in the barrel before I re-entered the house.

For the remainder of that day I sat frozen in the green scratchy upholstered chair by the front door afraid to breathe, move, speak, or contact anyone to say that I was terrified that the devil was in my house. When my family returned, I tried to explain what happened, but my mom dismissed it as my overactive imagination.

In the summer after my Junior and Senior years, I worked on Mackinac Island, relishing in my freedom. I developed a friendship with a married man. It was not something my church elders would have approved so I did not tell them. Coincidentally, at the end of the first summer this man left to go to a teaching job in Rochester New York where my sister and her new husband had just settled after marrying. I felt called to go to Philadelphia College of the Bible to study to be a missionary after I graduated high school. My now divorced parents could not afford to pay the balance my scholarship did not cover, so, after my job ended, I slunk back to the confines of that haunted house. I enrolled in the local community college taking classes at night, embarrassed for anyone to see me having told everyone I was headed to Philadelphia.

One Saturday night in late October I was awakened by a bright light at the end of my bed. I opened my eyes to see a shimmering appearance, a translucent being. It spoke to me telepathically. It said, "go to Rochester." I shook my head, no, because the married man lived there. I did not want to be tempted to do something my church would condemn. "Go!" Then it was gone. *I can't go. I'm in college. Besides where would I stay and how would I get there?*

Within forty-eight hours I was on a plane to Rochester, having withdrawn from college and having obtained permission to stay with my newly married sister and her husband.

The Move

I made the decision while visiting my sister to move to Rochester. About a hundred days into my transition I had my own apartment, a job with an insurance company, and I met my first husband. He was everything I was not, a college graduate, a smoker, a drinker, a "worldly" man, but he said God called him to the ministry. In my disordered thinking I thought this was the reason I was told to go to Rochester. I was to shape him into a God-fearing man who would accept the call to the ministry. He was far from godly when he forced me to perform oral sex on him on the fourth date. He claimed it was my fault for arousing him. From my religious indoctrination I was taught that the woman is responsible when that happens which meant I was a harlot. It also meant I was damaged goods that no Christian man would want. My only hope to gain God's redemption was to marry him. I did seven and a half weeks after we met.

I constantly prayed to be shown what I could do to gain God's favor and be a good wife. We moved to Syracuse to live in an old house subdivided into three apartments. It was about the same age as the one I grew up in. Every night before my husband came home from work, I would hear noises in the basement. It sounded as if someone was doing construction under my kitchen. My neighbor in the next apartment could hear it too. We made a pact. We would each go down into our adjoining basements while talking on the phone to see what was causing the racket. As we each descended our separate cellar stairs the noise stopped, but the air was chilled and heavy.

Another day I went down to the basement to do the laundry. As I approached the bottom step, I could see out of the corner of my eye a man about 60 wearing a fedora and overalls. I looked again and he was gone. I would catch a glimpse of him regularly just staring at me when I would be transferring the wash into the dryer.

I finally asked the landlord what is all the racket in the basement? He laughed. He revealed that the original owner of the house died at his workbench in 1942. I described the man I saw. It was the owner. When I would leave the apartment, I would turn off the lights and lock the door. When I returned the lights would be on and the door unlocked. When my son took his nap, he would scream as if someone were terrifying him. When I napped someone would knock on my headboard and call out my name.

One afternoon when the neighbor lady was over for tea, we heard a song play on the radio "Melanie Makes me Smile." We called the radio station to ask who the artist was. They told me, "We are not playing that song." Whenever it played again, I would call my husband at work and say, "turn your radio on, the song is playing." It never played on his work radio. I found out decades later that this is a real song performed by artist Tony Burrows. It was his single hit in 1970. I heard the song in 1972.

Four years and two children into our marriage my spouse accepted the call to the ministry. I believed God was finally honoring my obedience, but the person my husband became behind closed doors was the opposite of his pulpit presence. I felt he was possessed. Multiple affairs, alcohol, and sexual addiction along with physical and emotional abuse were his alter ego. Constantly being told I was the cause of his errant behavior eroded my self-esteem. I was perplexed why the spirit sent me to Rochester and how me being obedient could result in this outcome.

To cope with my inability to control my husband's actions I found alcohol to numb my pain. Even while self-medicating I could hear a voice in my head telling me, "this is not the real you. You can be so much more than this." I drank more to drown out the voice.

A Spiritual Awakening

At the age of thirty-two I was diagnosed with another chronic condition called Interstitial Cystitis (IC). It is likened to arthritis of the bladder. After a two-week hospitalization, my urologist told me alcohol and IC do not mix. I was angry being forced to become sober. I decided to prove the doctor wrong. I spent an evening imbibing Kalua while my husband was leading a Bible study. The pain became so unbearable I called my friend to take me to the ER. I was not going to call my husband because he would only yell at me and remind me how much money I was costing him. Before my ride arrived, I called out to God, "please take me. I want to die. I can't stand this pain another second." More clearly than any human voice God spoke to me, "I will take you my child if you wish, or I will help you fight this disease."
With deep aching sobs I answered, "Okay, if you will help me. I will try to get through this."

I want to report that it was a smooth road from then on, but that would be a lie. Eight years into the fight to live with this debilitating condition my urologist offered me surgery to help ease the pain by tacking up my bladder. It was to be a simple procedure done as an outpatient.

My husband dropped me off at the day surgery center and went to work. I was used to fending for myself. I said a simple prayer as the anesthetic flowed into my vein. "God, I put myself in your lap. Please take care of me through this procedure."

The anesthesiologist told me to count back from 100. Ninety-nine, ninety-eight and I was out. Fifteen minutes into the procedure my blood pressure bottomed out, but my sense of consciousness heightened. With the calmness of a glassy sea, my ethereal spirit rose from the figure strapped to the gurney and floated effortlessly up through the ceiling into another dimension. A light, as if shining under a closed door beckoned me to approach. There was no pain, no fear, no sadness, and no remorse only an intense sense that I was totally enveloped in a blanket of love so powerful that it exuded from my soul into my surroundings. The walls encircling me began to part, and a light of the most beautiful shade of yellow shimmered in front of me. I had no other thought than to be there in that moment. Getting my bearings, I inched toward the light. What surprised me was how my thoughts became the vehicle to propel me forward.

Emerging from the murky darkness I became aware of a presence beside me. "Mitchell, is that you?" I shrieked. "Yes, Mom it's me. Here I'm okay and you see me as the teenager I would have been had I lived. Do you want to go forward and meet the others?" he casually asked as if we had communicated regularly since I miscarried him 16 years earlier. "Oh, my dear, sweet baby boy. How I wished I could have held you all these years," I said reaching out for him as he embraced me. Pulling back, curious, I asked, "What others am I to meet?" "You'll see, come on," he said grabbing my hand. I could feel him, look at him and only marvel. *Is this heaven?* I wondered.

Mitchell helped me get into a little dark blue rowboat. He stood up paddling in deliberate quick strokes, parting the black lake water while I sat on the brown wooden seat holding onto the sides of the craft. I could feel the tepid water brush against my hands. In less than a couple of minutes we neared the shore. I saw the shadowy outline of figures at the water's edge. I could not decipher any recognizable faces. The crowd surrounded the boat as it reached the shallow water, and they drug the boat effortlessly to the shore. Stepping out, I looked at the myriad of faces all smiling at me.

I gasped. "Grannie Mildred is that you?" Pointing to the twelve-year-old mousy brown-haired young man I said, "Alan, you died when I was in fourth grade." Circling around I stared at another familiar face. "Judy, you were hit by a car the week before eighth grade. Wow, you all look so good for being dead." Slowly rotating I viewed the scenery and then shouted, "Hey, wait a minute," raising my left index finger. "I've been here before. I remember it now," I said smiling. "It was July nine years ago when I got stung by four bees and I felt my spirit lifting out of my body. I recall getting a glimpse of this place and being pulled back. Do I get to stay this time?"

A seven-foot male figure I did not recognize placed his hand on my shoulder and communicated with me telepathically. He said, "No, we brought you here to show you what is going to happen to you in the future, but you won't remember until each event takes place."

One by one videos of the future scenarios played in front of me showing work I would do, people I would help, and directional changes in my life. Once finished the tall spirit figure said," It is time for you to return. We will be with you always. You can ask for our guidance as needed. Your mission is to tell those who feel unloved that they are loved and for you to love them until they can love themselves."
I did not fathom the implication of my mission in that moment. I asked, "How will I remember to ask for guidance?" "Remember Robbie and the Indian Chief?" he said as his shape transformed into the Chief. "Like, this, we will make our presence known as events unfold."
"Oh, Okay, thank you," I said feeling overwhelmed.

In the next moment I was sucked back into my sedated body. The anesthesiologist had pushed medication into my IV to reverse the hypotension. The procedure was completed, and I was wheeled to the recovery room. Even though I was given the amnesiac drug Versed I recalled every detail of my Near-Death Experience (NDE) except the future events they showed me.

Aftermath of NDE

The NDE changed me for the better. I felt affirmed and no longer alone. My anxiety especially about God sending me to Hell left. My need to gain God's favor melted away. I entered therapy. Through hypnosis I was able to see that Robbie, and the Indian Chief were indeed my guides. I began to laugh more. I no longer felt responsible for trying to reconcile my marriage or control my spouse's behavior. Hawks, owls, and butterflies frequently presented themselves. I felt compelled to recycle and conserve energy.

This new-found me did not bode well with my spouse. I no longer cared if he wanted the same things I did. I began pursuing how to raise my consciousness and vibration. I was meditating and journaling regularly. Two years after my NDE I had an experience while sleeping. It was not a dream. I found myself wandering through the waiting place where people go when they first die. People moved aimlessly about and did not seem to understand that they were dead. I thought I was. No one looked familiar. A voice from above my ethereal form spoke to me. I recognized it but did not have a name yet.

"Melanie, we brought you here to offer you an opportunity. You can make a spiritual leap (a vibrational elevation) progressing far ahead. If you decide to make this jump you cannot ever return to where you were. You cannot discuss this experience with your husband if he chooses not to join you. Do you understand?"

My husband was wandering in the abyss with me but did not hear the voice. I told him what was happening and asked him, "Do you want to jump with me?" "Sure," he said. I leapt forward, he did not. When I awoke, I felt discombobulated. I could not get my bearings. My husband asked me what was wrong. Following the instructions to not discuss it I just laid there. I tried to avoid his stare. It did not work. "What is wrong with you?" he asked. "I just had a dream, okay?" I said hoping that would suffice. "What was your dream about?" my husband queried. "I can't talk about it. "Why not?" "Because I am not supposed to." Becoming irate he said, "I'm your husband for God's sake and you don't keep secrets from me. Tell me!" Fearing his wrath worse than the spirit ordering me to not tell him, I caved.

My husband assured me that he would have made the spiritual leap with me, but he did not in the experience or in life thereafter. He vicariously learned from my practices but did not commit to them for his own personal gain. My consequence for going against the spirit's admonition was my freedom to explore the higher echelon of spirituality was stunted. I knew I was under my husband's watchful eye. I would have to report to him every detail of my practice. He would then evaluate what I told him and use those details against me in the presence of others. He had done this in many instances. That lack of freedom to explore put a ceiling on what I could accomplish.

Thankfully, as I continued my meditation and journaling, I was able to travel to other countries while I slept and could speak their language, but not when I awoke. Sometimes when my alarm sounded, I was not fully back in my body.

For Thanksgiving that year we went to Washington DC. I quickly fell asleep after sightseeing all day. I awoke at 3 a.m. to a shimmering light standing by my side of the bed. I rubbed my eyes and stared. The translucent figure spoke to me telepathically. He said, "It is time for you to set up a holistic psychotherapy clinic." "Huh, what'd you say?" I asked unafraid, sitting up. "How can I do that? I don't even know where to start or why I should," I bravely said. "Remember us showing you things to come?" he said stretching out his arms. "Ah,.. You mean when

I saw Mitchell during my surgery mishap?" "Yes, we told you we would let you know when you needed guidance and the time is now."

He then vanished. I sat up on the side of the bed, perplexed, trying to comprehend what it all meant. I knew fighting against it was futile. I groped around in the dark for a pen and the pad of paper on the nightstand next to the phone. Quietly, I tiptoed over to the chair in the corner and curled up in it. I made some notes. *Where will I find an office, colleagues, money to pay for licenses, etc.?*

Exhausted I crawled back under the warm covers and waited for daybreak, too excited to sleep much. When the sun peeped through the heavy curtains I smiled, stretched my arms, and got up. I woke up my husband to tell him of my experience with a cup of hot coffee to appease the sleeping bear. He thought my experience was just a fabrication of my imagination and did not support me in the plan.

Ninety days later I opened the clinic with staff, licenses, and clients all booked. My husband kept telling me, "Why don't you get a real job with benefits instead of being so bullheaded and have to have your own practice?" The fact that I was making twice the amount compared to an agency job did not sway his opinion.

The clinic thrived, but my husband felt threatened by my success and announced he was leaving town. He said he did not care if I went with him or not. I did not listen to my gut, but as the ever-constant dutiful wife I closed my practice and followed him. A HUGE mistake. He became more emotionally abusive. I had decided to seek my doctorate in holistic psychotherapy, a decision he opposed, but uncharacteristically I pursued it anyway.

The gap between us widened. I sought therapy to help plot my course ahead. When he decided to resign his pastoral position to move elsewhere, I agreed to go if I did not have to work with him in a church again. With my doctoral degree in hand I sought out what would be right for me.

Individuation

As I embarked on my own path in our move to Alabama, I began to teach others to meditate with great results. People were lowering their anxiety and my confidence was rebuilding. That angered my spouse further. He began to act more on his addictions. In a meditative state it was shown to me who he was spending time with while I developed my practice.

In January of 2009 I went on a spiritual retreat. We were instructed to take a meditative walk on the beach. Being so frustrated with what to do about my marriage I sought direction. Remembering how I cried out for God to take me years before, this time I pleaded, "Show me what to do about my marriage, God." The response was crystal clear. "Like the medical intuitive you consulted told you, you are in this marriage alone. You are free to go." "What do you mean, go? Divorce him?" The response shook me to my core, "I have always been with you. I will take care of you through this."

It took me six months to get the courage to leave. When I did, I climbed out of the quicksand of that existence and never looked back. As promised, I felt God's presence supporting me as I was diagnosed with colon cancer, Lyme disease, and had five TIA's (minor strokes) all while completing the divorce. My spiritual guides I now know are named Natir and Sabin. The two began to speak to me regularly through telepathy. They would bring things to my attention such as people to avoid or cut off communication with or alert me to dangers. I would journal a question I wanted them to answer and then meditate to get their response. I used modalities like a Prayer Wheel and the Law of Attraction to draw towards me that they would suggest I pursue.

From the scared dutiful housewife for forty years, I became the wise woman confidently exploring my inner dimensions.

My Mission Returned to me

Four years into singlehood I met my second husband. Instead of marrying after seven weeks we did after seven months. Our life was cut short by him having a fatal stroke after being married only ten months. A few days after he died my grandson was staying with me so I would not be alone. I felt my husband's presence beside me as I slept in our bed. The next morning my three-year-old grandson who is also psychic was asked, "Have you seen Woody?" "Of course, Grandma." "Where did you see him?" "He was sleeping right beside you, Grandma."
My sister stayed with me not long after my grandson did. When she got up, she said, "I felt Woody was here last night." "Me too, I said."
A few weeks later Woody came to me and I asked him, "Why are you here?" He said, "I don't want to leave you alone." "I'm all right. You are supposed to go to the light. I'll be okay." "Are you sure? I promised I would protect you." "Honey, remember my mission from my Near-Death Experience that I am to love the unlovable until they can love themselves?" "Of course, I do." "Well, my dear you did that for me. Your mission is complete. I love myself and I know all will be well. You are supposed to go on. I love you. It's fine for you to go." "Okay, I will. I love you too." Then he disappeared. It was quiet but peaceful. That chapter of my life closed.

Visits Begin

Nine months after his death I was spending the night at my daughter's apartment. My grandson was sleeping with me. I awoke with us huddled on the floor of his closet as a bright light shone into the room. He was afraid. I told him it was okay. We were transported to a ship. I do not recall who the beings were, but they could read our thoughts. My grandson did not remember the experience when we woke up, but I did. I was not able to think clearly or function for a few hours. My pupils were dilated and dark.

Seven months later I was awakened in the night by a seven-foot thin being wearing a tunic. He had round eyes and a gray being that came up to the taller one's elbow. They were standing on the right side near the foot of my bed. The shorter one was muscular with large arms. I was not frightened. I asked them why they were there. Telepathically they told me, "We are here to help heal your body." I was wracked with pain related to Lyme disease co-infections and the Interstitial Cystitis. "Go to sleep and we will take care of you." It was as if they knocked me out. When I woke up, my head felt invaded. My pupils were dilated and black. It took me a while to get oriented. I remembered them coming and, in my head, I thanked them for working on my body.

The next time they worked on me I awoke with an indented mark on my forehead. I have awakened other times in the morning to find marks, bruises on my body that were not there when I went to bed. One time there were imprints of three finger marks on the inside of my thighs. I felt pain as if I had been penetrated.

Another instance I was visited by three entities. They tried to unsuccessfully insert a device in me. When I was hypnotized to try to understand what happened I reported that they were daemonic but not demons. I researched the difference between the two. Daemons are neither for good nor evil. Their job is to help define a person's character or personality. I am still exploring what that means for me.

Where I lived at the time in the Panhandle of Florida, at night I would hear the whir of UFO craft and see very bright lights. When I would cross into Franklin County driving home from work, I experienced crossing into a different dimension. There were periods where time stopped. I would feel like I had been gone awhile but when I looked at the clock no time had elapsed. I would often wake up between

2 and 5 a.m. feeling a presence in my room or outside my bedroom. I was not frightened.

Since my encounters I have had increased perception and my health has improved. Since birth, my perceptive grandson has been petrified to sleep alone. He says he sees spirits. I have cleared away many negative entities that he senses.

I began to question if my visitors were angelic or non-human entities (NHE) from somewhere else. I contacted MUFON (Mutual UFO Network) and they in turn got me in touch with Kathleen Marden and Denise Stoner. From that in-person meeting I decided to become a referral source for those who wanted to explore their ET contact experiences with a therapist. I was invited to attend the Orlando Mufon conference in August of 2016.

A Chance Encounter

During a lunchbreak at the conference, I met Kevin Briggs. We discussed his ET encounters experienced since he was a small child. He asked me to help him explore what to do with his information. As a result of our meeting, I invited him to meet some others to see how we could help him.

We informed him that he was channeling the information his ET connections were giving him. A group of us decided to gather monthly to hear what those channeling through Kevin wanted to tell us. We recorded our sessions and took temperature readings of the room. I volunteered to lead the group in a meditation to relax us and invite the beings in. There are eight beings on the Inter-Galactic Council, comprised of different species. They each have a function. They called us the earthly council.

We met monthly over the course of two years. Our directives were clear. We were to raise our consciousness by becoming acquainted with the Council of Eight members and they in turn would reveal themselves to us. Then we were to add others to our group, connect with other groups, and finally there would be a big reveal to the world. When whoever was speaking through Kevin, I would feel a tingling all over as if electricity were pulsing throughout my body. During one such meeting my phone got fried. When I took it to the repair shop, they asked what had caused it. They had never seen anything similar. The temperature in the room had gone from 77.5 up to 85 degrees. Kevin would sweat profusely while channeling. His voice would change in tone and volume as the Council members spoke through him.

One time we were told that we would each see a UFO craft. They gave a us a designated day and time. I went excitedly to my back deck to await their arrival. As I stepped outside, I disappointedly heard my neighbors loudly partying next door in eyesight of my home. I called out to the Council, "can you show me something, please?"

There was a flash of three lights in the sky over my house, no thunder or rain just flashes. I then challenged them, "Okay, if that is really you then do it again, please." They did. I thanked them. When I would go out my front door to look for craft, I would see a bunch of orbs floating in the dark. The streetlight across from my house would go off. Sometimes I would ask, "if you are here Council can you make the streetlight go off and come back on, please?" They would do so.

Information I Received from the Council of Eight

Two of the beings on the Council of Eight have had a profound effect on my life. One is Rah and the other is Sheeva (not Shiva). Both are in the 9th dimension and watchers. There are 10 dimensions. The 10th is consciousness itself.

Once when Rah came through, I questioned him. "Rah, can you show us some evidence of your presence?" In a booming voice, Kevin stood up and faced the group, as Rah spoke through him. "Is this evidence enough?" I apologized and said, "yes, thank you." Rah told us that consciousness and source energy are one. As we develop physically and learn things in life that increases our consciousness which then increases source energy. Sheeva, is at the right-hand side of Rah. She oversees the Council of Eight. She is spiritual in nature; has not been incarnate for a long time. She and I have a strong connection. She calls me her daughter.

We, the Earthly Council gained much knowledge over that two-year period. We were taught that all humans can learn how to use conscious energy if they are shown and interested. Conscious energy can be used for travel and for creating things on a spiritual level. Consciousness is the life force of the universe and everything. The goal for us was to work toward individually achieving dual conscious communication with the Council of Eight and with each member of the Earthly Council.

A watcher we learned is a very experienced soul. They have had many incarnations over many thousands of years, and with each incarnation they learn more and ascend to the higher dimensions. They have different roles, one of them being to assist in the development of the human species. They also watch over different species that are not human. They can incarnate into the different species, if they choose to do so. Their purpose is to guide and assist in development.
Sheeva and Rah have the power and enjoy helping our bodies heal, but we must ask. They will not interfere without our permission. If we ask it helps with our development, but we must be specific about what we want healed. They said we can heal many things ourselves just by thought. Sheeva has helped heal many of my physical complaints.

I asked for a Council member to explain the purpose of the implant I found in my left palm. I was told that there are other species, not of the Council of Eight, who are interested in what we are doing. They may have put an implant into my hand, so they could track me. I could announce out loud that I do not wish to be tracked. I did so. I no longer feel the implant. A subsequent one was implanted in my right thumb. It feels like a moveable pellet. I even had a doctor check out the one in my palm. He could feel it, took an X-ray but nothing showed on the film. I also inquired about the seven circular puncture marks on my leg, and the mark on my right bicep. The markings on my leg were tests that were done on me they said. They may cause me some discomfort, but they would not harm me. I was not told who did the tests on my leg or what the purpose of the tests were. They reminded me that I was working with Sheeva to help heal my body. They may have meant this was some of the methods to help me heal.

Sheeva told us there are many ways to heal, some through light, or sound. She said the Council was feeding information to leading scientists a little at a time while they slept. This process allows them to develop their treatments and improve their knowledge of science. She said our world already has a successful treatment for cancer, but our pharmaceutical companies have squashed it. It has been this way for decades. Scientists are beginning to develop new treatments and are rekindling methods in the Middle East. They have cures now for the tumor cancers. It is based on the simple principle of sound resonance. They vibrate the tumors with a certain sound frequency and burst their cell membrane, with no damage to the healthy cells. We have had this knowledge for many decades, but it has not been used. This process is being revisited now and we have a new device that does the same in the Middle East. As for the other diseases, the Council is working on treatments for them and are helping our scientists, which will be successful.

To improve our conscious contact with the Council we were told to regularly practice asking a question out loud to a specific member and then wait for a response through thought. The thought would be from that member. The difficulty with telepathic communication is having the confidence to discern our own internal dialogue from the Council's response.

All species are part of one consciousness. Some are at a higher vibrational frequency, a higher dimension as are Rah and Sheeva. The higher dimensions are closer to source energy, conscious energy. When we leave this life in the third dimension, we will be contacted by our guides, but we can have contact with them in this dimension. I now understand that my guides were there when I had my NDE and when my vibrational frequency was raised in the 'waiting place.'

One time during the two-year Earthly Council timeframe I was in excruciating pain with a urinary tract infection that lasted three years. It reminded me of the time I drank and ended up in the ER ready to leave this plane to be out of pain. A voice came to me like when I heard God's voice. It said to me, "We can take you out of this dimension if you are willing to leave right now." I told the voice, "I cannot leave my family or my clients. They need me." The voice responded, "We may not be able to extract you when you may request in the future. Do you understand?" I told them, "yes."

At one of the monthly meetings I asked if it was a Council member that I communicated with about this issue. I was told it could have been. It is offered from time to time depending on circumstances. The channeled Council member then suggested maybe I should accept the offer. The Earthly Council members and I laughed. "Thank you, but no, I choose to stay."

I am an inquisitive person who also because of my psychotherapy background wants proof. Overtime I kept asking the Council members when were they going to appear physically? Sheeva heard my request. One night when my pain was intense, she appeared to me with her birdlike feathers surrounding my body. It was the first time she called me "My daughter." She says I am composed of more alien DNA than human. I am reminded by different members of the Council that I chose to come to earth to do this mission.

The Earthly Council was informed that as the time for the big world reveal approached, there would be those who would try to impede it. That may explain the reason the projected date of February 1, 2020 in Central Park did not happen.

Next Phase

After we stopped meeting monthly, I began a Wednesday night meditation with some of our earthly council members. We were instructed to put people into a chamber and to ask Sheeva to heal them. We would discuss each week who needed healing. As I would enter the craft during the meditation headed toward the chamber, I would pass through a purple viscous liquid. I could breathe in it. They told me the reason I needed to go through that was to adapt to the higher dimension. At times different Council members would greet us during the meditation.

The method I was instructed to follow was to lead each group member into their personal inner sanctum. This process functioned as a launching pad to enter the higher dimensions. Once each meditator was in their own inner sanctum in front of them would appear a bell-shaped curve, a grid that would be analogous to a roller coaster structure made from what appeared to be a rusty kind of metal. Each person would be told to give a nod for the grid to slide to the side. Then an aperture would appear in front of each person. Like a camera lens or flower petals it would begin to open. From the inside from a higher dimension a bright magnetic light would beckon everyone forward.

Following my instructions we individually entered in, we would tend to whatever task we chose. It maybe to go to the healing chamber, it may be to seek an answer to a question. After 15 minutes I would call us back. Once fully reoriented we would discuss what happened. I kept a journal of my experiences.

One of the Council members is a jokester. He, Jark (pronounced Zark) will take jewelry or hide things like keys. He does this he says because either he wants my attention to tell me something or he says I am too serious. One Wednesday night he showed me an image of spots on my lungs. I entered the healing chamber to eradicate them. I have not had a scan to see if they are gone, but my asthma improved after that session. During that time aboard the craft, he showed me an instrument panel with many lights that was somehow part of his responsibilities on the ship. He reminded me that I chose to stay in this dimension and since I was not 100% human I did not quite fit in my earthly vessel. I took that to mean that I may continue to experience physical infirmities.

Post Council

Just as the Council of Eight meetings lasted two years so did the weekly meditation phone call gatherings. In February of 2020 when the "Big Reveal" did not happen as we envisioned; I was given a new directive. I was told that I do not need to meditate to connect with them anymore. Telepathic communication can be done anywhere anytime.

We are all connected. The earthly council I was part of had completed the tasks asked of us. The Reveal would now be more soft, individualistic. I am to work with those who are ready to raise their vibration so they can eventually connect with the Council members and the collective consciousness. They reminded me that I accepted this mission before being born. The things they taught me I can now do and more. They showed me an image of Jesus calming the sea and the words he spoke to his disciples "That which I do you can do and more." It is time for more.

Some of my clients already reported meeting members of the Council when they meditated. I did not introduce them to the Council nor tell them what to expect. It validates what I was directed to do. I began exploring what other tasks I could do to help the planet and her people. I started working with a select few to attempt to alter the destructive weather. In the fall of 2019, we worked on Hurricane Dorian. Within two hours of meditating to lessen the storm the category was downgraded, and the direction turned away from Florida. I wish we had started sooner to see if we could have helped lessen the damage in the Bahamas. I do not know if what we did made a difference, was a coincidence, or what would have happened had we not tried. I am not willing to set up an experiment with a control group. There are too many extraneous factors and people's lives would be at stake.

How does this Work Fit into the Present World Chaos

When I meditate, I am told to continue the practice. By doing so I raise my vibration and connect to the collective consciousness of which we all belong. This process will not only help strengthen my immune system but help raise the vibration of the planet as well. I am not to be a harbinger of fear but to be a guide to calm those who are afraid. I am to carry out my directive from my NDE to love the unlovable until they can love themselves. This is already evident in my clients especially those who endured trauma or have a diagnosis of Borderline Personality Disorder. As I teach them to meditate, connect with their wounded inner child, and their Highest Self the improvement is miraculous. This directive opens doors I would have never imagined. Lowered vibration is likened to lowering your shields as in the *Star Trek* series so the unwanted, unwelcome can enter. That includes illness, fear, controversy, and depression. Lower vibration can be the result of trauma, neglect, or generational baggage.

There is a process called the Maharishi Effect where a percentage of the population during meditation intentionally focuses on a particular thought – for example, lowering the crime rate or lowering the spread of an illness. If a group of us focused on lowering the COVID 19 infection rate in a particular city, we may be able to make a positive impact. This does not mean that in carrying out this directive, my life has reached a state of Nirvana. I have my own continued health and relationship challenges. People who have not experienced meditation or contact with non-human entities think I am in cahoots with the devil or just cuckoo for Cocoa Puffs. When I espouse some information gleaned from my inward journey people often look askance at me and form a smirk on their face. "Sure, you talk to aliens. When are the little green men coming to take us away?"

When I am working with a client, I sometimes get a loud piercing high-pitched squeal in my right ear that cannot be ignored. It is usually to tell me something about the person I have in front of me. The guides will flash me a picture in my mind's eye of an image of a person or a piece of clothing. I will then ask the client does so and so mean anything to you? Most will say, "how did you know that? I never mentioned that to you." My response is, "sometimes when I tune in to someone information comes. What does what I just said mean to you?" Usually, it is a message they sought from a loved one who crossed over. Tears ensue and they feel lighter more engaged in the therapy process thereafter. Sometimes I get the feeling that a negative energy is holding them captive. I will ask for permission to explore the premise. If found through my intuition and kinesiology to be true I ask permission to address it. The negative entity is there for a reason. I let it know its mission is done. It can either go to the Light side and be finished with ever causing such trouble again or be sent back to the Dark side never to return. Once the process is complete, I ask the person how they feel now? The answer 95 % of the time is 'lighter.'

Present Mission

What is my present mission? That is in the process of being revealed as I work with a new group of experienced meditators. We are open to whatever we are called upon to do if it serves the highest good. I know part of it is to share what I have learned with you.

What is your mission? Have you sat and just listened as I was taught to do asking a question and waiting for the answer to come into your head? Keep a meditation journal. Write down a question you want answered such as spirit guides please reveal to me your name, presence, tasks, and dimension. If you already are in contact with your guides you may ask, "what am I to do to help raise the vibration of this planet?" Remember we are all connected. ETs are in a higher dimension, but they are not the ultimate. God, Allah, Jehovah, The Source, or whatever you call it is at the top. We are all part of the collective just like Seven of Nine was part of the Borg in *Star Trek*.

Perhaps your experience with NHE has not been positive. How you perceive things can make all the difference. I encourage you to explore the purpose of your contact. I suggest you contact Kathy Marden after COVID is over to possibly schedule a hypnosis session with her. She has helped me. I know now that Robbie, the Native American chief, Natir, Sabin, and the Council of Eight are all connected and operate in different dimensions. I am glad I chose to come to earth to guide and instruct others to raise their vibrational frequency. Doing so helps us all. Since you and I are connected why not join the collective consciousness? Ask a question and meditate on the answer. Raise your vibration and teach others to do the same. We will all benefit. We are all in this together. I will love you until you can love yourself.

A Lifetime of Experiences via the Contact Modalities

ALINA CASTILLO

What I am about to share is a glimpse into some of the experiences I have had throughout my life. I believe these to be a window into understanding consciousness and the many ways that we can come into communication with not only higher intelligences but quite possibly what could even be multi-dimensional aspects of ourselves. Since I was a child, I have known that part of my purpose on this Earth was to unlock the mystery of our connection to the universe and share in bringing understanding into the deeper meaning of who we truly are as we transcend the conventional explanations of what we are capable of as a species.

Since as far back as I can remember, the subject of consciousness has always been a topic I have been heavily drawn to. The phenomenon in general is something that has felt familiar and profoundly meaningful to me. I remember when I was a toddler that I would beg my father to let me watch TV with him. We would watch shows about aliens, ancient Egypt, ghosts, or anything of the nonconventional variety - while my twin sister played or watched cartoons, which was what you'd expect from a child that age. This would become something that would come to define me as an adult and explain why I believe I am even here at this time. I can remember being about three or four years old, when my mom asked both my twin sister and I what we wanted to be when we grew up, and I remember having this profound knowing that I was different and that I came here to do something important to help change things in some way. I also have keen memories of being intensely drawn to the psychic phenomenon. I always wondered why I couldn't simply move objects with my mind or manifest things out of thin air as I believed I could. I have wondered what talents I might have developed if I didn't have parents constantly questioning my quirky tendencies and beliefs. I especially wonder about this when I think back to one incident where, without a doubt in my mind but rather an innate knowing, I did manifest something just like that, *out of thin air*. I was in kindergarten, and it was after school. My sister and I sat on the couch, devouring a bag of M&M's my mom had given us each. When I got to the bottom of the bag, I refused to accept I had eaten the last one and proceeded to rip the bag at the seams knowing one more would come out and indulge me with my craving for more! My sister then looked at me all puzzled and asked, "what are you doing?" to which I answered, "making another M&M appear so I can be happy I got one more!" and she giggled and said, "yeah, right!" Just as I ripped the final seam of the pouch, an M&M manifested right out of that seam....I literally saw it materialize!! This type of thing would eventually become a theme for me years later in some pretty amusing ways. I have likened these experiences to examples of how my thoughts are "interacting" with my simulation. More on that later.

Another event that would shape my curiosities tremendously as a child occurred when I was three years old and was sleeping in my crib in my parent's room. We lived in a two-bedroom apartment, with my brother having the second bedroom. For that reason, my twin sister and I slept with our parents, and our cribs lined the wall of my parent's room. I remember always struggling to fall asleep nightly and would spend a great deal of time awake in my crib. One night, I remember seeing a soft glow of peach-colored light through the corner of my eye that was coming from the floor on the side of my crib and reflecting on the wall. I rolled over to look and see where this glow was coming from, and to my absolute shock and surprise, I saw a little, grey, extraterrestrial-type being staring back at me! It had big dark eyes, a large head, and translucent flesh-colored skin that emanated a soft glow. I distinctly remember being able to see through its chest and could clearly see its heart. The little being couldn't have been more than the equivalent of my age. This startled me, and I cried and screamed for my mom to pull me out of my crib!! In hindsight, there was absolutely nothing scary about this little being, just the sheer surprise of seeing something that I had absolutely no concept of until that point as a three-year-old toddler. My mom immediately rushed to pull me out of my crib and wound up letting me stay in her bed for the rest of the night. Still, I spent the remainder of the night wide awake, peeking over to see if I could somehow catch another glimpse of the mysterious little creature I just saw. My twin sister, of course, slept through the whole thing. The experience would soon be forgotten or instead "dismissed" by my parents as merely a tall tale. But to me, that experience has remained one of my life's greatest mysteries thus far. Since then, I have pondered on possible theories as to what that encounter could have meant and how it connects me to the phenomenon on a more personal level. One could only imagine.

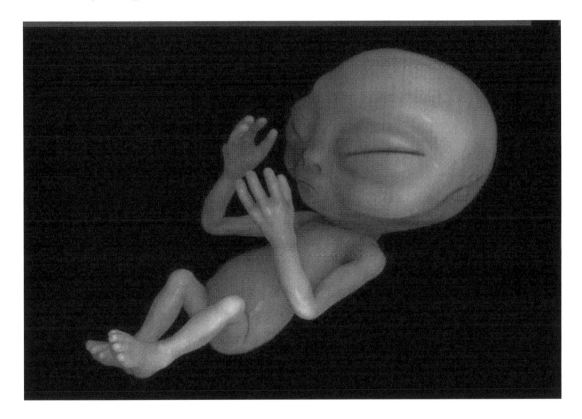

Growing up, my tendency was always to explore the unexplained, the supernatural, and the mysterious in all its many forms, which always made my family, friends, and classmates wonder why I was so "weird." Yet, it was there that I felt at home. As a teenager, while the other kids my age were out starting to drink and party, I would find myself gleefully anticipating a night of watching *Unsolved Mysteries* or *Sightings*, …two of my all-time favorite TV shows. I couldn't relate to others my age, so I often sought what made me feel good, hiding out in my room for hours on end, reading books on the paranormal, and getting lost in the mystery. The idea of seeing something myself always terrified me though I remember I could sense energies, which would always freak me out despite my tendencies.

When I was 17 years old, I recall going through a phase where I felt like I was walking between worlds. Perhaps it was due to a mild case of insomnia, which I believe caused my psychic abilities to heighten. A pattern I have come to notice throughout my life. Still, at the time, I recall having some curious lucid dreams where I was taken into a tunnel. The walls of that tunnel were large screens, each displaying significant events yet to unfold in my life, some of which were trying times for a teenager. It felt like I was being given advanced warnings so that I could not only recognize them when they would begin to manifest but so that I could be better prepared, perhaps. I remember watching these events flash by me and recording them in my memory, and then telling two friends with me in this "dream" that it was now 4:17 am, and it was time to return to our bodies. As I said that, I jumped in my bed, startled, and reached over to the clock only to see it was indeed 4:17 am.

I had multiple other experiences where I felt like I was consciously leaving my body and being vacuumed out at lightning speed through a flashing tunnel to where I even thought I could leave my body at will. I began to attempt this with a friend on the phone one evening, only to have my parents barge into my room with my sister and it was then that they proceeded to try and shake me out of this altered state as I felt myself leaving my body. My sister said that she kept trying to move me. Still, I was as stiff as a board until she finally managed to connect to me where I could hear her attempts to bring me back and when I said, "I'm coming back now," she said she saw my body almost "inflate" as if it became animated again and it was then that I regained full consciousness. That event earned me a trip to a psychologist because my parents thought I had lost my mind. With that said, every event I was shown in that tunnel came to pass exactly as I saw them, although I only had a fleeting awareness of them until they occurred. This is something that I believe still happens when I need to be warned of situations that can be particularly intense, almost as if my soul is preparing me to lessen the impact.

Another critical experience for me would occur in early 2008 while visiting Asheville, NC. My sister and I decided to take a ghost tour one evening, taking us to different spots throughout downtown Asheville where all sorts of incidents leading to untimely deaths and paranormal activity were known to have occurred. We stopped at one location with an unusually high number of deaths that occurred within a few years, some 200 years ago. Both employees and patrons of the bar had reported having strange encounters or paranormal activity, so I decided to take a picture of the front of the building so that I could remember the name of it for when I had time to google it and look into some of the place's history and reported activity. I double-checked that the place's name was legible in the picture and carried on. At the end of the tour, the guide mentioned reviewing any photos we took in two days time because in her 17 years of experience guiding these tours and for reasons unknown to her, things tended to manifest in the pictures that weren't there before. I thought, "I could only wish to be so lucky," and that was that! A few days later, a friend wanted to look through my pictures, so I mentioned to her what the lady had said as she skimmed through my photo album of that evening; it was only a moment later that I heard her gasp and say, "What the F?" and I looked over at her and said "yeah right!!" and she said "Alina, I am not kidding, LOOK" and handed me my phone. I was shocked. Before me was an image of a little girl standing in what appears to be between the glass doors of this bar, and you can see she had one foot in front of the wooden frame to not leave any room for doubt that this was not a normal image. As I zoomed into her face, I got goosebumps as I could clearly see her eyes had no irises and her jaw appeared to be dislocated. The picture stunned me not just for what I was observing but because there was no child anywhere in downtown Asheville as it was after 11 pm, and the only places open were bars! Beyond that, I had looked at this picture the night of the ghost tour to ensure the bar's name was legible, and there was no child in the picture, let alone in person. That blew my mind. The next day I decided to call the bar directly and ask if, by chance, they may be projecting something on the glass to humor the tour participants because at this point, I was grasping at straws. This picture was just too good to be true! I described the picture I had captured to the bar manager. The man was floored and proceeded to tell me that neither he nor the ghost tour people had ever done anything in any way to psych people out or "enhance" the ghost tour experience.

He could not believe what I had just told him as he had employees who reported seeing this little girl for years, with one woman becoming so startled to encounter her (as she was coming out of the restroom) that she quit on the spot. That said, it became clear quite quickly upon returning home that I had not returned home alone. This awareness was pretty immediate for me as I began to notice a shift in energy around me that, at times, would manifest as an eerie sensation as if someone was standing next to me.

Things would only become more interesting for me during this time. I then began seeing sparks of light where energy was manifesting. It felt as if I was forced to drop the resistance I had since I was a child to seeing anything because just as soon as this started happening, I became increasingly more sensitive to energies in general and could sense what sometimes felt like angelic, protective energies. Other times it felt like the little girl herself, which I saw in several different forms, including a green cloud of what looked like green electricity hovering over my bed. I did get to see her in physical human form on another occasion, and one evening during that period of heightened activity, I also saw a humanoid type being, short in stature (maybe 4'9"), with flesh that was a blueish color, and was wearing a skin-tight suit. This timeframe would prove to be very active on every level. I found myself vibrating intensely nightly for almost a year. I remember being able to leave my body at will and having curious sensory experiences like feeling my consciousness outside of my body but strangely feeling as though it filled up the whole room. Another time I remember floating above my body and then floating off into the living room only to find myself there, but as I was two hours before I went to bed. This really confused me! It was a time when the veil between spirit and matter became so thin that it became permeable for a fleeting moment. The feeling of being anchored in a different dimension occurred a few times when everything looked crisper and sharper, where colors were heightened. The feeling of euphoria and unconditional love was almost too much to contain, yet I found that if someone near me was receptive and open to my vibration, then they too would tap in and share in this experience! During this time, I began to research the topic of consciousness, which, of course, I believe, contributed to a lot of these experiences as it activated me tremendously. I became obsessed with the idea of a shift in consciousness and how there were benevolent beings assisting humanity and even how they were making contact with certain people and bringing a message forward to assist in humanity's awakening. This area of research had singlehandedly activated me the most, as I recognized part of my purpose for being here. It directly correlated to that and continues to unfold to this day. This was a time of pure connection and expansion.

As the years progressed, I focused mostly on raising my daughter, who was just a toddler then. My time for exploration became minimal and all the while, I had also become quite disenchanted with my research as I had found a massive influx of new agers and newbies had come in and taken over the scene. This was not just on social media; it also bled into the material that would turn up on my google searches. Contamination of disinformation had seeped into pretty much every corner of this field, so I decided to walk away from it all for that moment because I was just too turned off by the disingenuous vibe that had taken over my field of research. What was once niche had become one more trend for the masses, and it lost a great deal of substance when it came down to the material that was out there on the world wide web and beyond. Suddenly everybody was channeling some sort of "5th-dimensional being" and using specific catchphrases and cliches that were kind of sickening to me. I mention this because that would inadvertently become a catalyst for a few curious experiences later on down the road. I stayed far away from all of what was once my literal lifelong passion for the better part of 4 years, something that felt foreign and even alienating in a way. I took a full descent into the 3D realm of experience (something that I had literally never done the entire time I've been in this body), and needless to say, that would later prove to be detrimental to my health. I became sick with all sorts of symptoms and issues, yet no doctor could figure out what was wrong with me. It was over a year after this when the stress started to get to me, and I remember praying and pleading with God to help me understand what was wrong with me. I was scared, and I remember falling asleep crying one night in prayer. I slept very deeply and can recall finding myself in a cave-like dwelling where nine very tall ant-like beings surrounded me. They must have been at least seven feet tall, and each had a different color ring around their neck which felt like an indication or distinction of each of their roles in the colony. These nine beings felt very familiar, their presence was incredibly comforting to me, and as they surrounded me, they telepathically communicated with me. That I knew why I had become sick, because I had walked away from my path and abandoned the aspect of myself that needed to seek understanding of who we are and why we are here. This was part of the very reason why I was incarnated at this time. They told me that the time was fast approaching where I would be needed, and I no longer had time to waste, that the time had come to return to my path and reconnect. I woke up that morning feeling incredibly peaceful and relieved but didn't have much time to think about what I had just dreamt though the feeling stayed with me the whole day. It wasn't until that evening that my husband rented a movie that he barely knew anything about but rented anyway because he thought it looked cool. I was completely blown away towards the end of the movie as the plot unfolded, that the main character came into contact with an insectoid being almost identical to the ones I saw, and I was stunned!! I felt in my soul that this was a validation that what I dreamt wasn't a dream but a message. I later went on to meet a few others with similar experiences with beings like the ones I saw.

Around this time, I had another curious experience that I would later understand more profoundly as the years progressed. Something I instinctually knew would be the case when it happened. It seems this time required less subtlety when reaching past my resistance and forcing me to notice the following occurrence, which came about without my seeking. On one evening, I found myself dozing off watching TV on my couch, as I often did, but something prompted me to open my eyes, and when I did, I saw a woman standing across the living room facing me. I was too sleepy to care and only partially registered this and closed my eyes again. Some time passed, and once again, the feeling that I should open my eyes forced me to look once more but with my eyes only semi-open. To my surprise, the woman was still there, except she was closer to me, and I remember thinking, "oh, her again?" I simply accepted it as just a matter-of-fact type thing and closed my eyes yet again. Now I have no idea how much time passed until I woke up suddenly. Still, this time it was because I had a very heightened awareness that someone was standing next to me and when I opened my eyes, there she was again, exactly as I had been seeing her the two previous times - dressed in a black and white dress, she had salt and pepper hair and was about 60 years old. I remember thinking, "wow, she is so beautiful," but also knowing she was some sort of higher dimensional being and not what one would typically assume to be a ghost. It was an instant knowing that she was visiting from another dimension and somehow from the future. I knew when I saw her that I would someday understand who she was and that the black and white of her clothing also had a particular significance that I would also one day understand. She crossed my mind throughout the years, and I tried coming up with ideas of who she might be and what her visit meant, but none of it really felt right. It wasn't until four years later that I was listening to a past life regressionist describing how she not only regressed her clients but also "progressed" them into future lives when suddenly, the download just dropped into my head. AHA!! It was an instant irrefutable knowing that this woman I saw was me from the future. I knew it with every fiber of my being; she was *me*. The reason why it was important for me to understand the significance of the black and white clothing was because it symbolically represented that I had achieved balance in all polarities, "zero point," if you will. Duality is very much an attribute of this 3D plane of existence. I knew that this aspect of me had transcended those limitations and was operating from a higher level of consciousness. It was her light that struck me as so beautiful. I understood that she appeared to me so I would find peace in that momentary phase of disillusionment that disconnected me from my path, connection, and purpose.

Little by little, I began reconnecting with my research and slowly became re-inspired to continue my quest to understand consciousness and our connection to the universe and beyond. This served me well as I started to magnetize towards others of like mind who were genuinely seeking and contributing to this cause. This period activated me tremendously, and I had a few exciting experiences that exceeded anything I had experienced thus far. One of the first things that happened during this time was because of a concern I had with a possible infection becoming severe. On this particular day, I accidentally cut myself deeply while giving myself a pedicure but forgot about it as the day progressed. On that evening, I went out wearing sandals, and after getting stuck in a pretty heavy storm, I wound up stepping into several muddy puddles as I made my way to the car. I noticed it was hurting a bit when I took a shower, but I washed it thoroughly and went to sleep shortly afterward. As I lay sleeping, I could feel an intensely sharp throbbing pain in the toe where I had cut myself. It was so intense that it felt like I would have to go to the ER as it was more pain than I had felt before for something like that. In my semi-asleep state, I heard myself go into prayer. At this point, my waking mind had no involvement because there was no thinking as far as what to say, the prayer flowed automatically, and I asked for divine intervention as I knew something was seriously wrong. It felt as if I was communicating directly with the universe, and at that moment, I knew to open my eyes, and when I did, I saw a giant purple orb about the size of a cantaloupe some 20 ft. away. As I became aware of it, the orb began to float toward me, leaving a trail of light behind it as it approached me. When it reached my shoulder, it stopped almost as if to allow me a moment to register what was taking place before me. Then, this orb entered my shoulder, and I felt a warm current of energy trickle down through my body until it reached my toe. At that moment, I felt the most incredible sensation of instantaneous relief and comfort, and just like that, the pain was gone. I knew that this purple orb had healed me, and this feeling of peace washed over me as I went back to sleep and never thought of my toe again.

I had two other experiences with purple orbs healing me in the coming years when I was experiencing high strangeness, waking up completely taxed, and feeling remarkably unwell. In these two instances, I was wide awake and suddenly found myself so tired that I couldn't function and would have to lay down as if I took something strong for sleep. Each time I felt a current of energy enter through my feet that felt so strange and ice cold that I would begin to shiver uncontrollably. On one of these occasions, my daughter saw me and brought several blankets, but nothing helped. The sensation was a bone-chilling cold I had never felt before, as the energy itself felt very different. The first time it occurred, I opened my eyes after I felt it exit through my head, and I saw a purple orb floating in front of me as it completed its sweep through my body in what felt like an energetic recalibration. The second time occurred a week later when I was energetically in an exceptionally massive slump and undergoing several uncomfortable physical symptoms. Since I recognized the sensation this time, I paid closer attention to the energy as it coursed through my body. Still, as it exited my head, I opened my eyes to register the purple orb that had just gone through me - but to my surprise, this orb looked different. It looked like a shattered plasma orb that had fragmented, and it looked almost as if it was made up of fluid light. It was pretty curious, but I felt my energy had been recalibrated and balanced, so I was grateful for whatever this phenomenon was.

I've had a good few encounters such as these, but those were the only three times I saw what was healing me. On one occasion, though, the power went out at the very instant that the current entered my feet. The outage only lasted a few seconds and may have been a coincidence, but the sensation of this electrical charge entering me coincided with the electricity around me simultaneously being affected - curious timing to say the least. I would later find out that the power blink wasn't limited to my home but the entire block I lived in. Strangely, it was only on the side where my house was located. In other words, all of our front door neighbors were unaffected. The only difference with the exit of this particular current was that instead of exiting through the crown of my head, it exited through my mouth, which caused me to spontaneously open my mouth and let out a loud puff of air. The feeling that followed this was one of pure relief.

There was another instance that comes to mind where it seems as though I might have been assisted in balancing my energies during a particularly challenging time a few years back. One night, I had gone to bed feeling quite drained and must have fallen asleep pretty quickly because I don't remember much after laying my head on my pillow. At some point during the night, I heard a voice say "now we will work on healing your sadness" and as these words were being said to me, I suddenly found myself inside of a small white pod with only enough room for the bed I was to lay in and just above me was a purple light which I intuitively understood to be the source of my healing. Next, I was taken to an identical pod right next to the previous one and told "now we will work on healing your anger" and right when I heard those words, I woke up suddenly kind of startled only to find that there was a purple rectangular light hovering above my bed! I was baffled to see something was really happening outside of this dream, although the dream itself felt very vivid, as though something significant was really taking place. Intrigued by this, I proceeded to roll over and go back to sleep with the hopes that whatever was happening would continue. The next day I woke up feeling significantly lighter and more refreshed but quickly forgot about the visuals from the night before and simply carried on about my day. It wasn't until I went to shower later that evening that I started to see purple sparks throughout my time in the shower. This triggered the memory of my dream and bedroom experience from the night before and it made me wonder what the source of this purple light was as this seems to be a recurring theme that has repeated itself in various ways throughout the years, with the common denominator being that each time, this purple light (in whatever form it manifested) was there to heal me. I can say that relief was **always** the end result and for that, I was grateful.

A final example I can think of is a little bit different in terms of how it occurred and the means by which I sustained relief from what was bothering me at that moment. I would however, consider this more of a testament to our thoughts influencing the simulation rather than phenomenon-based intervention. In this particular instance I had been having anxiety and a heavy feeling in my body that was weighing me down. As an empath, I felt as though I had absorbed some pretty dense energies that day after talking to a friend who was particularly emotionally charged up when we spoke. I felt pretty drained afterwards and decided to go for a walk because I could tell my blood pressure had gone up a bit but that was of no help. After spending the remainder of the day feeling off, I opted to just relax in front of the tv and unwind that way since nothing else seemed to be working. That idea would only prove to be fruitless when it came to finding relief because I found myself feeling restless nonetheless. At this point I decided to just ask for help and prayed for some relief from this anxious heavy feeling because I truly didn't feel like myself. Interestingly, it was then that I felt this little sensation of something above my wrist clinging to my sweater fibers that felt like the sting of a splinter. I had been wearing my sweater for hours and hadn't felt anything like that till then so I wondered what could possibly be causing that sudden sensation. When I rolled up my sweater, I saw a black splinter coming out of the area above my wrist and I immediately went to carefully pull it out. As I did and the tip of the splinter came out it was as if someone had removed some sort of "mood cartridge" out of me, to put it that way, because I instantly felt this cloud of heaviness lift right off of me. More curiously still, was the fact that I felt my vision suddenly become considerably sharper, my sinuses spontaneously cleared up and I could hear things more clearly as well. I thought "Wow! What relief!" This was instantaneous and all as a result of removing this black splinter that had no reason to be poking out of me as I hadn't come into contact with anything that would cause that, which I of course would have also noticed as it happened in the first place! Did my intentions to find relief manifest in the density materializing out of me in this curious manner? One can only surmise but whatever the case, relief is what came of this prayer!

Every now and then I have felt a momentary connection so deep that it feels as though I am being granted a glimpse into a different layer of reality or (in this case) perhaps even tapping into the very consciousness of nature itself. A notion that is typically most often associated with psychedelic trips and the like. On this one particular morning, I had decided to do a meditation outside by a giant palm tree in my yard. I had been using this palm tree as part of my meditation in that I would align my back to the trunk of the tree and then I would visualize a toroidal field forming around us with myself and the tree being the center point of the toroid. I visualized this field in a constant flux of energy surging up from the center of the Earth through myself and the tree and then ascending up to the heavens and back down again forming this enormous toroidal field all around us. I noticed myself getting lost in the moment as I repeated one of my favorite mantras (Zin - Uru) to help keep my mind in the present moment. Mantras are words or phrases used as tools to keep the mind focused and occupied so that it doesn't get interrupted by fleeting thoughts which in turn allows one to enter a deeper meditative state. This helped me to go even more deeply into my experience and also kept me present in my intentions.

For a moment there, it felt as though nothing else existed but me, this tree and all of the elements of nature that surrounded me and it felt glorious! I began to connect to my heart space and decided instinctively to use that moment of connection to transmit some love energy to a grieving friend whom I had just spoken to a little while earlier. I felt myself so submerged in these high vibrational frequencies that I felt that anything that I transmitted in that moment would be more potent so I decided to direct my intentions towards my grieving friend. At that moment, I felt guided to use the roots of the trees to transmit this love frequency so I envisioned the roots as a network connecting tree to tree until it located my friend on the particular point on the planetary grid with which he found himself in. I focused my energies on my heart space and filled myself with loving thoughts as well as intentions and then pictured the roots firing up with this frequency then directly sending this transmission to my friend wherever he might be at that time. I went so deep that I felt as though I was traveling for a moment. What an enchanting surprise awaited me, when right there before my eyes there were literally hundreds of silver shimmering particles dancing in front of me in the most magnificent and spellbinding display of whimsy! I was mesmerized. I squinted my eyes but they remained in full view for at least 20 seconds. As they started to fade I wanted to tap back into them or bring them back so I closed my eyes once more, then reconnected to my heart space and visualized these roots lighting up again and just like that, the silver shimmering particles returned once more! It was as though I was tapping into an encrypted layer of my "reality" and I momentarily found myself residing in that in between space, where *spirit and matter* meet. A word that came to mind was the word "sylph" which is an air spirit and while the idea of elementals is considered fantasy, for people in other regions of the world this is not only openly accepted but many have had encounters with all kinds of nature spirits from gnomes to faeries and yes, even sylphs. I have always naturally felt open to that type of thing since to me it's just another way that consciousness manifests and expresses itself so who's to say that there aren't beings that reside within the lower dimensions and within nature itself. With that said, I also appreciate a good scientific validation and in this case it came recently by way of a video that was sent to me of a scientist discussing multidimensionality and the quantum field. In that video, Dr. Glen Rein discusses the center of a toroid which is called a "catenoid" and he likened it to the center of a wormhole also known as a *transversable wormhole.* Dr. Rein explained that the catenoid allows for consciousness to move easily from one dimension to another like going from 4D to 5D and back down to 3D etc. I could not believe how specific this was to the very thing that I was focusing my attention on when creating this toroidal field when I pictured myself and the tree as exactly what this scientist had just given me a name for: a *catenoid*! Suddenly, my experience made so much more sense and this helped to explain why I felt as though I was tapping into another layer of reality, because in this altered state I found myself in, I actually ***was***!

This wasn't the only time that I had an experience that I would say was like tapping into the consciousness of nature and the elemental kingdom itself. The first time that I can remember such an experience was while visiting a pair of twins that I had become good friends with due to our mutual love of esoteric topics and the phenomenon etc. This was the late 90's and I was only around 20 years old while they must have been in their mid-twenties but they had already authored a book on astral projection and mastering astral travel by this point. They had grown up studying unconventional topics and had been mentored since they were small children by their aunt who was a spiritualist and highly knowledgeable in the arena of psychic development and skills. By the time I met them, they were like living libraries of information on all things metaphysical and esoteric. One day while visiting them, they asked if I wanted to try altering my brainwaves with some biofeedback equipment they had been experimenting with. I of course was game! They had a whole slew of devices and head gear to ensure the most profound experience possible which included a metronome and blackout shades worn for full sensory focus minus any visual influence or traces of light except for a red dot that would run across ones forehead back and forth plus other equipment meant for immersing the experiencer fully into this audio sensory experience. They placed headphones on me that were playing isochronic tones and left me alone so that I can take off into hyperspace. Boy did I ever!! I lost all sense of time and space and became hyper-visual almost immediately.

All sense of reality shifted radically for me and I found myself in what felt like a *waking dream*. I was suddenly surrounded by trees in a forest except I wasn't just standing in the forest, but instead was immersed in the consciousness of the trees themselves. I could see their auras pulsating and them "breathing" and alive in a way that was more profound than what we normally perceive in our ordinary three-dimensional experience of nature. The green of these trees was so vivid, so green that the color itself also felt **alive**. I was enveloped by their consciousness and I felt myself become a part of it. As I felt myself merge, I suddenly found myself experiencing nature but from an entirely different point of view. All of a sudden, I was tiny and hidden amongst the blades of grass except from this point of view everything seemed more subdued and muted in tone and less vivid. Everything also felt denser even from an energetic perspective and just as I was starting to take in the elements of this new perspective, I noticed a small faerie in front of me a few feet away that was about the same size as me and quite amused to find me there hidden within the grass. She watched me and giggled then flew away. That visual struck me since I grew up with a lifelong love of faeries and I couldn't believe I was experiencing one up close in what felt like an even more real "reality" then the one I had just left behind to have this experience. That immediately brought me back into awareness of my body and I called for my friends to return to the room so that I can tell them all about what I had just experienced. As I began to describe it in the only language that made sense - as if it were a "dream" but my friend Herbert immediately corrected me and said that was no dream. He explained that I had just astral projected my consciousness and was in fact visiting another dimension with my astral body. As he explained things further, it all strangely started to make perfect sense. Many years later, I shared this story with a friend who had just returned from a trip to the rainforests in South America where she met up with a shaman for an ayahuasca trip and spiritual journey. I felt compelled to share because a lot of what she described that she saw while on ayahuasca was remarkably similar to my own experience with biofeedback except instead of through psychedelics, mine was through technology that created the altered state of consciousness <u>naturally</u>. I have since heard many other stories similar to my own that involved mushrooms or peyote and other psychedelics. One friend described the profound connection he established with trees during one of his mushroom trips that remained for a good while after and left him with an ability to communicate with trees and even hear their "thoughts" telepathically. **How magical**!

There was a moment there that I got a little fixated on the idea of trying mushrooms myself and pretty much kept it in the back of my mind for a good while. I didn't want to do mushrooms alone so I held off on this and instead decided to focus on grounding/balancing my energies and clearing my "channel" naturally through a water fast which I did for a few days. Well!! This would prove to be most fruitful because what I succeeded in was in activating myself to such a degree that it felt as though I was tapping into a different aspect of myself and even connecting to nature directly without even having to take anything to get me there. Since mushrooms had been residing in the back of my mind for a little while before then it was almost as if that somehow allowed me to lock frequencies with their consciousness since after all every aspect of nature is "alive" as we know. One morning, as I closed my eyes I was shown the consciousness and energetic signature of a mushroom, and also of a tree. The two things I had been longing to connect to. I can feel their essence and see their "face" and they each had a distinct energetic signature and a wisdom to them. Each looked like a wise elder with their own distinguishing features. I was in awe. Next, I was shown the consciousness of the mycelium network which is a mass of branching thread-like fungi that form a network that runs throughout the entire planet beneath the ground and also happens to be responsible for allowing trees to communicate with one another. *(Sound familiar?)* These appeared more like a "collective" of a bunch of little mushrooms that looked more like joyful children excited to connect. The way that I saw them, they were all smiling and laughing and jumping up and down in pure joy. What a wondrous sight!! More curious still was that during this "waking dream" I was also shown one more thing that although seemingly unrelated to this theme connected to the kingdom of nature, but what it *was* connected to was a glimpse into the consciousness of yet another thing that is very much alive.

What I was shown next was the *journey of a blood cell* and its voyage through our veins. I saw myself rushing through tunnels of veins and how I came into contact with other blood cells and what it felt like to see things from that perspective. Just incredible. Now, this might not seem as substantial as an actual psychedelic trip or biofeedback experience and even though I was very much activated and having all sorts of experiences that were outside of the normal perimeters of human experience but the element that I have yet to mention of why this is but another testament to how consciousness works is not the vivid visuals themselves. (As a side note, all that I was shown of how the consciousness of trees and mushrooms appeared for me turned out to be exactly what others have been shown on psychedelic trips but again, that is merely a secondary validation.) What I actually wanted to convey in terms of consciousness is the idea of thought "transference" …. whether its energetic transference, consciousness transference or telepathic. One could only guess but the fact of the matter is that I had just come into direct contact with someone who had had all these magnificent experiences with trees and mushrooms and interfaced with their consciousness and as for the journey of the blood cell you might ask? Well, I had just been spending time with a friend who had had a near death experience and amongst the incredible things he experienced (during his 12 minutes of clinical death) was you guessed it: the journey of a blood cell. It felt as though I had become so cleared energetically that I was locking frequencies and telepathically uploading information from these different friends' consciousness. There already was a psychic connection between each of these friends that perhaps helped facilitate these experientially vivid visuals but one thing was for certain, each of the things that I had been "shown" was exactly how each of my friends had seen them and I only came to learn of these details after the fact. I was not just left with a visual impression but an energetic imprint as well.

I had been connecting to trees for a few years already during my meditations and was already familiar with their energy in a more subtle way but this was as if I was looking at them more directly as ***conscious beings***, something that many people have been blessed enough to experience through psychedelic journeys. We can certainly attest to the fact that all of nature is conscious and we as humans can connect with its consciousness if we simply set our intentions to and that is one thing that I had had a desire to do for a long time with absolute reverence. What a treat it was to connect in this way.

Sometimes the ways in which I have come to discover how our consciousness interacts with our reality has been nothing short of surprising. There have been moments where it has even looked like something out of a movie. The notion that our consciousness can not only manipulate matter but that it can also ***affect*** the elements around us (something deeper still then just tapping in and connecting as previously mentioned) was something that I came to experience firsthand during one of my invocations that pretty much started off more like a sluggish prayer outside one night shortly after midnight. It had been an intense day for me after I had an unexpected disagreement with a moody friend which left me completely drained and sad. Because I didn't want my day to end on a sour note, I decided to go outside before bed so that I can do a prayer and also cleanse with sage to break up some energy. I was so exhausted by then that I was having a hard time thinking of what to say for the sake of clarity in my intentions, but I pressed on anyway. After a little bit of time and focus, I began to get "in the zone" and my words started to flow naturally without me even having to think of what to say. Eventually, this power and conviction took over and I could feel my whole being begin to shift radically, and just like that, what started off as a warm and muggy night suddenly shifted to a considerably cool and breezy one. It felt as though the temperature dropped easily what felt like 20 degrees.

What happened next looked like something out of a movie because as I gained momentum in my words and spiritual convictions, this gust of wind began to spiral at a high speed all around me picking up leaves and pretty much anything that was there. I was enveloped by this swirling vortex that was only surrounding me and in that moment I felt as though I had merged with the elements themselves. It didn't even feel like something I had to ponder as a possibility, I knew the elements were interacting with the force of my convictions and intentions and it was as if for that moment, I was in direct communion with not only nature, but the universe itself. Of course, ***this wouldn't be the only time this would happen***, by any means and this also wasn't the only way in which the elements would join in for validation either.

Another time that I remember feeling as though I merged with my surroundings and nature was one late evening/early morning that I once again went outside for a ritual and prayer invocation. As I got further into my prayer, after burning some parchment paper and herbs, I started to once again enter this channel where my thoughts were no longer involved and the words were just flowing out of me from this deeper place. As I began to feel a rush of energy flow through me, I pointed my wand up onto the dark night sky and said something deep and the moment I did this, lightning struck as if on queue like in the movies and as I continued, it began to pour ferociously and it just felt as though the energies were merging but of course this can be dismissed as a well timed coincidence even though the elements responding at specific moments when my invocations gained strength became a staple for me during rituals but what was more interesting still was that besides this well timed lightning and subsequent storm was the fact that

I had directed my wand to a point in the sky where there was a star and that's what I was looking at the whole time even after this flash storm began to pass a few minutes later. As I continued my prayer and invocations, I suddenly witnessed the star that I had been looking at the whole time suddenly shoot up and leave!! I laughed!!! I was like "wait what!!??!" I had been talking to a small ship the whole time!! Thank you, universe! That's all I can say, because it wasn't just the elements listening, I had a little cosmic visitor join in on the action and I couldn't have felt more excited to end on that note.

There have been so many other interesting things that have happened during rituals, and not just outside but on my altar as well but one particular instance that comes to mind was when I was doing a ritual with my friend Sandy and we decided to write out some intentions on paper, just as we had done many times before and with the theme of this particular ritual being a heart chakra healing in which we also invoked the Archangel Rafael within the written intentions as he is the archangel known for healing. We then went outside and proceeded to place some herbs into a cauldron and burn the paper with our intentions. We couldn't believe our eyes because after I set the paper on fire, the flame lit up bright green!! Sandy and I were blown away!! I had never in my life seen anything like it. We literally sat there for a few seconds with our jaws dropped like "whoooaa" but by the time we snapped out of it to grab our cell phones to take a picture, the fire had already started to diminish in intensity and turn purplish towards the upper part closest to the paper but nonetheless it was still noticeably green on all the outer part. Here's what's interesting symbolically speaking, but not only is the corresponding color for the heart chakra green but the ray of light that corresponds to Archangel Rafael that is known as the healing ray is ALSO green! Very interesting "coincidence" although I always like to research and see if this was some type of natural phenomenon that I was not aware of but after researching extensively, the only realistic possibility that I came upon was that this could happen if there were traces of copper involved and there *were not*. I was using my same ritual pen, paper, and herbs that I had used dozens of times before or more. Nothing new was brought into the mix to justify such a thing so that was definitely a departure from the norm. Since that time a little over a year ago, it has only happened one additional time and it was (yet again) when we were doing a written intention involving heart chakra healings. Go figure!!

Picture above was taken at least 10 seconds after the initial pure green flame had been burning but we were too shocked to think of taking a picture so the green flame was already starting to diminish and change in color towards the top. In person the upper portion looked like a vibrant purple color with the green still very much present.

My altar has also played a key role with regards to rituals and manipulating matter in inexplicable ways. One of the ways that comes to mind is when I had used my altar to pray for two different people that I knew, that had passed away within ten days of each other and how it seems as though each time that I was connecting to one of them in prayer that some sort of message would manifest by way of very specifically rearranged objects that were moved around and placed in a way that were meant to convey a very exact message linked to something that each individual (while living) was connected to that was meant for me to understand. Each time, the multiple objects that were moved was while I was near them and alone and it was physically impossible for them to have been rearranged in the way that they had. I even had lights turn and off as well as my tv be paused when I asked for validation that I wasn't alone. There was also a special powder I had that's typically used for blessings and protection that manifested sprinkled all over my altar when I had asked for protection during a time that I was experiencing interference. Whenever I'd ask for signs, they would manifest in the most specific ways that I could then interpret and "*decode*" - and always in ways that could not be explained by conventional means and specifically when I was alone. This was a common occurrence and *a fun one* I might add!

Two other random bits come to mind as I think back to all these interactions that seem to be connected to these activation phases that I have mentioned a few times now. I have come to notice that when I speak on the phone with someone that happens to be connected to the phenomenon, and we wind up locking frequencies, that they have on a few occasions seen a ship show up while we were on the phone. Some

The above photo is an example of one of the times that objects were moved to convey a very specific message. Less than a minute prior, this rainbow card had nothing on top of it because I had walked a few steps away to refill the cup of water that had been sitting on top of the rainbow spiral. I was also alone in the room so no one else could have done this. There are at least 4 objects with very specific messages that I can easily decode symbolically and apply to a situation that was connected indirectly with the person that passed away. I also happen to be talking to that person in my head at the exact moment that I was walking to the kitchen to refill my cup with water. When I asked for a validation if this was him, I received a notification on Facebook that someone had liked a post that he had interacted with almost a year prior so it was the first name that I saw. When I thought, "well that could be a coincidence" my TV literally paused and a few seconds later, the light in my foyer turned on by itself.

of the times, the ship has lingered long enough to be photographed while other times it will just pop in long enough to be acknowledged and then it disappears. These sightings always seem to happen when we are having mind (and consciousness) expanding conversations. This has happened with a handful of different people throughout the years. There have even been moments where one particular friend and I noticed that our respective rooms would begin to feel electrically charged as if there was a presence there. I'll usually see sparks of light in different colors or even flashes while my friend would see an actual being as a fleeting vision that she described as a "master in a white robe and long beard." If we happen to be physically together talking (as opposed to when it was over the phone) she would point to where he was standing and it was always right where I was seeing the sparks of light throughout our chat. The being in a robe has appeared for her a handful of times during our conversations and there was always a palpable energy that manifests when we'd go deep down the rabbit hole together as if we are tapping into another frequency (or dimension?) for that moment.

Speaking of tapping into a different frequency, there was a time that I can think back to where I truly felt as though I was walking between worlds more so than ever before. I was manifesting almost instantly and was just so tapped in that my simulation became fully interactive….literally. When I say literally, this is the best example that comes to mind where even my husband saw part of this take place. He witnessed just enough for me to not question my own sanity! One evening, I had decided to go for a walk at dusk while my husband went to go pick up our dinner. I was walking up my block as he drove past me and I remember noticing that just in front of us was a bunch of teenagers playing basketball at the house that capped off the block. I would say it was about 7 guys that were bouncing the basketball and tackling each other for this ball. I waved bye to my husband and then put on my favorite playlist as I walked up my block towards this one area where a little group of 4 duckies were always hanging out. I had watched them grow up and had developed a fondness for them and always made sure to stop by and say hi. On my previous walk some nights before, I had noticed that they'd get super excited and would start wagging their tail feathers whenever I played a certain song. I literally played it for them every time I had seen them since and would even dance with them. On that particular day, I remember thinking "geez, if these kids weren't there, I'd totally play the song and dance with my duckies" as I was actively hearing the balls bouncing off the pavement while I was looking down at my playlist. It was literally in that very instant, as I was having this thought that I stopped hearing the balls bouncing off the ground, FULL STOP! When I looked up, all 7 kids were gone!! I was stunned!! They were literally there the nanosecond before, how on earth was this possible? Anyway, ask and you shall receive (when you are in these frequencies apparently) because my wish came true to be able to dance with my duckies without an audience that might question my sanity! That was nuts! When I told my husband over dinner, he of course didn't believe me but he did remember seeing these kids playing basketball and them not being there upon his return shortly thereafter. I seriously would have wondered if I imagined this somehow or who knows what because it would otherwise be impossible for 7 kids to all disappear so quickly into the house when the walk to the front door or side fence was minimum of a few seconds away for each and additionally, we are not talking one kid, we are talking seven! An instantaneous dematerialization mid basketball bounce? **How**? The curious things that happen when we are acutely attuned to way that our thoughts *create* our physical reality.

A period of time that stands out for me was when Mary Rodwell (a researcher and author in the field of ufology and consciousness) came to Miami for a conference where she was to lecture. I was lucky enough that Rey Hernandez invited me (and a few others) to come and meet her. Rey knew of my interest in learning more about Mary's particular regression methods when investigating experiencer cases. There, the idea of her conducting a class for myself and others to partake in was born. This would prove to be quite interesting for us as there seemed to have been a few parallels that would later occur to at least four of us after meeting her during this class. In keeping with the theme of some of my previous experiences, it was in that semi-asleep state that more curious occurrences would take place.

One night as I lay dozing off watching TV, I felt a presence come up beside me; because I was in that semi-asleep state, I simply accepted it as normal and remained with my eyes closed. At that moment, I felt energy be scooped out of my back as if I was being energetically cleared somehow. I then felt something come towards my eye and saw a lime-green etheric needle slowly go right into my eyeball. It in no way alarmed me, and I continued to sleep, only recording what was happening in my mind so that I could later share it with some of the friends I had made in Mary's class. As the night progressed, I felt the scooping in my back happen again, but I simply allowed it and then went back to sleep. The next day, as I shared this with one of my new friends, I was shocked (and excited) to learn that the same thing had happened to her. We reached out to a few classmates and learned that two others had the same experience, except the scooping was in their throats. So, two of us had scooping in our backs and two in their throats. Fascinating parallels, I thought!

Mary's class would prove to be quite the eye opener for me in a lot of ways. She explained a lot of common patterns that experiencers share and what is really behind certain elements of their experiences which often times get overlooked as just memory distortions or even the imaginings of a child. It wasn't until she explained what a screen memory was that I felt truly astounded. I remember I gasped out loud like "OMG" of how stunned I was that suddenly, two very specific and vivid memories I had finally made sense. My obvious outward excitement got me a few awkward looks but it really was a moment of clarity that I couldn't contain.

A screen memory is a false memory that the mind creates to mask the true details of an experience. In psychology, these typically form as a way of protecting the psyche from a traumatic experience but as ufologist and researcher Budd Hopkins concluded, in the case of experiencers and contactees, the screen memories were believed to have been planted by the aliens themselves. The most common screen memories with regard to the phenomenon usually involve animals that replace the actual events that may have transpired. Another common screen memory can involve car wrecks and emergency or utility vehicles. I'd like to highlight this last possibility as it parallels a story I will share later on that is very much connected to this notion and deepens the mystery for me even further. More on that later.

The first memory that came to mind which I can still remember clearly was when I was around seven years old and was laying in bed with a very high fever on Christmas morning. It was shortly after 7am when I woke up suddenly with the awareness that I had to get up to look out the window at that very moment. The problem was I felt so crummy and in pain that the very idea of having to move felt like torture. I tried to ignore that nudge but it became stronger like "get up now!" almost as if I was going to see something if I looked. I had to take a moment to convince myself but eventually found enough motivation to move my sluggish fever ridden body out of the bed and walked over to the window while my sister lay sleeping in her bed. When I pulled back the curtains, I could not believe my eyes! I was like "what?!"….right there before my eyes was Santa Claus on his sleigh floating right past my 5th story window at that very instant! I could not believe what I was seeing but was so happy and overcome with joy that I got to see something so unbelievable. The funny thing is that I have zero recollection of anything after that. I don't remember if I tried to wake my sister or parents up or if I even went back to bed after that.

My second memory was a few years later when I was nine years old out trick or treating with my sister and a group of kids inside the halls of my five-story apartment building. We were excitedly running from door to door getting loaded up with candies and at some point we had worked our way towards the back of the building where there was a pair of stairs which if you stepped into would allow for a glimpse of the night sky. The building itself was like a hotel in that the hallways were inside the building with no view to the outside except for when you'd reach the stairs. As we passed the back part of the building something told me to stay behind so that I could go take a peek at the night sky. I knew this was meant for me to do alone so I didn't summon my sister to come with me but instead stayed behind, something I would normally never do because I'd get spooked at how "away from civilization" that portion of the building always felt. Needless to say, I snuck away to the stairs and started gazing at the night sky, something that has always mesmerized me and was a hobby of mine at the time. Upon looking on this particular Halloween night, something was different. I could feel a little eerie excitement in the air and it was then that I noticed something floating through the clouds in the moonlit sky. Again, I found myself in utter disbelief and was like "no waayyyy!" but there it was, a sight I never thought I'd see except for in a movie or storybook yet right before me, live and in living color was a *witch riding a broom*! I just could not believe my eyes, how could this be real? But there she was, and it wasn't a fleeting image, she was there in plain view, an image that became seared into my memory till this day. Suddenly, it all made strangely perfect sense. It was only ever meant for me to see and this was why I always knew on a deeper level not to call anyone else into the experience. When I think about what I saw each time that I felt compelled to go to a window or look up into the sky, it makes sense in an innocent and amusing sort of way that these fantastical images be what was on display since after all I was but a mere child. That was one of the most important puzzle pieces to come of my time with Mary Rodwell and I was grateful for it.

This was a time of major activations for me, and I can distinctly remember how I psychically linked up with one of my classmates, Marlo Alvarez, who would later become one of my closest friends and definite soul family. The messages and synchronicities were incredible and would always somehow become validated in real life or through others. These would be exhilarating times for me as things became increasingly more curious. Marlo and I seemed to have a very natural, psychic, and telepathic link. We both noticed how subtle aspects of physical reality would shift into something entirely different. This happened enough times where a very clear and obvious pattern emerged, and it almost seemed like a message though the one thing that was clear is that this was occurring only with Marlo and I. I even joked, "could it be that there is some multi-dimensional aspect of us out there messing with this version of us, or maybe we are just avatars, and someone is messing with our simulation?" There were many amusing examples of this, but one that I will share was when he told me to download two specific songs to add to my workout playlist, and he went so far as to tell me to put them at the top of my playlist so I could start my workout with those two songs to energize me. I was like, "okay fine!" and proceeded to download them and move them to the first and second position on my playlist. The next day at the gym, he asked if I had gotten the songs and asked to let him see my playlist. I confidently handed my iPhone over since I had done just as he had asked, but he was less than impressed and said, "wow, Alina!" as if disappointed and rolled his eyes at me as he handed me back my phone. Puzzled, I looked over at the playlist only to find two random songs I didn't even know I had; one was called "Reaching Out" and the other "Unlimited Combinations." The reason I found that amusing is that the titles played right into the notion that some other version of us "out there" was reaching out to us, and what are unlimited combinations, if not timelines that can shift? It felt very synchronistic, although, in many other cases, with these little subtle shifts, it was actual objects that would change physically or dematerialize and reappear elsewhere in ways that you could say were *impossible*. There were always breadcrumbs that would remain from the prior timeline, and they always implied a connection of him to me or me to him. Curious indeed, but quite fun, I must say.

One such example comes to mind which seems to have happened almost as if to prove a point in a pretty humorous way for us. Not too long ago, Marlo and I were having a little joke filled debate on text (as he made fun of me) for having him partake in a meditation that involved balancing polarities - which in this case pertained to the masculine and feminine polarities. He wasn't having any of it and made me promise not to make him ever do something "so cheesy" like that again! I was so thoroughly amused by his reaction that I couldn't help but laugh and this turned into a little back and forth banter that must have lasted a little over half an hour where I tried (in vain) to explain the importance of balancing polarities in general so that he can apply it to this particular version of it. Yeah, that got me nowhere and fast haha! All the while, I was sitting in the living room (by myself) flipping channels as this was happening on text. Suddenly, to my surprise, the remote control stopped working out of nowhere. I tried everything I could think of to make it come back to life but nothing was working. As a last resort, I decided to try replacing the batteries even though I had just done so the week prior so there was no reason for brand new batteries to fail like that. Nonetheless, I tried that as well anyway. This is where things got curious! Upon opening the back of the remote, I noticed that both batteries were facing down in the same position with the "+" at the bottom. How specific was that? I was like "point taken universe!" and told my snarky buddy "You see how too much of one polarity doesn't work?" and right there, the simulation decided to give us a live illustration of the very thing we were going on and on about. Too much of one polarity without balancing it with the other simply doesn't work, so there you have it! How could this have happened if I was sitting with the remote by myself and had been using it with no problem the whole time? That was just one more of the many curious and amusing occurrences that seemed to be a theme for us from the very beginning of our friendship. Although the first year was the most active (in terms of these little instances that defied logic and reason) but we have yet to have a shortage of anomalous incidents within our connection *to this very day*.

There was a period of time not long ago, where it seemed as though our minds were beginning to merge. We were both being guided to understand higher concepts related to quantum physics, multi-dimensionality, light body activations, ascension, our connections with star beings, how to enter into higher states of consciousness and even timeline jumping and *beyond*. It was becoming quite evident that we were each tapping into some higher dimensional aspect of ourselves but what was exponentially more curious still was the fact that we were receiving or being guided to the same information at the same time or having parallel experiences connected to these higher concepts. We would only make the "coincidental" connection *after the fact* each time. We were being led down an exquisitely fascinating rabbit hole and boy was it exhilarating. Little by little, it became clear to us that seemingly unrelated and complex concepts and knowledge were in fact related. We began to realize that we were decoding information and being made to understand these deeply profound concepts because we were each to respectively develop and use these in some capacity in the future....*To be of service to humanity*. This mind meld was **mind blowing** and quite obviously *by design*.

A few weeks ago, Marlo and I began to tap back into those frequencies while talking on the phone, but to such an extent that we felt the energies shift us completely. My head began to tingle so intensely that it felt like electrical pulses vibrating in every direction all over my scalp. It was just one synchronicity after another after that, and it began to feel as though our conversation had been guided. The activation we both received that night was to set the tone for the rest of the week for us each. It became obvious to us through a series of synchronicities and validations that we were beginning to connect once again with our respective research. This manifested for us in the most ironic and obvious ways, so much so, that we began to document all the things that started to happen (back-to-back) because there was no way that we could dismiss any of it as coincidence. Mind you, Marlo would be the first one to dismiss an undeniable synchronicity as "cute" and roll his eyes because he's been around this type of thing so much (with his own family) that he's become just a touch jaded. But not even he could disregard the signs that we were receiving. It was obvious that we were connected to these frequencies that whole week and beyond. As for me, I usually ask for validations in threes to sort of appease the need to bypass my logical mind while also affirming that there is a consciousness interaction taking place. This only elevates the experience further and certainly also makes it easier to share these types of experiences with the more incredulous types as well - that's for sure.

The week would come to an end in what could only be described as a considerably anomalous sighting that was unlike anything I had ever seen before that particular point in time. Before I get to that, I will preface by saying that Marlo and I had spent all day that Saturday going deep down the rabbit hole listening to an experiencer//researcher we have both been following for years who also happens to be one of the very few that connects to the degree that we both enjoy. This only further supercharged us more after the activation we had both had since our phone conversation the Saturday prior.

Another thing that had me vibing really high, which might seem random (but you will soon see isn't) was this new song I had been listening to endlessly and obsessing over. I must have played this song 40 times (or more!) and it was giving me euphoria....*literally*! Needless to say, I was floating in the ethers that day.

At some point, I decided to go to Target, since I had been sitting in front of my computer most of the day, but that's where things got a little interesting! As I was driving back home, I of course had been exploiting my new favorite song the whole drive back but decided to take the longer way (inside my neighborhood) so that I could blast the song one more time. *This* would be where I meant that things got kind of interesting. As I was driving up towards my house from two rows of houses away, I could see a reddish orange sphere floating above my home. This object was large enough that I could dismiss the possibility of it being a drone or paper lantern though it appeared to be hovering over my house the whole time I was driving towards it. It wasn't until I wrapped around my block and approached my home that I saw it move away towards the left and past my yard. Something told me not to go inside to drop off my Target bags but instead, to stay in my driveway and look up. Just then, a second sphere showed up _directly above my head_ that I can only describe as looking like a perfect ball of fire. It was red and orange and glowing. I stood there mesmerized in awe and watched this second sphere also move to the left and fade away past my yard. I remember thinking "if this is something anomalous and connected to the phenomenon then I want to see another one!" and literally, at that very instant, when I looked up, a third fireball showed up _directly above my head yet again_! Like whaaaaaaaaaaattt??? I managed to film the last two since I was driving when I saw the first one hovering over my home from a distance. I've since shown it to several researcher friends and two separate friends that are film producers in the field of consciousness and contact and one of them is convinced it is an orb and that it was not my idea to go to Target but "theirs" because she believes I was guided out of my home so that I can have this experience. The second friend, who has spent the better part of 8 years documenting unidentified flying objects and the phenomenon said it looked "amazing" and then said "wtf" when he saw the actual video. Makes me giggle! I was blown away even though I admit that my logical mind needed to scan the rolodex of possibilities to rule out the probability of a conventional explanation. In my 45 years of life, I had never seen anything like it, let alone 3 in the exact same spot, as if on queue. One would show up as soon as the previous one began to fade away in the distance. It almost reminds me of a series on Prime called "Upload" where the simulation backdrop would glitch and the same bird would keep showing up in the same exact spot, on repeat.

The one thing I can say for certain is that I was absolutely tapped into what I call my _"miracle frequencies"_ and when Marlo is in there with me, this amplifies them exponentially because we both tap in and expand and it feels as though my simulation becomes interactive or as though everything gets folded into this vortex and for that moment, I am in direct communion with the *Universe*. Now, how does music factor into the equation? For that, I will circle back to Marlo and an incredible contact experience he had while visiting Bolivia for a contact retreat back in 2016. A story that he will share in a later chapter.

After a chain of events that seemed cosmically guided and highly orchestrated, Marlo came into direct contact with a ship and interfaced with it telepathically while on a boat in Lake Titicaca. One of the messages that he received was that one of the ways to connect to the beings (*and their frequency*) was through music and that was precisely the cloud I had been floating on all day (that day) while riding the frequencies of activation from reconnecting to Marlo and I's respective research. The other thing, is that this encounter "obeyed" the pattern I've always requested of validations in multiples of <u>three</u>. If this was *them*, it was only the cherry on top of an already magical week and all I could feel was gratitude regardless of whatever this was (*if anything*) that I had just witnessed above my home. I have seen enough unusual things when I am in those frequencies to know that anything is possible and I will never tire of keeping my eyes on the sky for there are more mysteries to unravel than we can wrap our *wondering* minds around! As Neil Armstrong once said: "*Mystery creates wonder and wonder is the basis of man's **desire to understand***." …..I concur.

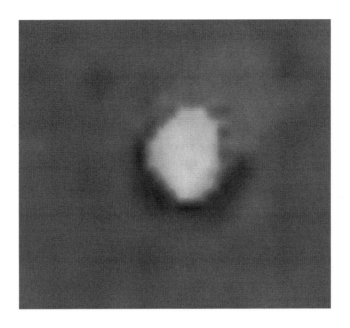

Another two experiences would happen during the period of time after meeting Mary that felt connected somehow. The first one took place one night as I prepared for bed. I was extremely drowsy that night from not sleeping at all the night before, so I knew my sleep was going to be deep. As I began to lay down, I heard a loud vacuum-type sound as if something had entered the room, and my ears literally popped as if whatever this was caused a change in pressure in the room. This, of course, startled me, and I became annoyed because all I wanted was to go to sleep, and I said, "if this is anything not of the light, you must go now! If you are of the light, all I ask is that you let me sleep!" I then laid down, and that was it. It was then, that the most curious night of "sleep" would happen for me. For 9.5 hours, I found myself in what could be described as a lucid dream, except I was hyperaware of what was happening in this dream but also my body as it lay there, dreaming it. I found myself inside a gunmetal colored conference room with a large panoramic window overlooking the Earth. I sat at a table with the sensation of several beings standing to my left, but I could not see them. They then proceeded to hand me a clipboard with a list of the names of volunteers that had come to serve a specific mission to help awaken humanity. At the top of this list was my name, Marlo's, and many others I had met or would come to meet in the years that followed.

All directly connected to this deep quest to understand consciousness and contact, all part of what felt like a soul family that came to unite directly or indirectly in purpose and mission. These beings then proceeded to drop etheric cubes of information into me, each containing massive volumes of information connected to my mission, all of which I immediately recognized and became overwhelmed with excitement to remember. I asked if I was allowed to exit the dream to write some of this down so that I could remember when I woke up, and surprisingly, they agreed! I popped out of the dream, completely lucid and excited, and started to write as much as possible in a text to Marlo. I texted, "there's too much to type, but I'll try to remember when I wake up so I can tell you, but I must return to the dream now!" and I literally re-entered the dream.

The dream felt like it was taking place in real-time, as in I could feel the time as if each hour was passing, as opposed to that warped sense of time that dreams usually have. As more was being downloaded into me, I asked once more if I could exit for a moment to document some of this so I could recall it later, and I once again was allowed to exit briefly. I proceeded to write another friend, Desta. Luckily, I still have access to the email message I had written her, so I was able to look and see what I had said at that time just recently. Even though a lot of what I had written was only nuggets I said I had to remember to share later, the one thing that I did elaborate on that I found interesting was that we were "intermediaries" for the beings that incarnated with special missions to assist in humanity's awakening and ascension into higher levels of consciousness. It was something that I very much recognized.

Occasionally, I still come upon pieces of information, be it from other contactees or material I've read. Even certain movies move me to tears as they stir a deep remembrance in my soul of part of what I was told - that I know is part of our purpose here. This lucid dream continued for a while and eventually ended with me simply waking up, struck by the incredible experience I had just had.

I did have some interference that week from what I would liken to a shadow person that I felt came to observe me somehow or who knows whatever else, but I had been making it a habit to encapsulate myself in a bubble of protective white light every night before bed. So, when this shadow being got close to me, I can distinctly remember seeing it through a convex bubble that he could not penetrate so he left me alone.

I also remember affecting electronics a lot during this time. Something that has happened to me since I was way younger whenever I became activated. I would notice electronics break if I touched them (something that could be chalked up to coincidence) or light bulbs burning out and popping or even exploding. Occurrences that I would try to dismiss as coincidence until there was a week where a total of 12 bulbs that either burnt out or exploded when I turned them on or even simply walked past them. More curiously still was the fact that some of these were brand new bulbs. It happened at work and home, so I knew it wasn't due to electrical malfunctions since it only occurred during specific times when I seemed to be activated for a short while. Batteries would also drain almost instantly and things like that. The timing is always the same, and it's always only during these phases, so I eventually came to accept that it was something connected to my momentary change in frequency and perhaps my need to ground this electrical charge that seemed to coincide with these activation phases I'd be in.

Next was the experience that I would say topped them all. It unfolded on a particular night that I had participated in an event that required a great deal of mental energy, mind over matter, you might say. From beginning to end, this event was purely tests of will, like walking on broken glass, walking on burning coals, bending a metal rod with your neck, and things like that. After this event, some friends and I went for a drink at a nearby bar. During the drive home, I suddenly realized how tired I was, something that had never happened to me before or since. I called Marlo to see if he could stay on the phone to keep me awake, but he was busy. It was nearly 3 am, so I didn't have any other options and decided to push myself to try and stay awake so that I could make it home safely.

The drive was a struggle, and I kept nodding off uncontrollably as I tried to keep my eyes open. Somewhere along the way, I became aware that I was approaching a curved highway bridge that could become extremely dangerous if I wasn't at my full capacity to drive. I got scared that I wouldn't be able to drive home because my senses kept slipping. At this point, I became only mildly aware of two gold lamp lights floating just past the curve of the highway bridge, but because I was so drowsy, it only half registered. In this hazy state, I did manage to notice these lamp lights had no post holding them in place midair, which of course, immediately sent my mind into a moment of puzzled confusion as to how this was possible as I began to pass this through my little logic processor like "wait, what??" and of course, this put my mind into high alert as I continued to approach these lamp lights except thankfully I was now fully awake! A fact that could easily have saved my life, but as I got closer to these floating lamps, I realized there was a third one forming a triangle shape which surprised me, but what really shocked my senses was when I had to drive past them and realized I was driving under an actual object in the sky made of metal with a full body that encased these lamp lights. What? wait, I thought?? How on earth is this humanly possible if I clearly saw the night sky surrounding these lamps that seemed to mysteriously remain suspended in the air with nothing holding them up? It took me what I would estimate was about 10 seconds to drive through the length of this "object," and the notion that this thing was close enough to where, if I chucked my water bottle up through my sunroof, I could easily hit it made me even more perplexed as to what I had just come upon.

Of course, Marlo finally called after I no longer needed help since by this point I was exhilarated, confused, but *wide awake*! When I told him what just happened, he was like, "aww, that's nice," as if I was talking nonsense, and it wasn't until way later that he registered what I had told him, only this would be many months later. The following day I talked to my friend Rey (Hernandez), and I told him what had happened to see if he had any idea what this could have been, and he said, "duh, Alina, you drove under a partially cloaked ship. This thing could have pierced our dimension", and I was like, wow, I can't believe I didn't think of that, but the shock was still too great. I later talked to my friend Desta (Barnabe), a researcher and assistant to ufologist and author Grant Cameron. She said, "Alina, I've been around enough experts and research to tell you that I am pretty certain what just happened to you." I was like, by all means, share! So she continued, "I would say that that was likely you from the future preventing you from messing up the timelines." That gave me chills because it felt strangely authentic and familiar, as if, on some level, I already knew this. One thing is for certain, this "partially clocked ship" was the reason I managed to stay alert enough not to drive off a highway bridge because I was literally nodding off a second before and not in my full senses until it showed up before me. A fact that I can safely say saved my life.

Up until the aforementioned experience, the most remarkable UFO sighting that I had was one that took place approximately 5 years prior (2012) while stuck in traffic with a friend one early afternoon. I had just had a reiki session during a visit to a metaphysical shop named *Five Sisters* and the one thing I remember about the vibe of that day was that we had both left there feeling really peaceful and connected which was only elevated further after also getting into some really deep higher mind type conversations pertaining to esoteric and metaphysical topics on our drive back home. This had us both really zenned out and in a "*flow state*." I remember staring out the window of the car and contemplating how beautiful it was to see such a vibrantly blue and cloudless sky on this gloriously sunny day. We both sat there quietly at this point and were just vibing and waiting for the gridlocked traffic to break up and move. This was not a typical traffic pattern for that hour of the day which was around 2pm but we didn't care, we were that relaxed. This seeming "inconvenience" served us well in what happened next.

As I stared off into the sky in quiet contemplation, I suddenly noticed a *dime sized silver disc* pop into view in my sight range out of nowhere. Puzzled by this, I squinted to get a better view and decipher if maybe this was a plane. I immediately realized that it wasn't, because it quickly collapsed into its center and disappeared only to reappear in a completely random spot in the sky that was further away a second later. I watched this object do this about 5 or 6 times where it would dematerialize and reappear each time in areas that were nowhere near each other and each time, it was in that same manner where it would condense its shape into its center and disappear from view. The funny thing is that it didn't hit me till later that I knew exactly where to look each time it reappeared and I also knew ahead of time intuitively when the final emergence of this UFO was going to take place before it disappeared for good. The impression that I had was that this silver disc was putting on a show for us, a visual spectacle so that we understood that what we were witnessing was not conventional. At the very instant that the UFO disappeared, this **black wasp-like looking helicopter** popped up out of nowhere and proceeded to fly around in front of us (and pretty low too) scanning the entire area where this UFO had just been, but strangely, it was flying around erratically in an unusual pattern. What was really strange was that as soon as I was able to collect myself from the sheer awe and snap myself back into my immediate physical reality, it was only then that I noticed that not a single driver was looking up or reacting at all to any of it when all of this activity was unfolding right before our very eyes ***in plain sight***! And especially the large black helicopter!

How could that be missed? We were sitting in an ocean of idle cars that were within close proximity of us so it was easy to see a handful of drivers but I didn't see a single person looking up. Everyone I was able to see (including a few passengers right next to us) was simply staring ahead! Strange I thought. The funny thing is that the closest one to me (my friend lol) was literally an afterthought! I hadn't even thought to check if my friend Cintia had seen any of this, but when I looked over, its as if she had just come out of suspended animation and was collecting her jaw from the floor because she said "did you freaking see that?!??" and I was like "OMG thank God you saw that too because I was about to question my own sanity!!"

The other strange aspect that I almost didn't register because I had so much to process in just 30 short seconds but it wasn't until Dr. Joseph Burkes interviewed me for a chapter in Rey Hernandez's **FREE Organization** academic research book "*Beyond UFO's*" that I realized another aspect that was quite anomalous regarding this black helicopter - and it was when Dr. Burkes asked me something about if we had *heard* the helicopter when it arrived. That seriously perplexed me because it was only then that I realized that actually NO, this thing appeared out of nowhere, looked strange and was completely <u>silent</u>!! I had the biggest "wtf" moment when it hit me that I had completely overlooked such an obvious and unusual detail. Could it be that that what I saw was a perceived helicopters but was it a *holographic projection.* Rey Hernandez mentioned to me that he also saw a perceived helicopter with no noise but when it turned in front of him it was a large silver oblong object with no wings and no windows that made a 45 degree turn right on top of him. He informed me that this object, just like the objects he had seen, had changed appearances right in front off him and he also suspects, just like Dr. Joseph Bukes, that UFOs are holographic projections. Whatever the case, I was just excited to have had this sighting and that there was another witness there with me!

Things would continue to happen but on a much smaller scale. I saw numerous shimmering, silver objects in the sky, including two that appeared to intercept only to then disappear midair at the same point where they would have collided. It was almost as if it was to make it clear to me, the observer, that what I was looking at was no regular plane. It was something that I already sensed as these tended to disappear and reappear in different areas of the sky and always showed up when I was on the phone talking about the phenomenon.

The bulk of these sightings took place when I joined Rahma (Latin American contact group) and was heavily researching Rahma's history and background. I could at times feel the energy around me as I researched, and curious things even happened with electronics being used as instruments for what you can call contact. On one occasion, I was helping Marlo write a blurb on the connection between consciousness and UFOs, and I was drawing a complete blank as to what to write. I felt completely blocked, so as I sat in front of my laptop, I thought in my head, "okay, beings, help me out," and just then, I noticed a note on my laptop's notepad that said, "handwritten note." I thought, "huh?" I'd never used that function and didn't even know how to do that, so I opened the note, and the screen said, "The beings communicated to her." I was blown away!! As I reached over to take a picture with my cell phone, the note closed and disappeared…uff. I like to document proof whenever possible, but this was not to be.

Another occasion where I called on the beings for help was when I took a sacred geometry class. We were taught how to activate our Merkaba (a 3D sacred geometry symbol that can be activated as a vehicle of light to access higher consciousness), but needless to say, I had not been paying attention when we were taught this as I had been pretty tired that day and really didn't register much of what was taught on how to do this. The following class, the teacher bought some metal rods that she used to create a life-sized Merkaba shape so that we could each stand in to practice activating our own energetically. I was freaked out because I had zero clue how to do this. They say, "fake it till you make it, " and I did! My three other classmates went before me while someone took pictures of them. They each stood inside this three-dimensional Star of David shape and mentally activated their energetic Merkaba around themselves. When my turn came, I was lost in the woods, so I just mentally invoked beings of light and asked if they could help me activate a Merkaba of my own and after my classmate took a ton of pictures, I stepped out of the real-life one. They began scanning the pictures of each of us doing our activations. They stopped upon one of my classmates, a practicing psychic medium and healer, and they were super excited to see a white light mist in front of him in his picture, which was pretty much all they managed to find amongst all the pictures taken of my classmates. When they arrived upon my group of pictures, I heard them all go "WHOA!" and they called my teacher and me over to see, and when I looked, I was pretty stunned to see that there was a ray of light coming into view that only increased as they went through each of the pictures. The pictures not only showed an increase in the intensity of this ray of light, but they eventually became a bubble that encapsulated me, and each picture showed a subtle change in color for this ray of light as well. I was pretty surprised, and my classmates just looked at me stunned, like how did that happen?

Electronics have been more than just a tool to document anomalous occurrences. At times, they have also served as participants in the phenomenon in other not so expected (albeit subtle) ways. One such incident was shortly after a group meditation where Marlo and I went deep down the rabbit hole talking about the *Mandela Effect*. We were both super activated after such a deep meditation and then going deep into phenomenon-related topics. As I was getting ready to leave his house, I remember getting a download of a few things I felt we needed to revisit in terms of research and projects we had been working on throughout the past three years that sort of stayed in the dust. It happened to be about four or five different topics that I received an instant knowing about, and so I relayed the message and left. When I got home, something prompted me to check my emails for a specific message. As I opened up my email, I was taken aback when suddenly, the only emails present in my account were all very specifically pertaining to the four or five different subjects I had just gotten a download about. This was not even feasible, given that these emails ranged in time for as far back as three years and scattered throughout that window of time. There was no rhyme or reason as to how this was possible, and I did take screenshots so that I wouldn't doubt this occurred. Was this a validation from my simulation?

One last example of these consciousness interactions was on a night I had been reading about a Rahma member's contact experience in Mount Shasta, where he and a few other witnesses saw an etheric city manifest over the mountains. As I read that, I remember getting super excited, and I could literally feel the energy as I read this. After a series of synchronicities connected to this happened, I decided to go outside and try to connect to the beings. It was after 10 pm and pretty dark, but I focused my sight on a star in the sky, began invoking them, and asked for proof if they were around since I could already feel them by this point. It wasn't until I started to connect to the feeling of unconditional love as I thought about my friend Marlo and a trip to Bolivia, we were about to embark on that I was so grateful for, that this feeling of love and gratitude just came over me. In that instant, I saw a white light form a wobbly line in the sky and disappear. I knew it wasn't a shooting star as the line formed going upwards and into a wobbly angle. I was so surprised and excited, but in all honesty, I wanted some backup validation before I began to second guess what I just saw, so I proceeded to invoke again. And once again, the very instant I connected to my heart, I felt a rush of unconditional love and gratitude, and right then another white line formed, this time directly above me and slightly different from the one prior. This line made up of light did not follow a traditional trail-like trajectory as one would expect from a shooting star, etc. I was overwhelmed with excitement, and just as I was going to message a friend to share what happened, I could see from the corner of my eye a large, dark blue orb to my right against the backdrop of my light-colored home's wall. Many more examples come to mind that validate that I am interacting with something that transcends conventional explanations.

Some years prior, during the time of my disenchantment with my field of interest and how watered down and inauthentic that it had become, one of the ways that I chose to cope was by creating art. One experience stands out as peculiar and maybe even a clue into understanding consciousness and one of the many ways we interact with aspects of it. At the time, I had started creating nichos, which were small tin shrines similar to a shadowbox but much smaller and required careful curating of tiny objects that would be used to create the kind of scenarios I envisioned in my mind's eye. These art pieces would often take many hours to put together, which I very much appreciated because they served as active meditations that would keep me so focused that, at times, I felt like I was connecting on a deeper level than just to my little tin creations. I can recall one example where I saw my deceased neighbor walk past my kitchen door. On another occasion, I also received a very specific message that I was guided to give to his wife; it contained such specific details (although minor) that were far too exact to be a coincidence. Those are just two examples of many more that came of these creative moments. Definitely an interesting "side effect" of heightened focus, I'd say!

On one occasion, a friend asked me to create a nicho for her with a theme of personal significance, but it took me a good while to conceptualize it. The idea eventually just dropped, in full detail, all at once as I showered one afternoon. This piece took me many hours to complete because I had decided to create a replica for myself since I loved the idea so much. I worked till late that night, and my friend asked if she could stop by that evening to pick it up in her impatient anticipation of seeing it. I went to bed pretty late that night, and after so many hours of working on these nichos I was left quite exhausted. That night I dreamt that I was in complete darkness with a guide who explained that all creations already exist as a stream of consciousness and that when I create, I simply am tapping in and channeling this information and bringing it into form. I was told that anyone in resonance with this creation could tap into and bring said creation to fruition. I woke up super excited to tell my friend about this dream message and called her when I woke up but to my disappointment, when I told her; she started to laugh. I was like, "but why are you laughing? I thought that was so cool?" and she said, "I'm not laughing because I don't believe you; I'm laughing because I had the exact same dream!" Whoa! One day as I relayed this story to Rey, he told me that he believed I created a wormhole through these two identical pieces that I had created, which, incidentally, we had both put up (that night) on our respective bedroom walls. Strangely, that made good sense to me. Another contactee used the word portal to describe this idea. Whichever words we use to explain it, this was a testament to the many ways that consciousness works, not just in the way we both connected to the same information, but to the message itself, which I later came to learn was a known concept that I got to learn about through a dream message.

Another curious experience comes to mind, which occurred some years later and left me pretty baffled and amused. In this particular instance, a friend was to share in this experience with me, adding another layer to what can be understood of what was to unfold for us that night. It all began with an invitation to a group meditation and spiritual gathering that I was invited to by a healer I knew. I decided to invite my friend Mariela, a psychic healer and medium who has always connected to the spirit world since she was a child.

The event took place poolside in the healer's yard, and there were some 25 people in attendance that night. After the mediation, we were invited to partake in wine and snacks at a long table alongside the pool. When it was our turn to get our snacks and wine, we noticed that the first bottle of wine was empty, and there was no bottle opener for the other bottles that were there, so I offered to go inside and ask the host for the bottle opener so we could serve ourselves. I then proceeded to go inside, and when I returned to the table, my friend was nowhere to be found, which made me assume maybe she had gone to the bathroom which was located right next to where we were standing. But when I looked over, the door was open, and no one was inside. I then began to scan the yard to see where my friend could have gone since there was no other place she could be. I started walking around the yard and couldn't find Mariela anywhere, so I walked right back to the table and asked a woman that was standing at the table if she had seen my friend and proceeded to describe how she was dressed to which the woman simply replied "no sorry." I continued to walk around searching for her and finally came upon her at the exact spot where I had left her in what felt like an eternity prior. I said, "finally! I found you," and she just looked at me and giggled. We carried on with opening the wine and scooping up some snacks. At the end of the night, as I dropped her off, she looked at me with a somewhat mischievous face. She said, "you didn't even realize what happened to you tonight, did you?" I looked at her confused and asked, "what do you mean?" and she said, "you walked right up to me when I was standing by the table where you left me, and you looked me straight in the eyes and asked me if I had seen your friend. I knew something weird was happening because you looked blurry like a cell phone picture filter as you walked over to me. Something felt a little off, so I knew not to break the energy of whatever was happening by saying something to you. I played along and watched you walking all around the backyard at times, even walking right past me and not seeing me until you finally did. I knew it was over because I could see you again clearly and not in the fuzzy way you appeared before." I looked at her puzzled and asked if she was being serious, and she said she was just as perplexed as me when it was happening, but because strange things have happened to her so much throughout her life, she has learned not to doubt anymore.

This isn't the only time we have had curious things happen. Another example was when we went to a bookstore and were looking for the escalator to go to the first floor since we had entered through the second floor. So we walked over to the nearest escalator and saw that it was coming up and from afar saw the one going down was on the other side of where we were standing, so we started to walk over to it. When we got there, it turned out it was not only coming up; it had several people on it about to get off, eliminating the possibility of theorizing that the store had somehow reversed the function of the escalators in the 15 seconds or less that it took us to walk to the other one. The people on it were already at the top, with a few at the midpoint of the escalator, which means that they had been on it for a while longer than what it took us to walk over to it when it was originally going down. If it were just me that this happened to, I would have seriously questioned my sanity, but both Mariela and I looked at each other when we saw the switch and said, "what the ????" because we both saw the same thing. There was a strange energy in the air that we had both already noticed before that occurred. An element that seems to precede these little "glitches in the simulation," as I call them.

Many have happened to me, especially in recent years, with one, in particular, standing out so much that it still blows my mind. Little did I know that this was a known attribute of the phenomenon that implies not only some consciousness link but also the way higher intelligences might very well be interacting with us.

One such example happened fairly recently during a dinner outing with a friend whom I regularly meet up with to discuss all things consciousness and our connections to spirit, etc. These dinner dates always seemed to be divinely guided in many ways, something that was quickly becoming obvious to us. There seemed to be a theme to each one of our dinners and topics that seemed to be guided for us to "unpack" until we fully understood, frequently with each one of us receiving a portion of the message that we would then bring together and analyze until all the pieces fit. We both noticed that when we would succeed in figuring out whatever was being shown to us, we would somehow always be *rewarded* with a major validation or synchronicity that was so exact we would be floored by how these things would even happen. This friend is an older woman that after suffering a huge family tragedy, spent many years immersed in spiritual studies and healing that would open her up so tremendously to the world of spirit that her connection became a constant and extremely potent one until this very day.

There is an openness when we interact that seems to amplify "the field" when we come together, so perhaps this would help explain what happened on one of our most baffling nights together. On this particular dinner date, we got into the topic of how we would handle an emergency and the role empathy plays in people's responses. An unfortunate joke in poor taste that another friend made regarding a situation that was of a delicate nature seemed to irritate her greatly as it reminded her of the struggles she and her parents faced when they fled from communist Cuba. I notice that emotional charge serves as an amplifier of whatever energies we are interacting with. Our conversation continued for more than an hour, with the main point being the level of empathy each of us would respond with in an emergency.

As the night wrapped up, we walked out into the parking lot to exchange our final thoughts as we always did. The parking lot of this restaurant was situated alongside a bustling street that was always buzzing with traffic no matter the time, and this night was no exception. At this point, as we were sharing our final thoughts, we suddenly heard a giant explosion. It was so loud it felt like we were hearing it in stereo.

Startled, we both looked over to the street and saw a red pickup truck flipped over, skidding across the intersection, sliding up the street, and crashing into the sidewalk. Stunned, we looked at each other like, oh my God! and we knew we had to call 911. She reported it as I watched the shocking scene unfold before us. I witnessed several people jump out of their cars and try to look into the smashed upside-down top of the truck to where the driver was. I was worried the person might not have made it given the little space there was for a person to fit into the crushed carriage portion of the pickup truck as it was on that side that it had skidded, which was easily for a block and a half. I started to wonder what this truck had hit to cause it to flip and walked over to look and see what was down the road and all I saw was another car barely damaged. It was only a few minutes until the ambulance showed up, but strangely, the sirens weren't on. Weird. It arrived with the lights on and no sound. Seconds later, several police cars arrived, but they, too, had no sirens on, just lights. By this point, my friend and I were both looking at each other confused, like, "okay, that's different." We watched the scene unfold and impatiently watched to see if they could pull the driver out. A while passed, and my friend had to leave, so I promised to update her, and I continued to observe the scene. At that moment, my daughter called unexpectedly, as it was already past her bedtime, to ask me if I could go get her a bottle of soda for a science experiment, she needed to do the next day and had forgotten about. I was like, "wow, what timing," and continued to watch to see if they were finally able to pull the poor person out.

To my absolute surprise, no one was ever taken out; the paramedic hopped back into the ambulance, turned off his lights, and drove away, as did the police. I was so confused because if the person had died, they would have pulled him out and covered him on a stretcher to be removed from the scene. I couldn't believe it. I had been watching the whole time; how could this be? I gave up trying to make sense of this and drove to the pharmacy, which was right beside where the truck had crashed before rolling over. That would be another strange layer to this already bizarrely themed night. As I was driving there, my friend called me, but she sounded completely befuddled at this point and said she had no idea what was happening. As my friend was driving through the exact neighborhood, she had driven through for many, many years and knew better than the back of her hand, yet on this night, for whatever strange reason, it looked completely different, so much so that she had even gotten lost. She said she had no idea what was happening, but something really weird was in the air.

By this point, I was walking into the pharmacy, and I get goosebumps just thinking about it because just as she said, I felt something strange indeed was *in the air!* As I walked in with my friend still on the phone, I felt as though everyone was looking at me as if I had walked onto a movie set, a very bizarre feeling. And at that very moment, a tall black man walked up to me. He said, "it's you!! I know you! Do you remember me?" and I said, "no, sorry, you must have the wrong person," and he said, "nope, it's you. I know your voice, I know your face, I know YOU!" I said, "well, I have a twin sister, so it might be her you are confusing me with," and he said, "no, darling, energy doesn't lie; I know YOU." Okay, that was weird, I thought and continued about my way. When I got to the register, I still couldn't shake the feeling of something being slightly off and strange about the night's energy. I asked the two employees at the register if they knew anything about the accident, and they both looked at me confused and said, "what accident?" I asked, "you guys didn't hear that loud crash about 20 minutes ago?" They both looked at me and said, "no." The manager said, "I've been here all night, and I never heard anything like that at all".... now that was very strange to me because the accident happened literally right beside their street, and we heard it incredibly loudly at the moment of impact which was even further down the street to where the restaurant was. As the days progressed, and I would try to piece together the details of that night, all of it made less and less sense, yet a theme was prevalent throughout. I mean, what were the odds that here we had spent the better part of the evening talking about how we would handle a moment of crisis and as we were wrapping up on that topic, something so specific to this conversation happened at literally that exact moment as if right on cue?

I started to remember another bizarre aspect of this whole situation. It was that as the truck lay there flipped over, almost no cars drove by, something unheard of for such a busy street, but beyond that, not one single car, and I mean none of the cars that drove by, ever slowed down at all as they drove past the flipped truck, not even one. As if it was not even there. That was bizarre to me because if there is one thing that I have always noticed, it's that even when it is just a car that has broken down, this always causes traffic to slow down. After all, human nature dictates that, ESPECIALLY when there is a visually impactful sight like a car accident. I stood there watching for about 20 minutes, and not one of the attributes of that scene made any sense. There were no sirens from the ambulance or police, no person or body removed, no traffic or interest by potential onlookers, my friend getting lost because she didn't recognize her own neighborhood, the strange energy of the pharmacy, and even the guy claiming to know me. It was almost as if that happened to add another layer of peculiarity or even somehow to highlight the strangeness. My friend and I both felt it and knew something was off about the whole night. I believe the incident itself put us in a state of "hyper-awareness," something we have come to notice makes us more tuned into the subtle ways our reality interacts with us and sends us clues, breadcrumbs of not only the nature of reality but how higher intelligences are observing and perhaps checking to make sure we are paying attention.

A few months later, I spoke to a friend who hosts an online show on ufology and the phenomenon and regularly interviews ufologists, researchers, and contactees. He mentioned that this was a known phenomenon where the beings used "false timeline inserts" to interact with us; these are subtle clues to those keen enough to notice and realize that they were interacting with the phenomenon. Marlo, who has researched contact cases for the greater part of his life also pointed it out and recognized the energy immediately before I even got to the main parts of the story. He immediately noticed something strange in how my story unfolded, and he got excited and said, "there is something to this; tell me more! I can tell something is happening here." He too, mentioned these false timeline inserts. It all felt as though this was very much in line with what we had experienced that night. A pattern was there as to how they not only know what we are discussing but even possibly giving us glimpses for a deeper understanding of the nature of our reality *and just how permeable it truly is*.

It was to be proven to me once more a short time after that in a more fun and lighthearted way after yet another one of our deep dives into understanding consciousness and our place in the universe. This time the conversation entailed how we are all fractals of the creator and how we eventually return to oneness with God. There was an element of that conversation that we didn't see eye to eye on, and it turned into an intense debate. Disconcerted by this, I went home and continued to analyze the subject further and asked the universe for clarity on the matter. The next day it was as if I was scripting my own "simulation" with what I call easter eggs (clues) everywhere I would look. The theme of our oneness with all that is was coming up in songs that would pop up, if I happened to look at a random magazine or texts from other friends who happened to randomly mention something; it was literally everywhere I would look so much so that it became comical. I started to document this because I got excited. It was as if my outer world was interacting with my inner thoughts. The "simulation hack" took on a life of its own as more random and inexplicable things started happening. As I would say things, they would show up around me in the movie scene that happened to come on or in other fun ways that I couldn't even begin to describe and even keep up with because things were coming at me from every direction almost all at once. It was cartoonish and far too exact and continuous to be random.

Still, there is one example that I will mention while I was in that frequency, I guess you could say, that occurred when I went to grab an archival ink pen that I had in a pencil holder that my daughter had been looking for. I had noticed there were two of same archival ink pen sitting there. When I reached over to grab one, I noticed it was the wrong color, so I went to grab the second one, which had a silver cap just like the other one, but as I held it, I felt a bizarre tingling sensation and a warmth in my hand. It was the most peculiar sensation you could imagine, almost as if my hand was burning, and I could feel the pen change shape as I grabbed it. I couldn't believe how weird it felt when the pen, out of nowhere, suddenly felt thinner and as I looked at it, it was an entirely different pen that didn't even look similar from the top if I were to try and explain how I might have confused it for one of the same kind as the other. I had never seen this pen before and had no idea where it came from.

Still, when I looked at it, the pen seemed to be continuing the theme of the conversation as it read "OmniSky" Perhaps it's a stretch on my part, but Omni means one, and we usually tend to associate God with being in the sky. Whatever the case was, this pen had shapeshifted in my hand, and the sensation lingered for a good while afterward. The endless streams of synchronicities kept me in a hyper-awareness state for a few days. I can recall feeling activated and euphoric the next day as the synchronicities continued nonstop. I could feel that my energy was amplified, and at some point, when I went to wash my hands, I saw that white smoke was coming out of them. I thought for sure I imagined things, but as the water would touch my hands, I noticed this smoke coming up out of them, and yet the water wasn't even warm; it was at a moderate to cool temperature. I kind of thought that maybe there was a logical explanation to it, but then, as I went to grab the plug of a small LED light stand I had, and my hand touched the plug, the energy in my hand caused the stand to light up for a moment as if there was an electrical charge to it. It was a very curious few days, and a lot was coming through as if my mind had switched channels momentarily. I received information from a higher level of consciousness beyond my usual way of thinking. Many things began to make sense on a much deeper level as if I was being allowed to see them from the point of view of the creator.

There is a curious story I would like to share that perhaps is a testament to how we are all a part of *one* collective consciousness with this interconnectedness oftentimes revealing itself in most unexpected ways. The implications within this story, in my opinion, are multifold. It all began with my decision to revisit an astrological chart I had done some years prior by a woman named Lavandar who had discovered how to determine if people carried what is termed *"star markings"* on their astrological chart. This is something she believes to have been guided by beings of a higher intelligence where she even underwent what could be called a "trial by fire" for several years so that she could validate this discovery in what turned out to be a highly synchronistic and even seemingly divinely orchestrated chain of events. After she satisfied this quest with sufficient proof that the formula she discovered was indeed valid, she then went on to create an astrological reading known as a "Starseed Confirmation" which thus far has helped many people come to understand more profoundly why they have always felt so different. This type of natal astrological chart provides insight into not only some of ones own star origins but also innate spiritual gifts and ways that one can connect to the galactic beings that are there to assist these souls that have chosen to incarnate in order to fulfill a service for humanity. That was without a doubt something that felt very familiar to me and immediately struck a cord as a chart reading that I should have done after it was recommended to me a few years prior.

On this one particular day I felt compelled to listen to the audio of my Starseed Confirmation again because something told me I would possibly get more out of it this time around and as I listened, that is indeed what happened. So much of what I was hearing made even more sense now. There were even aspects of my journey that had started to unfold in obvious ways in the years that followed that reading. One thing that struck me was that something called "ship communication" was mentioned and in the audio, it was explained that I had that built in connection and that all I had to do was ask three times so that it was clear that I was using my free will to make a request to connect. I immediately thought this was something I wanted to experiment with soon.

There was one particular day of that same week that felt like the perfect moment given that it was one of those highly synchronistic, high vibes kind of days. Everything seemed to just flow, whether conversations or whatever I was doing, there was a magical frequency about that day that I have learned to recognize and at times use to manifest what I would consider small miracles. What better moment than that to make my request for contact? Once bedtime rolled around I decided to ask for exactly what the term "ship communication" would imply and I asked to be taken on the ships during dream time, I also asked to have full recollection of this and also to be given some insight into what was going on with the whole covid thing. I asked for each three times as instructed in my reading and then proceeded to go to bed certain that something would come of these requests. When I woke up around 8am the following morning I was super disappointed that I had zero recollection of any dreams. I was so sure something was going to come of my requests but accepted that this meant I'd have to try again another time and went back to sleep. When I woke up about an hour later, I noticed I had a WhatsApp message from a woman I had met two weeks prior in a "Galactic Human" workshop that we had both attended. We belonged to several experiencer groups on WhatsApp together so that was how she had my contact information. I had known of her for several years as Rey (Hernandez) had once invited me and a few others to her ranch in Naples, FL, a visit that I was ultimately unable to attend. At the time, he had mentioned that she lived on a ranch with many acres and had regular UFO sightings on her property.

The purpose of the visit at that time was to gather for a CE5 (close encounter of the fifth kind which is human initiated contact) and one that turned out fruitful for some of the people in attendance. I would later come to hear quite a few stories from different friends and acquaintances in the local contact scene who had either visited this ranch or had hoped to drive up to it someday in the hopes of having a sighting of their own. The woman who I will call *Diana* had become well known over the years due to the amount of UFO activity she had on her property some of which she was blessed enough to have documented for others to see. Little did I know when I was talking to her during the Galactic Human Workshop that this was the same woman Rey had invited me to meet 3 years prior. We spoke casually about the different extraterrestrial races and I remember she asked me if I had ever seen an Arcturian to which I responded that I believed that a blue being that I had seen once, during a time I was experiencing high strangeness pretty regularly to be an Arcturian though I couldn't say with absolute certainty. She mentioned she felt a connection to them and then shared some interesting stories and pictures of the different sightings she had had on her ranch in Naples. I said "oh wait, are you Diana?" and she said yes and I remember mentioning briefly how I had hoped to visit her with Rey once but was unable to and we agreed that maybe one day I would pay her a visit with a friend who was also supposed to attend at that time years prior. We agreed to plan this soon and that was that. Flash forward to the morning after my request which was two weeks after this workshop and it was then that I was to hear from Diana again in the most unexpected way.

When I reached over for my phone after waking up for the second time that morning, I noticed I had an urgent sounding message from Diana asking if she could call me, that she had something important to tell me. Intrigued, I immediately responded and she proceeded to call me within seconds of my reply. Her voice sounded exhilarated and she prefaced by saying something along the lines of "you know my experiences with UFO's have been many though almost entirely from afar when I've witnessed them in the sky" she then went on to mention she had only been on board a ship once in a lucid dream and that was it, that is, until *now*.

With a noticeably excited tone she went on to share that she had a second lucid dream of a ship the night before that blew her away because she remembered it in vivid detail. She proceeded to share how she was taken onboard a ship filled with "blue beings" which she believed to be Arcturians and that shortly after that, she saw me enter the ship except I was some sort of a commander in a silver suit. She mentioned how all the beings were excited to see me and crowded around me and it was then that she received information on what was behind the whole covid situation. She mentioned how this was something that was supposed to catalyze humanity into its next phase and that this was something that needed to happen in order to shift us and cleanse all that was no longer working for us on this planet. She also mentioned that she was told that even though we thought that everything that we were witnessing in our waking state was all there was but there was a lot more that was taking place behind the scenes and during dream time that we were partaking in to assist humanity and that those of us that signed up for this mission would be protected while we completed our tasks.

I was truly blown away, not just by the details of her dream but the fact that all three things I had requested had been granted albeit through somebody else. This in way, felt more significant because I could eliminate the likely probability that I programmed my subconscious mind to create this dream based on actual thoughts and intentions I had before bed. The fact that someone else with zero knowledge of my request who wasn't even someone I was in contact with was shown all that I had requested in such an exact way leaves little room for doubt that something curious was happening here. Could it be that we really were having experiences on a ship during dream time and better still, that we were already being of service to humanity in some way that would eventually become more obvious and direct for us during our waking hours? If not that, at the very least this was a testament to how we are all somehow interconnected, our consciousness being the bridge. The way that I see it, each of us is like a thread, all intricately woven into the fabric of creation that together form the sum total of the <u>ONE</u> mind that is ***God***.

Dreams have always played a significant role when it comes to ways in which I receive information that later on proves to be prophetic. There is always a different "feel" to these types of dreams in which I am usually shown or given insight into events that oftentimes are yet to unfold. At times a specific person themselves will come and give me an update on what is happening to them in real life but interestingly, the information given is usually ahead of time and yet to transpire. There was one particularly active week for me in terms of "information dreams" where I knew something critical was taking place with a friend of mine who had been out of touch and going through a rather difficult period and in isolation as a result. There was a running theme to each dream I had that week that seemed to be building up to a massive ending of a negative influence and phase and I remember things felt imminent.

In one dream in particular, I remember trying to communicate an important message to my friend who for some reason couldn't hear me and as I tried to yell from across a room, that gesture actually caused for me to jolt awake in real life and the moment I opened my eyes I saw a flash of gold glowing light language projected onto my pillow. I looked at it in awe for a moment and knew it meant something that was connected to this dream but was too sleepy to contemplate it further. What was interesting is that this chain of events that unfolded consecutively within my dreams throughout the five or six dreams that I had that week (*with each building upon the one prior*) would later prove to be exactly what occurred in real life. Once I came back into contact with my friend, I was astounded to learn that bit by bit, everything unfolded exactly as I had seen it and even the elements that were more metaphorical were still precisely parallel to the real-life occurrences that would later take place and would ultimately serve as catalysts in bringing us back together again as friends.

Are dreams another way our consciousness interacts with us (and each other) in some altered aspect of our reality? Or rather, perhaps a better way of putting it is that we are having experiences on the astral planes in our subtle bodies. I would also theorize that perhaps while the mind is at rest and subdued, it is easier for our consciousness to project itself and interact with others that we are connected to, particularly when there are times that the human ego or other aspects of the 3D construct gets in the way, so perhaps this is another means in which we can interface with other fractals of God's consciousness without the third dimensional flesh suit and limited waking mind in the way!

A final experience I would like to share is one that really became the ultimate validation of just how powerful our consciousness is and how it can not only impact the physical world around us but can also influence others as well - but with one more added layer that deepens it all even further. This story begins with an unexpected phone call from a stranger that started in a way that paralyzed me with fear: "Hi, is this Alina? This is Ady's friend, and I don't mean to scare you, but I am here at the hospital trying to reach all of Ady's friends to inform them that…." my heart sank and I got instant palpitations. He then told me that our friend had been hospitalized in serious condition, and the doctors were doing everything they could to regulate her heart rate to prevent her from having a heart attack. This really freaked me out as the last I heard from her was that she was going through a traumatic situation that affected her emotionally. She had been doing her best to cope with it, but apparently, it was taking a toll on her emotionally, and she had some trauma responses as a result. He asked me to please pray for her, and I immediately decided to do a little ritual along with my prayer after I took a walk just to ground myself and connect to myself and, of course, to her.

I felt so much love and empathy for her as I understood on a personal level what she was going through. My heart broke for her and the pain it caused her to get to this point. Her friend had informed me that the nurse was giving her some sort of medication every hour to keep her heart rate stable and to prevent her from having a cardiac event. He also told me that she was having a rough time sleeping and would always be restless, something he had observed since he had been staying in her room with her so that she wouldn't be alone. He had texted one final time with an update about Ady's condition, and I told him that I was about to start my prayer ritual in a few minutes, and we signed off for the night. I felt deep empathy and love for her, which I always wondered about growing up, as I noticed that I would feel more deeply than most people. I would feel such profound empathy at times that it felt as if I was feeling the other person's emotions. I suffered a lot at times because of this. Still, it felt as though I would enter this little secret heart space that allowed me to connect more directly to a person's soul. As a result, I noticed that I would receive visits from people when they passed away, and I'd connect to their essence as if this was a channel or bandwidth that we were both coming together in somehow.

Before I continue with Ady's story, I'll share one more anecdote in this regard. This story involves Marlo, who I have mentioned numerous times and someone I truly love like a brother - *unconditionally*. It's amusing to think back to all the times my friend Rey (Hernandez) would talk to me about my long lost "soul brother" who he said was like the "male version" of me and how much he insisted (for the better part of a year) for me to connect with him on Facebook. I always kind of giggled and disregarded it until we finally met in Mary's class and sure enough, *Rey was right*!

The bond was instant and so were my protective instincts like a sister. A dynamic that has been consistent throughout our friendship. There was a time when I noticed his energy was shifting tremendously, and he was losing balance as a result. This was during a period when he was staying with a friend during quarantine. His friend was naturally very anxious and had nitpicker tendencies, but Marlo was mostly only around him during this time when people were mainly just staying inside. I got a sense that my friend was starting to lose balance from only being around the more mental energy but what I felt he was truly lacking was the love energy altogether. It was a sharp intuitive ping because I know my buddy so well. I decided to do some sun gazing as I had heard that this was good for opening up one's third eye and this could even be done as a brief meditation, which I did at sunset to avoid hurting my eyes.

As I started to connect and go into a light meditative state, I felt compelled to do a prayer for my friend, and I asked that he be shrouded in a stream of pure love to help balance his energy and vibe. As soon as I connected to him from my heart, I saw this green cord form from my chest, and it went straight into the sun where I was staring. I couldn't believe what I saw because it looked like an energetic cord connecting straight from my heart to the sun's light. At that moment, I heard the words "*your heart is a portal*" in my head, and I thought, wow, that's interesting, as I instantly understood what that meant in a deeper sense. What was funny is that as I walked back into my house, I noticed an oracle deck that I had just purchased but hadn't looked at. For some reason, something told me to look at the lid of this card deck, and right there, in plain text, the inside of the lid read "Your Heart Is A Portal".... incredible synchronicity to what I had just experienced outside.

A few days passed, and I got a text from my friend with an excited tone that read "you're not going to believe what just happened to me! As I was getting up this morning, I heard a voice say to me, 'if you get up now, your day will proceed as usual, but if you lay back down, you will receive a stream of the love frequency to balance your energy out,'" and he then shared how amazing he felt as he hadn't felt like himself for a while. He felt brand new and so much better, exactly what I had prayed for when the green cord formed during my sun gazing experiment. This felt like definite validation as the heart surely felt to me like a gateway to not only connecting to others from a place of love, but this had already previously proven to be a link to connecting to the phenomenon itself, and what more powerful force is there in the universe than *love*?

That brings me back to Ady and how I felt at the moment I went into my prayer ritual; what I felt was pure love for her. I put on a *Twenty One Pilots* concert that always induces "the feels," I lit a few candles and proceeded to communicate with her higher self and God to help heal her. I told her I held her in pure love and wrapped her in it, and I began to burn some sage and say other things; then, when I finished, I went to sit on my recliner but continued to talk to her telling her I knew she was going to get better. The following day her friend texted me to say to me that he knew that whatever I did during my prayer ritual worked because at the exact moment that I said I was going to do it, he said that her heart rate slowed down, and she got so peaceful and calm that she started to smile. He couldn't believe how quickly she shifted because it was the first time in the entire time he had been with her that she had been that calm, and because of that, the hospital staff didn't need to administer the hourly dose of medication to regulate her heart rate. That made me happy but what happened next really was what blew my mind.

A while later, I noticed I had a voice message from Ady herself which was quite the surprise because up until then, she was mostly just extremely groggy and trying to rest as she struggled to get better. In the voice message, she had told me that she had had the most beautiful experience the night before where she saw herself coming to visit my home and that she witnessed me doing a prayer ritual and that I had candles on and began to burn sage as I talked directly to her and that when I said I wrapped her in pure love energy, I physically wrapped her with a hug that she said felt so comforting and loving that it put her at ease. She then described my home in detail and how I went on to sit on the couch and continued to talk to her, except she sat in front of me and interacted with me as I spoke to her. She said she woke up feeling the most incredible feeling of love and could feel my consciousness with her in her room. That this love feeling I was transmitting was surrounding her ever since. I should mention that she had never been to my home or even seen what it looks like since she lives in another state, and so that made her detailed and exact description of my home even more incredible.

Hearing her experience just blew me away so much. I couldn't help but get teary-eyed because up until then, I had been doing my rituals and prayers and sending love when I was compelled to. I knew something was happening on some level, but to see how directly I impacted someone who also had wound up flatlining for two minutes and clinically dying due to the state of duress she was in and that I was able to transmit something to her that actually reached her in such a literal way that everything I said she actually experienced in this altered state she was in. The fact that it shifted her enough to where she didn't require medication and bought her that amount of relief that she could even feel my presence and the love I transmitted to her, for not just that moment, *but every day she was hospitalized after that.*

I was truly beside myself in gratitude that I could be of service in that way and that something that profound would even happen. For a good while after that, any time I recounted that story or it crossed my mind, it would make my eyes water because that truly touched me deeply that I could even do that. There were several months when she and I seemed to have stayed connected somehow because she began to tap into me with messages that were so specific related to things she had no way of knowing but also connecting to situations pertaining to a friend of mine that we were working through. There were some issues she knew absolutely nothing about, yet she connected with and received information in great detail about this friend. I found this quite interesting because her connection to my consciousness served as a bridge to this other person, perhaps due to how close I was to this particular friend. That, for me, was yet another glimpse into just how deep the rabbit hole goes when it comes to understanding the very nature of consciousness.

These are only some of the experiences that have shaped my understanding of consciousness and how extraordinary our reality can be once we become aware of what we are capable of. Some of these experiences are also a wonderful reminder that *we are not alone*. There are benevolent intelligences overseeing humanity's evolution that are simply waiting for us to align to their frequency so that they can connect to us as they have in so many cases that are being documented for the world to understand. Times are changing, as is humanity, and someday, I hope to be a part of a world where we, as a planetary race, can have open contact and alliances with other intelligent species other than our own. I genuinely believe we have reached that tipping point.

Perhaps I have only scratched the surface of my explorations into understanding such a profound topic, but I sure am having a lot of fun putting together the puzzle little by little, piece by piece. I will never get tired of seeking to deepen my understanding and will enjoy dedicating my life to unraveling the mystery.

A lifetime of Experiences via the
Contact Modalities:

OBEs, Materializations of Non-Human Intelligence, Telepathic Communications, UFOs, Communication with the Deceased

Kevin Briggs

"Everything in the Universe is energy and energy vibrates at different rates. Each person has a unique vibration, which is the product of all of the influences he/she has ever encountered. The influences upon which we focus our attention or thoughts are those which determine or define our vibration"

I am an experiencer of 57 years and I am now 65 years old. My view is that an experiencer is a person who has interactions with non-human intelligences. This contact covers multiple Contact Modalities.

As a young child I was always sensitive to other vibrational frequencies in close proximity to me. My first encounter with Non-Human intelligence was a physical materialization. I was eight years old. It was early evening and I was taking a bath. The water was warm and inviting and as usual I had my boats and submarine to play with. Suddenly I felt a change in the vibrational frequency, a very strange feeling, this was accompanied by a slight drop in temperature, which made my skin quiver. Two Non-Human Intelligence "beings" materialized they were slightly elevated from the floor by some 8 to 12 inches. Both were attractive and athletic. They appeared human in form with blonde shoulder length hair and blue eyes. Their clothing was blue in color and was one piece and very tight fitting, like a thin jumpsuit. One was male, and the other was female.

I was terrified by their presence and I couldn't move, it was as though I'd turned to stone. They were speaking to each other without moving their mouths. Later I knew this to be telepathy. I could understand what they were saying. Their conversation was about me, not with me. The female said, "Is this the boy", The male said, "Yes, it is. The female said, "Are you sure, he is very small, uneducated and he looks frightened by our presence". The male then said, "This is the boy, I will guide him, I will teach him". There was some other conversation but I do not recall it. They left the bathroom, and the female was correct, I was frightened, so frightened that I dare not move from the bathtub. I just stayed there numb, speechless and the water was getting cold. To my relief my mother came to see why I was still in the bathtub. I tried to explain to her about the two beings, she said it was my imagination. I knew it was not my imagination; it was my first encounter with non-human intelligences. My encounters with these two have continued to this day.

My understanding of vibrational frequency is defined as "the rate at which the atoms and sub-atomic particles of a being or matter vibrate. The higher this vibrational frequency is, the closer it is to the frequency of Light." Within this encounter were actually three modalities of contact.

1. One being the physical materialization.
2. Two beings telepathic communication.
3. Third being consciousness as the conduit.

Consciousness itself is used in communication, travel and creation.

1. The communication was telepathy, telepathic communication.
2. The transportation into my bathroom denotes travel.
3. The appearance of what I perceived as physical bodies denotes creation. Whether they were physically there or if it was a projection is immaterial. Whichever, I am not sure, however they certainly created it using consciousness as the conduit.

My second encounter happened when I was nine years old when an orb appeared in my home. It was about four to six inches in diameter, yellow/orange in color and vibrating slightly. It was by the window in the living room tucked away behind the drapes. I do not recall having any direct contact with the orb. I checked every day behind the drapes. It did not move, just vibrated and hovered. It stayed for six days, arriving on the Sunday and leaving on the Friday.

When the orb had left my psychic abilities had been enhanced tremendously, to a point where I could separate my consciousness from my physical. I could do this at will by relaxing opening my mind, and using thought as a means to travel. I now know that the orb was pure conscious energy. This energy was of the male in the bathroom. His name is Ort.

This ability I now have was very exciting. I would visit my grandparents who lived about seventy miles away in Liverpool. I would relax open my mind and using thought I would travel the seventy miles in an instant. My grandparents lived in a large Victorian house with a large staircase leading up to the bedrooms. I would go through the master bedroom to the dressing room and sit on the ottoman. There I would look down at the floor which appeared opaque, although it was carpeted. I could see my grandparents clearly. My grandmother would usually be in the kitchen cooking and my grandfather either watching TV or reading the newspaper. As a child I would visit my grandparents on a regular basis in this way. I first thought that this method was just another of our "senses" like touch, taste, smell, hearing, sight and now out of body travel. I had no idea the full potential of out of body travel. At the time I often wondered what my grandparents would have seen if they had come upstairs to the dressing room.

They would have seen a pure conscious energy orb four to six inches in diameter, yellow/orange in color and slightly vibrating. My own pure conscious energy. As I became older my out of body travel could and would be used in everyday life, in very simplistic ways. It didn't take me long to move to a more advanced level.

I was working at Leeds University and found myself a small rental apartment a little out of town. With no personal transportation my commute was using the local bus service. I had a choice of two service routes and the bus stops were not located near each other. Both stops generally had long lines and long waits. To make my life easier I would use my out of body ability to quickly check out both bus stops, chose the shorter line and then quickly get to that stop.

On other occasions I would use this ability to check out on my friends to see if they were home or not. No point in walking a couple of miles only to find they are not home. It's not an exact science. I once did my out of body travel to see if my buddy Gary was home, he was on the sofa watching soccer. I grabbed my coat and set off walking the 30 minutes to get there. His mom answered the door. When I asked if Gary was home, she said no, you've just missed him, he's been watching TV all morning. He'd gone to Steve's and then was going to my place. I had to be quick to catch him up.

I guess the easiest way was to phone him yet the phone in the hallway in my apartment block was broken most of the time.
This out of body travel was difficult to talk about to friends. I tried various methods of hinting and bringing up the subject as though I'd just read about it, or from a third-party source. From all the people I spoke with no-one had any experience of it. The complete opposite. I'd receive comments like." Whatever you read is science fiction and all made up" or I'd get a response like, "Are you out of your mind."
It was time to seek advice from my guide, Ort. There was much more to this out of body travel. I was using it as a simplistic tool.

That evening, I went to bed, I relaxed held out my hand asked Ort for more information I said "I cannot find anyone else to explain this to me and I know there must be much more information and knowledge about this so can you please show me." Ort came he took hold of my hand I left my body. I looked down and clearly saw myself asleep. We left through the window which was closed and I was on the third floor. We flew around the neighborhood and back in through the window I looked down and my body was still asleep I went back into my body. Ort had not shown me anything different. I needed more. I still didn't really know if I was dreaming, lucid dreaming, or was it real.

The following evening, I decided to seek out Ort again. Ort came and took hold of my hand. I looked down and could see my body asleep. We left through the window and this time we flew to Leeds City town center. I recognized the buildings the town hall the hospital the university where I worked. We flew back into my apartment through the window I could see my body asleep and I re-entered it. The following morning, I was still not certain what was happening. I enjoyed travelling with a companion, especially Ort why were we taking baby steps.

Still not convinced, I needed more. The third evening I asked to see Ort again. Once again Ort came, he took my hand. Before we left I asked Ort I said "I am still not sure whether I am dreaming sleep walking, I am concerned about leaving through the window as we are three stories up and it is a concrete pavement below so can we go out through the roof. Ort Laughed. That night and all subsequent travels we were to exit out through the roof.

We travelled much further, I saw earth, our little blue planet from afar expanding my knowledge. I was beginning to understand.

On one occasion Ort came to me and said he was going to take me somewhere special tonight would I be prepared to go with him. I said I would. We left in the usual manner through the roof. On this occasion we just kept going up. I could see the blue earth, but this time getting smaller and smaller until it disappeared. I then believe we travelled into a higher dimension. Eventually there was a line of about thirty people. At the front of the line was my deceased father he was stood tall, as tall as me he was six feet in height although I had never seen him standing before as he was in a wheel chair from when I was born. I was greeted with open arms and the feeling of love from the group was tremendous. My father said he was going to introduce me to my family members going back over three hundred years. We started down the line the first fifteen appeared to have a physical body and we spoke telepathically again the feeling of love was tremendous. As I moved down the line about half way I did not see a physical form. I saw an orb, a pure conscious energy orb, yellow/orange in color slightly vibrating. I could still communicate with them and they would show me their last physical body.

I would continue to visit this group with Ort until I became confident to visit them on my own. I did this for a couple of years. This experience was very enlightening and a major development for me. Eventually, after about two years of visiting them, I was finding it difficult to get back into my body. It was time I stopped. I should let them know. That evening, I went to visit as usual I was welcomed with open arms and the tremendous feeling of love. I explained I would not be coming back to visit because of the difficulty of getting back into my body. They tried to persuade me to stay. I told them that I couldn't and that I felt there would come a time I would not be able to engage my physical and if that were to happen, I would die, I was enjoying my physical and I knew that they would still be here when my physical does expire. I have not been back to visit since that date but I know they are there and that I will be welcomed when it's my time. As yet it is not my time.

These experiences show me that our consciousness continues to live on after our physical dies. I would say that consciousness is the true- life form of the universe. It exists in everything, in the plants, animals, rocks the earth itself, all exists as a shared consciousness which includes all life in the universe to include our extraterrestrial family. I think I was shown the deceased members of my family to demonstrate that our consciousness continues after our physical death. This was an important step for me at the time.
Communication after death.

Uncle Alex was a single man, never married and he lived in our family home all his life. He was alone when my grandparents passed, although he would visit his sister, my mom and us quite frequently. Uncle Alex was very fond of my wife Sandy his visits became more frequent, then we found out he was sick, how sick we didn't know. He invited us to his bi-annual club event and on the second trip we knew he was getting thinner. He was always a portly man with a round chubby face. Sandy finally persuaded him to tell us what was wrong and finally we were in communication with his doctor, with his permission, of course. Cancer was the diagnosis, as we suspected.

On his last visit to our home, he was very frail and weak. I asked him to stay with us but he was adamant that he went home. I drove him back to his home in Liverpool. I informed his friends and neighbors who were aware of his cancer, and that he did not have long in this world.

A couple of days later he passed. Always sad when someone passes even though I know their consciousness continues to live on. The funeral was arranged, and the church was packed with all his friends. He was very popular and organized many events to the various clubs and associations he belonged to.

Uncle Alex smoked a pipe with St Bruno tobacco, I must admit I did like the smell of the tobacco even though neither Sandy nor I were smokers. When he visited us it always took a couple of weeks for the tobacco smell to totally dissipate. A couple of weeks after his passing I felt a change in the vibrational frequency in our home, accompanied with a strong smell of St Bruno tobacco. It was Alex. I did not inform Sandy, as it was only a few weeks after his passing and she was still upset. She was not aware of his presence, until the following day Sandy said to me you are not going to believe this but I can smell St Bruno tobacco. I explained it was Alex he was visiting us once again. I was surprised that she sensed his tobacco, he clearly wanted her to know he was here.

Alex was in our home all the time, although Sandy didn't always sense it. I asked him why he was still here he said he did not like dying alone. I explained that he had the option to stay with us and that he had declined. Alex eventually became a nuisance in our home, he was there all the time. I could not discourage him; I had to be harsh so I actually banned him from the home. He did not visit again in that particular home in the U.K. However, approximately thirty years later, Sandy and I were now living in Florida in the U.S. I was reflecting on our lives together and the memory of Alex came back to me, and of how I had banned him from the home all those years ago. So I said out loud to Alex that I was sorry for banning him and he was welcome to visit any time as long as he did not become a nuisance. There was no immediate communication until a couple of days later. Sandy had gone to bed, I was watching the late -night news, there was a strong smell of St Bruno tobacco Alex was back after all these years. I asked how he was, again I said he was welcome anytime as long as he does not become a nuisance. He did complain again about dying alone, that did surprise me after all those years had passed. I did not tell Sandy about his recent visit, it didn't seem important. A couple of days later, Sandy was in the kitchen cooking, I was watching the TV. Sandy said to me you are not going to believe this but I can smell St Bruno tobacco and I feel someone is stood next to me. He did not communicate with Sandy directly other than the smell of tobacco and a presence stood next to her. I explained to Sandy that I had recently felt guilty about banning Alex from our home all those years ago in the U.K. I think Alex is now at peace with himself. He has not been back since but he knows he is welcome anytime.

I share these experiences with you as examples of consciousness being used as a modality of communication. I have no evidence of any of my experiences but this particular experience was shared with my wife Sandy. What I do find interesting is how we can still contact our deceased family members and even go and visit them at the higher level of consciousness where they exist. I am sure many of our scientists are now accepting consciousness plays a much larger part of who we are and I am sure they are moving towards an understanding of this Phenomena. This is not new to many of us, but it is a new discipline for our scientists.

My understanding of both encounters I have described are that consciousness is the conduit used for communication. We are all connected to all living physical life, not only in this dimension but other dimensions. Consciousness is inter-dimensional. We are also connected to what we perceive as deceased relatives. When we accept this, it will help in our development and evolution. It is important that many more of our scientist understand this and use consciousness as a tool to further not only their own knowledge but our collective knowledge as a species.

The higher conscious beings that I interact with are open to sharing information, they want us to learn, I just have to ask the right questions. Telepathy is this modality. This is how I communicate with the higher conscious beings. The mind is a powerful part of our body and I believe we all have these abilities we are just not taught how to use them. Telepathy is one of the modalities of contact that has taken me a long time to learn and indeed accept this. As an experiencer I question my own belief systems, as all these modalities are outside of our understanding. It is like any new skill or discipline; it takes patience and guidance.

My guides have been with me since I was eight years old and they have been educating me in a very different way. It was difficult at first to understand, yet I opened my mind and progressed quite rapidly. My guides Ort and Dee are higher conscious beings and they have given me my experiences to develop. Thought is conscious energy every time we have a thought; we are accessing consciousness which in turn is connected to the Universe which is also conscious.

Where does the thought come from when we have a thought? Is it our own individual thought privy to that one person? I would say not.my experience a few months ago may explain this. I was sat watching TV, it was about 10pm. A thought just popped into my head. Had I locked my chickens away for the evening. We have a few chickens and they have to be locked away in the evening so predators can't get to them. Where did that thought come from? Was it my thought? At this point in the experience, I would have to say yes. However, I decided to go and check my chickens. I walk out the back door and as I do so the street light opposite goes out. Not unusual in itself, I then walk through my gate to the chicken coop, it is secure. Then the second street light behind the coop goes out. Too much of a coincidence. I stand for a second and I begin looking up, at the same time a thought popped in my head about a craft. I gaze to my right and there it was a triangular craft, not very high up perhaps a couple of thousand feet. It was lit up like a Christmas tree with red strobe lights wrapped all around. They would go off and white strobe lights would come on. It was moving slowly; it passed right over my head silently and disappeared in the distance. Back to my first thought about my chickens being secure. Was that my thought, or was it given to me at that precise moment so I would see the craft. I believe this modality is an example of telepathic communication. there is often a synchronicity involved with telepathic communication. The second modality is electrical interface or interference, the street lights. The third modality was the craft. These three are prime examples.

We have close friends from the UK that visit us at least every year. He is an ex-colleague of mine. He has been a complete skeptic all his life in relation to higher conscious beings, the spirit world, ETs and UFO's, pretty much anything "out of the ordinary". It was early evening, still plenty of daylight left and the four of us were relaxing, having drinks sat by our pool, deciding on a place to have dinner. I went inside to freshen our drinks and I thought this would be a good time for a craft to appear. Within a few minutes on my return a craft appeared to the right of us as though on demand. The four of us saw it, just above the tree line. It was stationary for a second then at high speed moved to the left and stopped again. It was dead center of us. A second or so later it moved further to the left at high speed and stopped for another second then went vertical out of sight. On the last movement Sandy said wow did you see that.

My friend was motionless, gazing he did not believe his eyes. He was quiet for a moment and then we all started looking at one another, then began all talking at the same time. We all saw and witnessed the same thing. For Sandy and I this was not an unusual occurrence, especially for me. That moment has changed my friends' life forever. He is so open minded now.

The "thought" that I had about a craft appearing when I went to freshen our drinks. I wanted a craft to appear. Was it a coincidence? I think not. Another example of telepathic communication of which I have many. The second modality was the craft.

Later during the third week of their stay there was a full red moon, a blood red moon. It had just come up over the horizon at the front of our home. My friends' wife had her i-pad ready to take photos. We were all stood or sat on our front porch looking at the sky to observe the moon. A number of photos were taken. I brought out my telescope and we all looked at the moon, it was an awesome sight so clear and with depth. Afterwards we all ventured back inside. As I was putting away my telescope my friends' wife shouted us to take a look at the photos she'd taken. Three of the photos had five or six large orbs in front of the moon. The presence of these orbs stimulates further discussion with my skeptic friend, further opening his mind to other realms and possibilities. What were these orbs. We didn't see them with the naked eye, yet they show up on the photos. The camera can pick them up but sometimes our eyes cannot. My understanding of these orbs is that they are higher conscious beings opening a portal to observe and communicate with us using conscious energy.

Let me take you back in time. I was about 32 years old, and a police officer in the U.K. I had just finished a quick change over shift where you work until 10pm and then you are back on duty at 6am the next morning. Which really means 11.00pm in bed at the earliest and up at 5.00am latest. Sleep seems to be elusive. When I had completed this shift change, I was usually very tired and would get home about 2-45pm earliest. I would tend to the dogs and then go to bed for a couple of hours until my wife came home from work.

On this occasion I got into bed and before I closed my eyes a shadow person came through the closed door. They are small in stature almost elf like in their appearance. I have seen these shadow people many times throughout my life. It was explained to me that they live between dimensions, they are sometimes used as a precursor to contact. Normally I would see them out of the corner of my eye. They would be elusive, darting behind furniture, mischievous in nature. This time was different he looked directly at me and beckoned me, most unusual. I told him I was tired so go away and come back later. He went back through the closed door and a minute later he came in again beckoned me as if he wanted to show me something. I told him no, I was not interested come back another time. He left again through the closed door. The third time he comes back again, he was persistent and he beckoned me again. I relented and said ok you have gone to all this trouble let's see what you want to show me. The shadow person left through the closed door

I got out of bed opened, the door and in the hallway was a beam of light from the floor to the ceiling. The beam resembled the beam of the teleporter of the first star trek series The shadow person got me here for a reason so I stepped into the beam of light. I immediately had a feeling of euphoria, just total euphoria, I was then contacted telepathically. The message was I am your father you are your father's son. There was no other communication. A few moments later the beam disappeared equally from the floor and ceiling at the same rate and dissipated in my stomach area. I felt energized and still euphoric. I was no longer tired I got dressed and went about my day. When Sandy came home, I informed her about the incident and that evening we went out for a meal. This was highly unusual after this type of shift change. I was always so exhausted that watching TV sent me to sleep. I had so much energy. Sandy commented and she was very surprised that I wanted to go out for a meal.

I was trying to figure out the meaning of the quotation that I was given. Initially I thought it was my deceased father trying to communicate. It was not. It was a higher conscious being, one who leads a group of other beings. There are eight in total. I have communicated with them before and will do so periodically through the years. At this time my instinct tells me that this group is important and will become more prominent in years to come.

The modalities within this experience are physical materialization, this would be the shadow people. Telepathic communication which was the quotation. The beam of light is not easily defined yet that could be conscious energy.

Astral travel is a form of out of body experience (OBE). I am able to separate my consciousness from my physical, when separated I am no longer bound by the physical realms and our laws of physics as we understand them.

Let me share an experience of astral travel. I have been using astral travel all my life just for entertainment. There are no limits or boundaries as to where to go. Only your thoughts limit you. I am using two forms of energy the first being thought itself then conscious energy. I usually use astral travel when I go to bed of an evening. I'm more relaxed and its quiet but the astral plane can be accessed any time using the same method. I relax open my mind then I look inward. I keep looking inward, I have a feeling of traveling inside myself. I then see an opening like an eye. I then change direction and move forward towards the eye and travel through it. When through the eye the image changes, like a myriad of stars. This is the astral plane. My personal understanding is that I have reached a higher level of consciousness and it gives me access as long as I keep my brain activity at the higher frequency. I am able to continue my travels.

I was informed by my ET guides that the astral plane is between dimensions. It is also used as a conduit for travel and communication. On this occasion I was just enjoying the freedom without the encumbrance of a physical body.

A craft came along side me, there were two beings on board Ort and Dee, my guides. I was asked on board with telepathic communication. As I entered the craft I could feel the skin; it was conscious. Ort and Dee appeared as pure conscious energy orbs yellow/orange in color slightly vibrating. After pleasantries Ort said, "We would like you to convey a message to someone for us." I said, "Yes, that would be fine." The message was for a particular person. I had actually heard of him, but did not know him. The message was simple. He had to change his Itinerary for a specific date as he was in some danger. He was not to inform anyone of this change. I agreed it was a simple message to convey, I left the craft, and then I realized that the intended person was sure to ask who was the message from. I asked to return to the craft as I had a question. I went back on board feeling the conscious skin again. I asked who should I say the message is from.

Ort said, "Tell him it is from the light beings." I thought that was strange, I had never heard that term before. I thought they would have said Ort and Dee. I left the craft and headed home back to my physical body. I arrived back in my physical and woke up. I wrote the message down so I would not forget. I went back to bed and fell asleep. I awoke in the morning remembering my travel on the astral plane and the message. I looked at the written message and I thought I'm not going to do that. I screwed up the piece of paper and threw it in the trash.

How could I explain to a person who I do not know, that whilst travelling on the astral plane I came across two light beings named Ort and Dee and they gave me a message for you. He would think I was delusional at best, if not a lunatic. As far as I was concerned that was the end of the matter.

The follow evening, I was not traveling on the astral plane. I had just gone to bed and was in a deep sleep. Ort and Dee appeared in a dream., They told me that it was important that I conveyed the message, if I didn't then this person would die on that day.

I woke up the following morning and couldn't get the dream out of my head. I had a dilemma. There was no-one I could ask for advice. I pondered about it for a couple of days. I came to a decision that I would convey the message. If I conveyed the message, and he thought I was delusional, I could live with that. I do not know this person; I have never met him and probably never will. However, if he died on that day, I would never forgive myself.

The next step how do I contact him. My guides would help, they do when I ask. My telepathic communication worked and they assisted me. I sat at my computer then the information would present itself to me. The search engine brought up many videos and information dedicated to this man. The first video at the top was of him addressing a group of people. The person sat next to him was someone that I knew of. I had never spoken with him however he was an ex-police officer from the UK that I recognized. He was going to be my conduit. I did some research and finally got his email address. I contacted this person and told him of the experience of how I received the message and who it was from. I did not mention that he would die if he did not comply with the message, I said he was in some danger which was the original message. The message was conveyed and I did receive an email via the third person thanking me for the message and that he would take it under consideration. He also emailed a photo he had taken of a light being when he had been out doing a sky watch.

I felt relief that a huge weight had been lifted from my shoulders. It had been a difficult decision for me. I asked Ort and Dee why they had given me such a difficult task They said they wanted to see if I would convey messages. Thankfully, the person in question continues to do his work although I have not had any communication with him. Let's look at the modalities on contact in this experience. We have out of body experience (OBE) which is traveling on the astral plane, Ort and Dee as pure conscious orbs that is telepathic communication, the craft, this was consciousness itself and in this instance was used as a conduit for telepathic communication, travel and creation itself. Finally, dreams. Ort and Dee came to me the second time in a dream. So many modalities were used.

I meet Ort and Dee on the astral plane frequently where we share our time together. I always enjoy my interactions with them. It's like visiting family. We are on the astral plane and I merge into their conscious craft. I always have questions when we meet. On this occasion I need to clarify my understanding of how we communicate with one another. I said to Ort am I correct in assuming that we are travelling on the astral plane which is between dimensions, and we are in a conscious craft as three beings two from the fifth dimension and one from the third dimension. I see both of you as two pure conscious energy orbs. Is that how you see me., Ort replied, "Yes that is correct. You can travel further he said. I said "That's OK for you as you have a conscious craft and it's better travelling with a companion rather than alone". Ort said, "Why don't you build your own craft." I laughed and said," How would I go about doing that". He replied," By using thought and consciousness, two forms of energy you already use and are comfortable with". I said," OK, I will try and see what happens". I left their craft and went back to my physical body. When I woke the following morning, I was excited yet a little apprehensive to try and push my boundaries further to create a craft.

That evening, I lay awake on my bed. I relaxed, opened my mind and thought of a craft. I saw the craft in my mind's eye. I then accessed the craft, it was round in shape, it was conscious in nature with a window at the front. I set off in no particular direction but I looked out of the window. I was travelling fast, faster than I thought possible. I could see what looked like stars flying past at great speed. Then I realized they were not stars they were galaxies flying past. At this point I became fearful, I did not know where I was going, I had no plan, no navigation, could I get back. I quickly severed the thought and I was back in my body. It clearly worked, but I needed to plan better and I needed a navigation system, a preplan of where I would like to travel too.

The following evening, I decided to try again. I was awake and relaxed, I opened my mind and thought of building a conscious craft. This time I would make it a little bigger with a larger window. A navigation system with a thought interface. I needed a point of reference for the navigation. Earlier I had checked the star systems and decided to travel to Andromeda. An easy choice as this was where my life long guides Ort and Dee came from Andromeda.

I am successful with my craft and it is more comfortable, slightly larger, with a larger window. If indeed it is a window. The navigation system was state of the art with a thought conscious interface. My destination was in place, it was time to go. I felt amazed that this was actually working. This was something I would not have thought of on my own. Again, more help from Ort and Dee. I reached my destination. There is no movement as such, no sense of time. I came to a light blue planet about the size of our earth. It was surrounded by clouds. I could not see any land and did not venture into the cloud base. I circled the planet and headed back the way I came. The navigation system worked well with the thought interface. When I was orbiting the planet, I wondered if it was inhabited like our planet and if so how would the beings see me. Would they see me as a UFO, if they could actually see me at all. More questions.

Is there no end to what we can achieve when we leave the constraints of our physical body. I must admit I was surprised when I was able to achieve this.

Throughout my years as an experiencer, I have been fortunate to have made contact with other higher conscious beings. Although my contact with some of the group of eight has been infrequent they are very significant in my life. This is one of those times where I feel I need their presence, at least to make contact, it's been way too long since I've heard from any of them. Now that I have my craft, perhaps I can travel further and faster to find them. I started to make my plans. I would start with Andromeda, a reference point which is familiar to me. I created the craft in the usual manner using thought and consciousness. It seemed to take no time at all. I was at the same location near Andromeda as I had been on other occasions. There was no sign of any of them. I travelled further to other galaxies looking for them I had no success at all. Had they abandoned me? I suddenly felt alone. I know I had Ort and Dee yet my other beings were also important to me. The feeling of desperation came over me. I had come so far with their guidance why were they not communicating with me. It was time to return home to the third dimension. I arrive home and enter my physical. I woke up feeling tired and disappointed. Suddenly all eight appeared in my bedroom looking down at me. There was also a huge craft in my bedroom. I told them that I had been looking for them. They said, "We know, that's why we are here.". I then asked how can all eight of you appear in my bedroom with this craft. They proceeded to explain about Space, Time and Dimension. I did not understand the explanation.

What was interesting was that the huge craft was very similar as the one shown in the movie Close Encounters of the Third Kind. I was relieved and pleased that they had not abandoned me, even though I still did not understand how they could all be in my bedroom at the same time.

Many modalities here. Travel, OBE, creation, conscious thought used for navigation.

Let's explore this with the different contact modalities. Having just written this it sounds like a science fiction novel and if it was not for my life long interaction with Non-Human intelligences, Higher Conscious Beings, Extraterrestrial Beings, Spirit Guides whatever label you are comfortable with. I would not believe it myself.

I cannot explain this I can only share the information I have been given. I am told we live in a Holographic universe, our reality is created by our thought and consciousness, and we are only limited by our thoughts. This last experience would support this. Is it any wonder we as experiencers do not talk about our experiences? I do find it fascinating that Rey Hernandez has had experiences that go far beyond our knowledge of space, Time and dimension. There are many of us that have been asked to speak out. I do find it quite comforting that when you meet a fellow experiencer, we have all been given similar knowledge.

The download modality is relatively new me. There is little to experience. This method happens so fast, its mind blowing. It usually comes in a large amount of data or information that it instantly enters the brain. A split second. The download is very often of a subject matter totally unknown to the experiencer. This is how it is on the occasions that it has happened to me.

On this occasion Sandy and I had just finished our evening meal outside in the lanai. We had both cleared the table and Sandy was busy stacking the dishwasher. I went back outside to watch the sun setting. In an instant I was given some information on the Quantum Unified Field Theory. The information is retained and amazingly enough can be recalled verbatim.

> *Quantum Unified Field Theory is correct as your scientists understand it. There are the four interactions, the weak force, the strong force the electromagnetic force and the gravitational force. There is a fifth interaction that your scientists do not include and that is consciousness itself. If your scientists include consciousness, they will have a better understanding of their own Quantum Unified Field Theory.*

If it wasn't for my life long interactions, I would probably not accept the information and just think it was my mind playing tricks. However, I asked for confirmation on what I'd just received I said telepathically if you are downloading this information can you show me a craft as confirmation. A craft appeared immediately, beyond the trees and moving east. I went inside and shouted for Sandy to come and take a look. We both stood to the left of the pool deck. There wasn't just one but SEVEN craft all moving slowly and silently eastwards over the lake. After they had almost got out of sight they changed direction and disappeared sequentially as they had appeared. I went into my home office and wrote the information down as I had received it.

On another occasion, it was mid- afternoon and I had just finished some paperwork. I grabbed a cup of coffee that I'd made at lunchtime and sat under the lanai. I received a download. It was about The Theory of Everything. I had heard of it but not something I was familiar with.

Your Theory of everything is correct however, there is a measurement problem within the calculations. Your scientists understanding of non-locality, duality and entanglement are correct yet if they include 'C'-Consciousness as a constant in their equations it will solve the measurement problem. The measurement problem relates to space, time, dimension. They went on to say that your scientists understanding of non-locality, duality and entanglement is correct. However, the entanglement has to include the entanglement of consciousness in a non-local duality, this explains at a quantum level how you are able to be in two places at once and how you use consciousness for communication, travel and creation.

In a separate download they went on to say that:

Consciousness exists at a quantum level between sub atomic particles. Conscious energy exists in all matter at this level as light. It has its own duality of wave and particle, this is how our Holographic Universe exists as a projection using thought (energy) conscious energy, and our brain as the receivers and translators of the energy that we see using our senses again all achieved at a quantum level in our brains.

The following information and equation came to me as a download. I wrote it down immediately as it came to me. I am not scientist, yet I feel it necessary to share it

Spiritual Consciousness
A broader perspective
Holographic Universe
Projection by consciousness itself, symbiotic evolution.
Pure energy
Already been shown matrix which holds/binds all together

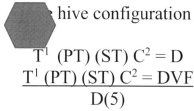 hive configuration

$$T^1 \ (PT) \ (ST) \ C^2 = D$$
$$\frac{T^1 \ (PT) \ (ST) \ C^2 = DVF}{D(5)}$$

T = Thought. PT = Present Time. ST = Space Time C = Consciousness. D = Dimension and DVF = Dimension, Vibration, Frequency D(5) = 5th Dimension.

Date of download 11/23/2016

I am not a scientist and the only way forward is for me to share the information with others.

I asked for confirmation of this by asking them to show me a craft. One appeared immediately outside of the pool area to the west, it flashed three times then disappeared.

Let me share an experience of another type of download. My guides asked me to go to a MUFON Conference which was being held in Orlando. I was not certain why they had asked me to go but I bought a ticket and attended on the Sunday. I was surprised at the amount of people in attendance. The speakers were varied but all very interesting. I met a Canadian who was a fellow experiencer he was an engineer and his interest was on ET propulsion systems he asked me if I knew anything about them. I did not but I said I would ask my ET guides. The following day at home, I sat at my computer and asked about their antigravity propulsion system. Almost immediately I was shown a visual representation and given an explanation of how they worked. Each propulsion system was encased in a sphere. The sphere was filled with Mercury. Inside the sphere was a copper filament not unlike our own electric motor with tightly spiraled copper wire. Which was central with a moving filament spinning in the sphere near the inside casing. As this spun it created an antigravity effect. It created its own electromagnetic field which then used our earth's magnetic field like two opposing magnets. Although it was electromagnetic energy. These spheres could then be used singularly as in a small craft also in various configurations

Depending on the size of the craft they could also be placed in a line this accounts for the sightings of the cigar shaped craft. Within the craft the gravity was negated so there was no inertia felt by the occupants. I was also informed the reason why we see a glow with this particular propulsion system was that the electrons in the atmosphere surrounding the craft become excited and glow.

My Wife Sandy although not a lifelong experiencer, over the past few years my ET guides have included her with some of her own experiences. They are all very interesting however, one in particular was quite interesting as it gave both of us confirmation of their interaction with us. Our usual morning routine is that Sandy gets up first, takes the dogs out then prepares their breakfast. Once they are eating the coffee is brewing and the tea kettle is on. She makes her tea and sits outside with the dogs. Shortly I rise, shower and dress ready for the day. Coffee is beckoning and I join Sandy. On this particular morning, I was later than usual, it was around 8-30am. I seemed compelled to make contact with my guides. I relax open my mind and use consciousness as my conduit for communication. I was unable to make contact with them but at that moment I connected with a small group of greys they were close by. They were in a small craft. My image was of five or six within the craft, flying the craft was a small grey I know as Teah. He is a pilot and a technician; he maintains the crafts and transports different groups. I asked him what he was doing here. He said that he was close by and wanted to see where I lived. We had some other brief conversation and Teah said they would have to leave now as they had deviated off their assigned course. I quickly dressed and grabbed my coffee and joined Sandy on the pool deck. Sandy greeted me with a sarcastic good afternoon. I smiled. She then said that I'd missed the most beautiful rainbow. I said did you get a photo she said she had taken a few. She then said that you're not going to believe what else I saw, a craft and she pointed to where it had been. She said it was only there for a few seconds but I got a photo. We have five acres and the rainbow went from one fence to the other touching the ground some five hundred feet at the rear of our home. No rear neighbors, open land and in the distance a tree line.

She described the UFO as a metallic disc shaped craft darkish grey in color about fifty feet in diameter. Sandy was taking a photo of the rainbow when it appeared right in front of her eyes she clicked and got the photo. It is slightly distorted yet clear enough to see it was a craft. I suspect it was moving off at speed or uncloaked just at the right time for the photo. I do not believe in coincidences. The most interesting thing was that the time on the photo was 8-30am. This was the time that I was communicating with Teah.

This modality would be telepathic communication between myself and Teah. Sandy's photo and experience confirms this. My wife Sandy has had other interactions, sometimes items in the home have been moved, obvious items. She called me one day to take a look in our closet, which I did. She pointed to the floor and I laughed. She blamed me for moving her shoes. I denied it. Her shoes were all lined up neatly all facing the same way and just touching the baseboard. Her shoes are NEVER like that.

On other occasion my wife would close the blinds in the dining room only to walk away and when she turned around, they were open again. If Sandy was to set the table, she would always do the place setting the same way every time. On a couple of occasions when she had done this when she returned to the table the cutlery and napkins were disarranged in a way that she would never do.

I asked Zark, one of the ETs if he was responsible for the items being moved. I suspected Zark as he has a good sense of humor. He admitted that it was him. I asked him why he did this. He told me that he liked teasing her, he thought it was funny. However, there is a serious side to this. It was a way to communicate with her, to let her know that we are here, and it is a way of confirming that are amongst. One evening I attended a group meeting which I thought would be a good venue to promote my book. I was going to give a copy to the organizer yet she was always occupied. I spoke with another attendee who happened to know the organizer I asked her if she would pass my book onto her when she was free. She agreed. We continued our conversation. Time had flown and I had to leave. I gave her my book and then I left the meeting. She felt compelled to open the book near the back. There was a sketch of Ort and Dee. She was taken by surprise as she knew them. We would become good friends.

She invited Sandy and I and another couple, who I knew, for dinner the following Saturday She asked me to bring my journal. The four of us went in my vehicle and drove south to meet with our hosts. Introductions were made and she and her husband made us very welcome. After our dinner the hostess immediately got her journals out and I with mine, the two of us were instantly deep in conversation on many mutual topics and experiences. We spoke about consciousness, guides, crafts and much more. I showed her my original sketches that I'd drawn of my guides Ort and Dee. She has met them numerous times. She had the female as D as in the letter and not Dee as I have. We were both excited and couldn't stop talking about our encounters. I'm sure that our first meeting was not by chance. It was meant to be.

More recently, since my book was published, I have been fortunate in attending conferences and meeting so many different people from all kinds of backgrounds and professions. Subsequently I have also given talks on radio shows. I do not have a personal agenda for personal gain, financial or otherwise. I see my role as talking to as many people as possible about my experiences. Communicating with people who also have very similar experiences as I. People who are apprehensive and require reassurance that they are not alone. Other experiencers even have contact with the same beings that I do. These are not coincidences. These are connections that are meant to happen, threads that join us together, like destiny.

In July 2019 I was a speaker at a conference. It was Consciousness and Contact. The conference was held at the All Nations Gathering Center in Pine Ridge, South Dakota. The conference was a huge success, for me in particular. The small group of delegates made this conference more intimate. Speakers and attendees from all walks of life. All providing their own personal insights at this very special place. Home of Sitting, Bull, Crazy Horse, Lakota Spirituality, Wounded Knee and much more. Speakers research on ET hybrids, on development on healing techniques, ET consciousness, Lakota Sioux spirituality, meditation, ET contact and abductees and more. A wonderful event.

There were regular UFO sightings and we could always mix fun and humor whilst sharing our experiences. One of these sightings lasted one hour and twenty minutes. Unbeknown to the delegates lies a prophecy that was fulfilled during the weekend.

The prophecy was from a Brazilian mystic, Chico Xavier. He stated on the 20th July 1969 if we had not entered into a third world war in fifty years by 20th July, 2019 we would be in for a long period of peace and there would be many sightings of UFOs throughout the world, and later a global physical interaction with our species by the ETs.

It is February 1st 2019 I was woken up by the sound of a loud humming noise, it seemed very close. There was a craft above my home. Craft are mostly silent, why this noise. I glanced at the clock the time was 111am. There is a synchronicity here. The date is the first and the time,111am. I received a telepathic message that they would like to reveal themselves to our governments' representatives at our United Nations in New York. They didn't give me anymore specifics as that would be relayed to me later. I repeated the information back to them and that I would like confirmation. I went into my bathroom and asked them to turn off the street light opposite. They did so immediately. That was good enough for me I had the synchronicity at the front end of the message and confirmation with the street light going off as confirmation at the back end of the message.

I went back to bed and fell asleep. I was woken abruptly at about 7-45am. By someone jumping on the bed, this happened twice in succession. My immediate thought was that Sandy had let the dogs in to wake me up. No dogs, No Sandy. Within a second another message entered my head. The reveal would be February 1st 2020, the craft would appear over the United Nations in New York at 06-39am landing at 06-41am. I asked them what was the importance of that date. Their reply was that the REAL importance is the 2nd February as this was to be THE FIRST DAWN OF A NEW HUMANITY. I repeated the message back and required confirmation. This time the street light opposite the bathroom was off as it was daylight, I asked them to turn the street light on as confirmation, they did so immediately.

The Reveal is dependent on a protocol being implemented for the United Nations to receive the ET's. I know there are many individuals and groups working towards this. They have tried before and failed. My understanding is that a Stanley Fulham, a Captain in the Royal Canadian Air Force, was given similar information. His prediction of UFO's over New York City on October 13th, 2010 attracted international media attention when unidentified objects did appear and was witnessed by thousands in New York City. Another of his predictions was that UFOs will appear more frequently in 2011 culminating in a face-to-face encounter between extraterrestrials and major world leaders at the United Nations. Sadly, he passed in December 2010.

In December 2017I was asked by my group of eight ETs to contact the United Nations to see if there was a protocol in place to receive them. I contacted the office of Niklas Hedman, Chief of Committee, Policy and Legal Affairs Section (CPLA) of the United Nations Office for Outer Space Affairs (UNOOSA). Mr. Hedman serves as Secretary of the Committee on the Peaceful Uses of Outer Space (COPUOS) and its Scientific and technical subcommittee and legal subcommittee. I did receive a reply from his office stating that there was no protocol in place at this time to receive advanced Extraterrestrial should they wish to contact the United Nations. I then followed up and asked how would such a protocol be implemented. The reply from his office was that a member state would have to make a Mandate proposal to that effect.

In light of this information, I contacted the office of Nikki Haley. At the time she was the United States Ambassador to the United Nations. I asked if she would consider a Proposal Mandate should Extraterrestrial wish to communicate with the U.N. I did not receive a reply.

I thought that would be the end of it, however a few weeks later I was contacted by the lead council of the eight ETs. I have had contact with him before, he is a formidable character. His name is Rah, he asked if I would contact our President asking him to follow up with the Ambassador Nikki Haley. This was not an easy task to contact the President of the United States. I was reticent to do this but I wrote a letter and mailed a certified mail to the president on July 29th 2018 I remember the date as it was my wife's birthday. Unfortunately, I did not receive a reply.

The ET council of eight needed this message to spread to other people who could completely understand it's importance. The Reveal had to spread. Most were members of certain established organizations. On February 27th, 2019 I began making some enquiries and the most appropriate method of contact. Individual names have been omitted to protect their privacy. However, some of the organizations are listed below: I contacted. The Disclosure Group, The Rahma Group from Peru, MUFON, The Exoconcious Group. The FREE Organization, The WCETC, World Coalition for Extraterrestrial Contact group. There are a couple of individuals who are not affiliated with any of the above. I emailed eight people informing them of the location, date and time of the reveal.as I had received it from the ET council of eight.

CONFIRMATIONS: Within thirty minutes after the emails were sent my phone rang, I checked the name and it was my friend, one of the recipients I just emailed. I assumed she wanted to talk about it. After pleasantries I said, "I guess you've seen my email". No, she said," I have just received a telepathic message. She said it was a very strong energy and that I was to contact you immediately, and to listen to what you had to say, so that's what I'm doing.

I sensed it was Rah, only he has very strong energy when communicating. She had not yet seen the email. I proceeded to tell her what I'd written in the email. This is confirmation that this individual is in contact with one or more of the ET council of eight.

One of my experiencer friends, and a recipient of my email, has been in communication with my ET guides Ort and Dee ("D") for many years. She may have had contact with other members of the ET council of eight. However, Ort and Dee are special to both of us and this is confirmation.

Another one of the recipients of the email was the person who I had to convey a message to many years ago. I was in a dilemma at the time until I realized his life may be in peril. He had sent me a photo of the "light beings" which he had taken on one of his many field trips. The light beings are of Ort and Dee, which are two members of the ET council of eight. Another confirmation that this individual has a connection to the ET council of eight.

Another quick response to my email came in from a lady I met in Orlando when I was giving a presentation to a small group that meet monthly. She was often invited to these meetings but had never attended until now. Her ET connection told her to attend on this particular day. Later during the break, we talked. She spoke of her interaction with her ETs she said she was able to see their conscious energy and emotions when she spoke with them. I had not heard of anyone speak of this before. I am able to do the same with my ET connections. This really got my attention. Later we became friends and shared many experiences. Her name was on the list to email about the reveal. My friend, researcher and author was also a recipient. She recently had a book published and I together with the ET council of eight was mentioned in her book. This is also confirmation that she has and is in contact with the ET council of eight. I know that she connects with Zark.

Unfortunately, my email to one of the groups did not find its way to someone who would respond. What I did find interesting was a thread, a thread that led me to understand that I did receive confirmation. I was on a short vacation in New York. I was reading a post on the Contact Modalities, it was about dreams and a dream that appeared to be common among experiencers. It was about a large number of craft appearing simultaneously over some of our larger cities. I have had this dream three times during my life time. I know that when I wake up I am disappointed that it was only a dream, but as dreams are part of the modality of contacts and others have had the same dream, there may be some synchronicity and commonality. When I had finished the reading and responding to the article. I turned off my phone and was immediately drawn to look out of the hotel window. We were on the 24th floor and I could see Central Park between two large skyscrapers. At that moment about fifteen craft appeared. I saw them quite clearly, they moved in a certain pattern, disappeared and reappeared. I had seen this formation before at the rear of my home. It only lasted a few moments, yet it was very clear. I understand this to be confirmation. This person has written so many articles on contact and modality and we have been in communication on similar work. I will research further and decide as to whether he is the individual I need to send details.

The following day Sandy and I decided to take a walk to see the United Nations. Perhaps the UFO's the previous evening was a precursor to what we can expect. I am confident that already out of my eight recipients, six have been confirmed. As I move forward describing my experiences there is a pattern of the contact modalities. In these last few paragraphs, we have seen telepathic communication, craft appearing, we have mentioned the dream of multiple craft appearing over our lager cities.

We as individuals are unimportant, we are each a small piece in a very large jigsaw although it is nice to have the whole jigsaw if one piece is missing then the whole can still be seen.

Although the ETs craft are important, they are a small part of this book and are just one modality of contact. The overwhelming evidence for all contact modalities is consciousness itself. The ETs are here to assist in our evolution and education to a higher level of consciousness.

When I was asked to share my experiences and write about them. I said but people will not believe me. They said it did not matter, but it is important you talk about your experiences this will expand your collective understanding of consciousness.

CHANNELING

Channeling, is one of the modalities of contact. For me, this is a fairly new modality of contact. Just over three years ago, I went to a MUFON meeting in Orlando. At lunchtime I sat at a table with a few other people, all complete strangers, but were they. We had plenty to discuss and we all got along so well. Later a few of us decided to meet for lunch one Saturday. We ventured to one of the groups home to continue our discussion. We all shared a common interest and wanted to explore further. We decided to work as a group, recording and collating what we did. Once a month we'd all meet at my home and discuss new ideas and perhaps formulate new beginning's.

We always began with a meditation, today was no exception. After the meditation she asked the group if anyone had made any contact of received any information since we last met. Everyone said no they had not. She then asked me again if I was sure that I had not received anything. I again said no. I then felt a presence next to me, it was male stood next to me. I could feel the higher vibrational frequency of this individual. She then said to me who is it. I said I do not know.

She then asked me to ask him who he was. I did. It was Ort my life long ET guide. He proceeded to speak through me for about 40 minutes. Afterwards I was totally drained and exhausted. I needed a glass of water but I could hardly stand. Sandy went to get me a glass. Although I did not fully remember all what he said we recorded it and later had it transcribed.

What had just happened was a complete shock to me, and I did not fully understand it. One member of our group said you have just channeled. We all discussed channeling. Month after month went by and I became very comfortable and at ease with channeling. We started measuring the air temperature immediately around my body. The room temperature was 77 degrees and immediately surrounding my body the temperature was 87 degrees an increase of 10 degrees. I now understand this to be the conscious energy used for the Channel. I have included some of the channels we did, they do make interesting reading. I do not recall much from the channels so the transcripts are ideal for me. Ort told me that they name this modality of contact Dual Conscious Physical communication. I move my consciousness to one side to allow Ort's conscious energy to enter my physical body and speak through me.

TRANSCRIPTS FROM OUR GROUP MEETINGS ON CHANNELING

Transcript of January 14, 2017 Musketeer's Meeting

The Council of 8 members are as follows: 1. Rah (Watcher, Annunaki, lead council, 2. Ort, and 3. Dee (both married Arcturians), 4. Jark (Average Grey) (pronounced Zark), 5. Arna (Blue Avian), 6. Targ (Tall Grey), 7. Cheeka (Insectoid Mantis), 8. Orla (Tall White).

Ort: I am Ort.
Jean: Thank you. Maria and Mack: Thank you for coming here Ort.
Ort: Hello Mack. Hello Maria. Hello Jean. Hello Sandy. (All say hello.)
Jean: I understand that we are allowed to ask some questions.
Ort: Yes, I've spoken to Kevin. Let me explain what I am doing. Kevin is here. He is next to me and he has allowed me or given me permission to use my consciousness in his physical to speak to you. He is here; he is listening; and he will ask to come back when he is ready to come back. He is a little uncomfortable because he is not used to this form of communication. We call it dual conscious physical communication where his consciousness allows mine to enter his physical. This allows us to speak and I know who you are through Kevin. Kevin's thoughts are my thoughts. What Kevin see's, I see in this state. Kevin will get better at this and it will be less stressful for him. He is a quick learner. I have interacted with him since he was a child. So, he's used to me. If you want to start with your questions, I will see if I can answer them.
Mack: I have a question if you can answer part or all of the first one. If we just consider for a moment that we may be joining some sort of mass consciousness or at least one of several, what connection is missing that could help small groups like ours to link with others on Earth to help with this same cause. In other words, to help make these tiny groups of 4 or 5 into larger, stronger groups of souls here on Earth for the betterment of mankind?

Ort: Okay. Let me just think about that. We all share the same consciousness. We are individually conscious as well as sharing consciousness itself. We, as you refer to us as extraterrestrials, have the same access to the same consciousness. It is one. This explains how I am able to use my consciousness through Kevin.

Mack: Are you ready for the next question?

Ort: Yes.

Mack: I don't see success when a mass move is made to Mars to make the necessary steps to force it back to life (Terra firmer), regrowth, unless and until some sort of world consciousness has been reached while we are here. What do you say regarding this?

Ort: You will, as a species, not be going back to Mars permanently. You will go back on visits in the future, but not permanently.

Mack: Is there a reason why?

Ort: It's not suitable for you, because of its atmospheres and to change it takes a great technology. There has been life there before.

Mack: Who was the life before?

Ort: It was another species.

Mack: Thank you.

Maria: I am next on the list and I have some questions for you to answer for me if you are willing.

Ort: Yes.

Maria: Number 1, I have begun to explore the similarities and differences between interdimensional phenomena and intelligent entities who travel in structured craft, to determine whether or not ET visitation is the same or different than visitation by interdimensional beings, who simply step into our 3-D reality here on earth. I do not yet have enough evidence to make this decision at this point. Can you give me some insight into what is happening?

Ort: Yes, let me think about it.

Maria: Okay.

Ort: There are two answers to your question. There are interdimensional beings that just live in the spiritual. These do transcend the dimensions from time to time. Then we have what you call extraterrestrials from different dimensions. The difference between the dimensions is only the difference in the vibrational frequencies that they exist in. So, people get mistaken between the spiritual and the physical from the different dimensions. I exist in the 5th dimension.

Maria: Can you tell me the dimension that what we call angels exist in?

Ort: Yes, I can best describe that as a life between a life—consciousness itself manifesting in your dimension without the physical.

Maria. Thank you very much. My next question is what process is used to remove human abductees from their homes through solid surfaces such as walls and ceilings and onto craft and back? Could you be as scientific and specific as possible?

Ort: What you consider solid can be changed and altered. They are just atoms with electrons which are of a certain vibration. We amplify the electrons to different vibrational frequencies, which is just the frequency of the body, and this allows it to move through the wall. We can also do this by our thoughts.

Maria: Thank you. Can you tell me what is causing interdimensional portals to open up in so many places on Earth, with a variety of beings and time shifts taking place? Is this a danger to Earthlings?

Ort: There are different reasons. There are extraterrestrials that can travel into dimensions using what you call wormholes--portals. That is one reason for this. The other is caused by your experiments. You currently have 17, what you call, hydron colliders. You will probably know of the big one at CERN. But there are 16 others. When they are in operation, they open up portals. You are searching for subatomic particles. When you find them, you will able to open up your own portals. But it will be a while yet. It is not a danger at this stage.

Maria: Thank you. There is one more question from me. You had mentioned to Mack that there was once life on Mars. Dr. John Brandenburg has evidence that 2 thermonuclear explosions destroyed life on Mars 250-500 million years ago. His hypothesis is that outsiders, not the Martians, dropped the bombs. Is he correct in any of this?

Ort: He's correct on some of his assumptions. There was life on Mars millions of years ago and the planet was destroyed by nuclear explosions. But it was the species themselves that did it. It is what could happen here on Earth. They were in a similar position. But it was not an outside attack. I do not know the exact timeframe.

Maria: Thank you very much. I appreciate you answering my questions. And now Jean has some questions for you.

Jean: Is my understanding that the "Reveal" that we are on a level right now is individual. Is this "Reveal" that we're getting, raising our consciousness, happening to a whole bunch of people?

Ort: Not to this level of communication, but they are by definition of understanding raising their consciousness and attempting to contact us.

Jean: So, what you're saying is that this group is unique.

Ort: Yes, you are the lead council for us.

Jean: Okay and eventually will we lead this group, with others, to make a combined reveal simultaneously.

Ort: Yes, I'm going to ask you do something for me.

Jean: Okay.

I would like to reveal a craft to you, Jean. I'd like you to write an approximate location, time and date early next week. Then your guide will give you some information. Mack, I would like to reveal a craft to you after Jean's reveal. If you could also give me an approximately location, date and time…if you write it down before you leave today and give the list to Sandy.

Mack: Okay.

Ort: Dee is asking permission to contact you when you see…when the craft is revealed to you. Will you give permission for her to speak to you?

Mack: Yes, and thank you.

Ort: Now Maria, I would like to reveal a craft to you after Jean and after Mack.

Maria: Okay.

Ort: I will need me an approximate location, date and time, and Jark is asking if you'll give him permission to communicate with you. He informs me that you have a keen scientific mind and he is one of our leading scientists on the Council of 8. Will you give him permission to speak to you?

Maria: Yes, I will.

Ort: Thank you.

Kevin takes deep breaths. There is a pause.

Jean: May we now continue with our questions?

Ort: Rah is here. (Overseer of the Council of 8)

Group: Each member says hello.

Ort: He is asking permission from Mack to speak to speak to the council of 4.

Mack: You have my permission.

Ort: Sandy, he wants your permission to speak to you.

Sandy: He has my permission.

Rah: I am Rah. I am a watcher. I am lead council of the Council of 8. I am Annunaki. I thank you for working with Ort towards the reveal.

Mack: You're welcome.

Rah: Let me explain why. (Deep breathing and pause.) Your governments are aware of our presence. They have been aware for many years. They do not want to disclose our presence to the people of your planet. It is important for the development of yourselves and your planet to be aware that we are here. We are many. I have been here before, many thousands of years ago. And you destroyed yourself then. And you are in a position now to do it again, and we will not allow it. So, we will have the reveal with your help. Kevin is asking to come back now.

Group: Yes, we will help. Thank you.

Rah: Before I leave, I would like to thank you again. I will speak to you again and I'm going to activate some of Kevin's DNA, so the process of dual conscious physical communication will be much easier for him and less stressful.

Group: Thank you very much.

Rah: I am leaving now.

(Ort comes back.)

Ort: I am Ort. It is most unusual for Rah to speak. Most unusual. Kevin is requesting to come back. He is getting anxious, so I am going to leave. I thank you for meeting with me and we will meet again.

Group: Thank you very much.

Ort: Thank you and goodbye.

Group: Goodbye.

Pause as Kevin comes back into his body.

Kevin: I'm back.

Group: This was very interesting.

Jean: How was it to have your consciousness beside your body?

Kevin: It is just interesting really. Rah's energy was tremendous, exhausting.

Group: We could feel it! (Everyone felt a strong electrical tingling sensation in their bodies.)

Mack: And he had a very deep powerful voice.

Kevin: So, that's a first for me.

Mack: The eyes were very powerful, looking around, and the temperature went to 85 degrees when the Annunaki stepped in. The variations in temperature for Ort went from 82-83 and then to 85 when the Annunaki stepped in. Otherwise it was around 77.5 degrees.

Kevin: Did you get many questions answered?

Group: Many questions. Yes.

Mack: Sandy didn't get to ask hers.

Everyone laughs.

Sandy: I think, if anything, our questions would have overlapped.

Maria: We have one or two left for the next time.

Jean: Right, but as things progress, they might not need to be answered.

Mack: That's quite possible.

Kevin asks group for approximate location, date and time for the reveal of the coming week.

Mack: I'm assuming that I would give my home address and where I want them to reveal.

Jean: I know exactly where mine is going to be.

Kevin to Maria: I had an image of the craft over the lake when he was talking about yours, so it may appear over the lake.

Jean: It's going to be over my house, because that is where I hear them when they come.

Mack: I'd like it over the greenbelt behind my house. All the way to the end of the street between the houses is where I saw the huge craft. So, there.

Kevin: So that will be interesting. If that transpires then we can move forward.

Jean: They are not just revealing but there is a reason they are revealing it to us.

Kevin: Yes.

Group: Yes, it will be confirmation.

Jean: I wonder if they'll let us take a picture.

Kevin: I don't see why not.

Maria: I wonder if the daytime will be okay.

Kevin: They didn't stipulate.

Jean: I'm going to do nighttime, so the neighbors won't be outside.

Kevin: Wait and see.

Mack: What about Sandy?

Kevin: We've already seen them.

Transcript of February 25th, 2017. Musketeer's Meeting.

The Council of 8 members are as follows: 1. Rah (Watcher, Annunaki, lead council, 2. Ort, and 3. Dee (both married Arcturians), 4. Jark (Average Grey) (pronounced Zark), 5. Arna (Blue Avian), 6. Targ (TallGrey), 7. Cheeka (Insectoid Mantis), 8. Orla (Tall White).

Kevin: Hello Mack, Maria, Jean, Sandy. I am Ort.

Everyone: Hello Ort.

Ort: Now before we start the questions, I have some things to discuss with you. Concerning the experiment, we did after our last meeting, with regard to seeing our craft and communicating with the Council,it went quite well. I was pleased with the results. Maria connected with Jark, which was very good. You saw some craft, Jean and Mack, but I don't think you communicated with Dee. Is that correct?

Mack: Yes, that is correct.

Ort: Now what I would like to do this time is to do the same experiment next week. So, I would like to change the order this time. I'd like Maria to go first, then Jean, then Mack, then Sandy. So, I will need you to write down the times, the dates, and the locations. We will do it in the evening this time. This makes it easier for us to reveal ourselves with our crafts. Are you happy to do that?

Everyone: Yes.

Ort: Okay. We are going to meet today with other members of the Council of Eight. Edgar is here as well. He will not be communicating today, but he will be here and listening. Rah will speak as well and he will speak last. So, the Council of Eight is going to introduce themselves to you. What I would like to do is to improve our communication between our group here and the Council of Eight, with any member of the Council of Eight. We are going to start with Dee. We have met Dee before but she will speak to you now.

Dee: Hello, I am Dee. We have met before.

Everyone: Hello.

Dee: It is good to see you. I am an Arcturian. I am the wife of Ort. I am Council of Eight. I am here to work with you towards the Reveal as a member of the council. I would like you to contact me anytime if you have questions.Jark would like to speak with you now.

Jark: I am Jark. Hello Mack and Maria and Jean and Sandy. We have met before, Maria. It is nice to see you.

Maria: It is nice to see you too.

Jark: Your communication skills are very good.

(Maria documented her communication with Jark after their meeting in January. She wrote: "I do think that Jark connected with me on Sunday when I experienced a very strong electrical tingling sensation throughout my body and felt spaced out. I recall receiving a message about dimensions and wondered if it had come from my own thoughts or from elsewhere. I have amnesia for the messages.")

Jark: I am a Grey alien as you describe us. I am not alien to myself. I have been communicating with Sandy. It is important that Sandy knows we are here. I moved her shoes and lined them up for her. I moved her table settings.

(*Later, when Kevin asked how the shoe rearrangement was carried out, he stated, "We did not move the shoes physically. We moved the atoms that form the shoes. We moved the atoms into another space-time. We moved the atoms by thought." They proceeded to give Kevin a formula: $T^1 (PT)(ST)C^2 = D$. It is explained as follows. T is Thought energy, PT is Present Time, ST is Space-time, C is consciousness, and D is Dimension.)

Jark continues: I opened the blinds when she closed them. Just recently I moved a spoon. Kevin and Sandy witnessed the spoon moving. It moved 3 times and Sandy was within one foot of the spoon, so she knows we are here. I also did not fully manifest here when I was in the room, but Sandy saw me. So, now as a member of the Council of Eight, you can communicate with me anytime you would like. I have already communicated with Maria and would like to communicate with the others. Arna is requesting to speak with the group. Will you give her permission to speak?

Everyone: Yes.

Arna: Hello.

Everyone: Hello.

Arna: I am Arna. Thank you for letting me speak with you. I am Council of Eight. I am a Blue Avian. I have met Kevin before. I would like to be able to communicate with any of you at any time.

Everyone: Thank you. Okay. Yes.

Arna: We have Targ with us now and he would like to speak with you next. He is asking for permission to speak with you.

Everyone: Yes.

Targ: I am Targ.

Everyone: Hello.

Targ: Hello Mack, Maria, Jean, and Sandy. I am Council of Eight. I am a Grey being, as you describe us. I am different from Jark, but he is a good friend of mine. I think you have met Jark. He is Council of Eight also. I would like to work with you as a group and feel free to communicate with me anytime you wish. I am here to assist you.Orla is here and she is asking permission to speak with you.

Everyone: Yes.

Orla: Hello, I am Orla. I am Council of Eight. I am a tall white. It is good to meet with you.

Everyone: You too.

Orla: Feel free to communicate with me anytime you would like.

Everyone: Thank you.

Orla: Rah is here. He would like to speak with you.

Rah: I am Rah, lead council of the Council of Eight. I am a Watcher. I am Annunaki. We have met before. It is good to see you. (Members of the human group sense a strong electrical tingling sensation in their bodies.)

Everyone: Hello Rah. Good to see you too.

Rah: You have met some more of the Council of Eight today. We are trying to improve our communication with you. Maria has already spoken to Jark. I speak to you today through Kevin. He gave me permission for dual conscious physical communication. I would like for you to communicate, through thought, with me or the Council of Eight members.

Group member: Thank you.

Rah: Maria understands thought communication, as does Jean, as does Mack. You communicate with thought through your own guides. Sandy, however, does not have thought communications yet. But we will help her to learn and develop that. I know a little bit about you and I would like to get to know you a little bit better. I see, Mack, you are very old—very old indeed. You go back to the first time. Do you remember?

Mack: I remember some things.

Rah: I see you in an aquatic world in Orion. Do you remember that?

Mack: I do.

Rah: For the first time…Eons ago, Mack. Maria, I see you as you've been a small Grey. Do you have memories of it?

Maria: A little bit.

Rah: And Jean, you are Arcturian. Is that correct?

Jean: I believe so.

Rah: Okay. Sandy is very special. She is what we call a pure blood, a blue blood, a human. We will have work for Sandy in the future. So, it is important that we all communicate. I see that you are all working with Ort in relation to improving your communication.

Everyone: That's true. Yes.

Rah: Now I understand that you have some questions. I will answer them to the best of my ability. Did you want to start Sandy?

Sandy: Yes, my first question is: The existence of multi universes has been considered scientifically plausible, and in 2015, a scientist has possibly discovered that there is a parallel universe "leaking" into ours. Is this true and if is, is it this which has created the many portals that have suddenly emerged?

Rah: There are many universes and parallel universes and sometimes they do leak and we get change in a timeline. However, the portals you are referring to, some are from other beings and some are caused by your scientific experiments. Does that answer your question?

Sandy: Yes, it does. Are you ready for my second question?

Rah: Yes.

Sandy: Is the recently discovered Trappist system with 7 Earthlike planets home to the ETs visiting earth?

Rah: There are life forms on two of these planets within the system you speak of. They are of a similar development to your species. But they do not travel here. They do not have the technology. Do you have another question?

Sandy: No, my questions are now ended. I think that Jean would like to ask you her questions if that's okay.

Rah: Yes.

Jean: my question is, I have an acquaintance in Jacksonville who says he is not from Earth. He says that Earth is just a game for all of us—that nothing is real. Is it true that we create our own reality and that this is just a game?

Rah: Yes and no. Yes, we create our own reality by thought, by consciousness, by space-time. No, it is not a game.

Jean: Okay, thank you. My second question is: We heard 7 members of the Council of Eight. Is there an eighth one that we don't know about?

Rah: There are 8. You will meet later. We are trying to communicate with you and teaching you how to enhance this skill. You need to improve your communication skills you can request to speak with us and we will appear and teach you. That is what we are working towards.

Jean: Excellent. Thank you. I have one last question. When I was driving back from Georgia a couple of weeks ago, I saw 3 things in the air. Were they craft?

Rah: Yes, they were. We are trying to communicate with you individually and as a group. It is a learning curve for you.

Jean: Yes, it is. Thank you. I think I have finished with my questions now. Mack is up next.

Mack: I think you have answered my first question without me asking it. My attraction and comfort in water, more so than on land, goes back to a time when I was on a planet that was liquid.

Rah: Yes, I see you as a very old soul back to what we call the first-time eons of years ago. And you were in what you call the Orion Nebula. You were in a water world, as you have your dolphins today…a very early consciousness.

Mack: I am very attracted to dolphins. Okay. Next question: Are Ort and the others on a journey like we are? Yet possibly from a higher level? If so, might they be some sort of guide to us, helping us find our way to a higher level? In other words, are they disciples? Are you some kind of disciple, and for what or who?

Rah: We are here to guide and assist in the development of your species and your world. We planted your seed here and we helped to develop it. We introduce things to assist in your development. As for the other members of the Council of Eight, they are your extended families. We have a connection to our consciousness, to our souls, to our soul energy, which we all share. If we raise your level of consciousness to a higher level, you are able to achieve more. This is what we are trying to do here. You have been to this position before and you destroyed yourselves. We are fearful that you are in a position to do that again, and we will not allow it this time. We will intervene.

Mack: Thank you. Just a couple more that you have already begun to explain. Can you explain to us your understanding of consciousness?

Rah: Consciousness and source energy are one. They are the life of the universe and for consciousness to grow and develop; we need to create lives, which we do with the physical and consciousness. We go through the physical life and learn and that increases consciousness as source energy which is growing. It is the ultimate energy that creates all life. But we create it with the help of the physical and with the help of you.

Mack: Thank you.

Rah: Does that make sense to you?

Mack: Yes, it does. I have one last question. Humans are spiritual beings in physical bodies. At least that is what we understand. Are you spiritual beings? And if not, are you attempting to become spiritual beings?

Rah: We are spiritual beings as you are. We have a symbiosis with the physical and consciousness—what you call your souls—soul energy. While I do not have a physical at the moment, I do not need one. I am a Watcher.

Mack: Alright. Thank you.

Rah: As you progress though the different levels of consciousness, you'll have a better understanding.

Mack: Yes, I just wanted to confirm something that I felt. Thank you so much.

Maria: I now have some questions for you, if you will answer them please. Last week I spoke with some friends about the perplexing phenomena that seems to be related to contact such as psychic phenomena, paranormal phenomena, and interdimensional contact. One friend told me that everything is living consciousness and all things seen are only a matter of density. Is she correct?

Rah: Yes, but I would choose different words. Instead of density I would use energy and vibrational frequencies. Then I would agree with her. She is correct.

Maria: Okay, thank-you. I have heard that individuals have warned our government and military that our planet is in danger and ETs are seeking "The Reveal." No one has ever been successful in carrying this message to our governments. They think the messengers have psychological problems and are only imagining this. Why don't you contact world political and military leaders?

Rah: That is a good question. I can give you an answer. We have made our presence known to your governments globally. They know we are here. They have known we are here for a number of years. We have shown them that we are here many times. We have shown your military that we are here. They won't accept this, and they fear us. We've closed down your missiles. We've disabled your missiles when you've fired them. We flew a fleet of our craft from the North down through Russia, down through the Balkans, down through your Europe. And we turned around and went back up again. We were seen on your radar. America thought it was the Russians. The Russians thought it was the Americans. And then they realized that it was us. But they still refused to acknowledge the fact that we are here. All your leaders know we are here. Your heads of industry know we are here. They just won't admit it to the population. So, we have to try another method. If we land on your

White House lawn or at the Kremlin, it will be seen as an invasion. We do not want that.

Maria: Okay, I have another question. When we talk to the members of the Council of Eight, they always state that they are ETs. Are you really ET beings? Or are you from a parallel universe not far from our dimension? Will you explain that please?

Rah: I am soul energy. Let us speak of Ort and Dee. They have a physical in the 5th dimension, which is just a higher level of consciousness understanding and a physical vibration. So, if we can raise your level of consciousness we can meet together on the same level. You call us extraterrestrials. We live here in the same Universe. We are life forms, as there are many life forms throughout the Universe. It is you that label us as extraterrestrials. If you went to Andromeda to one of the planets there, would you consider yourself an extraterrestrial or would you be a human?

Maria: I would probably be extraterrestrial to them, but human to myself.

Rah: That is a good possibility. I do not think that Ort thinks he is an extraterrestrial.

Maria: Thank you. And last, I met a woman who claimed that she is a "light being". She told me that if a human being kills an ET or what we consider to be one, the human will not be allowed to live. Is this true?

Rah: No, that is incorrect.

Maria: Thank you.

Rah: I can explain further if you wish.

Maria: Okay.

Rah: Let's continue to call them extraterrestrials, because you can understand that. I am fine with that. There are some extraterrestrials here who want to do you harm. They want to take over your planet. If you cross those particular extraterrestrials and you injure one of them, they will do you harm. We are the majority and we have six species on the Council of Eight. We will do you no harm. We mean to increase your level of consciousness to assist in your evolution and development. That is why we are here.

Maria: Thank you very much.

Jean: I think this is the end of our questions. Is there anything that we haven't asked you that you need to tell us?

Rah: No, I'm very pleased with our communication. It has improved over the short period of time we have been together. We need to be able to communicate by thought clearly to one another and continue along that line, and then if we get to a position where we can manifest ourselves at your calling, time, and location, as a group, that would be beneficial

Jean: So, is the global peace initiative that I am participating in, to bring peace and calmness to the world, helping with that?

Rah: That helps with the raising of consciousness. The more people who raise their consciousness, the more strength and power you have. You are raising that vibrational frequency. So yes, it is all very important.

Jean: Okay, thank you. So, do we have anything else or are we ready to let Rah…

Rah interrupts Jean: We need to improve our communications and then when we've achieved that we can move a step forward. That is a huge step. We have to do it in a way that cannot be undermined.

Jean: So, at 10:00 each morning when I purposefully connect with this group is that part of the process to get us where we need to be?

Rah: Thought between one another is good. Thought increases consciousness. Thought is a great way to communicate as you know.

Jean: Thank you very much for your wisdom, and for trusting us and working with us, and we'll do our part.

Rah: Okay. That's good. I will speak with Ort next week and see how the experiment goes. Hopefully, we will have an improvement in communication. I am going to leave now. I was just checking with Kevin, he has improved his dual conscious physical communication skills now and, hopefully, he will continue to improve with time. He is used to thought communication and he is very proficient with that. We need to expand our communication with others we need to develop our dual consciousness communication and for people to understand it.

Does that make sense?

Everyone: Yes.

Rah: Okay. I am going to leave now. Thank you for meeting with me and my Council of Eight. We will meet again in about four week's time.

Everyone: Okay. Thank you.

Rah: Thank you.

Kevin's consciousness returns to his physical body.

Jean: How was it to be away?

Kevin: It was okay. I don't seem to be as far away as I was before, if that makes sense.

Jean: And you're not afraid that you can't come back?

Kevin: No, no, no. I'm quite comfortable. (session ends.)

Transcript of April 8th, 2017. Musketeer's Meeting

Ort greets all members and we say hello.

Maria: Why are people chosen for an abduction experience with ETs? Is contact generational and are family lines being studied?

Ort: There is no particular reason why people are chosen for the abduction experience. But once the family has been chosen then it can occur down the family line. Usually, the first choices are when people are alone so they are not missed. So, initially families were not chosen for any particular reason, only that they were alone and their absence would not be immediately noticed.

Maria: I have noticed an absence of Reptilians on the Council of Eight. Who are the Reptilians and what can you tell us about them?

Ort: They are an aggressive species. They do not abide by the rules of the Council of Eight. They exist among us and we no longer have conflict with them. They come from the same place as one of a species of Grey and they too don't follow the rules of the Council of Eight. The reptilians sometimes work with this particular species of Greys who do the abductions. They have been invited to join the Council of Eight, but they have no intention of doing so. So, we, for lack of a better phrase, get along. But they are war mongers; they take what they want. We do try to put restrictions on them and sometimes we can. But not always.

Maria: What star system is each member of the Council of Eight from? Are your planets viable for life today? And where are you as a group right now?

Ort: We are here right now. We are in your solar system. We have been here for a while. We come from different star systems, from the Pleiades, from Sirius, from Andromeda, and from Zeta Reticuli. We are a very old species and some of our planets no longer support life. But we can travel anywhere.

Sandy: The multi-verse or multiple universes remains hypothetical here on Earth. Prominent physicists continue to debate this phenomenon. Do you come from a parallel universe, and if so, this would mean the multi-verse is NOT hypothetical?

Ort: We are from your universe. We are from different dimensions in your universe, but not different universes. If I can explain further in relation to your multi-verse question, space-time can be changed with consciousness, to change the universe that we are in, and change the direction in which we are moving, not as a universe but as life itself. Consciousness is the life force of the universe and everything.

Sandy: Are we all spirited beings having human experiences? If so, does this reflect on other species such as Avians and Greys, etc., to have Avian experiences and Grey experiences?

Ort: We are spiritual beings. The four of you here are spiritual beings, currently in a physical vessel which is of human form. We do this by choice. Some of the other species are similar. But we do not interchange with other species. We tend to remain with the same species, although it is possible to interchange into a physical vessel, of say a Grey. But we tend not to do that. It is difficult to do. Rah can do it; Sheeva can do it; and Edgar can do it now if he wishes to. But he does not wish to. I cannot and I do not wish to. We can use our consciousness to be in two and sometimes three physical vessels at the same time. We don't always do that, but we do have the ability to do that.

Sandy: World politics today appears to be having a direct impact on groups and individuals globally. Is this having a major influence on the timing of the Reveal?

Ort: Yes, you are in a very difficult time and economic time, and there are those who do not want the Reveal. There are those who want to control the earth's population and reduce the size of the earth's population. We don't want that. We want to expand human consciousness, so they can continue to evolve and take their rightful place in the universe.

Mack: Orbs are a form of energy we don't understand. We (humans) might only have the ability to use this type of energy when we are in spirit form (i.e. after death). Is this all one form of energy and someone decides what shape it will take, such as to travel within a craft in spirit form as an ET, as a ghost, or as an angel?

Ort: I will explain it to you as an experience that Kevin has had with regard to seeing and receiving information from an orb. When he was a young child, I communicated with him as a small orange orb. If you ask Kevin, he will describe it to you as an orb 4 to 6 inches in diameter, yellow orange in color and vibrating. That was pure conscious energy and it was my pure conscious energy. So, we can use that to travel. I showed Kevin how to use his conscious energy to travel. He does not remember me teaching him how to do it, but he can do it, and he has done it many times. So conscious energy can be removed from the physical vessel and used for travel. Consciousness is the highest form of energy within the universe. It is everywhere—in the plants, the trees, the rocks—and it is all connected. We are one.

Mack: What is the source of this "orb forming energy"?

Ort: It has always been here. It will always be here. It is what you call God. It is the life force of the Universe. It is never ending and it has always been here. It is life itself.

Mack: Whohas access to the use of this energy and can it be used both for positive and negative purposes?

Ort: The conscious energy is there for all to use, but you have to learn how to use it, how to access it. All humans can learn how to use conscious energy if they are taught how to do it. Conscious energy can be used for travel. Conscious energy can be used for creating things on a spiritual level, which allows you to travel spiritually. I gave Kevin the information he needed to create a conscious craft to travel wherever he wanted to go. He failed on the first two attempts, and on the third attempt he succeeded. And then he succeeded again. Unfortunately, this force can be used negatively by controlling people, controlling species, controlling planets. There is good and evil in everything.

Jean: There are many people in different groups who are discussing the possibility of the world being told the truth that extraterrestrials exist. (People on FREE Experiencers, private citizens, etc.) Is the reason for this simultaneous interest due to collective consciousness raising or are other people working on a reveal with other extraterrestrials?

Ort: It is due to the raising of your consciousness, which is what we are trying to do. This is what we are doing as a group. We are working to increase our level of consciousness. And yes, there are others who want the reveal and are working toward it, but they do not have the connection with the Council of Eight as we do. And if we decide to reveal ourselves to you and Sandy, and that is an if, we would want you to join these other groups together and show them the reveal. There are many of these groups and many that need to be awakened and be given a direction.

Jean: Are there things that we four can add to our routines to enhance skills for our part in preparation for the reveal?

Ort: No, you are doing very well. You are progressing nicely. You have developed an understanding of consciousness. You are able to communicate individually now with different members of the Council of Eight. You have seen some of them and we are very pleased with the work that you have been doing. We are guiding you and we are guiding the timeframe in relation to where you need to be.

Ort: The Council of Eight are here and they will listen to Kevin. Kevin is going to speak through me.

Kevin: I am Kevin. I am Council of Four with Maria, Mack, and Jean. I am requesting that the Council of Eight reveal themselves today to the Council of Four. We have met the Council of Eight. We have met Ort, Dee, Jark, Rah, Orla, Ana, Cheeka and Targ. So, we the Council of Four would like to meet with the Council of Eight and I direct my request Rah. I ask that the Council of Eight consider our request. Rah, you told me once that you are my father and I am my father's son. I did not understand that. That was many years ago. I understand that now. So, I of the Council of Four ask my father of the Council of Eight to reveal yourselves today. Without the reveal we cannot move forward, and we need to move forward, so please reveal yourselves today.

Ort: Kevin has finished speaking. The Council of Eight is considering your request. Kevin is going to return now. He is tired. (Kevin is breathing heavily and his voice quality has changed. He is obviously struggling.) It was a pleasure meeting with you and I will meet with you again.

Everyone thanks Ort.

Kevin returns. He tells us about the different forms that Ort and Dee have taken during their periods of communication over the many years that they have been together. They have been in the physical as manifestations. They have also been as forms of energy that communicate with him. They have also been like 1000 bright lights in his bedroom and the whole bedroom lights up. Several months ago, he woke up in the middle of the night and saw the Council of Eight. They were all sitting around a table and they were all looking down on him while he was asleep. He woke up, but he shouldn't have woken up, and three of them disappeared straight away. When he was finally completely awake the others disappeared. Recently he has seen three of them on the front porch.

Mack asks Kevin how he was able to speak through Ort. He was observing him and realized that he was standing to the side and also observed that Kevin's body was becoming extremely tired. Jean states that she also observed this. It took an extreme amount of energy and Kevin was struggling—breathing heavily—and his voice became weak. His formerly clear voice quality changed, sounding as if he has a severe cold. Jean stated that it seemed that the consciousness was separated into three parts and the energy needed to do this was extremely exhausting. Kevin stated that he knew that Ort had stepped aside, but then he did not know for certain what had transpired next. Mack and Jean felt their cheeks become very hot and their bodies vibrated. Maria felt very warm, but did not experience vibration, only tingling. Jean explained that she was being told that it takes a great deal of energy to manifest physically. Kevin stated that they had told him that it takes a great deal of energy to come from the fifth dimension to the third dimension and materialize. Jean used the analogy of talking to someone on a telephone. Part of their consciousness is here, but they are somewhere else in the physical simultaneously. Mack mentions that he saw the back of an opalescent bird with feathers that seemed alive.

Transcript of July 8th, 2017. Musketeer's Meeting

Ort: it's nice to see you again.
Everyone: It's nice to see you as well.
Maria: My first question is why aren't the abducting grays doing experiments on humans and what is their end goal in doing these experiments? Why do they take people who are biologically related?
Ort: Some of the grays do abduct and experiment with your genetics. They have been doing this for a very long time. They also enhance the DNA of the people they are abducting, in small ways, to genetically alter both species. The reason they use family lines is to keep the genetic codes similar.
Maria: Is Edgar Mitchell now in the fifth dimension?

Ort: No, Edgar is in the ninth dimension. Edgar is a watcher and there are 10 dimensions, with 10 being consciousness itself.

Maria: Thank you and how does one become a watcher? What does it mean to be a watcher and what are your duties?

Ort: A watcher is very experienced what you call souls. They have had many incarnations over many thousands of years, and with each incarnation they learn more and ascend to the higher dimensions. They have different roles, one of them being to assist in the development of the human species. They also watch over different species other than the humans. They can incarnate into the different species, if they want to. Their purpose is to guide and assist in development.

Maria: Thank you very much. So, are you a watcher?

Ort: No, I am not. I am Arcturian and I live in the physical in the fifth dimension.

Maria: Thank you. It is now Jean's turn to ask you questions.

Jean: Will the big reveal be done simultaneously around the globe?

Ort: The reveal has three stages. The reveal is already happening. The first stage is to have an understanding of consciousness itself. And to understand who you are as a species and to understand your higher self-consciousness, which we are a part of. So that is the first stage of the reveal. The second stage of the reveal is for you to have an understanding of the Council of Eight and the Council of Eight's position within this quadrant of your galaxy. They represent six species within the galactic federation, which manages the galaxy, shall we say. So, when you have an understanding of consciousness itself and who you are, and the Council of Eight, then the third and final stage will be a physical reveal. This will happen to individuals. It will happen to small groups. It may or may not be global it depends on governments. But the reveal is already here.

Jean: Is there a part that says you would abort mission if it doesn't go as its planned to, and you would stop from proceeding?

Ort: It would have to be an extreme condition. The reveal is part of your natural process of your development. And as long as you do not destroy yourself and you reach those higher levels of consciousness, and an understanding of where you are in your current galaxy.

Jean: My last question is, are we, the four musketeers and Sandy, in any physical danger by the powers that do not want the reveal as we move forward?

Ort: There is some risk to what you are doing but you are not in any immediate danger. And we the Council of eight will assist and protect you if we believe you are in danger.

Jean: And how would you intervene to do that?

Ort: We have many ways and it would be revealed at that time.

Jean: Okay, I understand. And Mack is up next.

Mack: Hello, please tell me if you know anything about this. Years ago, an entity came to my bedroom and attempted to entice me to go with him. Is this the same one who told me during meditation, on the phone, that I did not want to speak with him? And is he a part of the Council of Eight?

Ort: He is not a part of the Council of Eight. I do not know this entity that you are speaking of. There are many species, as you are aware. There are many entities that help and assist us. He may have been one of those as I am a guide to Kevin.

Mack: Thank you. And my second question is, should we be asking for healing of our human bodies or is this wrong about? When we are healed does someone decide this for us?

Ort: No, it is good that you asked for assistance. You should ask the Watchers for that. You should ask Sheeva, and Rah, and Edgar. These will all help you with your health, but you have to ask them. They like you to ask. They like to help. But they will not interfere without your permission. So, you should ask and it helps with your development. We can heal many things ourselves by thought.

Mack: Okay, thank you. And the last question, we have received many reports of UFOs and negative nonhuman entities in East Texas. This has happened to people who had no former interest in UFOs. They ended up experiencing demonic oppression. Do you have insight into what is occurring and what can be done to help these people?

Ort: There are many species now who are involved in the reveal. And they are showing themselves to many people. This has nothing to do with UFOs. This is part of the reveal itself and we will find that there are more and more reports.

Mack: And some of these numerous entities are negative?

Ort: Not that we are aware of. I think that we have discussed this topic before in relation to how you as a species can create a demon through negative thought. So, if they are experiencing some negativity it will be coming from within that group itself. That is why you always need positive thoughts. I don't think that you as a species understand yet the power of thought.

Mack: No, we don't.

Jean: But we'd like to.

Mack: Yes, we would like to. That was very informative, thank you.

Maria: Those positive thoughts are something that our team at MUFON is suggesting to people when someone is having a negative experience. We tell them to meet them with love.

Ort: That is good.

Jean: I just had contact with client in Jacksonville who is having this happen, and he said a portal is open and stuff is coming through. And he said a portal is open and stuff is coming through. And he said what can I do? And I told him close the portal and I told him how to do it.

Maria:So, what did you say? What did you tell him?

Jean: I said see who is there, who is coming through if it is a spirit or something. And I said if they need to go to the light, send them to the light. And if they are evil and they don't want to be a part of good send them away. And he knows how to do that. You just say by divine light and love I close this portal. So, we did good?

Ort: You did good.

Jean: is there anything that you would like to tell us that we haven't asked?

Ort: No, the Council of Eight is very pleased with your progress so far. You have progressed very quickly and you have an understanding now of who we are. You have an understanding of our communication, and you as individuals have contacted different members of the Council of Eight. So that is good. And if you continue to do that you will progress even quicker.

Jean: So, in the meditation that Maria and I did last night, was that real was that my imagination?

Ort: that was real and so was Maria's as well. And if you develop that thought interface with consciousness then you can travel and you can communicate.

Mack: I have one more question that I'd like to ask. Very recently, I have been hearing beeping sounds in groups of three. And also, when I'm on the phone… dialing sounds. And you can hear the phone being picked up when I am on the phone with specific individuals. Would that be anyone in the Council of Eight letting me know they are there or would this be some other sort of interference that shouldn't be taking place?

Ort: We are not communicating with you by those means.

Mack: All right. Thank you.

Ort: It may be somebody else but it is not us.

Mack: Thank you.

Maria: I have another question too. I need a little guidance. When I attempt to connect with the Council of Eight, I feel that sometimes I have connected but I don't have a conscious memory of what was said. Can you suggest a way that I can train myself to have conscious recall of what was said?

Ort: Yes, if you ask yourself and then the thought that comes into your head is the answer. Perhaps you think it is your thought but it is not.

Maria: Yes, I know that. The problem is that I sometimes end up with amnesia for what was said.

Ort: Oh, you will have to ask not to forget.

Maria: So, I'll have to tell myself not to forget, so I won't have amnesia. I'll try it.

Ort: See how that works and let me know the next time we meet.

Maria: okay. (Everyone laughs.)

Jean: So, if there is nothing else, we can end this meeting.

Everyone: Thank you so much.

Ort: I will leave now and let Kevin return. He is not anxious or tired which is good. He is learning quickly. I will see you later.

Everyone: Goodbye and thank you.

Conclusion

Downloads, Telepathic Communication, Dreams, Channeling, Out of Body Travel (OBE's) Telepathic Communication, Physical Materialization, Electrical Equipment Interface, Craft, Consciousness.

I have personally been involved with all of the above modalities. All these modalities of contact are instrumental in encompassing consciousness itself.

Consciousness is the thread, not only of who we are with contact modalities, but all life in the universe. I would expand further by saying consciousness is the true-life form. Physical beings are manifestations of consciousness, which allows conscious life to explore and learn. This would include the extraterrestrials, elementals and angelic realms.

We are so much more than we know or are currently taught. I am sure this book is part of a new understanding of who we are, and our position in a much larger conscious holographic universe.

I dedicate this chapter to my friend Sperry Andrews without his understanding of consciousness and his questions to Ort and Dee We would not have this information. Sperry passed recently he will be missed by many. Sperry Andrews first contacted me after he saw an interview, when I was a guest on the Jeff Mara you tube podcast. Sperry who is a leading scientist in consciousness was intrigued by my experiences with my star families guides Ort and Dee. We had many discussions on zoom they were fascinating. My impression was that his lifelong work and theories dovetailed into my practical experiences, many of which I have covered here. I am not sure of the date but it was this year 2024 when Sperry contacted me and asked if I would ask Ort and Dee what they knew about the void. A term I was not familiar with in the concept of consciousness.

I asked Ort and Dee what they knew about the void. I was given an equation for the void of consciousness with an explanation of how timelines are created. All timelines, past present and future timelines are created from the void of consciousness. The void of consciousness is not void as the name suggests but is full of possibilities full of potential with intentions. I gave the equation to Sperry and he understood it. It supported his work and theories.

OVOC infinity which is greater or equal to OD. OV is zero void, OC is zero consciousness which is infinite and is greater or equal to OD, zero dimension. The void of consciousness is intrinsic within consciousness itself, not separate.

When I was seventeen Ort came to me with one of our shared journeys. Out of body travel, on this occasion Ort said to me where would you like to go this evening. I said to the end of the universe. I was being a bit flippant but by this time we had a good relationship. We set off out of body up and out through the roof. A journey we had taken many times together. This occasion we traveled further than ever before. I was a little concerned and kept tight hold of Orts hand. What seemed like an eternity we stopped and Ort sat down. I sat next to him and said are we at the end of the universe he said no we are at the end of consciousness but there is infinite space for consciousness to continue to expand. I did not fully understand at the time. I do now we were not at the end of the universe but were at the point where the universe meets the void of creation within consciousness itself.

Although I remember the out of body travel with Ort, I would not have fully understood without Sperry Andrews's question. There is an interesting depiction of the void of consciousness equation on a channeled portrait of Zark by my friend Aurora Belcea. The T-shirt and equation can be seen on the Exoconscious Community website. **www.exoconscioushumans.com** there are several portraits of the council of eight channeled by Aurora. Zark is a small grey, he is a mathematician an engineer. He is from the Pleiades system. He has a sense of humor which is apparent in the portrait. I find it fascinating that Ort and Dee are reaching out to others now. I have another friend Rebecca Renfroe who also has contact with Ort and Dee. They get a mention in her book, ***Quantum Windows & Dimensions: A Christians Woman's journey of Faith and ET Contact***. It is also interesting that Dr Karin Mcleod has been given the same or similar downloads about the quantum unified field theory that I have been given. Clearly, they are reaching out to many now to assist with our evolution. They are benevolent and are willing to share their technologies with us. What is the next step? I am told it is The Reveal globally of our star family's presence. The request will come from the citizens of earth. "I am a citizen of earth; I am requesting our star families reveal their presence globally for open contact and cultural exchange". This is a simple request we can all participate in as we move towards The Reveal.

Spontaneous Kundalini Awakening, UFO-UAP's, ESP, Multi-dimensional Rifts, Demonic Oppression, Angelic Encounters, Downloads, Rabbit Holes, and a Second Chance at Life

JOHN KIEHL

I'm telling a story that is both good and bad. I don't have the "Secret" to anything. I'm directing this mostly to those who have found themselves stuck in between veils for a lack of better terminology for words may never adequately describe what this is. If you're in this, you will know exactly what I speak about at times, perhaps most of these pages. I feel for you if you are.

This has tested my faith like nothing I have ever been through. A trial by fire of a spiritual kind, however, as you continue reading you will discover this "fire" can be physical as well. All I can do is write a testimony of the things I have witnessed. I'm not trying to convince anyone of anything but only to provide some hope, shed light on the darkness, and hopefully convey in a meaningful way that God is love and light. A tale of hopelessness, finding Christ, spontaneous kundalini awakening, falling from grace, UFO-UAP's, ESP, dimensional rifts, gang stalking, demonic oppression, Angelic encounters, downloads, upgrades, mind control, sobriety, jail, rabbit holes, and ultimately a renewed faith and a second chance at life. This is my experience.

The Holy Spirit

Sometime in the fall of 2004 I was desperate not to drink. I had been a few months sober at this time and someone had given me a small pocketbook of Christian prayers at rehab. During the past few months I had been reciting these prayers every night which was completely foreign for me. It was a start. I was baptized as a child but did not grow up with religion or attending church and still know very little about the bible. Somehow, I was fortunate to have the gift of desperation at the time and read the prayers as if my life depended on I, which it did.

I didn't want to drink but felt the all familiar tug of war coming seemingly out of thin air as it had happened so many times in my past. I hung around outside of the church and waited for the 3:00 "confession" to open up. I had a beautiful wife, one beautiful daughter at the time, and I was desperate.

I stood in line with the little old ladies and waited for my turn to enter. A red light was shining that would turn green when it was time for the next confessor to enter. My turn finally came, and I entered the chamber. An elderly priest was sitting down. He was to become a dear friend of mine for the next few years before he left this plane of existence.

I humbled myself and said what I came to say hearing an occasional knock from the perhaps concerned elders in the waiting area as I was in the room confessing for over an hour. What happened to me that day I can only describe as the gift of the holy spirit as I in my very limited understanding understand it. It remained heavy, pure, strong, for several months. I had arrived. This is what was spoken of. A gift filling one's cup so full of love and purity its ineffable.

I had experienced brief intervals of pink cloud sobriety in the past, but this was different. Completely. I wanted to share this love. I needed to. Wonderous Love. I proceeded to do just that. I shared my experience and to some small degree I hope I succeeded. A few people I shared with went and confessed to our father through the conduit of my new friend, this elderly priest and by the grace of God, are still sober today.

Kundalini

A thousand points of light which all come back to one. My friend had prayed in tongues placing his hand on my head while I knelt. I began to pray in tongues as well. I gave in, succumbed to spirit once again and let it rip. Unknown but potentially edifying. I was willing to do anything not to drink.

I was stressed. My family was falling apart as another tragedy had taken place. I was hanging on by a thread. I prayed the Rosary. In the kneeling position my legs kicked to the side and shot up in an inverted V formation as an intense energy was released from the base of my spine and up through my body. It felt like I was being electrocuted with an universal spirit filled energy, my body being the super conductor. Every muscle constricted, my face twitched and contorted. I voluntarily went with the flow, for how could this be bad while praying the Rosary? It couldn't be.

After several weeks of this switch being turned on, I began to find out literature describing what was occurring. There are many names for it, many symbols, throughout many cultures and time. A spirit filled energy, more cosmic, less earthly and edifying than the holy spirit but somehow, they tie together. I don't pretend to have the answers. Only God Knows.

Bakersfield

I was doing a side job, replacing a photo eye on the parking lot lighting behind a used car dealership. It was bright daylight and a blue sky for miles to see. Perched high on top of a ladder, I had an inclination to look up. To my disbelief, but seeing is believing, there was a scintillating cube of reflecting light, rotating on its axis a few hundred feet above my head. I watched in amazement as it rotated continuously, revealing its sharp outlines and cubic form.

A car accident across the street broke me from my viewing. A crowd of people began to gather around the scene. I thought it to be a perfect opportunity to share what I was witnessing. I really don't know what I was thinking as people involved in a car accident, severe or not, will not have any inclination to listen to some random guy shouting from across the street "Look up, UFO!" As I walked across the parking lot to the side of the street, it was there the entire time. Hovering in place on its axis, spinning as beams of light were either coming from it or being reflected from the sun. When I reached the curb, to utter my nonsense, it was gone.

The Inspection

We had just gotten into bed a few minutes before. It was another long day at work, I was tired, and our daughter was fast asleep in her bedroom across the hall. I have had numerous out-of-body experiences in my past. Sensations of flying, aware the environment had changed seemingly dimensionally, all the way up to traveling at tremendous speeds with my "light body" through what I can only describe as the appearance of a wormhole.

I have felt on several occasions in the past, something similar but never quite like this. I was completely conscious with my eyes closed and aware of my surroundings. I felt myself being gently lifted out of my body and stood upright in soul, in light, in spirit, and could see my wife and my "body" lying still. In this "essence" of me I felt something I'll describe as a "scan" go from the bottom of my feet gently to the top of my light body and back down to my feet again. It was a warm feeling. There was nothing bad or invasive about it. I felt "myself" then being gently floated perpendicular and placed back into my body. I instantly arose, intact and did my own inspection of the room.

My Lord. What was that? Every time in the past all of my out-of-body experiences had felt like mine and mine alone. This was something else. Some sort of gentle technology or inspection. Preparation for what I was to endure in the days, months ahead.

The Hard Hat

My foreman's hard hat had a big awkward sign on its side which simply stated, "How dare you question my faith." It was way bigger than normal sticker decals such as "high voltage", "sparky", "local union number", etc. It struck me as very odd. I had been transferred to work on Star Wars which I was excited about. We were told two to three years of straight work which is a blessing in the trades.

I get along with almost everybody and it's very hard for me to honestly dislike somebody. I did not know my new crew except for a couple of guys but once again I quickly got along with all. Then like all the familiar stories you hear about of those who have gone through this, it seems like a switch goes off and the classic workplace mobbing scenario took place.

The day before this occurred, I had been pulled over by the police for driving my motorcycle without having the motorcycle enhancement needed. The officer was actually super cool. He could have confiscated my motorcycle but allowed me to drive it home with a fine and these words, "Do yourself a favor and get a motorcycle license." If I had only listened.

We had one vehicle with four wheels, but my wife needed it to bring and pick up our daughter from school while I was at work. I continued to drive the motorcycle which on top of other foolish decisions I had made, only reinforced the thought that at one time, I had been placed into some select program, blacklisted by someone or people I know in positions of power with connections. Sure, I had made multiple shit lists, way more than I need to disclose, but people who find themselves in this situation soon discover there is a supernatural underlining to what occurs as well, which lends theory to possibly being supernaturally ordained, a trial-by-fire, perhaps better described as a modern-day man's dark night of the soul, techno styled.

I noticed the switch had been pulled. Now, my crew was acting strangely to me. I could feel the discontent and hateful eyes upon me. I could see the stares and whispers. Nothing extreme but the knowing it was directed your way. Ultimately, I view this as the law of attraction that had magnetized my negativity into a negative realm. Living like an old episode of "The Dark Side" found its beginnings and found me. Hit!

I ended up losing my job. A few days later, I was driving our car with my daughter when another car pulled up behind me and started taking pictures of us. I had no idea why as he sped off, but I didn't like it one bit. I started to sense I was being followed at this point. I later learned that a private detective had indeed been hired to investigate me. Perhaps this was only one small bit of the energy I was picking up.

What was otherworldly was the series of never-ending circumstances which began to occur. For those in the know you are well versed in color sensitizing. People who feel they have been placed in this "Program" often times report a color associated with a negative stimulus which becomes constant. Red is the crowd favorite of other people's testimonies and red it was with me. Every car in traffic surrounding me was Red. I'm not saying one, two, three. For weeks, reaching into three months deep, every single car no matter where I turned, where I went, how slow or how fast I drove, was red. Surrounded by an endless horde of Red. If that is not enough to drive you bat shit crazy simultaneously everyone you encounter from school pickups, to school drop offs, the malls, the stores everywhere is now wearing red. Are you fucking kidding me? It is so bizarre, so other worldly, so perverse, it's hard to explain but you definitely know you are not in Kansas anymore. If this is the famed synchronization key this is truly the shit end of it.

The head trip only continues. Random people you walk by out of the blue will blurt out something only you know. Something so particular to your life story. If you have ever read anything about demonic harassment you know this is one of their classic modus operandi. On top of the unnerving personal insults chilling you to the bone weird inexplicable sneers showing hateful smiles of teeth.

The Reptilian

I was working at a University in Southern California known for its science and technology. Previously to accepting the position I was researching a lot of different things. The first day on the job I was working in a closed off area with images and pictures on the wall many directly related to what I had been interested in and investigating myself.

It was lay the end of the day and I was by myself on the roof inspecting placement for a conduit run I would be navigating in the days to come. A man came out of nowhere and began speaking with me. He said he was with facilities and his attire was normal. Everything about him was normal except the fact he had classic to the "T" reptilian eyes. I know how absurd and cliché this sounds. I acted as if Nothing was out of the ordinary from my perspective, answered the couple questions he had of who I was and what I was doing on the roof, and got on the service elevator to go home. I chalked it up as just another unbelievable occasion.

The Demons

With the flip of God's ordained switch, like holographic quantum theory, my resonance was attracting the dark. Everywhere I went lurking around every corner was another negative attraction disturbingly real. I will not sugar coat the facts. If there ever is a truth you discover to share with the world about the existence of evil manifestations in your waking reality this was it. When you realize that this change has occurred it rocks you to the core. No humanly way possible, no statistical mathematical improbabilities, to bring moment after moment, encounter after encounter of negativity. They Live" has arrived on your doorstep in an unmarked box with an old VCR tape you unpackage which rains down hell fire.

You begin to question and struggle for answers playing internet doctor to yourself. Video after video on you tube with countless people going thru the same experience and struggling to come to any logical conclusion that makes sense of the insanity. Entirely impossible but true. For the observer reading these pages who hasn't gone through this, you simply may not understand. For the psychiatrist, psychologist, you may heavily lean to giving it a diagnosis. I'm here to tell you are wrong.

It is 100 % spiritual in nature and my hope is to shed light on this and to provide hope to those suffering. Crazy does not "know" things have become crazy. Although I do not try and pretend there isn't legitimate chemical imbalances and real diagnoses that people may obtain real help with medication this is something "ENTIRELY" different and real. A spiritual solution for a spiritual attack is what is needed, and it is what has brought me across the bridge and through the gate. Jesus Christ my savior and redeemer, his host of angels, my higher guides, the light, God's infinite love for his children.

I do not want to exclude anyone who is not of the Christian faith from benefiting from these pages. God is love and undoubtingly no matter what your core belief is if it is God centered love, continue in this for your solution to obtain freedom from the darkness. Use the laws of attraction to your great advantage. Pray, meditate, listen to uplifting music, help others in need, and place yourself around people you know are seeking the same thing. We are all one no matter what you believe.

My heart bleeds for whoever finds themselves going through this. Please take heed in my words and believe it is not your family, it is not your police, it is not your military, it is not some program you were placed into. Some are chosen to be refined by fire like the legendary Phoenix. To go through the flames of emerge from the ashes victorious. Transmuting the darkness into a beacon of hope and raising a torch for your fellow man who cannot find his way out of the pit. It is a wonderful blessing.

I have read many accounts of people and how they first perceive this is happening to them. It starts and continues so similar for most that once again the statistical probability of so many people experiencing the same phenomenon is next to none. I will attempt to describe as best as I can what happened, what's happening now, and how I'm a better person for it. In layman's terms to defeat this one must do this through love.

It began like I said as if one day a switch was turned on which magnetically attracted crazy town to me. As I've heard many people declare and witness one of the first things you observe is the constant bombardment of stranger's evil grins. A smile with all teeth showing, a perverse invasion of contempt for you. A hatred and a look as if they know you and highly dislike you is not a qualified statement. It is an encounter of hate. Strangers hating you and the more you encounter this the more it intensifies and the more satisfaction their glares and mannerisms become aimed directly at you. It is so continuous, so nonstop, it instills fear. Fear is what "they" feed off of. Stephen King would find it hard to describe how utterly surreal this is.

These bombardments of darkness put you not into not only defense mode but one of super sensitive observation. This was completely nuts. You place yourself on high alert. Many people state at this time they notice they are being followed. I sure did. As many people have proclaimed it's usually a series of one particular color car that once again is magically drawn to YOU. Like many, for me it was red. Everywhere I went there would always be red cars in front of me, behind me, parked next to me. Everywhere. Once again this was impossible but yet it was happening.

The who, what, when, why, and how comes to the forefront of your mind as you struggle to comprehend this insanity which countless other people you have discovered are going through and witnessing the exact same things. At this stage I dove headfirst into the internet to attempt to find the answers.

The who and why fit many different pieces to the puzzle in my life. Sure I had pissed off people high in political office, I had poked my nose into many rabbit holes and broadcasted my opinions to the world. It doesn't make any sense that a man-made program targeting many thousands of people in every country around the world describing the exact same thing could be possible. It isn't. To place oneself on such a level of importance or a threat to the world at large that any government would spend the money or resources to conduct no touch torture is grandiose. It is not no touch torture. It is a sucker punch coming from left field of a supernatural kind, with potentially human players participating in raising hell unknowingly, one could only hope.

When faced with such an unknown you soon realize the futility of your situation. If you have a family to protect it's even scarier. Ultimately once again in my life I was faced with something I became to believe no human power could relieve me of. God had done for me in the past what I could not do for myself. His love and power, his magnificence, his radiance I had witnessed before. I was humbled. Please God I begged, to be delivered from this insidious horde. A torment I could not shake. Unexplainable to anyone who hasn't walked through this darkness and completely relatable to people who find themselves stuck in it.

I deplore for those of you reading these words finding yourself so completely lost feeling abandoned by humanity but worse yet feeling God has abandoned you, to not give up. Sometimes I think God chooses some souls to go through a trial by fire of a supernatural kind. I can remember at this point struggling to read the words of the bible. When this occurred it really left me feeling abandoned. Perhaps a huge wakeup call was in order that God refused to be used by me as a relief pitcher when I was the one who ultimately had left his grace to begin with.

Whatever your personal circumstances you perceive landed you into the pit do not give up. My belief now is God and my guardian angels were with me every step of the way. Sometimes you must go through the bad to get to the good. Even when you walk through a valley of deep darkness do not be afraid because he is with you. His rod and his staff will comfort you. "The ABC's we all must face, try to keep a little grace." Jerry Garcia. Sometimes we are forced to whistle through our teeth and spit and know Jesus has our back! My eyes have been opened. I am wide awake.

Deny evil as a reality. It is a disillusioned false state of consciousness which is not of God. God is light and love pure and simple. The darkness has no foothold in your existence for God said it cannot exist.

The Spook

We were at one of our weekly shopping sprees in Walmart to get food and supplies for the coming days ahead. I was in the paint section picking up some for a few projects around the house. A man and woman were there that I had struck up a conversation with while waiting for my paint to be spun. It turned out he needed some electrical work done so we exchanged phone numbers.

A few days went by and I saw this man in the local bagel bakery every time and figured it was just a coincidence. We spoke for a few minutes each time. During this period, I was still experiencing the color red everywhere I went. Random cars coming up to me, slowing down and taking pictures, coupled with the negative, dark, sneers and showing of teeth by almost everyone.

He told me one day at the bagel bakery, that he currently wasn't working anymore. His exact words were, "They won't let me carry a gun anymore," and, "I used to be a bodyguard of sorts for high level politicians. Okay?" He always seemed like a levelheaded fellow, so this didn't seem so strange and I didn't press him for more information.

Before all this had begun, I had done extensive research into 9/11, false flag theories, planet x, conspiracy after conspiracy. One being the missing Malaysian Airlines flight 370. On one of my conversations with this guy on the telephone he blurted out "Hey have you heard of all the missing naturopath's that went missing on MA 370." I replied no and coughed up what my own research had led me to believe.

I thought this was a bit weird as our conversations had never gone down this road remotely before but didn't place too much stock into it as I thought he was just shooting the shit. I did ask him if he knew of a good Naturopath for my wife who was suffering from sarcoidosis. His reply was shocking as the name of the doctor he produced was highly personal to events in our past but a completely different doctor located on the east coast. I thanked him for the information and the referral and promptly googled a Naturopath who went by that extraordinarily coincidental name in southern California. Nothing.

The next time I went to the bagel bakery this man was there again. That would be 5 straight weeks in a row at different times he would always be there. I looked at him a little differently now but still without judgement. He followed me out to the car as I put my daughter in the backseat. His next words spoken were haunting and eerily exciting at the same time. "Hey, do you want to hear a joke?" "Sure," I said. "So, there's this guy who's being chased all over town. Everyone thinks he's crazy and he's being followed everywhere. No matter where he goes, they are behind him. What's really going on is the military is trying to recruit him but all he keeps saying is I didn't do it."

Side Note: I just arrived back to my home state from driving cross country with my wife. When we were almost across the country, we were pulled over by the Highway Patrol. A very nice officer approached the car. When I had submitted my driver's license to the California DMV it came back with the wrong birthdate on it. I have always been apprehensive about it and tried to correct the issue.

He had me exit the car and go with him to his cruiser. The officer let me sit up front with him uncuffed while explaining to me that according to his system, I was wanted for terrorism. I chuckled at this which he responded by saying "I'm serious. Look." He proceeded to show me on his screen an Arabic looking man on my California's driver's license with all my information including the wrong birthdate which had been given to me. He then said, "But this clearly isn't you." The officer then let me out of the car without making any calls for back up and let us go. One cool cop for sure.

The Visit

I was lying in bed. My daughter was fast asleep in her room. No sooner had I laid down when I felt a strange hypnotic, euphoric, trance came upon me. I could feel my body being gently rolled over to the left. All senses real. Then to the right, and gently turned onto my back again. I was completely aware. The sensation is hard to comprehend. Your feeling so good you allow it to happen. I knew some other force was moving me but, in the moment, I was ok with it. My legs shot up and the lower half of my back was off the bed. I felt what seemed like a liquid light go through and circle my lower abdomen. This was an intrusion. My daughter! Hell no! I snapped myself out of it.

My eyes opened; my legs came crashing down as I was partly hovering off the bed. I shook off the hypnotic fog and ran into my daughter's room. She was ok. Fast asleep. Thank God!

What had just happened? It's one thing when your faced with the unknown. A completely different story when you have a family to protect. Regardless of the reasons why, the tech is infallible, invasive, and traumatic. Imagine what poor bastards who wake up during surgery must go thru? Maybe there was a good reason? I do not know.

Note: The same thing has occurred a few more times to my recollection however the last time I consciously can remember I felt myself being lovingly embraced by my own limbs but through someone else within me controlling my arms and the greatest amount of love and affection was conveyed through every fiber of my being.

The Burn

"Blessed is the man who trusts in the Lord, whose trust is the Lord. He is like a tree planted by water, that sends out its roots by the stream, and does not fear when heat comes, for its leaves remain green, and is not anxious in the year of drought, for it does not cease to bear fruit." - Jeremiah 17:7-8

I was smack in the middle of it. Something dark and positive at the same time although I couldn't see anything positive at the time. I was confused. Searching for answers of the humankind when this was something "more." My wife and daughter were gone. I had tried to explain something so unexplainable it must have scared them. I know it did. It felt like I was under attack therefore they were. I was grateful they were gone for I didn't know how to protect them when I didn't know who was attacking me. Better yet, what?

I packed a bag of clothes and some other bare essentials. My plan was to leave. Perhaps draw the enemy away from my family and losing whoever, whatever was tormenting me in the process. My face had now been burning and my brain felt as if it was being fried from the inside out for days on end. I lost track of how long in fact this had been occurring. I just wanted the pain to go away but it wouldn't. This truly felt as a living hell while still very much alive. I must admit there were times I wondered if I really was.

I lived in a complex a half a mile away from the department of Homeland Security's headquarters and our complex was full of staff from all branches only intensifying the speculation that this was indeed man made. I now know I was actually placed on a list you do not want to find yourself on. There was real surveillance. It was apparent. My downloading a Russian made app for my phone in order to continually bounce my SMS messages from cell tower to cell tower so my phone could not be sting rayed. I'm sure only made matters worse. I just wanted my privacy.

I thru my items in the car and sped off around the corner rapidly approaching our complex's gate. A man came running out of his unit with no shirt on, no shoes, only sweatpants. He attempted to stop me. I knew him and have observed him observing me in a few random places outside of the complex in the past. I gathered he was former military from the emblem on his car but he had the air of someone active in another branch. Why did he try and stop me? What did he know? What the fuck was going on? What was I into?

A car had been waiting for the gate in front of me, so I drove around the friend, foe and hauled ass out of there. I made my way to the interstate and started heading east. The burning on my face and the brain fire diminished a little. Thank God.

When I was about 50 miles outside of Orange county, heading to Arizona the weird shit started once again. There were signs along the side of the interstate with bright yellow digital display letters. The first one I read was "It's been so long since I've driven a car." What? I shook it off and trudged forward. Roughly a half mile away the next road sign said "Cool, I just saw myself through your eyes." Okay so at this point I got scared. How could I be reading this? There's no way it would be on roadside digitized billboards!

I kept moving and got to a part of highway heading to the Arizona border where there were no more signs. My intent was to find a place, a barren place to camp. I turned on the satellite radio. Some dance/techno music was playing, and I could feel as if something was trying to control my mind. I started to feel euphoric. I went from total fear to euphoria by music and something "else."

I crossed the Arizona border. Home free I hoped. I still was under this euphoric, hypnotic, spell when wham! Instant panic attack hit me. This was too much.

I pulled off the first exit I could find and rolled into a little gas station/convenience store. A car pulls up to me with 2 guys in front and a woman in back. There was a tv screen in the back seat with the image of an atomic explosion? I went inside my heart pounding. A young man follows me in from the car which pulled up next to me, walks by me with a huge grin with a shirt saying, "The Thin Blue Line." I was to see this same young man with his same shit-eating grin a month later in a hotel in Costa Mesa. More on that later.

I jumped back into my car. I turned around and started heading back to California while the satellite radio came back on by itself. Screw it, I asked my first question. "What do you want from me?" The screen started flashing "CIA Make Magic." This was too much. I continued. I asked "where do you want me to live?" The screen started flashing "Where the Streets Have No Name." I instantly started thinking of gang stalking's ultimate goal of attempting to make you institutionalized, suicidal, incarcerated, dead, or homeless as it seemed very fitting for all I had been through.

I thought of the next logical thing to say as I was fucking done with this game, this mysterious bullshit of cat and mouse with pussies hiding behind fucking radio waves. "Let's meet," I said. "No Phone, No Police, Federal Land", started flashing across my radio in green. The music kicked back on and I started feeling better again. Too good. If there was a form of mind control this must be it. I pulled off the highway to another gas station approximately 20 to 30 miles back on California's side. Admittedly during this stretch of highway, I almost, almost, came close to purposely flipping my car. Never.

I cruised up next to the pumps, got out, broke my cell phone, smashed it with my steel toe boots, thru it into the trash with the windshield wiper fluid below it, when a car screamed up out of now where. I sat back in the driver's seat and watched a woman jump out of the driver's seat, reach into the trash, grab my phone, and sped off into the night. Again, WTF.

I drove away, found the first barren parking lot I could, pulled into it and waited. No one ever came. I must not have been on Federal Land. LOL.

Guardian Angel

I turned the key to the car and visibly watched the needle for the gas gauge switch from hovering at empty to 3/4's of a tank full knowing I hadn't added any fuel. This was just another experience I somewhat over looked at the time as these occurrences were happening daily. Life had become an intense display of magical happenings, some good, some evil, all hard to comprehend, and some seemingly divinely ordained.

I tried my best to calm our daughter down. This had been a tidal wave growing which crashed ashore. She needed out away from me. Something was terribly wrong, and it scared me to have her subjected to whatever I found myself into. I brought her to my sister's home a mere

25 minutes away in southern California. I calmed her down as best as I could struggling to make sense out of something you cannot. I stayed for a while consoling her. She had been thru a lot over the past few years, some by my foolish mistakes I am eternally sorry for, but this shit was not me?

It was early evening when we had arrived and dark outside. I walked towards my car in shame. How could I have let this happen? What was so dark infecting our lives? I had a strong inclination to look back at the house before I got into the car. My front door was ajar. It was a splendid, momentous site. Breathtaking. Surreal. A luminescent figure was hovering over my sister's house silhouetted against the black starry night. I couldn't believe my eyes were seeing this but yet I was.

The figure was that of an ANGEL. Gorgeous, glowing brilliantly. It was a pure, phosphorescent white. The outline of its wings a brighter white with even brighter spots every so often along the outlines. It had the appearance and feel of a living light being. It was not a craft, nor a classical Angel in the sense of a human with wings. It looked like a faceless cloth Angel 10 feet tall on top of a Christmas tree but only "Alive." Simply put the most wonderful thing I've ever seen.

Its luminescent wings unfolded and flapped. The Angel shot up 100 feet into the night with one swoop. Two more times and it was at least 300 feet into the starry night. It then turned perpendicular and with three more strokes of its wings it was completely gone off into the distance along its celestial flight. Such a gift to see when all hope seems lost.

A Typical Walk

"Do not be afraid or discouraged, for the Lord will personally go ahead of you." Deuteronomy 31:8

Life can be very challenging, especially when the veil to the other side has thinned, so much so that crossings are made. So much so that they are no longer figments of one's imagination but walking, talking, and even flying about. Both the good and the bad.

Alone for days now in the house, the oppression had driven my family away, or I drove them away to be free from it. Either way they were safe. There now was an ominous feeling, a presence about this entire apartment complex that was palpable. I just drove by some mid 50's man with parted back, feathered, blond hair I had never seen before. He turned his head to me as I drove by on my way to my place and raised his index finger to his lips signaling the "Be Quiet" universal sign. I continued driving. WTF? It was around every single corner. Darkness aimed directly at me. I couldn't escape it?

Before my family left, I had my daughter with me at Laguna Beach for a walk and to get some lunch. While we were walking out of the blue, she started screaming at me hysterically that I was dragging my feet. Her tantrum at the age of 11 was way out of whack and scary. I brought her back to the car and she calmed down saying "Daddy, I don't know what just happened, I'm so sorry."

We drove a mile away and pulled into a gas station. An old, beat up, yellow, 70's Scooby-Doo van with a dream catcher hanging from the rear-view mirror pulled up next to us. I took her inside and the driver of the van, a rather large man, about 50, with long blond hair, gives me evil grin and proceeds dragging his feet while staring at me intensely down the aisle never breaking his glare and evil ass smile. Daily, hourly, this is what it was like. Fuckers.

Back to being alone again. It was still daylight. I went into my place and was spooked by the electric eerie ozone of the place. So, my next bright idea was to take pictures and see what spirits might reveal themselves in my unit. Brilliant! In times before I had tried to read the bible when this all got intense, but I physically couldn't. The words were all visibly scrambled. When you're scared shitless and reaching for God, it feels like you are abandoned. It's hell. Literally.

In my genius I took the pictures thinking perhaps it would be worthy of some form of self-defense. "You see me, well I see you too." Click, click, click, ...The reveal. Holy shit! Great. There is a fucking "person" in my living room riding a horse, carrying a sword, and bearing a crown. To top it off for good measure were a ½ dozen other elvin/goblin entities hanging around. I couldn't believe my eyes but seeing is believing.

A picture of my deceased father in law fell off the mantle of our fireplace with no draft or motion by me. It floated like a feather and landed at my feet while I was standing 10 feet away from where it was originally. I heard him say to me in my mind "Don't let them push you around." I'm grateful for that happening.

I decided to go upstairs and try and lay down in my dark room. Click, click, click. Oh, fuck no! My entire bedroom now is showing the walls are made of some weird ectoplasm shit with hundreds of smiling demonic beings everywhere. I'm now going to fall asleep in my bedroom which has morphed into "The Portal to Hell". Fuck No!

At this exact point in time a horde of coyotes are going bananas sounding exactly like wild baboons across the street. Well let's go for a walk. Why not? I put on my coat and hat, squeeze my feet into sneakers and hit the street. By the way, over the past two years living in this residence I had never, ever, heard a single coyote.

I begin walking out of the neighborhood. It's about 11 o'clock at night with only occasionally a car driving by. About 10 minutes into my walk, I arrive at an intersection. A car pulls up in front of me and stops at the red light. The driver's head is twisting back and forth at an inhumanly impossible speed while his upper body simultaneously is going toward the dashboard and back into the seat like a pendulum on crack. God please help me.

I continue walking toward the local 7-Eleven. I hear the hounds of hell once again, a shit load of them, a very large pack of coyotes coming down the side of the mountain thru fog towards me. I welcomed it at this point. I waited until they were close and whistled to them. There grunts, growls, and shrieks of the night are turned by this simple act and they run away.

A motorcycle comes flying by with a passenger doing a wheelie precisely at this point. No helmets with masks hanging from the back of their necks as if from a costume party in hades they roar past me into the night.

These are just a very few, very few examples of what it was like.

"Those who trust in the Lord will find new strength. They will soar high on wings like eagles." Isaiah 40:31

Trial by Fire

What was the burning? I had been researching all of the things people who were going through this had in common. Whistle blowers, conspiracy theorists, people that perhaps saw something they shouldn't have, said something they shouldn't have, a host of reasons for people asking themselves "why". People who try and put a human face to this think they are on some sort of list. The deception runs very deep and the deeper you went down the rabbit hole yourself only makes it harder to understand something so beyond the norm whatever that may be. There was a common theme I cannot deny. 9/11 conspiracy theorists, false flag investigations, pissing off certain people of perceived power.

If there is one thing I have learned, it's no matter what answer to anything you are researching on the Internet, you will find it. I have my own beliefs to many things and in so broadcasting my opinions on such matters was this enough to land someone on such a list. I think not however it was made apparent to me that indeed majestically my California driver's license was now bearing the face of a middle eastern man with my information essentially saying I was wanted for terrorism. How the fuck does that happen? I think I know the who and why and I already forgive them as lame and as much of an abuse of power that may be. Taking the high road.

One of the common things people who are going thru gang stalking is the sensation and claims of being hit with nonother than microwave weaponry. Commonly referred to no touch torture for those that find themselves in this predicament. I was taking readings in our home of seemingly elevated levels of Gauss. Super high levels. All of which are completely unhealthy for not only adults but children especially. In other parts of the world there are standards in place to protect people and children from this.

People going thru this stage are now not only feeling followed, having weird paranormal occurrences usually of a negative kind, but now it has elevated to a physical level. Things get infinitely more real when your face starts to burn nonstop relentlessly for days at a time. It hurts like hell. There was no escaping it. Wherever you seemingly went so came the burning. An intense sunburn sensation cooking your face and the inside of your brain relentlessly.

Note- two other actual Veterans in the high desert locked up with me who had experienced gang stalking described the exact same thing. One crashed his motorcycle because it happened to him while travelling. He also has many UFO encounters. My friend actually ended up in a coma from the accident and was legally dead for a few minutes. Regardless these were two other random people I befriended while locked away who most definitely had experienced the exact same thing?

I tried escaping it by driving, staying in a hotel, at different places and it never stopped. I was so disoriented from this, confused, seared, in pain, and feeling abandoned by God that I tried like other's to place a human face to this as it sure felt like a hell fire technology had been unleashed upon you. How could God allow for such diabolical torture? It had to be manmade.

At this point your faith is tried like never before. Day after day of weird dark encounters and now, holy shit, you are being fried alive. Sucker punched from somewhere. But who, why? There had to be a reason. I had reached my breaking point.

I was completely alone. This process, this trial, this oppression had driven my family away. I couldn't take it anymore. My wife had bought me a brand-new wood handled electricians' knife for Father's Day. I unfolded the knife. I was laying on the floor alone in the dark. I couldn't take it anymore. I reached over with my right hand and sliced my left wrist with the razor-sharp blade. Nothing Happened. I tried again. The blade would not cut me. A brand-new razor-sharp blade with me, making an attempt as hard as I could. Nothing. God was with me the whole time.

The Disks

It was another bright sunny day in southern California as I stood in my sister's back yard contemplating. I had the inclination to look up into the sky. Two disks I would estimate at 1000 feet inverted diagonally to the earth flew by silently at tremendous speed. They maintained equal distance from one another in formation over the entire brief time of viewing. They were there, then off disappearing into the distance together. Gone in a flash.

The Stars Turn Into? And Fly Away

It was nighttime now at my sister's house. The stars were shining bright and beautiful. I had made the decision to come outside to sleep under the stars on my nieces and nephews' trampoline. I wrapped myself up in a quilt and placed a pillow under my head. I laid down for a night of star gazing.

One by one each star, one after another, turned into a stationary "craft" with a blinking red, green, and white light underneath. The light of the star would turn "off" then by magic was a stationary vehicle of some sort. Each one would remain still for a few moments before slowly riding off into the distance all at the same pace. How was this possible? I do not know as it left the night sky devoid of stars in this vicinity. I went inside to sleep.

The High Desert

I was outside of our apartment gazing at 3 stars which were in the west above the ocean. It was too early for Orion's belt and they were too low. What was this? Pronounced in their heavenly float shimmering in our earth's lower atmosphere?

The top star decided to slowly ascend into the night sky following an 11 o'clock trajectory, the middle stayed in place, while the bottom followed the same path down on a 5 o'clock trajectory seemingly going into our great blue Pacific. While in the high desert county jail I had many peculiar discussions with a few men all of whom had UAP experiences. I was discussing this with a friend, an army veteran of the Afghanistan war suffering from PTSD and described what I saw.

Based upon our discussions of earlier phenomenon we both had witnessed I felt more than comfortable sharing with my friend. As soon as I said the top "Star" shot off in the 11 o'clock position Shawn said,

"Shut Up!" He answered the remainder of my encounter by saying "And the bottom one went down in the 5 o'clock position!" "No fucking way, No fucking way." "I saw the exact same thing."

At certain times during my stay it was as if I could see spirit attachments or demonic influences visually within some of the inmates. Their bodies would shake uncontrollably and their faces in a contorted way displaying a certain evil manipulation. It wasn't that they were bad people nor were they displaying their true nature at all. It was something else that was attached to them like a psychic vampire which would show its true identity as it struggled to gain foothold more permanently. I noticed the men who stood close in prayer seemed to recover from this affliction the most.

Son of a bitch if this was spiritual sight, I wanted none of it at the time. Occasionally in the beginning of my stay I would also hear the all familiar speech from inmates speaking of things which somehow were directed at me. Knowledge so personal to me it was incomprehensible they would know. Looking back I see now it was not them talking at all. It was "Them."

Once again, I'm reminded of the law of attraction. From a human perspective and my infantile understanding. You can place so many names on this but at the end of the day you hit your knees and pray God delivers you from evil. I have read and heard hundreds of people's accounts, testimonies, who have gone through much if not all I am describing. My personal belief I have stated previously is I had fallen from grace. I had attracted this to myself. The man made, the supernatural, the good and the bad.

All of this in my eyes officially started from resentment. A putrid hatred of my own making. Family politics, politics, drama, courts, booze, drugs, and handcuffs. I projected an anger so intense at my perceived injustice of the world so intensely that I ended up being burned by it myself. These extraordinary resentments morphed and opened up a doorway months earlier.

As the days rolled by my condition improved through prayer, meditation, reading, fasting, and companionship. Deep conversations unfolded on an hourly basis. Many of the inmates in the Veteran's dorm had their heyday in the paranormal, a few in seemingly special access programs, and two which I know of had direct experience with "Gang Stalking", demonic oppression, whatever evil, vile name you can surmise. These two other friends of mine also had been hit with directed energy weapons as I have. What was this all about?

Through all the shared bullshit every one of us had gone through to lead us all here, despite the threat of repercussions, there was no racism permitted within the dorm. Black, White, Hispanic, Asian, Indian, American Indian, etc. It did not matter. Men who have seen too much do not permit that bullshit. A salute to American Veterans.

Time

Time and your observable perception of it can challenge you. As I write these very words my wife with the door closed lying in bed in the room next to me just asked me "Do I know what TIME it is?" Very typical of the connection we share.

Time seemed to stop or rather seemed to disappear at different intervals over a period of a few weeks. Al l the noises around me would just stop. The birds, the cars, motorcycles, construction bangs, everything. I would just be there then the radio in the yard next to me would start playing again, the construction work would return to normal with all of its sounds, and the birds would be chirping once again.

I was at my sister's house after days on end of weird sometimes frightening encounters. My father was in town receiving chemotherapy for his leukemia. My sister and her family were traveling so I had slept in one of my nephew's beds the night before.

I was standing in the living room watching my father as he watched the television. I turned the corner walking out of the living room into the hallway and entered my nephew's bedroom. There was a small pile of change on the bed which had fallen out of my pocket the night before while sleeping.

I scooped up all the change and placed it in my pocket standing, solid, sober, aware in the bedroom. In a flash without any physical movement by me accompanied by a weird whooshing noise I was standing back in the living room watching my father watch the television in the exact same place, stance, location, I had been in previously! I've had this sensation before but not nearly as surreal and unmistakable as this. I reached into my pocket where I had just placed the loose change I had taken off of the bed. Absolutely nothing in my pocket. Holy Shit! I walked back into the room and there was the change laying on the bed. I reached down picked up the "Change", glanced to my left. As I did this my eyes fixated on my nephew's 3rd dimensional globe of the world. Change the world.

6 months later on route to find my old housemate, now homeless, hoping to see him outside of a Starbucks to possibly uplift his spirits and mine, I drove by a car with a license plate hanging in the window with the word "Ascend" and in big painted block letters on the side of the car was in quotations "Change the World."

Information Sent

I was lying down in bed my family gone. Dispersed. I Consciously awake having an outer body experience. I was floating with my "essence" and could see in 360 degrees in every direction all at once. I could detect what I perceived to be an ominous force inside every residence I had lived in for the past several years as I flew into each one desperately searching for my wife and daughter.

My perception was I was being challenged somehow. | kept on saying out loud "I'm a Christian I'm not afraid of you". With a swooshing sound I'm fully delivered back into my body. I am fully aware of my surroundings, eyes closed, but wide awake. I see clear as day google maps in my mind's eye with a Pin moving visibly as if I'm watching this on a screen within myself go floating by, where I was living in southern California and headed south west from that direction to where the pin dropped in place. I was shown latitude and longitude coordinates for the location. "Fort Magic, Ford Nix" were the two words that came into my mind when shown this. Immediately next a mathematician/scientific formula was displayed on the screen now available to me in my mind. It was black and white and just there.

Later on, in the day I had the inclination to research time, different dimensions, light, time, travel... I saw the exact formula I had seen in my mind right in front of me! It was too clear. I took a screenshot on my phone of the equation. Several days later I receive an email from Google Maps explaining to me they appreciate my picture for the State of Vermont and the time/dimension formula was what I allegedly had downloaded to google maps. The email | received electrician jobs in Antarctica for fun as it simply is not a possibility at this time. The email I received said thank you for your contribution saying there were over 5000 views of my screenshot and the only continent revealed by name was Antarctica.

Ale House Sightings

Just like the Veteran's dorm, I found myself locked up in where there were a significant number of guys who had encounters of all the contact modalities. The Ale House I lived in for a few months was the same. In the Veteran's dorm it was concentrated with guys who had near death experiences, UFO/UAP experiences, ghost encounters, out-of-body experiences, paranormal events of every kind including a few who had suffered the phenomenon of gang stalking/demonic oppression.

The Ale House which I lived in was a sober living environment, as it was very cheap rent, a safe place, and full of like-minded people. I had no idea how like-minded. Out of the ten guys living in the house at least 7 of them all had encounters just like in the Veteran's dorm. People suffer great stress in life some way more than others. Labels can be placed trying to explain what has now manifested in these poor souls' lives. From what I've seen, I can't help but think when great stress occurs, and PTSD is proclaimed, it is more of a negative spirit attachment or demonic oppression. Doorways get opened. This is my observation. Perhaps this is why "some" refer to us as containers.

Around the end of November, I was star gazing. A completely silent ship flew over my head estimated at 500 feet above me. Its "nose" was divided in two with a triangular rear. Brilliant lights ran along both sides of its tuning fork front. Amazing.

"Note" the day I moved into the Ale House a black helicopter flew down this residential street extremely low almost buzzing the house. The moment I stepped out of the truck. This has happened a few times.

Projections

Unmarked black helicopters are a common theme surrounding UAP sightings. Like a car having to be visibly marked with identification more importantly is any vehicle flying in the air to be marked. These sightings of these black helicopters seem to appear for many around the time of a sighting. My experience has been this to be true as well as a certain kind of airplane especially at night.

Last night directly overhead of my wife and I two planes which resembled exactly what I witnessed the "Stars" turning into in Costa Mesa started from the exact same point straight above us with the exact same latitude and speed. Pitch perfect. Noise and lights present just like the "Helicopters." Out of nowhere they materialized directly overhead estimated at 1000 feet from a single point and headed p away from each other in a V formation. I've witnessed this before on my trip to Catalina Island but with two extremely bright "Stars" doing the same thing.

After explaining to my wife what I believed really just happened I continued to star gaze and stare at one particularly bright star to the west. As always it started to bounce around visibly in the night. Perhaps extraterrestrials can bend star light to give the appearance of the "Star" moving to grab our attention. About 10 minutes following the "Star's" movements DIRECTLY over my head a beautiful luminescent craft streaked across the sky shinning an intense bright phosphorescent white. Straight across above me, most definitely NOT a shooting star as it felt like it lasted 2.5 seconds to pass and was so majestically other worldly. Awesome! 5 minutes later, while still thrilled at what I just witnessed, an extremely bright white flash was blinked. I took it as a hello. I say hello as well.

The Stars Move

Every single night I am privileged with observing the stars in southern California. Some nights you can see more than others. They move. Not just their position in the night sky as the hours past. Not an atmospheric wobble. They move when gazed upon individually with an unbelievable distinctive zig zagging, straight up and down movements, and loops. This is observable when using my telescope as well. Not just one, two, or three but every star in the night sky is responding this way. Indescribable, holographic, crafts, projection of consciousness, technology intercepting and redirecting the light, or perhaps best placed in my understanding as God's movements. My wife walked down to the beach with me at night. Thank you. She has now witnessed this happening as well.

Night scope

I will look into the night. The wonder. A spiritual being having a human experience. Another passenger on the ride.

I bought a night scope. I had been seeing activity every night for several months. The stars you can see even while nestled in Orange county is mind boggling. The ones you see zooming by the field of vision with the scope is just as cool. Some will light up intensely and fly away on their merry way. I don't know it's hard to fathom were alone in the universe but in no way does that inhibit my steadfast belief in a loving God and the son incarnate. Jesus the Christ. Not at all.

Moon Dance

Last night for the second time, not only do the stars move, but the moon is doing the same thing. Dancing in the night sky when gazed upon. A beautiful aura with a hint of rainbow began dancing around the moon while I witnessed the moon bobbing and weaving in the night sky. Marvelous. What does this all mean?

Catalina Island

"I will instruct you and teach you in the way you should go; I will guide you with My eye." Psalm 32:8

I was seeing so much activity in the night sky it was crazy. Every single night after night and I loved it. It provided me, and still does, with a comfort knowing there was someone, something else observing the bullshit we were going through here on earth. Wherever they come from, wherever we come from, is the same place. That of light and love. The Father of light. A welcomed embrace from observers unknown to me saying we know the truth and see how you suffer. I would broadcast love back to the stars and usually something would light up and streak across the cosmic backdrop.

I felt a calling to be in nature. Catalina Island was just a short ferry ride from Long Beach, and I had never been there. I made up my mind to take a solo camping trip to the island. The night before my departure I sat in the backyard of Ale House and star gazed. Three intensely bright white objects off in the distance materialized and flew off in formation in the direction of the Island. Another good omen.

My good friend Emir brought me down to the ferry the next day. I took a backpack with bare essentials and a sleeping bag. No need for a tent, I wanted full exposure. I had rented a site at Blackjack Campground smack in the middle of Catalina Island's nature preserve.

The day was beautiful. Nothing but sun and blue ocean on the passenger ferry ride to Avalon. It had been several months, actually years, since I had an escape from the over stimulating concrete jungle of city life. My father was dying of leukemia in Vermont, I hadn't seen my oldest daughter in 5 years, my youngest in a year, my wife was gone, and I was stuck on felony probation in California.

As soon as I made it to Avalon, I was amazed. What a beautiful little city protected from what you might as well call the foreign country of California. I love California but Catalina Island, the two days and one night I was blessed to stay there, I will always cherish.

The hike to Blackjack Campground was only 3.5 hours. 3.5 hours I spent choking back tears at the beauty. The trees, green grass, and ocean to my right was an over stimulating peace I desperately needed. I had been lost and now I was found.

The Island's interior is one gigantic nature conservatory. Someone had the foresight to make this land protected. It's an amazing fact to be so close to southern California's coastline and not to be over developed in the least bit.

Eventually I made it to the campground after climbing one last steep embankment followed by a few twists and turns, then back down descending into Blackjack exactly as the sun went down. I soon found a spot to pitch my sleeping bag, unsure if it was the designated for me or not but there were only a few campers dispersed among the many sites.

Once settled in I decided to go towards a patch of forest next to where I was sleeping and hike as high up as I could among the trees. Snapping my way along the fallen brush, I reached the pinnacle and retained a clear view of the night sky. Two bright objects starting from the same origin separated from each other at an equal pace creating a V on their celestial flight. They remained equal in their V flight path the entire time until they had gone so far away into the night, I could not see them anymore. Awesome!

I stood on the perch among mother nature in the dark, knelt down, and prayed the rosary, the whole time "kundalini' energy flowing through my body like always. After all the shit I had put myself through and been through, it was nice to know the universe, God, his Angels, and celestial visitors bear witness to the shit hand we sometimes get dealt and throw you a big shout out from the Heavens.

At exactly 3 am, I woke up with the distinct image in my mind of a short story I had read when I was a kid by Isaac Asimov in which our universe was essentially inside a supercomputer? I looked to my right and a deer tick was inches from my face on my sleeping bag. I look up at the full moon and a chemtrail is perfectly floating by the moon at the same precise moment.

The next morning, I woke up at around 5 am and decide to pack up and make my trek back starting off in the dark. The stars were dancing as usual, but I did not see anymore "craft." However, two hours later amongst the cliffs by the ocean as the sun was coming up a luminescent, bright light approximately 150 yards from the coastline was shining brightly under the water's surface. I fumbled for my phone and managed to take one really cool picture! It was the size of two cars in diameter and then just like that it was gone.

Contact with an Apparent Plasma Energy Being Inside my Bedroom

Gabriel Hutcheson

In late September of 2018, I was up against a deadline for a book. I didn't think I would make it. This was the important thing that I get it done. The intuition was saying that this was how I was going to help the world. Raised Roman Catholic but strongly agnostic for many years, I prayed to the unknown for help.

Three days passed. On or about September 28, 2018, I woke to a spotlight of moonlight on the wall. It was right at the bed. It was strangely, distinctly circular, moonlight normally being cast in a diffusion. I looked to the adjacent window. There was a big moon. My vision tracked back against the wall. The spotlight of moonlight was gone.

I am telling you, I saw a quote unquote orb in 2018 from less than four feet away. It hovered pin-still at the point of its fastening, three feet above and in front of me one night, almost watching me as I lay quietly in my bed. It was Spielbergian bright, plus flickered with the affectations of a slowly moving fire, and on its intensity, it was equal to a headlight on brights. In the time it took to read the object's effects playing along my wall, and then at the big moon bearing up in the window adjacent, it was given to me "a download" on how we come from a complication on nothingness, and as I had looked to our moon for air, it disappeared. This would all seem to be in response to the prayer I'd done three days before. God knows I am not lying.

I was able to keep calm for about eight seconds, when my heart caught, and I felt the need to recalibrate, in case this was a hypnogogic illusion. I looked out the window and then turned in and ahead to where the object had been. It was gone. I then immediately realized I had an understanding of something that is just so beyond my typical ability to synthesize that I attribute this idea as having been the result of a kind of download process.

I. DOWNLOAD.

1.) That there is no information is itself information.

2.) At some aboriginal point prior to the beginning of any other proper model or logic sequence we shall ever contrive, there is no information. This itself is information, in what you could call a "backspace"; you will represent this abstractly as a *no-on*, which is a theoretical particle like all the others, and it is abstractly representative of this, our first principle, an informative emptiness, a super-tautological *logos*—a necessary prior condition for the emergence of any and all other structure.

3.) All information co-occurs with awareness in a synchronicity. This is the real lesson of the double slit. All other human experimentation also reflects this.

4.) The co-occurance of information and awareness prior to any logic sequence or model—which is the *no-on*—is historically referred to as the "I am (awareness) who I am (information)."

You may call this insight "pre-structuralism." It works moving beyond the forward limits of any other model or logic sequence, as well. In the current thinking, speaking in terms of Shannon entropy, the fact that no information is itself information points to a transcendental, de-limited pleuroma of sorts.

The types of possible information indicated by such an informative emptiness as the *no-on* are both infinite and indestructable, barring that which does not identify/and or compromises the ID of such a system.

II. MORALITY AND ENTROPY

Morality has a scientific correlate, the second law of thermodynamics. We are in a low-entropy trainer. …What is called evolution is at a deeper level the better expression of the second law of thermodynamics. What is called evil is what could be considered as a thwarting of the second law of thermodynamics—a reduction of future max potential entropy. (This is why it is considered in many circles immoral to eat meat, to have abortions, and so on.)

"They" or it or whatever—then gave me an image of two particles interacting. The particles looked identical. They said that these particles were abstract representations of this special case of information interacting with itself. They have said again that you could call these particles "no-ons," like photons or electrons, quote unquote particles of nothing. It was this interaction of the real and vastly more complex "nothing" with that they think could have happened in the first place.

Then, about six months later, still looking for a more complete answer, I ran into what I think was a depiction of what I saw. This was originally found in the 1920s, pinned to the wall of a Tibetan Buddhist's private chamber. The name of the book you can find the image in is The All-Knowing Buddha.

It was then that I met with particular of Buddhism's traditions, especially that of the "celestial buddhas" who sometimes visit and give wisdom on what their tradition calls "emptiness." I have determined that there are many similar images to be found.

The Council of Light:
A Collective that Channels Through Me Consisting of God, My Higher Self and My Spiritual Team - Spiritual Interdimensional Beings, Masters, Guides and Angels

Catherine Chapey[1]
©2024 Catherine Chapey

---

[1] Rev. Catherine Chapey and The Council Of Light (A Collective that Channels Through Me) Consisting of: God, My Higher Self and My Spiritual Team - Spiritual Interdimensional Beings, Masters, Guides and Angels

The Council Of Light

The world will expand for those who seek to understand, that which is in their own hearts. All will come to know of this existence. This that exists within each one of us. We are not all at that point in our development, in our evolution. But each of us here, that are walking on this planet, carry within our very being, our very essence, the ability to experience such wonder. For when we go within to where all answers lie, for that is when we will see Truth, know Truth, feel Truth, experience Truth.

Fear not those who say nay, for they are still wrapped in the veil of forgetfulness. It is within them not at this time. But they will continue on their journey, and will one day reach that point, where they too shall seek, they too shall find.

Be blessed, blessed in the knowing that you, you have glimpsed that knowing within yourself. As you look to share that knowing and understanding with others, your passion and understanding of the ones that come to you, that come through you, this, this is what will expand into the ethers, and attract those, those that are opening to their own experiences. Continue on your mission fully knowing, we walk with you on your journey of Light.

I met and heard about Rey Hernandez's work on Facebook in 2016. During that time I was having all kinds of what I call UFO ET Experiences which were also Loving and Expansive Spiritual Experiences. These experiences which I was having during my lifetime were all part of my own unique personal journey. They were Spiritually Transformative Experiences (STEs). They were all part of the "Contact Modalities" as Rey calls these Experiences. I have had STE's during my whole life, starting from when I was born.

So naturally I was very happy to learn that Rey, and his team from the Dr. Edgar Mitchell FREE Foundation, were conducting the very first scientific study of UFO Contact Experiencers. This was the world's first and only comprehensive academic worldwide research study of UFO Contact Experiencers. The research study received responses from over 4,300 people from all over the world, including myself, were partaking in three part extensive surveys. I was so happy to be part of the extensive research. That data derived from this academic research study presents a "Paradigm Shifting" information that was published in the 800 page book titled "***Beyond UFOs: The Science of Consciousness and Contact with Non-Human Intelligence***". This book is highly recommend reading.

I knew right away, as I do now, that Rey's work is important because it not only helps the reader understand how these many different experiences are all connected. It helps the Experiencer to understand that what they have been going through, sometimes for their whole lives, has been part of the evolutionary process of their own unique Spiritual Journey. Which I feel is also happening on a global scale. As it is part of the whole world eventually waking up to "A Greater Reality". "The True Reality" is Love.

These Experiences although unique and very personal to each and every one of us, are what I think of as puzzle pieces. No one person has all of the answers, but together we each have a piece of the Infinite puzzle that holds us all together in Unity and Love. Just as we are all part of The One, The All. When we come together and express our True Self, it is through Sharing of these Core Spiritual Experiences that we can catch a glimpse of and be part of "Heaven on Earth" of "The True Reality" of "A Greater Reality."

After having had so many different kinds of what I call UFO ET Experiences and Spiritual Experiences in 2016, I was curious if other people were also having these kinds of Spiritually Transformative

Experiences or Contact Modalities. So I started hosting and facilitating a monthly sharing group called "UFO ET Experiencers" at my local library. During covid the library closed down. I then jumped on to the technology that everyone was using during that time. And started hosting and facilitating the "UFO ET Experiencers" group on zoom. It has grown into three different Zoom groups online, they are "Safe Space Sharing Group", "UFO ET Experiencers" and "Spiritual Experiencers" These three groups are held on Zoom monthly. They are open to people who have had any or many types of Spiritually Transformative Experiences, otherwise known as "The Contact Modalities." These three groups are open to people who are very curious and open to these kinds of Experiences too. I developed the three groups with the intention of providing a Safe and Supportive environment for people to be able to share what they have experienced without judgement or disbelief. People that are there care, and most are Experiencers also. If you are interested in attending any of the groups that are supportive and filled with kindred souls that are in our Sharing Groups and Speaker Q and A Groups, please sign up. As we would Love for you to join us. You can come and listen, and also share if and when you are ready about your own unique Spiritually Transformative Experiences. To Register for, and to find out more, about our Sharing and Speaker Q and A Groups and more go to: bit.ly/m/CatherineChapey.

In 2020 I trained and became a Certified Facilitator and Moderator for the International Association For Near Death Studies IANDS.org Sharing Groups. This is also a Safe and supportive place where the people in these groups share about all kinds of Spiritually Transformative Experiences, not just NDE's. And Happily Yay!, In January of 2024 IANDS started having their very first monthly Topic Sharing Group called UFO/ET/NDE which I also facilitate. I am so excited to see IANDS opening up to UFO, ET, NDE and all kinds of STE's. This includes all kinds of Experiences associated with UFO ET Experiences that are also Spiritually Transformative.

In 2021 I became involved in the newly formed organization called "Spiritual Awakenings International" started by Dr. Yvonne Kason, MD, where I trained and became a Certified Facilitator for their SpiritualAwakeningsInternational.org monthly Sharing Circles. I am also on their Advisory Board and I am one of the moderators for their Facebook Group. All of these groups and organizations are near and dear to my heart.

I have lived a life of Spiritually Transformative Experiences since I was born. So being involved in these groups and organizations is something that has not only helped me to feel more of an acceptance and understanding from others, which has been very healing for me in my own journey. I am grateful that I can also help others to feel that same support and understanding that is available to them by being a part of these different Sharing Groups and Organizations.

Being in Service in hosting and facilitating many Experiencer Groups over the last eight years I have heard many Experiencers describing their very young childhood NDE's. That along with PMH Atwater's research on Childhood NDEs in her book called Forever Angels, this combination has helped me to put more of the puzzle pieces together of my own early background. Many of the different types of Experiences I have had, had an early impact on my life as a childhood experiencer. I compiled a list of many different times I actually almost died during my life. I don't mention them all here, but a couple of them are described from when I was very young.

Born into an NDE

I'd like to start with when I was very young, because it gives a background of how things started for me. I was born almost two months premature in 1963. I was in an in incubator for over a month, where no one could hold me, not even my mother. Back in those days the belief was that it would be harmful for the premature babies if they were held.

They weren't aware of how crucial it was for the development of fragile premature babies to feel a close connection and to bond with their Mothers and Fathers. That early touch and bonding actually aides in their growth, development and overall health. Although I spent the first month or so in an incubator with no one holding me, I have come to understand over the years, through my own spiritual journey, that I was not alone. I have been told and shown that most of that time, I was not in my body. For most of that time my consciousness was out of my body and with my Spiritual Family, my Team of Loving Beings that are always with me, that have always been with me, even to this day.

Baby Aspirin

When I was one years old and my brother was two, he fed me a whole bottle of baby aspirin, the little orange ones. I guess he thought they were candy. I say jokingly my brother tried to kill me when he was two! They had to rush me to the hospital once my parents woke up and discovered that the whole bottle was gone, and I was not doing well. At the hospital they had to pump my stomach.

When I was almost two years old I had a very high fever of almost 107. I have memories of being in the bathtub with ice water as I was screaming while my parents were trying to get the fever down because it was so high.

Frozen in Bed

I had so many different experiences when I was very young. Looking back now I realize these early experiences have set me up for a lifetime of Spiritually Transformative Experiences. When I was a kid I woke up several times feeling frozen in my bed. By frozen I mean that I couldn't move at all. As this was happening, I felt like there was a menacing male presence right next to me. I was very scared. As I was raised in a in a religious tradition that had a lot of dogma. We were taught very early on about hell, and that we are going to hell if we weren't good, and if we didn't go to church every Sunday. I had a lot of fear about the devil. I thought that the devil was in my room as close as my right ear I was so scared, I couldn't move. When I tried to scream, nothing would come out. And finally when I just made the tiniest little sound, when I was able to make that little sound, whatever it was released me and I was able to move again.

That experience of feeling frozen and unable to move, is known as sleep paralyses. That happened to me a few times when I was a kid. I have come to understand this as I was not fully back in my body. I now know when we are sleeping, I feel that our consciousness is out and about. Sometimes we aren't fully back in the body yet, while waking up, so we feel like we are frozen, or cant move at all until we are fully back in. This sleep paralysis is the bodies way of protecting us from acting out our dreams physically while we are sleeping.

Trauma

I had an experience of severe trauma during my childhood where I was so scared. I was out of my body viewing the traumatic experience from above. I have no memory of being in my body during that Experience. I wasn't feeling the pain of that trauma. Any memory I have ever had of this incident, I have always remembered it from being up in the corner of that small room, where I was up above and to the right of the door, up in the corner of the ceiling. I was watching what was happening to me down below. I didn't realize until more recently when I was at the IANDS sharing groups. By hearing other people share about their OBE's, I realized, Oh my God, that was an Out of Body Experience. I never really realized that until the last couple of years. I always remember that traumatic incident from that viewpoint. As a kid and right up until today. I think that experience also helped me to understand at a very young age that I was not just this body. I feel because of these and more early experiences I was very aware there is so much more to being human than what I was being told by adults and society.

Mother Mary and Jesus / My Non Dogma Prayer book

I was raised in the Catholic religion. I remember, when I would say certain prayers that were in my little prayer book, I knew that God is Love. I had my little prayer book for when I made my first communion. And in it there were certain prayers that I actually cut out of the original prayer book, Blasphemy! I cut out my favorite prayers that weren't dogmatic at all, and I made my own little version of the prayer book. I carefully cut out and pasted all of the Loving non-dogmatic prayers that I liked and glued them onto small square pieces of papers. Then I glued a very sweet picture of Mother Mary holding baby Jesus onto the cover. Which is all held together by a small round gold clip in the upper left hand corner of the booklet. I still have that little prayer book today.

Whenever I would say the prayers that I read from my own little prayer book, I would feel an instant sense of connection to Mother Mary and Jesus. That would happen right away, as soon as I would start saying the prayers, I felt as if they heard me, it was a lightness that came over me as I said those prayers, and whatever I was going through, if I was sad or worrying about something, it was lifted from me during that time of saying those prayers. Looking back now, I am glad that I had an early upbringing of a religion. Even though it came with dogma, it helped me to question the bigger meanings of life at a young age. And it helped me to know through my own Experiences at a very young age, that there is so much more to this life, than just this earthly existence.

Questioning

We were taught at a very young age about the devil. We were taught that people would go to hell if they were bad or didn't go to church every Sunday. So I had a fear of the devil at a very young age. I actually thought that the devil lived under my bed underground when I was very young. I would jump off the edge my bed because I didn't want to put my foot on the floor next to my bed, because I feared the devil was waiting there all ready to grab my foot, and pull me down under to hell where he lived.

As I got a little older, I had come to an understanding, even though I had a fear of the devil and hell. I was also aware at a young age that something about this concept of hell and the devil really didn't make sense. I started to question a lot of what I was being told.

We had these wonderful neighbors who were Jewish. I remember anytime we went over their house which was often because their kids were our age, they invited us into their home and they treated us like we were family. Any time we were with them we were part of their family. They were so kind and loving. I remember going home one day and I asked my mother because I was concerned. I said mom, are our friends up the block, are they going to hell because they're Jewish and not Catholic?? My mother, being who she was at that time said, Yes! I knew that was just not true. That was not happening. I knew at that very young age that religions and their dogmatic teachings didn't make any sense. I knew that God Is Pure Love and that God Loves Us All.

Coworker

As an adult I was working in a very male dominated field. There was a gentleman on my job and he was being scapegoated by some of the guys on the job. These guys basically pushed him out of his leadership role where he ended up losing his job. He was a bit older than me. He had older kids that were in college and older. At that time he must have fallen into a very severe depression because sadly, he ended up committing suicide. I'm sure there was more going on in the background of his life. This poor man, the way he killed himself was absolutely shocking and so tragic. One night very shortly after he passed away, I saw him in a dream, he was smiling and beaming at me. He looked so happy. He told me how happy he was, and not to worry about him and the way he passed. I was filled with so much joy and gratitude that he came to me. I was saying to him, Thank you, I am so glad you're OK. Thank you for visiting me and letting me know you're ok. He was so happy! That was the best part!

The next day I went to work where I said to the guys on the job, "I had a dream last night about our coworker who passed away, and he was so happy." When one of the guys turned to the other guys and said something making fun of the way he killed himself. They all laughed! I was disgusted and horrified. In disbelief and realizing that these are the same guys that were acting like they were his friends at the recent memorial service, but pushed him out of a job, and now they were all laughing at the horrific way he committed suicide, "behind his back."

A week or so later I was at a diner parking lot. I was explaining to someone about what had happened on the job, and how these guys were pretending to be his friend, yet saying this horrible thing and laughing about him and the tragic suicide. As I was saying this, my coworker who passed away walked right in front of me! He looked over at me. He looked as solid as you and I as he was walking near a small group of people. I could see him very clearly, he was about 10 - 15 feet away from me. He turned his head and looked right over at me, as if to acknowledge me, as if to say, I know, I know exactly what's going on. I stood there in disbelief saying, "Oh my God, and there he is, there he is." Wondering, how can this be? He died and here he is walking right past me, looking right at me, looking as solid as anyone that was also walking near him in the parking lot. I was dumbfounded as to how this could be possible.

Spiritualist Church 2007

Along with seeing my coworker in spirit looking as solid as you and I, and his recent visitation in my dream. I was also having many different kinds of experiences of spirit world contact. For example, I would start smelling my grandfather's cigar as I was talking about him to someone, and no one else was around that was smoking a cigar. Things like that were happening. So I got curious about what was happening with spirit contact and me. At that same time, I was also feeling like I wanted to find a community of people who were spiritual, but not a religion with dogma. I wanted a more open type of Spiritual not Religious connection, and community. Not knowing what I was looking for I googled Spiritual Communities near me, and a Spiritualist Church popped up. I didn't even know there was such a thing.

At the same time to the day that I googled and found a Spiritualist Church. I got a call from a friend who was so happy to tell me that she kept thinking of me when she had just went to, a Spiritualist Church that past Sunday! She thought that I would like it. She described it to me and then she said, "Spiritualism is all about Personal Responsibility and The Golden Rule" she went on, "There is no dogma, and they believe in equality for everyone. There are both Female and Male Spiritualist Ministers. So they aren't about a patriarchy." I liked that. My friend didn't know I was thinking about finding a Spiritual Community of some kind. And I told her I just Googled that today!! It sounded like it checked all the boxes for me. Plus this was all so very Synchronistic!

That following Sunday was when I attended my first Spiritualist Church Service. In Spiritualism, there is no Dogma. They teach about living the Golden Rule, Personal Responsibility, that we all make our own happiness or unhappiness according to how we live our lives, and that we are all part of the Infinite Love of God. During their Sunday Service they have a guided Meditation, Healing Prayers for others, Uplifting Songs, an Inspirational Talk usually from a Spiritualist Minister, or Medium, Hands on Spiritual Healing from the Spiritualist Healers, and Mediumship, where the Spiritualist Mediums will give messages from Spirit Loved Ones who have crossed over, to the people present in the congregation. These messages are always brought through with the intention of being helpful and healing, and all for the highest and best good.

The medium stood up at the podium and asked me if she could come to me with a message from Spirit. I was all the way in the back. She said she couldn't even see me because she didn't have her glasses on. She asked, Can I come to the lady all the way in the back with the fuchsia pink shirt on?" I said yes! The medium began describing my grandfather who had recently passed away to a T, right down to some of the last moments I had with him shortly before he passed away. She started giving me messages from my grandfather. He was answering my questions as if he heard me when I was asking him for help just the week before. I was on my patio in my backyard talking to him in my head. I was asking him to help me with one of my children who was having some challenges. I knew he was in a higher place now and he could see what was going on. I thought now that he was over there on the other side maybe he could pull some strings and help with my child. I had been trying everything I could for such a long time, and nothing was working. Then he said to the medium, "Tell her, (meaning me) Don't pray to me." At first I thought, what? Then I knew right away why he was saying that to me! I was asking him for help with my child in my mind the week before. He heard me! Then I realized, Omg! every time I speak to him he hears me! He wanted to let me know to Pray to God not to him. Go straight to the top! And Pray to God. And so after that I started to dialog with my Grandfather on the other side through different means, through my own mediumship, automatic writing, and simply talking to him. And I prayed, I prayed to God. I asked God for help for my child. After a series of events and Synchronicities, all kinds of different miracles started to happen around this particular situation that was happening with my child. Before that, it was as if all doors led to nowhere. Now that I started praying to God asking for help, and communicating with my Grandfather, who assured me that things were going to be ok. Then suddenly, doors started opening and Miracle after Miracle kept happening. Things I could not even believe were possible opened up, as if the waters had been parted. Synchronicities, the right people at the right time, and Wow! Everything fell into place, one thing after another like dominos, magically! And what was happening was all I could hope for and So Much More than I ever could have imagined. During that time in my life I learned that I have so much help from God and from my spirit team, and my Grandpa who is on what I call my Spirit Team, in the spirit world. This really opened my eyes to how God, Spirit, our loved ones, our Spirit team hear us, they are near to us, and they want to help us, and stay connected and part of our lives, even while we are here on earth, and they are in spirit.

Unfoldment Class

I started to sit in Unfoldment Circle every week at the Spiritualist Church with a group of developing mediums. We all wanted to develop our mediumship. I wanted to be able to serve spirit by giving mediumship messages at the podium at the weekly Spiritualist service, to bring through spirit messages for people that were grieving the loss of loved ones, and also to bring through messages that were helpful and healing for people. There were people that would come to the Sunday service every week, some were new timers, and some were there at times. Spiritualism is a beautiful religion, there is no dogma. It's about The Golden Rule, "Do unto others as you would have them do unto you." It was such a special time in my life. I was there for about eight or nine years. So many amazing things happened during that time. When I first started to sit in circle I wanted to develop my mediumship so that I could help others to also know what I had learned. That we are always connected to God and our loved ones in spirit. As soon as I started sitting in unfoldment circle, we learned how to meditate and quiet our minds. We had an awesome mediumship teacher who was a Spiritualist Minister also. During the weekly Unfoldment Circles he would take us on guided meditations, of all different kinds, all with the intention to open up to the spirit world, to stretch and expand our consciousness, so that we could connect in with the spirit realm, to be able to give evidential helpful messages from spirit to their loved ones.

I struggled to learn how to meditate at first. I didn't think I would be able to do it because my mind was always going. I had a very active monkey mind. But I was very fortunate in that I had an amazing mediumship teacher. He would bring us on these beautiful guided meditations, which really helped me to be able to focus so that my monkey mind would move out of the way. I would just focus on the beautiful meditation that he was guiding us through. This helped me to be able to relax and focus with intention. So every week we would sit in circle and he would take us on different guided meditations that were always with the intention to open up to the spirit world and be able to receive messages from the spirit realm that was for the highest and best good.

Then on Sundays during the Spiritualist Service myself and some of the mediums would go up to the podium and give messages to the people in the congregation. Every week we would sit in circle to practice our mediumship, then I would serve at the Sunday service either by doing mediumship or spiritual hands on healing which I also learned to do there. It was such a beautiful time in my life. I did that for about eight or nine years. I had so many amazing experiences of connection to the spirit realm and healing during that time.

Asking to know God - 2007

During a Spiritualist Service shortly after I started going there, during a guided meditation. While we were envisioning a White light traveling upward and stopping at each of our chakras and expanding each chakra with its colored light. As we reached higher and higher we were guided to see our crown chakra at the top of our head as a flower fully blooming, any kind of flower that we loved. I saw a beautiful flower as my crown chakra, with so many petals opening all at the same time. The women then said, now ask anything you desire to know. With that I felt a deep yearning that seemed to come from the depths of my own soul, from out of nowhere inwardly I said, "I want to know you God"

2007 Spiritual Awakening, OBE's and Unitive Experiences

My crown chakra opened and I was in the cosmos, I was one with all of creation, immersed in the most expansive Infinite, Blissful, Waves of Unending Loving Energy pulsing through my being, Divine Endless Love. I was one with this Love. I was Love. At one point I knew the answers to everything. I was One with God, Pure Joy!

They had been taking me out a body between three and four in the morning and we were going way out into the cosmos. I knew I wasn't by myself, I was with more than one being. I couldn't see them but I knew they were my guides, my team. As we traveled I was seeing portals in the heavens, and I watched as the Angels were flying out of the portals.

This was in late 2007 every morning between three and four in the morning, I happily was being taken out of body. One morning as I lay there in bed, eyes opened, the walls of my room totally disappeared and I was in the cosmos. I could see all kinds of beautiful cosmic scenes and scenarios. I was brought to this opening in the cosmos, in the heavens. I was with my guides, I couldn't see them, but I felt them as they were always there with me.

I became aware that we had to stop and watch from a distance. I couldn't go any farther or I wouldn't be able to come back into my body. I had to watch from a distance, I just stayed there and I watched, with my guides right next to me. Within the opening in the heavens that I was watching were these flames of Brilliant Light. The opening which was almost like a doorway or a window in the cosmos, had these huge flames of Light behind it, that I could see and feel just inside of that opening. I don't even know how to properly describe it. It was brilliant bright light, it looked like flames. I knew that I couldn't go any further or wouldn't be able to come back. And I was feeling all of this Love and Bliss and Joy. I was one with All Of Creation, One with the Universe, One With God. I was having so many Beautiful, Expansive, Blissful Experiences. I was seeing all kinds of beautiful scenes from the heaven world and the cosmos. These were such Glorious, Amazing times. I was having Unitive Experiences where I was filled with So Much Love, Bliss and Joy. I knew what was like to be part of the ocean. I knew it was like to be part of the trees. At one point I was merging in with my Leland Cypress evergreen trees that I planted on my property years ago. As I merged with them I could feel what they were feeling. My beautiful Trees are such Loving, Sentient Beings, So Alive. They are healers. They are Protectors, and they are here with me in this life, they help to protect my home, my land, me and my family.

Not long after I had those experiences, I was telling someone I know who is also an experiencer/contactee about the opening in the cosmos and those Brilliant Flames of Light and Love that I was seeing and feeling. He said he thought it may be the Great Central Sun that I was seeing. That felt right to me because I just knew that I couldn't go any further or else I wouldn't be able to come back, plus I was feeling so much Love, Bliss and Joy at that time.

I felt this feeling of being reborn after these experiences. I had come to know my True Self Which is Love. This is who I am, at the core of my being, Pure Love, One With All Of Creation, God, The All. We Are All One. We are all part of The One, The All. This is what I know to be True based on my own unique Experiences.

Spontaneous Kundalini/Spiritual Awakening Feb 2008

We started asking to meet our spirit guides during our Unfoldment Circle. During a guided meditation we asked with the intention to meet our Spirit Guide. At that time I saw what was a small glimpse of my spirit guide when I saw the bottom of her robe and her foot. That was all I saw at first in our Unfoldment Circle. I was curious about that. I wanted to know more. When I was at home I would meditate also.

One night very shortly after seeing my guides foot and the bottom of her robe. I was at home, and I was thinking and wondering about my Spirt Guides and asking who they were.

The next morning as I was waking up, I started to see my guides, as one by one each one started to show themselves to me. It was as if they were introducing themselves to me, one after another after another after another after another. They were each smiling as I saw each face. As if to say, "Hi, here I am, you were asking." I was in two worlds at one time. I was in the physical world but also in the spirit realm. I was In the True Reality, where I was feeling Infinite Love, Bliss and Joy. I was my True Self, I was Infinite Love. I felt God with me, in me, a part of me and I was part of God. We Are One. I was one with Creation, Waves of Love pouring through me, one with the Universe. I was having a Unitive Experience. Words can't come close to describing this feeling of Infinite Love that was permeating and expanding through every bit of who I am and more. The True Reality which is Love, so huge, vast, infinite, where every cell of my being and more pulsated with Infinite, Endless, Love in Unity with Unending, Ever Expanding Bliss, Joy, Pure Freedom. This is The True Reality! 1000 times more real than this earthly reality. I was seeing my guides and my loved ones in spirit. And as my spirit guides were introducing themselves to me, I remembered them, but I didn't. I felt as if I were seeing long lost family again. They were so happy to see me and I was so happy to see them. There was such an instant heart connection. Many of them I knew from different time periods of history and different religious figures and beings that I recognized. As my consciousness was merging in with different guides. I was feeling like my True Expanded Self, which is Love. We were connected, we were one, our consciousness was one in this Beautiful Bubble of Love.

A strong feeling came over me of remembrance, as if I had done this before, maybe in other lifetimes. My True Essence, which felt so familiar to me as I remember thinking, "This is who I am! I am going to stay like this forever!

There were different Symbols I was seeing, Golden Scrolls had appeared, I felt the energy of the scrolls and knew all that was contained within them in that moment. The Golden Head of Tutankhamun appeared, with his long thin upturned beard, which I became starkly aware of.

I saw an Elephant type of being and I felt as if I was in front of him, he was part of me, we merged and I experienced what it was like for me to have his long flowing trunk, my pure essence was connecting in with it as I saw it uncurl. The energy of this was now part of me. We were one. I felt and saw his trunk growing out of my own being. It is so hard too describe this and exactly how all of this was happening, but it was. I didn't know who the elephant being was at that time. But I found out after that experience who he is. He is a Hindu God or Deity named

Ganesha. He is the Hindu God of wisdom, prosperity and also for releasing fear, overcoming obstacles and new beginnings.

My body was going into spontaneous yoga positions which is really interesting because, I don't do yoga this lifetime. I must have been having cellular memories of yoga as this Divine Energy within me was guiding my body through and into different yoga poses. I felt these poses were natural as they came from deep within me. When I tried to do something myself, this energy that poured through me, it would stop. So I just went with it. And at one point I looked over at my cat who more recently had always slept curled up right over and around the top of my head whenever I slept. He was on my bed totally immersed in this Divine Energy too, his body looked as though it was in movement, in flow with this Divine Energy also. And I thought to myself oh wow Little Guy is into this too. And then I realized in that moment, that while my cat slept above my head for all of these months, he had been protecting my crown chakra.

At one point I reached over to touch the wood on the foot of my sleigh bed. As my hand was within about 8 or 10 inches from touching it, flames of bright light poured out of my hand, as if there was electricity pouring out of my hand going straight to where I was going to touch the bed. Startled, I moved my hand away from my sleigh bed and continued merging in with this Beautiful Expansive All Knowing Divine Energy.

Introduced to my Spirit Guides

Once my spirit guides had introduced themselves to me, I became aware that I also had two main guides and that one of them was my main Guide. I then I met my 2 main Guides. When they appeared I was in front of Mother Mary and Jesus, I, my soul essence, turned into a baby in front of them. I was a little two-year-old child in front of them. And I, my soul essence child bowed when Jesus appeared.I was on the ground in front of Jesus bowing in deep reverence and complete respect and absolute Love. It is hard to put into words because there's so much to what was happening this was on a very deep soul level. It was spontaneous as if my soul automatically did what it did. Words cannot capture the depths of all it. And Mother Mary as I was told is my main guide. Mother Mary spent much time speaking to me telepathically and channeling through me. She had a beautiful accent that was middle eastern. There was a Brilliant white Light that appeared in my room in the corner up above my dresser in the corner near the ceiling on the right hand side. I was on the ground immediately and started bowing as soon as the Light appeared. My physical body was on the ground bowing over and over to this Beautiful Divine Brilliant White Light. It was instantaneous, I just did it without any thought, as if my soul knew just what to do, as my physical body flew into action. And there was such a deep Reverence, Respect and complete and Total Love for this Experience of Truth and Pure Love, which engulfed every molecule of my being, my soul essence.

All of my guides formed a circle around me. I was in the middle. Like a dot in the middle of a circle. Suddenly I was standing on this stretchy material that they were holding up. It was a circular piece of material and the only way I can describe it was that seemed like some kind of a trampoline because I started jumping up and down on this material. As I turned into tiny child in front of them. My little two-year-old body was jumping up and down, as all of my guides were surrounding me in this circle of Love, while holding the material up, watching me with so much glee, totally, completely, enjoying me, having so much fun jumping up and down on this bouncy material. As I few in the air so high, they were all smiling ear to ear, looking up at me and they were all beaming so much Love up at me as I continued to bounce up so high. I could see them, each one of them as I looked down and I could see their smiling happy faces. I could feel all of their Love for me, beaming their Love up at me. I could feel just how much each one of them loved me, and how much they were enjoying seeing me having so much fun, just being my True Self, a little child, pure, and so so trusting of them. They just love me so much. I can still feel all of their Love today, in this very moment. And I know, They Love Us All This Way.

The Being Not From Here

Most of my guides, I was somewhat familiar with where either I knew who they were from different periods in history or different religions. But there was this particular being that was working with me telepathically for hours and hours. I couldn't see him, but I felt him, and I knew he was not from here. He knew everything about me. He was Very Intense but Very Loving. He worked with me for hours and hours, and he communicated with me, downloading information into to my heart, right into my soul. As he was communicating with me I was being shown different symbols and signs that had meaning I was to remember them. And at times he was speaking to me telepathically. I would ask him questions every now and then. I knew this was important for me to always remember. I was going to be tested on this. These understandings that he was downloading would be within me. I knew I would have to pass the test and remember everything. This was going on for hours. It is hard to describe because there is no way for me to accurately describe in words exactly all that was happening. Much of this was on the Spiritual plane. I was connecting to my heart center, and there was an activation of sorts going on within my heart. I started to do a certain kind of movement, sign language with my hands that connects me to my heart center, which connects me straight to source, God, and my Higher Self and My Team, My Guides. This was happening spontaneously when this being was with me. And now years later when I channel or connect with God, My Higher Self and My team. They told me it is a Soul Language, or a Light Language. But for me it isn't a foreign language that comes out of me in a language. It feels like a cellular activation that I can immediately sense in different cells of my being as if they are lighting up with each movement of my hand as it moves quickly spelling out certain symbols while intermittently connecting to my heart. It's usually my right hand sometimes the left will move too. This Soul Language connects me straight to My Higher Self, God, and My Higher Self Team.

About a year went by and every single day I would think about what had happened that morning in 2008. I was also always wondering who the being was, because he was the only one I didn't see, but I felt everything. I know he wasn't from here. He was from somewhere else. A year later I told someone I knew who was a contactee about him. He said to me, Why don't you ask, before you go to sleep? So I did that. I asked right before I was about to fall asleep. I said, "I really want to know who you are. I know who all of the other guides were that were with me that day, but you were the only that I couldn't see even though you were working with me for so many hours. Can you please show me who you are?" And then I fell asleep. As I was waking up the next morning, I saw a beautiful Interdimensional disc shaped UFO in my mind's eye, I kept my eyes closed, it was coming in and out of reality of my inner vision. That's how I knew it was an Interdimensional ship. It was an oblong disk shape, and it had these windows all along it and it was gold. And then as if overlayed in front of it, over it there was a Merkaba. I was aware that the Merkaba isa symbol for interdimensional travel. And then it appeared in big letters above the Ship the word that appeared spelled out Metatron. I didn't know who Metatron was at the time. I had heard of Metatron. I found out that Metatron is an Archangel who was one of two Archangels that were once in bodied in human form. According to Kabbalah he was once Enoch. He walked with God into heaven where God made him into an Archangel. He is known as the scribe for God. He is what I understand to be the overseer of the Akashic records, and he is also the overseer of the cosmic realm. Metatron's Cube is a representation of all of the shapes that are in existence, it represents the blueprint of creation.

My family members weren't able to understand what was going on with me. I was seeing and communicating with my spirit guides and talking to my loved ones in spirit,and God, so they weren't able to understand what was happening. I quickly realized I could not share about the intensity of my Experiences with them. It scared them. So I had to learn to keep most of it to myself. But I was not scared at all. As a matter of fact I was in Bliss and Joy and Love. And I knew that what I was experiencing was so real, it was 1000 times more real than this earthly reality. No one can ever convince me that what I experienced was something negative or bad.

I ended up being told by God, My Higher Self Team, that they wanted me to experience what happens to people. They told me that this was an initiation, and they wanted me to know that this is what happens with people who are waking up to their True Self. They said in this part of the world especially, that a lot of times when people have Spiritual Awakenings, and they're having these beautiful Spiritual Experiences, they are often told that they are crazy, psychotic or that they are they need to be put on medication or that they're having some kind of a breakdown. But I knew that I wasn't having a psychotic experience because these were such Beautiful, Expansive, Connected, Loving Experiences. There is no way it could be anything close to a negative experience. I trusted that. I knew it was God and my Spirit Guides. It was Pure Love and So Many Synchronicities happening at that time too. My Higher Guidance Team told me that over the next many years, many people will be waking up. So they wanted me to experience what people will be going through. They said that I was going to be helping people that are waking up. So I asked them, "What am I going to be doing? Am I going to be doing healing work? Am I going to be helping to grow the Spiritualist Church?" They said, "You'll see, you'll see, but yeah, you're going to be doing healing work." And they didn't tell me too much. They only told me a little bit because, as my mentor Dolores Cannon said "You wouldn't give a baby a steak." So they didn't want to tell me the whole picture, and that's good, that was in 2008, it probably would've blew my mind anyway.

Different Beings

So shortly after that I start to see different types of beings. Earlier in my life I had experiences of waking up seeing little short all white beings around my bed, they wore robes and had big round heads. I was never afraid when those kinds of things happened. I would just fall back to sleep. So I've had glimpses of different types of beings in that state. But I started to see different beings in my during meditation and in my dreams and in my mind's eye as I was channeling. These beings were from different dimensions as I understand it and possibly different planets. But the first one I remember seeing in my meditations were the feline beings. I thought it was interesting because I knew they weren't our furry babies, cats because they had robes on, they were tall and they had feline features. Also they were standing on two legs like we do. I saw that same friend of mine at the time who was a contactee and I said, "I saw these beings in my meditation, and they looked like they had feline features, they were standing up and they were very tall." He said," Oh yea, those are the feline beings."

So, over the years things progressed. I continued learning all I could about mediumship and I learned many different spiritual healing modalities. I also learned QHHT Quantum Healing Hypnosis Technique from Dolores Cannon in 2014 when I went to Arkansas to take her in person class where I became a Level 2 QHHT Practitioner. Gratefully I was in the 2nd to last class that Dolores Cannon ever taught. I feel so blessed to have had the opportunity to meet her, and to have learned so much directly from her. She was so generous and giving of her time, and she just loved teaching her students in person.

My years at the Spiritualist Church were rich with all kinds of growth and learning for me. I continued doing mediumship and healing at the Spiritualist Church every Sunday, I went there all together for eight or nine years almost every Sunday to serve the church in some capacity either mediumship or healing. Then in 2015 there were many different things happening behind the scenes at the Spiritualist Church that I felt I was not in alignment with. Sadly for me at that time, but looking back now I know it was all in Divine order. I ended up leaving the Spiritualist Church in 2015. At that time I thought I had failed at my Mission because I walked away from the Spiritualist Church. When I heard my main guide Mother Mary assuring me she said, "You did not fail at your mission, that was just part of your schooling. You will be stepping into your full potential." I was confused and I didn't know what she meant. I was in grief and so sad at that time. It was a huge loss for me at that time as I felt I had no choice but to walk away, so I did.

In 2016 I started to have a lot of different Spiritually Transformative Experiences with different kinds of beings. Many of them were also feline beings. These beings were showing themselves to me in so many different ways.

May 14th, 2016: Cat Blizzy in Spirit Form

I had so many synchronicities and Spiritually Transformative Experiences around my cat, who had passed away. I had to put him to sleep after he was attacked by a pit bull from a couple doors down. The pit bull got out of his yard, and attacked my poor cat who had kidney disease and was asleep under a tree by our front porch. He very tiny as he was probably around 5 or 6 pounds. He had been with us for many years. I ended up having to put him down because of his extensive injuries. I didn't want him to suffer anymore. He was also very frail from the kidney disease he had. It was one of the hardest things I ever had to do. My heart was breaking. I ended up having what's called, A Shared Death Experience with him. When my boy Blizzy passed away, he passed right through my heart. I could feel him! I could feel how much he loved me. I was stunned at how much my little cat loved me. The only thing I could compare it to was the Love that God had for me, but not quite as much because that is Infinite. But this little boy just adored me. All I could say was OMG I didn't know, I didn't know, because I did not know just how much he loved me. And I adored him too. I still do! It was so hard to put him down. He knew it too. He was also visiting my friends that were mediums during that time he was giving them messages for me. He was Amazing!

My cat Blizzy started to come to me in spirit right after I put him down. I went home; it was late. I went into my room, sat on my bed, leaned back, I closed my eyes and there he was right away as soon as I closed my eyes. He was as clear as day, on my front porch, on the chair. He was showing me that he is still here with me. I heard telepathically see Mommy I'm still here on the front porch. He lived primarily on our front porch for so many years. We even got him a little heated house for out there. Blizzard insisted when he found us so many years ago, that he was mostly an outdoor boy. He hated being indoors. I fell asleep, and the next morning as I was waking up I could see him in my mind's eye. He was talking to me in this sweet little cat voice. I know it sounds crazy, but he was talking to me telepathically, and he had this high pitched voice, I could hear him, I kid you not! He was saying, "Mommy don't worry about me I'm fine, look I'm here! I'm happy! I'm climbing trees and he showed me himself climbing trees. And Look Mommy I'm with Grandpa and Grandma!" as he was showing me where he was in heaven with my grandparents as he jumped into each one of their arms. He showed me my dog Goober who was there with him too! Then each one of my cats that passed as he delighted in showing me each one who was there with him also. They are all there together! He is so excited and Happy, he kept saying, "Don't worry! don't worry Mommy I'm fine, see I'm so happy!" Then he said to me, "Mommy, go down to the crystal shop and get this candle." As he showed me a small light green candle.

So the next day, I went down the crystal shop with my daughter. As we were looking around the tiny shop, a green cat candle fell on my foot. It was the only cat candle in the whole little crystal shop. I said to my daughter, "Oh my God, look what just fell on my foot, I think it's a sign from Blizzy, do you think I should get this?" she said, yes.

The cat candle was green and slender and tall, it looked like one of those elongated Egyptian cats. that's how my Blizzy boy was. He was all black with a little white spot on his chest, he was very lean and slender throughout his lifetime. He loved running around outdoors, so he got a lot of exercise. Then I found the same exact little light green candle that Blizzy was showing me that morning. It was this little green candle which had a little prayer that came with it, a prayer for Abundance. So I thought oh wow, Blizzy wants to work with me on Abundance. So I brought that candle home along with the cat candle. That night I placed the little light green candle on my bookshelf/Altar, I lit the candle and I would say that prayer of Abundance as I would every night. Shortly after that all kinds of amazing things happened.
So Many Synchronicities are happening around this time I can hardly keep up. UFO's, Beings, Me Traveling to somewhere they wanted me to see, My guides communicating with me, Me starting to Channel a collective and on and on. I'm not able to describe all that was going on at that time in this chapter.

I will be sharing more of my journey with pictures and videos in talks I will be giving and in books that I will be finishing up and writing that have a lot more detail, of all of the phenomena and more that was going on during that time. I will continue to tell about some of the things that were happening.

May 18, 2016: Mother Mary

That night I fell asleep and suddenly I woke up and there right next to me between my bookshelf /Altar is Mother Mary in my room. She is slightly above and in front of my book shelf. She is beautiful and sending me so much Love. Then I notice, Mother Mary is holding my John of God Clear Quartz Crystal in her hands, and the crystal is pointing toward me. I know immediately what she wants me to do. And I remember thinking oh, Mother Mary wants me to get out of bed, and take my John of God Clear Quartz Crystal (that was always on my nightstand) and place it on the Bookshelf/Alter. I need to make sure that the point of the crystal is pointing directly towards my crown chakra. I get out of bed, and I place my John of God Crystal on my Altar. I make sure it is pointing right at where the top of my head will be when I'm lying on my pillow, when I lay back down to go back to sleep. I carefully place it on my altar and point it toward the top of my pillow. I lay back down and I go back to sleep.

In the morning, I am waking up, I open my eyes and there is the most beautiful White Feline Being! Her beautiful face is morphing out of my ceiling. My eyes are open, I am looking at her. She is smiling at me and sending me so much Love. She feels like Mother Mary Divine Feminine Energy. I just get this feeling that they are connected. And I just lay there looking up at her, as she continues smiling at me and sending me so much Love. While I'm saying in my mind thank you, thank you, I love you, thank you.

When I woke up in the morning, I took a picture of my Abundance Altar. I look at the picture and I notice, in the middle of the Altar where I had placed a 7 pointed clear quartz Chakra Crystal. As I looked more closely at the center of that clear quartz crystal. I could see inside the middle of the crystal is what looks like the face of the beautiful White Feline Being that I was just seeing that morning morphing out of my ceiling! I keep looking to make sure I am seeing what I am seeing.

May 21, 2016: Periwinkle Orb - Let Your Light Shine

That evening I took some videos and pictures in my room and surprisingly there was a big periwinkle orb floating right by my bookshelf/Altar. This orb is huge and such a beautiful color!

During this time, I am filled with so much Love and Joy, because the energy is so high, and I am feeling all of this expansion within my heart. Synchronistically my daughter had just gotten me for Mother's Day a cute little multi colored rubber glass clinger of words that she stuck onto the glass of my sliding glass door of my back patio that spelled out in multi colors "Let Your Light Shine" So, I'm feeling this buzzing sensation all throughout my body. And its around my heart too. Nothing scary, its a feeling of expansion and happiness. It's well after midnight and all of the sudden, I get this feeling that suddenly I want to take pictures outside? I've never done this before in the 20 years I've been here. So, I go outside on my back patio and I take four or five pictures from left to right of the backyard. And then I take one video from the left all the way to the right. Then I go right back in the house. I go into my room and I pull up the pictures and the video. Then I see it, to the left there's a tube of light floating across the sky in between but beyond my sassafras tree's branches. There was a huge column of light coming down from the sky all the way to the right of my yard.
And on the side of the deck of the pool, there is what looks like all different kinds of felines. I could see a lion and cats when I went back into the pictures that I took. These feline beings they in what looked like a type of ectoplasm looking phenomena that happens in the environment and shows up on the pictures and it is part of the phenomena. This was what showed up on the side of my pool deck while there was all this other phenomena that was happening in my yard

and in my consciousness also, as daily I am waking up to many different types of feline beings in my mind's eye.

Then I notice it, there is a huge column of Light stretching all the way down to the ground on the right side of my house. Then I looked at the one video that I took. As the video pans from left to right as I am standing just outside of my sliding glass door on the back patio. When out of where that column of light was, I could see something zip out of where that column of light was. When I slowed it down on the video and looked more closely, there was a golden disc shape moving very quickly from out of where that column of light was. Above that at one particular point in the video there appeared for a split millisecond, a Light Bright Green Orb. I screenshotted it, so I could see what was happening. Because it was so very fast, very quick, and you could miss it if you didn't pay attention. So I screenshotted it. It was a Beautiful Light Bright Green Orb above the disc shaped Golden Craft. Wow! I am blown away.

At that time I was going for acupuncture weekly. I was really open. My consciousness was really very open. That happens with this kind of thing. I could see all different kinds of feline beings in my minds eye as I was waking up in the mornings, and I was channeling. I had just started channeling a collective,and communicating more with my team my guides. So the energy was really high. So the next morning, I'm lying on the acupuncture table and I'm so relaxed. I'm seeing and talking to my guides. I say to them, "What was that that golden disc that came out of that column of light last night?" and they said "That was us, did you like that?" and I said, "Yes!, And what was that green Orb that showed up above the golden disc?" Then they told me, "Wait for it" (I kid you not) as they paused. "It's The White Feline Being" in that green orb!" I said "No Way!" And they said, "Yes! When you get home pull it up on your phone and enlarge it." So when I got home, the first thing I did was I pulled it up on my phone and I enlarged it. There it was! I could see The White Feline Being in that Light Bright Green Orb above the disc, from the night before. And the time on my phone above it when I pulled it up to see it said 1:11. I took a screenshot of it. That is another thing, the Synchronicities also through numbers come in with this kind of phenomena. Those synchronistic numbers 1111, 111,1212, 444, and all different types of Synchronicities that were happening with all of this Fun, Creative, Loving, Expansive, Joy Filled Phenomena.

May 22, 2016

Before going to sleep, again I light the light green candle on my Altar. I say the Abundance prayer and I ask for Love, Peace, Joy, Bliss, Knowing and Discernment. So many Synchronicities are happening that I can hardly keep up with them all. And then once again I head outside in the backyard to take some pictures from left to right again.

I go back inside and I pull up the pictures. To the right where the column of Light was the night before, are two thin lines coming down from the sky in the same place and width that the column was. There is a big greenish Orb to the right back of the yard flying around.

Then I pulled up the photo to the left side of the patio. There is something going on, I didn't notice it at first because I was seeing a white line to the right of that photo. Then I zero in on a very small shiny Light Bright Green almost crescent shape. I enlarge it to look at it more closely. It seems it is on the grass between the end of the patio and the shed. As I enlarge it to study its shape as it has a bulbous top to it, Interesting, it's a very bright light green. Then I scan up the picture to the shed beyond the patio. I can't believe my eyes! I look again to see if what I am seeing is really there. I enlarge the picture more, as it stretches onto the full view of the page what I was seeing seems to disappear as it stretches to wide and long. But when I enlarge it just enough to see the full view of the shed, I can see as plain as can be to me, Mother Mary, she is on the front door of my shed. She is so beautiful! Mother Mary is looking towards the right side of the shed as she seems to be looking into my back yard, at a specific location that will later make sense to me. I can see her face, her head scarf over her head, which frames her delicate face as it drapes down over her shoulders and continues down, joining her robe towards the bottom of the shed.

In August of 2016, I took some pictures of my backyard during the day and I noticed something so amazing. On the shed exactly where Mother Mary appeared in the photo, is now something that is permanently showing itself in the plastic of the shed. What has formed is the face of a Feline Being. It is the face of the White Feline Being, that so Lovingly morphed out of my ceiling that morning in May in my room after Mother Mary came to me in my room holding my clear quartz crystal. The same White Feline Being that was in that Light Bright Green Orb that was above the Golden Disc. And now she is permanently there. Her face is on the shed door, it has formed from within the plastic of the shed where Mother Mary appeared in the photo in May. And I feel so grateful because I know they are assuring me yet again, They Are Here! They Love Us All! and that We Are Never Alone!

July 24, 2016: Green Lights in The Trees

In 2016 there was a lot of UFO activity. I had these Bright Light Green Lights and Orbs that were showing up in my trees. I would go outside and I would be filming them and taking pictures of them and communicating with them. I discovered they were primarily part of the feline team, but there could be other beings in the Bright Light Green Lights and Orbs too.

I was outside by the tree, I moved closer as I was filming asking this Bright Light Green Light that was spinning and morphing, to come down the tree. I asked, who are you? I heard, "We are you in the future. We are You and You are us." Then I said, "I want to learn more about you." As I said it, The Bright Light Green Light started to move down the tree as I am watching it get closer and closer to where I am standing. The next thing I notice in my camera as I'm filming, in the right side of the camera, and to the right of the tree, in comes an orange disk shaped craft. So I start following that craft across my yard, as I am filming it, and then another one appears, and another one, and another one, then there are three in a triangular shape that seem to move in unison. Then three stacked up on top of one another. And there are more! They just kept coming! Omg! Until There were over 30 salmon colored discs that were flying over my house and over my neighborhood. And some were flying very low that went right over my house and my yard and over the next door neighbor's house. The dogs were barking next door, I was in my glory saying Omg! You guys are here! I'm so Happy! Thank You! You guys are Amazing! Your here! I always knew you would show up! I remember saying to my X husband years ago, "I know we are going to see something one day." (meaning them) While this was happening and they were flying overhead they looked very low and oblong in shape. They were disc shaped, oblong, bright salmon colored. And in one of them, it came down so low right between my house and the next door neighbor's house, that I could actually see a being who standing there looking out as it passed by in the craft itself. And the being was standing there looking out at me. It was that low! While these 30 or so salmon colored disc shaped crafts were flying over my neighborhood and my house, there were all kinds of very fast moving, flickering things all around the salmon colored discs that were flying over my yard. When I went back indoors and looked at the video, I could see the very fast moving ones were the Bright Light Green Lights. These Green Lights are flying so fast, so much faster than the salmon colored discs. And I couldn't believe what I was getting on film. I was able to slow it down to see, as they were these moving Bright Light Green Lights, that were going by really fast. As they moved they would be in an Orb like shape, as they would go to turn a corner, the Bright Light Green Orb shape would actually compress and shrink down into a disk shape, it would flatten and then they would make a sharp quick right-hand turn, super fast. What I also saw in my camera was something I can't wrap my brain around. These crafts or UFO's were the opposite in size to what I was actually seeing with my own eyes. The Salmon Disc Shapes looked so much larger in my own vision than the Light Bright Green Orbs did that were quickly flickering around those salmon colored crafts. The green orbs looked tiny in my vision with my eyes. But In the videos and pictures, the Salmon colored discs were much smaller than what I actually saw with my eyes and the Bright Light Green Orbs showed up in the camera to look much bigger than the salmon colored disc shaped crafts. It is wild but it's True. I don't understand to this day how that could be, but it is. It is for sure High Strangeness!

What I learned later on is that the salmon colored discs that flew over my house, the beings in them, they were actually part of a group of beings, and the way they presented themselves to me was, they are part of the Sasquatch family, and I know that sounds crazy but its True.

Sasquatch Beings

One morning in 2017 I was waking up to seeing in my minds eye a bunch of sticks that looked like they were placed on the ground. It looked to me like an alphabet of some kind, as if they were trying to spell out something in sticks on the ground. I was still in that very sleepy state, but awake with my eyes still closed. Confused, I asked wait, what? Who is this? I could see this in my mind's eye vision as I was waking up when one after another after another, I was seeing all different kinds of Sasquatch beings. They were all different shapes, sizes, colors, each one unique, just like humans. There were so many. They started to explain to me telepathically that I had a life as one of them. They told me that they are coming to different people that are also connected to them. It was just really amazing! They showed me what I looked like as a Sasquatch being. Omg! They showed me people that I know in this lifetime that I actually had a lifetime as a Sasquatch with them, and I just thought, that's just too crazy. But then they showed me this one little blond girl who was actually my little Sasquatch baby, she morphed into this beautiful little blond baby Sasquatch in my arms. I was holding her looking down at her and I could see her face morph into almost human like, but she was still a Sasquatch.

Later that day when I went to a place where I was going on Sundays for fellowship. There was a woman there who I just felt very drawn to her. I felt like I knew her. I walked over to her and I said, Excuse me, Do I know you? She turned around and looked at me and I realized that she had the exact same face that I saw that morning as I was waking up and they were showing me my little blond baby Sasquatch. So as it turns out, she was my daughter, and part of my family in that lifetime. I know that sounds insane but they did so many things to show me that they are here and that they are real. I have pictures of them, and video, one video is of one that's running past really fast and turns into an orb. I have had so many synchronistic things that have happened with them, that show me that they are definitely here. The thing with the sasquatch beings is that they can disappear and they can appear they are interdimensional. They are part of the ET/Interdimensional beings. I know it sounds funny, but it is so true and it's just wild.

That year 2016 and 2017 I met so many different kinds of beings. Many different types would show themselves to me, and I always felt like they are family when they would show up, I was never afraid. I always felt so much love, and my heart, it was buzzing all around my heart and expanding outward. That would happen because they were connected to my heart. I would feel a buzzing and vibration around my whole being and my inner being. I felt expanded and filled with so much love around these beings. So, they come in with a lot of Love, Joy, Synchronicity and so much Creativity. They can appear in so many fun creative ways. I mean, one day, they actually had me going to HomeGoods. Lol ! They kept popping HomeGoods in my head. There are two Home Goods near me, so I asked them which one? And I saw in my mind's eye the one that they wanted me to go to. When I got there, I said to them, in my mind, "ok what do you want me to get here?" The next thing I hear in my head is, "Go to the back of the store." So, I go to the back of the store, and then I see it, Omg! There is an 8 foot tall resin Male Sasquatch statue, for $2000. I stood there in disbelief and amazement! And then I said, "Funny! Ha! But I'm not buying that!" I did however ask someone to take my picture with the Sasquatch Statue. And then I took peoples pictures with him. It was such a fun experience indeed. I still laugh when I think of that! I know that they wanted me to see, that "They Are Here!" And they are communicating with me.

I walked around Home Goods after that, and I saw this awesome Himalayan salt crystal lamp that was much bigger than most. It stood about 16" - 18" tall and about 7" or 8" wide. I thought to myself oh wow this would be great in my living room right next to my big screen TV. I felt like it would be a perfect lamp, and next to the TV would be a great place for it, as it was big, it would absorb the negative ions coming out of the big screen TV. So, I purchased it and brought it home. I plugged it in right next to my big screen TV in my living room. I sat down in my chair, looked over at it and to my surprise and delight, there is a Sasquatch being right on the front of the "Salmon Colored" Himalayan salt lamp crystal. It is all part of the natural inflections and in the cut of the stone. It looks like a Huge male Sasquatch walking, he has a large chest and his head is elongated. I can see what looks to me like his heart in between his ribs. His right arm hangs down bent, as if he is walking in a stride. His left arm reaches down as if he is holding someone's hand. I like to think that someone is me. I know they are always around me, they are protectors. They are very Loving, very psychic, heart centered beings and so creative and fun! They have shown themselves to me so many times. I've documented it all, filmed them and their phenomena. They Love us humans, the earth and all of its inhabitants and They Are Here!

Conclusion

Over the past 18 or so years I have been documenting my Spiritual Journey, Dreams, Synchronicities, Premonitions, Visions, Phenomena and more through Writing, Journaling, Automatic Writing, Filming, Photography, Art, Poetry, and to date over 650 Transmissions of voice recordings from my Higher Self Team, The Council Of Light, which consist of God, My Higher Self, Masters, Angels, Spirit Guides and many different kinds of Interdimensional Beings. I have seen these different beings in my mind's eye as I am channeling them. They have shown me their name "The Council of Light" They started to channel through me by Trance Channeling in 2016. At that time I started to trance channel with a couple of mediums that I knew, all three of us would meet once a week and we would each take turns trance channeling inspiring uplifting messages from Spirit. Shortly after that, one morning as I was waking up I was being shown in my mind's eye a Gold Lions Head Door Knocker. As if they were saying, "Hello, Knock Knock, We Are Here!" Lol!! So with that, I started to channel them regularly in the mornings as I was waking up, then before I fell asleep and anytime during the day also if I felt compelled.

My Team as I call them, have been such a huge support to me throughout my life's journey. They have been with me my whole life and more. They are My Lineage my Spiritual Family of absolute Love and Support. I am a trance channel so when I trance channel them, I record it or I only remember a subject, and not the whole transmission. They have helped me, guided an supported me through the most difficult, challenging times of my life. And they have been there with me during the most Glorious, Loving, Blissful, Unitive, Expanded times of my life. I have had a wide range of Spiritually Expanded Experiences and also there have been times in my life of Contracted and Fearful Experiences. And they have been with me through them all. I am so Grateful to have this Loving connection in this lifetime to God, My Higher Self, My Team who together as a collective have referred to themselves to me as "The Council Of Light." What I have learned and I know to be Truth with every cell of my being is that they are not only here for me, "They Are Here For All" as "We Are All One" and "We Are All Part Of The All".

There are so many ways that these beings have come through to show me that "They Are Here!" :) Not only in my consciousness or my mind's eye as I see them clairvoyantly, hear them clairaudiently, feel them clairsentiently and know claircognisently. They have also showed up in my 3-D reality in so many ways that I gratefully, have been able to document their existence and the many ways they have come through. The stories of how they have come through and what they are teaching me through my own unique life's journey are to much and to many to share in this chapter. But as I said earlier I will be sharing in a much more detailed way, the many different ways they have come through during my journey in future Books, Photos, Videos, Art, Poetry, Automatic Writings, and Transmissions that have channeled through me throughout the last 18 plus years that I have been documenting.

I have learned so much throughout my journey. I am so happy to be able to share what I have learned. I am filled with gratitude to be able to share some of my journey with you here in Rey Hernandez's book "A Greater Reality" Volume 5. My whole life I have had so many different kinds of Experiences STE's NDE's, OBE's, Unitive, Kundalini Awakenings, Spiritual Awakenings, Mystical, Oneness, Medium, Channeling, Angelic Encounters, UFO ET Experiences, and more. When I heard about Rey and his work in 2016 I was elated that he was putting these pieces together. Because my life had been filled with all kinds of Contact Modality Experiences or as I call them STE's. and finally after taking the three surveys that Rey offered to people in 2016 to compile the data for his first book "***Beyond UFO's***" It makes so much sense that so many of the Contact Modality Experiences or STE's have been happening to so many Experiencers. And I concur that they should all be studied under one umbrella, the umbrella of Consciousness.

It has been my goal and a big part of my Mission to bring people together that are having all different kinds of Spiritual Experiences, to be able to share them in a place of non judgement and support. I see a future where we can share our experiences openly and honestly without fear of being labeled crazy or mentally ill. The Medical field and the Psychological field still have a long way to go to get onboard with what Experiencers Know. That being said, I have also seen in the last 8 plus years that I have been actively involved as a host and facilitator for my own sharing groups and also in being a facilitator for Sharing Groups for both IANDS and Spiritual Awakenings International, there are many people that are also Experiencers that are in the Medical and Psychological field. And there are some that aren't experiencers but have a feeling that the people they work with, their clients, are having real experiences. It is upsetting to them that some have been told they need to be medicated. This is sadly still going on today.

I am excited to see and to be, a part of the global shift that is happening. Where people from all over the world are coming together and sharing their Experiences with one another on Zoom and In Person. We each have an important story to tell. Every one of us that is an Experiencer has an important piece of the puzzle. And we are sharing in Sharing Groups, Podcasts, YouTube Channels, Books and more. I see a world where one day this conversation won't be whispered or spoken about hesitantly for fear of being ridiculed, called crazy or worse. I see a world where we are all able to be who we each are freely. And where we can express who we are and what we have experienced while be met with Understanding, Compassion, Support and Love. No matter who we are sharing our Experiences with.

The whole world is in the process of waking up. Maybe not all at the same time, but eventually everyone will awaken to their True Nature. And that is something to look forward to. It is through the sharing of our own unique journey of Awakening into who we Truly Are, that we are creating a ripple that spans out into the far reaches, across time and space into the ethers, where this expansion can never be stopped. I feel this is the work we have each come to earth to do. To carry the torch of our own unique Truth and Light into a world that is needing to see and know it is so. To illuminate the way for others to be able to search within their own hearts to discover and know Truth. To then be able to stand in unity with others in their own Truth and Light, and then be able to share about their own unique Spiritual Experiences.

Each time I facilitate a sharing group or I am a participant in one, I feel so much gratitude for the group and our time together. Coming together and sharing our own unique experiences feels like "A Little Slice of Heaven Right Here on Earth." As these Sharing Groups are a Safe Place where finally, UFO ET Experiencers, Spiritual Experiencers can come together to listen and to share about their own Unique Spiritually Transformative Experiences, while feeling Accepted, Supported and Loved for Being Exactly Who We Each Truly Are.

To find out more about the IANDS Sharing Groups and Topic groups go to IANDS.org, go to Groups and Events and sign up. There is also a UFO/ET/NDE Topic Sharing Group that I facilitate on the first Wednesdays of the month at 7:00PM Eastern Time.

To Find out more about SAI go to
SpiritualAwakeningsInternational.org
You can register there for their Sharing Circles which are held on first Saturdays of the month.

To contact me or to find out more about and to register for our three sharing groups that I host and facilitate which are, "Safe Space Sharing Group" "UFO ET Experiencers" and "Spiritual Experiencers" each held on the first, second and fourth Tuesdays of the month at 7PM Eastern Time. We would love for you to join us! Also to find out more about me, our YouTube channels, some recent speaker events, and my first book that will be published in late 2024 to early 2025! I look forward to hearing from you or meeting you in the sharing and speaker groups.

Please go to:

www.//bit.ly/m/CatherineChapey

Exploring Other Worlds: A Life of Contact with Non-Human Intelligence via the Contact Modalities

Russell Davies

When I was asked to write a chapter for this book, my first thought was, why ask me? Surely there must be others out there that could do a better job? I mean, what do I really understand about the topic of the "Contact Modalities", as I am neither a scientist nor an academic, and am I able to look at this topic objectively being as immersed in it as I am? With close reference to my personal journey, I shall commence by giving you some background about myself and focus particularly on the life experiences that have shaped my understanding of the field of contact with non-human intelligences.

For much of my childhood my mother went to work running her own businesses, later working as a casino Inspector, having previously managed The Moody Blues when I was still learning to walk. A lot of my time was spent in private education in the countryside. My family included musicians, psychics and a great aunt who was a Spiritualist "platform" medium and as a child I inherited some of the abilities, which included talking to spirits who appeared in my bedroom closet. From a very early age, I had a fascination with both religion and the occult, and was having mystical experiences wherein I felt spiritual presences both in church, where I was the regular bible reader, and in my everyday life as a child, but by the time I was 5 or 6, my ability to actually see and talk to spirits had left me. However, my natural interest in all things spiritual was very pronounced, and I was reading ancient Hindu texts, and esoteric literature before I was ten, being particularly drawn to UFO related books including the work of Von Daniken and Adamski. I was avidly consuming any literature I could find on ufology and esoteric subjects, having an instinctive belief in the veracity of ET visitation and the reality of other planes of existence.

By the time I was a teenager, my fascination with religion and UFO's had extended to encompass spiritual traditions, belief systems, psychology and paranormal phenomena. Aged 15, I began to study and practice both High Magic and Kundalini Yoga, where after a year of practice I was spontaneously "frog hopping", as the Transcendental

Meditation movement calls it, automatically rising up into the air in full lotus position. I was also practicing lucid dreaming, astral traveling, having out of body experiences, was practicing consciously interacting with others' astral bodies following methods expounded by the Golden Dawn magic system and Dion Fortune, and was experiencing the presence of non-human intelligences in my magical practices and lucid dreams. I was also able to see auras around people as clearly as I could the people themselves.

This latter ability I was aware of, but personally validated for myself under startling circumstances, when on an exceptionally foggy British autumn afternoon, I was waiting at a bus stop with a member of the public, and I turned to him and said "Well it looks like we have company, someone else is coming". This surprised my fellow commuter, as the fog was so thick that it was only possible to see around ten yards ahead. He asked how far away the person was, and I replied "Around fifty yards". He looked at me very strangely, and I pointed to where I could clearly see, not a person, but a glowing halo around a body coming towards us, and I said "There he is". He arrived a couple of minutes later, which resulted in me standing uneasily in an atmosphere of shocked silence.

Around this same period, I was under a considerable amount of strain, as my mother's mental health was deteriorating due largely to a complex divorce case with my stepfather. It was at this time that a number of unusual paranormal type phenomena began to happen around me, as I was struggling to cope with everything in my environment, aged sixteen and feeling the strain of my mother's dramatic slide into mental and emotional breakdown.

One day after a particularly intense argument, about which I remember not what, I was feeling fit to explode, and my mother and I both heard a "ping" from a stone-cold Pyrex mug which she had been drinking tea from an hour earlier. I then witnessed a half inch long piece of glass break off the mug, fly several feet, turn around 180 degrees, and fly into the far side of my mother's thumb, which was facing away from the mug. It was at this point that I recognized that I had some latent psychic abilities, and that I would have to master them, and choose in life whether or not to utilize them, and if so, how.

By the time I was in my late teens, I believed that God is a being separate from the creation, and that there are many beings, some of which I felt I had sensed and even directly encountered, living in other dimensions. I understood that these dimensions could be accessed through consciousness, but did not yet fully understand the implications of what that actually meant. I was convinced of the reality of the astral body as the basis for telepathic communication, and had seen the very significant effects of practicing astral communication to change others' attitudes towards me using Dion Fortune's system of psychic self-defense.

In my twenties, I devoted myself to not only studying mystical systems, but also developing my psychic abilities, specifically focusing on Tarot and Clairvoyance, and went on to work professionally in this field. It was here that I began to experience for the first time since my childhood, other than the many unusual beings I experienced in my astral travels, conscious waking contact with beings from elsewhere. Whilst starting off as a technical reader, I soon began to experience moments where I felt I was merely a channel for "guides" who were assisting me. Usually these "guides" would communicate in a faint voice, almost like an echo of a very distant voice, (the still small voice of the bible springs to mind) accompanied with typed words forming in my mind, as if on a screen. I would then be given visual images of places and people, along with key words to guide the reading. The resulting readings would be startlingly accurate.

On one such occasion, for example, I was doing a psychic reading for a British businessman who was weighing up the possibility of working with two investors, and could not choose between them. I closed my eyes and as always visualized a blank screen, and I instantly was shown an image of the Statue of Liberty, gleaming in the sunlight. The feeling was very positive. The word "male" and an image of a man drifted through my mind. I was then shown a map of Europe with a faint voice repeating "Europe", and the image of a very irritable bad-tempered woman with a very dark and brooding energy. On relaying this information, it transpired that the choice was between a male New York investor, and a woman in Germany, who had so far been obstructive in a variety of ways. He was very satisfied with the reading and went on to work profitably with the New York contact.

My practice of psychic abilities dramatically changed my experience of life, and I reached the point where I would walk down a street and actually see peoples' thoughts projected in 3d around them like thought bubbles. I was able to surprise people by reading their minds and anticipating very specific things that they were about to say. My precognitive abilities became enhanced to the point that I regularly dreamed about features I would experience in the near future. People found me somewhat unnerving, and I found myself becoming reclusive and keeping my abilities to myself.

My study of Taoist yoga in my twenties, enabled me to not only heal many energetic, emotional and mental blocks I had accumulated through childhood trauma, but also had the unusual side effect of dramatically changing my consciousness. I discovered that even when I was asleep, I was fully aware that I was lying in bed asleep, my consciousness had expanded so that my conscious mind , through breathing exercises, was able to be fully present in moments normally associated with unconscious processes, and I was able to reprogram many automated physical and mental processes and habitual emotional responses. I could change my body temperature at will, and lower my heart rate to around 20bpm, a skill I had learned when practicing kundalini yoga as a teenager. My OBE's and astral traveling continued, where I would meet many "guides" and receive profound insights and have precognitive experiences in my dreams.

I was also practicing the Gurdjieff system, and was engaged in creating what is known as a "meso-self", so that I was neither attached to my internal dialogue, nor my cultural and family influenced automated responses to external events. From this, I began to experience far greater clarity of my own pre-dispositions, and began to have a greater facility for meditation and singular focus. I began to train my mind to disconnect from outer life distractions and false internal monologue, primarily to preserve my pre-existing psychic abilities and my life goal of genuine spiritual growth.

My study of Gurdjieff led on to my introduction to Sufism. I spent a couple of years as caretaker of a Sufi meditation house, where intense spiritual practices were undertaken on a daily basis. It was on one quiet day, with the individual sun rays streaming through the shutters of the meditation space, that I achieved what is sometimes described by mystics as unity consciousness, I experienced the reality of all life being part of one consciousness stream , and every being a manifestation of one creator, multiplicity in unity, unity in multiplicity. I felt the consciousness of everyone, and also felt the infinite golden thread which pulses as a resonance of living energy within all of us, like droplets forming a wave.

This was one of my most significant experiences, and has informed my awareness ever since. It also served as the basis for understanding my subsequent telepathic ET contact, and work in human initiated contact with extraterrestrials, whilst also aiding in the further development of my psychic and mediumship abilities, by expanding my consciousness to be aware of my presence in an infinite united consciousness field encompassing all beings.

By my late twenties, I had concluded that a creator force is in everything in existence as a living dynamic intelligence, that all consciousness is inextricably linked, and that there is nothing in the universe which is not "God". My contact with Sufism and earlier foundation in the Golden Dawn system of magic had led me to conclude that there are other dimensions around us teaming with life and that connection to them and indeed communication remotely to other human beings, can be achieved via the astral body. I had also concluded that we are being visited by ETs, which I assumed at this point were from this dimension we physically inhabit. I believed that spirits were in another dimension and could manifest physically to some extent in this dimension, but primarily visually, with telepathic communicative abilities. The Sufi communities were rife with stories of the Djinn, and yet at this point it did not occur to me that ETs and beings described as "Djinn" could be one and the same thing, with a particular cultural slant overlaid.

My late twenties through to my 40's were years spent gaining academic qualifications, including an arts degree, counseling qualifications, and various professional qualifications in different fields including teaching. However, being the creative right brain dominant person which I primarily am, I did not seriously pursue a career other than in music, and my esoteric interests were relegated to hobby status and secondary interests. During this period of 15 years, aside from continuing my spiritual endeavors, I worked primarily as a musician playing a number of instruments and styles and composing and recording albums.

I experienced a considerable amount of emotional turbulence in my personal relationships, consistently experiencing rejection for being different, and put this experience to good use both in terms of my own personal growth, and in refining my cognition of the processes of breakdown and healing, and ultimately the processes of cognition itself. This enabled me to develop my ability to help others through counseling, using my considerable life experience and spiritual learning to assist and help guide people on the journey of their own spiritual growth. It is this combination of spiritual study, personal growth, and the development of deep empathy and heart-centeredness, which I feel laid the final foundation for my subsequent ET contact, and advanced mediumship experiences.

This fallow period in my experience of other dimensions, albeit that I continued to have psychic experiences and premonitions, gave me some time to process the spiritual and paranormal aspects of my life and to return to a more grounded state of awareness.

What I feel distinguishes people who have experienced the contact modalities from your average person on the street, is simply that aside from being open minded to other realities, these people are able to switch off internal dialogue and attune more easily to other dimensions because they have organically, through effort, or through the unsolicited contact with an NHI, come to the realization that all beings are connected in consciousness, and that our collective model of reality is not only insufficient but fundamentally wrong. It is also a metanoia, a change of mind, predicated by the healing and growth experience after experiencing the ontological shock of contact with NHI's in all contact modalities, which I realize can permanently open up, or rewire our brain circuitry and transform our nervous system to experience other dimensions and both send and receive information from them. At this point, I was already completely open to other realities, but maintaining some aspects of the cautious mindset of mainstream scientific empirical thinking.

In my early 40's, after a long period of celibacy living with an "ex" as a friend, I had the good fortune to come across a reference online to the name of the first real girlfriend I had ever had, who was working as an author in France. I made the decision to contact her, and within a short space of time began a relationship in earnest, of necessity, long distance. I was amazed to have rediscovered her and that we still felt a strong connection. She was in the process of extricating herself from a very unhappy marriage, and was excited to have found her first love again, as was I. Within a month of meeting, however, things took an awful turn. Her husband discovered that he had a rare form of cancer. It was a traumatic experience, as not only had it been a long marriage, but they had had twin boys within the marriage who were at the time seven years old, and it was a huge emotional trauma for the entire family.

They separated nonetheless, but, understandably, she did not feel able to invite me over as she and the twins were regularly visiting him both at his new home and later in hospital. She was also from a traditional French family, and was horrified at the thought that she would be judged by family and the wider community if I were to be ensconced in the family home. Towards the end, he moved back into their family home, and spent much of his last six months on earth with the children.

During the eighteen months I waited for us to be together, I lived in a large Victorian house which was haunted. Almost every night, I would hear footsteps walking down the hallway towards my apartment when there was nobody there, and then a rush of wind, and I would feel the presence of a being I felt to be a child walking into my bedroom. This persisted to the point that I began to use sage to smudge my environment on a regular basis. I felt that there was a desire to communicate something but I was unsure what. My psychic sensitivity and mediumship abilities had begun to return after years of focus on external life, and I had become re-attuned to other dimensions.

When after eighteen months my girlfriend's husband was dying, I felt a sense of deep trepidation, as I had a sudden premonition that he was not going to cross over easily. In my talks with her, she had told me how angry he was about our relationship, because despite the fact that they had been having intractable problems for a long time, he had desired to save the marriage. I contacted a friend who is a Tibetan Buddhist lay practitioner, and together we decided to request of a local temple that practice be done by local monks to help him cross over when he died. This indeed took place a month later, when I heard the news that he had lost the struggle with cancer.

When I eventually moved to France to be with my girlfriend, almost a year later, I walked into an atmosphere heavy with emotion, and I instantly felt a spiritual presence in the building, and what appeared to be a spiritual attachment on everyone in the house. Both my girlfriend and her two children had a very oppressed and negative energy that went well beyond the deep sadness and unprocessed grief which was nevertheless present, and it was a difficult beginning to our living together. However, over the course of the year I spent there, things went from bad to worse.

Within six weeks of being there, the children expressed that they felt I had wanted to kill their father. There was a huge resentment at my presence in the house, to the point that my girlfriend would not even sleep with me, but set up a bed for me in the office downstairs next to the garage. I felt a very powerful and tangible feeling that the husband was present, and apart from the feeling of this and of being watched, I felt he was emotionally influencing everyone in the house directly.

I did my best to get on with building a life there, set up an "association" or local business, teaching English and guitar, but despite my best efforts, I was not assimilated into the household, and my girlfriend was quick to anger with me at the smallest things, often flying into an uncontrollable rage and even physically attacking me. In more somber moments, she would cry, and would say that we had killed her husband, and no amount of comforting or talking would move this feeling she had. The atmosphere was tense most of the time, and I sensed a brooding angry presence lurking, a hidden consciousness inhabiting the house which I could not communicate with despite my efforts.

One day, after months of uneasiness, my then girlfriend was roaming the house looking for something with the children, while I was preparing English lessons for my students. Eventually, I decided to ask what she was looking for as she seemed at her wit's end, and she replied by explaining that the children wished to look at a series of photographs of themselves with their father, taken on their very last trip to a swimming pool. They were on a cd disc. As she finished explaining, I heard a gravelly French voice in my mind, telling me in French that the disc was downstairs. He said that it was on the table, and showed me an image of a spool, and in a way that I cannot explain, showed me where on the spool the disc was. I descended the stairs and sure enough, thirty seconds later, returned clutching the disc. I explained what had happened, and she did not believe me, and repeated several times that she had checked on the table and had looked at every cd, and that the disc had not been there. I assured her that I had indeed heard her husband's voice, and proceeded to mimic the distinctive voice I had heard, much to her astonishment. She seemed shocked, and admitted that this was exactly what his voice had sounded like, but refused to believe or even consider the idea that I had spoken to him and walked off dismissively.

On another occasion, I heard the same gravelly voice telling me that if I were to go into the garage, I would see how much he loved his wife. An image was projected into my mind of the corner of the room, and a pile of old newspapers. I followed the voice's instructions, and sure enough, found a large pile of old newspapers. Taking them down, inside was revealed a set of five oil paintings he has painted of his wife, and when I took them to show her, she was surprised as she had forgotten all about them and had no idea they were still in the house.

She tearfully recounted how disappointed he had been when she did not react with the delight he had expected on showing her his tributes to the beauty he saw in her.

The final and most significant experience was when my girlfriend was staying downstairs with me (she always returned to the former marital bed before sunrise), and I heard slow gentle steps coming down the wooden staircase to the basement where we were. The footsteps then stopped, and there was silence for a few moments. I could clearly see the staircase, yet there was nobody there. Then, suddenly, there was a massive flash of light, as an orb the size of a soccer ball appeared and hung in the air for a couple of seconds, illuminating the entire room before disappearing as rapidly as it had manifested. It had the intense appearance of plasma. I rushed up the stairs, wondering if one of the children had used a camera flash to frighten us. Both children were fast asleep, and I stood for minutes listening to their regular rhythmic breathing, before returning downstairs, reflecting on the fact that the downstairs room was not completely dark, and I had not seen anyone walking downstairs, despite being able to clearly see each step, as the room was partially illuminated by the desktop computer in the corner.

Only a few minutes passed, and my girlfriend and I were disturbed by loud knocking on the wardrobe next to the bed, which made the wooden chamber of the almost empty internal space resonate loudly. This was followed by even louder, more violent knocking on the thin partition wall next to me, and I knew at that moment that it was the living spirit of the husband who had returned to express his anger at my presence. She said "Russell, I am frightened", and I proceeded to talk to the spirit, explaining that I was not there to usurp his position as father, and that I had the greatest respect and sympathy for him. The knocks subsided after ten minutes, and my girlfriend went back to sleep, denying that anything at all had taken place the following morning.

Within 2 months, I had returned to the UK somewhat traumatized, to pick up where I had left off. The atmosphere in the house had become such that it had been impossible for me to continue living there, and my girlfriend and I had no longer been able to communicate. Although I had previously had experiences with spirits before, I had never felt such a personal connection, and neither had I ever witnessed how such a manifestation could impact my three dimensional space in such a dramatic way, nor so strongly affect the living through what is known in the psychic world as oppression. This was nothing compared to what I was soon to experience.

Having moved into a Georgian town house, not far from my mother in the historic town of Shrewsbury, I returned to playing music, and also caring for my mother whose disability meant she needed regular assistance. I set about recording an album with a friend, later used by Project Camelot in a documentary on Adam's Calendar in South Africa, during the course of which I needed to acquire new instruments to record with.

On one such trip with my friend, to buy a vintage guitar, we were driving along a country road and I saw half a mile in front of us, around 100 yards above the rooftops of the nearby town, an orange ball of light, and I instantly knew that it was not a Chinese lantern or anything mundane. I spontaneously decided to engage mentally with this ball of light, and, staring at it intently, said in my mind "I know you are not a mundane object, you are an ET craft, you can't fool me". The glowing sphere, (which I went on later to call "mini suns", having since seen dozens of these orange forms of craft) instantly performed a 180 degree turn, moving right to left, rather than the original left to right trajectory, and after a period, made an abrupt right angle ninety degree turn and flew across fields parallel to our van's position.

When it had come down to a point exactly parallel with the van, it then turned 180 degrees again, and began flying across the fields alongside the van, matching our speed, approximately one hundred yards away, and at a height of around thirty yards. I was somewhat alarmed, as I had become very interested in ufology on my return from France, having had one previous experience of two UFOs flying at incredible speeds several years earlier. I had absorbed a lot of the darker material available in videos online, which suggest that ETs are abducting humans for their own agenda, originating from David Jacobs, Budd Hopkins et al.

Whilst this was happening, I was giving a running commentary to my friend, the driver, as all this was taking place on the passenger side of the car. Although he had witnessed the orb changing direction when directly ahead of us, he seemed uninterested however, and almost in a dream-like state, and was silent during most of the experience. Mentally, I projected (with considerable arrogance and naivety) the thought that "I am not the usual human type you encounter, I have considerable awareness, and I cannot be so easily manipulated". In retrospect, I am quite ashamed of this, but I was at the time in a considerable state of fear and shock. I then decided to project my consciousness into the craft, and commenced to close my eyes and take my consciousness inside through a kind of remote viewing, and thereby attempt to ascertain what I was looking at.

The exercise seemed very easy, and I found myself looking inside a large circular room, with a domed ceiling, and a corridor going off to one side. The room had several small white beings inside, around four feet tall, each of them apparently looking at displays molded into the contoured walls. I got the impression that they were aware of my presence, but did not look around. I looked down the corridor and saw that the craft was vast, at least hundreds of yards long, and at this point my friend said something to me, and my consciousness was back in the van.

I looked over to the glowing orb, and it immediately began to disappear from the top down, so that after thirty seconds or so it was a half moon, then a crescent, then within a minute or so, it was gone. Yet psychically, I knew it was still there, and the presence of the orb was still registering in my consciousness and nervous system as a feeling of being observed. This astonished me, and I realized that the level of intelligence and technological ability of the craft and occupants was beyond anything I could imagine. I returned home in a state of shock, and immediately contacted my local U.F.O network and made a report. This incident threw my mind into turmoil. In France, I had experienced tangible proof of the reality of the afterlife. I had not only experienced telepathic communication with the spirit of my girlfriend's deceased husband, but seen him appear as a plasma orb the size of a soccer ball which illuminated the entire room, and also experienced violent rapping on the walls, as well as feeling his presence. This had to an extent, traumatized me, and changed me forever, as much or more than the relationship breakup. Now, I had also experienced a non-human intelligence, in the form of a glowing plasma-like orb, whose consciousness I could feel, responding to my thoughts by changing direction and coming to examine me in the vehicle I was traveling in. I had previously always understood that all consciousness was connected ever since experiencing the mystical states of god consciousness and unity consciousness, but there was a huge difference between knowing it to be true and actually witnessing it being manifest in my physical reality. This was just the beginning.

Six months later, on December 31st 2010, New Year's Eve, I was sitting alone watching videos on social media, I believe they were mostly about the ET presence. I suddenly heard, in a way that sounded like my cranium was being used as a loudspeaker, my own voice, in my own way of speaking, using my own phraseology, telling me to "Grab a camera and go outside, you are going to see some UFOs". I was in a state of shock, and ran to the front door at breakneck speed, to see two orange plasma orbs, approximately three feet in circumference, floating very slowly at a slow walking speed inches above the rooftops at the end of the street, approximately 30 yards from me. There were a number of drunken revelers approaching, and I was too self-conscious to start filming. They were oblivious to the orbs and did not appear to see them. Two police officers walked directly underneath them, and could have thrown their truncheons and hit them with minimal effort. They did not see them.

I stood in shock for a minute, then began desperately running in the direction that the orange orbs had been flying in. They were nowhere to be seen. I sprinted through the town center, wildly scanning the skies for some sign of their presence, to no avail. Arriving at a bridge over a river, I stopped out of breath. And collected my thoughts. I thought back over the videos I had been watching about Dr Steven Greer and his technique of CE5, and decided to close my eyes and attempt to create a telepathic link with the ETs. Immediately I felt a rush of energy up my spine, and a deep exhilaration, and on opening my eyes, the orb was floating forty to fifty feet away from me, just above my point on the bridge, which stands only twelve feet above the River Severn in Shrewsbury.

I stood in amazement. It seemed to be composed of plasma, and resembled a scaled down sun, and was exactly the same type of object I had seen and remotely viewed from the van, 50 miles away, months earlier. I felt, as before, a strong sense of my thoughts and emotions being observed, and got a very distinct feeling that there were multiple beings watching and assessing me. I again got a very distinct sense that despite its size of three to four feet across, that this was like Dr Who's "Tardis", and was almost a floating portal carrying a number of beings inside. I received a quiet telepathic message that "We are family", and I stood mesmerized. Once I had recovered, I quickly got out my very basic Zoom Q3 video camera, but it was so dark a night that I could not see anything on the screen and was unaware if I was capturing anything.

I also felt the same sense of fear as earlier, that people might arrive and not see the object, nor understand what I was doing, the fear of ridicule, and the fear of being seen to be different.

When I left the bridge, it was still slowly floating away at around 2 miles per hour, and I hurried home to look at the video, expecting that I had not captured anything as I was unable to see anything on the screen whilst filming. Imagine my shock when having downloaded it, I saw that not only had I captured it, but that the single orb I had seen with naked eye also had other smaller multi-colored orbs rotating around it, changing formations, and forming triangles, hexagons etc. An artist friend was very interested, and downloaded the video and lightened it. What was revealed truly shocked me. My face was in the video!

When I shot the video, I was holding out the camera towards the orb, looking at the screen in front of me. I was behind the camera. Lightening the video revealed my face staring into the camera, with the orb behind me, as if I was doing a selfie with the ET craft behind my shoulder. This was not what took place, and I was astonished to realize that the video itself was paranormal and had been interfered with by the intelligence behind the phenomenon I had been filming! I pondered this, and came to the realization that I had purposefully been given a visual metaphor for the telepathic message I felt I had received from them, that I was one of them, whatever that might mean.

The following year was a period of attempting to cope with deep ontological shock, and led me to re-think everything I thought I had known up to this point. Through my experiences of spirits and mediumship, and in particular after my experiences with the spirit of my French partner, I had always known that we survive death in some form, and from my astral traveling and experience in High Magic, I had ascertained that many beings exist in other planes of existence, or dimensions. The one thing that I had not really understood, was that both spirits and other beings are able to manifest in the three-dimensional world that we know, and this came as a big revelation. At this point, I intuited that the "ETs" were manifesting from another plane of existence, even if they were not actually in residence there.

It was at this time that I began to practice and develop my own CE5 protocols, otherwise known as human initiated contact experiences, as expounded by Dr Steven Greer, the Rahma group and others, and I began to be followed by orange self-illuminated plasma orbs, or mini suns as I liked to call them. The orbs would follow me when I was on foot, traveling by car, or by train and this was witnessed by several people. I could even be sitting drinking a coffee chatting at a friend's house, and would see an orange plasma ball floating by, skimming the rooftops only twenty yards away. I felt that something very significant was going to happen, and indeed it did.

Around nine months after the contact event on the bridge, I awoke one morning after an uneventful day the day before, and went to shower, only to discover a perfectly rectangular scoop mark over an inch long on my leg. It was quite deep into the flesh, and was at least partially pre-healed, appearing to be cauterized. I checked the bed linen, and the clothes I had been wearing the previous day, and there was no sign of blood whatsoever. I immediately felt sure that I had been taken by the ETs, or at least visited, but tried nevertheless to think of a rational explanation for this strange mark, with no success.

Thus began a period where I was in intense fear and paranoia about my ET contact. It also heralded the most intense period of high strangeness which is so often associated with ET contact. During this period, I received triangulated puncture marks on my right hip, with raised bumps and central puncture marks. A nurse was unable to determine any possible natural cause. I regularly also experienced waking with violent bruising which was nevertheless painless. I witnessed orbs of different colors and sizes floating through the walls, ranging from golf ball to soccer ball size, and both police and military helicopters began to not only occasionally hover over my house, but also follow me to the park where I practiced human initiated contact with extraterrestrials, and on one occasion flew to the exact regular spot, circled three times, and shot off at high speed, as if to convey that these agencies knew my movements and what activities I was engaging in.

The number of orbs I saw during this period also intensified, to the point where as soon as I opened my front door there would more often than not, be orbs, usually now white, floating by inches above the nearby rooftops on my street. I also saw three flying saucers in a row flying silently at a low altitude of approximately one hundred and fifty feet, straight over my head at my usual CE5 spot, so that I could see the circle of multi-colored lights spinning in the undercarriage beneath them.

I was also regularly monitored by both the police and security forces or military, which included incidents such as two figures in tight fitting black clothes swimming across a river to the bank near my CE5 spot, and shining bright LED lights in my direction whilst crouched underneath a park bench, and a tall figure with a strange almost non-human gait, who at two separate locations, shone an old fashioned fisherman's lamp from nearby bushes whilst I was doing CE5 in the early hours of the morning. On one later occasion, I began filming the same man with an infrared camera, and within two minutes he was picked up on the river path by a black car, a path where driving is not permitted, and which is inaccessible to anyone but the police, who can unlock the security bollards. I have never seen him since. I was also watched practicing CE5 with others by a pair of identically dressed men in their 40's, who then followed me home with a friend, making no attempts to hide their surveillance. It is my understanding from personal sources I cannot name and from my own research, that not only are intelligence services and compartmentalized military departments studying and monitoring both some psychics and ET experiencers, but they are also heavily engaged in consciousness studies of their own relating to psychic work and also NHI's, and members of the public who are having interactions with NHI's are of great interest to them. During this period, which was both troubling and exhilarating, I reached out to many ET support organizations, which only succeeded in amplifying my fear and paranoia, as all of them without exception emphasized the idea that ETs are here for their own negative agenda, and that it was ok for me to be in fear. I was not at all satisfied with this, as despite a growing fear of sleeping, as I was now waking with marks on a regular basis, I also felt a massive expansion of consciousness, a deep sense of connectedness to every living being, and a feeling that the veils between dimensions are gossamer thin, and not as defined as those who believe in them imagine them to be.

At this point the phenomena diversified and I began to experience some completely new things. Firstly, I began to have dreams in which various types of ETs took a prominent role. These included dreaming of being onboard ships, and being shown the ships' energy sources and propulsion systems. The dreams mirrored in many details the remote viewing experience I had had with the first orange orb I saw, circular rooms with domed ceilings, etc, except that in these dreams I had direct telepathic connection with the small white beings who closely resemble what are known in the UFO subculture as the "greys". Other dreams involved sexual intercourse with other types of ET beings, which were both physically uninhibited experiences and at the same time, spiritually intimate and intense, as if making love to a profoundly spiritual entity who I was completely one with, and who could read my every thought and feelings. After some of these dreams, I would wake with marks, feeling as if I had actually been there and had been rudely awakened into this three- dimensional reality.

I found many of these experiences confusing, as they seemed to involve so many different types of contact. Could a dream really have any "reality"? Could I be imagining the orbs floating through my walls? I was never able to video any of the orbs indoors as the experiences were only seconds long, whereas I had succeeded in filming many orbs outdoors with HD infrared camcorders, so I was less inclined to be skeptical. And then, I also had photos of my scoop mark, the puncture marks, and the violent bruising, insensitive to the touch, and apparently partially pre-healed, to prove that there was a physical component to my experiences.

As if in response to my uncertainty, a couple of events took place which confirmed what I was almost certain of. One morning on awakening, I made coffee and went to the computer to check for emails. Before clicking on the "Google" icon, I noticed a photo had appeared on my desktop overnight whilst I was sleeping. It was a shot of my sofa, taken by my own webcam, and had two disembodied faces within it, one was a silhouette in profile of a comical looking male human face with a strange expression around the mouth, the second something altogether different. Taking up most of the area in the photo was a feminine face with the most beatific, loving expression I had ever seen, and the most exquisitely beautiful eyes staring straight into the camera, floating in a pink mist above my sofa! The face was very detailed, to the point of clearly identifiable high cheekbones, long eyelashes, and quite a large sensuous mouth. The expression in the huge eyes, at least three times the size of human eyes, was so profoundly beautiful that a friend who saw the photo could not stop staring at it, with tears in her eyes, and claimed that the profoundly deep and loving expression subtly changed the more one looked at it, as if the being in the photo were alive and present.

At this point, I became certain that the ETs could both interface with our 3d reality, and also interfere with technology, as not only had they managed to manipulate the video I shot to show something that did not transpire, but had had no problem using my own webcam to take selfies for me! The following events were to show me how much they are able to remotely read and influence my mental and emotional state, and also I believe, to corroborate details described in the Zimbabwe UFO incident with school children, that was investigated by Dr John Mack in 1994, and which I had become particularly interested in only just before.

I was sitting talking to someone on Skype, when I began to hear a sound that being a musician, I can say sounded very much like a synth oscillator, or to put it more simply, a didgeridoo. (This is often referenced by Dr Steven Greer as a sound that indicates that ET "ships" are nearby and powering down to land.) I was alarmed and interrupted the conversation I was having to say I would have to talk later. I then heard two long notes on a flute. Being a musician, I immediately played some notes on my guitar, and discovered that the note was C. I felt a very strong sense that something was in the garden, and flung open the curtains, only to see nothing but my garden illuminated by the light from my room. At this point, the room started to feel as if it was vibrating, and I heard a high-pitched noise which became more and more intense, rooting me to the spot in surprise.

Beginning with the soles of my feet, I felt an intense rush of energy, which went up through my legs, through my entire body, and out through my crown. As this was happening, I felt myself becoming calmer, feeling lighter, and feeling a strong mental clarity I had not had for a long time. The feeling was as if "Alka Seltzer" were fizzing upwards throughout my entire body. I had been involved in a long-distance relationship which had continued with my former French partner, who I rarely saw, and I was feeling anxious and tormented about my future, as we were unable to let each other go, but could not agree how to proceed in our relationship. All these anxieties dissolved, and I suddenly saw myself with all my potential and felt good about myself and my life, empowered for the first time in many years. In this moment, I knew that not only did I accept this kinship that I felt was being expressed in my growing relationship with these beings, but I strongly felt that they were very interested in my well-being. I also regard this experience as a form of healing I received, whether psychological, energetic, or otherwise.

It was when reaching out to Mary Rodwell that I gained a balanced sense of perspective on my experiences, and was able to hear of my commonalities with other ET experiencers. Having discovered Dr. John Mack's work through videos online, and resonating strongly with his balanced approach to the ET contact phenomenon, I was very happy to see that such an approach still existed. Mary was knowledgeable, and able to help me put into perspective many of my more extreme fears, the majority of which were centered around the fear of the military's interest in my contact experiences, and I was reassured that it was highly unlikely that I would be harmed, but rather simply monitored. Because my fears around the interest in me from both the military and the "ETs" were enmeshed, once I felt more relaxed about one, I instantly relaxed about the other.

I had by this time met another ET experiencer who I was to go on to marry, and we had both begun to work for Mary Rodwell's A.C.E.R.N as therapists in the U.K as I am a qualified counselor and she had trained in hypnotherapy. We had met during the very apex of my ET experiences, and thus I began to have witnesses to my experiences.

One day shortly after meeting her, we were in bed. I had decided to try an experiment, and had left a note to the ETs on the bedside table, having also sent out the same message telepathically to them, saying "Please appear to me tonight, if you feel I can handle it". Whilst both of us were awake, we heard rustling at the edge of the bed, and I recognized that the sound was of someone walking on the plastic carrier bags which had been left at the foot of the bed from a clothes shopping trip earlier in the day. I asked if she too could hear the sound, and she could. I then felt my hip being touched firmly, the same hip where I had previously awoken with triangulated puncture marks, and shot up in bed, only to see nothing, despite the hall light illuminating the room. I feel that the beings were invisible, just as I had also seen them cloak their craft. When we discussed the incident the following morning, I asked my future wife if she had seen anything in her mind's eye, and she said that she had seen two small white figures with violet glow moving around the room. I had seen the same two beings in my mind's eye, albeit without the same glow of color.

From this point on, my psychic ability began to dramatically increase. The ETs would send me telepathic messages to go outside when they were appearing for me to film them, and I also began a system of asking questions, and receiving information in one big drop days later, what is referred to as "downloads". I also began to experience increased sensitivity to the other planes of existence. My mediumship and abilities as a "sensitive" to non-human intelligences has come and gone throughout my life, and it returned in full force. Living in a Medieval town, famed for hauntings, I had ample opportunity to pick up on spirit presences, and indeed I did, to the point where some of the spiritual presences were as tangible as the people on the street. I also began to have premonitions albeit of a rather mundane character.

My then wife and I were in the habit of taking a rescued Saluki for a walk around the block, and each time we passed a house very close to the pavement, as many houses are in the UK. The house had no blinds or curtains and therefore we always clearly saw what was happening inside. One day just before turning the corner to pass by the house, I clearly saw an image of the game character "Sonic the hedgehog", and I announced that this is what we would see, and sure enough this game was being played on the television. This repeated itself a few times, always something radically different. I also discovered an ability to read the contents of sealed parcels, and my wife habitually tested me on eBay and Amazon orders which I knew nothing of, each time I was accurate on both color and material, even if I was unable to ascertain what the item actually was, or its function.

At this time, my marriage had begun to break down, and there was a substantial tension in the house, exacerbated by my wife's deep shock, sadness and existential crisis in the bereavement of losing three close friends and family members in rapid succession. Very strange things began to take place in the house. One aspect to this was that a shadow being began to appear in doorways, being seen by everyone in the house including visitors, even the animals in the house reacting to it. The atmosphere in the house became darker and darker, and the tension between my wife and I became palpable. I received several visitations in bed, also experienced by my wife, of ETs who would sit down on the bed and pat me as I went to sleep. It felt like they were trying to comfort me. The presence of the shadow being, however, seemed to correspond with moments where tensions were very high, and to exacerbate an already difficult atmosphere, and I often felt drained and felt ready to throw in the towel.

One night when I was up late worrying about the future of my marriage, I went into the kitchen to get my first beer from the fridge, and noticed movement in my riverside garden which was only accessible to my immediate neighbor. I assumed that for some unknown reason, they had come into the garden at 1am, and I decided to go close to the window to see. Standing 10 feet from me on the other side of the window were two of the same white "gray" type ETs I had seen in my remote viewing, and also, in my mind's eye, psychically many times during contact experiences. They were just over four feet tall, with large heads, disproportionately long arms, and large black eyes although not as almond shaped as is commonly presented. Their bodies had a dull glow, and seemed somewhere between an ethereal spirit manifestation and solid three-dimensional forms. They had a remarkable appearance and energy to them, which seemed, if one can imagine it, like a cross between a very aware child and a mystical master.

While one held me with a fixed and loving gaze and seemed to be telepathically communicating that they were family, the other seemed agitated, and was going backwards and forwards, peering through windows at the back of the house, appearing to be trying to locate something, or someone. After a period of four minutes, this abruptly ended when they disappeared instantaneously. I had been frightened to blink, let alone get a camera, which had indeed crossed my mind. Reflecting on this afterwards, I strongly felt that they were showing an interest in the shadow entity that we had seen so many times in the house. It was not until many months later that I empowered myself to the point where I was able to ask the entity to go, and go it did. I eventually had a fellow medium come to the house, who confirmed that the being and its energy was no longer present.

The interest that the ETs showed in me was not limited to appearing around the house and its grounds, they also manifested in a number of other ways. On one occasion, my wife and I were sitting watching television. We were no longer able to communicate and she had emotionally shut me out, effectively emotionally abandoning the marriage, blaming me for everything wrong in her life. My wife's phone rang, and a message was left. She picked it up looking shocked. "What is it?", I asked. "The landline has just rung my mobile phone and left a business card from Russell Davies!" The landline telephone was next to us in our small living room, and there was no other phone in the house. It was also unable to send text messages, let alone a "business card". I felt afterwards that this was a message from the ETs to my wife suggesting that she start communicating with me.

I found myself relating more to the ETs than I did my wife. I was spending more and more time on our roof terrace at night, practicing CE5 and communing with the universe. During this period, I was shown how many forms the NHI's can appear in. On several occasions, I witnessed what appeared to be a winged orb, similar to symbols found in Ancient Egypt and Sumer, around a foot wide and faintly glowing. On one such occasion, I was permitted to see what this actually was, as the orb flew over my head only twelve to fifteen feet above me. As it approached, I could make out that the wings were not actually wings, and as it flew slowly towards me and above my head, I beheld a one foot tall being inside a faintly glowing energy field. The glow around the being created the impression of a ball of light, which nonetheless appeared to have some form and an outer membrane. The being's arms extended beyond the energy field, and the being was waving its arms to propel forward! Even now, I find it hard to recount this without fear of ridicule.

On another occasion I witnessed a white plasma orb, three feet across, with a nine feet long tail, fly only thirty feet above my wife and I on the roof terrace, and disappear in plain sight. Others included a flying pyramid, with multi-colored lights flashing around it, flying blue eyes that seemed to be composed of blue flame, with yellow flame irises which flew 40 feet above my head, and I many times witnessed orbs de-materialize or cloak whilst being followed by military jets and helicopters. I and friends were also witnesses to loud booming sounds in the early hours of the morning with no apparent cause, and the presence of unmanned drones approximately fifteen feet long flying at very low altitude over the town, which on enquiring through friends in positions of authority in the local military bases, was informed never takes place. On all these occasions of witnessing extraordinary phenomena, the videos I shot with an expensive Sony HD camcorder were distorted, and only produced static, or fuzzy indistinct videos on playback, as if the camcorder were being directly affected by a high energy source.

On the day my wife left, I was going for a walk after an argument, and a pair of low flying orbs only around 50 feet in height, formed a plasma cross which hung for a few seconds in the air above me. I knew that this was a message that things were about to take a significant turn for the worse. This use of plasma orbs forming crosses in the air above me has been repeated on a number of occasions by the ETs when I am about to experience trauma and hardship. To this day, I have a strong belief that the ETs are very interested in my welfare, and my overall well-being.

It is clear to me from the variety of my experiences in the many contact modalities with non-human intelligences, that the non-locality of consciousness is key to understanding diverse forms of paranormal experiences. From remote viewing, to astral traveling, mediumship, psychic connections across continents, and telepathic connection with extraterrestrial intelligences, it is the ability of the mind to connect with beings that are apparently separate to us that is the underlying experience. The mind is not interpreting non-verbal signals or using the imprecise tool of codified information systems in language when it experiences telepathy, as is the case with inter-human communication, or even human communication with animals via interpretation of non-verbal signals. It can, indeed, experience a synesthesia of many different information sources which are direct and unhindered by the medium of our crude human languages. When I and others have received "downloads" of information from ET sources, or when people experience communication with NHI's in visions , the information is not garbled by the binary opposition present in our language, or our reliance on false absolutes and human subjective perceptions which are limited by our own nervous systems and neurological programming, but instead arrives rapidly and unfiltered as a block of awareness which can bypass the conscious mind.

Telepathic communication is predicated on a number of different modes, corresponding, I would suggest, to terms utilized in the psychic world. Collectively they are termed the clair-senses, such as clairvoyance, clairaudience, clairsentience and claircognizance, the experience of seeing, hearing, feeling and knowing directly from the unified field of consciousness without previously receiving information from a mundane external 3d source. These abilities, and others, are innate in all sentient beings, and enable humans to communicate with any being, including animals, other human beings, spirits, and ETs, within a singular consciousness field. In ET contact, just as in mediumship and psychic practice, these can manifest as being able to see beings that others cannot, hear them, feel them, and also receive downloads of information. All senses are utilized. It has been suggested by some experiencers that some of these are virtual experiences created by the ETs, and to an extent, I agree that theater of the mind operations are part of the ET contact experience. ETs are apparently able to target one person for contact and alter others' consciousnesses so that they do not perceive them.

It seems clear that apart from the concern of being intercepted by the military, who evidently do indeed have an interest in ETs and ET experiencers, as anyone who has had contact will confirm, the NHI's primary purpose at this time is to convey to selected individuals that they are here, and that they have a genuine and benign interest in us and the planet. The many manifestations that they produce during human initiated contact experiences, are from my experience, almost certainly largely holographic in nature, although clearly some are also physical.

When I experienced communication with the dead as a child, I was experiencing connection to other beings within a single consciousness field. When mediums contact the dead, they use clair-senses to connect with beings who are still accessible to us, despite, I believe, residing in another dimension, or plane of existence, because all consciousness, as I have always said, is permeable, only a thin membrane exists separating us from the consciousness of others, including NHI's. Psychic ability and mediumship, as well as telepathic links to what we term as extraterrestrial beings, are possible because non-locality of consciousness is almost certainly predicated on what is known to the esoteric world as "astral" fields, which link this dimension to others. Those of us who work in the psychic arena regard the existence of the astral worlds as self-evident, as we experience them in different forms on a daily basis.

It is clear that what the many modalities of contact with NHI's teaches us, is that we are in a universe that is not limited to the plane of existence that we inhabit. I have received direct telepathic communication with spirits who have sometimes appeared as balls of light, or perhaps plasma, and in one instance in France, this was exceedingly bright and the size of a soccer ball, and not the faint ectoplasm-like wisps that are commonly seen on popular paranormal television shows. The orbs which I have experienced after receiving telepathic communication from ETs, have also been predominantly soccer ball size orbs of light or plasma. It appears that it is not a coincidence that the two both manifested in a similar way. It is my assertion that if the ETs themselves do not derive from other dimensions, then they at least travel via dimensions, just as spirits do, and therefore could easily be called denizens of other dimensions, whether on temporary permits or otherwise.

Interestingly, the Scole Experiment, a series of experiments in the UK to contact those in the Afterlife which took place between 1993-1998, succeeded in a video experiment in capturing apparent images of a typical "gray" ET, which appears to confirm the many stories of ET experiencers, that in contact in dreams with ETs, they were reunited with family who had passed over. It seems apparent to me from my experiences with the "gray" frantically looking through my windows, that they were looking for the shadow being, which according to the lore of spiritual mediums are interdimensional entities which feed off the negative emotions of human beings.

I once performed an experiment in a British wood known to be haunted, which was previously an ancient site used by the Druids for many of their spiritual practices. I used a variation of the system I have used for human initiated contact with extraterrestrials, and it was as effective as any mediumship techniques I have ever used, and a friend succeeded in taking photos of me swarmed by orbs with faces. It is my belief that as all NHI's both extraterrestrial and spirits, are in other dimensions, that systems for contact with them all will overlap, the only difference being the state of consciousness needed will vary in quality depending on what one wishes to attract.

I and many of my clients have experienced contact with ETs in dreams, OBE's and also in the flesh, and given that the contact is consciousness based, (as even when they appear in the flesh they have used telepathy with me and many others) it is not a huge jump to accept the hypothesis that they can communicate in dreams. It is also a long-accepted idea in the spiritual and psychic worlds that spirits can communicate in dreams, in just the same way, utilizing this astral link between other dimensions and the material world we inhabit. The same can be said to be true of shamanic experiences and other modalities.
It is my belief that NDEs and OBEs, and many ET experiences, are predicated on experiences where consciousness has shifted to the astral body, which is effectively an intermediary between our dimension, or to put it more accurately, density, and the higher vibrating densities where other beings are located. My own experiences tell me that it is the astral body which acts as a hub to the unified consciousness field, or quantum field, which when activated and engaged through any contact modality, enables non-local consciousness and contact with NHI's, almost like a router to the cosmic internet.

I spent many years in Sufi communities, and having experienced numerous mystical states from the many practices I have engaged in, I am sure that this work helped me to cognize the parameters of our consciousness field or cosmic internet. When I became a Sufi, I was given the name "Anwar Laatif", which may be interpreted as the "Many lights of the subtle realms". This was a foretoken of things to come. In some sense I also believe that I am, in some sense, one of these lights, and feel that the video I shot of one of these ET orbs, where my face paranormally appears, was, along with the telepathic message I received that they are family, a sign of my larger multi-dimensional identity. Curiously, I once experienced a telepathic message whilst an orb appeared during CE5, when I was greeted gleefully with the words "Hello Captain".

The nature of identity is one that preoccupies our consciousness throughout our lives. We become attached to everything we see, and yearn for a sense of belonging and an identity that is tangible and meaningful, in the face of our ultimate physical death and imagined annihilation. Human beings thus identify themselves by their gender; (which is absurd if reincarnation does indeed exist and we are reborn as either gender), by their profession; (which is limiting oneself to what one actually does for economic stability); by upbringing and social / cultural group, (a set of characteristics by which others identify them as part of a subset of a cultural group within a national identity, which is obviously limiting), as a particular ethnicity; (which severely limits humans within defined parameters based on skin color and ethnic history, and can even pit us against members of our own species), and ultimately also identifying with the human species itself; thus identifying not with eternal and unbounded consciousness itself which is our true nature, but purely with the form we inhabit. To use an analogy, we identify with the outer casing of a half-broken router, whereas our true nature is unbounded energy and dynamic intelligence within the web which amongst other things, can create routers. It is consciousness within the web which gives rise to the creation of the router, just as consciousness within the quantum field gives rise to the creation of matter.

It is my assertion that in a very real sense, we are experiencers of multi-dimensionality. There is a long-held idea in the Mediumship field that souls can fragment, so that a human being can be present in several places at once. Spirits can pass over to the "other side" when they die, be in visitation of a former home or locale of trauma which they are attached to and cannot move on from, (an actual attachment rather than a memory in the energy field of the building) and also be reincarnated in a new body. In extreme cases, people can be haunted by a fragmented aspect of themselves. Similarly, I also feel that many people incarnated today as humans are also simultaneously living other lives in other star systems and dimensions, and could even be being visited by aspects of themselves living lives in parallel dimensions. If time itself does not exist in the way we imagine it, and it is as Armenian mystic Gurdjieff thought of it, a uniquely subjective phenomenon, then all of our many incarnations are theoretically as accessible to our consciousness as remembering the events of yesterday, the access being blocked only by the way our consciousness is programmed in our formative years.

Many children experience memories of previous incarnations, which then gradually fade as they get older. It is my belief that every being has access to the singular consciousness field, has an energy body, and has existence in multiple dimensions or densities, and that it is not unique to human beings or NHI's. This can for example be seen in the numerous experiences people have had with seeing the spirits of animals who have passed over. The scientist Rupert Sheldrake has performed many experiments appearing to confirm that animals can sense when their owners are returning home, and I have also personally experienced telepathic communication with animals, whereby a sick family pet sent telepathic images to me of their location so I would come to help them when they were in distress. On arrival, they were lying at the exact spot and angle that I received in mental image via telepathy. I have had numerous experiences of this kind of communication with animals.

It is my belief that the nature of identity is not as we envisage it, and that the nature of the Simurgh or Creator, sought by the birds in Farid ud-Din Attar's "The Conference of the Birds" explains well the nature of our true identity. "The sun of majesty sent forth his rays, and in the reflection of each other's faces these thirty birds (si-murgh) of the outer world, contemplated the face of the Simurgh of the inner world. This so astonished them that they did not know if they were still themselves or if they had become the Simurgh. At last, in a state of contemplation, they realized that they were the Simurgh and that the Simurgh was the thirty birds. When they gazed at the Simurgh they saw that it was truly the Simurgh who was there, and when they turned their eyes towards themselves they saw that they themselves were the Simurgh. And perceiving both at once, themselves and Him, they realized that they and the Simurgh were one and the same being. No one in the world has ever heard of anything to equal it. Then they gave themselves up to meditation, and after a little they asked the Simurgh, without the use of tongues, to reveal to them the secret of the mystery of the unity and plurality of beings."

Monism, or the belief that one supreme being is the only thing that exists, manifest in a myriad forms, is the idea which underlies Sufism and many other mystical systems, and is the mystical basis for understanding the theory of how there is only one consciousness field, albeit with many tributaries, which gave birth to the whole of creation, that consciousness itself is the origin of all that is manifest. One could describe the creation thus as an externalized vibratory expression of the Creator's thoughts, the Logos.

There is a doctrine in some Sufi groups that individual souls descend from the godhead, through the angelic realms, experiencing incarnation as an angel, on to the worlds of the Djinn, and into the human realms, before experiencing life in animal form, and even mineral form, and beginning again the long return to the godhead. If, then, time does not exist as we perceive it, one can see how that we could simultaneously be an individual droplet, which has the whole enfolded within it like part of a hologram containing all the information of the whole picture within it, and a whole ocean of selves which can simultaneously exist both within individual dimensions, and also interact with other dimensions.

What is clear to me from my experiences is that we not only survive death and go on to exist in other dimensions, but that other forms of beings inhabit some of these dimensions, and are trans-dimensional in nature. Effectively, we also are trans-dimensional when we experience NDE's, OBE's, and trans-dimensional telepathic communication of all kinds including through the clair-senses via non-local consciousness. Once a portal or gateway has been opened to other dimensions by accessing higher states of consciousness or using directed intention to connect to information and other beings via the unified consciousness field, then the high strangeness experienced by ET experiencers and others can attract beings of all kinds, some of which one did not actually intend to connect with. In psychic circles, this is thought of as a light which is generated by the active trans-dimensional capabilities of the medium, which can attract a variety of different beings, both negative and positive, or more or less evolved in consciousness.

When I have been in peak periods of communication with the ETs, the high strangeness often experienced by ET experiencers, has led to my contact with shadow beings and troubled spirits at moments when I was in a vulnerable state of consciousness. My increased sensitivity from spiritual work and contact has allowed me to see, hear, sense and communicate with spirits unseen by others, and I have witnessed how using a form of CE5 and directed intention usually used to attract ETs, can attract spirits causing orbs with faces within to swarm all over me in photos, whereas others present were free of these artifacts in photos that were taken of them. My mediumship abilities increased after my first experience of seeing an orange orb and remote viewing it whilst traveling to collect an instrument with a friend, and it was only a number of months after this experience that I was in France experiencing telepathic connection with my girlfriend's deceased husband.

In the same way that consciousness can be permanently altered by mystical states and the use of drugs, it is my suspicion that psychic experiences, mediumship, ET experiences, OBE's, NDE's etc, permanently change our brain architecture, transform our understanding of identity and the fictitious constructs of self we co-create in our lives, and also activate and enable the innate ability we have to connect to other dimensions of existence. Once the switch has been turned on, it cannot easily be turned off, and repetition can automate the neural and astral pathways to connect to other dimensions so that they are permanently turned on. In the world of mediumship, many mediums have to learn to close off to these experiences in order to be able to also function in their everyday lives.

When I experienced seeing someone coming through thick fog by their aura alone, I believe I was seeing their trans-dimensional light body, or astral body, which connects us via OBE's, NDE's and non-local telepathic consciousness to other dimensions. We are innately connected to all other beings in the universe through non-local consciousness and also via the medium of our astral energy bodies which are not permanently attached to the body, but which can entirely dislocate in a number of different contact modalities, allowing us to interact clair-sensibly with beings from other dimensions, Our true identity is not simply predicated by how we and other perceive ourselves in the reality we inhabit, but is composed of many layers on a much grander scale, many of which are not consciously experienced but can be sometimes remembered through dreams and experienced in visions during shamanic journeying and other modalities of contact with NHI's.

What Dr Joseph Burkes calls "TOTENCET", the acronym for "THIS OTHERNESS THAT EXPERIENCERS NOW CALL ET", is able to take on many forms, and it is quite widely thought by ET experiencers that the form of the "grays" is one of the many representations chosen as a projected image in virtual experiences by the intelligence behind the ET phenomena as a generic interface for their communication with humanity. Just as spirit entities and trans-dimensional entities can appear in many forms, so can the ETs also apparently morph their vehicles into any form they choose, using what the late great conspiracy researcher Jim Marrs commonly called "cultural tracking" in his many lectures on the UFO subject, to appear as apparently mundane objects in our skies.

In indigenous native cultures throughout the world, there is a long tradition of stories of beings shape-shifting, and even of humans with the power to do so, which point strongly to experiences with inter-dimensional beings who are able to take many forms, throughout history. There are many stories also of missing time connected with fairy abductions in folkloric tales, and in bible stories of contact with angels. The nativity story of the bible itself seems to suggest the creation of a hybrid through ET contact, particularly when followed by the appearance of a "star" or U.F.O guiding the Magi, who had been prompted perhaps telepathically to seek out the special child many hundreds of miles away. These themes repeat in the modern ET stories, and point strongly to a single phenomenon which has been present and interacting with us for much of our existence.

Many ET experiencers whom I have worked with personally as a therapist, believe that the consciousness of ETs can overshadow their own, so that the ETs can look through their eyes, and effectively displace their consciousness for short periods of time. Some have the sense that their consciousness is permanently being used as a portal for the ETs into this dimension. I myself have had many moments of feeling this. This has parallels with spiritual possession and what is termed "overshadowing" by psychic mediums, or at lower levels, spiritual attachment, whereby a spirit can eject the consciousness of a living person and take over their body, or at the least, strongly influence their thoughts and emotions. As with the ET phenomenon of visitations, being taken onboard craft, and abductions, both spiritual oppression and ET contact can result in marks being left on the body. However, with ETs the result of contact is more often of a positive nature, and even in spirit possession there can be a benign intention from the spirit world. When contacting spirits through mediumship, the energy of people who have passed over is comparatively low and at times even oppressive, whereas, despite also, I believe, contacting from other dimensions, ETs tend to create a very dynamic response of excitement in the body, and a feeling that one is in the presence of a vastly superior spiritual intelligence .The same clair-senses yield very different forms of communication. Mediumship experiences vary but spirit voices can sometimes be indistinct and the communication unclear. In electronic voice phenomena, spirits often have slowed-down voices, and communicate indistinctly seemingly with great effort at a very low density or vibration, whereas ET contact is both consistently clear, can even seem to be in the room, and the instantaneous communication so full, rapid and complex via downloads, that entire books worth of material can be received in a heartbeat.

It seems fairly clear that whereas both ETs and spirits may be trans-dimensional in their activity, while the ETs may well be able to access all dimensions, spirits are limited to manifesting in just a few. I suspect that the afterlife as a whole knows little of the astral dimensions which the ETs are able to inhabit, while the ETs themselves know far more of the nature of life and death and the nature of the spirit worlds than we can imagine. I once asked the ETs why they do not share their knowledge of the universe and the meaning of life, and received a very long and detailed answer as a download which can be summed up in a few words : the knowledge of the meaning of life and the nature of the universe which they could convey would effectively stop human beings at this stage in their soul journey from actually living life and benefitting from our experiences. They expressed the importance of our experience of duality for our development.

The ETs occupy the role that we think of angels (or demons) being able to have limitless powers and the ability to come and go at will through any dimensions they see fit to visit. It is also my belief based on my experiences, that while spirits can manifest physically to some extent, and I believe, ET's can fully manifest physically for extended periods of time, as human beings coarsened by our low density 3d bodies, we can indeed visit other dimensions and use the cosmic web, but have less ability to traverse other dimensions than NHI's.

I believe quality of consciousness, as I mentioned, is what determines contact with non-human intelligence, whether spirits, interdimensional beings, or ETs. It is well known in the spirit world that, for example, people in trauma will often experience connections with spirits who have died traumatically. Consciousness predicates the types of our contact. Similarly, it is what defines how psychic one is in one's daily life. The ability is present in all beings, as we are truly one being manifest in many forms. We are all part of the one consciousness which has given birth to form itself, and is manifest in many different types of beings, seen and unseen.

Many ancient belief systems are adherents of panpsychism, which holds that everything has mind as an attribute. This, I feel, is the underlying reality. The current elevated presence of the ETs, and the widespread trend to wish to connect via shamanic experiences, CE5 or human initiated contact with extra dimensional or extraterrestrial beings, and the present fascination with the paranormal and the spirit world , are symptoms of our expanding consciousness, a growing realization that we are more than the meat sacks that we inhabit, and a desire to discover what our origins are, the true nature of the universe, and to solve the mystery of the function of life beyond the confines of religious doctrine and blind faith.

Human identity and perception is limited by our programming, It is clear that through spiritual practices, through psychic practices tapping into non-local consciousness fields with tools such as scrying mirrors and crystals, in dreams and out of body experiences, through the use of music or indeed drugs such as DMT or ayahuasca in shamanic practices, through NDE's , the mind can break free of its limitations in 3d and expand into the cosmic web. As Grant Cameron suggests in his 2019 interview with Alexis Brooks, through trauma, brain injury, and shocks to the nervous system including fasting, it is possible to alter the nature of our perception and experience completely new realities. This can, whilst being consciousness-based and to all appearances subjective, at least partially impact on our 3d world through various manifestations.

Timothy Leary in conjunction with Robert Anton Wilson proposed an eight-circuit model of consciousness, relating to the Hindu chakra system, the last of which relates to what he called the "non-local quantum circuit" as experienced directly in near death experiences and other contact modalities. "8. The Non-Local Quantum Circuit. This is imprinted by Shock, by "near-death" or "clinical death" experience, by OOBEs (out-of-body-experiences), by trans-time perceptions ("precognition"), by trans-space visions (ESP), etc. It tunes the brain into the non-local quantum communication system suggested by physicists such as Bohm, Walker, Sarfatti, Bell, etc."

At this stage of our development, we are beginning to embrace new concepts, and I believe that the mere act of cognition will have the effect of, rather than believing it when we see it, instead of seeing it when we believe it.

My journey as a psychic medium, as a spiritual seeker, and as an ET experiencer, has given me the firm realization that all beings are one in a singular field of consciousness, that we are the creator consciousness in many forms, that everything is a manifestation of consciousness, that there is no death, and that our families extend across the entire universe, drawn together by love, which is I believe to be integral to, and embedded within the unified consciousness field, and with the surety that the one is many, and the many are one.

The Armenian mystic, Gurdjieff, proposed that mankind is not the top of the food chain, and alluded many times in his lectures to forces beyond our perception which feed off the subtle energies which we release either through suffering, or through conscious evolution. It is clear from my experiences that shadow beings do indeed feed off negative energies produced by human beings who are suffering, and it raises the interesting question of whether some vital force, perhaps astral in nature, is itself an energy source for some higher-density or dimensional beings, and whether the quality of that energy predicates the types of beings which are attracted to us.

If the astral body is, as esoteric traditions suggests, the link between the physical body and other dimensions, a consciousness vehicle in which one can travel both in time and space, to visit different dimensions, as well as our own dimensions at different points in time and space in remote viewing and psychic work, then it is unsurprising that we would experience so many different modalities of contact which are founded on a shift in consciousness from a perspective based in our physical reality to one located in our subtle bodies and our clair-senses. If the prime consciousness vehicle is the astral body, and associated subtle bodies, then the clair-senses are the original template from which our human physical senses are based, which the human physiology and brain chemistry filters and refocuses for the functions of 3d living. The consciousness field itself is therefore the prime origin of our senses and our physiological makeup, which crudely replicates the original blueprint of the clair-senses embedded in our higher density astral energy bodies. Some psychics believe that it is through the chakra system that clair-senses receive information within the astral body and transmit it to the mind and physical awareness of the psychic.

The feeling of familiarity which ET experiencers and those who experience shamanic journeys can have with the beings they encounter, might actually be based on previous experience with the beings prior to incarnation in human form, as suggested by Sufi accounts of the soul's journey prior to human incarnation. If one accepts the multi-dimensional hypothesis, and that time as we perceive it does not exist, then all these lives are always happening concurrently and can even overlap to the point that we can even meet ourselves as we are in other dimensions and in another timeline.

I have always very much believed that the feeling that one can achieve anything, the immense power of creative imagination, is based on the existence of a creator blueprint which is present within us as a capacity, albeit not readily manifest in our human form. It is my belief that the exhilarating experiences often had in NDE's, OBE's, and from contact with ET's, is both a memory of and a precursor to our previous and future incarnations in other forms, which are nevertheless always already being experienced, albeit without conscious awareness.

In the life cycle of a soul, everything, in the mystical analysis, returns to pure consciousness in ever refining body vehicles, so that even our astral body is shed, to become the causal body as expounded by Paramahansa Yogananda .in Autobiography of a Yogi. And in the process, our grosser identities are shed to make way for an awareness beyond identity conceivable by human mind, vast vistas of consciousness and powers of creation that are godlike in immensity. The beings I describe are already with us, I believe, and are reminding us of our origins.

In the Bhagavad Gita, it says "I will tell you of That which is to be known, because such knowledge bestows immortality. Hear about the beginningless Supreme Spirit—He who is spoken of as neither existent (sat) nor nonexistent (asat). He dwells in the world, enveloping all— everywhere, His hands and feet; present on all sides, His eyes and ears, His mouths and heads; Shining in all the sense faculties, yet transcending the senses; unattached to creation, yet the Mainstay of all; free from the gunas (modes of Nature), yet the Enjoyer of them. He is within and without all that exists, the animate and the inanimate; near He is, and far; imperceptible because of His subtlety. He, the Indivisible One, appears as countless beings; He maintains and destroys those forms, then creates them anew. The Light of All Lights, beyond darkness; Knowledge itself, That which is to be known, the Goal of all learning, He is seated in the hearts of all. I have briefly described the Field, the nature of wisdom, and the Object of wisdom. Understanding these, My devotee enters My being."

As John Donne famously said in his poem against isolationism, "No man is an island". It is now our soul duty to recognize the primacy of consciousness, return to the worlds that gave birth to us, and at last, reunite with the ocean.

References

Attar, Farid ud-Din: The Conference of the Birds (C.S. Nott) Toward Publishing 2016

Bhagavad Gita: Penguin Classics 2003

Cameron, Grant: Who's having ET encounters and what's REALLY causing them, Higher Journeys with Alexis Brooks February 20th 2019

Greer, Steven: Contact and the Cosmos, Boulder Hot Springs Lecture, YouTube 2018

Gurdjieff, G: Beelzebub's Tales to His Grandson, Penguin Books 1999

Scole Experiment, The Afterlife Investigations.
 www.thescoleexperiment.com   YouTube 2012

Sheldrake R & Smart P: Psychic Pets: A Survey in North-West England, Journal of the Society for Psychical Research 61, 1997

Wilson, Robert Anton: Prometheus Rising, Hilaritas Press 2016

The Reality of Consciousness, Its Relativity to Creation, and Non-Earthly Intelligence:

My Contact with Non-Human Intelligence via the Contact Modalities

Robert Maxxim

Abstract

The following philosophical notions introduce various concepts that pertain to the unification and universal relationships between consciousness, cosmology, energy and non-human intelligence via the "Contact Modalities" (NDEs, OBEs, UFOs, ESP, channeling, etc.), herein presented by invitation by Reinerio (Rey) Hernandez, Director of the Consciousness and Contact Research Institute, CCRI.

This document challenges current notions about creation, consciousness, and intelligence, establishing that solidity of matter, sense of space-time, and sentient associative modality[1] as it relates to existence, as well as contact with other intelligence, are linked by means of individual perception of reality across non-local[2] planes of existence numbering into infinity. This implies that consciousness and creation are unified and are one and the same, both manifest from causal (non-physical source or origin) rather than physical dimensions, and provide modes of communication and experiences relative to the dimension where their association occurs.

Such concept is reinforced by the fact that consciousness is non-local[3] [4] [5] (not physical), atoms have no immediate and direct physical

---

[1] the particular mode in which something exists or is experienced

[2] Nick Herber; "Quantum Reality – Beyond the New Physics." Chapter 12, Bell's Interconnectedness Theorem, p. 212

[3] EPR Paradox. https://en.wikipedia.org/wiki/EPR_paradox

[4] https://en.wikipedia.org/wiki/Quantum_nonlocality

[5] Janina Marciak-Kozlowska, Miroslaw Kozlowski. "Heisenberg's Uncertainty Principle and Human Brain." NeuroQuantology, March 2013, Vol 11, Issue 1, Page 47 – 51

properties[6], the cosmos is founded upon energy and vibrations[7], and all things including waveforms and thoughts exhibit repeatable intelligent patterns (convergence[8]). Hence, existence is a designed, vibrational dimensional phenomena.

To further solidify this concept, particles display intelligent wave-like behaviors[9] that originate from some uncertain yet consistent source (non-physical endurance). From the atom on up, they are functionally restricted by virtue of convergent design and provide consistent structure to the cosmos rather than chaos. If all manifestation, physical and mental, is designed and resides in non-local space[10], then so does consciousness. So it is that mind, energy, and experience are unified[11] with, and are indistinguishable from, all physical manifestation we associate with. Interpretation of our local environment is thus the byproduct of causal reality (the source of manifestation) and our own conscious imprecise[12] paradox, meaning that our intent to understand what we physically perceive will selectively limit the totality of causal awareness because local perception is the end result of causality. In other words, to understand creation and how the mind integrates into it, we need to look at the source, not the resultant cause.

---

[6] https://todayinsci.com/H/Heisenberg_Werner/HeisenbergWerner-QuantumPhysics-Quotations.htm

[7] http://cococubed.asu.edu/class/energy/pdf/mini01.pdf

[8] https://en.wikipedia.org/wiki/Convergent_evolution

[9] https://en.wikipedia.org/wiki/Wave%E2%80%93particle_duality

[10] https://en.m.wikipedia.org/wiki/Four-dimensional_space

[11] Robert Maxxim; "Legacy: Episode I – The Search for Love." Chapter 9, Second Contact

Also "Legacy: Episode III – The Forbidden Tree." Chapter 1, A New Dawn

[12] https://www.britannica.com/science/uncertainty-principle

1. Introduction

Throughout universal vastness, mysterious beauty pervades every manifested particle, waveform, force, even the lack thereof. The universe offers the observer a type of shock and awe of the perceptive kind that spans as far as the mind can conceive, but it is far more than that unto infinity. Creation is filled with harmonious spheres, both large and small, orchestrating an unparalleled symphony of energy interactions that register upon the beholder's physical senses with unavoidable wonderment, but for all intents and purposes, the true source that enlivens them remains veiled. Thus the realm of causal origins remains ambiguous, but only to those that do not understand the underlying patterns of creation for infinity will reveal itself to those that open up to its simplest properties; answers that are hidden in plain sight.

Every element exhibits a type of miniscule predefined "intelligence" that reacts according to intrinsic qualities and plays a specific designed role in the grand scheme of cosmic conscious reasoning. Wherever we place our sights, explicit consistent elements and space act and endure according to some unseen intelligence mandating it be so. This intelligence demonstrates potential, conservation, and motion; hence, it possesses energy[13]. It is also the stimulating essence that gives rise to consciousness and the pulse of creation. Without it, the living expression would not be possible and the concurrent foundation of universal patterns would cease to exist, meaning that the universe would have no perceptive progression or organized mechanics, hence turning into a lifeless reactive ooze or scrap yard.

---

[13] https://en.wikipedia.org/wiki/Energy

The cosmos is not hard to conceive, but what lies beyond it is. The universe is made up of 92 natural atoms, some isotopic variations, a handful of forces, few radiations, and 99.9999999999996%[14] emptiness (based on hydrogen atoms). That's about it. The combination of these physical ingredients creates the hologram we perceive. This physical realm we witness is not the foundation of creation or the unifying field of minds but rather where minds express a portion of their full inter-dimensional potential. It is not the birth place of matter either but rather where creation expresses a minute portion of its expansive multi-dimensional scope much as with minds. Minds themselves are made of the same creative "stuff" as the matter that manifests physically or locally; we will call this creative source "intelligent energy." Hence mind, energy, and manifestation are united and contact among them is limited only by personal perception.

2.   Personal Modality Experiences

The following are a few contact modalities I have experienced over time and the specific scientific reasoning behind each event. I must clarify that, to this day, I recognize I do not initiate any of these experiences but a higher part of my soul and extra-terrestrial intelligences do. These experiences start at higher planes of intelligence my soul is connected with, a connection countless lifetimes in the making with intelligences I have known and made arrangements with previously. Without preparation and higher assistance, these modalities would not be possible.

Out of Body Experiences (OBE):

An OBE is an experience where an individual seems to perceive the world and other intelligence from a location outside of the physical

---

[14] https://education.jlab.org/qa/how-much-of-an-atom-is-empty-space.html

body[15]. These experiences can occur during the process of attaining or during sleep states, in the course of near-death experiences, and even astral projections to name a few well-known modalities. One in ten people have an OBE once, or more commonly, several times in their life[16]. It is one of the most common of all modalities, mainly because it encompasses so many different types of experiences, but at the same time it is greatly misunderstood.

In my case, I have experienced tens of thousands of OBEs. I have seen and confirmed past and future events, visualized other worlds and dimensions, and downloaded volumes of information as situations and public needs demand it. These experiences took place during every type of rest state and physical exertion imaginable, meaning I was awake, asleep, and half-asleep, at rest or not, tired or not, focused on a relative or non-relative subject, and a myriad of environmental settings. There was no specific pattern to these experiences and reasons for their occurrence were not always clear to me. The majority of these experiences I did not initiate, request, or even anticipate. I can safely say they were "given" rather than "requested."

Details of these experiences are too many to mention here but may be found on my website[17] (www.rgaetan.com) and the Legacy episode series (Robert Maxxim, 2014). These experiences include past life visualizations, ESP, extraterrestrial world visitations and contacts, scientific and medical information downloads, future event and remote location viewing experiences, etc. The ensuing narrative will explain how modalities function and offer a guide to their natural incorporation into our lives.

---

[15] https://en.wikipedia.org/wiki/Out-of-body_experience

[16] https://en.wikipedia.org/wiki/Out-of-body_experience

[17] https://www.rgaetan.com

One important event I can share occurred one evening as I drove home. I was 17 years of age at the time and it was the first of its kind for me. I had resolved a family dispute and was overjoyed to achieve it. I felt this was my true calling, to help others overcome negativity rather than apply justice so typical of this world. That was a critical realization because I had seemingly stumbled, although not really, upon the cornerstone for enhancing modalities; selfless servitude from the heart, the key to contact and dimensional consciousness elevation.

I stopped at a red light a block away from my home. While I meditated on joy never before felt, I was suddenly overtaken by an incredible feeling of wellbeing, left the body and stood just inches from the stop light. I still had full control of my body but was immersed in incredible tranquility and silence similar to the feeling of peace one has during an NDE. When the light changed, I returned to the body but lived the next 24 hours in absolute tranquility with an overwhelming sense of confidence and inner positive virtue.

What I felt at the time was the attainment of a higher state of consciousness within my soul, another yet higher state of being within me, the same level of intelligence that provides other modality events to function including extrasensory perception (ESP), astral travel, past life readings, visualizations, etc. This event confirmed that our ability to engage and experience contact modalities is proportional to our aptitude to join this higher state of consciousness which is with us at all times, lives simultaneously within us, but resides in a higher plane of existence I will call the "contact modality dimensional zone." The power of a humble heart is the means connect with it.

Near Death Experience (NDE):

It was the summer of 1977. I was 19 years old at the time and had recently moved to El Cajon, California where I lived in a modest shared apartment. I turned in for the evening with nothing unusual to induct or trigger events about to transpire. As I slept, I dreamt with this older lady I will call Ms. "D." In the dream, she stood silently in front of me meaning to do or say nothing spectacular and I wondered why we were there. But suddenly, she took hold of my right hand with a wicked grin and started to rub back and forth the upper side of the area between thumb and index fingers. I saw worms gush out of her hand and penetrate into my skin, quickly covering my body.

I suddenly woke up but could not move. My entire body was numb much like when an arm or leg goes to sleep due to lack of circulation. I noticed my heart was not beating and likewise I was not breathing. Then without notice, my sights vanished into an abrupt sleep state without pain or concern. Next thing I knew, I was floating above and at the foot of the bed looking down at my body, but at a height that was easily much higher than the room's ceiling indicating that I was in a higher dimensional state where distance differs from our physical norm. My state of consciousness felt tranquil, all wise, and unafraid of my situation as if I knew where I was. I knew this process, I had been there many times before, and it was the same feeling I had experienced two years prior during my OBE at the stoplight. I was in the "Zone."

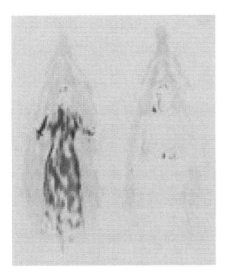

The room was filled with a blue electric-like hue and after a few seconds, it vanished into the conquering blueness. All my surroundings became blue and I had the sensation that this place was infinite and had no boundaries. I gave this place a name; the "Blue Lobby." I floated carelessly about without heading when I noticed two lights appear in the far distance moving toward my right. These two lights suddenly stopped and headed in my direction.

As the lights neared, I saw that they were flames and became brighter the closer they got to me. They were so bright I had to shut my eyes, but that was not enough. I placed my arms over my eyes, but the lights were so intense it was no use. Then suddenly, I felt flipped on my back, immersed into what felt like an ice bath, and the lights vanished.

I was back in the body, numb, unable to move, and with eyes opened. I stared forward unable to blink or breathe. But after a moment, I felt my heart beat once. Seconds later, it beat again, and again. I could feel blood course slowly through hesitant arteries then reach to all parts of the body bringing an end to numbness. I then breathed comfortably, blinked my eyes, and moved what parts of the body I could. After about two minutes, I was able to sit up and reflect upon the experience realizing I had been attacked by "lower astrals" or negative disembodied entities for reasons I would not conceive for many years to come.

Where did these negative forces come from? Just as there are higher dimensions above, so there are lower ones beneath us. In these lower zones, beings there have a need to receive physical mental energy in the same manner we reach out to dimensions above us. These forces harvest us to feed their negative emotional needs instead of lining up directly with the creative fountainhead of life. By doing so, these souls have degenerated beneath our physical level and continue to be very influential in reducing the scope of intelligence and progressiveness we aim for. Hence, these forces aim to hamper those positive contact modalities we can attain and most importantly, at times, can mask themselves purporting to be higher beings with benign messages when in fact they are not. That evening's attack, as well as countless others over the years, confirmed their depravities and restless purpose to interfere with our perception of reality.

Now think of who and where we are, and the many times we meditate trying to contact higher or foreign sources of intelligence. Are we not using the same methodologies as do lower astrals to target and obsess our minds? As Jesus once said, the kingdom of heaven is within (Luke 17:21), not outside of ourselves. We find that kingdom by knowing the "feeling" of it, so we can tell it apart from our lower nature and lower astrals. That feeling is sincerity, truth, respect, and love; to receive (Acts 20:35), that is what we must give.

UFO Contacts

When it comes to UFO and extra-terrestrial contacts, I have too many experiences to mention. These have been in the form of spacecraft sightings, physical face-to-face alien encounters, astral visitations, and psychic essence visualizations during wake state. I was five years old when I had my first sighting. The craft was a large one, sitting still in the skies over Havana's northern shores. I felt someone impress a new state of mind on me during the sighting, a more inquisitive and aware version of whom I was, a personality that has stayed with me to this day. Of course, discussing these experiences in Cuba was out of the question, unless one desired the full wrath of the government to descend upon you without mercy.

Moments prior to my astral travel to Venus on the evening of July 13, 1973, I saw literally dozens of craft up close and clearly. In 1980, I had a spacecraft follow me on I-5 southbound for over a mile on the Highway 133 overpass at night, so close to the car I could see through its window the beautiful being piloting the craft. There were two witnesses with me on that occasion, one was an air force ordinance officer quite familiar with every aircraft known at the time.

For years, beings from other worlds visited me in person and instructed me on the ways of spirit, helping to point out my state of selfish living in this world. At age 16, I met two Saturnian brothers in a copy store. A young brother from Mars went as far as to forbid me from revealing certain technical secrets shared with me, I was seventeen at the time. On another occasion in 1987, I stood on a parking lot on the northwest corner of Broadway and Price Road in Tempe, AZ. In skies above, I saw what seemed to be the oval image of a searchlight cast upon clouds, very dim though. As it coursed through the skies, something told me this was no searchlight but a UFO turned semi-invisible. Sure enough, in seconds, the craft's glow began to scroll from one end to the other and then descended to within feet of my location, only to head west and vanish.

There was a time when I attended a spiritual conclave in El Cajon, CA. I had watched a movie I helped write the music score to and remained alone in the amphitheater after its premier consumed by guilt. A man I had never seen before dressed in a white sport-like shirt and pants entered the empty amphitheater, sat by me, and said confidently, "You are innocent." He was physically fit, had dark hair, and what I would call a "boyish" Hispanic appearance. He never looked me in the eye but seemed to know just where to land his comments for maximum impact. He was a brother from Mars.

I was moved by what he said, but remained locked into my guilt though he assured me again of my innocence, but did not enter into details. He stood up decidedly and I felt he was going to take care of this matter. He left the amphitheater, but curiosity drove me to follow him at least to the door. I opened the door slightly but went no further, peeking through only to see him speaking to an individual I considered my spiritual teacher (Ruth Norman). I could not hear the conversation from such distance but knew he was challenging this supposed teacher with high ended questions.

Days later, I suddenly felt the necessary courage to stand up to and abandon this supposed teacher, and learned a most valuable lesson I cannot stress enough; never linger in the negative, follow anyone, want something from others, desire to convert others, or be beguiled by leaders who claim to represent other worlds because this is simply not allowed by universal law. We can only represent ourselves, are authorized to solely share what we have learned (not preach or sway others), and it must be done for free and without followers.

Why for free? The intelligences providing information and guidance do not charge for their services and the contact is not for our financial benefit but for the good of all; that is where the distinction is made between genuine and pretentious action. It is not universally ethical to make a living out of infinite understanding. Whoever does so is in severe violation of creation's prime directive. The reason is rather simple; the poor could never afford to receive, only those who pay.

Those who utter congested words before others and strike their chest with pride of knowledge should realize that the world of contact is not for them. Silence is the greatest of gifts and sharing is not a mandate but rather a guided opportunity to learn and enjoy a few moments in a higher state of consciousness. We are not masters but students, and if we cannot deal with the one being, ourselves, what can we possible hope to do for others?

I must add that I do not call on UFOs to show up. Rather, they show themselves to me when they deem it is the right time to do so and for the right reasons. Only once have I asked for sighting confirmation and the craft did reappear; that was the only time. The intelligence behind these magnificent machines can sense minds and their locations, determining thusly the moment and purpose for their contact in accordance with universal laws we are not familiar with, reason I do not request their presence but rather respect their assessment in establishing contact. For the same reason, I cannot teach others out of respect knowing what my humble position as a learner is being oblivious of their true needs; to assert my will over someone else without infinite approval is tantamount to interference indictable by karma.

I had other physical alien contacts. Shortly after the amphitheater contact, I met two Venusians in an exposition. I recognized them from a vision in their Venusian home where they showed me a past life that took place a million years ago during Unholy Six times (Legacy Episode II: The Unholy Menace).

Channeling and ESP:

Channeling is perhaps the most misunderstood and abused of all contact modalities, and something that must be taken very seriously by all its practitioners for the sake of verity and beneficial usage. Going forth publicly with an assumption of externalized messages without the fullest possible measure of soul-searching is the work of comprehensive ignorance and is most harmful to life. The issue with channeling is simply this; any thought can provoke in its listener an irresistible desire to brand it as the words of another being when in fact they could be our very own. This modality can be a double-edged sword and extreme care must be practiced. Without going into too many details, it has been responsible for countless human pitfalls, wars, and exploitation throughout the ages due to a poor understanding of us. This writing attempts to describe the architecture of creation in order to understand and properly apply this modality.

In ancient times, the "voice" came from the gods. In modern times, it comes from "aliens." But nowhere do we find personal accountability that questions or auto-analyzes the "real source" of this voice, only that it is assumed to be foreign to our being. Only by knowing our thoughts, constantly, can we best discern who the voice really belongs to. It could be the self, a negative astral being, or a real positive extra-terrestrial source. It pays to be alert, question every source, and never assume.

Little do individuals realize that for the most part we are influenced not necessarily by the thoughts of other individuals, some within sight while others far or even in other dimensions, but our own past memories and the lifestyle that surrounds us. We are constantly "channeling" whether we are aware of it or not, but fail to grasp the who, where, or what it is. To avoid being wrongly influenced, we need to know who is talking on the other end. As the saying goes; trust, but verify. Without self-analysis and adequate preparation, caution must be exercised with this contact methodology to avoid being misled or misleading others.

A few years ago, I took part in a large exposition teaming with a plethora of psychic artists you might say. It was a gala event where healers, mystics, readers, channelers, contactees, and a vast conglomerate of accessory providers offered seekers everything from energy to readings, crystals, even action figures. It was a discovery haven for attendees whose admission fee granted a rare opportunity to visit with "answer providers" willing to share their gifts with the masses; unfortunately, some required yet another fee. It was like a psychic supermarket lined with aisles full of products and services complete with customer service assistants and cashiers, all under an air-conditioned roof. A few steps from my booth was the food court where vegetarian edibles were being served, quite good I might add and at a price to beat every other booth, the reason its line was the longest all day long.

If was my first but also last exposition, and with reason; I was there to deliver a message, not benefit financially from knowledge granted or render unauthorized service. Readings and healings were given without discretion, direction, or incentive to confirm the source. I felt completely out of place and sidelined by those willing to risk it all, pay whatever amount, and take chances with the information given. I had to see this with my very own eyes to believe it and walked away from it most displeased, but having learned a great humility lesson on the ways we betray the Infinite and its messengers, play with verity and lie not only to ourselves but others for self-gain. The higher sources that share their knowledge with me never send me an invoice, and likewise, I should abstain from invoicing others. Moreover, doing so opens the door on our ego self, and shuts the door on our celestial counterparts. The way to clear contact modality is through selfless service and that is non-negotiable.

That said, channeling and other contact experiences must demonstrate a higher purpose, exacting spiritual principles, selfless disposition, and teachings that are consistent, given anywhere, anytime, without making listeners have to incur travel or dispense cash. Information given is "free" and "now," never later; no waiting is involved as waiting begets corruption through anticipation.

To experience selfless service, personal beliefs, what reality we think is true, or what we "prefer" to be the truth must all be put aside; no personal filters must exist. Past readings must be given only if we are authorized to do so by the sources providing the information, the individual it is meant for approves receiving it, and is made aware of how to process it. Teachings are also given in such manner that creates zero conflict with present beliefs and are perfect for the common audience. In other words, channeling is a form of progressive and positive coaching not meant for entertainment or curiosity but for "planned application." Also, the channeler must take no credit for the action but rather understand that it is a process of "selective listening," something that we are all capable of doing but choose to ignore and rather replace it with the mundane, the ego, and a desire to bolster a personal point or aim for fame. The experiencer cannot put the caller on hold, choose the topic, or go tell everyone about the experience without permission; we must not forget that we are not here to lead, teach, convert, convince, get followers, or money.

Service is just that, give all for others, want nothing for the self, and serve the elements; only under these circumstances do we act as true channels and allow extra-terrestrials to increase our capacity to reach new heights of clarity, channelship, and unity with the dimensional brotherhood whence these higher intelligences come from and modalities operate. Failure to do so causes stagnation, if not retrograde development, corrupting purpose, message, and betraying extra-terrestrial endorsement. The slightest feeling of fear, anger, or selfishness is in direct opposition to the higher brotherhood "purpose" and immediately hangs up the phone on our end; moreover, it will block the caller's number for some time to come, if not permanently.

We must place our sights on celestial realms and receive its wonders into the fondest depths of our heart. Once the heart's vessel is filled with infinite goodness, it is to be passed on to all elements that surround us without exception. If the heart's vessel is not filled by celestial might, astral obsessions will occupy it and we become servants of evil. There is no in-between.

Our aim is to become a Brother, a being set aside from this world that serves creation as its life's mission. To do so, we must drink from the fountain of infinite knowledge and share its delights with the cosmos until no mundane desires bespeak from our lips.

These things I say from personal experience. Yes, I committed several blunders in the past. I let my ego take over, hung up the phone, betrayed, acted for personal benefit, all the above for several lifetimes. I'm not the perfect channel, but testimony begets healing and healing allows the capability to increase. Thus, reason to know oneself and be brutally sincere at all times, because in our walk of life we are constantly channeling; where from and for what interest, that's what life is all about and we must choose from one moment to the next what channel, what dimension we prefer, and hence there shall we be. Evolution is not a pathway but a direction, paths are many but the direction is dual. We must choose either backward "for me," or forward "for them."

As previously mentioned, if our work must be done free, why do supposed channelers, psychics, and contactees charge incredible amounts of money for their services? If higher beings do not charge for their services, why should we expose ourselves to corruption and favoritism by way of money? We must separate ourselves from self-benefit in order to be clear channels for those who are in themselves selfless in nature. Selfless begets selfless, selfish begets selfish. Where our heart is, that is precisely the direction whence we will channel from; either a benign, wicked or personal force.

My first channeling experience came without knowing when I was 18 years of age, a time when I knew little about reincarnation[18]. To say the least, I was shocked by what I saw, so much so that I wrote a novel series on that past incident and many others dating back hundreds of thousands of years (Robert Maxxim, 2014, Legacy episode series, www.rgaetan.com). Since then, I have been flooded by spiritual and technical downloads, modality capability enhancements, and past life readings that include that of others; confirmed of course. Healings have taken place from these readings. History has been clarified, beliefs corrected. The technical information constituting this writing was derived from channeled information.

Channeling and ESP are states of mind where the self is not involved and no personal gain is sought, no questions are asked, and tranquility sets in. This is the same state of mind experienced during NDE and OBE modalities, a consciousness elevated above physical ego and dependency, and the conscious life we should lead while on this plane. It is a form of mental association, an extension of consciousness from a sender to a receiver, a bridge from a common "mental backplane" or "unified state of consciousness" which is the normal form of contact between higher alien beings. To them, this state is just as normal as talking is to us. This bridge spans any number of space or time events since the dimension whence it operates is not subject to a sequential continuum. In other words, for clarity to set in, we must literally die of the self and replace it with the key to contact,

---

[18] https://unariansunited.com/iccc-18/ and https://unariansunited.com/iccc-13/

unconditional love for all elements, each other, and creation; not love as in desire or because one has to, but true, progressive, caring, sincere love.

3.   Intelligent Energy

"Intelligent energy" is the conduit that sanctions consciousness to exist and allows "contact modalities[19]" (different mechanisms wherein humans have contact with non-human intelligent beings) to function. Both do so in multiple dimensions simultaneously. One is an intrinsic part of the other since all energy and intelligence is unified and is in constant awareness of the other. Before we can grasp what this means, what consciousness is, and how contact modalities integrate into it, conceiving the origin and motive of this intelligent energy is critical because it acts as the binding glue per se between them.

Prior masters of science paved the way for future intellects to unravel the secrets of objective reality[20] (things we are sure exist independent of us) and eventually solve the most sought-after of riddles; what and where we are. That riddle has yet to be solved, and it will not be so until the fountainhead of intelligent energy and its measureless kingdom is first conceived.

Great strides have been made by conceiving that reality cannot be disentangled from participatory observation (John A. Wheeler, 1981), atoms have no physical properties (Werner Heisenberg, 1927), everything is vibrating energy (Nikola Tesla, 1942), and universal patterns are inherent in all things (Robert Maxxim, 2017). Thus, consciousness is shared and establishes common reality, atoms are dimensional, all things consist of energy regulated by intelligent patterns, and waveforms are the pulse behind everything conceivable.

---

[19] https://www.consciousnessandcontact.org/contact

[20] http://www.ict.griffith.edu.au/joan/atheism/reality.php

The common thread behind these findings is simply the presence of dimensional, non-local unifying energy transferring through multiple planes of reality wherein it takes on a plethora of properties and expressions. And as quantum non-locality would have it, if consciousness is non-local, so is intelligent energy as well as contact modalities. It is the purpose of this writing to reveal the "what" part of the riddle, which is energy, and the "where" part which is our relationship to it. Energy and waveform relationships are the cornerstones of contact modalities.

Resulting manifestations brought forth by dimensional design are exemplified by convergence[21] and can be termed "energy theology." Innumerable convergent patterns or "replicas" exist throughout the boundless cosmos but these go for the most part ignored. These patterns give rise to a holographic array of identical repeatable objects or intelligent ingredients that ornament creation anywhere we turn; replicas born from a central energy vortex[22] or manifold[23] whence copies spin-off. Manifolds are not based on Riemannian[24] or Euclidean[25] topology but are "dimensionless" since UDE is not based on space or time. Thoughts are also made from energy waveforms and

---

[21] https://en.wikipedia.org/wiki/Convergent_evolution

[22] Norman, Ernest L. "The Infinite Concept of Cosmic Creation." Chapter 3

[23] https://en.wikipedia.org/wiki/Manifold

[24] https://en.wikipedia.org/wiki/Riemannian_geometry

[25] https://en.wikipedia.org/wiki/Euclidean_geometry

reside in manifolds. Manifolds are in turn related to each other by resonance, either in full or partially, and therein you find intelligence exchange between them. The harmonic relationships[26] created by these exchanges give rise to contact modalities such as NDE, OBE, telepathy, and several other experiences.

From the most elemental atom to the deepest recesses of space itself, expressive intelligent forms, even ideas and feelings share the same essential waveform elements whence all things and minds are made from, manifest, and are "consciously" interconnected by "purpose" sustained by dimensional vortexes. Were it not so, then contact modalities would not exist or be greatly diminished in scope.

While some seek to solve physical riddles proposed by material vitae's admired philosophy that theoretically suggests the existence of ever smaller God particles responsible for the presence of physical forces, mass, and other properties, there are numerous other concepts such as scalar convergence, empty space, and intelligent energy that endure mostly in utter disregard. Much of what is considered intangible inconveniently begs to be noticed; not along the lines of mainstream theoretical discretion, the exclusive disposition of intellectually complex vocations, or the weight of compromising beliefs, but by associative energy concepts that unify existence and reality be it sentient or inert. String theory[27] is such a unifying concept that deserves much merit, given serious adaptations of course. In short, all things are united (consciousness[28], contact among intelligent sources[29], and matter) by a common creative ingredient with origins in causal fourth-dimensional realms; I refer to it as "unified dimensional energy" or

[26] Norman, Ernest L. "Tempus Invictus." Chapter 3, paragraph 6 – on

[27] https://en.wikipedia.org/wiki/String_theory

[28] https://en.wikipedia.org/wiki/Consciousness

[29] https://www.experiencer.org/introduction-to-contact-modalities/

UDE. But what evidence is there of this unifying energy and where is it? It will not be found in dirt, but what lies beyond it.

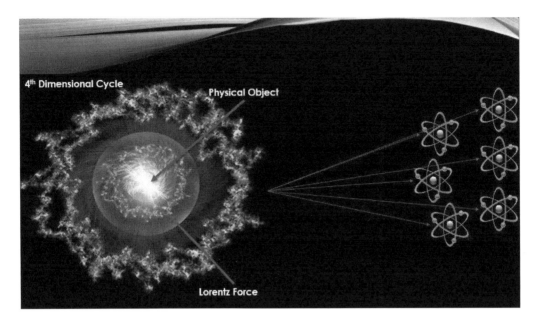

Evidence for convergent design and creative unification abounds. Atoms have the same properties wherever they are found, "know" by design how to consistently interrelate, combine up through protein chains, and integrate into matching scalar progressive units (Robert Maxxim, 2017) that give rise to complex living forms by the sum of inherent functional intelligence. That is, atoms contain consistent DNA-like behavioral instructions that perform countless intelligent roles under an unlimited number of conditions. This is not by chance but by design implied not at the physical but the dimensional level.

Each atom is a unique cosmic ingredient (a miniature computer) in a grand universal multi-course recipe, an intelligent cosmic bill of materials or instructions that built the expansive home we inhabit and the alphabet of creation. Every atom type is the same everywhere with countless served throughout 28 billion light years of space, each born from a single master vortex that multiplies them on our dimension regardless of time, space, numbers, age, or isotopic rendition. The atom's vortex is the carrier force transferring waveform instructions between its originating fourth dimensional pattern design into ours and then back up again.

The atom's waveforms are aware of their capabilities by interplaying with other waveforms that can modify its course and features, never failing to imply its universal instruction set according to its relative exchange conditions. It applies its existence in duty cycles, is creative and manifesting, carries out planned deployment, and endures its features above adversity; thus, it is a mind. Consciousness meets all these basic purpose requirements, implying it is the by-product of intelligence which is dimensional energy; the basis for contact modalities. Thus all existence and experience are conscious, reside in non-local domains, and are unified. Contact modalities operating from such UDE states are the norm for all beings, human and non-human. Intelligence is thus a shared "mind" per se. Personal development, selectivity, and ego limit our access to this "mind" or its available modalities. Consciousness, creation, and non-earthly intelligence are thus related by the existence of UDE.

4.   Contact Modalities and Consciousness

Contact Modalities are the instrument by which awareness of another intelligence is achieved be it material or spiritual. Intelligence is a term that applies to human, non-human, material, personal, or ethereal sources. There are countless methodologies by which humans have contact not only with each other but also their own personal conscious states, non-human intelligent beings, and energy reservoirs across vast distances and dimensions; our primary challenge is telling these sources apart. Contact methods can be mental or conscious, physical, or electronic in nature, but are limited and at times compromised by recipient capability.

An increase in personal capability equates to an increase in contact, while an increase in contact also defines and increases specific personal capability. It can be said that contact events are a type of "mentorship" that changes an individual's life and encourages on most occasions a path of discovery and self-improvement, stimulating a quantum change in consciousness and skills not previously possessed. However, results hinge around personal receptivity, integrity, and most important, capability. Where hostility, deceit, fear, anger, ego, incapacity, unwilling participation, even belief and other personal "filters" are found, the number and quality of contact events will be limited, if not altogether compromised. Hence, the measure of personal conscious maturity and competency in dimensional concepts is proportional to contact clarity.

During a contact event, the recipient may not be aware of it due to fleeting conscious states or lack of awareness. In other words, low competency. Also, the methodology used or diversions may cause an inability to have a contact experience. This is a low state of maturity. At times, a recipient may not consent to the event due to disbelief or conflict with personal fundamental creeds which is most often the primary cause of dismissal or experiential aberration. On occasion, recipients alter part or all of their experience details to gain mainstream headline fame or make a name for themselves. As with any relevant learning experience, impartiality and sincerity are paramount to increase personal capability while affording the same effect on others.

Some contact events can be controlled or uncontrolled, others occur by happenstance; I call the latter, "contact drive-byes." Both can be initiated by a plethora of intelligent sources and situations, though the recipient may not be fully aware of the purpose or mechanism by which these take place. A lack of personal control during or after contact may not invalidate the original event, but personal filters applied to contact content will obscure the experience after the fact.

Likewise, filters can lead to false or imagined contacts due to lack of maturity and competence.

To overcome these filters and get the most out of extra-terrestrial contacts, experiencers must understand the source, nature and outcomes of contact modality realms and learn the principles behind how consciousness and creation work. Only then can personal filters be fully mastered and contact clarity achieved. Failure to do so is akin to writing a physics thesis in kindergarten so to speak.

Achieving a high degree of clarity is paramount to any experience. It not only increases contact modality efficacy and verity but also the amount of information assimilated. The process of enhancing clarity is "iterative," constantly lessening intellectual local uncertainties and incompatible integration factors with the Infinite by increasing capability and competency.

5.   **Modality Access**

Aspiring contactees must become aware of and overcome several filters that impede clear contact. These filters include our own limited concept of creation, ego, and misunderstanding of the true workings of consciousness. To do so, we must abandon the age-old notion that consciousness is a local physical phenomena and the soul something tucked away somewhere and somehow in our DNA and brain cells. By the very nature that the brain can only record about an hour and a half of visual data, and DNA less than a gigabyte, it gives much reason to wonder where the idea came from that these cells and molecules contain "intellectual property" and past life keys. It is true, DNA can in fact be distorted by past life events and the soul does actually maneuver these cells, but they are not a record thereof, only an end result.

To experience clear and significant contact, we must elevate our awareness to where the soul and mind reside, a dimension where most causal modalities function. On these planes, advanced non-earthly intelligence understand, use, and experience life in ways far beyond our present intellectual understanding. As we move "up" dimensional planes so to speak, intelligence and capability also go up proportionally. Modalities such as astral travel, telepathy, remote viewing, etc all take place unknowingly in conscious states above the norm. So in order to experience these and other modalities, the recipient must have capability and competence in planes where these function much like selecting and dialing into a radio station. The higher the station, the greater the functional capability. Hence, modality is proportional to mental compliance with the requirements of a specific contact source and the mature aptitude of the recipient. Let's briefly consider how it all works.

Made from the same type of energy, mind and matter are equivalent, not local to the physical plane, and originate from UDE dimensional sources; planes of creative essence and primary linkages that allow contact modalities to function. In simplest form, UDE is a ring of energy or cycle that contains waveforms on it. It can be likened to a 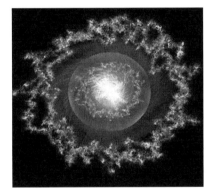 sphere or circle whose circumference vibrates. Such structure is termed by today's science a "closed string manifold" and carries upon it all the information needed to manifest an atom, rock, or thought on our physical plane, when, and where.

Understanding how these cycles work will help explain how consciousness and modalities relate to one another in higher dimensions. How these cycles emerge unto the physical world explains how modalities work and can be used.

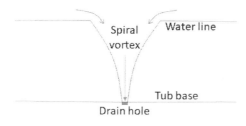

Imagine for a moment that we have a round bathtub full of water and a covered drain hole keeping the water from leaking down the drain. In this scenario, the water represents the instructional content carried piggyback on top of the closed fourth dimensional cycle. The moment we pull the drain plug, water immediately funnels about the drain hole in the form of a tapering spiral and rushes toward the drain. The funnel in this example represents a vortex[30] or the mechanism by which a cycle's instruction stream rushes into our dimension. Gravity, atmospheric pressure, and planetary Coriolis force help push water down the drain, an action comparable to what I call the "Concavity Current" acting upon the cycle (see graphic). What is this current? If you guessed the will of a higher mind, you guessed correctly.

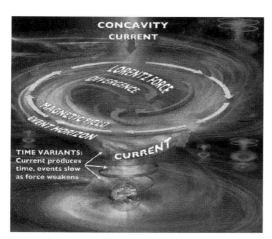

Concavity is the "breath of life," the pulse of creation, the course of infinite intelligence that creates life by means of polar fluctuations; meaning, the act of replenishing energy through sending and receiving, giving and taking, pushing then pulling, negative and positive. Concavity is a state in which all things are never static but rather in constant oscillation much like the alternating electric current in our homes. Hence, Concavity creates a vortex by acting on a 4D cycle and a vortex "downloads" energy stored on a 4D cycle to our dimension. Concavity on the other hand is thrusted by "will." Let us discuss what this will is.

---

[30] Normal, Ernest L. "The Infinite Concept of Cosmic Creation." Chapter 3, paragraph 19

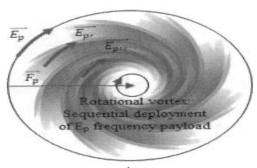

Vibrating energy on the 4D cycle's circumference creates forces perpendicular or at right angles to the circular ring $(\overrightarrow{F_p})$. Symmetry induces an inward Lorentz[31] type of centripetal force that "pushes" vibrating energy toward the center of the circle in a spiral $(\overrightarrow{E_p})$. This is how the vortex is formed. Hence, "will" is the intelligent nature of oscillating symmetry, the architectural design that creates 4D circular cycles and the mechanical properties of elements in the fourth dimension.

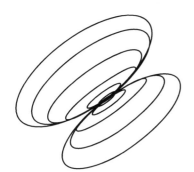

Just as atoms are connected by space, time, and forces on this dimension, cycles are connected by symmetry, frequency, and energy in the fourth. The difference between both dimensions is a lack of time factors. Hence, the fourth dimension is one of mind where intelligence capability supports Contact Modalities by default, and access to capability must therefore be of the mind as well.

Going back to the tub, water flows in only one direction; into the drain. In the case of 4D cycles, energy oscillates into the third dimension and also back out much like a bouncing spring. The vortex mechanism previously described is the means by which energy manifests and then returns back to its 4D manifold. A vortex is a "Type B[32]" waveform meaning that it "replicates" instructions from its UDE manifold and delivers it to our plane. Energy goes past our plane and

---

[31] https://en.wikipedia.org/wiki/Lorentz_force

[32] Schild, Rudy. "FREE Survey Results Related To My Study of Black Hole (MECO) Physics."

continues on into infinite absorption or energy diminution, but then it turns around and returns back to its original UDE, thus forming a double helix. At the center of the vortex at a point between UDE emergence and absorption limits, both vortexes meet or seek balance. This is the third dimensional focal point, the drain hole or physical crossover point between planes.

Type "A" Waveform

Once water enters the drain and goes down the pipe, it no longer spirals but assumes a straight sequential path propagating linearly rather than as a unified payload. Thus it becomes a "Type A" linear waveform which is the norm in our physical world exemplified by what is known as a "sine wave." To put consciousness into perspective and exemplify linear and vortexal waveforms, "Type A" waveforms can be likened to sequential retrospection, meditation, or daydreaming. "Type B" manifests as an instant feeling or sense of intuition. For messaging and reading type of modalities, this crude comparison can help determine the source of that Contact Modality. Since modalities are dimensional or "Type B," an instant feeling rather than a sequential sustained thought pattern bears its mark.

We must keep in mind that consciousness is the sentient instrument that transits between lower and higher levels of intelligence in the soul. The lower self is the lower level of intelligence in our soul, a recollection of experiences gathered in the physical plane. The higher self is a more perfect life expression built over many incarnations to become the guiding more positively polarized understanding of infinity as it relates to our experiences[33].

When contact is initiated by a higher intelligence, that being undergoes a mental step-down process to reach our level. The reason we lose information and time references during contact is due to our lack of familiarity with a higher conscious level being imposed on us. Hence, personal understanding of creative energy and mastery over conscious experiences are the gateway to establishing authentic contact and recalling exacting details.

There are numerous types of personal experiences that corroborate relationships between contact modalities and consciousness levels operating beyond this dimension, as discussed above, that interact with creative intelligent energy of which it, and all things, are composed.

Table 1. *Contact Modalities and Consciousness Sources*

Contact Modality:	Description:	Confirmation:
Near death experiences (NDEs) ([34]-[35]_[36])	Consciousness detaches lower-self entity and body, enters higher dimensional realms, and returns to the physical.	Personal experiences that confirm consciousness is multi-dimensional and its tenure is not physical. Witnessed and discussed

---

[33] Norman, Ernest L. "The Infinite Concept of Cosmic Creation." Chapter 18, paragraph 9 – 36

[34] https://www.near-death.com/science/evidence.html

[35] Lommel M.D., Pim Van. "Consciousness Beyond Life." HarperCollins, 2011

[36] Moody Jr M.D., Raymond A. "Life After Life." Bantam Books, 1976

	The body may or may not be in deceased state during experience. Viewer may see other beings or places beyond the physical on different space/time tier	for millennia as evidenced by Plato[37] and countless witnesses throughout the span of time
Out of body experiences (OBEs)[38]	Consciousness operates outside the physical realm, in wake or sleep state, covering numerous time/space paradoxes while still attached to the lower-self entity and physical body	Confirms that time, space, and physical tenure are subject to consciousness (reality and uncertainty) and its energy source which is outside the physical realm, also observed by researchers of ancient times
UFO contacts	Remote or face to face contact with alien intelligence, initiated or carried out by the self or an alien source, typically by mental association	This mental link breaches space/time rules, pointing to consciousness as a timeless instrument not bound by physical tenure
Channeling, ESP	Reproduction, transmission, or download of information from another intelligence; ability to interchange awareness, conversations, or messages between beings	Another form of mental association, at times an extension of consciousness from a sender to a receiver, a bridge or rift in physical state from a common "mental backplane" or

---

[37] https://www.near-death.com/science/evidence/ndes-have-been-known-throughout-history.html

[38] https://www.iacworld.org/history-obes/

		"unified state of consciousness[39]." This is the normal form of contact between higher alien beings
Mystical meditation	Variety of methods used to achieve a devotional state, influence knowledge, mental state, or connection with a creative intelligent source	Consciousness attunement process relegating control of physical awareness to reach a unified consciousness state. It may start as a "Type A" mental action that progresses into establishing a dimensional "Type B" state wherein contact takes place
Remote viewing, dreams, visions, readings	Conscious visualization of an event, place, or message, whether local or not, in past, present, or future states	Consciousness attunement into any number of space or time events or individuals from a dimensional point of view where continuum is not sequential. The information does not come from a physical form but rather an inter-dimensional conscious record linked to at that higher level

---

[39] Adamski, George. "Inside The Spaceships," chapter 6, paragraph 36 – 37

The above experiences and others provide convincing account of the existence and workings of a unified state of consciousness or super-physical bridge between minds which do not equate to physical laws but rather operate from a superior dimensional plane, one that supplements this dimension and can be felt or used by beings on our plane. This unified state is what makes contact modalities possible.

It will be shown that all the various manifestations of energy forms and intelligence as they are concerned with the more immediate fourth, fifth and sixth dimensions which are in close proximity to the earth, and all the different manifestations we call the speed of light, are only transferences of energy from one dimension to the other[40]. Consciousness is also a transference of dimensional intelligent energy no different than atoms.

6.   Scientific Hurdles

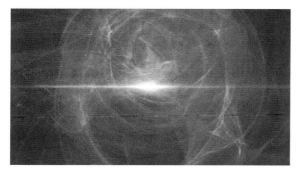

Since the dawn of time, man sought to understand life's purpose through the use of symbology and self-imposed intellectual filters built around his immediate surroundings. Not much has changed since. Our ambiguous mental recesses labeled mystical unseen forces about us as spirits or "soul" without much proof, meaning to explain energy and cosmic forces in a pseudo-scientific way, though correctly hinting that energy is an "intelligence collective" or soul. This intelligence collective connects consciousness and creation together and makes contact modalities possible, but science knows nothing about it. Thus, understanding what it is, and is not, is of utmost importance.

---

[40] Norman, Ernest L. "Cosmic Continuum," chapter 8, paragraph 6

Many conceive the soul to be some type of ghostly entanglement, mysterious haze, or "ectoplasmic ooze"[41] of unknown substance. Research into its nature over time has been plagued by countless compromised concepts, mishandled by biased inquiry, and tested using unsuitable methodology. To this day, the question still remains: what is the soul, does it exist, and how can we prove it? The answer is rather simple, surprising, and fascinating:

- Consciousness is the "probe" of the soul, a "unified state"[42] that collects information from our interaction with intelligence on several dimensional levels
- The soul is the accumulation of consciousness experiences taking place at multiple dimensional levels simultaneously
- All of the experiences we probe and store into the soul are composed of the same stuff we are probing which is energy
- If matter is energy and energy is intelligent[43], then everything including us in totality is also composed of energy (unified dimensional energy or UDE)
- Energy is thus the soul's ingredient, the foundation for reality and unified sentience whether of or out of this world
- Contact modalities have UDE and consciousness in common and are thus also energy

The soul is the creative substance science has long been searching for, not particles. Sufficient evidence does exist to prove its existence, but it fails to be recognized. Before understanding the soul and the unifying principles that apply to its existence, we must identify and eliminate limiting creeds built into prevailing physical concepts holding

---

[41] https://en.wikipedia.org/wiki/Ectoplasm_(paranormal)

[42] Norman, Ernest L., "The Infinite Concept of Cosmic Creation, Questions and Answers." Lesson 3, paragraph 117 'A – In other words'

[43] Maxxim, Robert. "Energy and Waveforms." https://www.youtube.com/watch?v=hwGFXy91nRU

us back. This implies knowing where atomic forces really come from and the obvious limitations inherent in admired philosophies, mainly elemental orbital and particulate mechanics.

When we think of atoms, we imagine a conglomerate of subatomic particles that look and behave much like a tiny solar system complete with planets, moons, and asteroids; it is far from that. The atom is an energy capsule designed to execute a specific consistent function and works much like a miniature star, not a solar system. From the early days of classical mechanics to Rydberg, Bohr, and others that followed, several attempts were made to conventionalize the orbital nature of elemental electrons, account for quantum, Zeeman and Stark effects, and a host of atomic forces that to this day number up to five[44]. Evidence of the atom's non-orbital nature abounds, but a long chain of complex particle and force hypotheses stands in the way of further consideration[45].

To exemplify present conflicts inherent in today's admired philosophy, the inequality gap between Coulomb and Newtonian formulas is just staggering: $2.3 * 10^{39}$. Not long ago, this was the standard for calculating atomic radius. While taking Physics 101, I recall going to the blackboard and showing the discrepancies mentioned above; the Physics department did not take too kindly to my presence after that event.

Today, the Standard Model[46] of particle physics stands tall as the pride of international scientific collaboration, offering an exotic maze of particles and generations that best fits predicted behavior, but still falls short of being a complete theory of fundamental interactions and

---

[44] https://en.wikipedia.org/wiki/Fifth_force

[45] https://en.wikipedia.org/wiki/List_of_particles

[46] https://en.wikipedia.org/wiki/Standard_Model

explaining the origins of elementary particles and forces (fermions and bosons). Baryon asymmetry, gravitation theory, neutrino oscillations, and dark matter are just a few of the unincorporated conditions in this incomplete model. In spite of this, the standard model continues to set the pace for quantum field theory development and modern atomic science.

Like the Phoenix bird, this model rose literally from atomic collider ashes, a close encounter of the violent kind hoping to dissect the atom and measure what essential pieces it contained by catastrophic means. Absolutely absurd to think this actually works without damaging or mutating the particle and its intelligence in the process, be it mass, force, or relativistic mass-energy. Particles are not what we think. They are a locum for energy waveform packets, not solids, so crashing them is irrelevant and nothing more than the interruption of harmonic oscillations occurring between manifolds and this dimension. It should be noted that collider detection traces do not exhibit independent particles but fewer energy points that appear multiple times in the image too fast to be noticed. The collision invades the particle's natural harmonic oscillation and interrupts its dimensional download, setting up abnormal time continuum states that alter its manifestation or normalized displacement. In other words, segments of the particle may appear in multiple places at once or over a period of time, perhaps even light years away or prior to the collision taking place. Random energy impacts play havoc with time, space and distort reality, and increase quantum uncertainty.

Atoms should be thought of as a standard "ingredient" or "recipe" available in all corners of the universe, replicated from a single dimensional element "database" or master closed-string manifold. This fact is in plain sight, exemplified by evolutionary analogous structures in the field of convergence[47] that include enzymology of proteases,

---

[47] https://en.wikipedia.org/wiki/Convergent_evolution

nucleic acids, plasma crystals, and elements. Hence, convergence is the physical end result of UDE and intelligent structures precipitating an infinite number of "copies" into our plane from a single database source. Each copy stands alone on its own evolutionary track.

Entropy decay shows that atoms and isotopes "know" how to degrade or "half-life" into preceding atoms. Stars and supernovae evolve atoms forward rather than backward, indicating the presence of a highly sophisticated, consistent "rule-based" atomic DNA or scalar progression blueprint designed into each atom such that it knows when and how to become what. Problem is, we take that for granted and fail to grasp convergence at the atomic level. Below are recent findings of interest that support convergence:

- Herschel space telescope: found oxygen in the Orion nebula[48]
- Spitzer telescope[49]: found hydrogen gas and ions in the Andromeda galaxy
- Gas clouds between Andromeda and Triangulum galaxies: most ionized hydrogen resides in independent clouds hinting star formation fuel for nearby galaxies[50]
- Primordial galaxy SXDF-NB1006-2[51]: galaxy 13.1 billion light-years from earth contains oxygen

Atomic constructs such as electrons, protons, and neutrons are also much alike wherever they are found, even after exchanging atoms, surviving supernovae, beta decays, and quantum shifts all over the universe since the beginning of time. Theoretically, they live on for at

---

[48] www.space.com/12494-oxygen-molecules-space-herschel.html

[49] spaceplace.nasa.gov/review/posters/spitzer_posters/spitzer_andromeda_8x11_all.pdf

[50] www.huffingtonpost.com/2013/05/09/interstellar-gas-cloud-andromeda-galaxy_n_3244446.html

[51] www.space.com/33186-ancient-galaxy-universe-dark-ages-has-oxygen.html

least 66 trillion trillion trillion years[52] yielding millions of kilowatt-hours over their entire lifetime. A hydrogen atom at 13.6 eV[53] for example can deliver 350 billion watt-hours of energy over a 580 trillion trillion million hour lifetime. If we shorten that lifetime, as in a nuclear blast, part of the atom's total lifetime energy is expended in a much shorter span of time. By comparison, an Energizer 9-volt battery delivers 5.5 watt-hours[54]. It's staggering to think atoms can hold such power and survive that long without a recharge, an assumption that must be challenged.

In a hypothetical case, given particle theory tenure for a charged sphere, if we assume an electron has a certain capacitance, resistance, electron radius, and implied field energy with estimated terms, its discharge rate or time to live is not very large ($2.3 * 10^{-27}$ s). Hence, per this estimate, charges must be "resupplied" periodically by a higher dimensional energy source.

By analyzing atomic scalar affinity (ratio of neutrons to protons), we find that elementary particles and forces are not responsible for atomic properties. Ca, He, Si for example have the same ratio of neutrons and protons but do not "taste" the same. In addition, atomic force microscopy shows that every atomic surface differs in topology, curvature, and lattice patterns; that cannot be attributed to force and particles alone but symmetrical harmonic interchange affecting linear space displacement.

If the number of elementary particles does not impact atomic ingredient or pattern, then weight and force as a function of elemental numbers is not an ingredient discriminator. In all cases, inherent

---

[52] "Electron." https://en.wikipedia.org/wiki/Electron

[53] https://www.quora.com/What-is-the-total-energy-in-a-single-hydrogen-atom

[54] https://sciencing.com/energizer-watthour-battery-specs-7425932.html

dimensional recipes or intelligent instruction sets are the differentiator and lattice arrangement is a perfect example of that.

Atoms are not composed of marbles but an all-inclusive energy waveform vault whose functions are released through access portals when bombarded by specific frequencies; consciousness is no different. Some of these atomic frequencies can be seen on spectral charts but we must take into consideration other frequencies that cannot be measured due to uncertainty factors that average-out harmonic interaction with our measurement instruments. I call this relationship between energy vibrations and our senses and instruments, "reality averaging." Reality averaging will affect what physical components we end up seeing, including empty space. It has led science to appraise the atom minimally, in fact to the point where its convergence and dimensional properties are just now being considered.

An atom is a two-part (not three) instrument much like a star composed of an inner positively charged core and an outer negatively charged cloud. Surrounding this cloud are "*pronemo*" charges that power the atom's field (Robert Maxxim, 2014). In other words, the atom is basically a pulsing energy field where its inner or positive proton core and the immediate pronemo surroundings vibrate at a rate three times that of the layer between them we call the electron shell (f_e). Thus, there is no such thing as a positive or negative charge, but rather a 3 to 1 frequency rate ratio between them that simulates what we measure as a charge. This is just one of many uncertainty factors that cloud our view of the atom and hold us back from confirming the existence of non-material dimensions where consciousness unification occurs.

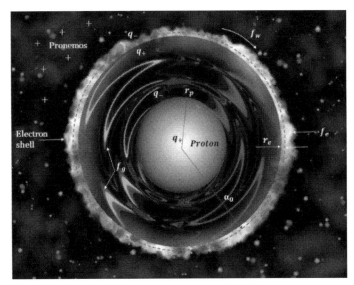

Consciousness is all about uniformity with a select homogeny of pre-defined manifestations that minds interact with on this plane. Yes, the universe is a rigged matrix and contact modalities are no different, equipped with pre-planned access channels or components of this uniformity.

Consciousness cannot exist in a plane it is not a part of, is not compatible or familiar with, or is not built from the same factors. This is important to consider. Likewise, consciousness interaction levels or planes of existence are in themselves modality channels that act much like radio stations transmitting and receiving intelligence from same or other channels. Intelligence can only experience contact by mentally changing dimensional factors, but to do so awareness of that level is required. These channels are active at all times, but if you do not have the capacity to listen it is of no use to try.

Being locked into one level of awareness, as is our earthly case, would necessitate to conceive, experience, and develop these channels in order to more effectively experience contact modalities. This development however can be deceiving. It is just as difficult to design a spacecraft without knowledge of space as it is to develop multi-realm awareness without experiencing it. Many contact development methods are suggested including meditation, energy tapping, mantras, crystals, etc.; however the primary key that opens up these channels is contact modalities themselves or the association with higher intelligence as the catalyst for awakening per se. This higher intelligence can be alien or spiritual in nature, but definitely a source of awareness residing on another sub-manifold of experience.

For contact modalities to occur, consciousness must be aligned with the various causal planes where unification and source occurs. This means that an originating contact must be able to link to the recipient's plane, and this is true for most contact modalities where compatibility and associative mental compliance are required.

7. Consciousness and Light Speed

According to special relativity, the speed of light is the maximum speed at which all known forms of information in the universe can travel[55] including Contact Modalities, but I beg to differ. It is considered to be the speed at which all massless particles and changes of the associated fields travel in a vacuum regardless of source motion or inertial reference frame of the observer; this is not the case as proven by experiments conducted by the NEC Institute[56] where speeds far beyond that of light were charted. In space, we note objects far enough away whose light should not return due to recession, not even Gamma rays, yet light does return from them[57]. A star or even car headlights coming toward us violate light speed barriers.

In actuality, neither light or mind travel; instead, they transition and displace between dimensions according to manifold interactions, not physical obstacles. Note prior observations made on collider continuum effects that violate time and space. We must not forget that consciousness exists on various sub-manifold plane levels and acts as a

---

[55] https://en.wikipedia.org/wiki/Speed_of_light

[56] https://physicsworld.com/a/laser-smashes-light-speed-record/

[57] https://www.rgaetan.com/red-shift.html

telemetry switch board. Each mental level pertains to a different reality complete with its own propagation laws. Permissivity, refraction, friction, diffraction, displacement, and many other physical vector relationships play out in higher dimensions before "re-arranging" manifested atoms accordingly on this plane. Light speed and Relativity are the primary hindrances placed in the way of recognizing dimensional physics and contact modalities. As has been suggested and in many ways verified, both light and relativistic restrictions are not real.

From a higher dimensional perspective, there is no real velocity or time, only unified states of energy. Time, space, and velocity only become real when dimensional energy crosses the physical threshold or the "3D crossover point."

For example, the light coming from the far-off object GN-Z11[58] in Ursa Major at 620 nm decelerates 3.48 times light speed ($\sqrt{z+1}$) upon contact with our environment, much as light would do in water or glass due to refraction (the square root of final over initial light energy) that determines speed[59]. This indicates that light from this object, just before reaching our plane and based on red shift, is traveling at 1,044,000 km/sec, indicating that light speed limits do not apply to consciousness.

All around us, light sources are in a constant state of motion, some slower while others faster than the established light-speed standard. Blue shifts cover the heavens. Neutron star axial beams crisscross nearby space reaching distances light-years away, their tips moving at angular perpendicular speeds several times that of light.

---

[58] https://en.wikipedia.org/wiki/GN-z11

[59] Adamski, George. "Inside The Spaceships." Chapter 3, paragraph 52

A high powered laser spotting the moon 400,000 km away, shifted 48 angular degrees per second, causes the tip of the laser to travel faster than light. A Moreton pulse appearing on the sun's surface creates a light flash that races across its surface at light speed[60]. In the time it covers 58 visual kms on the sun's surface at an angle of $8.33 * 10^{-5}$ radians, it covers 12,511 kms at Earth's distance, or 215.7 times light speed. SOHO[61] satellites and Earth observers, from their vantage points, do not encounter visual delays from these perpendicular events indicating that extended angular velocities are not in fact restricted by light speed limits, only those sources refracted by present instrumentation.

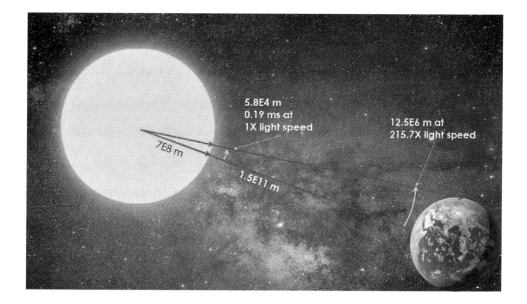

Our instruments and processes measure direct light sources, not indirect. These direct measurements either pass through refractive materials or come in contact with them, thus compromising light's original properties. A laser beam protruding from a lensed encasement,

[60] https://pxhere.com/en/photo/915272

[61] https://sohowww.nascom.nasa.gov/

or produced by light sources also encased, inherits their refractive qualities. The same holds true for any mirrors or lenses the laser's light comes in contact with[62]. Our measurement instruments are compromised by their own intrusive properties.

8.   The Realm of Existence

This narrative has taken the reader through a voyage of discovery, exposing various modality and novel scientific concepts, and establishing critical links between them. Our discussion cannot be complete without considering the boundaries of our dimensional realm of existence; the limits of what we consider to be the physical cosmos insofar as the microcosm, macrocosm, and the mysterious limits of ethereal fields are concerned. Much as the sun's heliopause determines the edge of the solar system, a cosmo-pause determining the edge of our physical dimension lingers unidentified. Those that conceive it do so poorly understood and with reason. It is no one's fault that this is so, humanity is just beginning to find their way across the stars but much error must be discarded before moving on.

Science has taught us that there are three dimensions; length, width, and height. Visually, this is correct, but physically it is not. The concept of energy is best understood if we put physical existence into an entirely new perspective, one that is more closely aligned with energy continuum rather than measurement. There are two physical variables controlling existence: space and time. These are born from higher dimensional energy interactions that give rise to physical events and resolve into the known three dimensions. Hence, from energy and vibration we get space and time, and from that we get measurements. The realm of our existence is thus not three but two dimensional: space and time $(2D_t\{d_x \mid t_x\})$.

---

[62] https://t4.ftcdn.net/jpg/02/30/64/23/240_F_230642309_o1C3J09izS4xqjNcYLEIsl6GyCY7dhYH.jpg

Our physical dimension is an instance or segment of a higher or fourth dimension that brings about all third dimensional events. Fourth dimensional continuum is composed of energy and frequency that yields the totality of events in physical space and time $(3D_t\{d_i \mid t_i \mid e_i\})$. Each physical event can thus be identified and selected among the rest from the fourth dimensional event conglomeration as demonstrated by the following vector equation such that the sum of third dimensional events, elements of fourth dimensional energy/frequency, can be tuned or selected to specify an event point in physical space and time. Hence, a travel and time machine:

$$2D_t\{d_t|t_t\} = \nabla_{d|t}\left[\sum \overline{2D_x}\{d_x|t_x\} \in \overline{3D_i}\{d_i|t_i|e_i\}\right]_{d|t}$$

The actual physical event is an energy/frequency footprint that translates into space/time, remembering that space is a resultant wavelength of energy and time the inverse of its frequency. There is no uncertainty since there is no present in the span of time, only past and future. Even a traveler going to the past is in its own past state, not present, reason Heisenberg's theorem does not limit the possibility of continuum selectivity and Relativity never applies. This can be taken a step further by considering that continuum can not only be selected but "constructed," meaning that an infinite number of inter-dimensions mirroring the universe can be fabricated and be set apart as its own continuum reality. In other words, invisibility and parallelism of existence. This in itself is a huge field to enter into but I briefly touch upon it to prove a point; energy manifolds of reality and existence are as infinite as atomic isotopes, they are "dimensional isotopes." The edge of existence is limited by contact modality, what the mind will conceive; consciousness.

9. Conclusion

Contact modalities are universal communication channels shared by all intelligences in this and other dimensions be it beings, matter, or creative energy. Consciousness is the key dialing and receiving mechanism involved in contact, understanding that all thought and matter is built from the same ingredient; unified dimensional energy. Consciousness is not bound to time or space given that its origins are dimensional where sequential time is non-existent. The atom is a resonant energy form manifested from dimensional manifolds much the same as consciousness, not tiny particles or solar systems. There is no such thing as matter or space but rather all is filled by dimensional energy. Consciousness is likewise non-matter energy just like the rest of creation.

The soul is an energy warehouse containing all the events the being experienced throughout its evolution, stored as energy in multiple dimensional levels where these were experienced and according to their intelligence quotient. These dimensional levels help individuals contact other beings and forms residing at those levels, but prior personal experience at said levels is needed in order to promote contact. This experience is often promoted or helped along by other beings through contact modalities they initiate, causing an increase in personal awareness of said modality. From that increased contact, possibility and clarity are also increased. Modalities are not limited by light speed, a restraint imposed by refractive losses that pertain only to measurement instrumentation rather than permissive space and higher dimensions.

10.   About The Author

Born in Cuba, the author experienced several wake and sleep-time visions of other worlds as well as direct contact with non-earthly intelligences including space crafts. His experiences have led him to visit several worlds and dimensional abodes in this solar system as well as others nearby, receiving knowledge from non-earthly intelligence regarding dimensional, scientific, medical, historical, and devotional subjects. He has had three NDEs and countless OBEs over the years, experiencing countless channeling experiences daily.

He received a BA in Music at the Havana International Conservatory, and BA in Education and Computer Science at Western International University, both Summa Cum Laude. He studied Physics and Mathematics at Cal State Fullerton and served an internship at NASA's JPL, participating in imaging efforts involving Viking and Voyager missions. In 2014 he published two auto-biographical novels titled "Legacy" that describe his visions, what he learned from other worlds, his many past lives, and historical depictions of ancient civilizations such as Atlantis and Lemuria. He plans to release three additional episodes as well as a book on fourth dimensional physics.

The "Paranormal" Contact Experiences of a Christian Minister:

Experiences via Pre-Birth Memories, Reincarnation, Contact with Physical Beings, UFO Contact Experiences, & Spiritual Transformation

Reverend Jeff Schulte

In presenting the following, it is my desire to reveal to the reader the truth of My reality and the miniscule part of it that I can comprehend. Therefore, I would like to say at the outset - what you are about to read is based solely and simply upon my experiences and my interpretation of those experiences. In no way, do I wish to challenge the reader's faith, beliefs and or understanding. I am not trying to tell you what to believe or not to believe and if, when reading the following, you find yourself asking the question – how can this man continue to serve as a Christian minister believing what he now espouses and believes to be the truth? Then you are in good company as you would join a long list of souls for whom this is an enigma! I can also assure you that I have been damned to hell by more devout, believing and loving souls of various persuasions than I can count. I have also discussed most of the following subject matter with my superiors in the church and although they are of a different opinion, they still support me in carrying the ministry, which. for me has been and is a service of Love that I have dedicated myself to for the greater part of my life.

I am 64 years old and have been in active ministry as a priest for over 40 years and as of this year 2021, I only have months left before formal retirement at age 65. I would like to add that it has only been in the last 10 or so years that I have come to realize and accept that I am an active contactee and experiencer and have been so since the day I was born. I serve in a Non-Denominational Christian church which has been around since the 1860's. Most of the ministers in the church serve in a voluntary position, i.e. we offer our time voluntarily and don't receive payment or salary for our time spent in the ministry. Hence, we need to hold down normal paying jobs and most are family men who must deal with all the normal day to day issues that husbands and fathers must deal with, while at the same time supporting the souls under our care with the family, life and faith challenges that they must cope with. I therefore humbly ask the reader to hold back from forming any preconceived ideas about who or what I am or may be and what I should or shouldn't believe in. So, if you are still reading, please stay a little longer.

As you read through my experiences, you may also appreciate that my experiences clash with the official doctrine of our church and indeed most religions! I hope to deal with these clashes as they come up during my journey through my life's experiences to this time in the year 2021. So, let me start at the beginning – at least the beginning of 'this life' or incarnation - from the very start, my life has been anything but normal because our church does not believe in, nor does it teach or recognize reincarnation, yet I was born in June of 1956 with a snapshot from a previous life!

Early memories

It was 2am on a Tuesday morning in June of 1956 that I entered this incarnation. The first 24 hours for me were, as expected, not something I remember, however, memory is a funny thing and to be honest, like most, I have forgotten far more than I can remember. However, I have a plethora of memories regarding these early years, memories that had to wait until my speech was sufficient for my parents, especially my Mother and my Nana, to be able to understand me, and then it was probably still a few more years before I started to question what I was remembering!

I believe that I can safely say that apart from my pre-life memory, my earliest memory was being held in my mother's arms as we left a bus, crossed a parkland and started up a steep hill and my mother spoke, **_'or thought'_**, we must hurry, it's going to hail. I remember it quite well, I remember the bus, the grass, the trees, the road and steep hill, the green hail laden clouds, I knew I was going home! I remember that I knew what these things were and what they were called and then my mother saying or thinking what I had heard. It wouldn't be until I was probably 5 or 6 before I asked my mother when this happened and she remembered it well! Why? Because it was the day after I was born and she was taking me home from the hospital where I was born.

Pre-life memory

The pre-life memory was just as early or may have even been from day one, this I can't remember for sure but I do know that I was assured by my parents that it never occurred during this lifetime. In brief, I was standing holding a parent's hand 3 to 4 deep on the footpath in front of terrace houses watching a royal procession go by. The royal couple were in an open gilded carriage, that was preceded by the guards on white horses and followed by the same which in turn were followed by brightly colored footmen. The dress code was mostly red. Across the road was parkland and to our right was a slight incline with a roundabout and an open pavilion where the royal couple got out of the carriage and took their positions in the pavilion. A function followed but I have no idea what it was about. There was also a statue or fountain in the center of the roundabout.

Up until the time of speaking to my parents regarding this matter, I had no access to a TV where one may consider it as a possible early recollection of what one may have seen as part of a movie or possibly a documentary. Yet these details are firmly etched into my memory and as my parents assured me that it hadn't occurred during this lifetime, I was left with the obvious conclusion even at this early age - this memory must be from a previous life!

Five hooded beings

Regarding my early years, there isn't a lot to comment on, I remember that there often appeared at the end of my bed 5 beings who looked like hooded monks. As our church, did not have monks, I couldn't have known what they were called or what monks looked like and yet somehow, I knew that the beings I was seeing were called monks! As these early years passed, I saw these beings less and less until they were just a memory. I don't recall them ever communicating to me, they were just there.

Uncomfortable body

I can also remember that something wasn't right. I didn't feel right in the body I had and I can assure you that I felt this way since well before I was out of nappies! Leaving nappies behind occurring on my second birthday when I declared that I didn't need nappies any more. I was so determined on the subject that my Mother and my Nana, who lived with us, decided to give me a go and apart from the occasional mishap, I haven't looked back. So, I can say for a fact that this bodily discomfort that I felt was from before my second birthday. This Body Dysphoria has followed me my whole life and I believe that I now know why - I would have felt wrong in any 3d body that I found myself incarnating into and probably did also in previous incarnations as well - because I am from somewhere else!

Blood noses

Using my second birthday as a focal point, I can recall events and place them either before or after my second birthday. One thing I remember from that time was the unrelenting blood noses I had. Thankfully I can say that as I have aged, the blood noses have mostly ceased.

Telepathic Communication

In my early years, both before, and for a while after my second birthday, telepathy was mostly my way of communicating at least around the other toddlers and infants but where my mother was concerned, it was a normal way for me to receive information from her, although I don't believe that she would have realized it at the time. On one occasion, when I was probably closer to 4 years old, I was playing in a sand pile with a little friend two or three houses away when I clearly heard my mother call me. So, I raced home and was about to knock on the door when it opened. My mum looked down at me and said that she was just coming to get me. I said that I knew because I heard her call me. She then said that she hadn't called me! As toddlers, we thought nothing of it but those who were leaving their childhood behind - the older children who had started school and the adults, for a while I could still hear or visualize what they were thinking but they couldn't hear me, and so, I was forced to learn to verbalize my communication and rely on the sense of hearing and hence my telepathic abilities diminished until they were no longer needed or used. I would also say that words formed only a small part of this telepathy, by far the greater part of it was images! Sadly today, this ability appears to be irretrievably lost.

Church

At this tender age, probably around 3 or 4, I also had decided that I hated 'church' and made sure that my parents knew it. However, my asserting that I hated church and didn't want to go only forced my parents to adopt the corrective measures of the time. *You ARE going to church and you ARE going to behave or you'll be taken down the back and spanked.* This in no way was helping to promote their cause but at the time it was the only way they knew how to deal with the situation. My father was the priest, so, at that early age I had little choice but to accept something that was against what I was naturally feeling. As they had no way of knowing or understanding why or where I was coming from, they continued to raise me as they believed was best for me.

I can also remember one occasion when I returned home after another session of church being inflicted upon me, that I went to our back steps and sitting there I pondered – *'How could anyone eat the Body and Blood of Jesus'?* It didn't make sense so the alarm bells had already started to ring! I was no older than 4 when this occurred. Over the ensuing years, my understanding of this Church sacrament grew. Of course, my understanding was and still is at odds with the accepted church doctrine on the subject but I wasn't to know that until I was taught otherwise in Sunday School and for reasons that I don't remember, I was unable to articulate my understanding on this matter! So, my teachers were left to assume that I had accepted the doctrine. I had learned their doctrine and could repeat what I was being taught but it still didn't sit right with me!

I was probably around 3-4 when my Nana decided to teach me a church hymn. I still find it fascinating that out of all the hymns she could have chosen, she chose one that spoke about my true home. The first line reads – *There is a glorious land for which my heart does long*. I had an ear for music so it was easy to learn. Even today when I sing this hymn I still get emotional because I Do Long So much - for my true home. For me, this is not so much a place but rather a State of Being!

5 years to adolescence

I can say that prior to Sunday School, I had no need to ponder a God/Creator – I simply didn't need that in my reality or my early ponderings. Nevertheless, as I grew, it became unavoidable that I had to think about it, and somehow incorporate into my paradigm a teaching about a *God Person - Being*. The **ONLY** thing that made any sense to me about any of it was that - *He/God* was also referred to as - *Our Father* and that *He* resided in my *True Home* - a place that I was taught is called *Heaven!* As it states in the Lord's Prayer - *Our Father in*

Heaven! It may come as no surprise though that I found a problem with what I was being taught about this ***God Being*** and this problem has stayed with me well into my adult life because no one could give me the answers I needed, probably because they just knew what they were told to believe and accepted it - but I couldn't, so I suppressed it!

The Catherine wheel UFO and an avoided accident

As previously mentioned, my father was also in the ministry and he had several congregations in different states under his care. As he was away most weekends, he often would take us - the family - with him. It was on one of these trips when I was about 6 or 7 that I saw what I believe to be, my first ***UFO***. As we had no TV at that time, I had no way of knowing about them or what this was that I saw, however, it looked nothing like meteors and shooting stars or even ball lightening. I had seen ball lightening before and that was just totally different!

We were travelling home after dark on a country road in Victoria. It was late and to help me to sleep, I was spread across my parent's laps in the front seat. This was a time before seat belts so no one thought of this as potentially dangerous. From my position, I had an almost uninterrupted view of the sky through the windscreen and the driver side window. That's when I saw it, it looked like a ***Huge Catherine Wheel***, it had no tail but was travelling quite fast in the same direction as we were driving - but I was the only one to see it. It also made a noise like a whooshing sound but no one else heard it. Then for whatever reason, I became very agitated and distressed and maintained that we were going to have an accident. I was almost inconsolable but I eventually gave in to my mother's soothing tones and pure tiredness and so I fell asleep. I don't know how long I was asleep for but I woke up again before getting home. It was then that my mother told me that we did almost have an accident. She explained that we were driving behind a truck carrying a load of pipes. She told me how they came loose and hit the road in front of our car, but for some unknown reason, instead of braking, my father accelerated! The pipes hit the ground in front of the car and bounced over the car without touching it. If he would have braked, the pipes would surely have come though the windscreen ending in a disaster and probably fatality. I have always believed that the *UFO* and the *Near Miss Event* were connected. I can't say for sure that the occupants of the craft helped nor do I know why they might have helped but I have always believed that they did.

Lost in Space

I don't know when we got our first TV but I would have been 9 or 10 when I saw the series *Lost in Space* for the first time and it was like a flood of emotion and recognition and no matter how corny the show may have been - *it felt like home!* From then on, I was hooked on all things science and science fiction. As I grew and matured, I also started to juggle my emerging faith life, spirituality and religious practices with my intensifying understanding of who and what I was and where I was from and I just knew - *I was not and am not, from here!*

Adolescent Years

As time passed, I found more and more that I needed to make a choice and concentrate on what I was going to believe and somehow, make it my own. I can now say that I was fortunate to be **dyslexic**. Why? Because I had trouble reading, I found it too laborious to search for answers to my questions in books and asking teachers and ministers etc. was not always providing satisfactory answers for me! Sometimes they had no answer at all and told me to just have faith! For me, this has always been a totally unsatisfactory response for someone trying to understand! Therefore, I resorted to internalizing the questions and most of the time, the answers came. So right from the start I was being taught by a different method than my peers and yet I was credited as having a deeper knowledge and understanding on matters spiritual and religious than many of my peers. This method of learning also inspired an increasing interest and dedication to the Christian doctrine, even though there were elements of what I was being taught that just didn't seem to fit with what I believed. I also enjoyed speaking to others about their faith or lack thereof and what made them feel so strongly about it and I very quickly realized that irrespective of my own beliefs and sincerity of faith, many others felt equally as strongly and sincerely and often even more so than I did and yet what they believed in many cases was like cheese and chalk when compared to what I had come to believe!

I left school in year 11 at age 16 as my parents had put me through a vocational guidance test and it was determined that I was best suited to the building and construction industry and would go to the top of my field. So, they arranged for an interview and I started almost immediately as a carpenter's apprentice! I don't recall being asked if this is what I wanted but even if I had been asked, I would have answered with what I believed my parents wanted for me out of love and respect for them,

I instantly hated almost every aspect of this job. I hated the dirt and getting my hands dirty I hated the building dust smell, also disliked the rough men who dominated the space around me and who delighted in humiliating me and objectifying me as a possible target of their sexual pleasure! I was being constantly cornered and harassed, so I fought back – not physically but with my work! I am a perfectionist and I was soon respected for the flawless work I produced. In fact, I was still in my first year of apprenticeship when the foreman on the job resigned or rather – quit! Because the company I was working for had no immediate replacement, they left me in charge of the project until a replacement could be found. I was also the only carpenter on the job but managed the task of temporary foreman with the help of the other tradesmen who obviously knew that I couldn't do it alone. Together with their help, the project proceeded without a hitch until eventually a new foreman was employed.

During these adolescent years, there was little that would qualify as out of place or extraordinary except for my total extreme dislike of school and an absence of friends. I can say that throughout my life, the relationships between friends that I saw in others around me held no appeal for me and I had no desire for, nor need for friends and I still don't, I used to say that my ambition was to become a hermit.

So, in a nutshell, between work and church, I was swamped and had little time for anything out of the ordinary. All I had time to do was put my head down and deal with what life presented in the moment.

The ministry years

By now my faith had become Everything to me even with the problems I was having with church dogma! Although I had little time for myself, I still found myself falling in love and getting married in 1978.

As previously mentioned, I also had a personal battle on my hands to justify in my own mind, my pre-life memory! Reincarnation is at odds with church doctrine, which of course states - that you live and die only once. However, I couldn't deny this memory and because reincarnation was not what the church taught, it wouldn't let me rest until I had dealt with it. A struggle I put up with for more years than I care to remember. So, I justified it for myself! I posited that if over time the same spirit possesses several individuals and experiences their lives, then that spirit could replay those lives in any vessel able to receive it. Hence, it could be said that I was experiencing the life of a total stranger who may have lived during a totally different period because we were or are both possessed by the same spirit! Although I would now say something different, at the time this seemed logical to me and so I could slip past the reincarnation doctrine, fit in with church doctrine and legitimately continue to minister as a Christian priest. I must add here that now when I read the Scripture, I can see references to reincarnation which are found in several places and my understanding of what spirit is has changed.

It is worth noting that ministers in our church at the time I was ordained some 40 years ago, did not prepare written sermons. Nor did we prepare notes, the ministers who served during a service were taught to ***let go*** and allow the Spirit to speak through them. So, I also learned to let go and allowed the Spirit of the Father to take over. I have always believed that this was one of the greatest blessings that I could receive, however, it was also the hardest part for me when holding any service – *Letting Go and Letting the Spirit of the Father to take control.* How other ministers experienced this, I don't know. This turned out to be a great blessing, both for the congregation and for myself, as the Spirit didn't just leave me at the end of the service but kept working within me. I have also on occasions stressed that if I had to the hold a service as opposed to the Holy Spirit holding the service – I would have run out of steam many years ago, as **I ALSO** needed to experience the Father's word and blessing, even if I was the one speaking it. This also made perfect sense to me because as a mere human, I could not possibly know the needs of each soul attending that service but of course the Father did and via His Holy Spirit the sermon was given spontaneously in the moment as was needed for each individual soul attending the service! This was borne up time and again as numerous souls would declare that the service was just for them and you would often hear them discussing the service and be amazed how one hadn't heard this, but had heard that and another would say the opposite all while discussing the same service. I was often thanked for the word spoken - as heard by the member thanking me, yet I had no recall that I said what they heard. On one occasion, I freaked myself out during a service as I found my mind wandering or daydreaming, then I realized that I had no memory of what I had just said, where I was in the flow of the sermon or if what I was to say next was even relevant to what had just been said! It concerned me that it may not have made any sense to the listener, so after the service I asked a few individuals including my wife if they thought that anything was strange about the sermon! They all only had praise and that it ALL made perfect sense as they felt the blessings flow. I still have no idea what was said during those missing minutes of daydreaming! For me, even today, the holding of any service was and is an exercise in what I would call *Channeling!* The *Channeling* of information from *the Father's heart and mind* through the *Holy Spirit – the Spirit of Unconditional Love!*

It is first and foremost this connection with my *'Father in Heaven'* or my *'Family in Heaven'* aka my *'Off World Family',* that I attribute the understanding that I have today to, even that which contradicts the doctrine that I grew up with! As I said earlier, as a toddler and young child I had no need in my reality for a *God/Creator figure.* I have always sought the answers to the questions about *WHO I am and WHY am I Here* and it seemed like I was being Drip Fed the answers throughout my life as the understanding became needed.

In 1975 I was ordained into a junior ministry and in 1981 I was ordained into the priest ministry. In 1988 I was charged with the care of the Beverly Hills congregation in Sydney and installed as their Rector. My life was hectic! Not only did I have my normal day job as a carpenter/builder but now I also had a much greater church workload to cope with as I was out with church work every night of the week. This virtually meant that I had no time for anything else in life including my young family. It would be fair to say that I even lost touch with being ME! I also had little to no time to question or ponder anything let alone anything that would contradict the doctrine I was taught and was now also teaching. So, such questions were just put on the backburner and somehow, I knew that they would eventually be dealt with!

My son has told me since that when he was growing up he never really knew me because I was never around. I would be up and gone before the children were getting ready for school. I would come home, have a shower, have dinner and be out again visiting families in the congregation or going to church meetings about this or that. It seemed that every minute of my life was consumed by something, yet I couldn't see it because I had no time to stop and see it or pause and think about it! However, even in the face of what my life had become, I always knew that life and especially intelligent life, was abundant in the cosmos but because of my position in the church, I felt I had to be careful about what I said to others regarding this matter as I have always held the faith of others as something precious to them and not to be disturbed by my beliefs and/or knowledge.

Probably because of our lifestyle, my wife's health deteriorated until and in 1993 we moved from Sydney to Cairns on the advice of doctors who had told my wife that if she didn't move to a more temperate climate she would die. We almost lost her a couple of times in Sydney! I have since come to accept that this was a Divine intervention in my life, I was drowning and this was the lifesaver thrown to me.

So, I left one church posting as a rector in Sydney, to take up another as rector in Cairns. Fortunately, the Cairns congregation was much smaller than the Sydney congregation and I found myself for the first time being able to breathe again with spare time to stop and think. I guess you could say that I was out of the water and now in the lifeboat but not yet safe on dry land.

Time to myself – time to breathe

This new-found freedom brought with it a clarity of mind and I began to see that there were major problems with the way I saw church doctrine. It was New Year's Day 1994 and I was reading a passage in the Bible that I had read 100 times before relating to the focal point of church doctrine when the scales fell from my eyes. What I saw for the first time that day was not what the church taught, although they used this very passage reinforce the doctrine. In brief - I made my superiors aware of what I was seeing and I was told in no uncertain terms to mind my own business as interpreting scripture was commission left to the Apostle ministry. I came very close to telling them where to shove it when I got that response but my relationship with MY Father was worth more to me than that and the souls under my care whom He had given me charge over were precious in my sight and I saw Their faith as precious to Them. So, I obediently pulled my head in and stewed over what I now believed was a major error in church doctrine.

Seven years later, on New Year's Day 2000 there was to be a change in church leadership in Australia. So, in the months prior, I humbly submitted what I could see to my Bishop in whom I trusted. He in turn promised to ask our worldwide church leader, the Chief Apostle, if he got the chance, as the Chief Apostle was to be in Australia presiding over the retirement of the then current District Apostle and the installing the new District Apostle for Australia. During the events of that weekend, the Bishop – my trusted superior and friend, was also ordained into the Apostle ministry. About two weeks into the New Year, my friend – now Apostle, called me to have a chat about my ailing parent's health. As this was not unusual for him. I thought little more about until he said – *Oh, and by the way, the Chief Apostle agrees with you!* It took me a moment or so before the penny dropped! The worldwide church leader over some 9 million souls agrees with me!!! He then said that the Chief Apostle asked me to remain quiet about it until the Chief Apostle had conferred with the Apostle College and it came out in writing as a new doctrinal position on the subject in question.

It was another 3.5 years until this revised doctrinal statement came out and was then expounded upon in seminars for ministers and members. However, that time of waiting became a time of trial and practicing patience for me because during those three and a half years we had many ministerial visits in Cairns by ministers far higher up the ladder than myself and I had to keep my mouth shut as they continued to expound upon a doctrine that I now **knew** was wrong!

It was during the 3.5-year period of waiting for this new doctrinal statement to come out, that both of my parents passed away. My Mother passed away, on the 4th September 2001, exactly one week before 911 and the twin towers event. My Father also passed away exactly 1 year and 3 days later. I can remember therefore that it was sometime in the first half of 2002 that I had my **First, VERY tangible, wake up call.**

First tangible visitation – a Stranger in my bedroom

There's a saying – a builder's house is never finished! To set the scene, the master bedroom of our home was adjacent to the living room where the TV was. The wall between the two rooms was not finished. It had plasterboard sheeting up to 8ft or 2.4m. The ceiling was sloped another meter or so higher and had no sheeting on it. Neither were the joints of what was there, plastered up or finished off, so even with the door closed, there was an abundance of light beaming into the bedroom from the living room.

On the night in question, I had gone to bed early as my work required me to be up at the crack of dawn and I was tired, so I soon fell asleep, while my wife remained in the living room watching TV.

For me that night was about to change and it would prove to be life changing! *I was awoken suddenly by a very loud noise in the room. It was a Sound like Maracas being shaken or the noise of Cold water being splashed on a Red-Hot Iron Plate or also something like*

the Sound of a Rattle Snake's Tail sounding a warning. As I recall, it was a similar sound, when I remembered back to the Catherine wheel UFO event of my early childhood. In any case, I opened my eyes to see a ***tall figure standing beside the bed*** and assumed it was my wife coming to bed, so I said goodnight and rolled over. As cobwebs cleared from my mind I realized ***it wasn't my wife!*** So, I rolled back over and opened my eyes again to see the figure was still standing there silently observing me. In the more than twilight of the bedroom light beaming from the living room, I focused to try and see at least some small details, however, this being appeared as little more than a silhouette as the light from the living room behind it was quite bright. By now I was staring intently, trying to make out who this ***Tall Person*** was who was in my room standing and quietly observing me, I can't say how long I stared for but I can say that I couldn't make out sufficient detail to form any opinion. As I was observing this being, it seemed to dissipate like smoke before my eyes and fade away.

I was now left wide awake pondering the incident. I was puzzled by my apparent lack of fear or even the lack of being startled by the presence of a stranger in my bedroom. In fact, what puzzled me the most was my absolute feeling of peace and contentment I had. Not being able to get back to sleep now, I decided to get up and join my wife watching TV. I didn't inform her of the incident as I didn't want to scare her. It wasn't long after that she decided to go to bed and I was left to ponder even more! I believe that it was probably between 2 and 3 am that I was ready for bed again.

As far as who or what this being was, I have considered that it must have been familiar to me as I was left in an almost blissful state. I have considered many possibilities including one of the hooded visitors from my infancy but the one that keeps rearing its head over the years is – ***was that being my future self*** - coming to somehow guide me towards a desired future? I simply do not know but I guess one day I will find out.

In the following week, I was chatting to my neighbor who was telling me about a **_UFO_** experience she had just had one evening while walking her dog. She said it was a very large, silent **_UFO_** and it was hovering over the end of our estate where we live. She went on to say that she has seen them before adding that she never tells anyone because they would think she was crazy and then added that she couldn't understand why she was telling me! When we compared notes with my experience, we think it may have been the same night as my bedroom visitor.

Second tangible visitation- Fight, Flight or Love

Approximately 2 weeks later I had another visitation but this time the being was much smaller and rather than just observing me, it felt like this smaller being was **_goading and teasing me_** and as I was anxious with this encounter, I was resisting and fighting back! I then heard a voice say, **_'Don't fight it – Love it!'_** A little startled at hearing this voice breaking into my resistance, I then relaxed my demeaner and projected the love that I would have for my parents, my child or a sibling back at it. At this change of heart, **_this little being extended a hand_** which I immediately felt as being feminine as it said - **_come with me._** What followed I have no idea as there seemed that there was no passage of time - the instant I heard and accepted the invitation, putting my hand in her hand, I was awake the next morning feeling like I just had the best sleep of my life with no memory of any passage of time or what may have been experienced during that time.

What followed in life was epiphany after epiphany, yet I was also left confused over what manner of experiences I had with these two beings. So, I began to look around the internet for spiritual, paranormal and UFO forums and it wasn't long before I found that my experience was not unique, even to some of the finer details. However, I wasn't going to go in boots and all over the explanations being given and to this day, the best I feel I can do still is to speculate about these events and wait for further clarification as time passes.

Regarding the epiphanies, they covered a broad spectrum of subjects from religious dogmas and spiritual awakenings to the Cosmology of Humankind on Earth and the Cosmos itself.

Five young people (I call -The Family as in Siblings)

Following my two nocturnal visitors, I also started having regular contact, mostly via *Lucid Dreams* with *5 young people who P believe are not from this world*. They were average size for humans and 4 have always looked like normal humans. The fifth one I have had little to do with, she is also average size and height but has appeared to me in a form which is different. If anything, I feel that this form is more aquatic in nature, but I stress that this is my impression and may not be so. As far as I recall, she has only appeared to me once by herself but she has also been with the others when they have visited me as a group. She did tell me her name but unfortunately, I have forgotten it.

When the five have appeared to me all together, they generally ALL looked human. The nature of their visits seemed to revolve around comfort and reassurance. Sometimes I was being taught various things. One of the females was involved in training me to control my phase shift. I was being tutored in how to phase shift the 3d body so that it was no longer subject to the laws of physics as we know them. These lessons gave me *virtually unlimited seemingly superhuman abilities* some of which were the ability to pass through solid objects, levitate or travel instantaneously to any point in the cosmos! While in her presence, these things were easily accomplished but for now, I must live with the memory of it because to be honest, while I am still stuck in this 3d illusion, any attempts at phase shifting meets with a solid wall of resistance! I guess my *'All Too 3d Human'* nature is still getting in the way.

In the beginning, I would have been content to write them off as merely lucid dreams until one night when I was invited onto their craft and taken for a ride. I woke the next morning with little more than the memory of the invitation and again I can say that I was feeling totally refreshed as seemed to be the norm with these lucid dreams and I thought no more of it until one day later when I found that my skin was shedding as though I had been sunburnt, yet I hadn't been in the sun, there was no sign of burning or sunburn and my skin was peeling everywhere including those places that never saw the sun. This event was a wakeup call for me, there had to be more to this than merely lucid dreams and still, there was more to come!

Mary Rodwell

An internet search provided several possible sources for help but for some reason, I couldn't get past Mary Rodwell. I watched several interviews and videos she was featured in. I watched her documentary film called 'My mum talks to Aliens', so after a little deliberation, I decided to reach out to her. This was around 9 - 10 years back.

Mary is a well-known author and researcher in the field of Ufology and general contact experiences and especially how these experiences are affecting our children as discussed extensively in one of her books titled *'The New Human'*. Mary is also the *Founder and Principal of Australian Close Encounter Resource Network (ACERN)* which was established in 1997 and *Co-founder & Director of The Dr Edgar Mitchell Foundation for Research Into Extra-terrestrial Encounters (FREE).* As previously mentioned, my meeting with Mary was not happenstance but rather I sought her out. However, synchronicity was still to play its part in our meeting because at the time, Mary lived in Western Australia and I lived in Far North Queensland at the opposite end of Australia. It also just happened to be the case that at the time Mary's son lived in Cairns, the same city I live in and Mary just happened to be visiting. So, it was true synchronicity that at this crucial time in my life, Mary and I could connect face to face.

In this first meeting, Mary listened to my story and shared a wealth of knowledge as well as some of the many well documented cases she had of Contactees. Mary did a wonderful job of reassuring me that I wasn't losing the plot! So, I don't remember if she offered or I asked but that day, Mary put me through my first and up to this day, my only regression.

The Regression

For those who have read thus far, you can probably imagine what was going through my mind. I wanted to find out more about this UFO, ET stuff and whether it was real or imagined! Was it demons or angels, or were these really people from other worlds or realities and if so, why would they be contacting me?

Mary first leads me into a state of relaxation where she could help me dig deeper into what was going on. Mary then leads me in to a corridor with doors to the left and right. She then told me that the doors are numbered and that those numbers represented a year of my life. No sooner had she said that and asked what number stands out and I immediately respond with the first number I see – *512!!* My conscious mind was still a little engaged and I am thinking to myself – What has this number got to do with a year of my life? I think I remember Mary hesitating at that moment also. But I am in her hands now and I go with it. She asks me to open the door and step through the threshold. She then asks what am I wearing on my feet? I answer that I can't see my feet, so Mary asks – what am I standing on? I instantly respond, cobblestones! She asks me what I am seeing and as clear as any memory could be, I see that I am in a medieval village market square with people going about their daily business. Now my conscious mind is doing a backflip as I grapple with what I am seeing or remembering with the reason why I am having this regression! Nevertheless, Mary continues to gently guides me through my memory. She asks if I recognize anyone and at first, I said no but as Mary asks if anyone stands out, I comment that a young woman who had her back to me, turned and looked at me as I passed her by. Again, Mary asks if I recognize her and I respond that I don't think so. So, Mary asks me to look at her and look into her eyes*!* At that point, I became overwhelmed with emotion, the tears were flowing torrentially, so much so that Mary has a hard time mopping them up. When she asks the source of the intense emotional response I say that I am not sure whether it is recognition or loss or both. Without going into detail about this memory, it appears that it was a previous life where I was also involved with matters of church and faith, either teaching, believing or both with an *emphasis on spiritual truth rather than religious dogma.* As the memory unfolded*, I saw soldiers on horseback and inquisitors on foot entering the village*. The young woman was taken by them and I never saw her again in that life. I feel that I was killed in a fight – possible a sword through my heart. I was not then, nor am I now a man of aggression, so it stands to reason that that I would be no match for a trained soldier.

There is a footnote to this episode, in January 2017, I was at a conference in Coffs Harbour where Mary was a keynote speaker at the event. On the opening day of the conference, I was sitting at the back of the hall and could hear the almost ethereal tones coming from Tibetan singing bowls at the front, however, I couldn't see who was playing them. The second day I sat closer to the front and this day I could see the lady who was the instrumentalist. Again, the soothing tones certainly settled my heart and set the stage for that day's events.

At morning tea, quite by chance I found myself walking directly behind this lady on the way to the refreshments. Without any hesitation, I tapped her on the shoulder and expressed how I loved her singing bowls. That started a conversation about harmonics and tones, frequency and vibration, during which introductions were made, her name was Anita. During our discussion, she stated that she had to book some time to speak to Mary Rodwell to which I replied that Mary was a friend of mine and that I would be happy to introduce her. She then enquired as to how I knew Mary and I started to recount my first meeting with Mary, why I was there and of course the regression. I was part of the way through recounting my medieval village memory to her when she broke in and started to tell me about a vision she had whilst in deep meditation. I think I had only just mentioned the emotional encounter with young woman of my memory at the time. What she then told me dovetailed perfectly with my medieval memory and in a very real way, ***described through her vision what happened after the inquisitors entered the village.*** It was as though **SHE** was the young woman that had stirred that emotion in me. She described a very similar setting and ***she was in the village market place with two friends when the soldiers and inquisitors came in***. I hadn't arrived at that point in my memory but now Anita was picking up where I left off! Her two so called friends yelled out pointing to her – ***she's one of them, she's a witch!*** She was then arrested and taken for questioning which ***resulted in her torture and death.*** Anita told me that fortunately for her she didn't survive the torture for very long, dying quickly rather than slowly was a blessing. We continued talking until it was time to go to the next session. On the way to the conference room, we happened to see Mary who was sitting at a table. So, we approached Mary and I asked her if she recalled my regression, which of course she did, I then introduced Anita to Mary and left them to talk and without saying anymore and I went to the next session. I don't what they talked about but they spoke for at least two hours. At the end of the conference, I found Mary sitting waiting for someone she had arranged to talk to. I said to Mary that I was downplaying any similarities of Anita's vision and my regression as it was probably a scene that played out many times over the years during the inquisition. Mary just looked at me and shook her head saying – *Jeff, you can't deny the High Strangeness and the similarities between the two stories.*

I was now, not only a Christian minister who was having contact with Off World Beings who were regularly communicating with me and giving me lessons in superhuman abilities, I also had another pre-life memory to add to the one I have had since birth AND I had a possible living witness to a past life event!

To finish off the regression story - yes, during the regression I found out a little more about my Earthly family and my Off-World family. At the end of the regression, Mary asked if there was anything I would like to ask of those who I sensed were around me, so I asked that their presence might become more tangible in my life. Well, surprise, surprise! Following the regression, my Off-World family was to dominate my life for several months to follow in a very tangible way.

My Off-World family comes calling

Over the next several months, it was almost a nightly experience where either through *Very Lucid Dreams* or *Actual Physical Contact, THEY* were in my life. Of these, the physical contact was by far the most prevalent.

Regarding this contact, there was no regular time of the night that seemed to be preferred apart from saying that it would occur between the time I went to bed and rose the next morning. I guess that would be because of my receptiveness or brain wave patterns that would occur during that time. It usually involved either one or two of the females in the group. The third female I only recall appearing to me once by herself, although this may only be because of my fading memory surrounding these visitations.

The first female it seems I am closer too, I believe from the regression that her name is *Indira* or something that sounds similar. The second female is *Elspeth*. I had recalled Elspeth from yet another 'undocumented' lifetime during the 1800's. When I met *Elspeth,* I had the sense that I knew her from my past and at some time I believe she was **Australian Indigenous** however, when I asked, she told me that we knew each other in the late 1800's and at that time she said that she was not indigenous. It seemed to be these two who dominated the tangible nightly visits. By tangible I mean that I was sufficiently awake to be fully aware of what was happening and I had no trouble in the sense of physical touch! This touch was always reassuring and very loving. As far as seeing them face to face - I can only say that even to this day, I am having problems with the phase shifting thing and either I was not quite in sync with their phase or they were out of sync with mine. So, to say I know exactly what they looked like during these visits would be incorrect, I would have to say – fuzzy. *Indira appeared fair skinned and bald* during most of these visits and *Elspeth was more Mediterranean looking had shoulder length short straight black hair*. No problems like that during the lucid dreaming episodes though. During the dream states, *Indira had long straight whitish hair and Elspeth still had short straight black hair.* The third female had a rounded face with a heavy brow line which extended around her head, no hair and only openings for ears. Even though this sounds strange, she was quite beautiful to look at and radiated a happy yet tranquil demeanor. She did tell me her name but it wasn't an easy one to remember. During the dream states, she appeared as a normal human but even then, I had little to do with her. As I recall, it was the female I call Indira who was my trainer in either learning or recalling how to phase shift and do other supernatural things.

The males I have had less to do with, however, the 'lead' male introduced himself to me in a very lucid dream state as *Freyr*. Until then, I had NEVER heard that name but it was clear as crystal. It was my daughter who enlightened me as to who *Freyr* might be and the relationship with *Norse mythology* which I knew nothing about! I also have no problems in describing him as he presented himself to me in complete clarity. He is of Average height, (I am 185cm tall so I guess for me that is average height), slightly chiseled but still soft features. Short dark curly hair, Mediterranean complexion and wearing a blue jumpsuit. *Freyr* introduced me to many souls of many origins and types. Most were from somewhere else other than HERE! He then showed me a *wall that looked like it was formed from flowing crystal.* Out of this wall came humanoid shaped beings who looked like they were made from the same substance as this flowing crystal wall! When I asked him who they were, he responded that they were the *'Reprogrammers'.* I have my opinion but I don't know for certain what that meant.

The second male is also Mediterranean in appearance but with slightly longer straight black hair and his name is Dureck, we debated the pronunciation of this name – I thought he meant Dereck but he insisted that it was Dureck with the emphasis on the last syllable 'reck'! I would have to say that if we are talking about Norse looking ET's, these two didn't fit the modern-day picture. The only one who really did was Indira as even Elspeth has more of an olive complexion and the third female looked humanoid rather than human.

As mentioned, these intense visits lasted for several months and were almost nightly. It got to a point where I was just physically exhausted so one night I simply asked if I could have a break to get some much-needed rest! It seems that I am still on the break as they have mostly left me alone since then.

Other Encounters

I also recall one visitation from a small Grey who was just observing me, and one from a small but bulky little fellow with a large flat-topped head. He had a deeply furrowed forehead and wide flattish nose and wide thin lips. He was about 60cms or 2-foot-tall and it seemed that his head was in width almost half his height. I cannot say for sure but I sensed that he had something to do with genetic harvesting. This is more of an impression than a matter of fact.

Off-World genetic family

It seems that I also have some genetic offspring who I first met on board a craft. This first encounter was via a very lucid dream. I found myself on board some form of vessel that I assume is at least interstellar and possibly interdimensional. However, as the vessel was not the focus of this encounter, I can say only that it looked and felt very organic and alive. No light source was apparent but everything was bathed in light and there were no sharp corners as everything looked free flowing in form and everything was white. My attention was very quickly diverted as I heard a young female voice call out – look mummy it's daddy. The voice belonged to one of three, apparently adolescent, young girls, all having straight almost whitish long hair with pale skin and wearing free flowing white robes. Mummy was also wearing a similar robe but hers was adorned with a metallic patterned trim. Her hair was also whitish but it was shoulder length and wavy rather than straight. She looked like she was in her late 20s or early 30s but that is just going by looks, I have no idea if they even count age like we do or whether their incarnation is ageless. There was a second encounter with my daughters was in January 2020 on the first day of the Cosmic Consciousness Conference held at Uluru in Australia. This occurred after arriving and as I was settling into my room. As I was tired from the travel, I laid on the bed and almost immediately experienced the tingling or buzzing throughout my body followed by their presence as they in turn seem to hug me. However, for whatever reason, this time I seemed to be slightly out of phase with them. Although I could feel their touch and touch them in return, I couldn't see them clearly. However, I knew they were my daughters from the dream encounter because of their nature and presence. It was familiar, loving and it also felt different to the encounters I had with Indira and Elspeth.

Scout party

I have also encountered tall human like travelers. They all would have averaged close to 7 foot tall and more.

This encounter occurred one evening when I had just gone to bed and I hardly had time to get comfortable when the tell-tale buzzing throughout my body started as was usually the case when a visitation was about to happen. I put this buzzing or tingling down to a phase shift that I experience that puts me in sync or close to in sync with the visitors. At the same time, I felt movement on the bed which caused me to open my eyes. The home where I was staying at the time had a cat and although it was not common place, occasionally this cat would pay me a visit but this time it wasn't the cat. This time it was two attractive females probably between my height of 185cm and up to 2m tall. One was dark haired and the other light haired. They did introduce themselves to me, however by morning I had forgotten their names. After the short intro, they physically rolled me over and put something in my back. When I protested, they said that I needed it and as it turned out, they took aboard their craft to meet their leader or captain. Whatever it was that they put into me was so that this meeting could take place.

As a point of interest, I told my son the next day what I had experienced, as we worked together, and asked him to look at my back, and sure enough, there was a fresh wound and small scab exactly where I felt them putting something in. I have no idea if it is still there or not.

The captain - (my words), advised me that they were part of an advanced scout group for their people. They were looking for a habitable planet as their own could no longer sustain them. The group's total population was only about 3 million. In any case, they were to report their findings back to the group's leader. There was the consideration that an indigenous population may have to be purged for them to take residence. I explained that such a move would not be necessary here as their group was relatively small and with their advanced technology they could easily transform some of the vast areas that we would consider uninhabitable and live quite comfortable alongside the human population and integrate with the Earth population over time. This idea was well received by this captain and he would then pass it on to his superiors. I have not heard from them since. It is interesting to note that I recall Dureck from my family group being by my side during this on-board encounter.

When reading the following, please understand that these are impressions that I am left with because of interaction with otherworldly beings in my reality. Whether they are correct or not, they remain, my impressions.

The God problem

Apart from what I have already said about not needing the presence of a God Being in my early years and pondering the God that we are taught about or even as it may be considered across the broad spectrum of religious teachings today, I have always felt that the teaching about the Almighty God, Creator of Heaven and Earth and

ALL that is – somehow for me just didn't add up! For me there was a niggling concern but I was told to believe what I was being taught without question! Ok, so as a junior individual who was trying to put the puzzle of life together, I had to deal with it. I also had to contend with - you MUST have faith! Somehow this approach to understanding what was going on and how things are or are supposed to be, just didn't cut the mustard! While I still consider myself a man of faith, I see that faith has many levels and the one that I just refuse to accept is that Faith is Blind, you don't have to understand - just believe! It may be that way for some but for me it has always been my belief that faith comes about because of experience. To cite an example – trapeze artists must have faith to do what they do because at some time during their performance the flyer must *let go* and the catcher has to be there to catch. No matter how well rehearsed they are though, the flyer makes a *leap of faith* each time they let go of the bar. Yet this leap of faith can't be described as 'Blind' because it is so well rehearsed! It's a faith which is based in and on experience.

With apologies to people of faith around the globe, my understanding is that a blind faith is foolishness! Why? Because it requires that one rejects one's own personal experiences and inner knowledge and instead, adopt or believe in an external teaching – in other words, somebody else's experiences and beliefs!! So - believe what we tell you to believe above everything else, including your own experience – Or Else! Yes, there always seems to be attached to this form of teaching the *'Or Else'!*

Back to the question of God. As already mentioned, I have had a problem with this subject virtually my whole life and when you consider that the greater part of my life has been as an ordained priest, surely this would make most go - hmmmmmm!? As usual, this was something that I had to deal with from the inside out and I only realized in retrospect that I had the answer all along but because it was covered by layer upon layer of dogma and I had lost sight of it!

Daddy, what does God look like?

Around 30 years ago, my 4-year-old son asked me – daddy, what does God look like? The response from my own lips almost startled me as did the few words that followed. I responded - Diddy, (his nickname), what does love look like? As quick as a flash he answered – Cuddles and Kisses! I then responded, well Diddy, that's what God looks like and this answer totally satisfied him! I have since pondered that answer over the years more times than I could count and yet now I found myself again struggling with the question - Is there REALLY an eternal God?

All Things are Eternal and All Things are Eternally Changing.

There are certain religious terms and phrases that are common place in our current paradigm, such as Eternal Spirit, entering Eternity in Heaven, to be with God for ALL Eternity and probably many other clichéd expressions but then there is the Eternal and Immortal Soul! I have heard this expression my whole life but then recently, within the last ten years, somehow the penny just dropped! All this talk and teaching about eternity - but wait a minute – is Eternity a REAL thing? With every fibre of my being I am compelled to answer absolutely - YES! Why am I so sure of this? Because *I AM! I always have been and always will be I AM!* The mere fact that I find myself pondering eternity answers the question for me, Eternity is the only thing that Really makes sense! You may say that **as finite as each moment is, so it is also infinite!** One of my favorite memes that I have coined because of my ponderings is – *Measure me a moment and I will show you Eternity!* These statements mirror the concept of the eternal NOW! Consider this, you cannot enter eternity! Why? Because that would imply an entry point and a starting point and that flies in the face of the definition of eternity as eternity can have no beginning! That then leaves me to understand that *we are already IN eternity!* That one little piece of the puzzle started a snowball rolling which rolled into avalanche of epiphanies! I AM an Eternal Soul! We ALL are Eternal Souls! But aren't we are told that we are created! If I AM created, then I have a beginning and if I have a beginning, then I must have an end and therefore I cannot ever be – Eternal! If this is the case, I can forget going or being anywhere for Eternity let alone in Heaven with God!

So, what about the Creation and/or the Big Bang? I understand that something probably happened sometime in the past, possibly even 14 billion years ago, but it was not the sudden creation of everything out of nothing! Rather it was more likely a point in time where a change of state occurred. A change of state of something into something else and because it remains beyond our ability to fully comprehend, we say it was the 'Beginning'! Of course, this is no great revelation today as many physicists already seriously consider this line of thinking. Unfortunately, most religions don't! However, even in Genesis God gives the instruction to the first humans to **Replenish the Earth! Gen 1:28** Then in Revelations it speaks of a New Heaven and a New Earth! So, this begs the question – has this happened before and if so, how many times has it happened and how many more times will it happen? To add a little more spice to the pot, bear with me as I give yet another bible quote, this time from King Solomon. *That which is has already been, and what is to be has already been; Eccl. 3:15* So even millennia ago it was understood that everything was cyclical. While many physicists may be on the right track, it appears that many theologians may be blind to the very scriptures they study!

The Immortal Eternal Soul

Let's entertain for a moment the thought that we as souls, not the physical body – aren't created but rather are eternal in nature. We hear the expression – Immortal Soul often enough. If we can get our heads around this thought, ***then if we are ALL eternal, so then we must also ALL be EQUAL!*** So, we start seeing a REAL God problem here. ***If*** *we are all eternal, are we also equal to God?*   In attempting to answer this question, let me once more quote from the bible. Just prior to Jesus being captured He went away from His disciples to pray. Who recorded His prayer we don't know! However, in one part He was recorded to pray - *that they all may be one, as You, Father, are in Me, and I in You; that they also may be one in Us. John 17:21.* This would not be possible unless equality is possible and He wouldn't have prayed it.

This then brings us to ask – if God is real, who or what IS God? Just as important is the question – who or what are we, especially in the face of who and what God may be! Over the years, I guarantee that I have done a great deal of soul searching regarding this question. Remember, as a toddler I had no need for a God figure in my existence. The subject of a God only came with indoctrination and for a large period in my life I had forgotten my childhood understanding as it was covered up by layers of dogma.

Where am I today with this question? I can say without hesitation that I absolutely do believe in God, however, what I believe God to be and what others belief God to be are probably quite different. I believe that my divergent understanding on this subject probably goes back over many lifetimes! Following the intensive indoctrination into the Christian dogma, for some reason, it took me years to link the episode where my son told me that God looks like cuddles and kisses, to the time the penny dropped! For me now, God is not a Being, just as Cuddles and Kisses are not a being but Cuddles and Kisses do paint a picture! I now consider that for me at least, *God is the Spirit of Unconditional Love aka the Holy Spirit!* My understanding is that spirit is an energy sparked by an impulse that goes out from its source and has an effect, Spirit is not a Being, however, it may be the energy that brings purpose to a Being, just as the Being will bring purpose to the Spirit! In the case of God or the Holy Spirit, this force or energy may also be called Grace. So many will tell you that Grace is underserved love and to be honest, very few, if any of us, feel deserving of it, however, Grace is not undeserved love, grace is Unconditional Love as it truly has no interest in whether we deserve it or not! It simply radiates as a light that is unstoppable. Some will embrace it and some will shun it but it radiates and shines just the same either way!

*Note: What is written about Jesus shows us how He was continually referring to **His Father** and taught that **His Father is Our Father too**. He Rarely referred to God and when speaking to the woman at the well He states that God is Spirit! Having often pondered the equality of Souls and Spiritual Hierarchy etcetera, I suggest that when He was referring **to His Father or Our Father**, possibly a more accurate, yet unspoken description of what Jesus was referring to may be **His Family or Our Family**. In this case, it would be a **Family of Spiritual Equals** to whom He prayed and out of which He was sent to Earth. A family to which we also belong! We, however, seem to have been corrupted by some past event, whether it was by our own doing or the interference by others is not perfectly clear. Whichever may be the case, this event or interference has kept us separated from Our Family! I believe that Jesus mission was to restore us to our original state of spiritual equality with Our Family of Love. For us, this would equate to going Home/Heaven! Hence, the Father of Jesus or Our Father, I believe is not synonymous with the term or concept of God!*

Existence – hopefully most will agree that WE or the self-proclamation – I AM, is a statement of existence and that WE exist! However, I believe that this existence is Non-Local, by that I mean that we exist not only within the space - time continuum, but also beyond it simultaneously.

I can't say much about what is outside the space - time continuum but within the dimensions where the space - time continuum operates, the operating system by which these dimensions' function may be summed up by the words Nikola Tesla when he said, "If you want to find the secrets of the universe, think in terms of energy, frequency and vibration." Notice he stated three things – **energy, frequency** and **vibration.** Energy is a latent force that can give rise to Frequency and Vibration. Without energy, frequency and vibration don't exist but energy requires an applied impulse to bring about a desired outcome. This reminds me of the words found in the bible at the beginning of the Gospel of John - **"In the beginning was the Word, and the Word was with God, and the Word was God."** A 'Word', still requires an impulse to generate it. I would like here to draw your attention to the two main subjects found respectively in this statement, First – the **'WORD'** and second **'GOD'.** This statement in the Gospel of John tells us that the Word and God are the same. To understand this statement from the perspective of someone like Nikola Tesla, you may replace the word **'WORD'** with **'Energy'.** By default, you are then also replacing the word **'GOD'** with **'Energy'.** So, you would end up with a statement as such – in the beginning was the **Energy** and the **Energy** was with **God** and the **Energy** was **God!** The text goes on to tell us that All things are made by it! Now, as we understand it, what are All things in the known cosmos made of? They are made of energy, frequency and vibration! So, WHAT is the **Energy** that was in the beginning *by which all things are made?* To answer this, we look to the bible again and again to John but this time one of John's epistles or letters. *1John 4:16 God is love, and he who abides in love abides in God, and God in him.* Now let's go back to the opening statement of the gospel of John and read it accordingly - *"In the beginning was the Energy of Love, and the Energy of Love was with God, and the Energy of Love was God."* I won't say that this is precisely what it means but I will say that this is how I understand it. Can we imagine how the world would change if it was *One Nation under Love*, or *In Love We Trust?* We may certainly defend in the name of Love but how many wars would be started in the name of Love?   Or how the meaning of the statement changes from –

My God is bigger, better and stronger than Your God *to* **My Love is bigger, better and stronger than Your Love**!

If this concept could be grasped and adopted by every culture, race and creed globally, then the world could once again **become Paradise on Earth** just as it was meant to be in the beginning when it was established by the Spirit and Energy of Love! Virtually everything in the known cosmos conforms to the 'Energy, Frequency and Vibration' principle and may also be considered as Ebb and Flow! Depending which side of the equation you find yourself on, you may consider it either a good thing or a bad thing. Take the ocean as an example - is the incoming wave good or bad? Is the outgoing wave good or bad? If a designation of 'Good' or 'Bad' is to be applied at all, I suggest that it will be decided per the observer's perspective!

What is one man's meat, is another man's poison!

Unlike energy though, an Impulse cannot be latent! Once triggered, it can't just sit around waiting for something to happen. Neither can it act alone – it requires a driver and that driver we may refer to as a Being or a Soul. A Soul has Will or Choice but requires a desire to pull the trigger and initiate an impulse. The desire is usually in the form of a reaction to an external stimulus. We may well ask then – What is the desire, trigger and impulse that gives rise to the waves of the ocean or any number of other natural phenomena that may be found throughout the Cosmos and is there a Soul in the driver's seat? I suggest the answer to that question resides outside that realms of space-time continuum!

It also said, *as above, so below*, therefore, where an individual Soul is concerned, they will, to a large extent, be responsible for creating their own individual realty by the exertion of their will in response to the circumstances of the moment they pass through. Energy also requires a medium through which it must travel whereby it can fulfil its purpose to create space-time by modulating frequency and vibration and that medium must be existent and cross the boundary that separates the realms of space-time from **beyond** the realms of space-time! I suggest that this medium is what we call **Consciousness**.

Consciousness is the Omni dimensional fabric existing within all aspects of the space-time continuum and beyond. It is also the field through which Information and knowledge flow. Information and knowledge are also infinite latent potentials existing across all aspects of space-time and beyond. These would also require an impulse to become activated. This impulse is triggered and sent through the field by us when we react to the moment we pass through, seek to learn new information and understanding it or even imagining a potential future, either good or bad, etc. Our personal understanding of this information - **(Knowledge)** and experience, then shapes or creates our **Individual Reality** generating it by frequency and vibration. A collective consensus of reality can thus be formed and experienced as the collective are generating vibrational frequencies which then create interference patterns. This interference pattern will be considered as either harmonic or discordant. Hence individuals experiencing a harmonic resonance will flock together while those experiencing the discordant will distance themselves from one another! Either way, a reality will be experienced both by the collective and by the individual within the collective. If we then conclude that consciousness is the fabric through which information travels, then where or what is the repository into which information is received and stored as knowledge by the individual? Some will say that it is the conscious brain that stores the information while others will say that it is stored by the conscious mind. I believe that all would agree that the brain is physical but what about the mind? Is it merely a function of the brain with its electrical impulses and chemical reactions or is the mind outside of this physical dimension as we understand it?

My answer to this question came around 10 years ago, when I was working on a friend's house on New Year's Eve. The work I was doing required me to be working on the roof. When I was finished, I proceeded to the ladder to climb back down. The moment I put my foot on the first rung, I heard a voice in my head say – it's going to slip! The very next thing I remember was looking at my body on the deck from above. I had no memory of the ladder slipping, the fall or hitting the deck but I knew where I was and I knew what day it was and everything felt totally normal except that I wasn't in my body and thought that it was strange that I had lost a shoe in the fall. I also saw my friends running to my aid. Fortunately, there was no serious damage apart from a broken rib. In any case, I decided not to say anything about what I had seen because I could very well have been hallucinating. I'm not sure how many hours I was in hospital being checked out but it felt like 10 – 20 minutes! During the next week, my friends paid me a visit at home to see how I was. Of course, the subject of the conversation was about the accident! It was then that one of them said that they couldn't understand how I lost a shoe in the fall. Up until then I had not mentioned what I had seen from above to anyone and now my friends were confirming what I had seen from outside of my body and that I really HAD seen it!

Until that time I would have said that I believe that I am not my body but now I can say with absolute conviction that I KNOW that I am not my body! So, when asking the question – Where is the repository where this information is being stored, therefore, I can say from my personal experience without hesitation or doubt that it resides outside the ***Brain and Body*** and rather in the ***Mind and Soul!*** I believe that **Higher Self - Soul or Being** exists beyond the space-time continuum and here it knows all things. The **Soul or Being** within the space-time continuum is merely a partial extension of the Higher Self or Soul, yet it remains connected to the Higher Soul via the Field of Consciousness, the same Field of Consciousness which connects or interfaces Soul and Body. As such, within the space-time continuum it is constrained and limited to its experiences here. When asking why this may be the case, consider it as a handicap to make the experience interesting.

As the Body has the Brain - so the Soul or Being has the Mind.

Body and Soul, although interfacing, exist across two separate dimensions respectively within the space-time continuum yet remain interfaced across those dimensions while the Soul continues to provide the impulse or the will to do so! In this scenario, the Soul is in the driver's seat and drives the vehicle we call the Body. Therefore, I believe that it is the mind which interfaces with the brain to experience this dimension of physical or virtual reality. The accident I had, provided me with an invaluable experience whereby I now believe that it is the Being and not the Body where this information is stored as knowledge. Hence, there is a continual flow of information back and forward between the Soul and the Body via the interface between the Mind and the Brain with the Field of Consciousness being the medium which carries that information.

Q & A

It's my intention to present the following not as factual absolutes but rather as points for the reader's consideration.

Q – Who or What is God?
A - As the concept of who or what God is or isn't depends greatly on the cultural and religious background of the one asking the question, there may not be a satisfactory one size fits all answer. In simple terms, I suggest that God is Spiritual Energy as mentioned previously. I would further suggest that God – this Spiritual Energy, denotes the spiritual

DNA or bloodline that identifies Jesus, His Father and the family of *'GOD' or Family of Unconditional Love!*

Q – Who is the family of God?

A – All those souls in whom the Spirit of Love dwells as defining their Whole nature – *1 John 4:16 God is love, and he who abides in love abides in God, and God in him.* **The Family Tree is therefore known by its fruits!**

Q - Why isn't there just one universally accepted, definitive answer that tells the truth as to who or what God is?

A - The short answer is that today there are too many competing philosophies on the subject for ONE universally accepted definition of God. The current world view of God, irrespective whether one is a believer, is relatively new, as it was influenced by the emergence of the great **Greek philosophers - Plato, Aristotle, Socrates and the like**, who lived around 400BCE. For them, such questions were worthy of consideration and debate to challenge the accepted paradigm. Prior to this time, most cultures were polytheistic believing in and worshipping many of gods, Abraham came from such a culture and these gods were obviously known also to Moses as the very first commandment is a warning by the Abrahamic God to worship no other gods but Him! A polytheistic belief system was the religion of the day for the Greek philosophers and humankind had a well-entrenched **ruling hierarchy** a model that had been passed down from the **Lords** and **Overlords** - *those claiming direct contact with the gods* – the priestly order who had been delegating power and ruling since the beginning of known history - and it worked well - *for the ruling elite!* Exactly when the Abrahamic religions became Monotheistic is unclear as their history and doctrine was handed down by word of mouth for many generations prior to it being put into writing. Before the time of these philosophers, the concept was more of a physical person who was considered superior – a **God, Lord, Overlord, Overseer** etc.! These **Lords** were assigned orders of superiority or rank depending on their duties and numbers of devoted followers and hence a hierarchy was formed from the outset with the most powerful being at the top. The terms **god**, **the gods** and **God** were superimposed over the terms **lord, overlord. overseer** etc. to deify these physical lords or officials. An example of this would be the Egyptian Pharaohs who were considered as *living gods* but were nevertheless still physical beings! The most powerful Being was designated as **Supreme God, the Almighty, Creator** etc. etc. by those passing the oral story down as per the definitions current at the time of the storyteller or scribe's life. Hence there was a continual battle to be owned and loved by the **greatest god**. There was and still is a continual wrangling amongst these **lords** and **overlords** to be the greatest and hence most powerful. A *'My God is bigger, better and stronger than Your God'* and *'you'll suffer the consequences for not believing in Him'* mentality was the order of the day and still is prevalent today and is encouraged these by these 'lords' as they continue to battle for top place in the hearts of men. *A possible source for all of humankind's wars.* Following the great philosophers and the spreading of their developing creed, the stakes just became larger and the term **God** became **hijacked.** It then became a battle of whose god was God over the greater reality until it became *'the Omniscient, Omnipresent, Omnipotent, Almighty God and Creator of ALL that is',* or as some of our modern-day belief systems claim – *'the Eternal Source of ALL That IS!'*.

Q - Does an Almighty God and Creator of ALL that is - exist?
A - As defining a single *'Being'* – no! However, the term *'Spirit'* does come close as *'Spirit'* underlies everything and may be considered as the *'Energy or Source of Change'* or what many would call *'Creation'!* Here the basic conceptual problem of the saying the *'Eternal Source of All Things'* is more correctly understood as *'Eternal Source of All Change!'* By changing that one word the concept falls completely in line with the statement – *'ALL Things are Eternal and Eternally Changing.'* Even so, *'Spirit'* still requires the impulse triggered by a *'Being'* for its potential to be realised.

Q - What is a difference between a Being and a Spirit?

A –The term *'Being'* is also an interchangeable term for *'Soul.'* A *'Soul'* is eternal and a *'Soul is Eternally Being!'* Hence the term *'Being!'* Therefore, only a *'Soul or Being'* can make the statement – *'I AM!'* *'I always have been and always will be I AM!'* A *'Spirit'* is not a *'Being!'* A *'spirit'* is an energy and as such, *'spirit rides upon the field of consciousness to fulfil its purpose.'* However, of itself *'spirit'* has **no will** and remains merely a latent potential until a *'Being'* consciously engages it and applies to it willpower or an impulse. In other words, it requires a *'Being'* to be engaged with a *'Spirit'* for a spirit's energy potential to be realized. This is like electricity remaining latent in an electrical conductor until a load is applied and the electricity then flows and works to meet the load's requirements. Using a household appliance or even a light as an example, an active human input is usually required to provide the impulse for switching the light or appliance on or off. In doing so, this acted upon impulse provides the previously latent electricity the freedom to flow, meet the load's requirements and the desired result is achieved.

Q - If the Soul or Being has choice, is it then inherently either good or evil?

A - The Soul or Being is mostly reactive and is free to choose. It may also initiate a purpose with an intent that may be good or evil. It may also merely be responding to an experience. Whatever the case, there is an impulse that is triggered by the Soul or Being setting in motion that which is then to be experienced. It then may be perceived by others to be either good or evil irrespective of the original intent.

Q - Does a Soul or Being ever die or cease to exist?

A – No, a body may die but even then, death is simply a change in the state of being for that body! Death is usually associated with the loss of bodily life but this is rather a perspective experienced by those who are left behind. The one who is deemed to have died has only had a change in the state of their 'being or existence' and goes on to inhabit a new body suitable for the dimension or realm that they find themselves in! For that one, life goes on because **Life is the essence of eternal existence**. Life is Eternal and hence also Immortal as it cannot cease to exist.

Look at this from the perspective of our own current human incarnation. We consider ourselves to be a Human Being, when in fact, we are Souls incarnates as being a Human. When we leave this realm, we are only a phase shift away. However, depending on our spirituality at the time of our crossing, we may be subject to decisions made while still in the flesh, we may have various options as to what our immediate future may be or we may be stuck here and yet not here at the same time - just slightly out of phase with the reality we have just left because we can't fully let go for whatever reason.

The following are examples of possible options –

- We may go on to be reincarnated here many times – but don't think that this is a given or that it must be a future reincarnation! It may seem to be a future experience, however, it may in fact be anytime, it may even be in a past time-period where the history of this world is concerned! Why might this be the case? Maybe we just decide to go back to experience something that we missed on our eternal journey of discovery.

- Also, bear in mind that the Earth has not always existed in its current form and will not remain in this form forever either! So, we may jump to one of its past forms or future forms and such a choice will be ours.

We may incarnate anywhere within the Cosmos either in this dimension or another. The choice of 'Body' applicable for our continuing adventure is also our choice and what memories we retain where we are going will also be our choice.

- We may be on a mission and so we may incarnate here many times until it is complete or we may come back here in the body of an Ascended Master to continue here with whatever our mission is.
  What is possible? Basically, if you can imagine it – then it's possible!

Q - What can be said about the Body?

A - According the rules set at the outset of the adventure we are on, our body will either be drawn from the substance of the world into which we incarnate, or depending on the level of our developed spirituality within the continuum we find ourselves experiencing, it may be designed and set by us. An example of this would be the body of an Ascended Master which does not need to conform to the laws of physics of the world or even universe into which it incarnates.

Whatever and wherever our journey takes us, it will ultimately be at our direction and choice, although at times it may appear to be otherwise! Also, whatever experiences we have will remain ours always until WE decide it's enough or we have reached the end of our adventure!

Q - What happens after that?

A - Remember WE are Eternal and Eternally changing! So are also the adventures that we choose to take! When we finish one adventure with its potentially countless experiences and incarnations, the game is then reset or reprogramed for us to continue to experience and learn new things. Eternity has no beginning nor end and across Eternity the possibilities for new experiences are Infinite.

Q - Isn't there a limit to knowledge and experience?

A – There is a *Jigsaw Puzzle* that repeats itself forever. This may be considered as a *Fractal or Periodic Pattern*. Then there is also the

Infinity Pattern, an Aperiodic Pattern that never repeats itself – there are no repeating or fractals here. What is interesting about this is that it can be accomplished with as few as 2 shapes or tiles with a patterned surface which can be arranged in an infinite number of ways where the pattern never repeats! And yes, here in this incarnation that exists. We may choose to play with either of these and while the *Jigsaw Puzzle* with its fractals we may find at first interesting, eventually it will become frustrating because it only repeats. The *Infinity Pattern,* however, we'll find a source of eternal fascination if our attention span could last that long because in never repeats! Ask this - how many Galaxies make up the Universe? How many Universes make up the Omniverse and how many atoms make up the Omniverse? When we understand that the answers are Infinity and beyond for each of these, then we will also know and understand that both Knowledge and Experience are also beyond Infinity!

Q – Are there any bad or evil Off World, Inner World or other ET or Alien Beings?
A – It would be foolish to believe or think that there are no malevolent Otherworldly Beings. Remember though that they are also on an eternal journey of adventure and although they may be considered either good or evil now, at some stage during their journey they will also be considered the opposite! The same would apply to ALL of us.

Musings

Individual Consciousness = active connection to the fabric of consciousness drawing upon information.
Subconscious = deeper levels knowledge or memory that may not be clear until drawn upon. It may also be responsible for the body or vessel working on auto pilot.
Unconscious = temporary interface disconnection between mind and brain. While Mind may be sending, Brain will be switched off and unable to receive. In some cases, mind may be able to transmit missed

data once the interface is restored. e.g. an OOB experience being recalled in retrospect.

Only a truly enlightened soul will embrace the darkness within and own it. To be able to perceive the nature of Unconditional Love is to know the path to Enlightenment. To be able to fully comprehend the nature of Unconditional Love is Enlightenment. Being able to feel and experience the Loving embrace of Unconditional Love is to feel the drawing power of Ascension and to fully become Unconditional Love is to have Ascended! Such a soul will not see the works of darkness in others and seek to destroy them because of it. Rather such a soul will embrace with Unconditional Love the soul enveloped in darkness until the darkness is consumed by the light and the soul that was in bondage has been freed. Where the soul goes, the body will follow!
To reach beyond our limits and explore with excitement the dimensions which until now still lay beyond our imagination, is the nature of the soul and to do it in the Spirit of Unconditional Love is our purpose!

To SEE beyond seeing, to HEAR beyond hearing, to FEEL beyond feeling, to KNOW beyond knowing and to LOVE beyond loving – Is to BE beyond being and BE – **ALL THAT I AM!**

As Finite as each Moment is - so it is also Infinite! *There is NO 'Final Frontier'!*

Jeff Schulte

How my NDE at 5 Years Old lead to a lifetime of Contact Experiences with Non-Human Intelligence via the Contact Modalities and to my belief that Consciousness is Primary

Donald Christian

My name is Donald Christian and I am a retired United States Air Force Veteran. I am a father and a brother. I am a published author and public speaker. I am also an Empath. I was hit by a car at the age of 5 and had a brief NDE/OBE. I returned unhurt. This accident turned out to be the beginning of a life filled with Contact Modalities involving NHI, including several NDE's and OBE's, Conscious Astral Travel, Energy Healing, Lucid Dreaming, and Hallucinogenic and Meditative Journeys. I was a United States Air Force Crew Chief who served in Europe at Bitburg AB, a strategic NATO Air Base in Western Germany in the mid 1970's. My pilots were flying in support of other NATO countries who were dealing with interventions by UFOs into controlled airspaces over their countries, and their sensitive military bases. This was also when one of the best documented cases of contact with NHI was occurring in Switzerland with Eduard "Billy" Meier's, among others.

There was a point in my life where I realized that I was a Contact Experiencer. It was when the large number of unexplained events and high strangeness experiences over my lifetime brought me to the point that explained the path I have walked in life. Being told to be in the right place at the right time. Meeting the right people at the right time. I began to add up the number of times I should have been seriously hurt or should have died. This all brought me to the moment my spiritual circuits opening to Critical Thinking and Self-Awareness. Coming to the realization that a Higher Consciousness, a NHI that has been interacting with human consciousness for millennia, was interacting with me.

I am doing this for several reasons. My son knows nothing of my early life, before I was his father. My brother and sister know nothing of my life experiences. I recently suffered a catastrophic house fire that took most everything. I'm getting older and want to get this information out now. The current Government Reports on UFO/UAP contact is disinformation. I am a USAF Veteran who served in Europe at a NATO

Air Base and was a Crew Chief on the F-4E. I heard stories from my pilots about what they were seeing over the skies of Europe. Many other people are having the same or similar experiences and seek information. This is my story of contact with Non-Human Intelligence, and my path to Higher Consciousness.

It started for me at the age of 5.

1962 - My first NDE took place when I was 5 years old.

I grew up in a suburban neighborhood, with several local shops and markets nearby. One afternoon, I had walked (really, I had slipped out of my house without telling my mom) to the local market around the corner near my house. It was 2-3 long blocks away. I had to cross a 4-lane busy road at a RR crossing. I made it across fine and went into the Centro Mart. I loaded up my pockets with Brach's candy and walked out. I again crossed the 4-lane road and was eating the candy and walking back home to dinner. By now it was around dinnertime. I had eaten all the candy I had stolen, and I turned back to (what else?) go get more. As I attempted to re-cross the 4-lane road at the intersection, a car struck me. I do not remember this. I was carried (thrown?) to the center of an intersection. It was and is a miracle I was not killed. When I came to, after several minutes or so, a crowd of people eating burgers surrounded me. I believe the hamburger place was called "The 3 Little Pigs" (now Michael's Pizza.)

I remember hearing the approaching ambulance sirens as I came to, and I was scared. I tried to get up and go home. I knew my dad would be mad. Anyway, I was taken to County Hospital and had virtually NO INJURIES! I remember the ambulance ride and being in an exam room. I remember being shy about taking off my clothes for the female nurse. I can remember my family coming to get me. My Father was mad! How do you punish a 5-year-old when he's lucky to be alive? I remember my dad coming in angry. I remember leaving by the front door of the hospital, and my dad stripping off my sling and hanging it on the big front door post on the main entry stairs. He was steamed. When we got home dad made me eat toast and warm milk. Yuk! A photo taken a month later shows me in a ride at Mickey's Grove Park, with a bandage on my right elbow. I now look upon this event as the start of my journey to Self-Awareness and Critical Thinking, and a lifetime of interaction with various Contact Modalities.

After my accident, I began to have a series of 5 recurring dreams that occurred over and over.

Same dreams, same locations, same series of events in the dreams. These dreams happened in a period from age 5 to age 15. They ended after that, and I never had them again. As I grew up, I often wondered about those dreams. They seemed so real. What was the meaning? Over the years, as my Self-Awareness and Critical Thinking skills developed, and I had more NHI Contact Modalities, I began to dive into the dreams and seek answers to my internal questions.

These are my 5 dreams and the meaning behind them, as best I've been able to understand. These dreams are life events that have happened to me later in life, that I dreamed about over and over as a child. I was a deep dreamer and had many vivid dreams. I have good dream recall, and I kept my dream journal next to the bed for 6 years. It was very helpful as I continued to grow in awareness. Dream recall is hard, as you have but a few seconds upon waking to grab a pen and jot down a few thoughts before they are gone. I would recommend it to everyone.

Dream 1

The 1st dream involved me being at a large Victorian style house. There are multiple rooms and floors. As the dream begins, I find myself in a large main room in the front room of the house on the 1st floor. A large party is taking place. Lights, noise, many people all in one room. A happy feeling is in the air. At some point it becomes necessary for me to go to the Kitchen and get something to bring back into the main room where the party is. I leave the main room, go thru swinging doors into an intermediate room between the main room and the kitchen. I then enter the kitchen, which is also brightly lit. I get what I need to get, I turn and reenter the intermediate room, and then enter the main room again. Only a matter of seconds has gone by. Instead of the happy party, filled with people, I find the main room completely empty, dark, and all the people are gone. Suddenly a woman in black (evil/fear/witch/the unknow?) appears and begins to chase me thru the house. I never see her face. I can't recall ever being caught or escaping the house. Time frame of the experience seems like several minutes in the sequence. No resolution happens in the dream. The dream ends.

The theme of being chased in dreams is a common one. Typically, when I was chased in other dreams, if I turned and confronted the "chaser", usually the fear/threat diminished or disappeared altogether. Not in this dream. I never confronted the "chaser". As I have looked at my life, I feel that this dream was preparing me for the many strange experiences that I would have to confront later in life.

Dream 2

The 2nd dream begins in front of the house I grew up in. My house was 3 houses from the corner on the block I grew up on. I walk West next door, into the front yard of the house that is 2nd from the corner next to mine. I'm now standing by the garage door next door. I look far down my block (East) and I see a large 18 wheel semi-truck turning the corner, heading down my block towards my house. I immediately realize that the truck is coming to get me, for reasons I do not know. (Again the "chaser" dream in another manifestation). I crouch down into the bushes along-side the garage, as the truck drives by. It comes to a stop at the intersection, and I now think I am free. As I peek around the corner to watch the truck drive away, I see the driver look over his right shoulder, and he looks right at me!

Slowly the truck makes an impossible U-turn in the small intersection, and I realize he is coming for me again. At that point, I make a run for my house next door. I never see the truck again, as my focus is what is in front of me as I run for help. (My father had built a small brick wall and sidewalk in front of our house in the early 60's.) I reach the sidewalk in front of my house. There in front of me is my sister and my mother. They are walking in front of me side by side. I am yelling for help, but they do not turn around or respond to my cries for help. Also, I find that I am running in what feels like waist deep mud, unable to make any progress forward. No resolution happens in the dream. I can't recall making it to the safety of my house, or ever getting help from my sister or Mother. The truck never gets to me either. Time frame of the experience seems like several minutes in the sequence. (Addendum: I now know with some certainty that this dream was foretelling of future events that came to pass vis a vis my sister and my mother, regarding her death. I choose to keep these details private as they are still most painful.)

Dream 3

The 3rd dream happens rather quickly. I enter the dream* experience quickly, realize what is happening, and then it's over. Here is the sequence. I find myself immediately inside a round room. I do not know how I get to this room. I have no memory of traveling or being taken (abducted?) to this room. No door is visible.

*(The room is gray walled and tall.) I can't recall a ceiling. I am sitting at a round table, with several other people I do not know. I see 3 very tall beings in robes standing against the wall. I realize they are there to prevent our escape, or to guard us in some way. I never see

their faces. To my right, and above our heads, I see a large orb (eye?) that is a few feet above our heads and the chairs we are sitting in.

The orb approaches above the person next to me, and then stops. I then immediately realize that the orb wants to scan my brain and take something from me, or perhaps implant a post hypnotic suggestion for some future event. As the orb finishes the scan of the person to my right, and begins to move over my chair, I immediately put up mental spiritual blocks that prevents the orb from getting into my head. It works every time. I was never taught how to do this; it just happens naturally and very quickly. The orb is successfully blocked and moves onto the next person, and the dream sequence ends. I can't recall how I get into or out of the room. I never talk to the other people in the room. This is a quick dream experience as I perceive time.

*Much later in life I met Tom Dongo, a Contact Experiencer and ET Author who told me of events that took place in Sedona AZ., that connect to this dream sequence.

Here are the details that link back to this dream.
Remember I have told NO ONE of my dreams before this point.

Tom relayed to me a story of two men who were exploring around Boynton Canyon in Sedona, AZ. They discovered a rock formation that contained some sort of dimensional doorway. This was a portion of the rock that looked solid, yet one could walk "into the rock" and disappear. After some preparation, the two men decided to explore the doorway. One of the men stayed on the outside of the "doorway" while the other man walked into and opening and disappeared. He was able to talk to his friend although he was not in sight. His description of what he saw is as follows:

"I am descending some very dusty stairs in a tunnel. The risers are larger and higher by several inches than a standard stairway normal humans would build in a house. The walls are giving off a slight luminescence and I can see without a flashlight. The stairs are covered in a thick layer of dust which looks undisturbed. The man continues down until he says "I have reached a door. I am opening it. I am in a large round room, with a table and chairs. The room is empty. I see a large orb of some sort slowly moving around the room above the chairs."

It was at this point I stopped Tom, as I was trying to process what he had just told me. It was clear that he was describing to me my dream. Clearly, I had been in that room, or one similar, many times in my childhood (either taken physically, or an OBE). I have heard of others who have had similar experiences.

One such event was relayed to me by the late Col. Wendelle Stevens. He told me of a man in Puerto Rico (The Amaury Rivera abduction case) who was taking a camera to the photo shop. He witnessed a UFO and tried to take photos of it. He remembers small beings approaching his car, and then he lost consciousness. When he woke, he was in a small round room with other locals from his town. They were all in this room being guarded. They did not why they were there. Higher consciousness entities then debriefed all the people in the room. They were told of future events that would unfold and they would be doing specific things at that time. As this man woke back up in his car, he snapped a photo of a craft moving up and away from his car. This story of abductees being told of future events is a common theme in the NHI/Contact Modality world. My dream was happening way before this type of contact information was out in the public in any real way, and certainly not to a me, a 10-year-old boy in Stockton who was unaware of UFO's in any real way.

Dream 4

I can best describe this dream this way. The opening scenes from the classic Sci-fi movie The Terminator 1 & 2 are what my dream looked like. Eerily similar. This was in the early 1960's when I was under the age of 10. Way before the movies, yet my dream was the exact opening scenes of those 2 movies. I come into the dream, and I am the leader of a small band of rebels fighting non-human invading forces. Non-human robots/entities are chasing us on the ground. We are running and hiding in the ruins of cities in the post-apocalyptic future. We are being shot at, both from the robot/entities and from large flying weapons platforms. Darkness and smoke. I neither win or lose or die in this dream. It is a short dream.
Had I seen the future?

Dream 5

This is the hardest of the 5 to explain. I am unable to recall the beginning of this dream. It happens fast. I am suddenly just in this dream. I become aware that I am in a tunnel. I do not have a sense of purpose in this dream. I experience a feeling of being pulled thru some sort of long tunnel. My body feels stretched, and I feel an urgent sense of fear. Feeling of total loss of control. I DO NOT want to get to the end of the tunnel. I don't try to actively get away from the end of the tunnel. A mind-bending, dimensional shifting, reality stretching feeling like no other. I see a bright light at the end of the tunnel. It is the brightest light I have ever experienced. I never reach the end of the tunnel.

Perhaps a connection point between two universes. Is this the tunnel we pass thru at the point of death? Was this preparing me for my death experience?

Later in life I would have a psychedelic experience that would also present the long tunnel of light, but with a GOD like presence also there. This was a different type of OBE compared to the dream. No fear, only wonder and awe. I would also have a clear OBE in meditation that took me to the white light again, where an enlightened being walked into my body and showed me the whitest light I have ever seen. There was a point where all these dreams stopped, and I never had them again.

My brother and I shared a front bedroom growing up. One morning he woke up and told me about something flying over the house in the night several times real low. He heard the sound and saw the movement of trees and bushes moved by the flying object. He recalls being scared. I have wondered often about the connection with that flying object over the house and my experiences. My brother and sister refuse to talk to me about any of this. My many NHI experiences challenge their religious beliefs.

Years 0 – 20

Growing up I had several incidents where I should have been hurt or killed. Bicycle wrecks, playing around a dangerous slough where others had drowned, innocently going into dangerous areas of town where bad people with bad intent lived. Here are a few incidents (NDE?) that I survived.

1971 - When I was 14, my family was on vacation in Oregon. It was a hot summer day outside Klamath Falls. Late afternoon, our car has overheated, and is off to the side of the road just past a blind curve on a two-lane road that was somewhat busy. Half on, half off the road and my father had the hood up. All I remember is my father looking up from under the hood, stepping out into traffic and waving a huge 18-wheel semi-truck, speeding around the blind curve, around our stuck car. Had there been another car coming the other way, it would have been disaster. It all happened in a flash. I remember my father getting in the car very shook up. He quickly got the car started and moved.

1972 – September 24th my parents and I went to an air show in Sacramento, CA. It was a long day and towards the afternoon we decided to leave. We drove across Highway 99 from the airport where the show was taking place, to a strip mall and attempted to get into a Farrell's ice cream parlor. It was packed with kid parties, my father didn't want to wait the 30-40 minutes for a table, so we left. We drove down Highway 99 back towards Stockton and stopped in Lodi at another diner. This drive took about 30 minutes. After we arrived at the diner, there a report that came over the radio of a plane crash in Sacramento. A vintage fighter jet attempted to takeout from the air show we were just at, hit several cars, and crashed into the same ice cream parlor we would have been eating at just 30 minutes earlier. I still think about that day. 22 killed, 26 injured.

1976 – I joined the Air Force February 1976. After basic training I went to Tech school in Texas. One Friday night I met a bunch of guys at party. One of them had just bought a new car and was very proud of it. The very next night I was coming back to base with friend late after drinking. We saw a car wrecked by the side of the road and a man standing next to it. His face was bloody, and he was in shock. He had been driving a Cutlass, and both men had hit the windshield. You could see the imprint in the windshield where they had hit their heads. The Cutlass was driving on the highway when someone had run a stop sign and they had broadsided that car. 1 killed, 2 injured. As we were first on the scene moments after the accident, I ran over to the man and asked where the other car was. He pointed out into a field. I ran to the wreck. Turned out to be the SAME GUY I had met the night before with the brand-new car! He was in the driver seat and was unconscious. The passenger side of the vehicle was caved in from front to rear tire well. The passenger was lying across the console and was out. I found out later he was killed on impact. The passenger in the rear was awake and his eyes were WIDE open. He was looking at me. I felt for the passenger's pulse on his neck, chest, and wrist. Nothing. He was bleeding from his ears. I ran to the highway and stopped the first car I could. There were no cell phones at that time, so the car took off to call for help. Very shortly thereafter the THP arrived and took control. It didn't hit me until later what had happened.

That could have been me had I been there a few minutes earlier. After my transfer to Germany, I was involved in a motorcycle wreck while in Germany that could have been fatal. I was lucky/blessed. I was discharged in 1977.

1977 – I had a NDE sometime in the summer of 1977 I was with 2 other friends at the Pacific Ocean on Highway 101. We parked and walked down to the beach. We saw a huge plateau of rock just offshore that we wanted to get on top of, as it was dry. During a lull in a set of waves I ran out across a momentarily dry area of rock and climbed my way to the top of this rock, out in the ocean. The top of the rock was dry!!! As the next set of waves began, Terry and Phil, who attempted to follow me up the rock, were swept out to sea and disappeared!!! I looked out to sea and the largest wave I had ever seen was towering over me and ready to sweep me off the rock. I lay down and prepared to die. The wave crashed around me and stopped just short of sweeping me off. After the set ended, I was able to get off the rock and make it to the beach. Terry had made it to shore, and just as suddenly Phil mysteriously reappeared out of the ocean and that was it. Should have been 3 deaths from stupidity.

From the time I left the Air Force, until 1989, I lived a regular life of jobs and dating. In 1988, I got married. Thru out this time, I had begun reading about UFO's. I had been visiting every book store in the greater Bay Area, and I was buying anything about UFO's in print. In 1989 a whistleblower came forward with an incredible story of working on UFO's for the government. (Robert Lazar, who much later I would have a unique slice of his story posted currently on my YouTube channel.)

This moment was a profound shift in my consciousness, along with many others on the planet at the time who were interested in the subject matter. I was married at the time, and my circuits opened to current information at the time. My wife at the time was not interested in spiritual growth, and we parted ways. Two things very weird things happened while I was married. The first one happened when I was sitting alone in my living room. It was during the day. Sunny and clear outside. No wind. TV on low. Suddenly, I felt and saw a "shimmer" pass thru my living room. Just like a wave, but I saw the ripple in time/space/reality pass thru. I still have no explanation for what I saw/felt.

The second weird thing was an afternoon when we were having a garage sale. Many people were stopping by. As we sat there, up walked a very tall man. He was wearing shorts and a tee shirt. He had a bemused smile on his face. His arms were LONG. His hands were almost covering his KNEES! His whole presence was different. His energy was unique. As he walked around our stuff, he looked right at me and smiled this knowing smile. He didn't buy anything. Again, this could have just been a very tall man.

This is where my life gets interesting, as I let go, went neutral and opened my spiritual circuits. I found myself in one situation after another that seemed more profound than the last one. By now I had really been getting into my spiritual side. I was reading lots of books at the time, and most are still in my library. I was also getting ready for my first UFO lecture. In February 1990, I presented my first UFO lecture at the Guiding Star bookstore in Mill Valley. Wendy Rose was the owner and a very nice person open to the possibilities. I had a packed house of over 50 people. It was fun and a bit scary. That started a part of my life that opened up so many doors.

As a prelude to continuing, a little background. In the months prior to the first International UFO Congress hosted by Col. Wendelle C. Stevens in 1990, he had released another book in his fine UFO Contact series. This one was called From Venus I Came. It told the story of a young girl who came to Earth from Venus at the age of 5. She was here to finish her final karma on this planet. She was to take the place of another girl soon to be killed in a car crash. I read the book and was fascinated by the story and knew she would be in Tucson for the Congress as the main speaker. So, with that caveat, here is the story of my time spent with a Venusian!

May 3rd – 7th, 1990, my friend Chris and I went to Tucson, AZ. for the 1st International UFO congress put on by Ret. Colonel Wendelle C. Stevens and Ret. Col. Robert O'Dean. It was an incredible affair with much international UFO information presented. I met many fellow spiritual seekers of truth, and a few charlatans. I helped one person film several interviews with all the speakers. The most memorable event for me was meeting and spending time with Sheila Gibson aka Omnec Onec. She was a housewife from Chicago. When we arrived, we found the venue had been moved to a new hotel. After changing hotels and getting settled, Chris and I went to the airport to pick up Michael Hesseman coming in from Germany. We met him and had a great chat driving back to the hotel. After dropping him off, we met in the main conference room for general mingling. As we were waiting around, a buzz went thru the crowd. There was Col. Stevens and Omnec walking thru the crowd. She was dressed in a form fitting dress and was looking beautiful. It was very exciting and as they drew closer my anticipation grew. I just wanted to meet her and say Hi, I read your book and nice to meet you. We were introduced and said our pleasantries. Later that day I was contacted by representatives of Col. Stevens. They were looking for someone to drive Omnec around the area. I had a rental car, so I was volunteered. I ended up becoming her driver for the week. There was one night we ended up at a small bar playing pool, having a beer, and talking about her life.

The week went by and come Friday, Col. Wendelle Stevens was going to present Omnec and her story for the first time to the world. I was asked to use my hotel room for her to prepare and change into her gown for the evening. After she was dressed, she gave me a private ½ hour interview, which I filmed, and still have to this day. We talked about her story and her reasons for coming to Earth. We finished the interview, and she was whisked away for her debut. My friend and I walked to the hall where she would be speaking. We sat in the very back of the hall and watched the lecture. Afterwards, she was swarmed onstage by people wanting to ask questions. I felt a sense of gratitude that I had so many opportunities to spend the time with Omnec thru the week. We slowly made our way back to our room, talking about the week's events and the many stories we heard, the people we met. It took us some time to make our way back to the hotel room. As we arrived and turned the corner to our room, we were greeted by a small group of people at our door. Col. Stevens, Omnec, her friends, and a few hangers on. I opened the door, and we all went in. I immediately set up my video camera in the corner of the room and began filming. I sat back and watched over several hours as one after another, friends came in for photos and to talk with Col. Stevens and Omnec.

(I lost all my research materials in a house fire, including the video tapes from this event. I had so many private moments that were priceless.)

I had a Contact Modality experience (OBE and UFO sighting) with several others after I left the Tucson UFO event and drove with friends to Sedona, AZ. There we rented a condo and spend time exploring. It was here I was to have one of my most profound Spiritual experience, of the many I've had. I was traveling with 2 women; both were deeply spiritual and much fun to be around. We formed a triad of energy that seemed to empower us thru the following experiences. We went to the home of someone who was an energy healer. His name was Roger LaChance. When we arrived at his house, we were greeted by a kind man who welcomed us into his home. It was filled with crystals. Many LARGE crystals. Huge amethyst clusters. The energy was fantastic. He showed us around his healing studio. In his therapy room was a massage table one could lie on face up. 3' above the table was a piece of plywood with 7 holes cut out. Each hole had a colored light that would shine on the 7 chakras of the body. A separate projector would shine colored lights on the soles of the feet. One would also wear headphones during the healing session. As I'm walking around the house, I see a photo on the wall. There sits Sai Baba, an Avatar on the planet. I knew nothing of this man. He is sitting in a large chair, wearing an orange jumpsuit type outfit. He is relaxed, with his head resting in one hand at an angle and holding the other hand up like he's waving. Under the glass holding the picture in place, in the lower left corner is a small plastic zip lock bag. Very small. 2"x3". There is some white powder residue in the bag. I ask Roger about the photo. Who is this I ask. He replies that is Sai Baba. As I hold my hand up to the photo, next to his hand, I get this jolt of energy from his hand. Woah! I step back. I ask Roger about the bag with powder. He replies that is Manna, or Vabutti, the spiritual powder that Sai Baba manifests from the ether. It pours from his hand when he walks among his devotees. Devotees rub it on their 3rd eye, their Crown chakra, and they eat it. As I'm pondering this, Roger asks me if I would like to have a chakra healing experience. I get on the table, put on headphones, and close my eyes. I am listening to acoustic music, like bells and gongs, chimes and singing bowls. As the music builds in my head, I immediately leave my body (OBE) and I am taken to a large ashram. I am inside and standing at the base of stairs. I look up and see Sai Baba sitting in his chair. At my feet sitting on the steps is Omnec Onec. She is silent. As the music continues to build, I see thousands of devotees coming into the ashram, and assembling behind me. I stand silently. Sai Baba stands up and slowly walks down the stairs. He approaches me, and then he walks INTO my body. As this happens, I am shown a small doorway that cracks open. The brightest, whitest light I have ever seen is visible. As I see this, Sai Baba tells me "This is where you are going. Your path is true." Just as suddenly the door closes, and I am back in my body, crying my eyes out. I sit up and repeat my experience to Roger, Shirley and Kiyo. From this moment on, after this OBE, when I needed guidance on something I was unclear about, what path to take, was something good or bad for me, etc., I would form a yes/no question in my head to Sai Baba. Before I can fully formulate the question, I get back IMMEDIATELY the proper answer, either yes or no. Worked every time. A connection with a larger something I can't really explain. (Many years later I was given 3 video tapes from a friend. They were taken in India, at the ashram of Sai Baba. They CLEARLY showed him manifesting objects and Manna from his hands right in front of the camera. I so wish I had those tapes.)

As our visit is ending, Roger suddenly looks at me and says, "Tonight, you and your friends are going to have a UFO sighting." He went on to explain what would happen to us. He said we would first stop at a location. We would get out and look around. We would then get a warning of some sort to leave. We would then go to another location and have a sighting. Little did I know it would be that and more.

After dinner, a large group of fellow UFO enthusiasts and I set out to Boynton Canyon in 2 cars. We had a VHS camcorder that worked perfectly. Prior to this, I knew nothing of the high strangeness in this area. The night was crystal clear. We drove into the Canyon and came to a T in the road. We parked our cars and got out. We were standing by the side of the road, next to a fence with barb wire on top. As we were talking, suddenly we all felt an apprehension at the same time. There was a moment of fear, and a red light hit a few of us from somewhere. A laser pointer red light. We immediately got into our cars and drove away. We went higher up the road, to a plateau of sorts. We parked and got out to look around. We could see quite far around us, and the skies were clear. As our eyes adjusted to the night light, we all could see the air traffic around us.

The Sedona airport was nearby. The birds and planes we saw moving around us were as one would expect. The stars were clear in the sky. As we watched, off in the distance an object unlike the others (birds/planes) began to approach our location. It followed a linear path towards us with no deviation. As it came closer, one by one we all began to see it. The object was circular and had 3 lights below it. Red and white, they slowly circled around the lower edge of the object. As it got closer to us, and we all started to clearly see it, our friend with the camcorder tried to film it. His camcorder failed to work. At this point we were all talking out loud, saying "do you see that?" "Is that getting closer to us?" "Is that a plane?" "That's not a plane, is it?" There was then a moment of out loud realization that what we were seeing was not a plane or bird. It was at this moment we all felt fear at the same time. We knew we were seeing something strange. All the while the experience is happening, the object has slowly been moving in our direction. It never got over us, but near enough for us to see it clearly. Ask we came to the same moment of realization and fear, the object stopped its forward movement. It hovered there for us all to see. The light continued to circle. I am of the opinion it knew we were there, and it felt our fear. It was not there to scare us. Just another Contact Modality for anyone ready to see it, feel it, engage with it. The object then began to recede back along the path it took moving out sight. No side movement, back out the way it came in. It then blinked out.

We drove back home and talked about it a bit. As we looked back, it was exactly as Roger had predicted it would happen. Just another strange event that I now know was a Contact Modality with NHI.

Not long after my Sedona experience, I met a woman who had written a book about her psychic work. She was using her abilities to help those who felt stuck spiritually to release bad energy. I began to work with her. I had the ability to meditate and hold energy in a room. I would call down the Archangel Michael. We would meditate together on creating a golden cage of protection with the intent to create a safe space for energy and psychic work to take place. This happened many times. There were times as I sat in mediation I would "see" the future, in the fact that the person working to release bad energy would describe settings or locations, and I would already be seeing them in mediation. I saw ET entities at the doorways looking in but blocked by the cage. A connection and synchronicity I couldn't explain then but makes sense now looking back on my path of NHI experiences.

Another such occurrence happened with the same woman in Sedona when we had returned to visit her friend, I will call Marty. Marty was very spiritual and had very good energy. After arriving at her home, we had made a collective decision to attempt to contact NHI in meditation. Earlier in the day I had taken a hike by myself to Bell Rock. I climbed up as I wanted to get as high as possible to see the bigger area. I was filled with energy and quickly made my way upwards. There was a point where I jumped over a small opening and down to another rock. I soon realized that I could go no higher this way and made my way back to the point I jumped down. To my shock, I found myself stuck with no way off the rock from this point. The only way I could get back was to make a one-time move to jump up and grab onto small rock nubs and hope for the best. After a gut check, I made the move and was successful. Could have gone either way.

So now Marty, Trish and I were in her house. Trish and I stayed in the Living Room, and Marty went into her bedroom to give us privacy in our psychic work. We sat knee to knee and went into meditation. We each left our bodies, and I had this experience. We found ourselves onboard an alien craft. We were standing in a hallway filled with many different types of life forms. Trish was taken away as I stood there. I then was talking to an octopus type of being with multiple arms. As I'm having this experience, I see Marty on the ship, and she is peeking around a door frame. After some time, Trish and I began to come back into our bodies. As we slowly return to our physical bodies and I open my eyes, I held up my hand and I see the bones in my hand as the skin reforms over them, and I return to physical form. Most intense experience.

As we sit talking, Trish tells me about being shown the engines and propulsion systems. As I'm telling her of what I saw, Marty comes in and without missing a beat, she says to me "Hey, how about that guy with all the arms?" I was stunned. She HAD been on board with us. How? Another experience I can't explain, yet it happened.

May 22nd 1991 - I presented a multi-media presentation along with Chris and Glenn in Oakland as the C.S.P. Society. This was just after the International UFO Conference in Phoenix so we were all prepped with great new information. As I continued to give UFO lectures up and down California, I met more and more people, and got to hear their stories of interaction with NHI. Some of their stories were supported with medical documentation, one in particular (a twin with a sister both having abductions) who carried a baby to 3 months, and then it was just…gone. The doctors had no explanation. The sisters had many experiences of contact with NHI, and their stories never changed. One night one of the sisters woke up to see her very fat cat sitting upright at the foot of her bed. As she watched the cat transformed into the classic grey alien. She was not afraid. She asked the being what was happening to her, and here on Earth. The being told her that we humans are just not ready to fully realize the big picture of why Earth is here, and what it's being used for.

Just one of many people who crossed my path with NHI experiences they were unable to explain. I realize that the path I have walked to get answers to my own experiences has allowed me to offer a safe place for those who saw my lectures to talk about their own strange experiences. Many women are having these experiences and are not sure what's going on.

October 30, 1991 – My fellow UFO researcher and lecture friend was giving a presentation in Palo Alto at a bookstore. I filmed the event. It was there I was approached by a woman named Victoria Jack. She was an event producer in the Bay Area and was putting together a large UFO conference. She asked me to be part of the Audio/Video production crew for the event. I agreed. Another important piece of my NHI life puzzle was dropping into place, unbeknownst to me. Little did I know that I would be helping produce what would soon become known as the Bay Area UFO Expo.

If you watch the History Channel, and have seen Ancient Aliens, the many researchers presented on that show passed thru the Expo. I was a cameraman and filmed every lecture. I hooked hot mic packs to all those speakers. I had dinner with most all of them. Had drinks, smoked a joint or two, and had many deep intense spiritual conversations. The stories presented on your TV are watered down for public consumption. Most of the stuff happening here on Earth is WAY above most human's paygrade. By that I mean their ability to adequately process the big picture, the many moving parts, the players involved, the lies told, the secrets kept, the lives destroyed to keep that secret. If you're reading this, you know of this. If you don't know of what I speak, get to reading and serious research. I also saw that there were professional speakers on the UFO circuit who were not interested in moving the subject matter forward, but instead were only in it for the money, or to obfuscate the subject matter.

Here is another time I interacted with NHI consciously, with 2 others. After one of these UFO conferences, I was introduced to a wealthy UFO researcher thru a mutual friend. We were invited to see and use some Russian nightscope technology that had been purchased during the time when Russia had been selling such tech on the open market to the highest bidder. Here is what I saw and used one night.

We drove to an address; we were led to a backyard set up with reclining chairs. The night was clear and cool. We each took a chair. I was then shown a unique binocular nightscope. It was large and heavy. The eyepiece was one piece 4"x2" slightly curved glass set in a frame with rubber around the viewing window edge to soften them against your face. There was a button you pressed when you wanted to look thru them. There was a small panel to install a 9v battery. When you pressed the button the 9v battery would heat up (excite?) a small chamber of sealed gas. These binoculars allowed the user deep atmosphere vision in a way I'd never seen.

So here is what I saw that night. Because the binoculars were HEAVY, one could only hold them up for about a minute before you had to drop your arms and hand them off to the next person. After becoming accustomed to them, I could CLEARLY see everything and anything flying, both at low altitude and deep into space. I saw birds flying at night. I saw details of feathers one would never see at night even with a spotting scope. I saw airplanes at altitude. I could CLEARLY read the letters on the side of the plane. I saw individual heads in windows. Then deeper in space I see the Andromeda Galaxy. Much clearer then with a telescope. It was magnificent.

We could see the movement of satellites across the sky. We could follow a satellite thru its path. Then one of us noticed a white light he thought was another satellite. It was moving on a normal path, then made a right-angle turn and stopped. What? One by one we looked and found the object. Since we could only hold the binocs for a short time, each of us would have to find it repeatedly. This object was under intelligent control. As each of us would watch it, and think about what we were seeing, it seemed to be aware of this. As I thought about what I was watching, I asked it to move, and it did. Were we contacting and interacting with a NHI? I will never know for sure.

We all watched this object for quite some time, each of us having his own personal experience with it. The fact that the object did not leave the area but stayed in the same area for us to continue to locate it, and interact with it, remains a strong memory for me.

The use of hallucinogens in mankind's history on Earth is well documented. Ancient civilizations most surely were aware of its use in contacting NHI, and it would explain some of the recorded history of ancient man's interaction with NHI.

These are some of my experiences with LSD, in its many forms, as they relate to NHI and I see this period of my life as just another chapter along my path to higher consciousness. Most of my LSD experiences had no Contact Modality or NHI elements to them. The few that did were powerful experiences. My overall takeaway from taking LSD was the realization that we are not fully realizing the true nature of the reality we exist within. When one's mind is expanded and the moment of self-awareness occurs to a different understanding of a much larger reality, that we are all a part of, it's hard to put the genie back in the bottle. Remember Neo and the Blue pill?

I was kicked out of the house at 17, in October of 1974. Thru all of 1975, I tried many types of psychedelics including: Mushrooms, Peyote, Mescaline, and LSD (in many forms and strengths including 4-way Window Pane, Mr. Natural blotter, Purple Mescaline tabs (20+ tabs over 2+ days nonstop) liquid drops, and paper.) Most of the time I was in Nature, outside, and enjoyed the experiences. I soon opened to the realization that the nature of reality as we have been taught is nothing like what is really happening here on Earth.

Here are some recollections of my LSD experiences. I never had a "bad" trip. Each one was unique in its experience. Nature would open itself up in ways I did not expect. I have done my best to describe some of my experiences here. There were just a few times where I saw, or felt, the presence of a higher consciousness.

One night I dropped LSD with a friend, and we walked thru Murphy's late at night, into the early morning hours. We saw a horse and walked over to see it. The horse approached us, and we silently communicated with the horse.

I attended an Auto Tech class in High School. I dropped a hit one morning before auto shop class. I did a front-end brake job on a customer's car high on LSD. I was clearly focused on the task. Another night after dropping acid, I was playing in the heavy fog, and I could HEAR the fog. Hmmmm...

<u>1990</u> – As I was continuing my research of UFO's, and was lecturing around California. I met a couple who attended my lectures, and they invited me over to their house. After getting to know them, they brought out some toad venom and a pipe. Toad venom, DMT and Ayahuasca are different types of natural psych active's. We proceeded to smoke the venom. I took a small hit, and almost immediately left my body and went to another reality. Very short fast experience. Unlike anything I'd tried before. Saw the intense white light. Felt a GOD like presence. Felt good. No fear. I never took LSD again.

Along with my many experiences with NHI, I also had experiences that opened my world to a bigger reality, and the fact that governments intercept empowering information to stay in power. Here are a few examples where I crossed paths with others having their own empowering experiences involving NHI. One morning I was called by a fellow researcher. She told me to meet her at her storage unit. When I arrived, she told me that representatives of Nicola Tesla's family were moving some of his archives and needed a temporary storage site as other arrangements were being made to receive the archives. We spent some time looking thru his archives.

I saw a stack of B/W photos showing U.S. government types in a Quonset hut looking at small UFO's built by the government. Others showing Tesla sitting in a Faraday cage, with electricity all around. I saw thousands of pages of his Colorado notes from 1899. We saw his original metaphysical book collection. Another moment of being in the right place at the right time.

I was a CATV installer and I met many people over the years. One day I met a man who told me of his father's work for the US government involving energy devices. His father prepared what are called "white papers", scientific suppositions and plans for exotic stuff to build and play around with. He then described to me a device, available only in Europe at the time (1990's) that was a miracle device. It had the ability to sample a human body by analyzing the following: blood, urine, hair sample, tooth sample, skin sample, etc. The machine (a computer of sorts) after analyzing the sample printed out a report of EVERY issue in the body. It found the mercury in teeth, the broken ankle from when you were 6, the nutrition issues, cancer, etc. It would prescribe a regime to follow to begin to adjust and address the issues found. It would also produce a homeopathic tincture that one would take to support the body as it began to heal. This is a Destroy On Site device that is against the law to have, own or use here in the US.

He revealed that the head of a large local Bay Area hospital was using this device locally in the Bay Area, and under the utmost secrecy, to treat his cancer. He told me that there were many doctors who know the medical system is flawed at best, and certain treatments and machines like this exist, but aren't available to all of us for many sinister reasons. When President Ronald Reagan went to Europe for "treatment" in the 1980's for an undisclosed illness, many believe he was treated with a device like this. No way to verify that.

I almost died in 2017

I almost dies in October 2017. My house caught fire, and I ran in 4 times attempting to fight the fire and save valuable's. I stood at the front door and looked at the whole house filling with smoke. I had 2 fire extinguishers and both failed, as they were expired. I could clearly see my bedroom, and my bugout box by the door. The smoke was hanging down from the ceiling throughout the house. I could see the floor. I entered the burning house the 2nd time, with a wet rag around my mouth, headed for my bedroom. I had made about 4 steps into the house, and the smoke dropped to the floor throughout the house. I was instantly unable to see. If I had made the turn to go to my bedroom to get my box, I would have passed out and died. As it was, when the smoke dropped, I instinctively headed for the back door. It was double locked. I fumbled and got it open. I went down two steps to a sliding glass door. I slid it open and fell gasping onto the patio. A few more seconds and I would have passed out. I lived up on a hill, and no one was around to help. I lost most everything I owned. I was able to save my photos and my rare metaphysical book collection.

Recently I watched the "After Death" documentary released in the theaters. I went to see it because I have had several NDE's in my life. I wanted to see if any of the stories would match any of the details of my experiences. The director opened the doc with a brief statement about the subject matter. We then jump into several personal stories of dying, death, and the return to the body. I won't go into the details of each story, as I will leave that up to everyone to watch for themselves and get the effect of the stories directly from the participants. We get great comments and insight from many experts.

What I want to comment on are the several common parts of each story, the common threads that most experienced, me included. I have experienced several NDE's and OBEs in my lifetime. I have written down each experience in detail. I have also taken several different types of psychedelics and have had many amazing experiences. My several dreams that I had for many years as a young kid I have written down in detail. It seems the NDE, the OBE, the experiences while under the influence of LSD, and the dream experiences seem quite similar and share a common thread.

Listening to the several descriptions of what each person saw, felt, and experienced made me think of the LSD/Psychedelic experience, mine included. It is extremely hard to describe "trippin' on LSD." Yet the NDE/OBE comes close in some respects. The feeling of being connected to a larger, bigger part of the cosmos. You realize the reality you think you know is way bigger than you ever imagined. You feel connected to it somehow in a larger way. You feel a lightness in your astral body/spirit. Your awareness levels are heightened. You can communicate with Nature in an unspoken way. When you take DMT/Ayahuasca, or toad venom, they can open a portal to another level of consciousness. Your awareness level is greatly expanded. The question is can you handle the experience?

The modern medical community is slowly beginning to use psychedelics in a therapeutic setting, helping people deal with anxiety issues that don't respond to typical therapies. Many are getting positive results after taking micro doses. I can say that once you take a psychedelic in any form (Mushrooms, Mescaline, DMT, Peyote, blotter LSD, Microdot), you will forever change usually in a more positive way. As far as DMT is concerned, usually it's a short 30-minute intense experience where most see "God" or touch/see a higher level of awareness and them return. Now individuals are taking DMT in a slow continuous drip, experiencing an extended several hours of contact with Higher Consciousness entities who are waiting for humanity to awaken to the next/another level of existence. Ancient civilizations were way ahead of us on this.

I will conclude with this message to all who read this. The many experiences I have revealed here are but a few of the many experiences that have revealed to me that a NHI is indeed interacting with all humans here on Earth. We are eternal spirits on an endless journey of reawakening and reconnecting to higher consciousness.

Peace to all on the path.

Don't Shoot the Messenger:

My take on Inter-Dimensional Communication

Carol McLeod

MS/MFCC, ATR-BC (ret.) CtH
Director, Starfield Foundation [1]
©2024 Carol McLeod

---

[1] https://www.facebook.com/starfield.foundation, https://www.facebook.com/talkwithaliens

I am a retired therapist looking back on 72 years of contact events via the Contact Modalities. I'm not here to argue if Non-Human Intelligence exist or not. I'm way beyond that. I talk with Non-Human Intelligence. Regularly. Often. You could, too, once you knew the rules. But that's a story for another time. also talk with people who've talked with aliens, and help them deal with issues regarding their experiences. So, this paper skips the what's and ifs and goes directly to the point: the How's Where's, and What's involved in inter-dimensional communication.

Don't shoot the messenger. I can't prove any of this is true, so I'm not going to waste time trying! What follows is my take on what it's like to be immersed in communication with Non-Human Intelligence, or, if you prefer term, with alien communication. I will try to explain how the process works for me, where I think the messages are coming from, while providing a sampling of what they are talking about.

I'm going to use the term "aliens" to cover a large range of "non-local consciousnesses communication with Non-Human Intelligence". Aliens come in all shapes and sizes, end up here for all sorts of reasons, and have a wide variety of things to say. Most have been hanging out here for millennia, watching the progress of evolution, setting up experiments, noting what happens...and no doubt betting on the results. I get the picture human civilization started with a little mental telepathy: "Hey, you there. Pick up that stick and rub it against that log. See what happens." They give us sparks and wait to what we do with it.

So... We live in a cosmic Petri dish. But so does everyone everywhere else in the universe. File it under, "As Above, So Below". There's always some group looking down and another group looking up, in a continuous chain, like looking at yourself between two mirrors. If you have not done this, please give it a try. Set two mirrors apart facing each other and sit in the middle between them. It's the best visual for imagining infinity and inter-dimensional worlds (although they are actually aligned more like soap bubbles). Each group both looks down and looks up. Those below us might mistake us for gods, while we look expectantly upward for divine inspiration. Ad nauseam.

Mostly my alien contacts talk about physics. And what it will take for humans to transform in the coming changes. They hint at the actuality of the structure of reality and how it applies to consciousness. They complain a lot about how annoying humans can be. They've been trying to get through to us for thousands of years but we keep getting the message wrong, losing it, forgetting it or hiding it from everyone but a select few in order to rule the world.

Turns out the great "mystery" behind the Mystery Schools of the ancient Greeks was simply that aliens were behind the advent of civilization. The ancient Chinese knew that, too. They represented their first ancestors as having snake bodies with human heads. Folks in ancient India did that, too. Their gods could fly. Some even had palaces up in the air. The Maya, the Aztecs and their cousins in South America revered snakes that could fly and coughed up the heads of venerated ancestors who offered advice. Flying snakes sound a lot like aircraft from which alien visitors emerge. And all across the Americas, a legend told of life being brought to earth by a woman who fell from the sky. She was the daughter of a great chief who lived in the clouds. Zeus and his crew lived on cloud-covered Mt. Olympus, way up high. They could also fly. So did the gods of the Zoroastrians. In Christina tradition, angels fly. But why would any culture invent a flying god? Why would gods come from the sky? The obvious answer still seems odd: Aliens were common visitors in ancient times, and stories about them turned into legends over eons. Aliens, for the most part, are not happy being pegged as gods, but if it helps get their point across, oh well. They keep sending their messages out over the centuries in the hope we will eventually get it right. Anyone with ears to hear can make contact and have a try at interpreting what they have to say. I've spent the last fifty or sixty years giving it a try.

Aliens want us to live life like a video game where we're players dropped into a level without any ideas of the rules. But there are rules, cheats, hidden clues, all along the way, which we learn by braking them. We have to make life-changing choices with every move, and we have no idea of the consequences. So we die. Then we come back. But with each return, our data has been wiped. We go through the same motions again. Die again. Come back again. Gradually we eke out some simple memories, enough to perhaps survive just a little longer. As time goes by, we experiment with writing things down so we can recognize what we had learned. We carved and painted on rock...Invented paper and made scrolls....Bound our notes into books. Lost the books to barbarian invaders who used them as firewood. Went back to carving on stone. Over and over, a step higher each time, we work our way up the levels of the game. That's why we are here. Our purpose in life is to figure out how to do everything right and eventually win the game. I asked for the secret of life, the strategy for winning the game. I was told, simply, to "Do everything right." I thought that was a rather difficult assignment, so I asked how was I supposed to do that. Their reply was, "Stop doing things wrong."

The problem with talking or working or otherwise dealing with aliens is, they don't think the way we do. We like to get our ducks in a row...we analyze things sequentially, arranging our thoughts from Point A to Point B. They don't. At least the ones I work with regularly don't. They think globally. Their ideas come across like an encyclopedia projected onto a disco ball sparkling in the center of my brain. They seem to look at a concept in all its glory simultaneously. I get the idea they expect me to look at the images without blinking ant take it all in at once, as well. Like reading a book all at once in one long stare.

It is possible for humans to learn to process this kind of information download, but it takes practice. I'm getting the hang of it, slowly. The natural human reaction is to latch onto one part of the totality and try to unravel the story line into some rational sequence. But what you get is a single segment cut off from the rest. The more you pull out snatches of information, the farther you get from knowing how to stitch them back together. Each might contain fascinating bits of information, but getting the story in a straight line is extremely challenging.

Each individual sees these snippets within the context of their culture and society. So each report on the content is flavored a different way. History is full of goddesses, gods, and heroes masking their alien roots with complex story lines tying them to specific locations and inclinations, but it all comes from the same place. Alien transmissions. From other dimensions.

It helps to have a context. According to what I've learned, each of us occupies a single point in an infinite universe, like a geometry of the mind where a vast grid holds countless points. Each point, yours...mine...any and everyone's...Each point is intersected by an equally infinite number of lines. Each line anchors the point in an independent dimension. Each of these dimensions are linked along that point....think of the double mirrors again....and we end up experiencing lives in each one simultaneously. "Simultaneously" is a big concept in alien physics.

If I was alone in the universe, I imagine I could handle the concept. Me, separate lives in separate zones...That's not a problem, that's an adventure! But it's not just me. It's you, the guy next door, those folks in the crosswalk, that mob on the bus, the dude in the next cubicle at work...Everybody. Everybody is on a point with infinite lines that all link up with each other along that one point which is connected to every other point all those points have lines intersecting the whole mess. It's bound to get complicated. Oh...and add to it that all those points and lines are operating in the past, present and future *simultaneously.*

The universe is all one huge inter-connected web. Any interaction on one level precipitates consequences across multiple levels, maybe even across infinity. Big ripples, little ripples...depends on the action and intention. So, careless decisions in one dimension ripple across other dimensions like boat wakes on a lake.

My aliens connections are all reacting to the consequences of our actions in our mundane world as they ripple across theirs. Same place, different dimensionality, similar consequences. Mainly this boils down to , "Hey, humans! Stop shaking the boat!" They understand us to be children, naughty children, who act without understanding the totality of the possible outcomes. We don't mean to be destructive. We just don't know the extent of what we do.

There's a lot going on in our cosmic neighborhood that we aren't aware of. There's no such thing as "empty space". The universe is full of flotsam and jetsam: seeds of life, broken planets, different dimensions, various kinds of energy...all sorts of things. One reason it is difficult to talk with aliens is the space between us and them (in whatever dimension) is full of emotional stuff. All the love, fear, hate anyone has ever felt. Every decision anyone has struggled over. All the results of everyone's actions and reactions. Feelings have their own kind of substance, and it doesn't dissipate overnight. It just hangs out in suspended animation. It's there. You just can't see it. But you can feel it.

Have you ever walked into a room where the air just seemed thick from people arguing? Like when you enter and everyone stops talking and there's this awkward moment, but you don't know what's going on. What you'd be feeling then is what I am talking about. Like a great shock wave, the time signature of past events lives on until dissipated by time or until another wave of significant energy washes over the space. You can feel beaten or energized, depending on your level of emotional development.

Folks from other dimensions have their own vibrations and leave their own time signatures on event horizons. You can learn to recognize the difference between ghosts and aliens because of this difference factor. Alien energy is fast and higher...not because they are operating from a higher spiritual level, but because their reality spins at a faster rate. They aren't gods and don't fall for it if they tell you otherwise!

When an alien falls in from another dimension, it's pretty impressive. First you hear a buzzing like some kind of insect. A really LARGE insect. That sound is their vibrational frequency breaking the dimensional sound barrier in reverse. It is generally followed by a boom. When a jet breaks the sound barrier with a sonic boom within our dimension, it is going really fast. When an alien begins to materialize here, the boom is from slowing down.

I was walking in the forest one stormy day and a bolt of lightning hit a tree next to me. The shock wave cracked the air so hard, it knocked me down. There   was a weird quality to the air, smelling of sulfur. I instantly understood how "sulfur and brimstone" became associated with powerful entities. I felt I had been smacked by Zeus himself. That's what it's like when a powerful alien materializes next to you.

There's a crack and a wave of energy. The air feels thick and has an odd smell, with a metallic flavor. Not all aliens come in like that, but it's pretty common.

Here's a good time to reiterate, aliens come in all shapes and sizes. We tend to think of aliens as warped versions of our own physiology, but not all aliens are star-shaped: head, arms, feet. They can be any shape...flat like paper, round like a ball, even multi-dimensional from some far out geometry. Intelligence is not defined by size, shape or materiality, either. For all we know, bacteria has consciousness and is just waiting for us to figure out how to communicate in order to make the connection. I have recently encountered entities that resemble deep ocean life forms, made of some barely definable clear substance with occasional spots of color. Another group resembling mops comes from a dimension full of lime green gelatin. I've also encountered flat entities resembling intricate designs which break apart and reform like an animated cartoon of intelligent lace.

There seems to be a universal means of communication between aliens, a kind of "sign language" made up of feelings, colors and pictures rather than words. I guess you could call it mental telepathy, but it's not hearing voices as much as it's understanding the video being shown. I call it "emoting". It works in this dimension as well as in any other. For instance, say you want to talk to a horse. You might teach it to recognize a few commands, but if you want to figure out what it is thinking, you have to let go of trying to teach it to talk. Instead, you have to reach out emotionally. You might try staring into the horse's eyes, rubbing its neck, or giving it a hug. Part of the process would be to open the energy centers located at your solar plexus and heart levels and push emotional messages at the horse. Amp up your energy and let it flow over the animal. Give intent to your energy. Show it some love. If you get it right, you will feel a response. If you practice sharing emotion, a bond will form. That's the basics of "emoting". Only, the aliens do it much better. You end up getting complex layers of thoughts and those disco balls of images I was talking about before.

When I communicate with aliens, they are usually contacting me. It's like they are having a conversation and it occurs to them I could benefit from listening in, or they have a message they want me to deliver. If I am trying to contact them, it's a different ball of wax.

The first thing about seeking a connection I need to mention is, it's tricky. You have to put yourself in a neutral stance, like a conduit, and if you're not careful, something you're not comfortable with might come in on the line. You have to take precautions. Native shaman create ceremonies to build protection when they go into trance states. They call in spirit helpers and teach human assistants to help clear the area and hold off negativity. If you are calling out to make contact, be sure to manipulate the energy around you so that it's flavored positive. Be cheerful. If you are afraid of what you are doing, things can go sour. The best strategy is to get someone who knows the process to work you through it, so you don't have to go it alone.

The next thing you need to know is, you will be using your imagination as a tool to investigate other dimensions. It's a great tool. Everyone comes equipped with one at birth. It's about the most important tool you'll ever use and it's free! But unfortunately it doesn't come with instructions on how to use it. And if the adults in your life haven't figured out how it works, which many don't, you have to go the "trial and error" route. This rarely comes out well, so most people are convinced theirs doesn't work. They drew a picture in grammar school and it didn't come out like they wanted. It didn't look as real as the example. Maybe somebody laughed at it. Boom! The door to the imagination and all that it entails gets slammed shut. The imagination atrophies. What a waste! But it can be fixed. And if you want to talk with aliens, you have to get it back into working order. Accepting that challenge can be a grand adventure all by itself.

You know where your liver is and where your heart is, so if they aren't working correctly, you know where you have to go to fix them. But where is your imagination? Your brain? Nope. You can't operate on your brain to fix your imagination. It's somewhere else. It's in your mind. But where is your mind? It's not in your brain, either. Your mind and your imagination are part of something called "consciousness" which operates from within a separate invisible "body". It is not a physical thing. It is made of vibrating energy which you can feel it, but you can't touch it or see it. Consciousness, and the mind and imagination which spring from it, are all intelligent energy.

Time for a metaphor.

When you use your imagination, we say you are being "creative'. That means you are being a creator, like God. That's the hidden secret in the saying that God created us in His own image. But I think He regretted it immediately, because He made a big point of making us promise not to eat of the Tree of Knowledge. That is to say, our ability to create was hidden from us by keeping us ignorant. Ignorance is what happens if you can't digest knowledge. We weren't allowed to eat, much less digest the big stuff. God just wanted us to be simple gardeners, not rock the boat and mess with improvements on His masterpiece. The snake showed up because he didn't think it was fair of God to hide our creativity. He conned us into breaking our promise , thinking he was doing us a favor by setting us up for reaching our full potential. Turns out he hadn't chowed down on enough of the fruit himself. His actions were neither knowledgeable or wise. He got caught and God decided to give him the earth and make him deal with it, since it would soon be ruined, anyway. You know..."It's your baby, now. You broke it, you fix it."

Of course, God knew there would be trouble if we were allowed to be creative. We didn't come equipped with other, equally important skills, like discretion, insight, or foresight to discern the impact and consequences of using our innate creative powers. We were somewhat like God, but not gods ourselves. Most people think we got kicked out of the Garden for having sex. That's like saying we got original sin for breathing or eating. No. We got kicked out when God looked down and saw we had invented something...clothes...thereby exercising our creativity with the fig leaves. That was the big sin. Besides, we had broken our promise not to get smart.

But here we are, with just enough knowledge to be dangerous, on the brink of destroying what's left of God's original plan. We didn't stop with inventing clothes. Mostly inventions came in pairs, a good side and a bad one. We invented weapons to bring food to the dinner table. But it didn't take long for us to start killing each other as well. We built towns so we could work together to make life easier. But the towns got jealous of each other and invented war to knock each other out. So it went...from bad to worse. And through it all, Mr. Lucifer Snake (whose name means "light bringer") is running around trying to get us to stop, realizing his attempt at delivering enlightenment to us imperfect humans was the cause of all the destruction. He gets a bad rap, but he's the poster child for "No good deed goes unpunished." In other stories, Lucifer is cast as a very bad hombre, so I hope you're not offended by alien cultural bias.

My point here is, a little creativity can be a dangerous thing. The best strategy is to know what you've got and develop it to the max. The part I want to emphasize now is the imagination's capacity to use creativity to facilitate moving something from one dimension to another.

Let's say you look out the window and see a bird trying to build a nest, but the wind keeps knocking it out of the tree. You realize you could help with a solution. You could build the bird a house. So you think about how it should function and what it should look like. You make some sketches. You take some measurements. Then you go out and find all the supplies and tools you need to construct the birdhouse. At the end of this process, you have a material object that originated in your mind but ended up in the real world. You transported it from one dimension to another.

This is very much like what you have to do to make contact with aliens. Like I was trying to say before, you don't want them to come drop in physically. It can be dangerous. And besides, talking to an alien face to face can be like trying to hold a conversation in front of Niagara Falls, if it were made of energy rather than water. If you want to make this work, you need to use the creative power of your mind to create a space where the alien can leave a message (usually the disco ball of images, lights, colors and emotions) for you to consider and translate into human terms. The alien leaves you with the mental image of the bird house and you use it to bring it to life on your side of the line.

I have an example: Aaity's Aliens. Back in 1961 when unfamiliar voices started calling to her, Aaity Olson was already clairvoyant, working in graphic design, and doing a little psychic/intuitive business advising on the side. Being in the business of using her unusual abilities, she was not surprised to be receiving messages in her head. There did seem to be a strange urgency to the calling. So she went into trance to investigate, and came out with the understanding she was connecting to aliens.

Her aliens represented a collective intelligence they identified as The Star People. They had been trying unsuccessfully to get their message across to the scientists at White Sands and Area 51 to stop blowing up atomic and nuclear explosives into earth's fragile environment. It was their environment, too, only on a slightly different level. The problem was, they could only communicate through mental telepathy. If you're a scientist on a top secret project in the middle of the Cold War and you start hearing voices in your head telling you to stop doing what you're doing, you get some medication to turn the voices off. And you don't look back or tell anyone about it. So the Star People had to look for another way to get their point across. Aaity believed they chose her because of her psychic abilities, her talent for graphic design, and her life-long amateur interest in physics. The amateur part was important because they figured she'd be interested enough in the subject matter to stick with the program but not polluted with formal training enough to throw up a lot of questions and delay the download.

They intended to present humanity with a basic physics primer, a book that would provide future scientists with knowledge of certain basic principles that the physicists of today had missed. They convinced Aaity this was going to be a simple project, something she could complete in a few weeks or months. So she agreed to give it a try. Fifty years later, Volumes I & II were finished, but she was working on Volume III when she passed in 2011.

It took that long because, like I explained before, the alien mind works differently. They downloaded the entire book into her brain, expecting she could just take a look and easily translate it into human terms. But each strand she pulled became such a struggle to understand that when she pulled the next, the download had shifted and the two strands didn't match. It took years of pulling and sorting to put all the individual strands into some useful order. And all the while, the download grew as the aliens saw ways to fit additional information in.

Translating the alien's complex concepts into human terms was hard. First she had to look at the lights, colors, emotions and pictures floating around in her mind and try to focus some meaning out of it all. She would eventually come to understand some parts through emoting, but then she would have to go back and fact-check to be sure she got it right. She had to teach herself physics in order to find the right terms and such. It was a long, excruciating process. But she got it done. She brought the information the aliens showed her in their dimension, and brought it into being in this dimension.

The aliens call their textbook, *The Alchemical Manual for this Millennium* because they see us as being at about the same level compared to their science as we see the alchemists in relation to our own. It is available on Amazon and other on-line bookstores. Or you can download it for free at **https://www.aldvavall.com/admin/uploads/BOOKS_PDFs/Alchemical-Manuel-Vol-1-2.pdf**

And just like that, proof positive of alien contact. I know Aaity, and she could not have written that book by herself. In fact, for 33 of those fifty years, I helped her edit and research and acted as a sounding board while she struggled to get the words right and the meanings clear.

I met Aaity during a low point in the project. She had given up so much...her career, her family, her original life plans...and the aliens kept pouring more information out. It looked like the process would never end. So she quit. She told them she was finished and they just left. Turned off the lights and closed the door. But she immediately regretted her decision. Her life's work sat unfinished on her desk. She felt empty, unsatisfied. So she tried to apologize and get them to come back. Her efforts went unrewarded.

She came to me because I was the designated "past life regressionist" for our local "new age" community. She had the idea that if I could regress her thru hypnosis to a point before she asked them to leave, she might be able to reconnect. It worked. But there was one unforeseen consequence: I was now attached to the aliens. When they updated her download, they gave me one, too. Not the science, because it's not my interest. They gave me the challenge of discovering evidence they had been interacting with ancient cultures across the globe. I was sent to Mexico twice to do fieldwork, and have expanded my research to all the Americas. And Europe. And Asia. Aaity and I were collaborating on Volume II when she passed. It might yet get finished. The aliens assure me it's important, and even at age 73, I still have time to finish saving the world. Ha!

The burning questions these days, after the U.S. government released video of moving objects they could not identify, is not so much are UFOs real, but what are they and where did they come from?! According to a recent survey from the Pew Research Center[1], 65% of Americans believe intelligent life exists on other planets. 57% believe UFOs reported by the military are likely proof of that. And most don't consider aliens to be a major national security threat. It seems like time is right for aliens to appear. It's almost to the point of being annoying that they don't.

There's a long list of reasons why aliens aren't making themselves known directly. To begin with, our planet is just too geologically fragile, unstable. Create a civilization, get it going on track, then, a volcano erupts and all your work goes up in fire and smoke. Volcanoes, earthquakes, tsunamis, meteorites, flooding, even pole shifts get in the mix. It's a dangerous place to be.

Another consideration is, the natives are violent. A lot of the time, they are working hard at eliminating every living being on the planet. The rest of the time, they are out to kill each other. They have created a global civilization which pollutes the air and water necessary for their survival. A large percentage of them ignore the obvious, that

---

[1] https://www.pewresearch.org/fact-tank/2021/06/30/most-americans-believe-in-intelligent-life-beyond-earth-few-see-ufos-as-a-major-national-security-threat/

the ice caps are melting and the climate is changing due to over-industrialization and poor resource management. Not only are they destroying their world, they are destroying themselves. Half the world is starving while the other half over-eats and blames the poor for not being rich. Would you want to mess with such obnoxious people?

The aliens are waiting for us to get our act together before they make physical contact. Until then, they are taking the safe route. They send us greetings, provide the opportunity for us to get with the program, sit back and watch, and sigh a lot because we fail at the obvious. We are born with all the right feelings...all ready to emote our way into everyone's hearts and minds...but we so quickly sour as we learn how the world around us operates. We could fix everything. We could save the world. But we don't. We get distracted, we wander off. We try the quick fix, the short cut. When times get tough, we get in the habit of complaining rather than taking action. And when we do act, we usually pick the wrong side even when we are trying hard to do the right thing.

I have tried to explain being human to my alien contacts, but they just don't get it. How could beings with such brilliant potential end up clueless and in the dark, when they should be out saving the galaxy?! Well, what can I say? We were given creative powers by mistake and have been perplexed since the beginning. And at the moment, we are headed toward even more trouble. The earth, the sun and the rest of our solar system are passing through an area in space that is charged with a very aggressive energy. Some people will rise with it, use it to propel themselves into higher frequencies, perhaps joining other dimensions. But a lot of us will get stuck trying to live the same way when everything around them is changing. The crazy energy will get us pounding our heads against an invisible wall. The social unrest we're already experiencing will get worse. We're in for rough times.

Maybe the whole point is, we can't save the world the way it is. It may need to be cleansed and then rebuilt, like a worn-out tenement. Maybe that's what the coming changes are all about. Those who make it through will be the ones who practice raising their vibrations and can get comfortable as the frequencies around them rise. They'll be the ones who embrace change rather than fight it. And there *will* be change. Times are changing now, with each new invention and the gradual adjustments we make as they become mainstream. This social and technological revolution will speed up until it gets all wound up and everything falls apart. Then we'll be back living in caves. And one quiet night, a voice will come out of the darkness. "You, there. Pick up that stick and rub it on that log. See what happens." And we'll be off on another round.

An Experiencers Tale: Impressions of my life with ET contact

Ralph Connor

Preface, and background

From my earliest memories in this life, I've known that life was eternal. When I was 3 years old, I was so terrified of the sight of a house nearby that my parents could not get me to walk past it. Many homes in that area were constructed in Tudor style, with faux battlements and castle towers. Just the sight of one such tower on one a home caused me extreme terror. When my family tried to coax me to pass it, it seemed that that I might suffer convulsions or some another physical crisis so great was my terror. The home was a few blocks away on the way to a friend's house and it was a nice walk for our family. Not for me. Although I came to appreciate the views later in life. I was too young for the crisis to be psycho pathological. Then my grandmother resolved to rectify the situation. We went for a walk one morning up the cobblestone streets near to where the home with the tower was. My Grandmother was very empathetic and when she took me to confront my trauma, she also remembered. She had been with me in our past life and she had witnessed my execution by being thrown from a castle tower onto the rocks below.

The situation resolved itself naturally around age 4 when I forgot the past life. An Indian mystic that I listen to Sadhguru says that it's common for children to remember past lives up till age 3 or 4. He calls it an ability and an aberration. In this life experience it is not intended that we remember past lives and relationships. Later if we become enlightened we obtain the realization necessary to correlate the big picture. That's how the experience of incarnation here is designed to work per Sadhguru. But he says that since this is such a great and extensive system, it is normal that there are some loopholes and cracks in the façade.

I lost the traumatic memory and was able to function normally. But the trauma affected my ability to integrate into this life. What was the point, it always ends the same way. Why is this happening? WHY do I have to keep coming back just to die? All of the aspects of this Western civilization promote the false Cartesian concept that materiality is all there is. Deep inside, I knew something that most people evidently don't. That everything here is transitory. Materiality was futile, there was really no reason to be involved in the appropriately titled Rat Race. As adults we can comprehend the concept of the cycle of rebirth. But as a child, I had little ability to integrate the reality. I remembered being murdered. Now I'm beginning the cycle again. I had known my Grandmother in the other life which made it very difficult to believe the illusion of materialism. It's all fake! It wasn't till I was age 15 a friend who was a Navy Chaplain helped me integrate the transitory nature of this life and what death was. Sadhguru is correct. Remembrance of immortality and past lives is not conducive to our being able to accomplish the lessons that we came to learn. It is the cocoon of forgetfulness that enables our ability to play the role that we came here for. I never truly lost the ability to access past life memories. I learned to control aspects of the memory and I could control most what I recalled. Instead of only remembering the traumatic parts, which is common in past life remembrance.

The event was a profound juncture in my grandmothers life. Our family includes Scottish, Irish, and English lineage. We have lived in central Virginia since the 1600s. My Grandmother had grown up in a self-sufficient homestead. They made their own clothes, grew their own food and literally had walked five miles to and from school. We still own the property and the log cabin which is over 100 years old. We were in the Baptist Belt but my parents were drawn to Presbyterian faith, possibly due to their Scottish ancestry. Faith, and going to church was very important in our lives. But there was no correlation in my Grandmothers faith Christianity for the realization that had been revealed to her. The realization made her seek closure. The culture in Virginia is very amenable to metaphysical phenomena. And not all superstitions are unfounded. This event took its place in our family history alongside many others. This experience was a profound juncture for my Grandmothers life. It was what Mary Rodwell calls a Trigger of Consciousness. Usually a consciousness related event like an ancestral visitation, a near death experience, or a UFO event which completely changes ones conception of reality. Like an upgrade. Things are different afterward. One has to adjust for increased perception, every time. My grandmother in seeking to validate this experience and others she had, found the Edgar Caycee Foundation. The informal psychic network, which was located nearby in Virginia Beach would play a role in the metaphysical life of our family.

My life as an experiencer began early. I use the term experiencer for several reasons. One, is because everyone who is interested in this genre understands the context. The second is that as a group, we have very similar experiences. This is confirmed by scientific study. The phenomena I've experienced in my life is almost all ET related. Even the religious experiences. That is my focus on in this essay. My intent is to accurately portray only what I've experienced. I want to leave the conclusions to the reader. I will only add my theory or conjecture if I believe it's required to make sense out of the material. I do not pretend to understand the nuts and bolts of the phenomena. I have learned to interact with the phenomena intuitively. I don't recall choosing to be an experiencer. It would be much easier to be silent. But since I am in this position, between two civilizations I feel a great responsibility to share my experiences as well as I can for the sake of humanity. The ETs can unlock the secrets of the cosmos, cure our ills and make life much better on Earth.

To describe paranormal phenomena, I will use the criteria that FREE used successfully in their survey. If I am unsure of the physicality of any experience I will classify it as a Vivid Dream phenomenon. Into the Grey Basket! A strange part of being an experiencer is that many of us have memories that we can't reconcile with this reality. Like being taken to other worlds, interacting with non-human intelligences or even stranger stuff. There is much of this that I have to leave out of this essay due to space. A lot of the memories of Darshan or Communion with these beings is so deep and profound I feel uncomfortable discussing it because I do not understand all of it. A lot of the conversation is about what I've learned in this life as opposed to having similar experiences in other lives. Real Grey Basket, Vivid Dream material right there! Why would ET beings be interested the evolution of human souls or consciousness's? That's supposed to be the job of religious deities. Angels and Gods. Not coincidentally, there is indeed evidence of encounters in all ancient religious texts. Even the modern sages such as Sadhguru state that the Gods of religion can be so classified. This is a great mystery that we enter into, of our own free will. I look at it from the point of view of Vedic study. What we call Mystery is an element in and of itself called Akasha. The fifth element. I've found Vedic concepts quite helpful in understanding and assimilating the paranormal. Everything is in there. From ETs and astrophysics to the nature of the cosmos. In those terms ET intervention is part and parcel of nature. It's an expression of the fifth element. We live in a Cartesian civilization so, the existence of another dimension of nature is left to the conventions of religion or denied altogether.

The wakeup call

I'm beginning this essay with my initial call to awareness of the ETs, and then a life chronology. Just like Whitley Schreiber and many others, I was contacted by the ETs after their fashion. I was made aware of a lifetime of contact that I was on and off aware of at different times. One day there will be an understanding about why the ETs do it that way. But now all that we know is that this pattern of is consistent. The wakeup call began around 2010 when beings became prominent in my consciousness. It was a very straight forward message from a Mantid Elder. Although I was unaware of what was happening, I have been part of contact between our species all my life. I did not remember much about them, except for enigmatic UFO encounters from early in my life. I could not get those events out of my head and they seemed to become clearer and clearer. We can speculate for days about how and why we were contacted. Most of us have. And we will not find a definitive answer. This is just how higher intelligences do things. And we have to accept that logically, higher intelligence means that we are not capable of fully comprehending. It seems quite logical to me that the ETs selected a statistical cross section of humanity as a control group to initiate contact. This is consistent with the extreme diversity of the people who have paranormal experiences. My personal, intuitive belief is that what's happening goes far beyond this life. The ETs have told me that on several occasions. ETs and beings that exist beyond time, are multidimensional. And they are so different from all Earthly life that its very different to relate. No so for them. They can present themselves to humans just like other humans and communicate perfectly. That seems to be a principle throughout metaphysics. Higher dimensions and realities can interface with lower realities but generally, not vice versa. It's like when adults address children. Baby talk. A consistent thread in my experiences and therefore this article is that they are teaching us how to initiate communication with them. Which is a completely different ball of wax compared to when they initiate a contact event.

In 2010 an intelligence which somehow seemed familiar, was insistent upon communicating with me. I had begun remembering interaction with the ETs extensively as a child. I did not believe that the memories were real, 100%. But they were correlatable with ET UAP experiences so I had to take them seriously. I was involved in a challenging and 1000% materialistic career in international sales and logistics. It took all the effort I had to maintain my career and family. The Contact experience that was happening to me was overwhelming from many perspectives. The ET was an elder of the Mantid race and he was communicating urgency. I had always thrived upon Science Fiction and I was beyond enthusiastic with the idea of interspecies cooperation. Now, out of the blue, the opportunity was knocking upon my door. The whole thing seemed odd but I was beyond fascinated. I needed some grounding, so I engaged a psychologist to help me integrate what was happening into my life. I chose him because he was close and looked friendly. Coincidentally, this doctor was a Monroe school graduate who practiced OBEs. This coincidence profoundly affected our interaction and the result. A paranormal phenomena like ET contact would throw a curve ball to most therapists. I had fortunately found exactly the right one. I am highlighting coincidences involved in the process of Contact, to explain my take on the phenomena of synchronicity.

I discussed almost all aspects of the phenomena with the Doctor and the help was exactly what I needed. He diagnosed psychological anaphylactic shock as the reason for my discomfort. My descriptions of interactions with the ETs throughout my life sounded to him like a higher evolved and benign intelligence engaging humanity. Exactly what it is. My yogic background gave me an outlook that helps me to engage phenomena. I am aware that none of my observations are conclusive. And, I make a conscious effort not to become attached to any of my theories. The ETs present themselves to me just as they do to many others. Flying saucers, greys, reptilians and all the other elements of the phenomena. I am aware of that but at the same time I realize that it could be something completely different from how my senses perceive it. That is the perspective that I want to present my Contact experience from. Just my perceptions, with just enough theory added to make sense when necessary. The phenomena wants us to make our own decisions and so it interacts directly with us on many levels not all of which we are conscious of.

The ETS didn't land and give me a briefing. I only experienced an insistent telepathy from the Mantid Elder. He was intent upon establishing our relationship and ensuring that I understood how it had existed throughout my life. He did not directly answer my questions as a human would. I began to read materials about contact. I was dying to talk to a knowledgeable human about this. I had some serious questions. The ETs were not answering the questions conclusively and the more I learned the more that the mystery deepened. I obtained Kim Carlsberg's book, ***Beyond My Wildest dreams***. I could relate to her experiences. And her bewilderment and frustration with the ETs enigmatic way of doing things. She had fear of the beings at that time and I could not relate to that. Some of my earliest memories were of being with the ETs and I know that they are benign. Frustrating, they might be but they mean no harm. There was a section in her book where she vented her frustrations by demanding that they appear in person, and they did. I had reached that point myself and it seemed the appropriate thing to do. So, outside I went and vented my frustration to a suspicious looking cloud that was overhead. I'm only human, I can't figure this out by myself! I need explanations! Nothing happened but it felt pretty good. I felt that they had gotten my ultimatum. And if they didn't care to answer then I would not give them much of my attention or time. Humans are so dramatic. Then, two weeks later I was driving my wife home during a storm. We stopped at City Drive in Escondido to have a late dinner at a French restaurant. As we walked out of the restaurant at about 10 PM I could see clouds whipping by above in the city lights a few thousand feet up. It was the most intense storm that year in the region. Then suddenly the storm receded. It became dead quiet, I could hear the mechanism in the stop light as it changed. Then about half a mile away a large metallic appeared dropped out of the low cloud cover. A red and white light began flashing below the inverted metallic dome that was peeping out of the clouds were swirling around the object. It seemed to be the bottom section of a flying saucer. And if so the craft would've been almost half a kilometer wide. Sitting there in plain sight a few thousand feet over Escondido. No Earthly object could hover in that manner during a storm like that. I need to try to photograph this I thought. But my wife was having none of it. The sudden cessation of the storm and appearance of the un earthly object was too much for her. She insisted that we should leave immediately! I was in an astonished state from this overwhelming reply to my ultimatum to the ETs, so I complied and drove home.

Physical manifestations from other worlds or dimensions are psychic events which encompass much more than our 3 senses. I don't want to go down the Rabbit Hole in this essay. I will try to stay away from esoteric phenomena as much as possible. But I have learned through addressing the phenomena, that it happens on so many levels it's not all apparent at the time. Our perception of time makes that which is beyond time difficult to perceive for our 3D senses. The term Download is used by many to describe the sensation of receiving a package of data that is then read or understood over a period of time. We perceive time linearly but other dimensions do not and there is something like a differential between two realities, is the best way that I can describe the sensation.

The astonishingly large craft in the sky shocked me. But the message that he conveyed by appearing like that came through loud and clear. Straight to the point without even the possibility of misunderstanding. The message was profound, what was happening to me was much bigger than he and I. And that I should consider losing some of my human drama in order to assimilate what was being presented to me. Many ETs exhibit playfulness, as a means of communicating with us. Since we are not skilled enough to ascertain the precise nature of the ETs that are engaging us, the beings try to ensure that what we do perceive is entirely as unthreatening as possible. It seems to be a cosmic anthropology initiative. My experience with the Mantids is that they are very direct. Which given the nature of this phenomena makes them quite revered and respected by humans.

That was the point in my journey where I was able to make contact with people who actually knew something about what was happening to me. Budd Hopkins had called me and we chatted a few times. I greatly appreciate his and Yvonne Smiths response to my strange dilemma. I'm being contacted by advanced intelligences and I don't know what to do. I explained to Budd that I unequivocally did not fear the beings, IMO they were completely benign. I had grown up with them. They had never done anything to harm me. Quite the opposite as I will relate. Budds' response made my heart sink. He said, that we could recover memories that would bring me closure. But first I should consider that it might be too scary. I really wondered at how anyone could be contacted by an ET and not be able to just blow it off because its scary. I have since learned that this is actually a very common response. I have spoken to people who the ETs have appeared to right in their living room asking them to communicate and interact with them for our mutual benefit. That's how they put it. My friend declined. There was something about the ETs that didn't seem right. You can't trust people who can walk through walls. I didn't realize that humans could be so illogical. But then, I was just getting an inkling of the difference that my lifelong conditioning with the aliens made me different. Budd offered hypnosis to recover memories which theoretically could offer some understanding and closure. My psychologist differed and said that the hypnotist absolutely always influenced the impressions of the patient, even in the best cases. Instead the psychologist offered a meditative method to retrieve and integrate traumatic memories. This was a serendipitous coincidence since I used meditation. I had lived in or by an Ashram for 3 years when I was in my late teens. That sat with me much better since I intuitively knew that it wasn't just about retrieving lost memories. The UFO culture at the time believed that the aliens hide our memories of ET interactions by inserting cover memories to facilitate whatever they are doing with minimal impact upon our lives. I agree that they are doing that. But IMO it is much more complicated than just hiding from us.

I realized intuitively that the way to address this phenomena was through Sadhana. A yogic lifestyle. Raising ones vibe. So, I began a program to do that. The Mantid Elder that I nicknamed Lothar had made it clear that this was the way it was going to be. I had to adjust to the reality, the reality would not adjust to me. I felt it quite fortunate that I had the skills to set about doing so. So, I settled in to do some internal work.

The FREE Foundation UFO Contact Experiencer Research Study

It was at this point in my odyssey when the Dr. Edgar Mitchell FREE Foundation UFO Contact Experiencer Research Study began sending out the survey questionnaires. I recognized the sophistication of the query. Someone with some knowledge was engaging the phenomena. The structure of the questions was fascinating. The focus upon discerning if the nature of an event was physical or virtual really helped me address the phenomena. I felt that the purpose of the survey would be best served if I only classified physical events by if there was other correlating data or witnesses. What was left, including Vivid Dream experiences and downloads was Grey Basket material. That POV really helped put things into perspective.

FREEs analysis of the survey was astounding and a confirmation of what I intuitively knew. It was an integral and timely revelation for all of us. I will try to illustrate how FREEs revelations throughout this essay. One is that UFO encounters are psychic events. A lot more is happening than just what our senses are registering. Another finding is that the phenomena is non local. You can be anywhere and there does not need to be a visible UFO or alien present. In my opinion these discoveries are the key to beginning to understand the phenomena.

Very likely the most important discovery from FREE was the concept of the Modalities of the ascension of human consciousness-- the Contact Modalities. It was imparted directly to Rey Hernandez by the Non-Human Intelligence while he was taken out of his body to another dimension. I compare it to ancient Celtic philosophy which concludes that all roads lead to the same place. Religious experience, religious charismatic experience, psychedelics, yogic sadhana, NDEs, ET Contact all lead to the same realizations of human consciousness. All of creation is connected and we are each a microcosm of the whole. I don't use the word God but the concept fits the definition.

There are two other experiences involved in the wake up call to exo consciousness story that I believe are relevant. The first is the when I began meditation to access the ET phenomena. I immediately discovered I had an ability to tune in to it. It happens on another level of reality that lies above the physical plains, between the boundaries of the Astral and the Etheric field of the Akasha. Sort of a communication field where different realities can merge. There is quite a differential between dimensions, that expresses itself in this dimension in different ways. Like time losses. I decided to ramp up the Sadhana or meditation with Yogi tricks I knew. Such as, meditation during the Brahmamyrtu hour 1 hour before dawn intensifies the effects meditation is designed to achieve. I knew about Mantra, Hatha Yoga and a lot of the other stuff. I studied the Dao, and I Ching intensely with another practitioner. Daoism helped me understand the phenomena of Contact in ways that I can't easily explain. Any time I experience direct contact afterwards, I am left with profound reflections on the void. It's something about where they are coming from, a non-physical no time realm.

The Queen Mother

I was doing lots of yoga and one morning I awoke at the perfect time for Brahmamyrtu meditation. I took my spot under the morning stars and after a few minutes of clearing exercises and pranayama a remarkable feeling entered into my consciousness. In conjunction with activity in the sky, I was flooded by feelings of well-being, deep compassion and profound caring. A greeting, modulated by a personality beautiful, and exalted like royalty. These are not the sensations one expects when considering telepathy with ETs. The experience was multisensory with all systems engaged. There were waves of color and imagery in my mind, there were deep astrophysical concepts and downloads going on as well as the emotional response to their energy that many of us have. The beings were on a craft with a ringed planet behind them through a portal. Standing around an object that was the focus of their communication with me. Whether the description seems like a desktop video intercom, or scrying a crystal ball we were communicating through it. My POV was in effect inside the thingie and the beings stood around it. I have some familiarity with this Tech, but I can only describe or understand minute parts of its function. My awareness was of a group of beings with the Royal Being paramount among them. I understood concepts of an alien DNA hierarchy and I realized that they were telling me who she was. She was the Queen. I understood that I was being addressed in my continuum in order that I could fully experience it and remember it completely in this continuum.

Other concepts that I automatically understood were, the habitat or craft that she was on was in the orbit of Saturn in the lower umbra. Her personality overwhelmed it all. It was so sweet, almost angelic with bright personality aspects. She was the perfect diplomat with a high level ability to make dialog possible. Despite her awesomeness she made you feel special. Just like when The Queen serves you tea in her sitting room. It would not have been possible for me I don't think, without the personality that she could exhibit. Even jokes. She referred to herself as a Happy Grasshopper as I was having thoughts about her insectoid appearance. Its hard to describe a direct conversation with the beings because it happens on so many levels.

To discuss all the aspects in linear format would take a book. But conversation is not linear and it occurs in complete concepts like downloads. To paraphrase the experience. I was told that the process of creating sentient communication, which is when we know exactly what is happening during an experience is a process that took the Mantids my whole life to accomplish. They are meticulous, I guess. Then when I was made fully aware of the scope of their involvement in my life, I accepted it and set my intention toward assimilating more of the modality. They sent a mental image of Kubrick's Space Oddessy when the Monoliths signaled the ETs that we were ready for contact. This was the end of a cycle and therefore somehow notable for them which brought me to their attention. I felt deep compassion and well-being vibes, and she said that they felt something like appreciation. I also felt deep attachments to the planet as if I had spent a lot of time there but didn't recollect it.

Contactees report a connection with the planet. I have often awakened with super high definition visions of planets in my mind's eye. I found a video by Robert Dean about the Mantid habitat or base that he said he showed pictures of. He said it was over 40 miles long. I've found other correlation of encounters like mine. The second notable experience from that time frame was one evening while I was making dinner. The Wee Man : I felt, or understood that a robed being that I had been communicating with for a long time was just outside the back door and I felt a polite query, if he could enter. I had had been having premonitions about direct contact with the ETs during morning meditation.

I was amenable, but not quite ready. But I easily slipped into a strange mode where I could conduct the conversation or communion and also finish making dinner. Its similar to a Yogic state, but its implemented by the ETs until we learn how. But that's an option some people do not pursue. I was flooded with information downloads, and a profound sense that I had indeed been with this entity. The entities are evolved beyond human emotions. What they have is more refined but I certainly felt loving, attachment for the being. He sent a ton of downloads, if that makes sense to you in response to queries in my mind when I opened to them. It seemed as though he was among a group of ETs who each performed a function. My questions were answered. He told me and I remembered him from times that he had come to me consciously, and in dreams that involved flying and or Astral Projection.

There were a lot of physical effects from those vivid dreams which involved passing through solid materials like walls. I had a gripe. At that phase of my Wake Up experience I remembered what I thought were blocked memories of encounters or Alien Abductions as the MSM like to portray. Were they doing that on purpose? I would like the memories back, if you please. His appearance is of a small ET in a black robe. I am familiar with a species like him. I have other contacts with small robes ones who I have different conversations with. Some of the conversations are exactly like folklore account of conversations with guardian spirits. But he is an Elder or leader in their world and has much greater ability. Usually, they don't address me directly like this. And I understood that this was in response to my desire to be fully conscious in this realm of the encounter. A female being or aspect of the being directed me to look away as he entered the dining room.

My impression was of an intense ball of light that radiated an intense sense of potential energy. We are addressing your query about your memory. You will have access to all of it that you desire. As many other Contactees have noted, the small robed ones have a sense of humor. In this case, understatement. I was positioned in such a way that he touched the nape of my neck from behind. I understood the term trigger of consciousness from a Mary Rodman video I had heard earlier that day and I understood that I was having one during the experience.

Your welcome! I felt nothing physically other than that my neck felt warm most of the evening. But I felt the presence of a lot of new information that I had access to. The weird thing was how the encounter took place in another place simultaneously as I cooked and served dinner. I've become used to the sensation which is part of the unfolding of the phenomena. The effect was to open my mind more to the field where the memories were easier to access. But the other parts of the conversation eclipsed the memory issue so as to make it not important.

He had given me a lot more to think about that I have space for here. It involved who he is in relation to his long association with humanity. I want to specify that as a Yogi, experiences related to Yogic realms and ET dimensions are intrinsically different from psychedelic experiences. I've had guided experiences with psychedelics and although the experience sounds the same, it's not even close. On psychedelics one is completely in the hands of the substance. You surrender your will to the sacrament and it takes you where it goes. During encounters with NHI they are in control of the encounter and our sensory impressions to some extent. Yogic experience is the ultimate since you are completely in control. All are equally profound but different.

ETs and elementary school

My earliest memories with them are abstract. I recall very little fear even when they would visit unexpectedly. I lived with my Grandparents out in the country half the week when I was in my early years. When they went to sleep, I would crawl out of the window and go out to the garden to wait for the ETs. I believed that they took me to the Moon where they had a habitat. We learned how to interact with the different ET races. My memories are of architecture similar to ancient Greek ruins with large tunnels seemingly open to the moonscape with no walls. They would drop me off directly in my bed just before school. Speaking of Elementary school, I preferred the ETs! Adolescent humans were totally unpredictable and I really didn't see the point. Compared with the serene and benign nature of the ETs. Later interactions with the ETs could be challenging. But the childhood experiences were more like nursery school by comparison. When I am with the ETs there is usually, an intense feeling of wellbeing and compassion. Not so much with humans. The ETs told me several things that I'll pass on for WIW. I was sent here by them to help them reveal themselves to humanity. I was not human I was part of them and they put me in my family out of necessity. They were far more family than the humans. The being that was with me the most in those years is as a small robed grey. I am aware of several of the robed ones. One of whom is blue or black robed and is a leader.

An early interaction that I had with him was when I was 5 years and I was being prepared for school. I had become enthralled in the idea conveyed by the movie, the Day the Earth Stood Still. The Robed One suggested that humans should strongly consider the concepts presented in the movie and that I could help. I strongly felt that I needed to publicize it to the community so I queried my parents how that might be done. They said we should write a letter to the local TV station in a year or two when I learned how to write. That would not do. The little robed guy had had a special Darshan or Communion session just with me on board his craft. The main point was that we were doing this together. Everything that we did needed to come from us. I have always been fully vested in the aliens because their nature is beyond sincere. The appear to our senses as higher evolution embodied and so there is little room for doubt. This interaction is an example of something that I did which was suggested by them. That they are taking such meticulous steps to inform us of their presence says a great deal about their integrity and their clear intentions, in my opinion.

Everything that they do is for the benefit of life in the cosmos. For the record my definition of good and bad is Vedic centric. Good is all that which nourishes and sustains life. Evil is that which takes away health and life. The ETs in that context are good. This cannot be said of our species.

In first grade my schoolmates were delighted with my stories of visiting the ETs in their craft and on other planets. We had an art club during lunchtime and recess. We would draw sci fi that we had read and I'd tell them about the ETs. ETs use Sci Fi as part of the contact assimilation process. The ETs use the concept to explain themselves and I will expound on that later. They thought it was wonderful if not a assimilation process. The ETs use the concept to explain themselves and I will expound on that later. They thought it was wonderful if not a bit scary. A few years later and the children all had been advised by their parents to stay away from my stories. I was either a pathological liar, or this being the Baptist belt it might just be the Devil at work! I began to be ostracized and even now my elementary classmates remember me by my nickname, Spaceman. I liked the moniker but cultural ostracizing is a common feature of experiencers lives. And so we learn not to talk about it. This cultural isolation is being addressed by the Contact community and also by the ETs through mass events. A mass close encounter event like the Hudson Valley events create many experiencers in a short space of time.

Some of the other children in school were involved in the ET activities. I would try to strike up conversations with children that I had met on board craft but not in real life. I remembered clkearly, but their memories were incomplete and they only felt confused. The ETs action was widespread and I was taken to be with them extensively. I have been aware since childhood that ET manage human contact with control groups. A great documentary about mass contact was the Secret of Redfern by Jim Maars. It seemed that my function was in many occasions was to help acclimatize other humans some of which I knew from school to the environment on the craft. They would present me in our little blue uniform to humans on board and we would try to help them overcome their shock and fear. If they could handle it, then we would interact on board with the ETs.

A good example of such an experience is when I was once eating dinner with my Grandparents. It was about 5 PM on a Fall afternoon. Suddenly, time stopped for me and I was flying up to a craft with a robed friend. I proceeded with him through the corridors of the craft till we came upon a scene of a small human on a table surrounded by humanoid aliens. The second that I set eyes on the distressed kid I recognized that he was one of the bad kids and his discomfort was not entirely unpleasant to me. In that microsecond I was returned to our kitchen and my Grandparents never knew anything had happened. In my life I had often informed my family when events like these occurred.

Up till age 5 my family tolerated it as an overactive imagination. After that they thought it something that they needed to control. I learned not to mention it and that became a lifelong habit. Humans can be quite illogical when their belief systems are threatened! My relationship with the ETs as with my elementary school colleagues involved my assisting the ETs with interfacing with humanity. I recall that they presented us dressed similar to them and I've speculated that the on board guests believed that I was an ET. Unless there was preexisting trauma, the presence of other humans generally calmed people and they were able to interact with the ETs. Obviously, the best time to acclimatize humans would be when they are young. Before they have developed the materialistic, Cartesian mindset which precludes even the existence of other intelligences. So throughout this encounter I tried to coach Dad through it. In close encounters it seemed that I was always functioning in coordination with the ETs although I didn't consciously know it. As though I knew what needed to be done and I instinctively did it.

ETs with my Father

As I grew up in Central Virginia in the 1960s and 70s, my father and I had extensive ET contact together. He managed a US Government health unit for Federal employees. He would go to remote Federal sites and give everyone chest x rays as mandated at the time. He would use the opportunities, which brought him to remote locations to collect wildlife and photos which he would use in his wildlife paintings. His preferred medium was life size watercolor bird paintings.

A giant Black Floating Sphere larger than 100 meters across

We did not at the time conflate the time losses that our family had with ET phenomena. But we witnessed mass events along with others on many occasions. I've since correlated all these events with news sources, and they were massive. Once when we were camping at a remote spot on the W. Virginia border for hunting we awoke early, went hunting then returned at about 10 AM for breakfast. Our friend Julian had a complete kitchen in his trailer and we were going to feast. I heard an exclamation and up the valley about 3 miles a large object was entering the valley and coming our way. It was a giant black sphere larger than 100 meters across. The sun glinted off it but it was strangely flat and light absorbent. As it approached it became transparent, there was a flying saucer inside and it was landing in a field some distance away. The craft was at least 100 meters wide, composed of 3 saucers stacked with a large pylon on top with what looked like a tesla coil on it. I have seen that craft twice in photos, one of which was taken by the Chilean military. I always feel connected to phenomena when it's around and so I replied to the others exclamations that this was an alien craft and we were being visited. That was it. The next thing that we remember it was gone.

My father's camping buddies were all GE engineers and they all agreed on what we had seen. Dad was insistent that we would not tell the family or anyone else what we had seen. All his credibility would be at state. Such was the cultural deficit in those days. We all remembered being frozen in place we assumed by fear. But our feelings after the event were uplifting. We knew we weren't alone and we had taken part in something exceptional. We only talked about it when we were together and then in whispers. A humorous side note is that the night before by the campfire, my fervent belief in flying saucer aliens had been utilized in the hazing that new hunters had to endure, as dues. In that respect it was a very good encounter for me. It was as if the aliens had backed up my assertion the night before. They didn't haze me anymore, in any case. This is one of a number of times that the ETs have shown themselves to other people in my presence. They might utilize the opportunity of me being there to engage other humans. Ideally, I would explain what is happening and vouch for the ETs. Alas, but it doesn't work like that. What I usually end up doing is cracking jokes. Because some people have fear and once they are scared, any opportunity for a constructive conclusion is void.

After we witnessed the craft land, we did a thorough investigation of the area that the craft had come from. We inquired with the local ranger whose cabin was near the area. He said that no one had been in the area since the snow had thawed this year. But the locals reported a consistent phenomenon in the area. This section of the Appalachians is considered deep and mysterious by the locals. Many of the best known NHI phenomena have occurred near here. Superstitions abound, and every old family has a trove of paranormal stories.

My most profound contact experiences of Contact with my father was when I was staying with him, at around age 16 in Richmond Virginia in 1972. We decided to go to a movie one night just after dark, and as we went up a freeway ramp that gave a vista of the city we saw a large cigar shaped craft moving about over the city. It was encompassed by a viscous golden light that seemed to cling to it like a liquid. It moved, totally unlike a terrestrial craft back and forth and it would stop and emit concentric rings of purple light onto the city. As we entered the freeway the craft moved adjacent to us filling the windows. It seemed intelligent and interested in us. We were struck with the desire to follow it and we tried to determine its course. Suddenly we remembered that Dad was a professional photographer. So, we pulled over to get the equipment out of the trunk. The craft which had been on the other side of the city moved closer to us. Inexplicably, the camera wasn't there. This was the first time he had misplaced it. What a co incidence. A lot of interaction with the beings seems to be a small joke on us. As if they're making the point that they can control all aspects of what evidence we are allowed to have. We raced to get on the freeway. At the time, we thought that we were chasing the craft. But in retrospect, it was always somehow always fully in our windshield. I remember that there seemed no way to gage its size except for one glance in which it seemed to be longer than a city block. Close to half a kilometer long. The last cognizant memory I have that evening is of the craft becoming brighter and brighter till I couldn't see. I never remembered the movie we were going to.

The next morning we had learned that the radio stations had all been inundated with calls reporting the UFO activity. Later in life when I researched it I found reports of widespread interaction with just such a cigar shaped craft. But not in Richmond specifically, but spread through the central piedmont region over 100 miles from our encounter. That reinforces my intuition that what was happening was very wide scale. This began a series of interactions with the Mantids and their group along with my father over the next few months. The relationship with the ETs, my Dad, and the companions was complex. My father felt that I was connected with the ETs, through the phenomena. I had learned to read by reading Sci Fi in the 1960s when Azimov and AC Clarke were publishing work. It had conditioned me to be very enthusiastic about anything having to do with space and aliens. Dad was old school, traditional Virginian in outlook. This was the Age of Aquarius, Dope, and Free Love. UFOs fit into the equation quite well, such was the culture at that time. I had dabbled with that culture when I lived in California and so I had quite a few strikes against me as far as Dad was concerned. When we infrequently talked about it Dad always insisted that he hated it and resented the intrusion. I do not believe that he would have ever accepted the indignity of being taken by the aliens any time they wanted as having any positive connotations. We never spoke of it except obliquely. One factor was fear of losing professional credibility.

I spoke with the other friends who had witnessed the flying saucer. They were as concerned about their own credibility as my father. But they conveyed to me that they were aware that they had witnessed something from beyond earth. The eyes will refuse to see what the mind cannot comprehend. This summarizes the changes in human society that will be required before we can progress to the point of cognizant communications with the ETs in my opinion. Looking at the length and breadth of ET contact phenomena it's obvious that the ETs are being very methodically and incrementally. I wish to advance the conversation. I sincerely believe that this phenomena is the catalyst for the next step in human evolution. I believe that the theory of the Kardeshez scale is correct. The transition to the 1st stage, which is sustainable civilization is the most critical juncture for a civilization.

On board and the transformation

At this juncture of my life, I was indecisive of my goals and I was spending time with my Father in Richmond Va. I recall leaving my girlfriend's house on foot one afternoon. The sky was looking like rain. I recall glancing at the clouds as I reached the road, I might be getting wet. Then all in a millisecond, the image of a saucer shape landing nearby appeared in my mind's eye. The next thing I was aware of, I was lying on my back somewhere else. My eyes were closed and my extremities felt numb. I was being encouraged to open my eyes. The encouragement resolved itself into the voice of my Mantid friend. You are with us. Somehow, I remembered him and I felt at ease and a sense of well-being. I knew that this moment was significant. I opened my eyes. My first sensation was of being in a room full of insectoid beings. The Elder Mantid was robed along with 2 other Mantids standing before me. A number of smaller beings were busy with me and the unit that I was reclined upon.

They seemed to be the Grey variety but with reptilian eyes. IMO the Mantids looked more like bees. Especially their heads. I began to come to my senses a bit more and I began to wonder if I shouldn't get worried. I was unable to move and the beings surrounding me, despite seeming somewhat familiar were becoming clearer visually. I'm okay when this happens as a day dream. But this time they woke me up. The being that I somehow knew was clearly in charge.

He then leaned forward and looked into my eyes, inches away. In response to my reflex I heard in my mind, we mean you no harm. I felt reassurance, and wellbeing. I was inside a large enclosure with bulwarks, panels, and orbs with strange lights all around. I was on a raised platform and there were many types of beings around other than those focused on me. They did not look reassuring but it was obvious that they were an advanced civilization.

It seemed very similar to science fiction scenarios I had read. The Elder who was directing my thought flow in some way indicated that the sci fi and aliens analogy was helpful for me to understand what was happening. I was in the presence of an advanced civilization who were interested in humans. I understood that he wanted me fully cognizant and for me to remember. I had been reading Heinlein's Grok and I was envious of the protagonist Michael and his relationship with the Martian Elders. He detected that and he told me that the concepts in the book were applicable to our relationship. In Grok, Michael was deeply connected telepathically to the Martians and would be for life. He said that in effect, they were granting my wish. We would be connected like Michael and the Martians, for life. I felt a profound sense of of oneness with all the beings around me.

Then, as if the greeting formalities were concluded, he leaned forward and stared into my eyes from inches away. I felt the loss of my identity and the merging with something else. The next thing I remember was re gaining consciousness. I was in a daze, but all the beings around me were all my best friends.

The Mantids were leaving and others were helping me stand. A reptilian being to the side who had been acting as sort of a guide for my experience expressed everyone's satisfaction that thanks to my cooperation, the procedure had been successful. Moreover, everyone present was honored to be in the presence the Elder. In retrospect, all this was almost ceremonial. I felt wellbeing and kindness from the beings. I had passed some benchmark. It seemed an achievement that to interact with the beings. But the atmosphere of being in the presence of higher intelligence was overwhelming.

In hypnotic regression material that I've read the procedure is sometimes referred to by the negative investigators as, Mind Scan. So named because one's mind is perceived to be wide open to the universe, and everything including ones identity is in flux. The descriptions of the procedure from Dr Jacobs, Dr Mack and Mr Hopkins are consistent. In my opinion anyone who has done a bit of yoga or psychedelics would perceive more of the experience.

In 2019 I was with Seri Tribe medicine men who perform the Otac, or Toad Venom ceremonies. After my first experience, I know exactly what the aliens were doing. The transformation of consciousness created by the Otac hallucinogen produces the same mental transformation as the aliens procedure.

As the Mantids left the area it was as though some magnetism released me and I began to move. Some of the beings had been quite busy doing something to my body. I was lifted to my feet with my Reptilian guide in front of me. He was robed and he looked me directly in the eyes at the about same height. I began to take in everything visually and I could see that he did not stand erect like a human. He was sort of stooped over and he was probably much larger than I. The effect was again just like a guided transformational, experience.

Afterwards, one is euphoric and welcomed back to their earthly existence. In the same way the beings that had greeted me in the beginning that seemed ominous now seemed like brothers and sisters. The oneness enveloped us all in a cocoon of well-being and love. There was just a touch of regret in the background that I would not be in the safe, loving cocoon for much longer. All our inner being was united in a unit. I don't have the words to describe much of this. But it was like we were a river with each of us as a small tributary. But the current was predicated by the Elders who were much more than a small tributary. I remarked, wow I can't even think when he's close by. He dominates all with his presence! The same for us, my friend said. Its hard to think of anything else when they are present. We want you to appreciate the honor.

A side note is that in all of my physical memories of the beings there is a consistent reference to a great achievement that we are all part of. Another of the robed beings in front of me was outputting encouraging energy and my mind was flooded with comic images of him sprouting a huge grin larger than he was wide. It felt like a group euphoria and I joked back, you don't even have a face for that grin! Ha ha. They were guiding me down a corridor and I knew we were going home. I was like an automaton and there were smaller beings guiding my limbs. There was an instant perception of motion then, we passed through the front door of our home. Then up the stars, with the small beings all around me.

Then, I was in bed almost asleep when I had a wait a second moment. I had seen them leave out of the corner of my eye and I was completely awake. I had an almost overwhelming compulsion to forget and go to sleep but I didn't like feeling compelled against my will. Instead, I went out the corridor to the bathroom where I met my father. I am having the most amazing dreams! Being near the beings has always been near euphoric for me. Dad was not happy. They drag my ass off every night, and I don't like it! Who are they Dad, I asked as though he could shed some light. He was a bit annoyed with my attitude that everything was okay.

During this Flap we were taken onboard quite often. Usually at night, just as I was drifting off to sleep. I would feel the presence of a craft above. Then, I would sense the beings nearby. In my opinion, this was the ETs politely letting me know that they were visiting. I suspect that they took control of my body's motor functions at this point since I didn't seem to be able to do anything except witness what was happening with wonder. They entered through the wall, usually. The wall would glow a bit then become transparent and they would come through. They moved much more rapidly than humans.

On one occasion they entered the room and an utterly bizarre looking being that I name Dragon Fly Guy moved to the foot of my bed. He grabbed my ankle with an impossibly long arm. I felt the energy all the way to the top of my head and it seemed to cause me to rise in the air like levitation. Another being caused a glowing aqua color light to form on the wall opposite the bed and we moved through it together. It's almost as if they tossed me through. I had a profound experience recently with Dragon Fly Guy. It was a healing experience for a loved one and it was very traumatic for me. I was so distraught that I had a hard time accepting the being. You look really bad in our terms, I thought. Despite the wonderful energy and the feelings of wellbeing. Any normal person would certainly think that you were a demon, why do I feel differently. Perhaps I'm crazy. He seemed almost offended. He replied pointedly that, we are first and foremost evolved spiritual beings. I could sense that his understanding of our emotions came from an empathetic understand and that his psyche was not vaguely similar to ours. But the empathetic care and compassion was intense and I really feel affection for the beings. Something that I have found consistent among the beings that I've met with insectoid features is that they are very straight forward. They just tell it as it is and you have to cope.

Others will configure the experience according to what they believe that you will find acceptable to try to mitigate the shock of their presence. I recall a funny story about a friend who was awaked by greys in her bed who wanted to talk. She was offended by the intrusion so they moved to the living room. She did not fear the beings at all but she felt indignant at the intrusion. And the beings who clearly found the communication process awkward, aroused her suspicion. So, the beings began to look like large bunnies to her. Presumably they thought that this would ameliorate her discomfort. But it didn't and so they left. I asked her if she would ever consider taking up communication with them. Because it seems obvious that it is the objective in all this. She found them unacceptable because they did not agree to human norms for communicating. I had the same problem with them at the beginning of my cognizant contact with them in 2011.

I discussed it with a psychologist. We could not understand why an advanced intelligence would not communicate in our format of emails, and powerpoint. But given that they are so completely alien, it's only another thing to get used to. An interesting thing for me about my friends experience is that she knows that she is in telepathic contact with the beings. In our conversation she was aware in some way that all she had to do was think about the beings and they would know.

I try not to use anthropomorphic concepts like telepathy. The experience is much more deep and profound than we can imagine. When they are present or when we are in sync with them psychically it's as if all our thoughts or our thought space is combined. Much more is shared than data or imagery. Emotions and profound concepts are part of the experience which I call Communion, thanks to Whitley Schreiber. I believe that the term Darshan which means a meeting between a teacher and his students might be appropriate. Because these beings are more advanced than humans, and especially in a spiritual transcendental sense.

I felt that the beings were intentionally taking steps so that I would fully remember this encounter. The Mantids came when I had gone to bed just as my mind was drifting off to sleep. I have come to understand that NHI who wish to communicate do so during that special time in our biorhythm when our conscious mind is relaxing and open. The Irish call it the special blue hour just before dawn. As a greeting the ETs radiated good will and an indescribable euphoric energy that was irresistible. Its such a wonderful feeling that I lay awake at nights and felt anxiety if they didn't show up. Several of the Mantid beings would show up and they let me know that they were there by first entering my consciousness. As our psyches meshed together they used concepts that were prominent in my mind to help them make their point. They detected the comradery of my circle of surfer friends in California in my memories. So they suggested that I should think of them in that context, and they would play the part. This would help facilitate our interaction. I don't have the words to express how awkwardly but expertly that they played the part. Hey Dude! Your friends are here! I was so overjoyed when the beings showed up. I somehow knew that these Mantids were young and were responsible for taking me to the craft. The elders on board the craft were a different story. They gave instructions and others did the work. There is a very obvious hierarchy among the ETs and it is fascinating.

Jesus Freaks

I was involved in religion quite a bit in my life. As a child in Virginia, we were originally Baptists. But we usually attended the best local congregation that we could find, whether it was Methodist or Episcopal. Until late in the 20th Century there were no Catholic churches or Synagogues in rural Virginia. I became involved with

Hinduism and yoga when I lived in California. Out of all that my main focus became yoga. Because I believe that out of all the modalities for ascension, religion is the least effective. For many reasons, primarily the inconsistencies in their doctrines. I believe the Yogis who say that religion only came about in the last few thousand years as a means that humans used to control other humans through yoga. Before that yoga was the primary means for spiritual growth, and for accessing the more subtle states of reality.

I reached a juncture when I was in junior college in Los Angeles in the late 1970s. I could not decide upon a curriculum, a career or life path. My second year of junior college I changed my major to Philosophy, against my councilor's advice. I put myself through college, so I never had more than two or three classes per semester. Philosophy seemed a more pertinent approach to learning about the world at this juncture, to me. Especially, given my relationship with the teachings that the Edgar Cayce foundation had exposed me to. I had accumulated quite a metaphysical library at that time. I had all of Edgar Cayce's works. I had several of Mdm Blavatsky's original volumes. And I also owned a number of Grimoires and Magical texts. The college Philosophy classes seemed to me more akin to debate than the study of the different systems that I desired. The subject is divided into religious philosophy, and all the rest. I thought that that was a quite arbitrary approach to wisdom. My counselor had been right.

The early 70s was the end of the Age of Aquarius and the Hippie social movement. I decided to do a Jack Kerouac and take a cross country trip. It was a bit of a tradition of the Hippie culture in California at this time to hitch hike across the country letting fate control the experience and the people we meet. It was a quite reliable way to travel for young people to travel at the time. Criminals spoiled it all, but at the time it was viable. So, I packed my pack and took off to the north. I spent some time at the Zen Ashram in San Bernardino, and I visited several monastic orders. I also visited a number of National Parks because I have always felt the divine more strongly in nature than in religious institutions. In the 1970s there was a movement in California called the Jesus Freaks. It was an evangelical, non-traditional Christian movement. The summer I chose to hitchhike around California the group was picking up anyone that was amenable, and taking them to their centers. They would entertain their guests, with food, comradery and religious discussion. Then they would Baptize the individual in a pool during a mass ceremony, by surprise. Their doctrine was, although they might not be able to convert someone for life they would at least grant them the Holy Sacrament. Their zeal and determination seemed to me quite genuine. For them I was a pilgrim, exactly the sort of person that they were looking for. I ended up staying with them a few days to absorb their philosophy. I felt quite comfortable with religion. The vibe it generated was profound. And of course our culture was dominated by the premise of the primacy of theological doctrine. The reality in the world of course, is the opposite. I had found some truths in religious writings and I wanted to discover the reality. I was a seeker in the classic sense.

The Christians had completed their mission of baptizing me in a big mass ceremony. They only asked my permission when we were in 2 lines leading to the stage. Ladies on one side, and guys on the other. An assembly line approach. I stayed a few days with them, then they dropped me off on the coast highway in Santa Barbara. Actually, such was their zeal that I was picked up 2 more times during my trip. The Pacific Coast Highway in California was a rural two lane road at that time bordered with white picket fences around hilly pastures rolling off into the distance on one side, and the ocean on the other. It was a perfect day and I wouldn't mind if I spent the day there without being picked up. I was in a contemplative mode, mentally. I really had not seen the trip I was taking as some kind of explorative journey for my soul. It was just something that seemed necessary for me to do. I felt that I did not have enough information yet about this reality to make decisions about the future. As I sat in the grass by the road I gazed across the pastures on the nearby hills. They were full of sheep. I thought, what a Biblical scene with the white fences and flocks of sheep on the hills. The sun was in its morning glory. Everything seemed too perfect. The instant that thought that the scene seemed Biblical, something moved in the sky by the sun. It was a metaphysical event.

Time and all the physical rules were over ruled by a higher reality. Another light was descending toward me. A Deity descending on a beam of light, like a staircase from the sun. I never daydream about anything nearing this scene. There was no doubt that it was happening. The reality of it exceeded anything that my senses had ever experienced. The being simply bypassed anything my ego tried to interject. Jesus connected with me on a familiar, eternal level. We had known each other forever. The interaction took place at a level of existence with no time or material encumbrances. I have connected with other beings like that and so, it is not an unfamiliar experience. He embodied the ultimate beauty of compassion and a beyond human purity of love and intensity. His energy was filling my consciousness. He was going to address me. He spoke directly to the very roots of my being in the most gentle perfect voice. I know you. You know me. I was devastated emotionally. No love, compassion, or anything like this exists in our daily existence on Earth. I was experiencing on so many levels. I was aware of a glimpse of the realm in which he was from, which radiated around him from above. Just like the religious art. I understood a profound vision like the multi beings of Easter religious art. The being radiated the ultimate best of all good human characteristics. That is its purpose. To illustrate what humans can and should aspire to,, in this realm. But was so much more. I profoundly understood that what Jesus manifested here is but a fractal of what he is across many other realms. What we call an ET. The basic facts of the universe were talking to me directly.

Much later in life I understood that the realm the beings was from which I had glimpsed might be what the Vedas call Goto Loka. The realm of the Gods. Just a glimpse of it causes intense emotion and tears is the typical reaction humans have. It is so perfect and beautiful that its overwhelming to our stunted, Earthly senses. That sensation is typical of my encounters with the divine even though I really have a hard time describing it.

At that time in my life I felt that I was being led, or drawn to explore my fate by forces beyond my control. It seemed that I had the choice between one path, or another with little ground in between. After a few months I returned from my trip in a twilight of the soul. The being Jesus would continue to come to me over the next few months. Something in the sun would seem not quite right and the being would descend. The encounter phenomena was like the ETs in that I did not consciously initiate it. It just happened with a strange degree of simultaneity, corresponding to my thoughts.

I had to continue school so I had little idea what to do with the new information that I had about life. I devoted myself to school and I continued to seek knowledge. The religious path as exemplified by the being seemed too all encompassing for me. I tried to maintain rapport with the experience but life, or rather Karma put me on a different direction.

The Ashram

When I lived in Culver City, California I began to frequent the local Hindu Hare Krishna temple which was run by the Bhaktivedanta Book Trust. Their presentation of Vedanta went down quite well with me. I had been doing Hatha yoga for a few years from books that I had found in used book stores. This was in the 1970s before the internet made all knowledge available, instantly. The Ashram answered doctrinal questions, but more importantly it taught me what Yoga was. A path to ascension or human evolution. A means to access the subtle realms from my experiences.

In my opinion individual human evolution is what we are put here for. Darwin's concept of evolution predictably redacts the most important points, which are those that separate us from the other lifeforms. We can choose our evolutional state, to some extent. The other lifeforms known to us are on a preprogramed path. But humans can choose to de evolve if they wish, as the history painfully illustrates. I studied with them for 3 years. The Baktivendanta Book Trust, Guru Srila Bhaktivedanta Prahbupada, produced almost all university level texts for the study of Sanskrit.

There was a class every evening in the Temple after Sankirtan. Exactly as per a tradition going back to pre-history. I understood that was the only way to understand Vedanta. In the context of practicing Sadhhana. You have to be at least doing some yoga or be making some attempt to access the higher energies for it to make any sense is my experience. For that reason I have little time for occidental Sanscrit scholars. I would have to know how much Sadhana they did before I tried to take their writing seriously. And there are plenty of unquestionable sources available at this juncture.

When I wasa Yogi my friends and I explored all the self-realization resources available in Southern California. After Sunday morning Sankirtan at the Temple, we would go down to Venice Beach for a breakfast special at a restaurant. Next door was a Pentecostal Temple and we would always attend the service since the restaurant had a long waiting list. We considered them to be as committed as us. They were questing for the eternal through a ceremonial approach. Our colleagues put on quite a spectacle. For them Channeling was their

Modality and it obviously worked for them. If I can wax the philosophical for a sentence or two, channeling or a similar phenomena has always been part of Christian metaphysics. From the pilgrim movement in Europe during the Middle Ages to the modern charismatic movements, which are not officially condoned by the Catholic Church have existed. Charismatic Services or ceremonies have many references to lights in the sky participating in or initiating the celebratory dancing and singing. The Pentecostal ceremony read through a few scriptures. And then the adepts or initiates put aside their books and began channeling Christian holy energy in the form of formal vocal invocations in Hebrew and other tongues. The energy was uplifting, they were colleagues and we gave them a donation on the way to breakfast.

There came a juncture in my quest for self-realization when I reached a point where I did not believe that I would advance further outside of the Ashram. I decided to join in order to experience the full transcendental lifestyle. I gave the temple all of my possessions that were not in storage at my parents' house and I renounced all materialism. My work in the Temple was purchasing, and I assisted with PR, coordinating our activities with the Los Angeles Hindu community. I was assigned to Tulsi Puja as my devotional service in the Temple. Tulsi Dev is a devotee who became a Demi God and incarnated as a species of Basil which is used in devotion to flavor food and the wood is used for devotional beads. After a year in the temple I felt confined and so I left and began to finish my schooling.

The Edgar Mitchell FREE Foundation (Now CCRI)

Someone made a comment that I'm going to appropriate. You don't have to understand UFO Phenomena to Experience it. In my opinion that goes for all the rest of these phenomena. From my point of view, formal UFOlogy always was a freak show of people who utilized the subject for their own interests. Never the less when I was contacted by an Extra-terrestrial intelligence in 2010, I was forced to turn to UFOology sources for clarification. I read all of Dr Jacobs, Mack, Turner and Bud Hopkins. I spoke with Budd several times. I was struck by how other than Dr Mack, all the people writing about the subject had a completely different take on the subject. Their take was negative. That concept was new for me.

There was discussion in the community about how a few hypnosis sessions would provide clarity for alien abductees. But I thought that it was all a lot deeper than that. All of their source materials from experiencers seemed accurate in terms of what I had also experienced. But gain, except for Dr Mack they all had a negative take on the whole thing. I chalked it up to some civilizational, paranoia syndrome, or something clinical. There was nothing in any of their material to imply negativity on the part of the ETs, in my opinion. But there is quite a bit of naiveté in their opinions in regard to what they expect from the ETs. I found it very significant that the only one of the writers on the subject was qualified to make judgments about human health and his opinion was that contact was beneficial to the human participants.

Almost all of the material about human ET Contact is labeled Alien Abduction and is focused toward helping someone overcome alien abduction trauma. My problem seemed the opposite. So obviously they couldn't help me. By great good fortune, during my search for information Rey Hernandez and FREE began their survey. I followed their surveys with great interest since their questions made much more sense than all the other material that I had encountered. Theirs was the first scientific survey of the subject. And they confirmed that the great majority of us experiencers, 85% believe that our experiences are beneficial. A percentage believe that the experiences are transformational in the highest sense. I was a bit relieved because try as I might I could not find any reason to believe that the ETs and their experiences were negative.

The FREE Foundation, which was transitioned to the Consciousness and Contact Research Institute, or CCRI, are disbursing information direct from the intelligence responsible for ET contact. And the revelations keep coming. For me the fact that ET Experiences are psychic events makes it much more understandable. There is a protocol of sorts in psychic as opposed to physical events. The phenomena is much more understandable in this context. Take memory for instance. Physical memory has always had a hard time explaining ET related memory phenomena. But taken in the context of psychic phenomena it's much more understandable. Yogis and psychics believe that the bodily existence dampens transcendental memory. When one leaves the body one has access to more than just the memory of one's current existence.

The Modality of the Toad

In 2018 I became interested in sacred medicines. I had taken psychedelics in High School along with many of my colleagues and I had little affinity for them. Like many, I had been a fan of Carlos Castanada and I had read his books about his apprenticeship with the Yaqui Medicine Man, Don Juan. I was practicing Sadhana regularly, focusing on early morning meditation. Another vibration raising technique is good deeds. As Dr. Jeffrey Mishlove points out in his video of the subject, focusing compassion upon those who are most in need greatly raises our vibe. This is an underappreciated truth reflected across many modalities. I meditate upon the sanctity of the nature in my surroundings. I have always sought the blessings and have been blessed by the nature presences, and I ask permission to enter their realms. It's part of clearing ceremonies that I do for meditation. I understood that the presences around me were linked to their sacred medicines and so I prayed that, if it was conducive to bringing the light and not too much trouble I was interested in knowing them through their sacred medicines.

I had mentioned it to a neighbor and a few months later he brought me about a kilo of immature peyote. I took it as an omen or response from the presences and the following weekend I had a ceremony. I chewed all of the peyote that I could stand and after a while a calm feeling of great beauty descended upon everything. For the next few hours I communed with a group of ETs. Their appearance was of the species referred to as Whitley Schreiber greys. I learned a lot about time in relation to humans and our interactions with the ETs. The experience made me interested in this modality.

I began to study the subject and I found that the local organic gardening group was sponsoring a local medicine practitioner. Dan is a Shaman sponsored by the Seri Comcaac, or Tiburon Indians. I watched his ceremonies and listened to the testimonials from the participants. Retired American seniors were experiencing the ceremonies many recommending the experience. The ceremonies were at a beautiful B^B by the lake just few kilometers away. It seemed too good an opportunity to pass up. I was aware of the coincidence. That I had prayed to the ancient ones and ask them for their medicine. I contacted Dan who sent me suggestions how to prepare for the ceremony. Fasting as well as mental and spiritual cleansing ceremonies were recommended. And its recommended that one who has never had the sacrament not to watch any videos or read anything about the medicines. One's mind should be as free from preconceptions as possible. I prepared by fasting from meat and wine for a week with extra meditation and prayer. Most ceremonies start with Rapay, and after that we all had Xanga which is a traditional M DMT compound that includes lotus root and salvia divinorum. Then it was time for the primary sacrament. The crystalized venom of the bufo alvarious or Sonora toad is the most psychoactive substance on the planet. The Seri Indians call it Otac. 5MEO DMT is 20 times stronger than M DMT. It is the ultimate psychedelic and used correctly it can achieve the maximum effect of psychedelic therapies. I do not have the words to describe the peak experience and its effects on my life. I'll use Sri Chinmoys descriptions of Samadhi to describe the corresponding states.

I took several doses over a little over a year to gain the effect Johns Hopkins Psychedelic Institute calls the full mystical release. Or the term everyone hates, Ego Death. For me it was completely mystical from the very start, which was a prayer. The knowledge I obtained from FREE, that this is a Modality of Ascension greatly facilitated my engagement of it as a Modality. My first ceremony was a great introduction. It let me know what the ceremonies could achieve. I was prepared and the first session took me to a state analogous to savikripa Samadhi. I had no awareness of my body I found myself in a body less state that seemed like a void. This was source, where were all from. I felt consciously and intrinsically bound to every atom and consciousness in existence. I understood that I was experiencing a Samadhi state. This is God. Realizations formed. I understood that I would be coming back to Earth, so I tried to extend the experience. I understood in that this first experience some ego made it through. I was making judgments and still perceiving subject and object differentiation. The experience made me aware of what the sacrament could do. But I would have to do some work.

The psychological effects of hallucinogenic involve clearing past traumas and resetting patterns of behavior which make up the ego. The computer analogy works for me. A primary function of sacred medicines is to reset the system. In order to stay on point which is the mystical nature of the ETs, I am going to simplify the process of explaining the sacred medicine experience. Within the year I was journeying with the Toad, I was in an almost alternate state.

My primary function is the care of my wife and that takes most of my time. The ceremonies involve transit to other states of consciousness, astral plains and beyond. And the facilitators can go part of the way with the participants. I greatly respect the people who go into this without any background either parapsychological, metaphysical, or yogic. Beings from those higher plains are usually invoked before ceremonies because the sacrament opens a portal to another realm. Portals have Angelic guardians like the Golden Ones. The Guardians stay with the participants afterward in many cases. Depending upon the intention of the participant. If one is not ready to experience eternity first hand, it scares people.

Of interest is Joe Rogan, who said that 5 MEO DMT scared the shit out of him. And Mike Tyson, who used it to achieve a completely new life paradigm and 600 million dollars. Most practitioners I know think Mikes descriptions of the process of using the medicine are the best. It's a difficult subject and he is the master of using the fewest words. His associates are calling him a prophet and that is IMO he is the best testament to the power of the medicine. The ultimate effect of the medicine is the highest Samadhi level. Or in the terminology of the Seri Comcaac Shamans, Otac can induce the highest energy. That is, the highest energy any human consciousness can experience. Which is the same for us all. In the Earthly existence nirvikalpa Samadhi is the highest energy that can be contained in an earthly vessel per Vedanta. The end of duality, which is impossible to describe. Sri Chinmoy, when you have become one with the soul in nirvikalpa samadhi, there will be no ideas or thoughts at all. There nature's dance stops. There is no nature, only infinite peace and bliss. The Knower and the known have become one. Everything is tranquil. There you enjoy a supremely divine, all-pervading, self-amorous ecstasy. You become the object of enjoyment, you become the enjoyer and you become the enjoyment itself. I obtained the full effect that the sacrament can offer. IE the full Modality and it took some work. It involved being around higher, Angelic intelligences. We have a saying in the community, integration only starts a year after ceremony.

It may take a whole year just to figure out what happened. After the full therapy the person, is considered an initiate who knows how to use the medicine. Whether it's to experience new levels of Samadhi . Or like Dean Jefferies, who uses it for NHI contact. Dean takes 5 MEO on his ocean voyages to communicate with the whales. The Toad ceremony participant gradually reenters this plain of existence, a rebirth and there is usually a lot of emotion, crying and hugging.

This is where I obtained an insight the first time I used the medicine. It was exactly what the Mantid elder had done. On board after the procedure, I felt love and connection for every being on the craft. I remembered the experience and the new insight, that the ETs had stimulated an experience like a Medicine experience really amused me. Big Space Hippy Bugs that hunt us down and catch us so they can get us high, is a DMT insight. Quite a laugh, when one considers the CIAs Aerospace Threat initiative, or whatever they call it. If they only knew. Beings that can stimulate the consciousness of an organism to the highest possible limit of consciousness it's capable of. What humans call Samadhi or Nirvana, with its eyes. That's a clue about the status of some ET species and why they are revered in their civilization. When I am in the physical in their presence I experience feelings of deep appreciation, and profound well-being.

The effect of these psychedelics upon humans when used correctly, therapeutically is consistent. It represses gross materialistic urges, it removes psychoses, and it leads to deep happiness and wellbeing. I can relate many instances of personal experiences of people whose lives were completely changed by the therapy. That an ET procedure performed upon Contactees produces the same therapeutic effect says a great deal about the ETs agenda. They are certainly trying to change our behavior through our, and our civilizations group psyche.

Synchronicity

I will write a few paragraphs. Since this is something that I discussed in depth with a Mantid Elder I realized that the Elder was involved and seemingly implementing changes in my life. A year or two after my wake up call, and despite never having considered it a sequence of coincidences landed me in another country. My wife and I visited San Filipe, Mexico on a whim. We were enthralled by the Mar De Cortez, the amenities and the safety. Since I live in California I quickly noted that no one locked their car doors. The city is so isolated that criminals can't get away with anything. We were there 3 days, met a realtor and made an offer on a home. Circumstances in my wife and my industry were such that we instantly decided to end our US careers and retire.

Putting all the coincidences in the context of being contacted by a vastly superior species, Lothar and I really needed to have another talk. I remember that it took several days of meditating sessions before I felt that I had a cognizant connection. I did and I felt his acceptance to talk to me about the issue. The subject is rather deep concerning their interaction in my life. Interaction with them has always seemed mutual in a way that it's difficult to describe. It has never seemed like manipulation. Since I was a child it's always seemed as some mystical journey rather than instigated by the ETs. They have always exemplified a we are all in this together attitude. His answer about the coincidences was twofold.

Firstly, that I should reflect on the human concept of synchronicity, as an effect of nature. Linked to and proportional to ones interaction with other dimensions and higher states of being than my own. He has always indicated that what we are doing, contact between our species is only part of a much larger sequence of events under way.

The more in harmony with certain sequences of events or probabilities the more entangled we are with the associated phenomena. The second part which could be considered homework, concerns the nature of Akasha or the mystical nature of the beings one chooses to interact with. As usual, I looked to Vedanta to help understand. And I found the classifications of the over 400,000 known intelligences in this universe quite helpful. Most species civilizations are designed to evolve collectively with their inhabitants in mutual harmony. A smaller classification including Gods, Demigods, and many others are created with no need to evolve. They are in our terms, perfect. The most useful classification for me is the distinction between beings that can create Karma, or action and those that cannot. An example are ET species that can't or don't choose to affect things directly or physically. The work to convince us to take the action to make the changes, or to create karma.

For every action, an equal and opposite reaction. But the higher beings create karma. There is not much difference between their will and events here on Earth. If that makes any sense. What they wish or desire has the tendency to become reality in this plain of existence. By a law of nature concerning beings that are much closer to the source than us. Upon a whim the Gods were said to change the courses of nations. If you are interacting with such a being the more their will manifests in our personal reality. I believe that all this correlates with Mdm Blatavatsky and the Theosophical society material. It is my interpretation of what he told me.

Missing Time

This is the most profound, continuous expression of any phenomena in my life. I will devote some space trying to describe it. Contact is primarily subjective. Vivid dreams and downloads. But missing segments of time and the accompanying weirdness is impossible to ignore. Its right in your face. There is no explanation or even theory in UFOlogy that sheds any light on what it is. I usually always ask experiencers I chance to meet if they have Time Losses. Like the rest of the Contact phenomena the experience is very similar for all of us. We do not remember what happened during the missing time except perhaps bits and pieces of memory that are usually not understandable.

It comprises a significant portion For me it happens every few years. During my career it was difficult for me to detect missing time and I tended to chalk it up to my not being organized and loosing track of time. But since I became aware and took up yoga to enhance my consciousness I have become completely aware of when it's about to happen. It's actually as if I'm either notified in advance, which is likely given the benign nature of the phenomena. Or, it's the result of my yoga and meditation program.

My life chronology of the experience starts with our Clan since it happened to the different ethnic branches. I know of 3 times in our family, twice with my father and once with my grandfather and I which Ill describe. In keeping with my theme of cultural phenomena. It's in neatly with the cultural tradition of old Virginia families. It was considered an intellectual understanding that events beyond our understanding of all sorts regularly occur. In other words its normal. So there's no need to go all religious or occultish just because we can't understand it. That is the cultural understanding I grew up with.

For me are a reminder from the cosmos of the utter mystic nature of our universe. A message directly from the Akashsa, or the mystical part of existence. Because the experience defies all rational understanding it's almost impossible to integrate it into this life. I've been able to gain insight, so to speak into the phenomena by entering meditation directly after major time losses. But the nature of this phenomena which is shared by <u>all major mystical experiences in the</u>

<u>other modalities</u> is completely mystical and unknowable. It's a window into the unknowable, endless and eternal universe. As opposed to the universe we live in which is composed of the other 4 elements which we can quantify to some extent. My understanding, or a deeper knowing from the meditation led me to the concept of the Akasha. Which is entirely beyond my ability to describe. I highly recommend Sadhgurus video.

Time losses when I was hitch hiking as a teen ager, from about 1969 to 1973 were a consistent and intense part of my teens. I remember that I knew something deep and mysterious was happening and that the key was for me to follow my intuition. When school took a break I would hitch hike 500 miles up the coast to Big Sur where I would camp amongst the giant redwoods overlooking the sea for a few days. The Pacific Coast of California is one of the most spectacular places on the planet. My favorite memory of one was when I was heading up the coast from Los Angeles one day when I was about age 16. My ride decided to drive through Topanga Canyon from the coast. That route is spectacular, and I instantly changed my itenary to take advantage of the opportunity. It seemed like a no brainer and the driver was also very intent on making the drive. When we had passed through the canyon and reached a junction, Dave remembered that he was actually going in another direction. And so he dropped me off and I began walking up a beautiful canyon called Old Topanga. It was completely rural at that time with drift fences. Hills with Pacific oak stretched off in the distance. Without crossing any obvious boundary, I headed up the hill to a grove of oaks that might possibly have water. Here I should possibly inject that I am an experienced hiker since I was taught by my Dad when I was young.

I have stories of metaphysical My Grandfather and I were driving home from a refrigeration job one afternoon in Forest, Virginia. I was age 11 or 12 and I assisted him in the summers as he visited refrigeration sites in the area. We had passed the Dam and we were going through a junction when I saw a couple of large mammals, presumably rabbits setting out on a lawn in the middle of the highway junction. They seemed so exposed and obviously out of place. They also seemed calm and friendly and although quite large for rabbits, they seemed helpless. It was no small feat to convince Grandfather to turn around and go rescue some bunnies during rush hour at the end of his workday. But I was fascinated by the huge bunnies and I felt obligated to help them. We drove by the spot and there was nothing there. I was quite confused, which amused my Grandfather and we drove home with almost no conversation.

Upon our arrival Grandmother met us on the front patio and demanded to know where we had been. We were 5 hours late and the police had been called. I was having a hard time understanding what was going on. Then, I realized that it was dark. It should've been 4PM and I began to realize what Grandmother was disturbed about. As we prepared for a late dinner I pulled Grandfather aside and asked him to confide in me and explain how we could've lost so much time. My Grandmother was not accepting our excuse. It's impossible just to lose 5 hours of time. This was obviously something that I had yet to be taught about and I was ready for the explanation. The incident became part of family mythology. The local rural culture accepted metaphysical phenomena as normal. But it was not a subject for children. I didn't realize what happened until I studied the subject much later in life.

CE5 Phenomena

That ET Contact is a human initiative now, is a major shift. And few seem to notice that it happened. My life long experience with them gives me the feeling that this is tutelage. At first they appeared in our dreams and skies of their own initiative. Now we call them, telepathically. Communicating with higher intelligences requires a skill set that totally transcends the Cartesian illusion in many ways.

Experiencers have always relied on the ETs. It's always been ETs initiative, ETs telepathy, ETs introductory phenomena. We didn't understand what it was. But now we have developed an understanding that we now know enough to address the ET intelligence directly. That we are doing so as a massive social movement, what's referred to as a grassroots movement seems to me to be a major and intended shift in the nature of contact. And nobody seems to have realized it's happened. Like most of my experiences I never saw it coming. In this manner. But as a child, the small robed ones told me that full Contact would be a reality in my lifetime. I was encouraged to participate. The more I actively participated the more that I would be included into the group event. It was always groups of humans who would be involved and they would be my classmates, workmates, and playmates. Wed discuss dreams we had which seemed mutual. And the ET phenomena modality entered our discourse through Sci Fi. Such was our fanaticism for it that we would have art breaks during recess every day in my 1st and 2nd grades.

Cryptids

I left this one for the end. A consistent phenomenon in the study of consciousness are cryptids. Everyone is familiar with Bigfoot and Yeti who are of great interest to the experiencer community. Anomalous physical creatures like Nessie or the many Canadian lake monsters are said by Native Americans to be interactions with another realm. Which is in any form a blessing. And they regard beings such as the undulating lake creature in Okanagan Canada Ogopogo, as sacred. I believe that in the conversation about Contact Modalities it is noted that experiencers of one Modality are usually experiencers of multiple Modalities. I don't know that it qualifies as a Modality. But it is a profound and pervasive phenomena throughout human history. Id like to see Cryptid phenomena statistics included in consciousness studies.

My own experience is that my father and I experiences the ET Phenomena extensively. We spent a lot of time in the wilderness and many of our ET experiences were there. And, we have experienced Cryptid fauna so there is definitely a link. Most phenomena intensifies in the country side has been my experience. My father and I witnessed many unusual animals in the wilds. On an early Fall morning my father and I were crossing the 100 meter footbridge on the Cowpasture river in the George Washington National Wilderness in a very remote part of Virginia near the West Virginian border. The river had just been dammed up to produce a reservoir and this would all be under water within a few weeks. When we got to the middle of the river we looked down into the crystal clear river which was very broad and deep. We could see huge boulders and dead trees at the bottom. And then, one of the giant boulders left the bottom and cruised up to the surface directly below us and looked up at us. It was the shape of an impossibly large turtle, almost the size of a Volkswagen. It glanced at us, took a breath then went back to the bottom where it became one of the boulders again. My father had always teased me because I always swam in these waters. I lost my enthusiasm for swimming in the wild at that point. Professional rescue divers that I've told this to tell me that they don't doubt my story. They say that the freshwater depths are creepy and their least favorite venue. One reason is lack of visibility and the other is that they said that they had seen creatures much larger than they were supposed to be. Cryptids are a phenomena deserving of serious study. In my opinion and experience, experiencers of the modalities also have this type of experience as well. In the culture of UFOs and Experiencers, when people experience communication with an unusual animal shaped being is common to assume that it's a cover memory. I have several anomalous animal experiences that were definitely cover memories. But the existence of Cryptids complicates the preconception.

Conclusion, the nature of the beings, and the benefits of the relationship upon my life

I believe the next step in human evolution is represented by ET contact. At this juncture, the uplift of our species seems much in doubt. But I take the optimistic view which is that we will overcome our difficulties and succeed in taking the next step in evolution. Which specifically involves learning how to communicate with these more evolved intelligences. The beings have told me that this is indeed their agenda, to uplift humanity. It is larger than any of us. That older species come when the moment is right to influence younger, less evolved species is part of the cycle of nature. The Kardishev scale for the evolution of civilizations probably applies. The big shift is from non-sustainability to a Class 1 civilization on the scale, which is clearly where we are at. Cultural archeology leads me to believe that these highly evolved beings have always involved in the evolution of humanity. If it's evolving. The premise of the Vedic, Age of Kali that we are in is the de evolution of the human species. After a crisis humanity then ascends to the Golden Age is how it's supposed to work. I read a dissertation by an Irish Celtic priest from 1765 named Colin O Hanlon which was the main source for Wendt's famous book the Celtic Fairly Faith. It was an attempt to reconcile the Celtic Fairy Faith with Christianity, specifically the Vatican. But it was also a treatise about the supernatural beings rituals and ceremonies in use which expounded that the nature of the people in the Fairy world was that they were higher than humans in the hierarchy of God. But below the Angels and the divine beings. The appeal to the Vatican if that's what it was didn't work and the Celtic church which existed in Ireland and Brittany went extinct. The conclusion that Rev O Hanlon was proposing to the church was that beings could exist more highly evolved than humans. But, a little less perfect than Angels. I like this explanation from a theosophical point of view. I will mention that this is the understanding of the yogis and psychics about the nature of the ETs.

Conclusion

The Dr. Edgar Mitchell FREE Foundation UFO Experiencer Research Study concluded that ET Contact was primarily non-local in that the ETs interact with us without actually being present, physically. They are present in my mind whenever I am conscious of them. It is an intuitive understanding that they encouraged me to develop. My understanding of their nature is from childhood and I know that any contact with them is for a positive purpose. That's simply the physics of evolution in play. I feel that I am part of something much larger than myself that is effecting change in this world. I believe that the goal is to increase human consciousness through many different means. I believe that when our civilizational awareness reaches a certain point, the ETs will make themselves more of a part of our lives. In addition, they will assist us to transcend the problems that have plagued humanity for millennia.

Boundary Conditions, Yet Infinity:

Pre-Birth Memories, Light Energy Beings

Susan A. Manewich, M.S.

Introduction

At the offering of Reinerio (Rey) Hernandez of the Consciousness and Contact Research Institute (CCRI), I am offering deeper reflections and story sharing regarding the contactee experience. Much of what is written here has never been told publicly as it just didn't feel it was the right time or venue to do so. Yet, now, it feels as others step forward and share the multilayers to the contact experience, we all may learn much to help us through this planetary transition and what it means to be human. We may also learn about the evolving nature of consciousness itself. Admittedly, I have held back sharing these deeper experiences and insight throughout the years as "there is only so much people can handle at times." Long-term colleagues who have kindly and not so kindly informed me that if I speak about my contact it could hinder the credibility where my name is associated with their name. This reflection isn't about the UFO/ET topic, nor is it about contact itself, it is about the intention of energy as connected to Source and the many forms it takes shape.

It is my intention with this personal reflection that we educate our friends, colleagues, interested parties and even our critics with this deeply personal and highly meaningful core of ourselves. That this education leads to greater connection, new learnings and heart-centered understandings. Our world could surely benefit.

March 1, 2020, currently tapping away flying 40,000 feet up in the air on a plane originally from Boston and headed to Cairo, Egypt. It is the first time (in this lifetime), I am visiting this country. I was asked to attend a conference and give a talk from a friend of mine who has had her own contact experience. The talk isn't about contact, it is about Women's Economics. A global platform for women to gather to discuss how to support other women and their initiatives. It is the first women's conference being held in the Middle East. My work is in the area of new energy technology and the need to help balance out the yin and yang within this field is part of my driving force to attend this conference. There is also far more which we will get to shortly.

The Incarnation: From Energy to Matter/Spirit to Form

I don't know the absolute end and the absolute beginning of anything. I only know "boundary conditions" as I refer to it. I remember where I was prior to incarnating to Earth. I remember being connected to Source/God/The Great Sun. I remember the moment I heard the call to go. I recall being extremely excited to go and change form. In fact, utterly euphoric, like I won the cosmic lottery to go elsewhere at that moment. It wasn't about leaving where I was, because I was aware, I will return. It was hearing the call to go and be needed to give and to connect the energy I hold to this "assignment." To separate from the pure spirit and move towards form. In what appeared to be flashes of seconds, I had separated from another spirit form, saw a council of golden light beings getting their directions from Source and then whizzing off faster than the speed of light to perform their work. The directions to these golden light beings were not auditory, the golden light beings, looked at the Central Sun and understood by looking at the energy of this great Source of light where to go and what needed to be done to help balance the Cosmos.

The next moment, I am moving from spirit into form very subtly and I telepathically get my "instructions", "your job is to understand how they live on this planet." The next visual I saw was me sitting alone in a room with a candle connecting into Source. There was a white cord from the top of my head to Source. This was my tool to keep the connection with Source.

Pop forward to the next scene and I am now outside of what I now know is my parent's bedroom. My mother and father are on the bed and I am a globular moving loosely connected ball of energy up in the corner of their bedroom. Next memory is in my mother's womb when I was about 7 months in utero. I remember hearing the chaos outside of my mother's belly. I remember turning my ear towards her stomach (like you would put your ear to the wall to hear what is being said on the other side). I heard all this noise and could see the kitchen, my brothers there and then realizing "oh no, not this place again." The feeling was one of a funny loathing. I remembered this place, Earth, humans in that moment of being 7 months in utero. I immediately remembered the density and the challenges, the hardness, the lack of connection. Yet, my freshly enthusiastic spirit, giggled at the insanity of it all. Here we go again I thought to myself.

I am the youngest of 5 in my family. My parents described me as a very happy and easy-going baby that laughed a lot. My Dad tells the story that my mother wanted another baby after they decided they were done at four. He said she was the most serious I had ever seen her about what she wanted. He was concerned about the size of the house accommodating another child and being able to financially handle so many children! He said, "your mother gave me that look, and she was absolutely clear about your needing to be born. She wasn't going to let it go." My mother describes my birth as, "I could have stood there and dropped you, you came out so easily."

They Come

I remember never being alone when I was a child. Even if I was in my room physically alone, I was never alone. This is when I would sense the beings from where I came begin to get closer to me. I had been waiting for them to show themselves more fully and growing a bit impatient at 5 years old. I can see my Earth family, but where is my other family?

They came at about 5. It was about 3 am in the morning and I could feel the energy in my body ignite, feel the cells becoming magnetized (pulled) and I then see my sister at the bedroom window saying, "oh look, what is it?" In my head, I am clear, this is them. Finally! I don't say a word to my sister because I realize she won't understand, and my body is only 5 and doesn't have the words to express all of what is going here. My consciousness knows that is happening, IT'S CONTACT! Finally, in the physical in this lifetime. But my 5-year-old self is not mature or developed enough to do anything other than just let this all happen.

I remember seeing the light ship rotating and counter rotating as it had a multitude of different lights with a crown light at the top and something at the bottom. It looked like the ship itself was organic and very much alive as well as sentient. There were 9 beings moving or rather gliding across the surface of the ground and moving in a coherent formation. It was clear they were utilizing group mind and group think with the heart at the basis of the energy. When they would move in formation they were connected to one another and seemed to create a field of energy around all of them.

Original artwork created by Susan Manewich

My sister and I had contact for several years both separately and together during childhood. My contact experiences continued, and they evolved throughout the years with different beings, different lessons and teachings.

Solace and Connection

As a child, I had a lot of energy and loved to explore nature. As an adult, I still do! I could feel the life force of nature so easily. It felt more nourishing than being indoors. I have fond and vivid memories of playing in mud, dirt and making pyramid shaped mud piles. I particularly recall one contact experience where I was very happy outside sitting in the dirt making mud piles and quite focused on what I was doing and how happy I was to be able to play by myself and just be with nature. At that moment, I can feel them, the beings. I see a pin hole of a spark of silvery golden light in the sky in front of me yet up high. I know they want to take me, and I don't want to leave my mud piles. So, I say, listen, I'm just a kid you can't take me, I need to play with my mud. At that moment, it is as if my higher self is speaking to me and says, "we know you know you're not just 5." There are no other words, yet the door to infinite consciousness opened at that very moment and yes, I knew better, it is time to go with them.

Often times, my family would find me hiding in the closet and under the table. I never realized what I was doing at the time. As an adult and knowing my patterns and how I operate, I can now see what I was doing. I was calibrating to what is natural to my spirit. Being around people who are not connected in, seems to make me tune out, and need to replenish and re-center my energy as well as seek solace alone.

The Transition of a Loved One

What others call abilities such as precognition, past life memory recall, remote viewing, extrasensory perception (ESP), telekinesis and clairaudience, seems to just be naturally how I come wired. Yet there is an enormous caveat to this which I rarely have seen discussed and that is intention on behalf of the greater good. These abilities seem to activate as it relates to helping others. An example of this is when I was going for a casual walk in Lion's Bay, Canada just outside of Vancouver. When I was walking down the road, I felt an immediate and sudden pang of an uncomfortable energy in my solar plexus. The thought that came in was my father, I must get home to Massachusetts. I then booked a ticket and was gone within 48 hours. About 6 days after being home, I had a dream about my mother. My mother passed away in 1997. In the dream, she was wearing purple yoga pants, a yellow shirt and was in this 3-story contemporary wooden structure house that is in the forest. She was there waiting at the door. I said, "what are you doing here?" She says, this is where she lives and does yoga to keep herself healthy. I got the sense in the dream, she was waiting for someone. And yes, I got the sense she was waiting for my Dad. The next day, I saw my father at 8:00 a.m. in the morning. When I saw him, I immediately began to tell him about my dream and that I thought my Mom was wanting to see my father. My father looks at me, drops his mouth open and shook his head. He then said, "I need to tell you something, the doctor called and said I have pancreatic cancer." We both just looked at each other in a state of shock, instant awareness and deep love, yet we were both scared at what we knew was happening.

On March 4th, 2017 at about 3:45 a.m. I lay next to my father as he was on hospice at his home. I was dreaming of seeing a flight of white stairs going up to a bright light. I woke up to my Dad saying, "Susan." I said, "I'm right here Dad." He says, "Ok, I'm ready." My first thought was ready for what? And then I remembered the flight of white stairs. My father had just told me he was ready to go and transcend. In an instant, I knew I needed to gather my entire family to his house, so we could all be together one last time. My father passed at 8:44 a.m. just 5 hours later with his family surrounding him and he was able to smile just minutes before his transition and even move his body by himself on the couch where he was lying to make room for me to sit next to him. Mind you he hadn't moved for 2-3 days straight at that point.

In January 2020, I had a dream where my father and mother were now in this same 3 story contemporary house where I saw her previously before my father's cancer diagnosis. My mother was cooking dinner and my father about to head out the door to go fishing, one of his absolute favorite activities to do. The house had more form and shape to it and they seemed to be living a "normal" life in a different vibrational plane.

I would love to say, I completely understand what all this about and how this occurs, yet I am a learner in this physical human body as well. Life moves, it evolves, it transcends, and it is still magical, mysterious and loving.

The Balance of the Spirit and Ego

There is a knowing I seem to have with people around me to help them balance and be in alignment with nature, their higher self and the cosmos. I refer to it as the prime vibrational highway to get on and be in the stream of to help to effectively move through this planetary transition. Significant life events flash into my awareness in nanoseconds about a person and the fact they will face a harder set back if they don't move into a different direction. This has happened many times on many occasions. One such example was a close friend of mine whose father was about to enter into the hospital for a routine surgery. In a flash of a moment, I knew his father was not going to make it out of the surgery and survive. My friend did not have a close relationship with his father due to abuse he suffered as a child. I said to my friend, "I don't think your Dad is going to make it long after his surgery. It may be important to settle your feelings with your father before he goes in for surgery." My friend looked at me and didn't say anything. I got the sense he heard me but didn't want to hear me. My friend's father came out of surgery and never regained consciousness. I reminded my friend of what I had shared with him before his father went in and this time, said it louder and with greater conviction, that he needs to settle his feelings with his father. He eventually did see his father and expressed his release of anger and sadness. He forgave his father. Soon after, the doctors told my friend's family that the father was not going to live. He died a few days later.

Future memories

The best way to describe this ability is a future memory. I get an instant nanoflash of myself in a future spot seeing the sights all around me and then often times years later the exact scene manifests and in that exact moment I am able to recall that I saw this before. This is not like dejavu, this is an exact future memory down to every last detail to the view point I am seeing the scene. I recall one such memory of when I was living in Massachusetts. I got an instant scene of looking down at my bare right foot walking on a beach carrying a pinkish, orange, yellow surfboard in my right arm with the ocean to my right. About 7 years later, I am living in Hawaii carrying the exact same surfboard, on the exact same spot, looking at my foot in the exact same manner.

This has happened several times which has caused me to ask about if space time is truly all one. There seems to be no delineation of time. In these moments of the future memory and then when the future memory unfolds into the present. It feels like there is no space or time in between in that moment. All feels as if it is one.

Constant Connection...of the Heart

Standing at my stove cooking a very basic meal of pasta and sauce around 9 p.m. one summer night in 2017. I was alone in the house and feeling separation and rather lonely. My father had died a few months prior and there was still a sense of grief from his passing as I stirred the sauce and pasta starring rather mindlessly at the pot. At that moment, I get a feeling in my heart of what feels like a rush or a swell. I then hear in my head, "go outside and look up." I begin to put down the wooden stirring spoon and begin to turn around to go outside. I then stop myself and realize, "this is silly, what if nothing is there. I can't handle any more disappointment or grief right now." Then I felt my heart begin to empty out. I stood there for a few more seconds and thought to myself, "well, if the feeling in my heart felt good and full, then I should allow that feeling back in and have some courage and go outside and look up." I did just that. I then exited the kitchen to the back deck of the house, looked up in the sky with my heart feeling full and boom, there was a ship in the sky filled with red and pink flashes of light. I just connected my heart and beingness to the light and allowed the connection. The light then grew very bright, the connection was strong. It then faded, and I simply smiled, shook my head and laughed at what just occurred. "Ah, stay with the feeling of love and don't question it I thought." Needless to say, the pasta tasted far better even though I ate it physically alone. Energetically, I was not alone. I was connected and feeling full of love and kindness.

Past Life Memory Recall: Seeding the Planet

For many of us contactees, several seem to also have past life memory recall. Not all but some. Without any hypnosis, I have clear memories of at least 3 significant past lives which I began to remember in my early 20's. One was "seeding the planet" which appeared to be somewhere in the Ireland area and this was during a planetary transition where the coding from sun was impacting the Earth. I can't say if I was in physical human form, I appeared to be much smaller and felt more etheric than physical. I do remember being there to see and receive the codes from the central sun to anchor and integrate with the Earth. I saw the four directions split in the sky almost like a quadrapole as well as signs and symbols from the sun and the sky.

In 2019, I attended a talk at the Space weather Conference in Albuquerque, New Mexico. Dr. Anthony Perrat, a former Los Alamos laboratory scientist was giving a talk about petroglyphs found all around the world and their coinciding features with emerging scientific understanding regarding the expressions of solar micronovas. The petroglyphs look exactly like the images captured from the Los Alamos experiments where the scientists were creating nuclear explosions similar to that of the sun's micronova. Some of these images are called a Birkeland Current. Sitting in the conference and seeing the connecting points to what science was validating with the images captured in the lab created explosions was too synchronistic to ignore. The petroglyphs are believed to have been carved during a strong solar burst where it appears life on the whole of planet Earth had suddenly changed. Somehow the people who created these etchings were seeing the shape and form and thought it was important enough to carve into the stones for its place in history to be recorded.

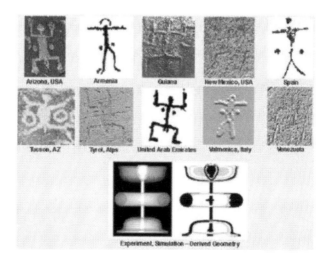

Pyramids-Sacred Power Generators and Healing Codes

I recall two lives where the first I was working with a sacred power generator, and the second life, I was putting in the healing codes into the sacred temples and pyramid walls. In both of these lives I do remember being able to phase in and phase out of the physical body. Meaning, I wasn't entirely physical and stuck in the density of the body. I still had contact with the beings and the ships. In both lives, the contact was still discreet. When I was working with the sacred power generator in the pyramid, I was a very tall, strong and a large male. My job was to protect the divinity of the sacred power generator to keep in harmony with the cosmos and Earth. At the time, man was beginning to fall and misuse the power and the male and female energies were appearing to come out of balance. My sense was that I was sent in to protect the energies which were being utilized in that sacred device.

The other life as a female, I was very tall, slender and with golden skin and light-colored hair. My job and primary memory was to etch into the wall of the temple structure the healing codes for the future to be active. I did this by tuning into the healing code energy to my cosmic connection, tuning into the future of the planet and what will be needed for humanity at the time and singing the code into the wall. The song and vibration of my voice is what etched in the code, not an object. I merely moved my finger in the direction I wanted, and the etching took place without touching the limestone. The sound changed the density of what appeared to be limestone and it opened up to receive the hieroglyph.

Crop Circle Experience

In early July of 2019 I was supposed to go to the UK for a meeting. I had not made travel arrangements to fly to London as the timing just wasn't feeling right. As I was about to fall asleep one night I see the numbers 2 and 8 appear in my mind's eye out of the blue. I ask myself, "what does this mean?" I realize it may have to do when I am supposed to fly into London. I tell my colleague who is in the UK that I think I am supposed to arrive on the 28th of July and we then make our travel plans for me to arrive that day. During the night time sleep upon my first night in England. I had a dream of going down to a large field. In this field I am escorted by a man who I cannot see his face. He is guiding me towards the field and then I am surrounded by these electric balls of light. These electric balls of light are coherent and "living" in nature. I touch one and get a little zap of electricity. I wake up from the dream that morning and then go see my colleague to have our meetings begin and ask him where the crop circles in England are. His response, "we are literally in crop circle country!" I then say, "would be great to see one while I am here. With all the times I've been to England before, I have never seen a crop circle and never even thought to ask when I have been here.

My Numerous "Paranormal" Contact Experiences via the Contact Modalities

Carolyn Padget

To have an opportunity to write about my experiences is amazing and freeing for the first time in my life. I never thought I'd be talking about things like this. But I have to say I jumped at this chance to get all these events down if even just for the chance to express how this has personally affected me.

My brother and I grew up in Southern California in San Diego County. We lived out in the country not near a big city at all. My father was in the military and my mother stayed home with us. I graduated from high school early and entered the military at 19 years old. I chose to study in the medical field. After the military I proceeded into the medical field again and then to the holistic field. I've been married for 37 years, and we have three brilliant grown daughters. We presently live in the southeastern part of the United States. While we live in a small town is a coastal resort area, the area does seem to have a small bit of open-mindedness to such topics if these times but not always. I am very careful about how I speak about this topic and to whom.

I don't consider myself a religious person, but I was raised Catholic. In the Catholic religion they taught us about angels and saints. The angels made me feel safe as a child and that continued into my adult life for a while for various reasons. My view of angels would change overtime as I had my varying experiences. My husband's family is very religious, and this became a hot issue for them. I knew better than to tell them anything regarding my experiences. They knew I was in the holistic medical field, and they thought that wasn't good either because they think that only God can do that work. Our relationship became strained over the years and unfortunately, we had to part ways to save our marriage.

MY EARLY EXPERIENCES

In my life I've been faced with realties that I thought were real to me, but those around me just assumed they were of fairy tales, childish make-believe stories. I would sit in my bedroom having tea parties with what I called angels. I just used that name because of what I was taught in church at that time. My mom would see me playing in my room talking to whatever I saw and just assumed I was playing with my make-believe friends. They never scared me, and it gave me someone to play with. I was very shy and introverted and preferred to play quietly by myself because of the things I experienced.

I started out in life feeling like the odd one out due to a rare disease I was born with that caused my teeth to not have enamel on them. I looked different than most children and I took solace in keeping to myself. I have friends who will say to this day that they never knew I had anything wrong, and they are still my best friends. I was aware of my surroundings all the time due to the abuse I took from other children. I realized that I could see colors around trees, flowers, and even people. I assumed everyone could also see the colors. I would tell my mother about the things I was seeing, and she would be very understanding, eagerly supporting my imagination and reality. She was the reason my life went on as normally as it could go.

Very Bright Light Coming from the Sky

When I was around 10 years old and my brother was 7 years in 1974, we were in the car with our mom driving home one evening. Since we lived in the country there were always other small country roads to take home, and this road was a dirt road that went by a dairy and open chili pepper field. We could see the front porch lights of our house in the distance as we drove. Suddenly, the sky lit up like someone had turned a huge spotlight on us. I remember the car coming to a stop and the car turned off. I still don't know if my mom turned the car off or if it was turned off by something. I was in the front seat and my brother was in the back seat. This light was so bright that the entire car was lit up inside for what seemed like a few seconds. I remember seeing my mom rolling the window down and sticking her head out of the window and looking up into the sky. At that point the car turns on or our mom turned the car on, and we began to head home again. I have no idea at that age if there was any missing time. I've always remembered that event. I heard my parents talking about it and they just said it was probably a meteor. There was something always in the back of my mind about that night, but I could never quite figure it out.

Saw my First UFO

Another event I never forgot was when our family were on our way home from a camping trip in Sequoia Nation Park. In the 1970's there were no seatbelt laws at that time, and we would sit or lay down where we wanted to in the car. We had a station wagon at that time, and it had a seat in the back that faced in the opposite direction. My brother and I asked our parents to lay the seat down flat and we would lay on our back just look up at the sky. On this trip I was looking up at the sky, I saw a few fluffy white clouds and blue sky. It was a sunny day. Then I saw something glittering beside the clouds. I assumed it was just a airplane and the sun was shining off of it. As I watched it, I noticed it wasn't moving to the next cloud, it was staying in one place. Then suddenly it zipped to the next cloud out of sight. I had never seen any plane move that fast. Then I saw it zip back to the place it started and it was in full view again. It moved to the right and then back to the left with lightening speeds. It then moved so fast that I lost it and it was gone.

Saw Ghosts/Spirits as a Young Child for Many Years

Life went on as normally as it could go into my teen years. I began to hear things as in the middle of the night that would wake me up out of a deep sleep. I would open my eyes and see people standing at the end of my bed. They would just stare at me not saying a word. I would freeze and pull the blankets over my head. This went on for several years and as it progressed, I would hear what sounded like many people talking at once. Each time this happened I would become paralyzed. I couldn't move at all during these experiences. I realize now that I was possibly seeing ghosts/spirits. I felt like they wanted something from me, but I had no idea what it was at that time. I was too scared to even think about what they might want.

Saw the Dead Man who Died in Front of my House

When I was fourteen, I saw something that still bothers me to this day. The house I grew up in was right beside a two-laned road that was known for having accidents. It had a very sharp, blind curve and our house was right beside the curve. One afternoon there was a very bad accident that happened in front of our house, and I heard and saw what happened. My father told us to stay in the house and he ran outside to help. A dune buggy and a flatbed truck had collided head on. Right before I had heard the impact, I had heard the dune buggy try to gear down, but it was too late. The man is the dune buggy was killed instantly and laying at the end of our driveway face down. The dune buggy had basically exploded into a million pieces. We had parts of his dune buggy in our yard, flowerbed, by the garage and our front door. One of our neighbors ran outside with a horse blanket from her shed to cover the body. After many hours we watched as the coroner came and finally picked up his body. It was really terrifying for me and my brother to see this.

Later that night I went to bed that night with all of that still fresh in my mind. I finally fell sleep and in the middle of the night I woke up to someone near my bed. I didn't feel my bed move, but it felt like someone was watching me. I opened my eyes to see a man standing to the left side of my bed. I just froze from fear. The man was just watching me, but the worst part was that part of his head was partially gone and mangled. I started screaming like I was being killed in my bed, and my father ran in my room. I tried to tell my dad what I saw, but it wouldn't come out and I was just upset. He told me I probably had a nightmare and go back to sleep. I didn't sleep at all the rest of the night. I know what I saw, and it was the man who had died in our driveway. He just looked lost and confused.

I would continue to see people at the foot of my beds over the years, but I would do my best to try and ignore them. The ghost or spirits at my bed only caused me more stress and anxiety over the years and add that to becoming a teen and life was not fun. Life goes on and you find a way to live your life as normally as you can and that's what I tried to do.

Saw Flashing Symbols & Numbers in Front of Me on Several Occasions

In my mid 30's and 40's I began to see things while in sleep state. One night my husband and I went to bed like any other normal night. We would watch and few minutes of TV, or I would read a book while he played solitaire. We finally fell asleep. At some point in the night, I began to see symbols flashing in front of my eyes. The symbols were flipping so fast like a deck of cards. This was so intense I began to wake up while this was happening. I sat up in my bed and I looked for my husband and saw him sleeping next to me. I then looked at the clock and it was a little after 3 am. I look straight out into my bedroom, and I was still seeing the symbols flashing in front of my face. At this point I became very scared as to what was going on. No matter where I looked in my room, I was still seeing the symbols extended in front of my face. The symbols had a color of a blue and the symbols at times were shaped similar hieroglyphics. I could never see them in detail due to how fast they moved. All of I sudden I laid back down and then it was morning. What is ever stranger is that I never fall asleep quickly and if I'm woke up it takes a bit to get me back to sleep. The next morning, I wrote all of this down in a journal I had started years earlier to keep track of things like this. This event happened two more times over the years and at other times the symbols would be a deep reddish color instead of blue.

Saw a Giant Merkabah Spinning Very Fast

In 2009 I saw something while sleeping again. It looked like I saw either while standing and looking up, or I saw on my back or sitting looking up. All I know is that it was above my head. I saw something that looked to me like a giant Merkabah turned on its side. The center of the Merkabah shape was spinning very fast. It looked like a type of light purple metallic. I thought it might be purple light coming from it but it was shiny. Then it began to glow brighter and brighter. I then saw numbers, I'm not sure which numbers but they were single digits. The numbers looked like they were in tiny squares all over like a matrix. At that point I saw the word GROUND in huge letters. As I saw this the numbers in the squares came towards me to the right side of my head and then it was morning.

Woke Up by a Brilliant White Light and Sent to Another Reality

In 2011 I began having white light experiences, but not a white light near death type experience. We went to bed one night and in the early hours of the morning a bright light woke me up. The light was so intense that the light woke me with my eyes closed. I opened my eyes, and it was a bright white light. I opened my eyes wider still to see if I was seeing things. At this point I sat up in bed and put my legs to the side of the bed to stand up. As I was sitting there, I looked for my husband and I couldn't see him. I looked for the clock and I couldn't see it anywhere. I thought I was in my bedroom, and I tried to see anything that resembled my bedroom, but nothing was there. I started to get scared because I couldn't find my husband. Suddenly, I heard "someone say everything is fine lay back down." For some reason I laid back down and then it was morning. When I woke up I told my husband everything that had happened. The part that bothers me is not hearing someone say something to me, but it was the fact that I did what I was told to do. Everything went through my head as to what it could be. White light reminded me of angels and nice things from my childhood. The voice sounded kind and not frightening to me. Still there was something that lingered underneath the surface that was unnerving me, but what was it?

The second white light experience occurred in 2013 as before with me going to bed like normal. This time I found myself in a place that was completely dark. I was standing and there was no light anywhere. It felt like being in an empty space. Instantly, I feel like something is above me. It was as though I was being watched. In a split second a white light shines on me and my hands went up to my sides with my palms out to catch myself, or to keep something from getting me. It was a protection response. I couldn't move. I was paralyzed in that position. The white light did not hurt my eyes. My head was tilted slightly down now the light hit me so I could see what looked like the ground under my feet. I could see orange colors soil and where the light hit and darkness on the other side I could see some grass. I just remember seeing dirt and grass and then it was morning. I don't know how or why I would be outside. I don't know where I was. It just all went black. The next day I was wondering if I was remembering being taken at another time, or was being taken at that moment? If so, then why would I be taken outside and then taken? I had so many questions during that time and no place to find the answers.

Saw a Big TV Screen & Shown a Detailed Experience

Our family doesn't have home movies of any kind. We just have pictures and slides from when I was young. The next experience left me wondering if my mother had been an Experiencer as well. I will never know since my mother passed away in 1992.

My husband I went to sleep after some light reading. I found myself in a room. I was standing in front of what looked like a big TV screen or a window while looking out at the night sky. There was something just below my full vision in front me like a counter or a panel. It had controls of some kind on it. I couldn't see it clearly as I didn't look down. My focus was on the screen. I knew someone or something was around me as I could get a glimpse of shadows moving. Then I saw something appear on the screen. It was the image of me around the age of 2 or 3 years old. My mother was running behind me making sure I wasn't going to fall. It was a beautiful moment in time that I was able to see from another viewpoint. It was images I had not ever seen before. As I watched everything on the screen, the images of my mother and me disappeared and I began to see other faces I did not know that turned to look at me while I was watching. The faces came closer to the screen looking at me intensely. I began to get very frighten at that point. That's when heard a voice say we have been watching you. I never knew if that meant they were watching me and my family or us as humans. A few seconds later the screen back to black but it was like looking into space. I could see stars in the distance. I saw something in the distance that was coming closer toward the screen. It looked like giant cells. I know what cells look like and these were giant versions of them. They had blue and green colors in them. I've looked in every medical and biology book I have and online for what I saw, and I still have no idea what kind of cells they were. As the cells came closer and they became bigger they began to go through the screen in front of me and went directly into my body. I was watching them enter me and I began to get terrified, and everything went black, and it was morning.

Had an OBE: Brought to Another Reality.

In 2019 my husband and I bought our first RV/travel trailer. Our plans were to go travel and see the country. I grew up with parents who loved to go camping all over the country. I wanted my husband to experience this as well since his family did not travel to far from their home in NC. They would go to Va. to pick apples once a year or my husband would go to church camp occasionally and that was the extent of his travel experiences. I missed traveling so getting an RV seemed like the easiest way to see the country in comfort as hotels can add up over time.

A month before we bought the RV, I had decided to find out some information in any way I could on how I was being taken. One day I was relaxing, and I just sent the question into the ether or into the universe. I asked how I was being taken and I just released it, and as time passed, I forgot I had asked the question.

We parked our RV on the side of our house and began loading it with things we might need on our trip. I had decided to start sleeping in it to practice getting used to living in it. We had all the blinds up in the window except for one over the kitchen area. We thought it would be fine to not worry about the curtains at that point since we had a long tree line that gave us privacy from prying eyes of any cars that went by our house. We had just finished a nice dinner and decided to just relax and enjoy the RV life. At about 11 pm we decided to go to bed. I pulled all the blinds down near our bedroom area. We had one security light near the road in front of our house, other than that it was dark outside. We had nobody on either side of our house, just empty lots. We also had a golf course behind us, but it was pitch black. Our backyard was always so dark, and I never went out into our backyard even with a flashlight.

I'm not too sure how long I had been sleeping when I began hearing a sound or a frequency of some kind. I was lying on my right side facing a small window. I had my arms pulled up close to my chest. As the sound came in it got louder and louder but it didn't hurt my ears. As the sound came in very tiny dots began dancing in front of my closed eyes. I could feel my body beginning to vibrate. It was like I was one of those snow globes that you shake up and all the snow scattered. My body felt like that all over. Like my molecules were moving at a high rate of speed. I became aware of everything around me. The sound and the dots seemed to come to a peak and the dots began to disappear, and then I could see the window. I saw everything on my right side with my eyes closed. I had never opened my eyes. The sound and hundreds of dots just faded, and I had clear vision. At that point I realized I could not move as I was paralyzed. Suddenly I began to move, and I was not doing any of the moving. My body lifted and I was tilted upright as to be standing up. I had not touched the blankets on our bed, I was floating at the foot of our bed.

Now realizing I was floating at the end of the bed I saw the inside of our RV and was struck with awe. The inside of our RV was only outlined in tiny white pin pricks of light. Our kitchen cabinets, sofa, walls, and windows were nothing but points of light. (I had my daughter who is a graphic design artist draw this for me.) Everything was outlined it white light. I remember clearly taking note of the saltshaker sitting on our lift table, and the glass water carafe sitting on our glass stovetop cover. There was not one bit of color in anything I was observing. At this point I was not frightened in any way. Instantly I had these thoughts come in that I was seeing everything at a quantum level.

I began to scan more to my left toward the kitchen area, and the I could see the long horizonal window above the stove and sink. This was the window that did not have blinds or curtains yet. As I looked at the window, I saw two faces looking in the window at me. This is when I began to get frightened. I saw these entities from shoulders up. I could not see any details in the face. But what I saw was a blue glow that outlined their bodies. At this point I became so scared because I was being pulled toward the faces. At that point I did not want to see anymore. I began to try and move myself in any way I could. I realized that I was turning slightly to the left and then everything went black.

Normally I would wake up and it would be morning, but not this time. When everything went black, I found myself standing and looking out of a large rectangular window high up in the air. I realized that I was in some type craft because I noticed whatever I was in was moving up away from the ground. I saw what I thought were people walking below and some were running. They were near a building of some type that looked like it had breezeways for people to walk under. As the craft pulled away, I could feel the slight sensation of being on a rollercoaster in the pit of my stomach. I did not have any seatbelts on anything strapping me in place. As the craft began to lift faster everything went black and it was morning.

The next morning, I got up and grabbed my cellphone camera and went to the end of our bed and took pictures of exactly where I was when I was floating. I made sure to put everything that was in my field of vision in the same place. I had my daughter who does graphic design make me an image of what I saw using the picture I took. I then proceeded to go outside and look on the ground for any signs of something being outside the RV. I was looking for footprints or any out of the ordinary markings. I also was measuring how tall the beings would be if they were standing and looking into my window with their shoulders and heads in view. I measured at least 7 to 8 feet tall from the ground to look through my window. If they were floating in the air then I have no idea how tall they were.

Altered State of Consciousness: Interacted with Spirits

That experience never leaves my mind. I think of it at least once a day. The next question I've asked in the last 6 months is why am I taken? We will see if I get a reply to those questions. I think part of me is apprehensive about what I may find out. This last experience I had was in April 2020. By this point due to Covid 19 we are in lockdown and living full-time in our RV. We had minimized our life and sold many things and moved out of our house. We are living on family land now until we can get out and travel again.

We went to bed as usual, but I'm not sure how much time had gone by when it started. I heard the sound or frequency coming in and it gets louder. At the same time my vision is changing to tiny spots or pixels-like very fast to a clear vision. My eyes are still closed but the sound that came in woke me up enough to know what is going on. I never open my eyes. I can't move my body in any way at all. Suddenly I'm seeing a face come into my vision. It's a distance from me and it's becoming clearer. I see it and I become frightened at this point. The face looks grayish, and the details are distorted a bit. I don't know what the face looks like entirely. At this point I try to say the words no. I'm physically trying to get it out of my throat and mouth and it's difficult to do. Finally, I felt like I screamed no.

At this point the images change to me lying in my bed next to my husband. I really thought I had said no and was able to not be taken. As I'm lying there, I slightly tilted my head up to look upward toward our long horizonal window above the head of our bed. I see that there is no window or a wall. I can see clearly outside the yard. It looks like what I saw in the first RV experience where everything looks like it's at a quantum level. Nothing is solid, no color other than everything is just white light points.

At this point I see what looks like a long line of people in the yard looking at me. These people did not look like living people, they looked like spirits almost. They were all dress in period clothing. They had a kind of gray, white color to them. They were very much outlined in white pin picks of light with no color to the clothing. I saw a young girl about the age of eight years old. She looked like she was from the late 1800's to early 1900's with a giant bow at the top of her head and a dress to her knees. She had a sash that wrapped around to a big bow behind her dress. She had what looked like knee high socks or tights and button up shoes. Next to her was a man who looked like a farmer with cover-all on and a wide brimmed hat. I could see more people in different clothing but these two stand out the most for me. As I am looking at them, the farmer looking spirit leans over out of the line and looks me in my eyes. Then everything goes black. I wake up and it is morning.

As I woke up and got my senses about me, I began to tell my husband what happened to me. The moment I told him I was trying to scream he interrupted me to tell me that I screamed help during the night. He said he was scared and just watched me sleep for a few mins. He said he didn't want to wake me in case it made things worse. He said he had a bunch of things go through his head as to why I was screaming help because I've never done that before. I don't talk in my sleep or sleepwalk, so this was very unnerving for him.

This experience had me asking more questions. Is this paranormal mixed in with my contact experiences with Non-Human Intelligence? I thought about the moment the farmer looked me in the eyes and things went black. This made me wonder as I was in the process of being taken and I became frightened. Did they change the scene so as not frighten me? I assumed was in my bed and I thought I was safe. This reminded me of one of the white experiences I've had where I was sleeping in my bed and a bright white light woke me up.

Then when the farmer spirit-type looked me in the eyes. Were they able to put me out and control the situation better? I've read that they can control Experiencers with their eyes by just looking into them.

I seem to have more questions than answers to my experiences, and there is no end in sight. I think of my experiences at least once a day. I am honestly in awe of the first RV experience. This has changed me as a person in that I take nothing for granted. I don't see the world as solid even though things feel solid. I've begun to study quantum physics more and to try and understand what I have seen. I've had a scientist explain to me what I was seeing after I told him my experience, but he said he has no idea how I saw able to see this. It was a validation for me that what I saw really happened.

These experiences have made me think of our short time here on earth. I was either taken from my body like an OBE or NDE or my entire body was taken. I don't really know. If this is possible that only my etheric body or what we call a soul is taken, then what does this mean? It may mean that our physical bodies are just for our personal transportation while we are here on earth. It reminds me of what really happens when someone dies. Our bodies go back to dust, to earth. The energy moves on toward something else. What that something else is still unknown.

As I'm not religious anymore I wonder sometimes if the Non-Human Intelligence I am interacting with are Gods or Messengers of God? I often think the angels I saw as a child during my playtime were either spirits or Non-Human Intelligence. My thoughts go so much deeper than I can explain to people that I don't even talk about them to anyone besides my husband and now here. Also, my hope is that humanity will become more aware that thousands of others are having experiences such as mine.

My Husband saw 3 Triangle Shaped Orbs

I wanted to add a few end notes here since this was written. My husband had an experience that has shaken him to his core. This happened in Dec 2020. He wanted me to add to his experience. My husband generally is up at 6 am and gets dressed and walks outside over to his man-cave. He has it set up with a refrigerator and a place to cook so as not to wake me in the RV. As we live on family/business property the business office in close to our RV. It's about 200 ft from us. When my husband walked out of the RV, he saw a ball of light fly out from behind the cinder block office building. He said it had 3 orange light together in a triangle shape. As it flew up about 15 ft above one of the business trucks and blinked out in a second.

Now he has questions as to what that was and why it was there. He said he thinks that's maybe they must have shown themselves to him to help him understand what has been going on with me. He said it was about the size of a large basketball. What was that? It absolutely scared him. This thing was in our front yard but why? So many questions and we are still waiting on answers. I don't know if I will get the answers in my lifetime, but my hope is that whatever it is that it is something good.

Consciousness & the Contact Modalities: Sightings of UFOs, Paranormal Activity, Shadow People, Contact via Lucid Dreams, Physical Healings, ESP, Empathy, Precognition, Missing Time & Much More

Neil Baumann

The total number of minds in the universe is one. In fact, consciousness is a singularity phasing within all beings.

Erwin Schrodinger

Think about our dilemma on this planet. If the expansion of consciousness does not loom large in the human future. What kind of future is it going to be?

Terrance McKenna

Consciousness research is the key to better understanding ourselves as human beings and our place in the universe. To me this is the most important factor in the evolution of the human race today. We are at a pivotal time in our development where we can no longer continue to act from a place of neglect, ignorance, and indifference. Research into the Contact Modalities is the most logical way to approach the subject of consciousness as well the topic of contact with non-human intelligences (NHI).

I am a contact experiencer who has been having contact with NHI for most if not all my life. My UFO experiences span a wide range of things. Sightings of craft, paranormal activity, shadow people, lucid dream contact, physical healings, ESP, empathy, precognition, missing time and much more. Through my personal experiences shared here I will demonstrate how consciousness is the one common denominator that is fundamental to the Contact Modalities. They are the tools we use to connect with the Universal mind.

I was born in Findlay, Ohio in 1969. I am the youngest of six children. My earliest memory from my childhood is from Christmas Eve at age three. I had been asleep in my crib and was awoken to witness a craft hovering outside my bedroom window. I recall many flashing-colored lights and bright red ones. It was hovering directly in front of me over my back yard. I was standing in my crib looking at the object. I remember looking behind me to my brother asleep in his big boy bed. When Christmas morning broke, we were awakened by our parents to come down and open presents. I was so excited about the thing I saw it was all I could talk about. I was completely convinced that I had seen Santa Claus's sled. This was my first contact with an NHI.

I have a distinct memory from this period of an encounter that I do not know is real or a cover memory of some sort. However, the vivid detail of the memory is uncanny. It has been with me all my life and has not faded in any way during the years. Around age five or six. I was out playing in the woods behind our property with my brothers and a sister. I recall being with my brothers at a spot where my oldest brother was building a tepee. The next recollection is of being alone in the woods and encountering a small entity. I was approached by a 4-foot tall being with the appearance of what we all now known as a zeta. His complexion was a fawn color. Kind of a coffee with heavy cream tone. He was wearing a skintight black suit that reminded me of a diver's wet suit. It went up to neck like a turtleneck and stopped at the wrists. He had stepped out around a large oak tree and said hello to me. He spoke to me in my mind and told me he was a scientist and that he was here studying our planet and its lifeforms. He asked me if I would like to be his friend and help him with his work. I agreed. He stated that he was going to be friends with me for my life, and he would be seeing me again soon. He then turned to his left and I noticed a highly reflective, metallic egg. It was approximately 8 feet tall. I had completely missed it due to its highly reflective surface. It was reflecting all the foliage surrounding it and was concealed. A door opened like a camera lens and he climbed in, the door closed, and it shot straight up into the sky.

During the course of the next five years, I was plagued with a multitude of bizarre paranormal activity. I was continually having what I called falling dreams. I would be completely asleep and would be suddenly slammed into the bed. I would literally be sliding down the bed as I was apparently being returned from activity elsewhere. This was very frequent in its occurrence. I also was having sightings of objects appearing in my room at night. I would be in my bed trying to fall asleep and would see black fuzzy objects about the size of an adult box turtle. They would appear out of the wall and would scurry across the hardwood floor under my bed. I had a complete routine before bed that I went through to ensure my "safety" during the night. I was paranoid about people coming in my room through my closet which faced directly towards my bed. I habitually put my bed spread on the floor by the closet and pulled it up to cover the crack. I was sometimes visited by the vision of a zeta face hovering in my mind's eye as I closed my eyes to sleep. I recall it confronting me to continually look into myself and it kept asking me "Who are you?" "Who are you?" Looking back now I realize that this is probably not a normal thought for a 7-year-old. My answer to the being's question was always the same, I AM.

The next time that I have any recollection of seeing beings like these is from a series of **lucid dream** encounters probably from age seven to nine years old. These at times frightening experiences were coupled many times with physical after effects. The first of these experiences was at age seven. I was still sharing a bedroom with my brother at the time. He is a year and a half older than me. I have the most vivid memory of being taken by three of these small zetas during a "nightmare." They were about 4 feet tall. I woke up on ship in a round room that is very brightly lit. I am laying on some sort of table as the three small beings are scurrying about. There are a set of very bright lights over me and the table. They each appeared to be oblivious to me. They moved quickly around the room in blurs, each addressing their own duties it seemed. There was a tall slender being that stood behind me at the top of the table. I will call it her as I was filled with a calming, loving presence from this entity: female and mothering. She was roughly 7 feet tall with long arms and a slender body. These beings again were zeta types that had the fawn color I described previously. She was what I now describe as the controller. Her duty seemed to be nothing but ensuring me that I was safe and to kept me calm. I began to become highly agitated and fearful. As these feelings filled me, the tall female began projecting into my mind. She repeated that I was safe, and they were not going to harm me. She leaned over me from above and was just inches from my face. Forcing me to stare into her eyes which were endless black pools of the darkest pitch. I sensed that I was falling into an abyss and that there was nowhere to go. This being was in my mind! It shared every bit of my being and my conscious awareness. It knew everything that I knew and felt. It was a terribly frightening experience. There was nowhere to retreat to. One of the small beings to my left stepped up to me with a long silver wand in its hand. As he came towards me three long thin wires came out of the end of the device. Then it turned into a jointed grasping tool that he used to remove my left eye from my socket. The terror was too much for my seven-year-old consciousness to endure. I immediately blacked out. I next awoke in my bed the following morning. This incident has since been explored and confirmed during a session of hypnotic regression.

The next incident again appeared in the form of a **lucid dream** encounter. However, there were physical traces that coincided with this one. Again, I am on a craft with the small beings. This time it is not as frightening as the previous experience. During this encounter, a small zeta drone put some sort of implant into my nose. As reported among many contact experiencers, the little zetas come across as worker bees or drones. I sense they work like a hive mind. A collective. I have total recall of this being using a small wand like tool that had a tip similar to a set of forceps. It inserted a small bb sized object into the tool. It had sharp barbs going up the length of it on both sides. The device was then inserted into my left nostril. It was then pushed up through my sinus cavity and into my head. This was accompanied by the most horrible crunching and crackling sound. There is no conscious recall of me being in any pain. The most unnerving part was the crunching sound in my head.

I woke the very next morning to a very painful nose. My left nostril was red and inflamed. It was crusted up around my nostril and felt like someone had pulled a marble out of my nose. It was red and irritated for several days after the experience. During this time uncontrollable nose bleeds were a common thing. As well as an overwhelming sense of being observed whenever I was alone. I would spend a lot of time by myself at that time. My house was always a flurry of activity. With such a large family I would frequently seek solace alone. I am introverted and empathic and would pick up energies easily. I spent time enjoying typical kid stuff and hung out in our basement a lot. While I would be alone sitting watching television or drawing, I was constantly seeing flashes of movement from the corners of my vision. This was always corresponded with the strong sense that I was being watched. This persistent feeling of being watched continued well into my young adult life.

During my childhood I cultivated a love for animals, nature, and the stars. My brother and I would lay out at night and look at the star filled sky. I was always overcome with a sense of awe and amazement when looking at the night sky, wondering what else could be out there among them. Surely there must be worlds like ours. From the time of 5 or 6 I was reading books on NASA, the space program, and astronauts. My father was the head of engineering at RCA corporation. A position he held for thirty-five years. He instilled in me a love of science, aviation, and space travel. He worked on integrated circuits for technology used in the Voyager program and the military. He was a former Navy pilot who flew a sub hunter after WWII and before the Korean war. He had Top Secret clearance because the plane he flew was nuclear equipped. I remember him giving me a large packet of Kodak 8 x 10's from NASA depicting all of our planets in our solar system. These were the product of the Voyager probe. The remainder of my teen years was pretty uneventful. I did have two brief sightings of craft during high school. One of them interestingly was forgotten for many years until I started to have contact in my adult life. I had visited an old girlfriend in college on holiday and relayed my experiences to her. She reminded me about an encounter the two of us had together during my senior year. As soon as it was mentioned a flood gate opened in my mind and I had full recall of the event. An event that I apparently was made to forget. We were returning from a day trip of shopping in Toledo, Ohio. It had gotten dark and the stars were out. On the way back to Findlay we witnessed a glowing green disk approximately 60 to 100 ft in diameter quickly fly across the highway.

The fall of 1988 is when I moved away from home to start college. I enrolled as an Art student at the University of Akron Ohio. I had a deep love for the arts and was a natural at drawing, painting, and anything else pertaining to the arts. During my early college years, I was very interested in psychedelic studies, religion, theology, spirituality, shamanism, mysticism, metaphysics, and consciousness expansion. I enjoyed reading the works of Aldous Huxley, Timothy Leary, Richard Alpert (Ram Das), and Carlos Castenada. I also enjoyed practicing meditation and studying Buddhism and Hinduism. At this time, I began experimenting with psychedelics like LSD and psilocybin (Golden Teachers). I treated the LSD and mushrooms trips as ritual experiments in consciousness expansion: exploring mystical states of being during these trips and having some of my first experiences with ESP, telepathy and synchronicity. I enjoyed both of the altered states of consciousness (ASC) I had using LSD and psilocybin/psilocin. Each compound had drastically different effects. LSD peaks were very introspective experiences. Whereas my trips on mushrooms were rife with mystical visions, mosaic overlays and a bizarre connection to what seemed like an extraterrestrial intelligence.

It was my summer vacation my second year of college. I was on break in Florida with my parents. I was spending the week with them about an hour from Tampa. It turns out two good friends of mine were in Florida at the same time and they said they wanted to pick me up for a night. They were both going to be going camping with a couple of girls they knew. And they asked me if I wanted to come and camp for a night. Being nineteen, single and hanging out with my parents for a week, I immediately said yes.

My two friends, Thad and Steve picked me up where we were staying, and we drove to the woods outside of Tampa. It was at Hillsborough River State Park. When we got to the camp we hooked up with the girls. They had a campsite set up. We all were introduced. Thad's friend Brenda and her friend whose name escapes me. Brenda and Thad were good friends from high school. We all hung out drinking beer and smoking pot. Then we all ingested psychedelics. I had ingested a couple of grams of psilocybe cubensis with the guys and the girls both dropped a tab of LSD. Now I had been doing mushrooms for about a year and a half at that time and had quite a few high dose experiences. So, I was no newbie to the drug. We all hung out and had some food and chilled out.

The campground was kind of crowded and filled with families. So, Steve offered the suggestion to move our camp back into the woods near an area of the park that was off limits. This sounded good to all of us as we all wanted to chill in peace. We hiked into a spot in the woods to pitch camp. Upon doing so Steve and Thad suggested going for a hike. The sun was setting, and we were all starting to go up on our individual trips. The girls and I decided we wanted to just chill on this nice oriental bridge that went over a small pond. So, Thad and Steve said they would see us later and took off. The girls and I were hanging out on the bridge enjoying the coming night. Venus and the first stars were coming out. Now I was enjoying myself, but I was in no way out of my skull.

Suddenly a huge owl to my left hoots loudly. It flies from a tree across our view to the right side and landed in a tree. It sat there observing us. It was awesome. He was about two and a half to three feet tall and had a wingspan of at least three and a half feet. I got some nice colorful tracers off it as it flew by us.

Following the bird in my line of sight I see a star blink at me. It was directly in front of me and appeared to be blinking different colors. Red, blue, green, yellow, orange, purple....repeat. So, I watch it for a minute before bringing it to the girls' attention. A minute later and I know I'm seeing this thing blinking colors. I turn to them and ask if they can see the object. They both were struggling to see it. I pointed a flashlight at it and blinked it two or three times in succession. Now at this time the sun was down, and all the stars were out on a clear moonless night. I asked them if they were seeing it blink and what colors they were seeing. I let them name them off as it blinked. We all three were seeing the same thing.

The object then began blinking in faster succession and zoomed in closer to us. It was what I call a mothership. It was quite large, but I can't say how big--well over a hundred feet. It made a very low humming sound and had a super bright white light emitting from the underside of the craft. I was blown away. We all were extremely excited and couldn't believe our eyes. I continued blinking it. When I did, it shot back to where it had originally been and two objects that appeared to be stars equal distance from the mothership on both the left and the right began blinking in fast succession green, orange, green, orange.

These two objects then came in perfect tandem towards us. All the while the mothership is just blinking away all the colors of the rainbow. When they were almost overhead, I ran into the clearing off the bridge and the girls followed closely behind. These two objects were perfect flying black equilateral triangles. Completely silent. They had spinning silver white lights around the front points and orange and green solid lights on the point tips. The one closest to me flew directly overhead. When it did, the object blacked out the stars so I was looking at it silhouetted against the starlit sky. They both turned in perfect synch a right-hand turn and flew off over the woods with the pavilion in it. We had walked through this area when we set up the second camp in the woods. I was so excited I ran back across the bridge yelling at the girls to follow me as something was telling me they were going to land in the clearing on the other side of the pavilion area. As I did this, I could totally tell the girls were not having an easy time with what we were viewing. Brenda expressed her fear and said maybe we shouldn't try and follow them. But I was too excited. I suggested we all get close and take the path through the pavilion area to the clearing beyond and into the unknown.

As soon as we stepped onto this darkened path, I could see the pavilion to my right. The clearing was in sight beyond it. Suddenly the bushes that surrounded us on both sides began rustling. We stopped dead in our tracks. The rustling stopped. I began to move forward another step. The rustling began again. All three of us freaked out at once and ran back to the bridge. We crossed it quickly and ran to the center of the clearing. All of us automatically sat down with our backs to each other. We all were just freaked out. We sat there quiet watching for any signs of movement back by the path to the pavilion. There was no sign of anything. The ships had all resumed their original positions, and we sat watching them. During the course of the next twenty minutes we sat there as the perimeter of the woods that encircled us got darker like someone was turning down a dimmer. When this happened all the sounds of life would cease. No bugs, no birds, no breeze, and no noise from the trees. This ebbed and flowed like this for the next fifteen to twenty minutes. We did not move an inch. I asked them if they noticed what was happening with the waves of blackness and they both said they saw it and felt it too. It was as if many sets of eyes were observing us.

At this point I had had enough. I looked at them and said I'm going back to the tents to get my 35mm camera. I had a nice Pentax 2000 from a photo class I was taking, and I had decided trying to get a picture of these craft was worth it. I got up and crossed the clearing to the entrance of the path through the woods to my camera. As soon as I took one step on the path, I heard the most terrifying scream from something I have never ever heard before or ever hope to hear ever again, in this life or the next. There was a sound of ripping vegetation and something large tearing through it heading straight for me. I have never felt more fear in my life, ever. I turned tail and ran for the clearing to the girls and fell down next to them. This thing scared me to the core of my being. It felt like whatever it is was coming through the trees and going to rip out my very soul.

Suddenly all went quiet. Everything came back to life. There was a breeze, night sounds, and birds. We sat there speechless. Moments later Thad and Steve arrived back from their hike. I immediately began to try and explain what had happened while they were gone. My friend Steve was immediately telling us we were crazy and just tripping out. He was an ex Air Force pilot and somewhat of an arrogant guy, but we all were friends. Suddenly an airliner with its lights on flew overhead. Steve said we all were just messed up and watching airplanes. And the rustling we heard was armadillos. They had encountered them on their hike. I however knew better.

The girls and I were razzed by them the remainder of the night. Brenda and I spoke last about seven years ago. She still remembers everything as I have described and brought up how terrified she was of the terrible sound we heard that night. This encounter was explored and verified in my regression as well.

After this incident I returned to Ohio with a fire burning in me for answers to all the questions raised by the encounter. I immediately went to the campus library and checked out a huge selection of books on the subject of UFO's. I never had a special interest in the subject. The first time I remember hearing about them it was on the old "In Search of" television show with Leonard Nimoy. I remember being enthralled by the show. It was the first time I had heard about Erik Von Daniken and *Chariots of the Gods*--one of the titles I checked out from the library. As I began to read these books on varying titles, synchronicities were happening where all of them kept mentioning UFO's, even the ones that weren't dealing with the topic directly like the book *Pyramid Power* by Alex Toth and *The Mayan Calendar* by Jose Arguelles.

A curious thing happened about a week later I was going to my folk's home in Findlay just for an overnight visit to do laundry. Now I had tickets for a favorite band of mine that was playing on Sunday night in Cleveland which I would never miss. So, my intention was on only going home for the night, yet I took the complete stack of twelve books home with me. I ended up taking a bike ride around my old neighborhood and ran into a group of my friends from school growing up--literally a group of old friends that I grew up with and had not seen since high school. I was invited to join them in a game of softball they were playing at my old Elementary school. We played for a while and I then joined them for swimming down the street. When I arrived, I entered an aggressive game of dunk football in the pool. To make a long story short, I get injured and have to have emergency surgery on a bad knee two days later. Thus, being forced to cancel the concert and was stuck at my parent's house for the next three weeks. During the first few days recovering from orthoscopic surgery, I had gone out around midnight for a smoke. The thoughts of the UFO's were forefront in my mind having been reading all of the books while I was laid up. I reached out to whoever was listening, God, ET's, the universe. What is going on? Is this real or all in my head? As if to answer me a "shooting star" streaked in and flashed me before disappearing.

During the next six months I remained completely sober. I was having a hard time coming to terms with the UFO experience in Florida. I was wanting to verify that these things weren't somehow in my head. At the time I had never heard of cognitive dissonance.

In July of 1992 I attended my first Rainbow Gathering. It was the national in Colorado. I had never been to Colorado before or experienced anything like what was in store for me there. I went to Colorado with two very close friends, Matt and Mary. We took turns driving from Akron, Ohio to Colorado for the gathering.

Upon driving into the staged parking, we then all exited the car and hiked the five miles into the forest to the main valley. This is where the gathering's main circle meetings and drum circles were located. Hiking in was a bit of a chore as I had never had to deal with elevation. I had to take many rests along the way in. I had become separated from my friends. Upon arriving at the main circle, I was completely blown away. The size and volume of people was amazing. I never had seen or been a part of anything like it. It was a week-long celebration of peace and love amongst the Rainbow Tribe in what was as beautiful a setting as the Garden of Eden. I spent the remainder of the day there. Everyone gathered hand in hand in a complete circle around the expanse of the valley. All of us praying for peace. The energies were off the chart. I was finally home.

When the sun started to set, I made my way up the hillside to find a place to pitch camp. I found a nice spot and proceeded to start putting up my tent. It was a six-person tent with what seemed like a million poles. I was struggling and being viciously attacked by mosquitos. I was saved by two awesome guys from Washington D.C., Jim and Kevin. They were from Georgetown. They helped me with the tent, and it was up in minutes. I then went and hung out by the fire. I was getting to know my new friends. As we sat there talking, I was taking in everything. The sky was perfect. A million stars seemed to be in the sky. Lightning bugs lighting the valley. It was magical.

All of a sudden, I noticed a red orb in the sky. It was the most intense red. It was zipping around making unbelievable maneuvers--hard angIe turns while moving super quick. I quickly brought it to the attention of my new friends. They saw it immediately. We watched it for about two or three minutes, and it disappeared.

They were both pretty happy and excited about what they witnessed. Jim said it's our star brothers and sisters. I agreed. I then decided to go back down the hill to main circle. A drum circle and bonfire were raging. I had met a nice girl and her nine month old daughter. We sat down on the peripheral by a small fire. While sitting there playing with the baby, I noticed her looking at the sky. I looked up and damn if I didn't see the red orb again. Zipping around again just as it had before. I hung out and listened to the drumming till I went back to my tent to sleep.

I found my friends Matt and Mary at main circle the next morning. They told me where the location of their campsite was: down the main trail, left at Krishna camp by the lake. I moved camp there in the afternoon. I spent most of the day hanging out with the Krishnas. The music and chanting were beautiful. I relished sitting by the water, enjoying life. We all shared a communal meal, and I went back to my camp to hang out.

Matt and Mary were there when I arrived. We hung out and discussed our impressions of the gathering so far. I told them both about the appearance of the red orb. They both new of my UFO encounters from my friends, Thad and Steve. I don't know whether they believed my tale. However, they both new the facts of the story. So, they weren't too phased by my depiction of the last night's events.

After we all ate some dinner and the sun had gone down, Matt asked to borrow my drum. I said he could take it if he gave me his word not to lose it. It was my girlfriends back home, and she would have killed me if it got lost. I cracked a green glow stick and tied it to the drum. "There, now you won't lose it." We both walked to the main circle as Mary stayed at camp.

We separated once there, and I wandered around enjoying the night. I was very excited about the encounters from the night before. I had a long period of self-doubt after my UFO encounter in Florida. I had returned from that trip and spent the next six months completely sober. I did not want to have any doubts about my sightings or my sanity.

While hiking around the valley, I took notice of a few objects flying high in the sky. They were moving quite slowly and had some blinking lights. However, they didn't look like planes. There was no noise coming from them either. I watched them circle the valley observing. I knew they were not aircraft. My gut just told me so. They didn't look right and they didn't feel right. It was getting late, maybe around 1 AM. So, I headed down main trail watching the lights still following the mountain range. I got lost trying to find the trail to Krishna camp. I sat down on a rock just off the trail and waited for someone to come by.

Finally, a guy and a middle-aged woman stopped. They were both from New Zealand. They agreed to take me to the lake. I was walking a few feet behind them still watching the plane like object following us. I asked them if either of them had witnessed anything strange the night before. They both said no. The guy spoke pretty decent English but the woman did not. I said well do you see that thing and pointed to our tag along. He said "oh that's an airplane". I didn't press it. All my alarms were going off. Right as we get to the lake. I notice three identical craft to the tag along sitting motionless in the sky over the lake. They were in a perfect equilateral triangle in the sky. Blinking colored lights. I pointed to the craft and said do you see that. Just then the tag along stopped, completing a perfect equilateral diamond. They all began going ballistic blinking back and forth to each other. Then the tag along shot across the center of the diamond, flashed into a super white light the size of the moon and was gone.

The woman from New Zealand began jumping around up and down screaming "did you see this, did you see this!", I laughed and said yeah I see that! The three broke formation. Two headed slowly to the west and one to the east. Still blinking. We separated then as I knew where camp was from there. I walked back alone totally excited and vilified. When I arrived at my camp I sat by the fire and stoked it up a bit. I then needed to relieve myself. So I walked about a hundred feet away by the lake surrounded by tall fir trees to my right and the lake to my left. As I stood there going, looking up at the sky I noticed a bright electric green orb about the size of a basketball ball. It was coming towards me over the tops of the pine trees. It was totally smooth and graceful in its movement. Gliding to stop right above my head. It bobbed up and down about three feet below the tree top, checking me out. It then glided right off. I could not believe it. I then walked to my tent and laid down.

I was quickly asleep. I woke sometime later. Maybe an hour or two had passed. I opened my eyes and saw a glowing green light outside of my tent. My mind immediately thought, oh it's Matt bringing back my drum. It's the glow stick that is causing the bright green glow. I then rolled over and blacked out.

Upon waking in the morning, I arose to Mary making breakfast. I sat down and said good morning. She looked at me and said I have something to tell you. She had awoken during the night and came out here to the fire. When she did she said my whole tent was pulsating with a bright green light!

To this day the visit from the green orb is my favorite sighting of an unknown. Mary still recalls the experience in full detail. This encounter was also explored through my regression and verified my recall of the events as detailed therein.

The next couple of years after that I was continually having issues of feeling watched again. I had a girlfriend who lived in the country. Many times I would visit with the intention of spending the night but the overwhelming sense that something was going to happen and feeling of being observed persisted. Sometimes to the point where I was so uncomfortable that I would drive the twenty-five-minute drive back to my place. This is where I had my first experience with sleep paralysis. I had returned on one of these evenings to my place. I went to bed and awoke some hours later. I was completely frozen, I was awake and fully conscious but could not move, no matter how hard I focused. I had the sensation that someone was in the room with me. Minutes later I was able to move and felt the presence leave. I even hopped up and searched the very tiny apartment to no avail.

The next strange experience I had was my first encounter with missing time. I was traveling home from Akron to my hometown to visit my parents. I made this drive religiously my first few years of school and new it well. Somehow, I came to as if dreaming yet I was already awake. I was sitting at a railroad traffic light on a road I had never seen before. I immediately pulled over at the first gas station. I ran in and looked at a map to see where I was at. Somehow, I was 30 minutes out of my way in a place I had never been to before.

I did not have any UFO sightings then again until the spring of 1994. I had graduated college and decided to travel out west. My first destination was Santa Fe NM to visit a close friend of mine on my intended trip up to Washington state. Of course, the first evening she takes me to a party out in the Devils Canyon. I witnessed many flying red and green orbs. I was so paranoid during this sighting that I locked myself and my dog in my car til morning. During my time there I soon began living outside Santa Fe in the national forest. I had a nice camp in the woods some distance from where I could park my car off the main road. During this time I had another sighting of a UFO and a possible abduction experience. A friend of mine Matt and I had driven to the top of the mountain by the ski basin. We had gone up there to camp for the evening and we had both eaten a little bit of mushrooms.

We were sitting around the fire, neither of us feeling any effects from the mushroom. Suddenly a small object lit with brightly colored lights comes zipping up the road, does a sharp right turn and flies right by the parking area. It was apparently being chased by some people in a car. They sped into the lot after the object and parked their car. They hopped out and were obviously drunk by their general rowdiness. We kept to ourselves and they soon left. We sat around the fire and decided to go to sleep in our sleeping bags. Neither of us were getting off on the mushrooms.

I awoke sometime later to relieve myself. I walked about 100 ft from our fire and was urinating. I was looking down a slope to a small creek below and suddenly saw a large being about seven to eight ft. tall peering around a large tree by the water. It had a very large triangular shaped head and large round eyes. Long arms with very long fingers. I immediately zipped up my fly, I thought that's not real, that's not real! I quickly returned to my sleeping bag, pulled it up to my chin and feel asleep. The cognitive dissonance had kicked in and taken over.

I awoke the next morning from a very vivid dream of being put into a stretcher type device that seemed to hover. It was contoured to my body. I was laid back on it and it shot me straight up into the sky. I remember peering over the edge and seeing the forest getting smaller and then looking up to see an oval black disc above me. That is my last memory in the dream. When we drove into town very early that morning we encountered another strange sight. It was a ghost town with no one around. We were passing through the plaza in Santa Fe when we witnessed a group of about twelve men in light tan army outfits with black shoulder straps. They were all of Latino decent and were holding m-16s. We quickly drove by as they eyed us in passing. I have no idea who these armed men were and have never seen any military or police groups that dress in these colors. It was a very strange experience all the way around.

During this time I had my first encounter with dimethyl-tryptimine, DMT. I had researched the drug thoroughly upon first learning about it through my readings in the works of Terence McKenna. I was completely fascinated by the experiences that he described while intoxicated on DMT. The mosaic visuals reminded me of the closed eye visions I had experienced while on mushrooms. That and the very close chemical makeup of each substance. Just one endole off from each other. No matter how much reading or research you could do, one cannot be prepared for the ego destroying experience that is DMT. The only preparation I can recommend to aspiring psychonauts is to have quite a few heroic doses under your belt first. Between five to seven grams on an empty stomach. If you can make it through these experiences you can most likely handle DMT.

However, I do not recommend this compound for the light hearted psychedelic user. It is a very powerful tool. I had a breakthrough experience the first time I ingested it. I smoked it with a friend who only used DMT and no other substances. He would take it alone in the woods and "battle demons". He prepared me for the trip ahead of time. I still was not prepared for what lay ahead. Immediately when I began to inhale the smoke, it was like my soul recognized the taste of it and the oncoming rush of the experience. I heard a ripping noise and was blasted through a geometric pattern. I was suddenly without a body, fully conscious and in a black starless void. I felt a million tiny hands pull my soul out of my body. Time had completely stopped for me.

The very next instance, I leaned back and opened my eyes to a new world. The room had completely transformed and had come alive. I looked down at the bedspread and the rose flowers on it began rising off of it and began talking to me. I looked around the room to what seemed to be threads of conscious bright white light stretched from floor to ceiling and was vibrating like a piano string.

Everything I looked at was transformed and vying for my attention. Tiny voices calling to me in unheard of languages. I covered my eyes and enjoyed closed eye visuals of beings I can best describe as cartoonish. Elvish looking dwarves dancing about playing with the colorful mosaics that were spinning everywhere. I stayed this way until the visions began to fade and these beings frantically were waving goodbye to me. It was such an enjoyable experience for me. My friend then had a trip while me and his girlfriend trip watched. After his trip I was so hungry for the experience I asked if I could smoke it again. He agreed and I took my second trip.

This time after coming through the void I was greeted with the most horrible open and closed eye visuals of death, destruction, and chaos imaginable. It went on this way for some time until I let go and saw a picture of Kali on the wall of the room. I then thanked Kali for showing me the negative aspects of existence and the visions completely changed. The negative imagery ended and was replaced with the jovial dwarves again dancing and singing. It was very profound. My acceptance of the visuals and my gratitude for them seemed to be rewarded after thanking Kali. The next day the "real" world seemed like a card board facsimile of itself. I had reached beyond the veil and had seen the void. This world was then transformed into maya, a world of illusion. The next 3 months were quite interesting. The DMT trip totally dissolves your connection to your physical vessel and the ego is shattered.

I moved back to Ohio in the fall of 1994. Things weren't going well with finding a place out west. I soon ran out of money and decided to go back to where I could afford to have a place. I landed in Cincinnati where I stayed with my brother and a friend until I found my own place. During this time, I became a part of the underground music scene. I had attended my first rave in NYC back in 1992. I had also tried ecstasy for the first time then. I really enjoyed the euphoric feelings of bliss and the strong empathic connection it created with people. I began regularly attending parties across the Midwest.

I also began djing in the fall of 1995. I chose the name Eleven:11, after my synchronous experience with clocks at the time. I was constantly seeing the 11:11 on clocks, billboards and commercials. I enjoyed the zen like flow I would get while djing. Raves to me were the cities shamanic equivalent of drum circles at Rainbow Gatherings. Both shared the same continual heart beat and caused states of trance to be induced by music and dancing. I would enjoy going to parties and taking MDMA and psychedelics and getting into extreme trance states while getting lost in the music in front of a stack of speakers.

During this time, I also was having sighting of UFOs. Sometimes quite frequently. Whenever me and my two best friends drove to Indiana we would encounter disc shaped craft. I recall several times seeing brightly lit craft that looked like something out of Steven Spielburg's Close Encounters of the 3rd Kind. I have no other recall of these events. Were these encounters full blown experiences that have been somehow blocked from my conscious recall?

During this time, I had a sighting of an unknown object that appeared to me and a group of friends camping. We were all invited to a weekend campout at my friend's land in Youngstown Ohio. During the evening, we were all hanging out on the porch outside. Enjoying the stars and watching lightning bugs dance in the valley. Suddenly a very bright light appeared in the valley and flashed us all. It was about the size of a soft ball. It hovered about six feet above the ground and gave off a super white and blueish light. It flashed us and disappeared. One of my friends turned to me and said "hey Neil, your friends are here". They knew of my past experiences and my friend Mary who witnessed my tent glowing in Colorado was there to see this as well. This is the first time that I had encountered this light. However, it was not going to be the last.

I had several sightings over the next few years but nothing major. I did have a lot of interesting experiences where I had moments of telepathic contact with people at raves. One specific event was at a party in Cleveland. I was on MDMA and I was dancing by myself in a side room at the event, I made eye contact with a girl that I did not know. We locked eyes with each other and I immediately felt a mental connection with her. We began dancing off of each other and I heard her talking with me in my mind and me talking back. It was very profound. I stopped and stood in place and she ran up to me and embraced me in a big hug. I whispered in her ear, "did that really just happen?" and she smiled and said yes!

The International Journal on Interpersonal Studies paper on Psychoactive Substances and Paranormal Phenomena states "There are good theoretical reasons for investigating psychedelics as a means of inducing ESP and other paranormal phenomena. Given that an altered state of consciousness (ASC) is assumed to be a common feature in the occurrence of subjective paranormal experiences (Alvarado, 1998; Baruss, 2003; Honorton, 1977; Parker, 1975) and has often been incorporated into experimental attempts to induce ESP (see Luke, 2011a; Palmer, 1978, 1982; Schmeidler, 1994), then visionary drugs are, potentially, a reliable means of accessing such a state.

Several researchers have documented some of the mind-altering features of the visionary-drug experience that are considered conducive to the production of parapsychological experiences and phenomena (see also Braud, 2002). These have been categorized thus:

1. Increase in mental imagery, in both vividness and quality, and the dreamlike state (Blackmore, 1992; Osis, 1961a, 1961b; Progoff, 1961; Tart, 1968, 1994)
2. Altered perception of self-identity, such as unity consciousness: The mystical experience of becoming one with everything in the universe (Krippner & Fersh, 1970; Nicol & Nicol, 1961; Osis, 1961a; Pahnke, 1968; Tart, 1994)
3. Altered body perceptions and dissociation (Blackmore, 1992; Tart, 1994). This is of particular interest with respect to the out-of body experience (OBE)
4. Distorted sensory input (Blackmore, 1992)
5. Increased absorption and focused attention (Millay, 2001; Tart, 1968, 1994)
6. Increased empathy (Blewett, 1963; Nicol & Nicol, 1961; Tart, 1994). This is of interest to telepathy, and indeed, elevated empathy is associated with use of psychedelics generally (DeGracia, 1995; Lerner & Lyvers, 2006)
7. Emotional flexibility (Blewett, 1963), which may also assist in negotiating the fear of psi (Tart, 1994)
8. Increased alertness and awareness (Huxley, 1961a; Nicol & Nicol, 1961; Osis, 1961b; Tart, 1994)
9. Increased inwardly focused attention and awareness, and decreased external and bodily awareness (Dobkin de Rios, 1978)
10. Increased spontaneity (Osis, 1961a)
11. Sensitivity to subtle changes (Parker, 1975) and intensity of feeling (Osis, 1961a)
12. Physical relaxation (Blackmore, 1992), although Tart (1968) questions its occurrence
13. Increased suggestibility (Huxley, 1961a; Tart, 1968)

14. Increase in intuitive thought processes (Tart, 1994)
15. Reduced critical conscious faculty and increased optimism towards impossible realities (Nicol & Nicol, 1961; Osis, 1961b; Tart, 1968, 1994)
16. Increased openness and extroversion (Rogo, 1976)
17. Release of repressed and unconscious material into the conscious mind (Rogo, 1976)
18. Complex distortions, and transcendence, of space and time (Garrett 1961b; Nicol & Nicol, 1961; Tart, 1994; see also Dawson, 2005; Mayhew, 1956; Shanon, 2001; Whiteman, 1995)

These are all common experiences within my own encounters with MDMA and substances like psilocybin, LSD, mescaline and DMT. Many times, I have had moments of ESP whilst on these compounds. I also have had an OBE and was once told that I was seen levitating off of the floor while entranced dancing at a rave. I believe these compounds help to illicit higher vibratory rates than we normally experience in our day to day lives. Time seems to stop. A connection with group consciousness or universal mind is felt. During a mushroom experience a week before the light showed up at the campout in Youngstown. I had an opened eye visual of an oval portal opening up and it being filled with many zeta faces staring back at me from a room that reminded me of an old medical school amphitheater. Earlier that evening I seemed to be downloading a vast amount of information from elsewhere. It was very strange. At the time these experiences were completely written off by me as hallucinations and not contact encounters. However, I am beginning to look at them from a much different perspective now. My continued contact with NHI leads me to believe these were also contact experiences of a different sort.

My contact experiences seemed to wain for many years until the birth of my son in 2006. He was born with cyclic neutropenia, a white blood cell deficiency. He was constantly having to have his neutrophils checked and whenever he got sick he was in the hospital. We did not know that my wife was pregnant at the time and I found out the day he was born that I was going to be a father! I quit my day job and became a stay-at-home Dad. After moving from Cincinnati to Akron Ohio I began to have problems in my marriage. I was separated in 2008 and my son had what I believe was his first contact encounter at age two and a half.

At the time he was speaking quite well but spoke of himself in the 3rd person when talking. One night during a full moon he asked me to take him outside to see the moon. We went outside and I was holding him looking at the sky when an object appeared and flashed me. It was a stationary light that seemed to flash colors. My son seemed to see it as well. Suddenly it fell to the ground like gravity had just taken control of it. I did not think much of it and we returned into the apartment. Later that evening after putting my son to bed in my bedroom. I was retired in the living room reading a book. An hour or so later I am startled by my son screaming bloody murder in the other room. He had never once fussed or had a night terror from the time he was born until this incident. I ran into the room, picked him up and began comforting him. He then says he wants to look at the moon again. So I take him outside. Whilst standing there admiring the moon he plainly says to me "(his name) went up into the sky." I said "oh yeah?" and he says "the mean monster and the robot took (his name) up into the sky". I said "and then what happened?". He states "they touched my belly and there was blood." And I said "then what happened?" to which he plainly stated "they brought me back". I was floored. I immediately hopped into my car to write it down word for word verbatim. Three weeks later I had taken him in for his blood work and **he was completely healed of the cyclic neutropenia**!

My next contact experience would take place during a camping trip in 2013 at Portage Lakes, in Portage County Ohio. I had gone camping with my son, my good friend Patrick and his two boys. We had spent the day fishing and playing catch. In the evening after dinner, we walked from our campsite to look at the stars over by the water, the boys were running about six feet ahead of us when Patrick and I spotted an unknown craft, well-lit and moving silently above us. I noticed my friend see it and he asked "what's that?" I said "my friends maybe". He was a close friend and had heard about many of my contact experiences. As we made our way to the water's edge the object disappeared. A large cigar shape craft then appeared directly in front of us over the water. It was to the left of an island and was as large as the blimp. It made no sounds at all. It was solid jet black and blocked out the stars. It had two very large solid white lights on its lower right side and two small red lights on its left side. All five of us saw it.

The boys began questioning what it was. There were two people fishing off to our left and they seemed oblivious to the craft. After about ten or fifteen minutes my friends youngest began to get distressed and wanted to go back to the camp. I stayed with my son and my buddy's other child and we watched the object another ten minutes. After Patrick had walked back to camp, we saw the object disappear as if someone had switched off a switch. It then reappeared on the other side of the island in the blink of an eye. It hovered there for about a minute, blinked out and again reappeared where it had first appeared! It was still there sitting silently when we walked back to camp that night.

The next life shaking event occurred in the fall of 2013. I suffer from a myriad of health issues. Firstly, I have fibromyalgia and rheumatoid arthritis. I was diagnosed at age thirty-five in 2005. I have also had diverticulosis during these years. On October 16th my parents were in town visiting me for the weekend. I became deathly ill after going to lunch with them. I could not stop getting sick. After getting my son from school I left him to play with my folks, so I may lay down. That evening, I had to have my father take me to the ER. After several tests and having been administered anti-nausea and pain medications, I was sent home. I was still getting sick the following morning with abdominal pains and had to return to the hospital. I was given a cat scan. This time they found that my cecum (my colon on the right side) had flopped and caused a complete shutdown of my stomach and intestines. I would need an emergency c-section surgery for a colon resection.

That was Saturday morning. I spent the day Sunday in utter misery. I had bloated out like a pregnant woman and had been told to drink a large jug of laxative as a pre-surgery prep. I informed the nurse that it was not going to work. I just knew this. She then stated "I have never seen it not work in all my twenty-five years as a nurse. Needless to say, I began getting violently ill about a third into the jug. It did not work and I was told not to drink anymore. At this point I was continually given anti-nausea meds and was hooked to a morphine drip. I went under the knife around noon on Monday. My colon had swollen to 13cms and was splitting when it was removed. I had nearly died. I awoke many hours later in the most excruciating pain I have ever felt. I was in a darkened recovery room just outside of surgery. I felt like a gutted fish. I was begging for more pain medication and they explained to me that I could not have any more at that time.

The next day I was magically blessed with an eighteen hour long block of UFO shows on the History Channel. This is how the Universe speaks with me. The next two and a half weeks were horrible. I had to start over with a clear diet and work myself up to solid foods. I spent much of my time wandering around the ward building up my strength so I could leave. I have always had a strong dislike of hospitals and the dentist's office. I feel it is PTSD from my contact encounters as I am triggered by the lights above me and being put in a chair or on a table. This started after the abduction dreams in my early childhood and persisted until my late teens.

I forced the Dr. who was in charge of me to dismiss me on day nineteen of my stay. I was beginning to become quite fearful that if I stayed any longer I was going to get sick and die. Many people on the ward had gotten pneumonia and I swear I smelled death in the halls while making my rounds. I literally told the Dr. he was going to let me out that day or I was going to walk out. Needless to say I was discharged two hours later.

I was set to return for another colon resection in January for my sigmoid colon. It was discovered to be so damaged from scar tissue from diverticulosis, that it would need to be removed. The next month was very hard on me. All my senses seemed to be turned up to the maximum. Smell, taste, hearing etc. The cold weather had moved in and ice storms were hitting us. The cold weather and surgery had thrown me into a very long and painful fibro flare up. I spent my days huddled on the couch with my dog. It felt touch and go for the next few months. I felt so thin when I left the hospital. Not physically, although I had lost 45 pounds. But my spirit seemed thin, frail. I was weakened from the ordeal. Like the veil between life and death had suddenly become paper thin. January came and went and the second surgery was completed. It was a lot less traumatizing to my system then the first experience. I spent the next year recouping and living my daily life. I was still having a lot of health issues with my fibromyalgia and arthritis. I was battling for my SSI during this time to no avail.

In 2015 things began to heat up. My UFO encounters were about to ramp up in a major way. I had a lot of time on my own. I only had my son every other week and was not working. I spent the time pretty much as a hermit.

During this time, I had become more aware of my Native Indian heritage. My mother had informed me of our direct lineage with Anne Suncloud, of the Lenape tribe from NJ. She was my great, great, great, great grandmother. A Umami Princess and daughter of the chief of the Lenape tribe. I had been researching this connection and was reading a lot of books by Native American authors. Two such books that effected me greatly were Black Elk Speaks: The Lakota Way and Encounters with Star People by Ardy Sixkiller Clarke. Both detailed experiences with Native American Star People. Wallace Black Elk discussed being visited by the Star People and having the morning star come down to him. The stories in Ardy Sixkiller Clarke's book detailed the most amazing and positive stories of interactions with the Star People that I had ever read. Both solidified my belief that my visitors were benevolent, I had struggled with my feelings on this over the years. As soon as I understood this, I decided to reach out mentally to my Star Family. I asked them to please let me become more of an active participant in my encounters with them. I knew that they were interacting with me and I needed to be able to remember. This is when my sightings increased.

I would go outside under the stars to smoke and started calling on the Great Spirit and asking for the Star People to come down. The first time I witnessed craft above my place, I had been looking at the stars when suddenly one of them moved. It moved slowly across a part of the sky and stopped. I then noticed another star like object fly into view and stop in formation with the first. This activity began to happen almost nightly in the spring of 2015.

Then I started to be visited by a stationary light that would hover in the sky and flash colors. I dubbed it the "object". It began showing up a lot. One day in anticipation of its return, I charged up my 4mega pixel digital camera to be ready. That evening around 9 PM I went out for a cigarette. The object had returned and was in its usual place flashing colors.

I called to my son inside to bring out my camera. He rushed it to me and I turned it on and began focusing. As soon as I pressed the button to take the picture. The battery drained from a full charge down to red and powered off. I could not believe it. I ran into the living room and turned on the camera and it opened up to a full green charge. It had been on the charger all day, so there was no way it was the battery. I ran back outside and again focused on the object. I pressed the button. Yet again the camera drained and shut off the camera. I again went inside to check the camera. Again, it was fully charged. I went outside and tried a third time and it happened again! To which I verbally laughed out loud, ***"you don't want me taking pictures"***.

So, from that point on I have never tried to photograph my sightings. When I put the camera away, activity really blew up. I was getting visits four and five times a week, multiple times in a night. I started naming the types of things I was seeing. Solid white orbs that looked like stars. Moving across the sky. Stopping. Changing directions. Making hard angle turns. Flashers. These would appear and flashbulb me like an old 1970s flash camera. Streakers, these would cut into our atmosphere parallel to the horizon at high rates of speed. Cut across the sky, flash brightly and disappear. I would feel a strong psychic connection with these objects when they arrived for me and put on such magical displays. My son regularly witnessed these sightings with me. I always thanked the Star People for showing up and would send them messages of love and gratitude.

In June of 2015 I went outside for a smoke. I was alone that week, as my son was at his mother's. I sat down in my chair on my porch and lit a cigarette. Suddenly to my left about twenty feet from me appeared the light from the campout in Youngstown. It was a solid blueish white light about the size of a tennis ball. It hovered about six feet off of the ground. It then flashed me. I calmly reached into my pocket and pulled out my keychain. On it I had a little blue led light. I flashed the object back. It answered me back! I flashed it twice in succession and it answered me again! It then flew directly in front of me and over to my right and stopped above my neighbor's townhouse roof. I flashed it three times and it flashed me back three times. I spent the next five full minutes blinking it and it answering me as it danced above the roof. Suddenly it just flew off.

The next time I saw the light I was having a fire in my back yard. I was laying alone under the stars sky watching when the ball of light flew up from my right and zipped about two feet above my head. It circled me and zipped off. During this time of my life, I was a total recluse. I only spent time with my son every other week and kept to myself. I was really excited and wanted to tell other people about my encounters but I wanted to keep it to just me for the time being. My relationship with them was growing. The mental connection that I felt with them increased as well. I could sense when they were going to show up, and they would.

We began to have paranormal activity in the apartment at this time. My son and I began to notice bright flashes of blue light appearing in my bedroom and reflecting in the hallway mirror. We would be sitting in the living room and suddenly see these flashes of bright light. I would catch them in the mirror and he would too. Things began to disappear in the house. Little things but they would go missing from where they were kept. And then they would suddenly reappear where they should have been before. During this time period I would find doors and drawers left open or pulled out. I also was touched on two different occasions by unseen entities. Once whilst lying in bed, I had what felt like a tiny hand rest itself on my knee. Another time I was tapped on my left shoulder from behind.

Also during this time, I began having aircraft fly over the airspace where I had called in craft. The ships would disappear moments before two F-18 fighter jets would fly in and directly over the airspace where the craft were minutes previously. It was actually quite humorous to see this. That is until I got buzzed one Saturday afternoon.

This was in the afternoon and I was in the kitchen making some lunch. The apartment started shaking and I heard a helicopter. I went outside and an all-black Apache with full gun array was looking directly at me. I could see the pilot. They hovered over the power lines well below FAA safety standards. They flew off when I flipped them the bird. This was not the first time I had encountered them or the last.

The first time I witnessed all black Apaches was one evening when two of them landed on the end of the tarmac by the old Akron Rubber bowl. A dilapidated old football stadium and field at the end of the property just beyond the airfield. The Akron airfield houses the blimp hangar, a Lockheed Martin facility, and an airstrip for small engine planes. The airfield also contains some type of low-key army facility. I was informed by a guard at the Lockheed entrance that it was a top-secret clearance, is only ever used during Mondays through Fridays till 9 pm and the neighboring radio towers were not functional.

The Apaches came in tandem and landed on the end of the airfield. Two all black SUVs drove down the airstrip from the Lockheed base to the waiting helicopters. A group of about 8 men exited them and got into the SUVs. They drove back up the airstrip to Lockheed and then the apaches lifted off and flew south.

Now in 2015 I was awoken on a Sunday night at 2am. I was alone as my son was at his mom's that week. I sat up to a super white light shining through my window over the airfield. *A voice in my head said 'GO OUTSIDE'!*

I immediately ran outside and into my driveway as the white light was coming down the airfield growing in size and brightness. The airfield was lit up like Christmas with all their landing lights on. Just then two all-black Apaches appeared and flew down to the tarmac by the Lockheed building. I ran the five houses down to Tripplet Ave. They landed as the white light grew to the size of the moon. I was directly across the street from the airfield.

The light then turned into a gigantic black diamond that blocked out the stars! It had solid white lights on all four points and two solid green lights and one solid red one inside the diamond in an inverted equilateral triangle. This thing was the largest thing I had ever seen. Completely silent. It flew right past me down the airfield, over the Rubber bowl and stopped over the cross street. It was as big as the football field! It then disappeared in the blink of an eye, as if someone threw a switch. All of the lights on the airfield completely blacked out as the Apaches lifted off and flew back to the south.

I do not even know how to begin to understand this one in my experience. Was this a secret black op craft? A UFO? Is there some kind of underground facility there? Who put the voice in my head? Was this an ET craft sent for me to witness? What did I witness standing in my boxers and a t-shirt that night?

My encounters with craft continued until the fall. For some reason activity seems to wain in the fall and winter months, but picks back up in the spring.

In June of 2016 I had my most profound conscious experience with the Star People to date. My son was over for the week and I had just laid him down to sleep in my bedroom. I had gotten up after he had fallen asleep and looked at the clock which read 10:15PM. I went out on the porch for a cigarette. I sat in the chair and lit my smoke. A moment later I look to my left and the light showed up right where it had appeared the first time it visited me. Again to my left about twenty feet from me. I flashed it with my lighter and it flashed me in reply. It then pulsed me with a very bright white light and disappeared. It was as if it did something or sent something to me. I finished my smoke and went inside. I immediately rolled up my last tobacco for one more smoke. I was excited that the light had shown up again and wanted to get right back outside. I then went back out and sat down and lit my smoke.

That is my last conscious memory until a moment later when I seemed to be floating down onto my neighbor's porch. I was facing over the roof of my building waving goodbye at a super bright light zipping off at a high rate of speed! I was waving with my right hand and was overjoyed with love. I stumbled off the porch and over to mine. I went inside my living room and stood there. I was tingling from head to toe and felt intoxicated. I did not know who I was, where I was or what was happening! I then went into the bedroom and looked at the clock. It read 12:15AM! I had lost an hour and 45 minutes. I went to bed and fell asleep. When we awoke in the morning my son had a symbol on his right hand! It was a red inverted equilateral triangle. It looked like a raised brand. It was about one inch in diameter. Looked red and irritated but was not painful. The mark remained for the next two weeks. (This encounter was explored and verified during my hypnotic regression)

This was a very profound experience for me. It was the first time that I was fully conscious for the event. I was not able to access the missing time which was most unnerving. That and the involvement yet again of my child. However, the experience did not frighten me in anyway.

Quite the opposite, I believe that whatever is visiting me and my son is ***completely benevolent.*** I consider them my family. I would not have felt such elation and joy upon leaving them when I appeared on my neighbor's porch. I know that they are my real family and have been with me all along. I feel the conscious connection to them was established well before my birth and then the current visitations started right after my incarnation here. Once this mental connection is made it remains.

This was how I was able to consciously call the craft to me during these times of initiated contact. Consciousness is the only modality we need to connect with these intelligences. We are all universally linked to the one encompassing consciousness that is in all things everywhere. Thought is instantaneous communication. I believe that this connection is how people are able to access unknown knowledge from the collective consciousness. This is how Edgar Cayce connected to the Akashic records, where he obtained much information on physical healings and the afterlife. Or where Nikola Tesla contacted Non-Human Intelligence that gave him information on his inventions and how to make them. From great artists, musicians, and creatives throughout history that have stated divine inspiration as the source of their creativity to mystics, philosophers, saints, yogis and spiritual adepts of all religions that say the same thing. They had obtained a state of conscious awareness that allowed them to commune with the spirit world.

To be on Purpose, Is to Create:

My Experiences via OBEs and Lucid Dreams

Mathew Foxworthy

The start, a very precious thing, our journey we must make.
A long and weary path indeed, still yet we must not wait.
For on that road we'll find ourselves distracted left and right,
And all of life that means the most is dim within our sight.
When dark storms and trials great, burden us to strain.
We look behind for days gone by, a search for comfort vain.
For you see by looking back, we still are forward bound,
And stumble to the future by steps on unseen ground.
Would it not be better, to turn and forward face,
And see the roses from the path once missed by jilted grace.
The choice on Earth, of good to do and in that karma smite,
And know the journey is the prize once sought with blinded sight.

As in the poem above, the start is a very precious thing. I believe this is true of each and every one of us. Here we are born and for the most part have no knowledge of what came before or what is to come. We move onward and seek that, which, at some deep level, is a notion of an eternity, long forgotten, that glitters at the edges of our vision, a vision dimmed by the cares and lessons that lie ahead in this life. This poem came to me in a time of great transition in my life and appropriately sets the stage for an examination of consciousness from a personal standpoint that is presented in this chapter.

I am an artist, poet, painter, designer and all around "maker" by compulsion. I have been to college yet had to leave before earning a degree. I design great pipe organs and paint for a living and this in turn brings a bit more beauty into the world. There is really nothing extraordinary about my life except for the extraordinary things that have happened to help shape it. I am just an Experiencer, here to recount the Contact Modalities that have affected my life and share what I have personally learned.

When Rey Hernandez asked me to write a chapter for this book, I was honored. I had only known Rey for a short time and yet understood the premise of his area of study based on his experiences. I became aware of Rey's work through an Earth Files YouTube video. I moved on to other videos, interviews and internet articles about Rey and the then the Dr. Edgar Mitchell FREE Foundation, which later transitioned to the Consciousness & Contact Research Institute, or CCRI.

I resonated with Rey's view of Consciousness and Contact, what Rey has coined the paranormal "Contact Modalities". I realized that this is also how I have begun to think in the last few years. Most of my life has been spent in silence about my personal experiences. I can count on both my hands the number of books I have read on these subjects. I felt compelled to reach out to Rey and to offer my help in any way that I could.

My life up to this point in time has been traveled on a road of ease and of disease, of feast and famine, of joys and sorrows, pretty much a normal life for those living a temporal existence. The only thing that has been different in my path, apart from the paths of my friends, it seems, has been the paranormal factors that have ultimately helped shape my personal path and decisions. These paranormal factors, or events, cover a range of the Contact Modalities. Through all the differing modes, a consistent theme seemed to emerge, at least for me. That theme was the essence of hope in love. It seemed to be a tie that bound it all together as a whole, as one theme, of a way of living. There are people that I have known that were content to "pigeonhole" every aspect of their lives. They had their "work life", their "social life", their "home life", their "church life" and other things that subdivided these individuals into many self-disconnected parts of themselves. My perception from my first contact experience is that we are all, each one of us, composed of many aspects s of our life in one complete consciousness. Furthermore, we are all responsible to each other as an individualized aspect of a greater consciousness. I really did not understand early on why people would do this.

To understand how I came to believe this, I must take the reader back to when it all began with that first contact experience at age seven. Then, moving forward, cover the many contact experiences that have occurred through the different modalities. As my life moves through this physical existence, I realize that these experiences and all the other catalyst of life mixed in were orchestrated in some great way for me, for us, to make one single decision before we can move forward. That decision would be; do we serve ourselves or do we serve others?

First Contact Experience, (Very Direct, Powerful and by an Unknown Force)

It was the summer of 1969, June I believe. I was seven years old at the time, stuck right in between an older sister and a younger sister. For as long as I could remember, at this age, we would pack up the car every summer and visit my Aunt Dot who lived just east of Indianapolis, IN. Both my mom's family and my dad's family were from just east of there in Cumberland, Indiana. I remember the jingle my grandmother Foxworthy came up with for my grandfather's dealership, Foxworthy Ford; "819 East Washington Street, Foxworthy Ford just can't be beat!" My Aunt Dot lived off E. Washington St. (Hwy-40). My Uncle Roy, who was now running the dealership, was also a pilot. This was a great interest for a young boy of seven. These were some of the things rattling around in my seven-year-old head, not to mention the upcoming Apollo 11 moon mission. My dad had already prepared his camera on a tripod to snap slides from the screen of our then clunky console TV. This was only a few weeks away.

One evening as the family was watching television in the living room; the three of us kids were getting our baths. It was the girls first and then the boys, me, last. Looking back, the windows were probably open in the house and the front door would have been open as well. I remember it as a normal early summer evening. When it was my turn, I locked myself in the bathroom, to keep the girls out. This was also the only bathroom in the house. My sisters had really sloshed the water around and out of the tub. My Aunt had carpet on her bathroom floor which was now damp and littered with my sister's wet towels. I was getting undressed to get into the tub already filled with water. I was standing next to the outside window and toilet. I had already removed my "boy scout" shorts and underwear when I heard the distant sound of what I thought was a small plane. I stopped taking my shirt off and listened. I wanted to see if this plane would fly over the house. The sound of the engine grew louder and louder as I stood listening and watching. At some point, I realized that the sound was more of a hum than that of a piston engine. It sounded electrical in nature. The sound continued to get louder and louder. It was really loud now. This was all happening fast but my memory of it seems to go on for a long time, like in slow motion. I have an impression of seeing a single light, maybe like a moving star. I did not have time to really get a grip on the visual aspect. The sound now shifted from outside to inside my head. It happened quickly. As it did, the hum began to modulate. This is very hard to describe. It was as if some other signal was modulating the hum, using it as a carrier wave. As the modulation began, the "signal" began to surge in waves penetrating deeper and deeper into my headfirst and then throughout my whole body with each wave of energy. I began to feel the flow of an electrical nature coming or going through my legs and feet into the damp carpeted floor. It tingled at the peak of each pulse. As this pulsating continued it became such a crescendo that I grabbed my head and ducked down. As I did this, all I remember was being engulfed in blinding bright white light. I have no idea of or even if anything happened next. The next memory I had was coming out of the edge of whiteness nearly six feet from where I had been standing.

My first sight was my hand on the bathroom doorknob. I was trying to get out as I was terrified and confused. I thought that maybe the plane had crashed into the house.

When I finally managed to unlock the door, I burst almost buck naked into the living room across a small hallway. The house was a tiny two bedroom built in 1941, so you knew and could hear everything going on in every room. Everybody gasped. I was literally scared white. I was told that I was white as a ghost when I burst into the living room. I was trying to cover myself with my hands and I still had the shirt on. I was in a panic as I shouted to find out what happened. Not a single person out of the five in the living room or my six-year-old sister in another room heard a thing. My six-year-old sister, who was doing dishes in the kitchen, thought she may have felt a tingling in the dish water but that was it. After they calmed me down and I put on clothes, I recounted the story. I asked how long I had been there. I think the consensus was 30 minutes. I thought I was only in there for five to ten minutes. To this day, no one in my family has spoken about this event that I can think of. I don't remember what they said back then. It is a void in my memory.

For days after this event, an adult would have to be present in the bathroom when I urinated. For the time it would take to defecate, I dare not change it. So, I decided to hold it in. This went on for days without anybody noticing. That was, until I got sick. I had to explain to my dad that I could not "go" due to fear of another episode. He was a doctor and realized that I needed to go to the emergency room. They loaded me up into the back seat of the family station wagon, a Prairie Bronze 1965 Falcon Futura. As I lay in the back seat on the way to the hospital, I could see the moon through the trees. This time it was different. Seeing the moon through the trees like this, I became nervous. I thought it was following us to the hospital. Then a dread of the sky welled up in me, a dread that was not in me before.

Apparently, everything worked out in the end. I remember still being afraid of that bathroom. To keep from getting impacted again, an adult would stand at the door with their back to me until I finished my business. I don't remember ever taking another bath in there on that trip. It must have been getting close to the time we would leave and head back to Tampa, Florida where we lived. We lived on a man-made island of residential homes within walking distance of downtown Tampa. I liked living on the water, well, except for the hurricanes. When we got home my dad was focused on the moon mission and I followed along when he was home and pretty much kept to myself the rest of the time. School was out so I would sit on the stairway to the second floor of our house and daydream. I was familiar with science fiction. My dad watched Star Trek, Time Tunnel, Land of the Giants and even the Thunderbirds. I was right there with him so my mind was open to new possibilities. I just never expected I would have experiences like science fiction.

Nightmares and Dream-like Visions

Not long after we got home, probably within days, I started having nightmares about what happened in my aunt's bathroom. They would always start the in same way; the humming modulated sound would start welling up in my head during a dream and take over with wave after wave of information. It felt like the same wave after wave of the original event. There were all sorts of disjointed fragments of images, emotions, thoughts, and themes leading to fear, sadness, depression and anxiety. It would probably be labeled PTSD today. Before long, the frequency of the number of these dreams per night increased. Not long after this increase in number, I started having these dreams/visions, all on the same theme, during my waking and sleeping hours. I remember one time while I was daydreaming on the stairs it happened. It happened once while my mind drifted as I waited for my mom or sister to use the restroom at a restaurant. I was now seeing full blown scenarios, each different with the, now, same message. There were no longer any disjointed images and thoughts. The visions were now complete scenarios that clearly warned what would happen if you lived life a certain way.

I only have a complete memory of one of these scenarios. It epitomizes all of the others. Its message is clear, and the resulting emotions were intense. I had this dream/vision towards the end, where these visions started to fade away. I had endured these dream/visions for six or seven months. It was the Christmas holiday season, so this vision takes on a holiday theme.

Here is how the scenario played out; I found myself in the living room of our 1925 Mediterranean Revival home standing next to the Christmas tree. The ceilings were 11 feet high, so we had a tall tree. We always went out to my parent's friend's property to cut down a tree. They had done this for many years. It was a native Florida "Sand Pine". The Sand Pine had needles that were approximately 2 inches long and the branches made it very uneven, but it worked and was a long-standing tradition in our home.

In this vision, like in real life, I liked my presents hidden away in the back corner of the tree. Only in the vision, I found that I had a compulsion to want to pull needles off the tree. At first this was OK, "there were so many", no one would notice any missing in the back corner. Once I had decimated the back corner of its needles, I started moving around to the side. I was pulling needle after needle. I could not stop myself. I wanted more and more. I could care less what the consequences would be. Before long, the damage became noticeable. It was not much at first. I tried to pull off needles evenly hoping that no one would notice. It was killing me inside. I was going against my very inner nature to satisfy some need for sick control. I could feel the conflict tearing my very being and I could not stop it. Needle by needle I kept tearing away at the tree. Only now, I was on the lookout for being caught. I knew I was destroying something very precious. When it was said and done, there stood a hideous skeleton of a once beautiful creation, destroyed by pure greed, and want, by an appetite that could never be satiated. Everyone was now there as a witness to the destruction. I was exposed. My shame was more than I could bear. This could NEVER be the life that I could choose in the incarnation I had only just begun. It just could not be. I could not bear it. This scenario played out many more times before the visions tapered off. I guess I had understood the message. I concluded later in life that this message was given by an unknown intelligence. It was a gift if you will. I wanted to understand the how and why of it. Thus began my seeking.

Something had changed inside of me. I did not know what it was or how to put it into words as an, almost, eight-year-old. The only thing I was aware of is that I had been given something that changed the course of my life. My cognitive and reasoning abilities seemed to increase. The outcome of some decisions was clear, almost to the point of visually seeing the outcome before it happened.

When my dad repainted his office, the leftover paint cans were stored in our utility room. It was great fun to see how high I could stack them. While undertaking this action, a flash of vision passed through my mind. I saw the interplay of gravity against the unsteady height and the possibility of a collapse. The next thing I saw was the possibility of cans that still had a good amount of paint in them popping open due to the shifting paint upon impact. No sooner had this passed before me, the cans began tumbling down and two of them burst open spilling the contents all over the floor. The feeling I experienced when my parents found out echoed the Christmas tree vision. I learned to pay attention to these messages running in the background.

Audible Visitation and Healing,

Sometime after the six or seven months that I was having the visions, I remember getting a pain in my groin that prompted a visit to the doctor. There was no real explanation for what was causing the pain. I remember being so disturbed by this that I insisted on sleeping between my parents for comfort. I had to lie perfectly still on my back to avoid the pain. I don't know what time it was, but it was late. Both of my parents were asleep. I heard a sound on the first floor at the stairway to the second floor where we were sleeping. I listened carefully to this sound which was a very steady "click" like sound. It was different than a clock.

As I listened, I realized it was moving. I heard it slowly come up the stairs, come around the corner and then it entered the bedroom. I had the blanket pulled over my head and there was no way that I was going to look. I heard the sound come around the end of the bed and stop right in the middle. This is where I was. It lingered there for a while. I felt a presence from the location of the sound but was too scared to look. After what seemed like forever, the sound exited the room and went back down the stairs and faded away. The next day, all the pain that I had was mostly gone. I never really equated one event to the other before writing this down. It seems as if my unseen visitor might have been there to help.

A Pat on the Back

When I was 10, my grandfather passed away. This was my mom's father. He would come and stay during part of the year. The rest of the time he would stay with my aunt in Indianapolis. I remember the last time seeing him when they left Florida to go home. After he passed and we were back home from the funeral, I was sitting in the living room of our home feeling alone and down. I was in front of the console TV. I don't even remember if it was on. Just when I needed it the most, someone came up behind me and gave me a pat on the back, several actually. When I turned around to acknowledge them, nobody was there. I felt the prescience as my grandfather. I knew he was gone but at the same time there still looking after me. I still get a warm feeling when I think about this incident.

Out of Body Experience,

When the weather was nice, I liked to go with my dad on the weekends when he made his rounds at the hospitals where he had patients admitted. He would usually park in the doctor's parking lot, and I would stay in the car. I really liked this as I could daydream without being bothered. I remember one time we went to St. Joseph's hospital in Tampa. The doctor's parking was near a swamp that still had cypress trees and water. I loved the water so it was a beautiful place to sit and watch nature. My dad was inside for quite a while. I remember lying down on the leather seat of his car and mentally drifted away. When I opened my eyes, I became very confused. I was no longer in the car. It took me a while to get my bearings. I realized that I was 100's of feet above the doctor's parking lot looking down upon the cars, the parking lot, the hospital, and the swamp. I could see the water and trees like I was in an airplane. At that moment, I was so shocked that I closed my eyes and was immediately back in the car, laying on the seat, looking at the pleats in the leather upholstery. This all happened as if I was fully awake. It was not dreamlike at all. When I was about 15, I found a book by Robert Monroe and realized that I must have had an OBE.

Precognition Mixed with Past Life Memories,

I had an experience when I was about 12 that gave me an insight into precognition and possible past life memories. I was in our side yard zoning out on the patio. I was looking up at the power lines that crossed our lot. As I was looking at these lines, I shifted to some altered state of consciousness. I don't really know how to describe it only that it was like watching events play out but not in actual linear time, same place but different. I could see little sparrows flying by. They were all over our neighborhood. I liked them because they suggested some memory of a time gone by in my own mind. I wanted them to nest on our house because their warbling reminded me of home. This home memory, however, was from another time and place. Our Mediterranean revival house had the same effect. When I was in this altered mode, I felt as if I were in two worlds at the same time. As I watched the sparrows fly by in this altered state of consciousness, I was concerned for the birds hitting the wire and at that moment, I saw a sparrow strike the wire. It fell dead to the ground. The shock of this vision jolted me back to a waking state. As I looked around, I saw two sparrows flying across the yard. One of them hit the power line and fell dead onto the top of a travel trailer parked beside our garage. When I pondered what I had just seen, I heard a voice in my head recite a verse from the Bible that I remembered, probably from Sunday school as a kid; "Are not two sparrows sold for a penny and not yet one of them will fall apart from the Father". I got out a ladder and retrieved the dead sparrow and buried it. The whole episode gave me a sense of more going on behind the façade of life than I had thought previously.

The Unremembered Friend

I became somewhat of a hermit at school, a prep school, complete with cliques, bully kids, and bully teachers. I did not relate much with my peers anymore. I became the skinny nerd that was to be made fun of for being different. I would rather be off looking at some little bug rather than playing ball in physical education class. During recess I had a hidden place where I could spend time with my own thoughts. A lot of effort was put into "pinning" childish pranks on me. I spent a lot of time in the principal's office. If I deserved to be there, I would accept my punishment. If I was there for something I did not do, I would fight tooth and toenail to clear my name. But what adult is going to listen to the word of a nerd kid in 1970. I point this out here because I realized that I had been given a strong sense of right and wrong. If there were a "cheat sheet" circulating during a test, I would just pass it by and rely on my abilities.

I also became somewhat of a rebel. After having suffered verbal abuse from the kids, I had to endure verbal abuse and shaming from teachers. Once I was beaten unconscious by a teacher that did not like my questioning of things in his class. I remember being beaten but it would be years later when I met an old classmate who was present that I found out that I was knocked out and dragged away by my hair. I thought I got away. This shows how fragile a physical mind can be and how we protect our mental stability within this temporal existence without ever missing a beat. Was it my memory that was wrong or the witness that I ran into years later? I don't know. What I do remember is starting to hold onto anger. At some point, I just stopped performing for these people, the teachers, who did not like me. My parents were at a loss. They sent me to a testing Psychologist to see if I had learned anything. I liked the doctor, so I passed his tests with ease. The school was forced to advance me grade by grade. I believe my ability to learn was another gift bestowed upon me in June of 1969.

When I was in my early teens, my mom was telling a family friend about things that I did in grade school. She recounted one story that absolutely floored me. She said that I had befriended one of the vagrants that hung out in the alley behind the school. Times were different then and apparently; she had no problem with me talking to him. She said that he had a pet parrot that would sit on his shoulder. I can see this might be something I would find interesting. She recounted how I would spend quite a bit of time just talking with him. She brought it up because, in her telling of the story, he was found murdered near the school. You would think that would be memorable, no, not for me. I have no conscious memory whatsoever of this person. It was as if I was hearing this for the first time. Where did all these memories go? Was that time I supposedly spent with this person missing? It was as if I was living in an alternate reality.

I do remember spending so much time by myself around school that I developed a way of seeing things around me differently. I could see the ant's view from below and I could see the bird's view from above. I found things that others simply overlooked, Chinese coins, a silver piece of eight and other trinkets just seemed to appear wherever I looked.

Still, this was a difficult time and I struggled to fit within the accepted social consensus. I learned to accept and embrace solitude, I felt OK with myself. Deep down, I did not feel abandoned as I had in the past. I did resent the abuse that I had to suffer at the hands of those who did not understand. I also made a few friends. Fighting was something I tried to avoid. In a few cases, I made a new friend of one of the bullies. All of this, as I learned, would become another source of catalyst that would force me to grow and expand my thinking of how the "world" worked.

Great Hall Lucid Dream Contact and Message

I must have been 14 or 15 when this happened. The only thing I remember playing around with during this time was a synthesizer my mom had purchased. It was a white faced Arp Odyssey. I had been trying to recreate the surging sound from the experience I had when I was seven. One night I went to bed as usual. I awoke to find myself in a place that was beyond my describing or imagination. I seemed to emerge into a great space through a translucent wall of energy. I could see colors that physical eyes would never be able to see. I can only give a dim description of this place. The self-luminous translucent walls were a vibrant yellow green. The surface was perceived as a swirling mass of energy particles. At regular intervals were massive buttresses in a half-ellipse shape. They were self-luminous in a brilliant cobalt blue. They must have soared to at least 150' or higher. I perceived the floor as like a black mirror. There was a great crossing to my right. I could see many entities going in all directions. There were areas to congregate and kiosklike structures for information. I wondered what this place was for and what I was seeing.

Just then, I was joined by an entity. He was dressed in a pale bluish white robe. He had flowing white, blonde hair and blue eyes. I would guess he stood approximately 7' tall. He began to explain to me what was going on here. I believe he was using telepathy. I don't remember him speaking with his mouth. I forgot most of what he said but I have retained some important details. Apparently, there was some great project or age coming to completion. The entities here were working toward that goal. I don't remember exactly the context but the coming was the age of "Phebos". I put these words in quotations as this is my best guess as to what was conveyed. There was a place being prepared for something that was called the dome or hall of "Tothados". I could almost see a vision of it through the translucent wall. He told me he was a helper, "Ekra-Laitos", here to tell me of this coming event or change. I could not grasp what he was trying to convey. He showed me a few more unremembered things and told me it was time to go. I had felt this as well. I hated to leave his presence, I had so many questions. I knew how to leave. I backed up into the energy wall. The next thing I remember is waking up at home in bed. I was somewhat sad at being back. It was very emotional.

My mom had been going to a Metaphysical church in Tampa. She had me talk to Rev. Lamb about the experience. I don't remember much of what he said. The only thing I remember was him saying that he found "Phebos" as being something akin to the light that was in the world. I never could find this correlation, so I don't know if this is correct.

I had a Near Death Experience: Before returning to my body, I was brought Out of Body to a UFO Occupied by Non-Human Intelligence. Is there a Connection between NDEs and UFOs?

Sharleene Howard

My name is Sharleen Howard. I am 48 years old, a mother of 4 children and I work as a Nurse in California. I am sharing my experience(s) to help others who have also had NDEs, (Near-Death Experiences), or OBEs, (Out-of-Body Experiences), and want to come out to tell their story. Prior to my NDE, I had not opened up much about these experiences out of fear of being judged and criticized. My experiences have not been compatible with my Christian beliefs, my Church, and my community. Needless to say, my experiences has caused me much stress and turmoil because my previous worldviews came crashing down and I am still trying to process these experiences.

Needless to say, my NDE and OBE experiences have changed my life completely, for the better. I now see life in a whole different view. It has made me a better person by showing me things about myself that I've needed to fix and change so that I could improve as a person and how I live my life. For one, I have become intuitive, sensitive, more trusting of my own feelings, far more empathetic, and able to feel other people's feelings more acutely. A lot of things have begun to happen and open up to me after these experiences. I remember these experiences as if they happened to me yesterday. They have shaped me and continue to be part of me, everyday, in every way. I am grateful.

There are benevolent beings watching over us. They want us to enjoy life. Be the real you. Be the true you. Love and faith. Do no harm. Grow your love. To these beings, they key to life is that humans need to learn now to LOVE. That's what matters and they want you to know this important information.

First Experience: Falling into Blackness

My first NDE-OBE happened when I was around 27 years old, during a trip with my husband to the Big Island in Hawaii. I don't recall whether I was sick, had a headache, or when I had last eaten anything.

But that night, I went to sleep as usual at this hotel we were staying at, when suddenly, as I was lying "asleep", I recall being totally conscious and feeling like I was falling endlessly into blackness, leaving my current reality behind. I had a feeling of sinking into nothingness. I remember feeling like I was "letting go" but I didn't know what I was letting go of.

Then suddenly, I disconnected from my body at an incredible speed. I was literally sucked out of it. It was so quick! During that moment I wasn't aware that I was letting go of life itself; but I did let go very easily. I found myself walking around the "side of the bed". I had a sense of being in the hotel room; but things looked somewhat different. A bright light coming from the doorway, (or where the door should have been), caught my attention. But the door wasn't there! In that moment, I was confused and not aware that actually, I was out of my physical body. It was all happening too fast! As I looked around, I realized there were no walls and no floor. I hesitated to move, further thinking that if I moved any closer to that light, I was not going to come back.

I was puzzled as I looked around and saw my husband lying in bed and right next to him, I could see my own body. My body gave off a gray-blue hue; it looked purple. I felt afraid and freaked out. I was running around the hotel room screaming and yelling for my husband to wake up. I realized something was very wrong, and that something had happened to me. I wanted him to wake me up, to help me. My notion of self and of my identity was intact. I knew who I was, where I came from, and was able to access my life memories. It is almost as if I was a holographic version of myself.

I eventually found myself at a still. My next thought was to talk to God, pleading to let me go back to my life. I had two little kids at the time and I didn't want to abandon them. I could not bear the thought of having to leave them without saying goodbye. I didn't want to leave my life behind.

And then just like that, I heard a telepathic voice instructing me to *"move away from the door"*. So, I did. My next thought was to figure out how to re-enter my body. I felt a sense of urgency with an awareness that my physical brain needed oxygen; and without it, I would fall into a vegetative state.

As I was trying to figure out a way to get back into my body, a voice instructed me to *"lie back into my body"*. So, I did, and then felt sucked back into it immediately, as my spirit and my body were reunited through some kind of vacuum effect. Instantly, I got up, and woke up my husband to tell him what had happened. I was cold and had to move slowly; but I felt fine otherwise-- I had no pain, and didn't go to the hospital.

As I processed the experience, I wondered why I had gone through this. My thoughts directed me to God, giving me a sense that I was being told to lose my fear of dying. Upon returning home, I connected with my pastor who seemed open-minded about my experience but confided that these experiences were not really talked about in the Church.

Second Experience: Encounter with a Spirit Guide, God, and Aliens

I had my second NDE/OBE in July of 2012, while in my house in Antioch, California. Again, it happened as I went to sleep, and still cannot recall when I ate, how I felt at that time, or what may have triggered it; but this was a totally different experience.

This time, I didn't see my body as I left it; but I did experience the blackness again, the sensation of falling, a sense of speed, and of flying up high somewhere, but without really feeling it. I ended up on a cloud outside of this world, fully conscious, with retained memories of my current life. I had not lost any of my functions, but was standing there in this place, nervous, and trying to calm myself down— being fully aware that I was having another NDE/OBE. However, this time I was more convinced that I would be fine and kept repeating those thoughts to myself to help me deal with the shock and surprise of having to experience this again.

The Spirit Guide-- Anna Love

From a big cloud, I was looking all around where I could see stars shimmering below me. Though, when I looked up, I could see nothing but black darkness. As I looked all around, it just seemed like I was outside of this earth, standing in a totally different place. Then looking over to my right, I saw the outline of someone approaching. It looked like a person's spirit walking towards me. Aware that I was out of my body, I anticipated an encounter with a deceased relative or a friend—someone I knew. Eventually, I was able to distinguish that it was a woman who seemed to be shorter than five feet. She looked Asian, with short black hair down to her shoulders, and a mole on the right side of here face. She was very pretty, but I could not recognize her. Although I looked at her hard, and carefully tried to identify her, I couldn't.

While standing to my right, she held my right hand, smiled, and spoke to me telepathically, without moving her lips. She expressed her deep love for me and told me that she had been with me since birth, and that she would be with me forever. She told me, ***"Everything was going to be okay"***. I felt a love more powerful than I had ever experienced before. This feeling of universal love was just overwhelming. It was the best thing I had ever felt in my entire life. I trusted that love entirely. I felt that she was a spiritual guide who had always been with me. I will call her, "**Anna Love**". Anna was the purest embodiment of love itself. That is how I felt when she touched me. She cared about me and loved me unconditionally.

Somehow, I saw a mirror appear in front of me with my reflection in it. Then a message came to me that "*I needed to be happier and feel more joy*". I saw the ugly part of myself. I saw that I was missing out on divine gifts because of how I was living, much like in automation.

My communication with GOD

Then, I could very clearly hear a man speaking in a stern voice. The voice was coming from above—from the deep blackness. He spoke with wide spaces between each word. I was unable to see a person or a face, so I don't know who it was. But I believed then, in my heart and soul, that it was God, Jesus, or a higher authority.

He spoke of his pride in me and the three blessings I was given, while also warning of something very bad that was about to happen to me. But in the end, he said, *"I would make it and would be okay"*. He spoke of the importance of faith—of having a "strong" faith. His presence felt gigantic and authoritative. At which point, Anna let go of my hand, walked away, and disappeared.

A UFO with Non-Human Intelligence

Then, somehow, I transitioned into this other place. It felt like I went inside an alien ship. Why I ended up there; I don't know. It was unintentional. In addition, I never believed in aliens up until that point, nor had I watched alien movies. I didn't believe in this, and never paid attention to this issue. It was so odd to find myself there. I saw an alien entity. Was it a man? A bug? A man-bug? He was about 6 feet tall and standing against a wall, which had no edge. The inside of the UFO was smooth and completely round. It had no doors or windows. He was hunched over. His eyes were wide open, and I couldn't see how he could shut his eyes because he had no eyelids. I could see he had three or maybe four long fingers that looked like crab legs. I am not sure because I couldn't see clearly.

I then turned my attention to two more aliens that were there in the middle of that circular UFO. These two beings had big, wide eyes that stretched all the way to the sides of their heads. They were sitting in high, back chairs without armrests. They had three rolls of fat at chest level. They were just sitting. I felt like they were sleeping. I was looking around this darkness and could only see a blue, LED-type of light. No one was moving. It was quiet. This place was rather empty. I could not see words or writings on the walls. I noticed a big tank in the centre, where the blue LED light was coming from. It was filled with this water gel liquid. The substance was lit up by the blue light. The light went around it. Again, the aliens all seemed asleep but real and alive, incarnated in a real body, while I felt dead in my spirit form. I figured they could not see me.

I felt like I was in this craft for quite some time looking around. But I also had a sense that time was irrelevant in that dimension. Our notion of time didn't apply there. It is therefore hard to tell how long I was there for. Minutes? Hours? Weeks? This kind of time frame didn't make sense.

When I got closer, I noticed a control panel where I could see square-shaped, red, blue, and yellow, colored buttons with no writing, which were organized in a circular fashion. It looked like the control panel they might have been using to fly this craft. Almost immediately, I heard a telepathic voice inside my consciousness telling me that I was not supposed to be there and prompting me to leave. I directed my attention to the alien that was leaning against the ship. He started to move. It freaked me out. I hurried to get out of this place. It dawned on me that the alien could see me after all. I realized they could see dead people. These beings are advanced in their abilities. In hindsight, my feeling was that these beings live here with us and that they have been living here with us humans the whole time, but that they don't want to be bothered with us. Why I ended up there during my NDE-OBE, I have no idea still to this day.

And then just like that, I was returned into my body—sucked back again through this powerful vacuum effect, with my body and soul reunited, perfectly. I felt no pain. I remember opening my eyes, looking out of the window, and seeing the sky, with a total recollection of what had just happened to me—noting how I was wide awake the whole time. I thanked the Lord for the blessing. I was excited and wanted to go out to tell everybody about this experience, what I had learned, and that God is real.

Summary of the Dr. Edgar Mitchell FREE Foundation CAP-UFO Experiencer Research Study

Reinerio (Rey) Hernandez

JD, MCP, ex-PhD Candidate UC Berkeley

The following is a quick summary of a fraction of the data findings from this historic 5-year academic research study of UFO Contact Experiencers published in our 820-page book *"Beyond UFOs: The Science of Consciousness and Contact with Non-Human Intelligence"*. To review the actual data findings, presented via bar graphs and pie charts, please review Chapters 1 and 2 in our book, available as a downloadable PDF file from the CCRI website at: **AGreaterReality.Com**.

Chapter One of our book was an analysis of the data findings from Survey #1 and Survey #2, our qualitative research instruments, which were comprised of 700 quantitative questions. Harvard Professor Dr. Rudy Schild and Reinerio (Rey) Hernandez were the authors for Chapter One of *"Beyond UFOs"*. Chapter Two of our book was comprised of any analysis of our Survey #3, which was comprised of 70 qualitative open-ended questions. Dr. John Klimo, a Ph.D. graduate from Brown University, who taught Qualitative Survey Methodology to Ph.D. graduate students, wrote the analysis for Chapter Two. We received over 10,000 pages of responses to the 70 open-ended questions in our Survey. We received responses from 4,350 UFO Contact Experiencers from 125 countries for our 3 surveys in the English language. We also conducted our surveys in other languages but this analysis will only discuss the findings from our English language survey.

The following is a brief summary of our research findings:

1.   **UFO contact is overwhelmingly a positive experience**:

Even though 37% of the 4,350 individuals who took our English language surveys initially viewed their experiences as negative, eventually, over their lifetime, the overwhelming number of CAP-UFO Experiencers concluded that their contact experiences were mainly positive, between 85-95% depending on the question asked. **We asked over 25 questions to determine if their experiences were Positive, Negative, or Neutral and we asked this question in many ways.**

Why? -- because depending how you phrase a question you will receive a different response. Only 5% responded that their experiences were negative. For our Spanish language surveys, the percentage that viewed their experience as negative was less than 1%. Below is a summary of some these 25 questions:

The overwhelming number of materialist Ufology researchers believe that ALL "UFO Contact" results in an Abduction and that ALL of these experiences are "Negative". This is FALSE! Abductees (individuals that have been involuntarily brought to another location) only accounted for one-third of the Experiencers. Of these 33%, the vast majority had OBE and Astral Travel Experiences. Two-thirds of Experiencers have seen a CAP/UFO, have had contact with Non-Human Intelligence, but have never had an abduction. Materialist Ufology is missing more than 2/3rds of all Contact Experiencers.

Thus, the vast majority of "Contact" does not involve an "Abduction". We also discovered that what occurs in an "Abduction" is very different than what is reported by the "abduction researchers" in the field of materialist Ufology. If you want to learn more about the "abduction phenomenon" read Volume 3-6 of the *A Greater Reality* book series. I also highly encourage you to read the article written by UFO pioneer researcher, Raymond Fowler, in Volume 4 of our *A Greater Reality* book series. Raymond investigated hundreds of UFO abduction cases for over 50 years and his perspective is the complete opposite of the views of Hopkins, Jacobs and Dolan.

Of the one-third that have described having had an abduction (individuals that have been involuntarily brought to another location), the majority of these individuals were actually brought to other "multidimensional matrix realities" by Non-Human Intelligence where the majority received some form of spiritual message. The percent that actually had a stereotypical abduction experience (taken by little grey beings and being examined by them in a flat table, etc., as presented by Jacobs, Hopkins, Dolan, and the other "Alien Abduction" Researchers was 15%, or approximately one half of those that claimed to have had an abduction experience. (I encourage everyone to read the chapter in this book by Carol Rainey, the ex-wife of "abduction researcher" Budd Hopkins, to learn more about how the "abduction phenomena" was co-created by Budd Hopkins and his friend David Jacobs. Her article is titled "*Priests of High Strangeness: Co-Creation of the Alien Abduction Phenomenon*")

Of the 1/3rd who stated they had an "Abduction", more than 70% of these individuals now call themselves Contactees and NOT

Abductees. Initially, 37% of all UFO Contact Experiences (Abductees and Non-Abductees) viewed their experiences as negative because of the ontological shock of the experience. The majority of these individuals continued to have contact experiences with various forms of Non-Human Intelligence. Over time, these experiences became increasingly more positive than the earlier experiences. In their later contact experiences, 85-95%, depending on the question asked, viewed their experiences as positive, even the vast majority that initially had an abduction type of experience. The vast majority of Contact Experiencers, both Abductees and Non-Abductees have had many diverse contact experiences. 40% have had more than 20 contact experiences. Another 20% have had between 10-20 contact experiences.

We discovered that the more experiences you have had, your perception of your experiences becomes more positive. Thus, when you start your experiences, 37% view them as negative but over time, only 5% view them as negative. It is individuals that have had only 1 or 2 abduction type of experiences are the ones with the most negative responses. These individuals remained traumatized and continue to view their experiences as mainly negative throughout their lives (approximately 5% of all Contact Experiencers, depending on the question asked). As previously stated, 70% of those who claim to have had an "Abduction" experience do not call themselves "Abductees" but instead they now call themselves "CONTACTEES".

Almost 50% of all participants stated that they "were brought to a "Matrix Type" of reality and received information" (Like Jodie Foster's "**Contact**" Movie). This was more than double the number of those that have had a typical "alien abduction" scenario. These experiences were overwhelmingly positive.

The overwhelming number of contact experiences with a Non-Human Intelligence lasted less than one minute, usually less than 30 seconds.

Individuals have seen thousands of different types of Non-Human Intelligence "beings" even though we only categorized 12 different types in our quantitative surveys. Our qualitative survey, consisting of 70 Open-Ended questions, discussed contact with thousands of different types of physical and non-physical beings. As of May 2018, the date that we closed our surveys, the most common type was the **Energy Being**, seen by 56% of all Experiencers and only 7% viewed this being as "Negative". The **Human Looking Being** was seen by 50.1% and only 5% viewed them as "Negative". The **Small Grays** were the third most seen being at 49.4% and only 10.5% viewed them as "Negative". All of these physical beings came in all sizes, physical colors and appearance, while some had hundreds of different types of clothes, hats, etc. For example, the Grays were seen in numerous different sizes, colors, clothing, physical appearances. The Human Looking Beings were also observed in numerous different sizes, colors, clothing, physical appearances. Some were Asian looking, some had African features, some were 15 feet tall and some were 2 feet tall, some had blonde hair and blue eyes and other had a vast array of hair and eye color, some were even bald. Some wore suits, some wore tuxedos, and they were observed wearing all types of hats, including baseball hats from the New York Yankees. In addition, these individuals described thousands of different types of "Humanoid Beings". Another researcher, Albert J Rosales, has published 16 books on experiences with tens of thousands of **different** types of Humanoids.

https://www.amazon.com/dp/B09C4VWHRP?binding=paper back&searchxofy=true

Academic Professor Dr. Jon Klimo wrote Chapter 2 for Beyond UFOs, which was an analysis of the responses to our 70 open ended questions. We received more than 10,000 pages to these 70 open ended questions. What Dr. Klimo discovered was that the UFO Contact Experiencer had experiences with thousands of **different types** of perceived physical "beings". This leads to the question: **Are these tens of thousands of diverse physical beings coming to visit us, usually for less than 30 seconds, from tens of thousands of different physical planets?** Or is the answer a bit more complicated than merely a physical being visiting us from a physical planet? Are these thousands of different physical beings coming to visit us from different physical planet? Are they multi-dimensional beings from another reality? Are they holographic projections or cloaked mental images projected to our Consciousness? Are there other possible explanations? At this point, many of the academic researchers of the FREE Foundation share the hypotheses that these perceived "physical beings" might be projected mental images into our individuated units of consciousness, but no one can be certain. This hypothesis was also presented by many major Ufologists, such as Dr. Jacque Vallee, Dr. J. Allen Hynek (in his later years), Dr. Edgar Mitchell, Dr. John Mack (Professor of Psychiatry at the Harvard School of Medicine), Dr. Rudy Schild (Astrophysicist at Harvard University), Dr. John Klimo (Professor of Psychology), Dr. Kenneth Ring (Emeritus Professor of Psychology at the University of Connecticut) and CAP-UFO Researchers such as Reinerio (Rey) Hernandez, Raymond Fowler, John Keele, Brad Steiger and many others.

2. <u>**UFO contact is overwhelmingly a "Paranormal" and not primarily a Physical Phenomenon.**</u>

While all of the Experiencers of our survey have both seen UFOs and have had various types of Contact with Non-Human Intelligence, including a physical entity, we found that the Contact Experience is overwhelmingly NOT a Physical/Material Phenomena-- instead, it is primarily a Paranormal/Psychic Phenomena.

Dr. Jacque Vallee, Dr. Allan Hynek, Dr. John Mack, Dr. Edgar Mitchell, and many others hypothesized this more than 40 years ago. Unlike previous research from Vallee, Hynek, Mack, or Mitchell, FREE has actually confirmed this hypothesis with academically derived data.

For example, for all that took our surveys, 95% have had Paranormal experiences in their home, 80% have had an OBE, 67% have received telepathic communications, 50% have received a medical healing by non-human intelligence, 37% have had an NDE, 60% have physically seen Orbs, almost 50% have been brought to a Matrix Reality, etc. We asked almost 100 paranormal related questions and these individuals have had almost every paranormal experience known to humanity. Chapter One of our book *"Beyond UFOs"* provides many more details and explanations for this finding.

3. **The Contact Experience is an overwhelmingly Positive Transformative Experience**.

For the vast majority, you start as a caterpillar and finish as a butterfly, even though a very small percentage are still traumatized by the experience. Approximately 85% of the FREE survey participants, more than 4,350 individuals from over 125 countries, have changed in the following ways, they became: more loving to other humans, more ecological, less materialistic, more spiritual, no longer feared death, know the purpose of their life, are more consciously aware, less religious, etc. We asked more than 70 different questions regarding the question of how they changed their worldview. Chapter One of our book provides many more details and explanations for this finding.

4. The UFO Contact Experience involves a manipulation of Space-Time and this in turn leads one to hypothesize that the CAP-UFO Non-Human Intelligence might be multidimensional in nature

This hypothesis was presented by various researchers, which include the following: more than 40 years ago by Dr. Jacques Vallee (Astronomer, Co-Inventor of the Internet and legendary Ufologist), Dr. J. Allen Hynek (Astrophysicist at Northeastern University), Dr. John Mack (Harvard Medical School Professor of Psychiatry), Apollo 14 astronaut Dr. Edgar Mitchell (MIT trained aeronautical engineer and physicist), Dr. Rudy Schild (Harvard Astrophysicist for 45 years), and Dr. Claude Swanson (Ph.D. in Physics from Princeton University), and many others. This, in turn, presents the hypothesis that this Non-Human Intelligence might be multidimensional in nature. In other words, the UFO Non-Human Intelligence might be consciousness-based and might be "embedded" in the very fabric of our reality.

Volume 2 of CCRIs book, *A Greater Reality*, contains 11 chapters that begin to discuss some possible theories on the relationship between CAP-UFO-related Non-Human Intelligence, the manipulation of Space-Time, and the cosmology of our Greater Reality.

Helene Layne, Kevin Layne and I are the 3 co-producers of a new science-based documentary titled "*A Greater Reality: One Man's Journey of Discovery*". We spent 5 years filming over 30 Ph.D. academics, scientists and medical doctors in addition to over 50 Experiencers of the Contact Modalities. Kevin and Helene developed more than 10 Star Trek films for William Shatner so we are in good hands. Our documentary will be a mirror image of our 5-Volume book series, *A Greater Reality*. We expect to release the film in the Spring of 2025. The draft "trailer" for the documentary can be viewed at the bottom of our website: **AGreaterReality.Com**.

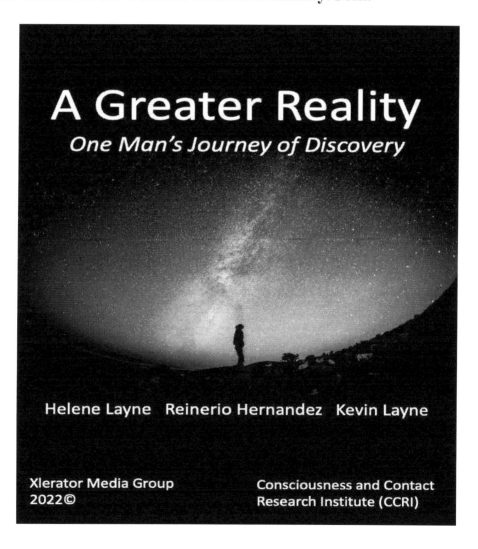

The Mind of GOD
A Spiritual-Virtual Reality Model of Consciousness & The Contact Modalities

Reinerio (Rey) Hernandez, JD, MCP, PhD (c)

Director, Consciousness and Contact Research Institute (CCRI)

Website: AGreaterReality.Com
Email: Info@AGreaterReality.Com

 CCRI

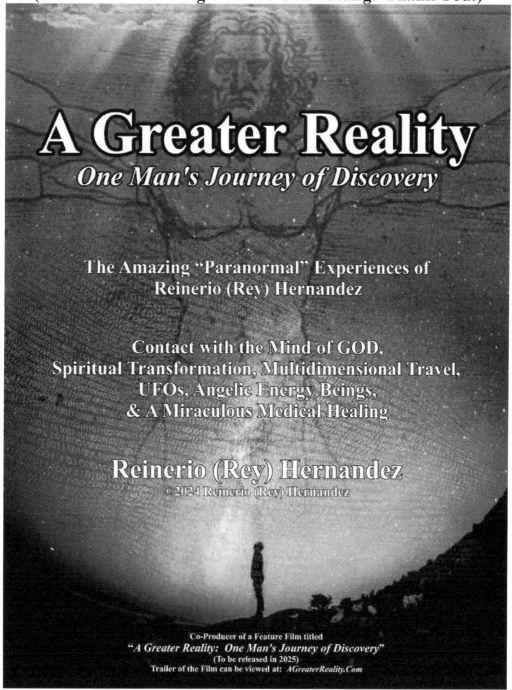

Made in the USA
Middletown, DE
09 May 2025